# Window Systems for High-Performance Buildings

John Carmody
Stephen Selkowitz
Eleanor S. Lee
Dariush Arasteh
Todd Willmert

## Additional Contributors

Carl Wagus
William Lingnell
The Weidt Group
Robert Clear
Robert Sullivan
Kerry Haglund
William Weber

W.W. Norton & Company
New York • London

For information about permission to reproduce selections from this book, write to Permissions, W. W. Norton & Company, Inc., 500 Fifth Avenue, New York, NY 10110

Manufacturing by Quebecor World Kingsport
Book design by John Carmody and Kerry Haglund
Production Manager: Leeann Graham

Library of Congress Cataloging-in-Publication Data

Window systems for high performance buildings / authors, John Carmody . . . [et al.]
        p. cm.
    Includes bibliographical references and index.
    **ISBN: 0-393-73121-9**
    1. Windows. 2. Commercial buildings – Equipment and supplies.
I. Carmody, John.

TH2275.W5643 2003
725'.2—dc21                                                2003059929

W. W. Norton & Company, Inc., 500 Fifth Avenue,
New York, N.Y. 10110
www.wwnorton.com
W. W. Norton & Company Ltd., Castle House, 75/76 Wells St.,
London W1T 3QT

0 9 8 7 6 5 4 3 2 1

# Contents

# CHAPTER 7. Window Design for Schools 297

# CHAPTER 8. Case Studies 330

# Appendices

# Glossary 375

# References and Bibliography 384

# Index 394

# Acknowledgments

This book was developed with support from the U.S. Department of Energy's Windows and Glazing Research Program within the Office of Building Technology, Community and State Programs. In partnership with the building industry, the U.S. Department of Energy supports a range of research, development, and demonstration programs, as well as education and market transformation projects, designed to accelerate the introduction and use of new energy-saving building technologies—including many of those described in this book.

Many people contributed their time and talent toward the completion of this project. The book would not have been possible without the continued encouragement and support of Sam Taylor at the U.S. Department of Energy. Sam has overseen the project through its many phases and helped shape the final product. In the later phases, Marc LaFrance at U.S. DOE was also very supportive in making completion of the project possible.

There are a number of individuals, listed on the title page as additional contributors, who added significant material and effort toward this book:

- Carl Wagus, Technical Director of American Architectural Manufacturers Association, and William Lingnell, Lingnell Consulting Services, wrote the technical issues section in Chapter 2. They provided guidance and comments in other sections of the book as well.

- At the Lawrence Berkeley National Laboratory (LBNL), two individuals provided expertise in key areas. Robert Clear worked with Eleanor Lee to develop the methodology used to compare window alternatives across many attributes. Robert Sullivan assisted in the development of the thermal comfort analysis tool.

- From the University of Minnesota's Center for Sustainable Building Research (CSBR), two individuals made major contributions. Kerry Haglund, did the graphic design and illustrations, and was invaluable in putting the entire project together. William G. Weber, Jr., assisted with data analysis and the development of graphics and architectural guidelines.

- The Weidt Group, an energy consulting firm in Minnesota, contributed to Chapter 7 with computer simulations and the analysis of window alternatives for schools. The Weidt Group team included Prasad Vaidya, Tom McDougall, Doug Maddox, and Autif Sayyed.

We are also indebted to other colleagues at CSBR and LBNL. At CSBR, Dr. James Wise (also of Eco*Integrations), offered insight and material for the human factors portion of the book. At LBNL, Lei Zhou, Christian Kohler, Robin Mitchell, Joe Huang, Rebecca Powles, Howdy Goudey, Fred Winkelmann, and Fred Buhl gave valuable assistance. Thanks also to graduate student research assistant, Vorapat Inkarojrit, and post-doctoral student, Vineeta Pal.

A number of people in the research and design professional communities provided helpful comments and suggestions. These included John Hogan, Department of Construction and Land Use, City of Seattle; Dragan Curcija, University of Massachusetts; Oyvind Aschehoug, Norwegian University of Science and Technology; Gregg Ander, Southern California Edison; as well as Gail Brager and Charlie Huizenga, both of the Department of Architecture, University of California, Berkeley.

Key individuals in the window and building industry also provided invaluable comments and material for the book. These include Mike Manteghi, TRACO; Richard Voreis, Consulting Collaborative; Joel Berman, Mechoshade; Michael Myser, Sage Electrochromics, Inc.; Lee Assenheimer, Tecton Products; Tom Mifflin, Wausau Window and Wall Systems; Don McCann and Dan Wacek, Viracon; Ken Moody, Velux-America; John Meade, Southwall; Greg McKenna, Kawneer; Raj Goyal and Bill Martin, Graham Architectural; Patrick Muessig, Azon; Valerie Block, Dupont; James Benney, NFRC; and Gary Curtis, Westwall Group.

The Chapter 8 case studies were made possible by the contributions and insights of several architects, engineers, and researchers. These include Philippe Dordai, Hillier; Danny Parker, Florida Solar Energy Center; Richard Jensen, will bruder architects, ltd.; Michael Holtz, Architectural Energy Corporation; Jim Toothaker, Consultant, High Performance Green Building Services; Marcus Sheffer, Energy Opportunities; John A. Boecker, L. Robert Kimball & Associates; Kerry Hegedus, NBBJ; Stefania Canta, Renzo Piano Building Workshop; and both Maurya McClintock and Andrew Sedgwick of Arup.

This book has benefited greatly from the suggestions and editing of Nancy Green at W.W. Norton. We appreciate her patience during the long process of completing this project.

John Carmody, CSBR
Stephen Selkowitz, LBNL
Eleanor S. Lee, LBNL
Dariush Arasteh, LBNL
Todd Willmert, CSBR

# CHAPTER 1

# Introduction to Windows in High-performance Buildings

## The Importance of Windows

Windows are one of the most significant elements in the design of any building. Whether present as relatively small punched openings in the facade or as a completely glazed curtain wall, windows are usually a dominant feature of a building's appearance. Windows can appear highly reflective, darkly opaque, or transparent, revealing or hiding activity within the building. Their color, transparency, and reflected patterns can change with the time of day and weather.

Although appearance is important in architectural design, the traditional purpose of windows was to provide light, view, and fresh air for the occupants. As completely sealed, mechanically ventilated, and electrically lit commercial buildings became the norm in the last half of the twentieth century, the role of the window in addressing occupant needs declined. There is a growing recognition, however, that while light and air can be provided by other means, the benefits of windows are highly valued and contribute to the satisfaction, health, and productivity of building occupants. In addition to the

*Figure 1-1. Alcoa Building in Pittsburgh, PA. Architect: The Design Alliance Architects; Photo: Courtesy of Viracon*

trend toward more human-centered design, there is an urgent need for significant improvements in building energy performance in the immediate future.

One challenge in designing facades and selecting windows in commercial buildings is balancing design and human issues and with numerous technical criteria and costs. Technical issues such as structure, moisture control, acoustics, and security require complex trade-offs. Increasingly, costs are being viewed in a life cycle context that accounts for the impact of a window on long-term operational, maintenance, and replacement costs as well as the initial expense. A critical concept that weaves together all of these concerns is *high-performance design*, also referred to as *sustainable design* or *green design*. Generally, high-performance design is intended to produce buildings that are energy-efficient, healthy, economical in the long run, and that use resources wisely to minimize environmental impact. An important concept in achieving these goals is *integrated design* that regards the entire building and its occupants as an interactive system.

The purpose of this book, therefore, is to provide design professionals with more comprehensive information on the energy, interior environment, and technical impacts of window design decisions in commercial buildings. To do this, the current advances in window technology and tools for evaluating choices must be understood. The building industry has needed a comprehensive reference that describes both the fenestration design options and the performance of such systems in commercial buildings. This book provides this critical information and performance data so that architects and engineers may begin to understand the implications of design choices on building performance.

It is not enough to know that window choices have an impact on energy use and environmental quality—the critical question is, to what degree do windows impact these factors compared to other conventional design options? A fundamental barrier to the implementation of high-performance facade design is this lack of information and knowledge, particularly at the early design stages, and the lack of tools allowing designers to quickly understand complex, interrelated building performance issues. The knowledge base for these tools must be built, in part, from evaluation of actual buildings.

The remainder of this chapter includes further background on energy use, human-centered design, and life cycle costs related to windows, as well as high-performance commercial building design in general. This is followed by a brief overview of emerging technologies and trends. Finally, the scope and organization of the book are addressed.

## ENERGY EFFICIENCY

In addition to having a dominant influence on a building's appearance and interior environment, windows can be one of the most important components impacting its energy use, peak electricity demand, and environmental consequences. Heat gain and heat loss through windows can represent a significant portion of a building's heating and cooling loads. By providing natural light, windows can reduce electric lighting loads, as long as effective dimming controls for light fixtures are employed. Proper window selection and design can also cut peak electricity and cooling loads, thereby avoiding costly

*Figure 1-2. Exterior of Occidental Chemical Corporation, in Niagara Falls, NY, showing the double-envelope curtain wall with louvers within cavity. Architect: Cannon Design; Photo: Cannon Design*

*Introduction to Windows in High-performance Buildings*

peak demand charges and easing the need for new power plants. In addition, high-performance windows impact mechanical systems, not only contributing to reduced operation expense but also to potential equipment downsizing, saving capital costs.

Commercial buildings account for 16 percent of all U.S. energy consumption (15.4 quadrillion Btus out of a total of 92.6 Quads). Windows are responsible for 1.1 Quads of energy for heating and cooling commercial buildings, while lighting accounts for 3.83 Quads. If it is assumed that 25 percent of lighting energy use could be affected by daylighting (about 0.96 Quads), then windows in commercial buildings account for about 2 Quads total per year, or over 2 percent of the total national energy consumption. Based on these figures, windows represent over 12 percent of all energy use in commercial buildings in the United States. If the residential building sector is included, windows account for nearly 5 Quads, or over 5 percent of the total national energy use.

## HUMAN-CENTERED DESIGN

In the United States, many buildings continue to be designed with large central cores and relatively few perimeter spaces with windows. Windowless offices and schools have become commonplace in the last fifty years. Windows, if present, are seldom operable and thus cannot provide natural ventilation. They are often darkly tinted or reflective to cut glare and heat gain, but also reducing the amenity of light and view for occupants. These trends continue, and are worse in some cases. For instance, glare makes computer monitor use uncomfortable, leading to the specification of dark glazing as a remedy.

Because light and air can now be provided through electric and mechanical systems, the traditional, principle role of windows has been undermined, lessening their significance in most commercial buildings today. This shift, of course, fails to address the sometimes less measurable, but critical importance of providing a healthy, productive, stimulating, and attractive interior environment. Daylight has qualities that simply cannot be replicated by electric light. The changing intensity, direction, and color of natural light connects us to the weather, season, and time of day. Views through windows, especially those including elements from nature, contribute to the well-being of occupants as well as improve their sense of orientation and feeling of spaciousness. Windows that open can provide fresh air and a connection to the outdoors in addition to giving occupants a sense of controlling their own environment. In effect, windows introduce variety and sensory stimulation that is missing in totally enclosed environments.

In some European countries the trend is to require that all workers be within a certain distance of a window and that it is operable. Of course, the benefits of daylight, view, and natural ventilation can only be achieved with careful design that mitigates and controls the potential negative effects of windows, such as increased glare and reduced thermal comfort. Current research demonstrates that windows and daylight play important roles in creating a more positive interior environment that improves occupants' productivity and well-being.

*Figure 1-3. Walter Library Reading Room at the University of Minnesota. In traditional buildings, large high windows offer natural illumination and a connection to the outdoors. Photo: Courtesy of the University of Minnesota; Photo: Tom Foley*

## LIFE CYCLE COSTS

Windows, of course, are also important in buildings because of their cost. The initial expense of windows is generally more than an equal area of opaque facade, but the need for or desirability of some type of window usually does not require justification. A more important issue is defending additional cost to provide more windows or higher-performance windows. Yet, the operating energy and maintenance costs of the building usually outweigh the initial costs by a factor of about ten to one. Moreover, the expense of occupant salaries within the building is typically many times more than the operating costs. The window's initial cost drives many decisions, but it is small in comparison to other more critical features.

Since windows can have a significant impact on the operating costs, health, productivity and occupant well-being, a broadly focused life cycle analysis must be used. Such analysis must include monetary, environmental, and human impacts of building design choices. Durability is also a key issue in any life cycle analysis. Window frames, glazings, and sealants may have different useful lives. Yet, window systems are expected to last at least 20–30 years and they can often be much more expensive and difficult to replace than other building systems. Maintaining energy performance properties over the life of the window is an essential aspect of window durability.

## High-performance Sustainable Design

In recent years, there has been a growing awareness of the impact buildings have on environmental degradation, both in the United States and abroad. According to the World Watch Institute, "as much as a tenth of the global economy is dedicated to buildings: to construction, operating, and equipping our built environment. This economic activity uses even larger shares, one-sixth to one-half, of the world's wood, minerals, water, and energy. Blame for much of the environmental damage occurring today, from destruction of forests and rivers to air and water pollution and climate destabilization, must be placed squarely at the doorsteps of modern buildings. Many buildings do harm on the inside as well: they subject us to unhealthy air or alienating physical environments, making us both less healthy and less productive than we are capable of being" (Roodman and Lensson, 1995).

In response to these concerns, interest has grown in pursuing *high-performance*, *sustainable*, or *green* design. These terms can be used somewhat interchangeably, although definitions vary. As defined in the Brundtland Report for the United Nations, "Sustainable development involves . . . meeting the needs of the present without compromising the ability of future generations to meet their own needs."

The *American Institute of Architects Handbook* states that ". . . sustainability refers to the ability of a society, ecosystem, or any such ongoing system to continue functioning into the indefinite future . . . . For architecture, this means design that delivers buildings and communities with lower environmental impacts while enhancing health, productivity, community, and quality of life." In fact, the definition of green, sustainable, or high-performance design will continue to evolve as it is practiced more widely.

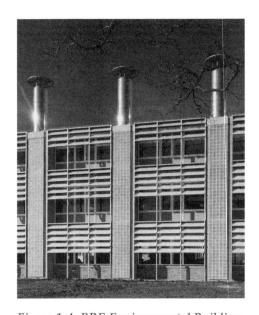

*Figure 1-4. BRE Environmental Building in Garston, UK. Aside from the glass in its operable windows, glass louvers are used as sun control elements and glass blocks are integral to the solar chimneys. Architect: Feilden Clegg; Photo: Colt International*

## BENEFITS OF HIGH-PERFORMANCE SUSTAINABLE DESIGN

There are sustainable design benefits for the building owner, the building occupant, the community where the facility is built, and for society as a whole.

*Reduced operating expenditures for energy:* Employing more energy-efficient systems and elements will result in operating savings from decreased energy consumption.

*Reduced operation and maintenance costs:* By using more durable low-maintenance materials and systems, facility operating costs will be lowered through savings in labor, waste handling, and streamlining of maintenance procedures.

*Personnel expenditure reductions:* Healthy, comfortable work environments can lead to less absenteeism and increased employee retention. There are also potential improvements in performance and productivity.

*Reduced costs for managing change:* By designing structures and systems that are flexible and adaptable to other uses, costs of periodic reorganization and renovation decline.

*Healthy, comfortable work environments:* Indoor air quality and other human factors issues such as daylight and view will improve to ensure occupant comfort as well as productivity.

*Positive effect on surrounding community:* By preserving ecosystems and minimizing impact on the land, sustainable buildings enhance their communities. Siting of buildings also can support sustainable community transportation and land use patterns.

*Reduced municipal operating expenditures:* More sustainably designed buildings decrease the amount of waste going to landfills during construction and operation. They also reduce loads on water and wastewater treatment facilities.

*Reduced infrastructure costs:* More sustainably designed buildings ease the demand for new power plants, expanded water and sewer systems, and more wastewater treatment capacity.

*Environmental benefits:* Sustainable designs have a reduced impact on global warming, as well as soil, air, and water degradation. They also promote the preservation and responsible use of valued ecosystems, like forests.

*Emissions reduction/clean air:* Cleaner air results from decreased consumption of fossil fuels, with lower emissions of carbon dioxide, sulfur dioxide, oxides of nitrogen, mercury, and particulates.

*National security:* By reducing energy use, we ease our dependency on foreign oil.

Strategies to achieve these benefits generally fall into the categories of site selection and design, water, energy, indoor environment, and material and resource conservation. Windows clearly play a major role in achieving energy and indoor environment goals, and also impact material resource issues.

## THE BUILDING LIFE CYCLE PROCESS

Although window systems are important in terms of appearance, interior environment, energy, environmental impacts, and life cycle costs, they are seldom designed holistically with all these issues in mind. For instance, architect and building owner usually pay considerable attention to exterior design features, the window seen as an aesthetic element. Because of their impact on thermal loads, mechanical engineers focus on selecting windows to control solar heat gains, meet energy codes, and downsize equipment. Balancing these different interests and criteria in an integrated manner is a tremendous challenge.

The entire design team and owner are typically involved in managing the project's initial costs, with "cost" only considered in a limited manner. Including life cycle costs in the design process that account for operating and maintenance costs, as well as environmental impacts, is an emerging trend, but is not universally practiced. In addition, the quality of the interior environment as it affects the health, productivity, and well-being of occupants is only beginning to be understood. In fact, the occupants of the building are often left out of the design process altogether.

Achieving high-performance, sustainable design is not just a matter of employing the right strategies. It requires a different design and construction process; the entire life cycle of the building must be considered. Some of the most important concepts are described below:

### Predesign

*Work as a team from the beginning.* Educate the entire team on high-performance design and examine good precedents. Conduct a workshop that involves the architect, engineers, owner, facility managers, occupants, and contractor, if available at this stage.

*Set sustainable design goals early.* Establishing energy use targets has an important impact on window design and selection. Goals must also be determined for the interior environmental quality of the building. This includes whether future occupants desire outside views, daylight, operating windows, and individualized control over their environment. Requirements for glare control and thermal comfort must also be set. Of course, different criteria will be set for different types of spaces. Sustainable design goals such as reducing VOCs for better indoor air quality and using materials with low environmental impacts may also affect the choice of window and frame materials.

*Document design intent.* As personnel and job responsibilities shift throughout the building life cycle, documentation is critical. Ensure that design intentions are documented from the early stages of design through construction and occupancy.

### Design

*Use an integrated design approach.* A critical aspect of sustainable design is that it is not simply a checklist of disconnected strategies or actions. It mirrors ecological systems in that all parts are interconnected and interdependent at many levels. For example, an im-

*Figure 1-5. Building life cycle*

*Introduction to Windows in High-performance Buildings*

proved window system results in greater thermal comfort and reduced energy use for heating and cooling. The same window system can also be optimized to provide daylighting which allows for less electric lighting, further reducing energy use. In addition, the improved window design can contribute to downsizing the mechanical system.

*Use computer simulation tools.* During schematic design and design development it is essential to calculate performance and compare alternatives. In the computer analysis, include the impact on energy use, peak loads, daylight, glare, and thermal comfort. Use life cycle analysis to make choices.

*Design to optimize for multiple objectives.* In the design development phase, consider the impact of window choice on energy, peak load, daylight, glare, view, and thermal comfort. Design the facade as an integrated system that may include shading devices, light shelves, and other components.

*Meet all technical requirements.* Select and detail windows to address structural, thermal, moisture, acoustical, safety, and durability issues. Design for low maintenance, easy access, and constructability.

*Specify NFRC certified windows.* Use the National Fenestration Rating Council procedures and specifications to ensure energy-efficient window properties based on the whole window (combined frame and glazing).

*Design for flexibility and adaptability.* Recognize that the structural shell and envelope of a building have a longer life than the mechanical systems, lights, and furnishings. For example, creating spaces with high ceilings that can maximize daylight penetration and choosing windows that transmit daylight are more likely to accommodate future uses and new technologies.

*Think of the future.* Design and select windows to optimize for future technologies. For example, lighting control systems that dim fixtures when there is sufficient daylight can save considerable energy, but are not always implemented because of cost or reliability concerns. Even though such systems may not be installed initially, they are likely to be installed at some point in the building life as costs and technologies improve. Therefore, selecting a window with a higher daylight transmission and zoning lighting circuits according to distance from the window would optimize for this likely future condition.

*Figure 1-6. Street scene of Potsdamer Platz in Berlin, with Debis Tower in background. Architect: Renzo Piano Building Workshop; Photo: Vincent Mosh*

## Construction

*Ensure careful construction and installation.* Build to ensure that all critical performance aspects of windows and related systems can be fully realized.

*Commission all systems.* Commission to verify operation of critical window-related systems including daylight sensors and controls, if installed.

*Verify design intent.* Ensure that design intentions are properly executed in all aspects of construction.

## Occupancy

*Monitor energy performance.* Continuously monitor energy performance and operate for continuous improvement.

*Conduct post occupancy evaluations.* Determine occupant satisfaction with ventilation, glare, thermal comfort, daylight, lighting, acoustics, and individual control. Feed results back to modify existing spaces and feed forward to impact the design of new facilities.

*Clean and maintain.* Performance suffers if the building systems and elements are not properly cared for.

*Complete the life cycle.* Reuse and recycle components and materials at the end of their useful life.


# Emerging Window Technologies, Systems, and Design Strategies

Simultaneously meeting the goals of energy efficiency while providing daylight, views, and other amenities of windows has traditionally been a problem. Uncoated single-pane windows are a great source of unwanted heat loss and heat gain, while dark tints and reflective coatings reduce light and view. In the last 20 years, the energy-efficient properties of windows have been improved by innovations in glass coatings, gas fills, low-conductance spacers and frames, and suspended plastic films that result in multiple glazing layers. Most notable in optimizing energy and indoor environmental concerns are spectrally selective low-E coatings that keep out most of the solar heat gain but transmit most of the daylight.

These improvements to standard windows are only one aspect of developments that have the promise of transforming windows into dynamically changing elements that provide a filter for light, heat, air, view, and sound. New technologies such as motorized shading systems and electrochromic glazing make it possible for windows to optimize energy use and interior environmental conditions. Building-integrated photovoltaic systems (often part of the glazing system) can make building facades a net energy producer as well.

Recently, there has been a wave of innovation by architects and manufacturers exploring advanced facade systems. These systems are actively designed to manage energy flows, view, and comfort. One type of advanced facade of current interest is the double-envelope system, which utilizes two walls of glazing separated by a ventilated cavity. Automated shading systems, daylight redirection devices, and methods of natural ventilation are often included in these complex systems.

Windows and facades are at the cutting edge of new technologies in buildings. With their importance to both the building appearance and interior environment, windows and facades are likely to play a central role in defining future architectural design. Even the best windows used routinely today still impose energy and environmental impacts on buildings. Emerging and future technologies could reduce energy impacts to "zero" and ultimately provide energy benefits to buildings in the form of daylight, passive solar gains, or electricity from photovoltaics.

# Scope and Organization

The term *commercial building* is used in this book to refer to any nonresidential structure. This includes offices, hotels, restaurants, retail and entertainment facilities, as well as institutional uses such as museums, libraries, schools, and hospitals. Also included are laboratory, manufacturing, and warehouse facilities. Much of the general information about window systems and their performance applies to all building types, however there are obvious differences between these so-called *commercial* functions in terms of their specific energy performance patterns, occupancy requirements, and the desired number and appearance of windows.

Throughout most of this book, the impact of window design decisions will be shown mainly for office buildings, which represent 50 percent of all nonresidential building floor area in the United States. The impact of window design decisions is shown in Chapter 7 for school classrooms. While many of the general trends will be similar for offices and other building uses, it is always important to use computer tools to analyze the window design impacts for a specific building type, climate, and configuration.

Energy use and other performance measures are typically determined for new construction examples in the book. Improving or replacing windows in the existing commercial building stock is also extremely important to reduce national energy consumption and its environmental consequences. General information on window systems and performance applies to both new and existing buildings. The differences lie in the specific impact on energy performance and the costs of installing the windows. Approaches such as applying high-performance films to existing windows are likely to be more cost effective than complete window replacement, but must be examined in a total life cycle context.

The term *window system* in this book refers to all three major types used in commercial buildings. These are:

1. Manufactured window units placed into rough openings in a building facade. These are built in a factory and include typical aluminum and steel frame commercial units as well as wood, vinyl, fiberglass, and other composite frame materials associated with small commercial and residential construction.

2. Curtain walls that form the entire building skin and are typically hung from the structural floors. These are commonly constructed on site and are made up of vision glass panels serving normal window functions and opaque spandrel panels set into a structural frame. Increasingly, preassembled curtain wall units are delivered to the job site.

3. Storefront windows found on the lower levels of buildings. Also assembled on site, these are intended to provide maximum view into and out of the building and often include glazed entrance doors. Unlike curtain walls, which by-pass floor levels, storefront windows are typically inset between floors.

The greatest differences between manufactured window units and curtain walls, other than the method of assembly, are the structure and appearance. Energy and other performance aspects of the vision glass sections can be similar. Storefront glazing differs in that high transparency and low reflectivity are often desired qualities. In many cases storefront glazing is shaded under canopies or arcade type roofs.

The term *facade system* is used in this book to refer to all of the elements that are part of a facade. For example, external and internal shading devices and daylight redirecting elements such as light shelves are all considered parts of the facade system. Advanced facade systems may have multiple layers of glazings and shading elements and may also incorporate ventilated cavities. While the focus of this book is on systems typically installed in vertical walls, many of the principles are generally relevant to skylights and sloped glazings in commercial buildings.

The book is organized to guide the reader through general design issues and technologies to their application in specific settings. Chapter 2 addresses three sets of design issues related to windows— energy, human factors, and technical concerns. Chapter 3 provides an introduction to existing and emerging window technologies and facade systems. Chapter 4 describes a decision-making process for design and selection of windows. Knowledge of issues, technologies, and design approaches is useful, but the actual impact of these elements on a building with a specific set of conditions reveals the relative importance and interaction of all these factors. Chapters 5 and 6 methodically present the impact of many design variables (orientation, window area, shading devices, lighting controls, and glazing type) on several performance indicators (energy use, peak loads, daylight, view, glare control, and thermal comfort) for office spaces in typical cold and hot U.S. climates (represented by Chicago and Houston). This information is presented in a format designed to aid the decision-making process. Chapter 7 provides similar information for schools. Finally, in Chapter 8, presents case studies of recent innovative examples of window and facade design in commercial buildings.

# CHAPTER 2

# Basic Issues in Window Selection and Design

## Introduction

Typically, aesthetics and costs are major factors in making design decisions about windows in commercial buildings. The need to reduce unwanted heat loss and heat gain has been the major energy-related issue in window design and selection. In addition, window design is influenced by various functional requirements like air- and water-tightness, as well as structural and acoustical performance. More recently, new driving forces have emerged in commercial window design and selection: human factors, environmental impact, and a more holistic understanding of building energy use. There is a need for an integrated approach to window design and selection that takes into account this expanded set of issues.

The purpose of this chapter is to describe certain key issues involved in window design and selection. The chapter is divided into three sections: energy-related issues, human factors issues, and technical issues. Aesthetics of window and facade design are not explicitly discussed here, but are left to the judgment of the architect and owner. Specific window system costs (initial, operating, and maintenance) are beyond the scope of this book and must be addressed on a case by case basis to be accurate, however energy use information is provided that indicates relative operating cost. Chapter 3 will examine how these properties apply to specific window materials and assemblies. Chapters 4–7 integrates this information into a decision making process.

*Figure 2-1. Minneapolis Community and Technical College, Wheelock Whitney Library. Architect: Cuningham Group; Photo: Peter Kerze*

# Energy-related Issues

The book's main purpose is to guide architects and engineers toward making more energy-efficient choices about windows in commercial buildings. One reason this is not a simple task is the broad range of building types, functions, and sizes included in the term *commercial buildings*. These variables fundamentally impact energy use patterns of the building and the role windows play within it. This book focuses on one of the main building types—office buildings. Fortunately, the energy impacts of window decisions can be examined in smaller building modules (called zones), and then applied to a variety of building sizes and configurations. This section of the chapter includes the energy-related properties of windows, their effect on the design and performance of commercial buildings, and the effect of energy codes on window design.

## ENERGY-RELATED PROPERTIES OF WINDOWS

This section serves as an introduction to the energy performance of window units. First, there is a brief introduction to the basic mechanisms of heat transfer and the key properties of glazing that affect energy performance: transmittance, reflectance, absorptance, and emittance. Then the commonly used energy-related properties of windows are identified—insulating value (U-factor), ability to control heat gain from solar radiation (SHGC and SC), visible light transmittance (VT), and ability to control air leakage.

### Heat Transfer Mechanisms and Glazing Properties Related to Radiant Energy Transfer

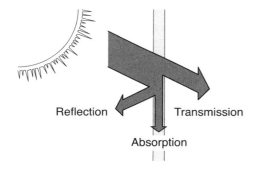

*Figure 2-2. Solar radiation through a glazing material is either reflected, transmitted or absorbed*

Most window and facade assemblies consist of glazing and frame components. Glazing may be a single pane of glass (or plastic) or multiple panes with air spaces in between. These multiple layer units, referred to as insulating glazing units (IGU), include spacers around the edge and sometimes low-conductance gases in the spaces between glazings. Coatings and tints affect the performance of the glazing. The IGU is placed within a frame of aluminum, steel, wood, plastic, or some hybrid or composite material. Some curtain wall systems using structural sealants and other special fittings have no exterior frame.

Heat flows through a window assembly in three ways: conduction, convection, and radiation. Conduction is heat traveling through a solid, liquid or gas. Convection is the transfer of heat by the movement of gases or liquids, like warm air rising from a candle flame. Radiation is the movement of energy through space without relying on conduction through the air or by movement of the air, the way you feel the heat of a fire.

When there is a temperature difference across an object (i.e., when a window separates a cold outdoors from a warm interior or a hot outside from a conditioned interior space), heat transfer will occur via these three physical mechanisms: conduction through glass and solid frame materials, convection/conduction through air spaces, and longwave radiation between glass surfaces on either side of an air gap. This temperature-driven heat transfer is quantified by the term U-factor and is discussed in the section on insulating value.

There are two distinct types of radiation or radiation heat transfer:

- Long-wave radiation heat transfer refers to radiant heat transfer between objects at room or outdoor environmental temperatures. These temperatures emit radiation in the range of 3–50 microns.

- Short-wave radiation heat transfer refers to radiation from the sun (which is at a temperature of 6000K) and occurs in the 0.3–2.5 micron range. This range includes the ultraviolet, visible, and solar-infrared radiation (Figure 2-3).

Even though the physical process is the same, there is no overlap between these two wavelength ranges. Coatings that control the passage of long wave or solar radiation in these ranges, through transmission and/or reflection, can contribute significantly to energy savings and have been the subject of significant innovations in recent years. Glazing types vary in their transparency to different parts of the visible spectrum. For example, a glass that appears tinted green as you look through it toward the outdoors transmits more sunlight from the green portion of the visible spectrum and absorbs or reflects more of the other colors. Similarly, a bronze-tinted glass absorbs or reflects the blues and greens and transmits the warmer colors. Neutral gray tints absorb or reflect most colors equally.

This same principle applies outside the visible spectrum. Most glass is partially transparent to at least some ultraviolet radiation, while plastics are commonly more opaque to ultraviolet. Glass is opaque to long-wave infrared radiation but generally transparent to solar-infrared radiation. Strategic utilization of these variations has

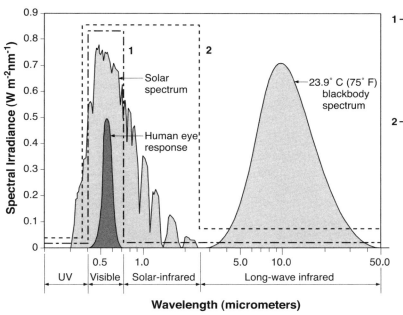

1 — - — Idealized transmittance of a glazing with a low-E coating designed for low solar heat gain. Visible light is transmitted and solar-infrared radiation is reflected. Long-wave infrared radiation is reflected back into the interior. This approach is suitable for commercial buildings in almost all climates.

2 - - - - Idealized transmittance of a glazing with a low-E coating designed for high solar heat gain. Visible light and solar-infrared radiation are transmitted. Long-wave infrared radiation is reflected back into the interior. This approach is more commonly used for residential windows in cold climates.

Note: As shown by the solar spectrum in the figure, sunlight is composed of electromagnetic radiation of many wavelengths, ranging from short-wave invisible ultraviolet to the visible spectrum to the longer, invisible solar-infrared waves.

*Figure 2-3. Ideal spectral transmittance for glazings in different climates (Source: McCluney, 1996)*

made for some high-performance glazing products. The four basic properties of glazing that affect radiant energy transfer—transmittance, reflectance, absorptance, and emittance—are described below.

## Transmittance

Transmittance refers to the percentage of radiation that can pass through glazing. Transmittance can be defined for different types of light or energy, e.g., *visible transmittance, UV transmittance,* or *total solar energy transmittance.*

Transmission of visible light determines the effectiveness of a type of glass in providing daylight and a clear view through the window. For example, tinted glass has a lower visible transmittance than clear glass. While the human eye is sensitive to light at wavelengths from about 0.4 to 0.7 microns, its peak sensitivity is at 0.55, with lower sensitivity at the red and blue ends of the spectrum. This is referred to as the photopic sensitivity of the eye.

More than half of the sun's energy is invisible to the eye. Most reaches us as near-infrared with a few percent in the ultraviolet (UV) spectrum. Thus, *total solar energy transmittance* describes how the glazing responds to a much broader part of the spectrum and is more useful in characterizing the quantity of total solar energy transmitted by the glazing.

With the recent advances in glazing technology, manufacturers can control how glazing materials behave in these different areas of the spectrum. The basic properties of the substrate material (glass or plastic) can be altered, and coatings can be added to the surfaces of the substrates. For example, a window optimized for daylighting and for reducing overall solar heat gains should transmit an adequate amount of light in the visible portion of the spectrum, while excluding unnecessary heat gain from the near-infrared part of the electro-magnetic spectrum.

*Figure 2-4. Sunlight transmitted and reflected by ¼-inch clear glass as a function of the incident angle*

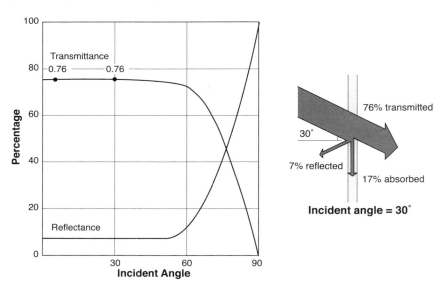

## Reflectance

Just as some light reflects off of the surface of water, some light will always be reflected at every glass surface. A specular reflection from a smooth glass surface is a mirrorlike reflection similar to the image of yourself you see reflected in a store window. The natural reflectivity of glass is dependent on the type of glazing material, the quality of the glass surface, the presence of coatings, and the angle of incidence of the light. Today, virtually all glass manufactured in the United States is float glass, which reflects 4 percent of visible light at each glass-air interface or 8 percent total for a single pane of clear, uncoated glass. The sharper the angle at which the light strikes, however, the more the light is reflected rather than transmitted or absorbed (Figure 2-4). Even clear glass reflects 50 percent or more of the sunlight striking it at incident angles greater than about 80 degrees. (The incident angle is formed with respect to a line perpendicular to the glass surface.)

The reflectivity of various glass types becomes especially apparent during low light conditions. The surface on the brighter side acts like a mirror because the amount of light passing through the window from the darker side is less than the amount of light being reflected from the lighter side. This effect can be noticed from the outside during the day and from the inside during the night. For special applications when these surface reflections are undesirable (i.e., viewing merchandise through a store window on a bright day), special coatings can virtually eliminate this reflective effect.

Most common coatings reflect in all regions of the spectrum. However, in the past twenty years, researchers have learned a great deal about the design of coatings that can be applied to glass and plastic to preferentially reflect only selected wavelengths of radiant energy. Varying the reflectance of far-infrared and near-infrared energy has formed the basis for high-performance low-E coatings (see Chapter 3).

## Absorptance

Energy that is not transmitted through the glass or reflected off its surfaces is absorbed. Once glass has absorbed any radiant energy, the energy is transformed into heat, raising the glass temperature.

Typical ¼-inch clear glass absorbs only about 7 percent of sunlight at a normal angle of incidence (also a 30-degree angle of incidence, as shown in Figure 2-4). The absorptance of glass is increased by glass additives that absorb solar energy. If they absorb visible light, the glass appears dark. If they absorb ultraviolet radiation or near-infrared, there will be little or no change in visual appearance. Clear glass absorbs very little visible light, while dark-tinted glass absorbs a considerable amount (Figure 2-5). The absorbed energy is converted into heat, warming the glass. Thus, when "heat-absorbing" glass is in the sun, it feels much hotter to the touch than clear glass. Tints are generally gray, bronze, or blue-green and were traditionally used to lower the solar heat gain coefficient and to control glare. Since they block some of the sun's energy, they reduce the cooling load placed on the building and its air-conditioning equipment. The effectiveness of heat-absorbing single glazing is significantly reduced if cool, conditioned air flows across the glass. Absorption is not the most efficient way to reduce cooling loads, as discussed later.

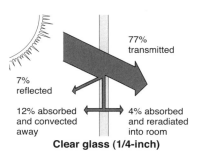

**Clear glass (1/4-inch)**

77% transmitted
7% reflected
12% absorbed and convected away
4% absorbed and reradiated into room

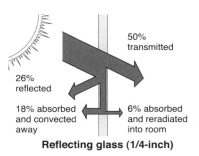

**Reflecting glass (1/4-inch)**

50% transmitted
26% reflected
18% absorbed and convected away
6% absorbed and reradiated into room

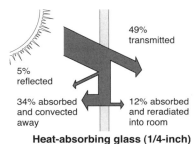

**Heat-absorbing glass (1/4-inch)**

49% transmitted
5% reflected
34% absorbed and convected away
12% absorbed and reradiated into room

*Figure 2-5. Solar energy transmission through three types of glass under standard ASHRAE summer conditions*

All glass and most plastics, however, are generally very absorptive of long-wave infrared energy. This property is best illustrated in the use of clear glass for greenhouses, where it allows the transmission of intense solar energy but blocks the retransmission of the low-temperature heat energy generated inside the greenhouse and radiated back to the glass.

*Emittance*

When solar energy is absorbed by glass, it is either convected away by moving air or reradiated by the glass surface. This ability of a material to radiate energy is called its *emissivity*. Window glass, along with all other objects, typically emit, or radiate, heat in the form of long-wave far-infrared energy. The wavelength of the long-wave far-infrared energy varies with the temperature of the surface. This emission of radiant heat is one of the important heat transfer pathways for a window. Thus, reducing the window's emission of heat can greatly improve its insulating properties.

Standard clear glass has an emittance of 0.84 over the long-wave infrared portion of the spectrum, meaning that it emits 84 percent of the energy possible for an object at room temperature. It also means that for long-wave radiation striking the surface of the glass, 84 percent is absorbed and only 16 percent is reflected. By comparison, low-E glass coatings have an emittance as low as 0.04. This glazing would emit only 4 percent of the energy possible at its temperature, and thus reflect 96 percent of the incident long-wave infrared radiation.

## DETERMINING ENERGY-RELATED PROPERTIES OF WINDOWS

There are four properties of windows that are the basis for quantifying energy performance:

- **U-factor.** When there is a temperature difference between inside and outside, heat is lost or gained through the window frame and glazing by the combined effects of conduction, convection, and long-wave radiation. The U-factor of a window assembly represents its overall heat transfer rate or insulating value.

- **Solar Heat Gain Coefficient.** Regardless of outside temperature, heat can be gained through windows by direct or indirect solar radiation. The ability to control this heat gain through windows is characterized in terms of the solar heat gain coefficient (SHGC) or shading coefficient (SC) of the window.

- **Visible Transmittance.** Visible transmittance (VT), also referred to as visible light transmittance (VLT), is an optical property that indicates the amount of visible light transmitted through the glass. It affects energy by providing daylight that creates the opportunity to reduce electric lighting and its associated cooling loads.

- **Air Leakage.** Heat loss and gain also occur by air leakage through cracks around sashes and frames of the window assembly. This effect is often quantified in terms of the amount of air (cubic feet or cubic meters per minute) passing through a unit area of window (square foot or square meter) under given pressure conditions.

These four concepts—as well as Light-to-Solar-Gain ratio, a ratio of VT/SHGC—have been standardized within the glazing industry, and allow accurate comparison of windows.

## Insulating Value (U-factor)

For windows, a principle energy concern is their ability to control heat loss. Heat flows from warmer to cooler bodies, thus from the inside face of a window to the outside in winter, reversing direction in summer. Overall heat flow from the warmer to cooler side of a window unit is a complex interaction of all three basic heat transfer mechanisms—conduction, convection, and long-wave radiation (Figure 2-6). A window assembly's capacity to resist this heat transfer is referred to as its *insulating value*.

Conduction occurs directly through glass, and the air cavity within double-glazed IGUs, as well as through a window's spacers and frames. Some frame materials, like wood, have relatively low conduction rates. The higher conduction rates of other materials, like metals, have to be mitigated with discontinuities or thermal breaks in the frame to avoid energy loss.

Convection within a window unit occurs in three places: the interior and exterior glazing surfaces, and within the air cavity between glazing layers. On the interior, a cold interior glazing surface chills the adjacent air. This denser cold air then falls, starting a convection current. People often perceive this air flow as a draft caused by leaky windows, instead of recognizing that the remedy correctly lies with a window that provides a warmer glass surface (Figure 2-6). On the exterior, the air film against the glazing contributes to the window's insulating value. As wind blows (convection), the effectiveness of this air film is diminished, contributing to a higher heat rate loss. Within the air cavity, temperature-induced convection currents facilitate heat transfer. By adjusting the cavity width, adding more cavities, or choosing a gas fill that insulates better than air, windows can be designed to reduce this effect.

All objects emit invisible thermal radiation, with warmer objects emitting more than colder ones. Through radiant exchange, the objects in the room, and especially the people (who are often the warmest objects), radiate their heat to the colder window. People often feel the chill from this radiant heat loss, especially on the exposed skin of their hands and faces, but they attribute the chill to cool room air rather than to a cold window surface. Similarly, if the glass temperature is higher than skin temperature, which occurs when the sun shines on heat-absorbing glass, heat will be radiated from the glass to the body, potentially producing thermal discomfort.

The complex interaction between conduction, convection, and radiation is perhaps best illustrated by the fact that the thermal performance of a roof window or skylight changes according to its mounting angle. Convective exchange on the inner and outer glazing surfaces, as well as that within the air cavity, is affected by this slope.

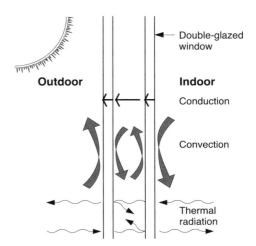

*Figure 2-6. Components of heat transfer through a window that are related to U-factor*

Also, skylights and roof windows oriented toward the cold night sky lose more radiant heat at night than windows viewing warmer objects, such as the ground, adjacent buildings, and vegetation.

*Determining Insulating Value*

The U-factor (also referred to as U-value) is the standard way to quantify overall heat flow. For windows, it expresses the total heat transfer coefficient of the system (in Btu/hr-sf-°F), and includes conductive, convective, and radiative heat transfer. It represents the heat flow per hour (in Btus per hour or watts) through each square foot of window for a 1 degree Fahrenheit temperature difference between the indoor and outdoor air temperature. The insulating value or R-value (resistance to heat transfer) is the reciprocal of the total U-factor (R=1/U). The higher the R-value of a material, the higher the insulating value; the smaller the U-factor, the lower the rate of heat flow.

Given that the thermal properties and the various materials within a window unit, the U-factor is commonly expressed in two ways:

- The U-factor of the total window assembly combines the insulating value of the glazing proper, the edge effects in the IGU, and the window frame and sash.

- The center-of-glass U-factor assumes that heat flows perpendicular to the window plane, without addressing the impact of the frame edge effects and material.

*Figure 2-7. U-factors for typical glazings and windows*

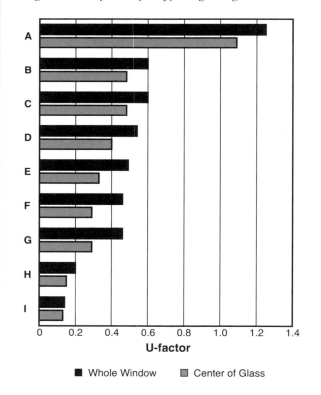

| Whole Window | Center of Glass |

**Window A**
single glazing
clear
U = 1.25
SHGC = 0.72
VT = 0.71

**Window B**
double glazing
clear
U = 0.60
SHGC = 0.60
VT = 0.63

**Window C**
double glazing
bronze tint
U = 0.60
SHGC = 0.42
VT = 0.38

**Window D**
double glazing
reflective coating
U = 0.54
SHGC = 0.17
VT = 0.10

**Window E**
double glazing
low-E, bronze tint
U = 0.49
SHGC = 0.39
VT = 0.36

**Window F**
double glazing
spec. selective low-E tint
U = 0.46
SHGC = 0.27
VT = 0.43

**Window G**
double glazing
spec. selective low-E clear
U = 0.46
SHGC = 0.34
VT = 0.57

**Window H**
triple glazing
1 low-E layer, clear
U = 0.20
SHGC = 0.22
VT = 0.37

**Window I**
quadruple glazing
2 low-E layers, clear
U = 0.14
SHGC = 0.20
VT = 0.34

U = U-factor in Btu/hr-sf-°F
SHGC = solar heat gain coefficient
VT = visible transmittance
All window properties are for the whole window, Windows A–G have aluminum frames (all but A are thermally broken). Windows H and I have insulated frames. See Appendix A.

The U-factor of the glazing portion of the window unit is affected primarily by the total number of glazing layers, their dimension, the type of gas within their cavity, and the characteristic of coatings on the various glazing surfaces. As windows are complex three-dimensional assemblies, in which materials and cross sections change in a relatively short distance, it is limiting, however, to simply consider glazing. For example, metal spacers at the edge of an IGU have a much higher heat flow than the center of the insulating glass, which causes increased heat loss along the outer edge of the glass.

### Overall U-factor

The relative impact of these "edge effects" becomes more important as the insulating value of the entire assembly increases, and in small units where the ratio of edge to center-of-glass area is high. Since the U-factors vary for the glass, edge-of-glass zone, and frame, it can be misleading to compare the U-factors of windows from different manufacturers if they are not carefully and consistently described. Calculation methods developed by the National Fenestration Rating Council (NFRC) address this concern.

In addition to the thermal properties of window assembly materials, weather conditions, such as interior/exterior temperature differential and wind speed, also impact U-factor. Window manufacturers typically list a winter U-factor for determined under relatively harsh conditions: 15 mph wind, 70 degrees Fahrenheit indoors, 0 degrees Fahrenheit outdoors. A specific set of assumptions and procedures must be followed to calculate the overall U-factor of a window unit using the NFRC method. For instance, the NFRC values are for a standard window size-the actual U-factor of a specific unit varies with size. Originally developed for manufactured window units, new methods are available to determine the U-factor of site-built assemblies.

Figure 2-7 indicates the center-of-glass U-factor and the overall U-factor for several types of window units. Window A has an aluminum frame with no thermal break resulting in a very high frame U-factor in the range of 1.7–2.4. Windows B–G have an aluminum frame with a thermal break. The resulting frame U-factor of 0.8–1.3 is always higher than the relatively low center-of-glass U-factors for double-glazed windows. The frame and center-of-glass U-factors for Windows H and I are closer because of the insulated frames which have U-factors in the 0.2–0.4 range.

The U-factor of a window unit is rated based on a vertical position. A change in mounting angle affects a window's U-factor. The same unit installed on a sloped roof at 20 degrees from horizontal would have a U-factor 10–20 percent higher than in the vertical position (under winter conditions).

### Effect of U-factor on Energy Use

Figure 2-8 illustrates the effect of window U-factor on annual heating energy use in a typical south-facing perimeter zone in Chicago. While heating use increases significantly with U-factor, it is also influenced by solar heat gain coefficient (described in the following section). In general, most heating in nonresidential buildings occurs during unoccupied hours, especially during the morning warm-up period

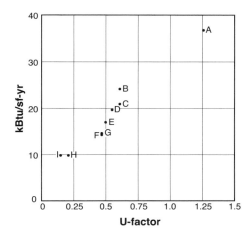

*Figure 2-8. Heating energy use by U-factor for a perimeter zone*

All cases are south-facing with a 0.30 window-to-wall ratio and no shading for an office in Chicago, Illinois. The window-to-wall ratio is calculated by dividing window area (36 sf) by gross exterior wall area (120 sf). Numbers are expressed per sf within a 15-foot-deep perimeter zone. The nine window types indicated here are described throughout the chapter.

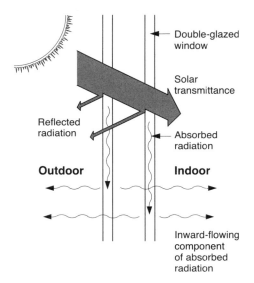

*Figure 2-9. Simplified view of the components of solar heat gain. Heat gain includes the transmitted solar energy and the inward flowing component of absorbed radiation*

**Window A**
single glazing
clear
U = 1.25
SHGC = 0.72
VT = 0.71

**Window B**
double glazing
clear
U = 0.60
SHGC = 0.60
VT = 0.63

**Window C**
double glazing
bronze tint
U = 0.60
SHGC = 0.42
VT = 0.38

**Window D**
double glazing
reflective coating
U = 0.54
SHGC = 0.17
VT = 0.10

**Window E**
double glazing
low-E, bronze tint
U = 0.49
SHGC = 0.39
VT = 0.36

**Window F**
double glazing
spec. selective low-E tint
U = 0.46
SHGC = 0.27
VT = 0.43

**Window G**
double glazing
spec. selective low-E clear
U = 0.46
SHGC = 0.34
VT = 0.57

**Window H**
triple glazing
1 low-E layer, clear
U = 0.20
SHGC = 0.22
VT = 0.37

**Window I**
quadruple glazing
2 low-E layers, clear
U = 0.14
SHGC = 0.20
VT = 0.34

U = U-factor in Btu/hr-sf-∘F
SHGC = solar heat gain coefficient
VT = visible transmittance
All window properties are for the whole window. Windows A–G have aluminum frames (all but A are thermally broken). Windows H and I have insulated frames. See Appendix A.

(5–8 A.M.) before people have arrived and before lights and equipment are turned on. Heating may also occur during occupied hours in all zones in colder climates and in north-facing zones in moderate climates.

## Solar Radiation Control

The second major energy-performance characteristic of windows is the ability to control solar heat gain through the glazing. Solar heat gain through windows is a significant factor in determining the cooling load of many commercial buildings. The origin of solar heat gain is the direct and diffuse radiation coming from the sun and the sky (or reflected from the ground and other surfaces). Some radiation is directly transmitted through the glazing to the building interior, and some may be absorbed in the glazing and indirectly admitted to the inside. Some radiation absorbed by the frame will also contribute to overall window solar heat gain factor. Other thermal (nonsolar) heat transfer effects are included in the U-factor of the window.

### Determining Solar Heat Gain

There are two metrics for quantifying the solar radiation passing through a window: solar heat gain coefficient (SHGC) and shading coefficient (SC). In both cases, the solar heat gain is the combination of directly transmitted radiation and the inward-flowing portion of absorbed radiation (Figure 2-9). However, SHGC and SC have a different basis for comparison.

*Figure 2-10. Solar heat gain characteristics of typical glazings and windows*

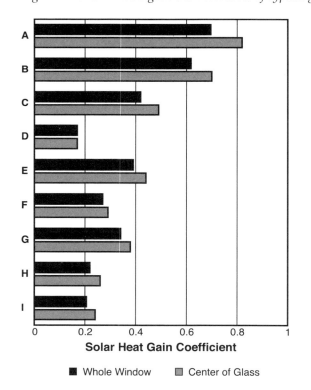

## Shading Coefficient

Until the mid-1990s, the shading coefficient (SC) was the primary term used to characterize the solar control properties of glass. Although replaced by NFRC and ASHRAE with the solar heat gain coefficient (SHGC), it is still referenced in books and product literature, and is expressed as a dimensionless number from 0 to 1—high shading coefficient means high solar gain, while a low shading coefficient means low solar gain.

The SC was originally developed as a single number that could be used to compare glazing solar control under a wide range of conditions. Its simplicity, however, is offset by its inaccuracies. For instance, the shading coefficient (SC) is only defined for the glazing portion of the window and does not include frame effects. It represents the ratio of solar heat gain through the system relative to that through ⅛-inch clear glass at normal incidence. The SC has also been used to characterize performance over a wide range of sun positions; however, there is some potential loss in accuracy when applied to sun positions at high angles to the glass

The SC value is strongly influenced by the type of glass selected. The shading coefficient can also include the effects of any integral part of the window system that reduces the flow of solar heat, such as multiple glazing layers, reflective coatings, or blinds between layers of glass.

## Solar Heat Gain Coefficient

Window standards are now moving away from *shading coefficient* to *solar heat gain coefficient* (SHGC), which is defined as that fraction of incident solar radiation that actually enters a building through the window assembly as heat gain. The SHGC is influenced by all the same factors as the SC, but since it can be applied to the entire window assembly, the SHGC is also affected by shading from the frame as well as the ratio of glazing and frame. The solar heat gain coefficient is expressed as a dimensionless number from 0 to 1. A high coefficient signifies high heat gain, while a low coefficient means low heat gain.

For any glazing, the SHGC is always lower than the SC. To perform an approximate conversion from SC to SHGC, multiply the SC value by 0.87. Total window SHGC is used throughout this book except in some case studies where glass is specified using SC. Typical SHGC values for the whole window unit and center of glass are shown in Figure 2-10. Since the frame area has a very low SHGC, the overall window SHGC is lower than the center-of-glass value.

## Energy Effects of SHGC

Figure 2-11 illustrates the effect of solar heat gain coefficient on electricity costs in a typical office perimeter zone in Chicago. Electricity use increases as the SHGC increases when no daylight controls are used. With daylighting controls, there are exceptions. The reflective window with the lowest SHGC does not have the best energy performance because its low VT makes it detrimental to daylighting.

*Figure 2-11. Annual electricity use by SHGC for a perimeter zone*

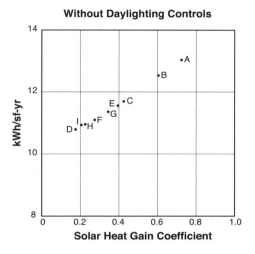

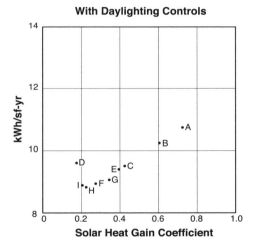

All cases are south-facing with a 0.30 window-to-wall ratio and no shading for an office in Chicago, Illinois. The window-to-wall ratio is calculated by dividing window area (36 sf) by gross exterior wall area (120 sf). Numbers are expressed per sf within a 15-foot-deep perimeter zone. The nine window types indicated here are described throughout the chapter.

## Visible Transmittance

Visible transmittance (VT), also referred to as visible light transmittance (VLT), is the amount of light in the visible portion of the spectrum that passes through a glazing material. A higher VT means there is more daylight in a space which, if designed properly, can offset electric lighting and its associated cooling loads. Visible transmittance of glazing ranges from above 90 percent for uncoated water-white clear glass to less than 10 percent for highly reflective coatings on tinted glass

Visible transmittance is influenced by the glazing type, the number of panes, and any glass coatings. These effects are discussed in more detail in Chapter 3 in conjunction with a review of various glazing and coating technologies. Typical visible transmittance values for the whole window unit and center of glass are shown in Figure 2-12. VT values for the whole window are always less than center-of-glass values since the VT of the frame is zero.

## Light-to-Solar-Gain Ratio

In the past, windows that reduced solar gain (with tints and coatings) also reduced visible transmittance. However, new high-performance tinted glass and low-solar-gain low-E coatings have made it possible to reduce solar heat gain with little reduction in visible transmittance. Because the concept of separating solar gain control and light control is so important, measures have been developed to reflect this. The term *luminous efficacy* ($k_e$), which is VT/SC, was first developed. Since

**Window A**
single glazing
clear
U = 1.25
SHGC = 0.72
VT = 0.71

**Window B**
double glazing
clear
U = 0.60
SHGC = 0.60
VT = 0.63

**Window C**
double glazing
bronze tint
U = 0.60
SHGC = 0.42
VT = 0.38

**Window D**
double glazing
reflective coating
U = 0.54
SHGC = 0.17
VT = 0.10

**Window E**
double glazing
low-E, bronze tint
U = 0.49
SHGC = 0.39
VT = 0.36

**Window F**
double glazing
spec. selective low-E tint
U = 0.46
SHGC = 0.27
VT = 0.43

**Window G**
double glazing
spec. selective low-E clear
U = 0.46
SHGC = 0.34
VT = 0.57

**Window H**
triple glazing
1 low-E layer, clear
U = 0.20
SHGC = 0.22
VT = 0.37

**Window I**
quadruple glazing
2 low-E layers, clear
U = 0.14
SHGC = 0.20
VT = 0.34

U = U-factor in Btu/hr-sf-°F
SHGC = solar heat gain coefficient
VT = visible transmittance
All window properties are for the whole window, Windows A–G have aluminum frames (all but A are thermally broken). Windows H and I have insulated frames. See Appendix A.

*Figure 2-12. Visible transmittance characteristics of typical glazings and windows*

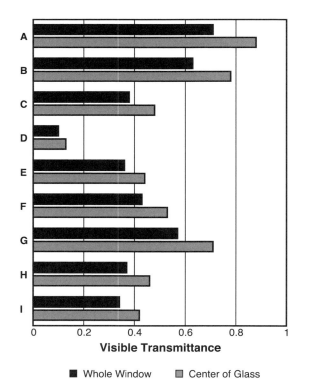

**Visible Transmittance**

■ Whole Window     ▨ Center of Glass

*Basic Issues in Window Selection and Design*

SC is being replaced by SHGC, the term *light-to-solar-gain ratio* (LSG) is now referred to in ASHRAE publications. LSG values for typical windows are shown in Figure 2-13.

The LSG ratio is defined as a ratio between visible transmittance (VT) and solar heat gain coefficient (SHGC). For example, looking at whole window properties, a double-glazed unit with clear glass (Window B) has a visible transmittance (VT) of 0.63 and a solar heat gain coefficient (SHGC) of 0.62, so the LSG is VT/SHGC = 1.02. Bronze-tinted glass in a double-glazed unit (Window C) has a visible transmittance of 0.38 and a solar heat gain coefficient of 0.42, which results in an LSG ratio of 0.90. This illustrates that while the bronze tint lowers the SHGC, it lowers the VT even more compared to clear glass. The double-glazed unit with a high-performance tint (Window F) has a relatively high VT of 0.43 but a lower SHGC of 0.27, resulting in an LSG of 1.59—significantly better than the bronze tint. A clear double-glazed unit with a low-solar-gain low-E coating (Window G) reduces the SHGC significantly, to 0.34, but retains a relatively high VT of 0.57, producing an LSG ratio of 1.87—far superior to those for clear or tinted glass.

Figure 2-14 shows the SHGC and VT properties for typical glazings used in this book in graph format. Windows F, G, H, and I perform best with LSG ratios higher than one. Window D has the lowest LSG ratio. The light-to-solar gain ratio is an indicator of performance, but does not directly correlate with actual energy use. As will be demonstrated in Chapters 5 and 6, optimal energy performance is derived from a complex set of interacting window properties and design conditions.

*Figure 2-14. SHGC and VT for common glazing types*

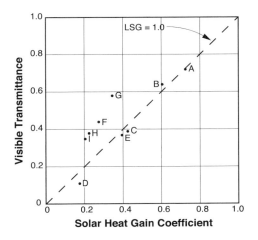

*Figure 2-13. Light-to-solar-gain ratio of typical glazings and windows*

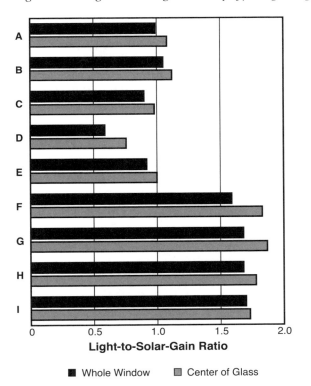

*Figure 2-15. Summary of properties of typical windows*
See Appendix A for further descriptions. Air leakage is not shown. It is assumed to be the same for all fixed windows.

| Window | Number of Glazings | Frame | U-factor | | SHGC | | VT | | LSG | |
|---|---|---|---|---|---|---|---|---|---|---|
| | | | Overall | COG | Overall | COG | Overall | COG | Overall | COG |
| A  Clear | 1 | Aluminum | 1.25 | 1.09 | 0.72 | 0.82 | 0.71 | 0.88 | 0.99 | 1.08 |
| B  Clear | 2 | Alum-TB | 0.60 | 0.48 | 0.60 | 0.70 | 0.63 | 0.78 | 1.05 | 1.12 |
| C  Bronze tint | 2 | Alum-TB | 0.60 | 0.48 | 0.42 | 0.49 | 0.38 | 0.48 | 0.90 | 0.98 |
| D  Reflective | 2 | Alum-TB | 0.54 | 0.40 | 0.17 | 0.17 | 0.10 | 0.13 | 0.59 | 0.76 |
| E  Low-E bronze tint | 2 | Alum-TB | 0.49 | 0.33 | 0.39 | 0.44 | 0.36 | 0.44 | 0.92 | 1.01 |
| F  Selective low-E tint | 2 | Alum-TB | 0.46 | 0.29 | 0.27 | 0.29 | 0.43 | 0.53 | 1.59 | 1.83 |
| G  Clear with selective low-E | 2 | Alum-TB | 0.46 | 0.29 | 0.34 | 0.38 | 0.57 | 0.71 | 1.68 | 1.87 |
| H  Clear with 1 low-E layer | 3 | Insulated | 0.20 | 0.15 | 0.22 | 0.26 | 0.37 | 0.46 | 1.68 | 1.78 |
| I  Clear with 2 low-E layers | 4 | Insulated | 0.14 | 0.13 | 0.20 | 0.24 | 0.34 | 0.42 | 1.70 | 1.73 |

## Air Leakage (Infiltration)

Whenever there is a pressure difference between the inside and outside (driven by wind or temperature difference), air will flow through cracks between window assembly components. The air leakage properties of window systems contribute to the overall building air infiltration. Infiltration leads to increased heating or cooling loads when the outdoor air entering the building needs to be heated or cooled. Air leakage also contributes to summer cooling loads by raising the interior humidity level. Operable windows can be responsible for air leakage between sash and frame elements as well as at the window/wall joint. Tight sealing and weatherstripping of windows, sashes, and frames is of paramount importance in controlling air leakage.

The use of fixed windows helps to reduce air leakage because these windows are easier to seal and keep tight. Operable windows, which are also more susceptible to air leakage, are not necessary for ventilation in most commercial buildings but are desired by occupants for control. Operable window units with low air-leakage rates feature mechanical closures that positively clamp the window shut against the wind. For this reason, compression-seal windows such as awning, hopper, and casement designs are generally more effectively weatherstripped than are sliding-seal windows. Sliding windows rely on wiper-type weatherstripping, which is more subject to wear over time.

The level of infiltration depends upon local climate conditions, particularly wind conditions and microclimates surrounding the building. In reality, infiltration varies widely with wind-driven and temperature-driven pressure changes. Cracks and air spaces left in the window assembly can also account for considerable infiltration. Insulating and sealing these areas during construction can be very important in controlling air leakage. A proper installation ensures that the main air barrier of the wall construction is effectively sealed to the window or skylight assembly so that continuity of the air barrier is maintained.

## OVERVIEW OF ENERGY USE IN BUILDINGS

### The Concept of Zones

All commercial buildings are divided into thermal zones, which represent areas of the building served by different heating, cooling, and ventilating systems. There are also lighting control zones, which may not correspond to mechanical system zones (see the following section on lighting controls). A mechanical system zone may operate like a separate building, receiving heating, cooling, and ventilation from either its own packaged unit or a central system as needed.

The reason for dividing a building into zones is that different spaces have different temperature and outside air requirements or different operating schedules, and therefore require separate control. For example, a highly ventilated auditorium and a storage room with almost no ventilation would require separate zones. Separate zones are also needed for a north-facing space which may require heat in winter at the same time a south-facing space requires none because it is heated by the sun. Similarly, an interior zone with no windows may require cooling at the same time a perimeter zone with windows requires heating.

Some buildings, such as a small school with long narrow wings of classrooms, may have mostly perimeter zones, while others, such as a massive office block, may only have a small percentage of spaces on the perimeter (Figure 2-16). The use of a court or atrium in the center of a building creates *interior perimeter zones* that have some of the characteristics of both. If the atrium is large and well daylit, these interior perimeter zones can behave like exterior perimeter zones with respect to light and view. If the atrium is fully conditioned, there may be no heat loss or gain or air movement as there would be through an exterior wall. On the other hand, an atrium may be unconditioned or a semi-conditioned buffer space that behaves more like the outdoors with moderate temperature fluctuations and perhaps fresh air available.

### Energy Use in Commercial Buildings

The main energy end uses in commercial buildings are lighting, space heating, space cooling, equipment (plug loads such as task lighting, computers, copiers, etc.), auxiliary equipment (such as fans and pumps), and domestic hot water. The percentage of total building energy use dedicated to each of these end uses is dependent on the building type, design, and climate (Figure 2-17). Almost all commercial building types have a significant percentage of their total energy use dedicated to electric lighting, typically from 20 percent in hotels or motels up to 55 percent in retail stores.

Space conditioning is typically another dominant energy end use for most commercial building types. The split between cooling versus heating varies with building type. A warehouse and high-rise residential unit with low internal loads from people and equipment will have low cooling and high heating energy use requirements. A large new commercial office building will typically have high cooling and low heating energy use requirements. Small offices, new or old, have almost equal heating and cooling energy use requirements.

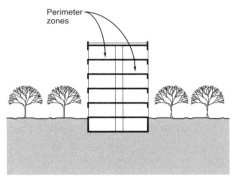

Building containing mostly perimeter zones

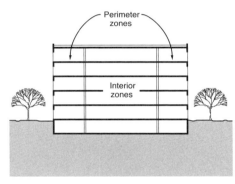

Building containing both perimeter and interior zones

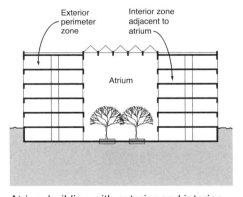

Atrium building with exterior and interior perimeter zones

*Figure 2-16. Building zones*

*Figure 2-17. Total energy end uses for different building types*
Data are given for the entire existing U.S. building stock (old and new buildings throughout the U.S.).
Data have been normalized using a site-source efficiency of 0.33 for electricity end uses and 1.0 for
natural gas end uses. Source: EIA, *A Look at Commercial Buildings in 1995: Characteristics, Energy
Consumption, and Energy Expenditures*, Oct. 1998, Table EU-2, p. 311.

| Principal Building Activity | Heating | Cooling | Lighting | Equipment | Ventilation | Refrig. | Water Heating | Cooking | Other |
|---|---|---|---|---|---|---|---|---|---|
| Education | 26% | 11% | 37% | 3% | 4% | 2% | 14% | 1% | 2% |
| Food sales | 5% | 7% | 19% | 1% | 2% | 61% | 2% | 1% | 1% |
| Food service | 7% | 13% | 25% | 2% | 4% | 22% | 6% | 18% | 3% |
| Health care | 14% | 8% | 30% | 12% | 5% | 4% | 16% | 3% | 9% |
| Lodging | 11% | 12% | 34% | 6% | 2% | 3% | 25% | 3% | 4% |
| Mercantile and service | 21% | 12% | 48% | 6% | 5% | 2% | 3% | 1% | 3% |
| Office | 11% | 13% | 40% | 21% | 7% | 1% | 4% | 1% | 2% |
| Public assembly | 29% | 10% | 35% | 4% | 6% | 3% | 9% | 2% | 2% |
| Public order and safety | 18% | 12% | 31% | 11% | 4% | 0% | 15% | 0% | 8% |
| Religious worship | 43% | 10% | 27% | 2% | 5% | 3% | 6% | 1% | 2% |
| Warehouse and storage | 22% | 4% | 41% | 18% | 1% | 7% | 3% | 0% | 5% |

As mentioned above, perimeter zones are more subject to thermal variation because of direct exposure to the outdoor climate. If the perimeter zone has windows or skylights, thermal variation will be even greater. On the other hand, conditioning core zones typically involves offsetting internal heat loads from people and equipment (lightings, computers, copiers, etc.) with cooling. Core zones often require cooling even in colder climates. Depending on how well the perimeter zone is designed to buffer against the negative effects of solar radiation and outdoor air temperature swings or to take advantage of daylight to offset interior lighting requirements, the energy use intensity (per square foot annual energy use) of perimeter zones can be greater or less than core zones.

A deep floor plan that has a high percentage of core-to-perimeter-zone area is often characterized as *internally load dominated* because the total energy use of the core zone is greater than the total energy use of all perimeter zones due to the greater core floor area. Buildings with a greater percentage of perimeter zone area are referred to as *climate-dominated* or *skin-dominated* buildings. A building may be internal-load dominated during occupied hours and external-load dominated during off hours when people are gone and lights are turned off. It is not uncommon for some commercial buildings to be in a year round cooling mode combined, during occupied hours, with some perimeter heating near windows.

## The Effect of Windows on Heating and Cooling

In a perimeter zone, the window's role is significant. Because windows modulate heat, light, and fresh air, they have an important influence on the energy use and people in the perimeter zone, even if it is a small percentage of the total building floor area. If enclosed rooms such as private offices are on the building perimeter, then these automatically define the perimeter zone by their depth, usually 10 to 20 feet. In larger spaces, such as an open office area, the depth of the perimeter zone can vary. The heating and cooling effects may influence up to 20–30 feet from the window depending on how deeply direct sun penetrates. Typically, however, thermal impacts due to cold or hot window surfaces affect occupants close to the window wall, depending on design. Daylight may also penetrate deeply into the space if there is direct sun, but the daylighting zone for electric lighting control is typically not more than 10–15 feet. The desire of occupants for daylight, view, and fresh air is leading to buildings that are thinner in profile with more perimeter and fewer interior zones.

Window area is one important variable affecting energy performance. Throughout the book, this is referred to in terms of the window-to-wall ratio. If a 36-square-foot window is placed in a 10-foot-wide office with a floor-to-floor height of 12 feet, the window-to-wall ratio (WWR) is 0.30 (36 divided by 120).

As shown in Figures 2-18 and 2-19, a typical perimeter office has heat gains or heat losses through the roof, walls, skylights, and windows. The impact of window choice on annual energy use is illustrated in Figure 2-20 for a 15-foot-deep south-facing perimeter zone in Chicago. Heating energy use diminishes considerably as the window U-factor improves from 1.25 (Window A—clear single glazing) to 0.14 Btu/hr-sf-°F (Window I—quadruple-glazed unit). High-performance windows also reduce cooling energy use. Figure 2-20 illustrates that in Chicago, lower electricity use for cooling corresponds to windows with lower SHGC (both lighting and other equipment use the same amount of electricity in all cases). Although the effect is not shown here, operating windows may reduce mechanical cooling costs by providing natural ventilation during certain periods of the year in some climates.

Figure 2-20 also shows total energy use (combined heating fuel and electricity use). In this analysis, total energy use is determined by multiplying electricity use by three to reflect losses during generation and transmission. This is added to the natural gas energy for heating. This 3-to-1 ratio reflects the greater primary energy required to generate and distribute electricity. While not precise, it also reflects the cost difference between the two energy sources in many places in the United States, making it a rough estimate of the energy cost difference between glazing types. Throughout the book, this method

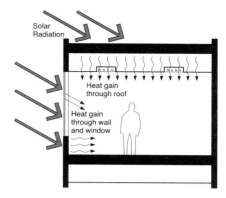

*Figure 2-18. In perimeter zones, heat gain occurs through windows and exterior surfaces*

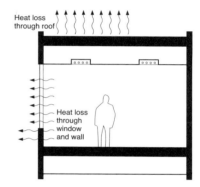

*Figure 2-19. When outside temperatures are colder, heat loss occurs through windows and exterior surfaces of perimeter zones*

*Figure 2-20. Annual energy use comparison for nine window types*
All cases are south-facing with no shading and a window-to-wall ratio of 0.30. Numbers are expressed per square foot within a 15-foot-deep perimeter zone. Results were computed using DOE-2.1E for a typical office building in Chicago, Illinois (Appendix A).

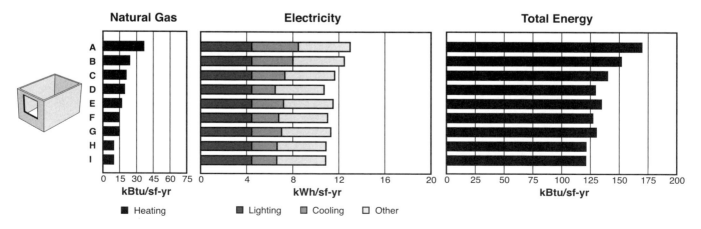

is used to calculate total energy use. Energy costs throughout the U.S. can vary by a factor of ten, so the use of this approximate value to combine heating and cooling does not significantly skew the calculations. Actual cost differences must be calculated using local fuel and electricity prices and they must reflect peak demand charges to be accurate.

## The Effect of Windows on Lighting Energy Use

In addition to transmitting heat gains and losses, windows and skylights also transmit light. Typically, this natural light is a desirable amenity but the electric lights continue to burn, resulting in no energy savings (Figure 2-21). In recent years, methods and technologies have emerged to better use this daylight so that electric lighting use is reduced as much as possible. Daylight is brought into the building by sidelighting with windows or toplighting with skylights, roof monitors, or clerestory windows. The examples throughout this book focus on sidelighting but the general concepts and performance issues apply to toplighting as well.

In order to reduce lighting energy use, the lighting system must be designed to respond to daylight from windows and skylights. This is referred to as an integrated daylight/electric light system. For example, since daylight is greater nearer the windows, lighting circuits should be zoned so that the fixtures near the windows can be controlled separately from those further away (Figure 2-22). This should always be done in new buildings since it is likely that automated lighting control systems will become the norm during the life of the building. For on-off switching, a person can then turn the lights off nearest the window and keep the lights on deeper into the room. Within a light fixture, the individual fluorescent tubes can also be switched separately. For example, in a four-lamp fixture, the outer two lamps can be designed to switch separately from the inner two lamps. This allows the occupant to tune light levels according to available daylight from 100 to 50 percent to no electric lighting. This is often referred to as two-step switching. Three-step switching is accomplished with three-lamp fixtures operated at 100, 66, or 33 percent (or completely off).

For higher-end applications, there are commercially available systems that enable a person to dim the electric lights with a remote controller. Lighting control can be automated for greater reliability, since often people cannot be counted on to switch the lights. Portions of the electric lighting are switched off or dimmed automatically in response to a photosensor in the same way that a thermostat regulates temperature. These systems are more expensive than simple switching and the technology is constantly evolving. Their installation and operation must be carefully monitored to ensure the projected savings.

## Energy Performance of Light Control Strategies

Figure 2-23 illustrates the energy impact of a range of daylight control systems for three windows in a south-facing perimeter zone in Chicago and Houston. Compared to the cases where there are no daylight controls, considerable reductions in electric lighting energy occur for all window types. Daylight typically provides much more light per unit of heat than electric lighting. It can also be noted that

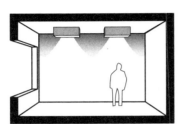

*Figure 2-21. Without separately switched lights near windows, electric lights remain on even with sufficient daylight*

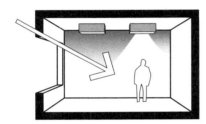

*Figure 2-22. With sufficient daylight, photosensors cause electric lights near windows to dim or turn off*

*Basic Issues in Window Selection and Design*

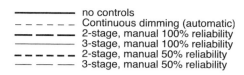

*Figure 2-23. Total annual energy use comparison by lighting control type*

All cases are south-facing with no shading and a window-to-wall ratio of 0.30. Numbers are expressed per square foot within a 15-foot-deep perimeter zone. Results were computed using DOE-2.1E for a typical office building (Appendix A).

Legend:
- no controls
- Continuous dimming (automatic)
- 2-stage, manual 100% reliability
- 3-stage, manual 100% reliability
- 2-stage, manual 50% reliability
- 3-stage, manual 50% reliability

## Chicago

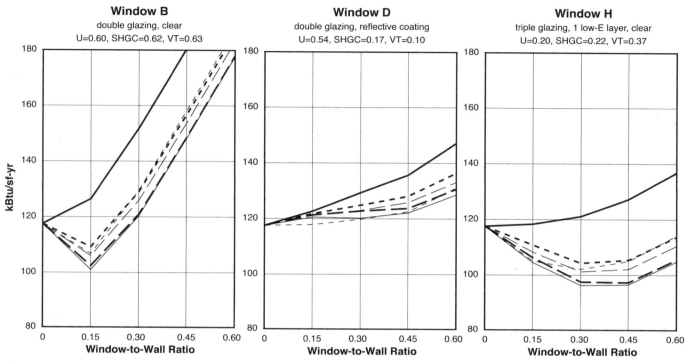

## Houston

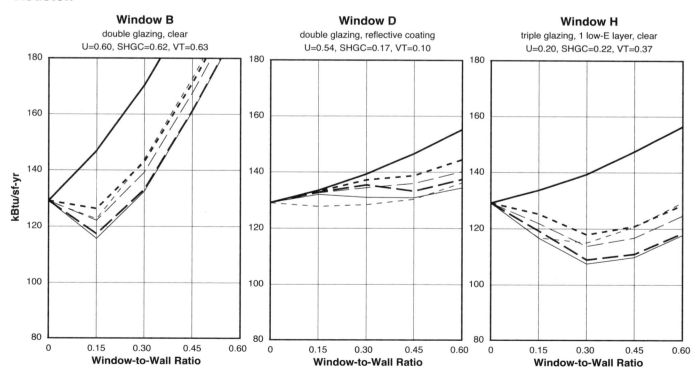

without as much heat gain from the lights, cooling energy use declines slightly, and heating energy use slightly rises in many cases. As will be shown in Chapters 5 and 6, this holds true for other orientations as well.

Five types of lighting control are shown in Figure 2-23 in addition to the base case with no controls. Continuous dimming shows the case where lights are dimmed in response to daylight so that the total workplane illuminance is 50 footcandles or more at a distance 10 feet from the window. The remaining four cases illustrate two and three-step switching with either 50 or 100 percent occupant reliability. If the occupant is always present and reliably switches the lights in response to daylight so that the total workplane illuminance is 50 footcandles or more at a distance 10 feet from the window, this is referred to as 100 percent reliability. If the occupant only switches the lights half the time, this is referred to as 50 percent reliability. Three window types are shown with a broad range of visible transmittance.

With Window B in this example, continuous dimming and the two- or three-step switching with 50 percent reliability yields nearly the same annual energy use and peak demand in both Chicago and Houston climates. With Window D, continuous dimming yields the least annual energy use compared to the other switching strategies for window areas less than WWR=0.45, while for larger window areas greater than WWR=0.45, its performance is comparable to the two- or three-stage switching with 100 percent reliability. With Window H, continuous dimming is comparable to the 100 percent reliability switching strategies for smaller window areas while for larger windows, it is comparable to the 50 percent reliability switching strategies.

Of course, occupants switching lights with 100 percent reliability is unrealistic, but it illustrates the best case. Note that continuous dimming will yield performance that is either comparable in performance to an optimal manual switching strategy with 100 percent or 50 percent reliability depending on the window size and type. This data can provide readers with a measure of relative performance when reviewing the performance data for continuous dimming given in Chapters 5 and 6. The continuous dimming controls assume conditions with reliable dimmable ballasts controlled by daylight sensors.

Window D with a very low VT (0.10) does not allow as much daylight to enter the space; consequently, the electric lights remain on more often. At larger window areas, enough daylight enters so that lighting control strategies become beneficial. This illustrates the classic trade-off that must be made when using dark tinted or reflective glazings—cooling energy is saved by reducing heat gain, but daylight is diminished as well, resulting in less savings from reduced electric lighting. Higher-performance windows that rely on selective low-E coatings (such as Window H) keep out the heat but allow sufficient daylight, maximizing energy savings. This interaction between the building envelope and lighting system is one of the key synergistic opportunities in developing high-performance buildings. The design and selection of windows is a pivotal aspect of this integrated design approach.

Figure 2-24 illustrates the effect of lighting control strategies on peak demand in Chicago and Houston. In both climates, peak demand reductions can be achieved with any daylight control strategy at any window area with high-VT Window B. Peak demand reductions begin

*Basic Issues in Window Selection and Design*

*Figure 2-24. Peak demand comparison by lighting control type*

All cases are south-facing with no shading and a window-to-wall ratio of 0.30. Numbers are expressed per square foot within a 15-foot-deep perimeter zone. Results were computed using DOE-2.1E for a typical office building (Appendix A).

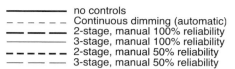

— no controls
— — — — — Continuous dimming (automatic)
━ ━ ━ 2-stage, manual 100% reliability
———— 3-stage, manual 100% reliability
■ ■ ■ ■ 2-stage, manual 50% reliability
— — — 3-stage, manual 50% reliability

## Chicago

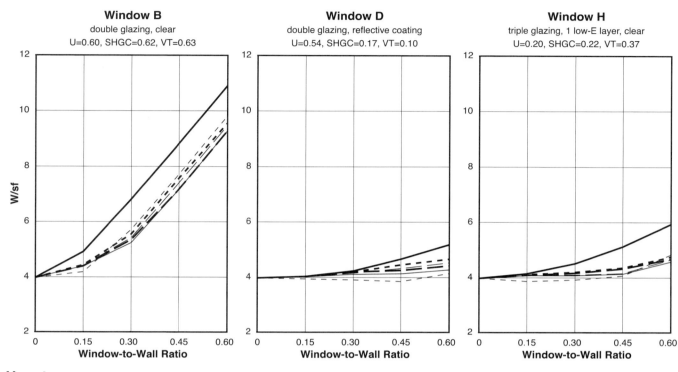

**Window B**
double glazing, clear
U=0.60, SHGC=0.62, VT=0.63

**Window D**
double glazing, reflective coating
U=0.54, SHGC=0.17, VT=0.10

**Window H**
triple glazing, 1 low-E layer, clear
U=0.20, SHGC=0.22, VT=0.37

## Houston

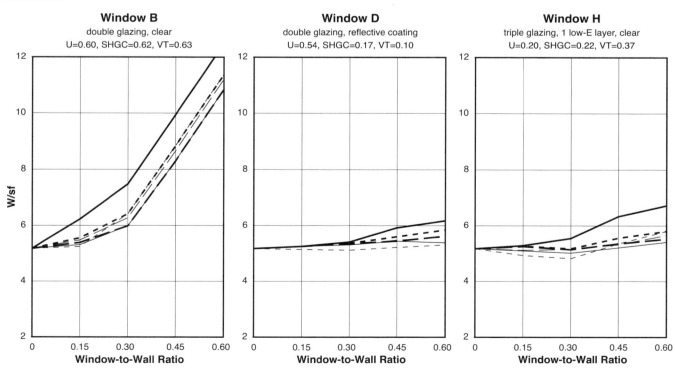

**Window B**
double glazing, clear
U=0.60, SHGC=0.62, VT=0.63

**Window D**
double glazing, reflective coating
U=0.54, SHGC=0.17, VT=0.10

**Window H**
triple glazing, 1 low-E layer, clear
U=0.20, SHGC=0.22, VT=0.37

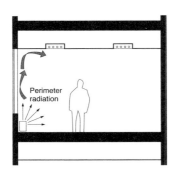

*Figure 2-25. Perimeter heat provided near windows may not be necessary with high-performance windows*

*Figure 2-26. Heat loss through different windows*

| Window | U-factor | Heat loss per linear foot |
|:---:|:---:|:---:|
| A | 1.25 | 695 |
| B | 0.60 | 340 |
| C | 0.60 | 340 |
| D | 0.54 | 307 |
| E | 0.49 | 280 |
| F | 0.46 | 263 |
| G | 0.46 | 263 |
| H | 0.20 | 121 |
| I | 0.14 | 88 |

All cases have a 0.60 window-to-wall ratio for an office in Chicago, Illinois. The winter design temperature used in the calculation is −6°F. The nine window types indicated here are described throughout the chapter.

to occur with Window H above WWR=0.15 and Window D above WWR=0.30. The benefits are less with very low-VT Window D.

In reality, there can be a range of performance depending on the design and operation of the lighting system. Studies have shown that manual switching and continuous dimming can yield significant savings but, in the case of dimming, savings are not routine. Today's dimmable ballasts and light sensors are not widely utilized as they are costly and difficult to specify, although this is changing rapidly. Throughout the book, continuous dimming is used as a basis for making window design and selection decisions.

Since the window system has a relatively long life, it should be designed based on the assumption that even if daylight control systems are not installed now, they will be in the future. As more information becomes available, more designers will attempt to maximize daylight to take advantage of its energy saving and human factors benefits. Light redirecting elements may also provide sufficient daylight deep in a perimeter space. This allows more electric lights to be switched off, not just those near the windows (see case studies in Chapter 8). A similar effect can occur with toplighting and borrowed light that bring daylight deeper into the room (see Chapter 3).

### The Effect of Windows on Mechanical System Design

Traditionally, windows have affected mechanical system design in two ways—they have made perimeter heating and cooling necessary and they have increased the size of the mechanical equipment for both heating and cooling. Areas near conventional windows have usually been places of the greatest temperature variation and discomfort in a building. While a majority of the heating and cooling in commercial buildings is delivered from the ceiling through forced air HVAC systems, additional radiant and convective perimeter heating and cooling is often required near windows (Figure 2-25).

Today, a high-performance window with a low U-factor and SHGC reduces the heat loss and gain through the windows significantly and comfort is improved because glass temperatures remain closer to room temperature (i.e. Windows F–I in Figure 2-26). Conventional practice has been to use baseboard heating in many applications. As windows become more insulating (lower U-factor), baseboard heating may be replaced with slot diffusers delivering heated air above the window. With highly insulating windows, a perimeter heating system may not be required at all. Specific design depends on climate, application, and local engineering practices. The Cambria Office Facility in Ebensburg, Pennsylvania, is an example of the integrated design concept of using highly insulated windows to eliminate perimeter heating and downsize the mechanical system for a net initial cost savings (see Chapter 8).

The second impact of high-performance windows is the reduction of the mechanical system size due to lower peak heating and cooling loads. This also can lead to reduced initial costs. Peak load reductions mean smaller chillers and boilers, smaller ducts, and smaller fans. In addition, since peak electric demand usually occurs on the hottest summer days when demand charges are highest, windows that reduce peak loads can result in cost savings as well. Reduced peak loads also lessen the need for additional power plant capacity.

*Basic Issues in Window Selection and Design*

*Figure 2-27. Peak demand comparison for nine window types*
All cases are south-facing with no shading and a window-to-wall ratio of 0.30. Numbers are expressed per square foot within a 15-foot-deep perimeter zone. Results were computed using DOE-2.1E for a typical office building in Chicago, Illinois (Appendix A).

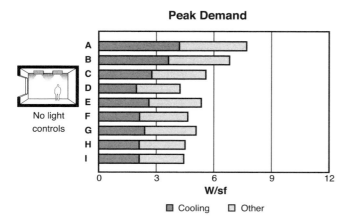

**Peak Demand**

W/sf

■ Cooling □ Other

No light controls

| Window A | Window F |
|---|---|
| single glazing | double glazing |
| clear | spec. selective low-E tint |
| U = 1.25 | U = 0.46 |
| SHGC = 0.72 | SHGC = 0.27 |
| VT = 0.71 | VT = 0.43 |
| **Window B** | **Window G** |
| double glazing | double glazing |
| clear | spec. selective low-E clear |
| U = 0.60 | U = 0.46 |
| SHGC = 0.60 | SHGC = 0.34 |
| VT = 0.63 | VT = 0.57 |
| **Window C** | **Window H** |
| double glazing | triple glazing |
| bronze tint | 1 low-E layer, clear |
| U = 0.60 | U = 0.20 |
| SHGC = 0.42 | SHGC = 0.22 |
| VT = 0.38 | VT = 0.37 |
| **Window D** | **Window I** |
| double glazing | quadruple glazing |
| reflective coating | 2 low-E layers, clear |
| U = 0.54 | U = 0.14 |
| SHGC = 0.17 | SHGC = 0.20 |
| VT = 0.10 | VT = 0.34 |
| **Window E** | |
| double glazing | |
| low-E, bronze tint | |
| U = 0.49 | |
| SHGC = 0.39 | |
| VT = 0.36 | |

U = U-factor in Btu/hr-sf-°F
SHGC = solar heat gain coefficient
VT = visible transmittance
All window properties are for the whole window, Windows A–G have aluminum frames (all but A are thermally broken). Windows H and I have insulated frames. See Appendix A.

Figure 2-27 illustrates the peak demand impact with nine window types in a south-facing perimeter zone in Chicago. Improving the SHGC and U-factor of the window has the largest impact on reducing peak demand. If daylighting controls are used in the perimeter zones, peak demand is reduced even further for a given window type.

This interrelationship between windows, mechanical system, and lighting system again illustrates the potential benefits of the integrated systems approach to design. Even though higher-performance windows and daylight controls may cost more initially, they may be offset by reduced costs for the mechanical system components and the elimination of perimeter heating. In addition, operating costs will be less and people are likely to be more comfortable and productive.

## ENERGY CODES AND STANDARDS

Energy codes and standards are one of the main tools used to improve energy efficiency in buildings. In most places in the United States, the commonly referenced energy code is ASHRAE Standard 90.1-2001. This code has two paths—the Building Envelope Option with prescriptive limitations on allowable window area and window properties (maximum U-factor and SHGC), or a performance approach called the Building Envelope Trade-off Option can be used to meet a total envelope performance. This latter option allows for greater design flexibility in window area and attributes, and provides credit for higher VT windows that enhance daylighting.

While the performance approach has a number of benefits, the prescriptive requirements give a good general sense of the limitations that codes place on window design and selection. The prescriptive part of ASHRAE 90.1-2001 indicates the following:

- The total vertical fenestration area, including the glass plus frame, must be less than 50 percent of the gross exterior wall area of the building. The total skylight area must be less than 5 percent of the total gross roof area.

*Figure 2-28. Allowable U-factor and SHGC for 26 climates—ASHRAE 90.1-1999*

| ZONE | HDD65 | CDD50 | Maximum allowable U-factor at a given WWR | | | | | Maximum allowable SHGC, all orientations at a given WWR | | | | |
|---|---|---|---|---|---|---|---|---|---|---|---|---|
| | | | 0-10% | >10-20% | >20-30% | >30-40% | >40-50% | 0-10% | >10-20% | >20-30% | >30-40% | >40-50% |
| 1 | 0-900 | 10801+ | 1.22 | 1.22 | 1.22 | 1.22 | 1.22 | 0.19 | 0.19 | 0.19 | 0.19 | 0.14 |
| 2 | 0-900 | 9001-10800 | 1.22 | 1.22 | 1.22 | 1.22 | 1.22 | 0.25 | 0.25 | 0.25 | 0.25 | 0.19 |
| 3 | 0-900 | 7201-9000 | 1.22 | 1.22 | 1.22 | 1.22 | 1.22 | 0.40 | 0.25 | 0.25 | 0.25 | 0.19 |
| 4 | 0-900 | 0-7200 | 1.22 | 1.22 | 1.22 | 1.22 | 1.22 | 0.61 | 0.40 | 0.40 | 0.40 | 0.31 |
| 5 | 901-1800 | 7201+ | 1.22 | 1.22 | 1.22 | 1.22 | 1.22 | 0.25 | 0.25 | 0.25 | 0.25 | 0.17 |
| 6 | 901-1800 | 5401-7200 | 1.22 | 1.22 | 1.22 | 1.22 | 1.22 | 0.39 | 0.25 | 0.25 | 0.25 | 0.17 |
| 7 | 901-1800 | 0-5400 | 1.22 | 1.22 | 1.22 | 1.22 | 1.22 | 0.61 | 0.61 | 0.44 | 0.44 | 0.31 |
| 8 | 1702-2700 | 5401+ | 1.22 | 1.22 | 1.22 | 1.22 | 1.22 | 0.39 | 0.25 | 0.25 | 0.25 | 0.15 |
| 9 | 1801-2700 | 0-5400 | 1.22 | 1.22 | 1.22 | 1.22 | 1.22 | 0.61 | 0.39 | 0.39 | 0.34 | 0.20 |
| 10 | 2701-3600 | 5401+ | 0.57 | 0.57 | 0.57 | 0.57 | 0.46 | 0.39 | 0.25 | 0.25 | 0.25 | 0.19 |
| 11 | 2701-3600 | 3601-5400 | 0.57 | 0.57 | 0.57 | 0.57 | 0.46 | 0.39 | 0.39 | 0.39 | 0.39 | 0.27 |
| 12 | 2701-3600 | 0-3600 | 1.22 | 1.22 | 1.22 | 1.22 | 0.73 | 0.61 | 0.61 | 0.61 | 0.39 | 0.39 |
| 13 | 3601-5400 | 3601+ | 0.57 | 0.57 | 0.57 | 0.57 | 0.46 | 0.39 | 0.39 | 0.39 | 0.39 | 0.25 |
| 14 | 3601-5400 | 1801-3600 | 0.57 | 0.57 | 0.57 | 0.57 | 0.46 | 0.49 | 0.39 | 0.39 | 0.39 | 0.26 |
| 15 | 3601-5400 | 0-1800 | 0.57 | 0.57 | 0.57 | 0.57 | 0.46 | 0.49 | 0.49 | 0.49 | 0.49 | 0.36 |
| 16 | 5401-7200 | 3601+ | 0.57 | 0.57 | 0.57 | 0.57 | 0.46 | 0.39 | 0.39 | 0.39 | 0.39 | 0.23 |
| 17 | 5401-7200 | 1801-3600 | 0.57 | 0.57 | 0.57 | 0.57 | 0.46 | 0.49 | 0.39 | 0.39 | 0.39 | 0.26 |
| 18 | 5401-7200 | 0-1800 | 0.57 | 0.57 | 0.57 | 0.57 | 0.46 | 0.49 | 0.49 | 0.49 | 0.49 | 0.36 |
| 19 | 7201-9000 | 1801+ | 0.57 | 0.57 | 0.57 | 0.57 | 0.46 | 0.49 | 0.39 | 0.39 | 0.39 | 0.26 |
| 20 | 7201-9000 | 0-1800 | 0.57 | 0.57 | 0.57 | 0.57 | 0.46 | 0.49 | 0.49 | 0.49 | 0.49 | 0.36 |
| 21 | 9001-10800 | 1801+ | 0.46 | 0.46 | 0.46 | 0.46 | 0.35 | 0.46 | 0.46 | 0.36 | 0.36 | 0.32 |
| 22 | 9001-10800 | 0-1800 | 0.57 | 0.57 | 0.57 | 0.57 | 0.46 | 0.49 | 0.49 | 0.49 | 0.49 | 0.36 |
| 23 | 10801-12600 | 0+ | 0.46 | 0.46 | 0.46 | 0.46 | 0.35 | NR | NR | NR | NR | NR |
| 24 | 12601-16200 | 0+ | 0.46 | 0.46 | 0.46 | 0.46 | 0.35 | NR | NR | NR | NR | NR |
| 25 | 16201-19800 | 0+ | 0.43 | 0.43 | 0.43 | 0.43 | 0.33 | NR | NR | NR | NR | NR |
| 26 | 19801+ | 0+ | 0.32 | 0.32 | 0.32 | 0.32 | 0.25 | NR | NR | NR | NR | NR |

All windows are fixed. Higher SHGCs are allowable for
north-facing orientations (see ASHRAE 90.1-1999).
NR=no requirement, U-factor is in Btu/hr-sf-˚F

- The allowable window area can be increased to 75 percent at street level if the first story is not higher than 20 feet and has a continuous overhang with a projection factor of 0.5 (the depth of the overhang=0.5 x the window height).

- The U-factor and SHGC of all types of fenestration cannot exceed limits prescribed for the appropriate climate zone. Distinct requirements are given for fixed and operable vertical glazing as well as different types of skylights. A higher SHGC level is allowed for north-facing windows. Windows with higher SHGC levels can also be used when there are permanent projections (overhangs) over the window.

Figure 2-28 shows a simplified set of U-factor and SHGC requirements for fixed vertical windows in twenty-six climates. Figures 2-29 and 2-30 show which of the nine windows used throughout the book meets the code in Chicago and Houston. If a window does not meet the code but can meet it with a permanent projection (overhang), the minimum projection factor is given in the table. Windows used in this table are typical examples, but a specific window may perform differently, resulting in a more or less stringent requirement. The performance-based approach gives wide latitude to incorporate extensive glazing areas if the appropriate high-performance windows are used.

*Basic Issues in Window Selection and Design*

*Figure 2-29. Ability of typical windows in Chicago to meet ASHRAE Standard 90.1-1999*

PF = Projection Factor (depth of overhang/height of window). PF=0.50+ means that glazing will meet standard if there is a projection factor of 0.50 or more. The PF for overhangs modeled in Chapters 5 and 6 are either 0.47 (shallow) or 0.70 (deep) for WWR=0.15–0.60 corresponding to profile angles of 65° or 55°. U-factor is in Btu/hr-sf-°F

| Window | Number of Glazings | U-factor (Overall) | SHGC (Overall) | Window-to-Wall Ratio | | | | |
|---|---|---|---|---|---|---|---|---|
| | | | | 0–10% | 10–20% | 20–30% | 30–40% | 40–50% |
| A  Clear | 1 | 1.25 | 0.72 | no | no | no | no | no |
| B  Clear | 2 | 0.60 | 0.60 | no | no | no | no | no |
| C  Bronze tint | 2 | 0.60 | 0.42 | no | no | no | no | no |
| D  Reflective | 2 | 0.54 | 0.17 | yes | yes | yes | yes | yes |
| E  Low-E bronze tint | 2 | 0.49 | 0.39 | yes | yes | yes | yes | yes |
| F  Selective low-E tint | 2 | 0.46 | 0.27 | yes | yes | yes | yes | yes |
| G  Clear with selective low-E | 2 | 0.46 | 0.34 | yes | yes | yes | yes | yes |
| H  Clear with 1 low-E layer | 3 | 0.20 | 0.22 | yes | yes | yes | yes | yes |
| I  Clear with 2 low-E layers | 4 | 0.14 | 0.20 | yes | yes | yes | yes | yes |
| Maximum U-factor for Chicago | | | | 0.57 | 0.57 | 0.57 | 0.57 | 0.57 |
| Maximum SHGC for Chicago | | | | 0.49 | 0.39 | 0.39 | 0.39 | 0.39 |

*Figure 2-30. Ability of typical windows in Houston to meet ASHRAE Standard 90.1-1999*

PF = Projection Factor (depth of overhang/height of window). PF=0.50+ means that glazing will meet standard if there is a projection factor of 0.50 or more. The PF for overhangs modeled in Chapters 5 and 6 are either 0.47 (shallow) or 0.70 (deep) for WWR=0.15–0.60 corresponding to profile angles of 65° or 55°. Although Window F with a SHGC of 0.27 requires a projection factor of 0.10 or more, there are many selective tints in this category that are below SHGC of 0.25 and do not require a projection. U-factor is in Btu/hr-sf-°F

| Window | Number of Glazings | U-factor (Overall) | SHGC (Overall) | Window-to-Wall Ratio | | | | |
|---|---|---|---|---|---|---|---|---|
| | | | | 0–10% | 10–20% | 20–30% | 30–40% | 40–50% |
| A  Clear | 1 | 1.25 | 0.72 | no | no | no | no | no |
| B  Clear | 2 | 0.60 | 0.60 | PF=0.50+ | no | no | no | no |
| C  Bronze tint | 2 | 0.60 | 0.42 | PF=0.10+ | PF=0.60+ | PF=0.60+ | PF=0.60+ | no |
| D  Reflective | 2 | 0.54 | 0.17 | yes | yes | yes | yes | yes |
| E  Low-E bronze tint | 2 | 0.49 | 0.39 | yes | PF=0.50+ | PF=0.50+ | PF=0.10+ | PF=0.90+ |
| F  Selective low-E tint | 2 | 0.46 | 0.27 | yes | PF=0.10+ | PF=0.10+ | PF=0.10+ | PF=0.10+ |
| G  Clear with selective low-E | 2 | 0.46 | 0.34 | yes | PF=0.30+ | PF=0.30+ | PF=0.30+ | PF=0.80+ |
| H  Clear with 1 low-E layer | 3 | 0.20 | 0.22 | yes | yes | yes | yes | PF=0.30+ |
| I  Clear with 2 low-E layers | 4 | 0.14 | 0.20 | yes | yes | yes | yes | PF=0.30+ |
| Maximum U-factor for Houston | | | | 1.22 | 1.22 | 1.22 | 1.22 | 1.22 |
| Maximum SHGC for Houston | | | | 0.39 | 0.25 | 0.25 | 0.25 | 0.17 |

# Human Factors Issues

Delivering a truly high-performance building is not just a matter of using less energy and meeting a number of technical and environmental criteria. The building must be high performance with respect to the people who occupy it as well, contributing to the health, well-being, and productivity of those who live or work in or visit it. Windows play an important role in achieving these goals because they directly affect several interior design attributes such as daylight, glare, view, and thermal comfort. Whether windows are operable and occupants can individually control light, heat, and air flow also contribute to both psychological and physical well being. In this section, four of these interior design attributes are described and are later used to evaluate window options in Chapters 5 and 6.

Using a single index to represent a window's impact on the interior environment of a perimeter space is challenging because comfort, daylight, and glare conditions may vary considerably throughout a day or a year. In addition, an attribute like daylight has qualitative aspects that are difficult to measure. Similarly, view has two distinct benefits—the spaciousness provided as well as the content of the view. Methods of comparing the windows based on average or weighted conditions with respect to thermal comfort, daylight, glare, and view have been included as part of this analysis; however, it is important to recognize that more detailed analysis is useful in design and window selection. The metrics identified here form part of the analysis and decision making process discussed in Chapters 4–6.

## DAYLIGHT

A recent study suggests "that the frequently reported desire for windows in the workplace is more than a matter of simple preference. Underpinning this preference is a fundamental issue of emotional and psychological well-being" (Leather et al. 1998). Daylight is an important part of this desire for windows. The changing direction, intensity, and even color of daylight are stimulating and connect people to the time of day and the natural world. Recent studies have suggested numerous benefits including links between daylight and increased sales in retail facilities and better performance in schools (Boyce et. al., 2003, Edwards and Torcellini 2002, Heschong 1999).

Windows, of course, permit daylight to enter a space. The design of a window and choice of glazing can dramatically affect the quantity and quality of daylight in a space and how it is experienced. To illustrate this point, a series of DOE-2.1E computer simulations were conducted on perimeter zones in office buildings. Figure 2-32 indicates the average annual workplane illuminance in a south-facing perimeter office in Chicago with moderately sized windows (WWR=0.30) at a point ten feet from the window. Average daylight illuminance is relatively high in this example because at the more northerly latitude in Chicago, the lower sun angle penetrates a south-facing facade more deeply than in more southerly latitudes, and there is no interior shading assumed in these calculations. Most visual tasks require only 30–70 footcandles. Figure 2-31 shows there is great variability in daylight illuminance with different window types. For example, the reflective glazing (Window D) has a very low VT and provides much less daylight than any other option. Figure 2-32 shows that the average annual daylight illuminance linearly related to the product of the window-to-wall ratio and visible transmittance (VT*WWR). Larger windows with low-transmission glass can have the same average daylight illuminance as small windows with high-transmission glass. South-facing windows generally have more daylight levels than north-, east-, and west-facing windows because of direct sun. Higher latitudes have greater average daylight levels on the south than lower latitude locations.

Simply using average annual daylight illuminance as an indicator of the presence of daylight can be misleading. Another measure of the effectiveness of daylight is to determine the percentage of time the illumination is above 50 footcandles (an adequate level of general office lighting) at a given location within the space. Figure 2-33 indicates that daylight levels exceeding 50 footcandles occur at least 70 percent of the time ten feet from the window for all cases except

**Window A**
single glazing
clear
U = 1.25
SHGC = 0.72
VT = 0.71

**Window B**
double glazing
clear
U = 0.60
SHGC = 0.60
VT = 0.63

**Window C**
double glazing
bronze tint
U = 0.60
SHGC = 0.42
VT = 0.38

**Window D**
double glazing
reflective coating
U = 0.54
SHGC = 0.17
VT = 0.10

**Window E**
double glazing
low-E, bronze tint
U = 0.49
SHGC = 0.39
VT = 0.36

**Window F**
double glazing
spec. selective low-E tint
U = 0.46
SHGC = 0.27
VT = 0.43

**Window G**
double glazing
spec. selective low-E clear
U = 0.46
SHGC = 0.34
VT = 0.57

**Window H**
triple glazing
1 low-E layer, clear
U = 0.20
SHGC = 0.22
VT = 0.37

**Window I**
quadruple glazing
2 low-E layers, clear
U = 0.14
SHGC = 0.20
VT = 0.34

U = U-factor in Btu/hr-sf-°F
SHGC = solar heat gain coefficient
VT = visible transmittance
All window properties are for the whole window, Windows A–G have aluminum frames (all but A are thermally broken). Windows H and I have insulated frames. See Appendix A.

*Figure 2-31. Average annual daylight illuminance in a perimeter zone*
Average daylight illuminance is calculated at a point 10 feet from the window. All cases are south-facing with no shading and a window-to-wall ratio of 0.30. Results were computed using DOE-2.1E for a typical office building in Chicago, Illinois (Appendix A).

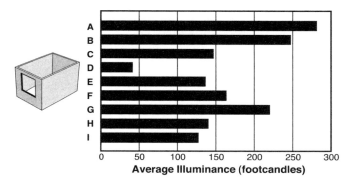

Average Illuminance (footcandles)

North
East
South
West

*Figure 2-32. Average annual daylight illuminance compared to the product of WWR and VT*

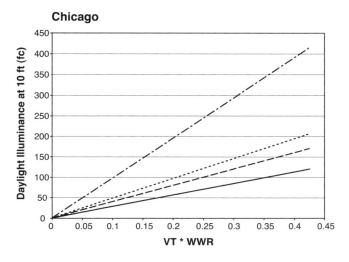

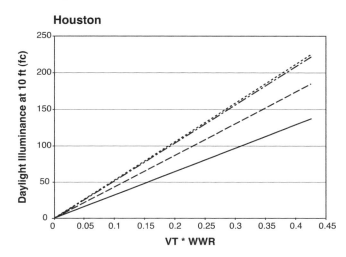

Window D. This occurs in part because it is assumed there is no control of direct sunlight with shades or blinds.

There is an additional reason that simply using average daylight illuminance as an indicator does not reflect the true impact on humans. The perceived brightness of the interior due to daylight is not directly proportional to the amount of daylight. For example, a window that results in an average illuminance of 60 footcandles may be perceived as considerably brighter than one that produces 20 footcandles. However, a window resulting in an average illuminance of 300 footcandles is not necessarily perceived as three times brighter than one with 100 footcandles. In order to make a meaningful comparison between windows on a 0–10 scale that reflects the visual impact of brightness on human beings, a brightness index was developed (see Appendix A). Figure 2-34 illustrates the brightness index for the same set of nine windows shown in the previous figure. The relative ranking of the windows remains the same but the differences are not so extreme. The percentage of time over 50 footcandles (Figure 2-33) has a very similar pattern to the brightness index (Figure 2-34). The brightness index is used to compare windows on a 0-10 scale in later chapters.

**Window A**
single glazing
clear
U = 1.25
SHGC = 0.72
VT = 0.71

**Window B**
double glazing
clear
U = 0.60
SHGC = 0.60
VT = 0.63

**Window C**
double glazing
bronze tint
U = 0.60
SHGC = 0.42
VT = 0.38

**Window D**
double glazing
reflective coating
U = 0.54
SHGC = 0.17
VT = 0.10

**Window E**
double glazing
low-E, bronze tint
U = 0.49
SHGC = 0.39
VT = 0.36

**Window F**
double glazing
spec. selective low-E tint
U = 0.46
SHGC = 0.27
VT = 0.43

**Window G**
double glazing
spec. selective low-E clear
U = 0.46
SHGC = 0.34
VT = 0.57

**Window H**
triple glazing
1 low-E layer, clear
U = 0.20
SHGC = 0.22
VT = 0.37

**Window I**
quadruple glazing
2 low-E layers, clear
U = 0.14
SHGC = 0.20
VT = 0.34

U = U-factor in Btu/hr-sf-°F
SHGC = solar heat gain coefficient
VT = visible transmittance
All window properties are for the whole window, Windows A–G have aluminum frames (all but A are thermally broken). Windows H and I have insulated frames. See Appendix A.

*Figure 2-33. Percent of annual sunlight hours that daylight is over 50 footcandles in a perimeter zone*
Percent time over 50 footcandles is calculated at a point 10 feet from the window. All cases are south-facing with no shading and a window-to-wall ratio of 0.30. Results were computed using DOE-2.1E for a typical office building in Chicago, Illinois (Appendix A).

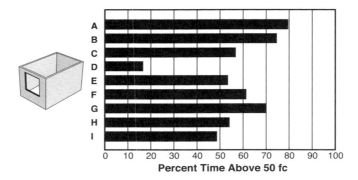

*Figure 2-34. Brightness index*
Brightness index is calculated at a point 10 feet from the window. All cases are south-facing with no shading and a window-to-wall ratio of 0.30. Results were computed for a typical office building in Chicago, Illinois (Appendix A).

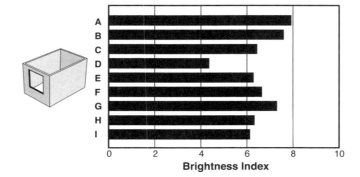

*Basic Issues in Window Selection and Design*

As is shown in Chapters 5 and 6, shading devices reduce the amount of daylight in non-south-facing orientations. In reality, north-facing zones might even yield more useful daylight than other orientations since there is less need to deploy interior shades to control glare and direct sun.

While the measures shown in Figures 2-31 and 2-34 are good general indicators, they are taken at one point in the center of the space 10 feet from the window. This approach does not illustrate the variation in light levels that occurs across a room. Figure 2-35 shows the spatial distribution of daylight at noon on June 21 in a south-facing perimeter zone with six window types. The differences between cases is due to the variations in the visible transmittance of the windows. The contours illustrate the intense daylight near the windows that diminishes rapidly moving away from a window. This lack

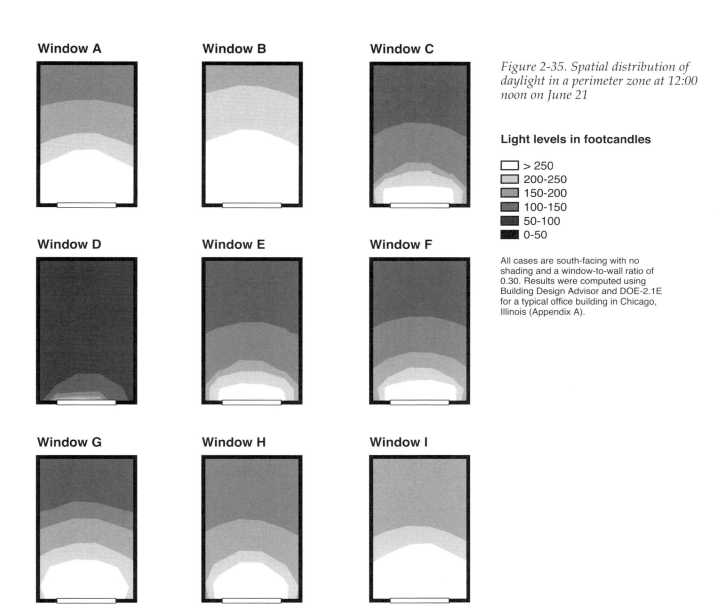

*Figure 2-35. Spatial distribution of daylight in a perimeter zone at 12:00 noon on June 21*

**Light levels in footcandles**

☐ > 250
▨ 200-250
▨ 150-200
▨ 100-150
▨ 50-100
▨ 0-50

All cases are south-facing with no shading and a window-to-wall ratio of 0.30. Results were computed using Building Design Advisor and DOE-2.1E for a typical office building in Chicago, Illinois (Appendix A).

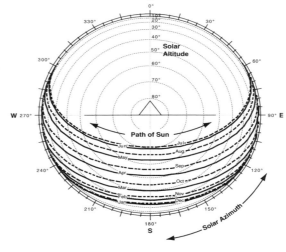

*Figure 2-36. Sun path diagram for Chicago (41° North latitude)*

Source: Solar Tool, Square One Research Pty Ltd., www.squ1.com

*Figure 2-37. Distribution of daylight at different times—Chicago*

**Light levels in footcandles**

- ☐ > 250
- ☐ 200-250
- ☐ 150-200
- ☐ 100-150
- ☐ 50-100
- ☐ 0-50

All cases are south-facing with no shading and a window-to-wall ratio of 0.30. Results were computed using Building Design Advisor and DOE-2.1E for a typical office building in Chicago, Illinois (Appendix A). All cases use:

**Window G**
double glazing
spec. selective low-E clear
U = 0.46
SHGC = 0.34
VT = 0.57

**June 21**

9:00 A.M.  12:00 NOON  3:00 P.M.

**March 21 or September 21**

9:00 A.M.  12:00 NOON  3:00 P.M.

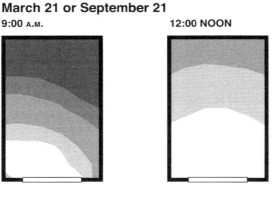 

**December 21**

9:00 A.M.  12:00 NOON  3:00 P.M.

*Basic Issues in Window Selection and Design*

of uniform light distribution is particularly notable at noon with an unshaded, south-facing window.

There are strategies to remedy this imbalance. For instance, light-colored surfaces within a room can provide good daylight distribution. Techniques, such as light shelves, can extend the daylight zone (see Chapter 3). If properly designed, light shelves reduce daylight illuminance near the windows and increase it further into the room. Introducing daylight from a second source—either a window on another wall or through toplighting—can also help balance daylight in a room, addressing the uneven distribution that occurs with sidelighting from one source.

Daylight illuminance not only varies depending on location within a space; it also varies with the time of day and season of the year. The variation in the location of the sun depends on specific location—Figure 2-36 show the sun path diagrams for 41 degrees North latitude (Chicago). Figure 2-37 illustrates the considerable differences in daylight intensity and distribution that occur at different times of day throughout the year with an unshaded south-facing window in Chicago.

Daylight design is far more sophisticated than simply providing a window with a high enough visible transmittance. More daylight does not necessarily equate to better lighting conditions. It is a matter of balancing daylight admission with glare control, as well as providing uniform light distribution. Remember that the usability of daylight is dependent on the task. For some tasks requiring a high level of visual acuity not subject to glare, the brighter the interior the better. For computer tasks, particularly with older CRT screens, reducing and controlling illuminance levels is better.

## GLARE

Too much daylight can produce excessive glare, which is particularly undesirable in computer work environments. Glare results when the source of the light is too intense for the naked eye to handle. As the eye attempts to even out the contrast between the task and the surrounding surfaces, the muscles of the eye have to work harder and more frequently. Tired eyes and increased levels of stress result. Glare within the range that the eye can handle is called *discomfort glare*; glare preventing us from doing a task is called *disability glare*. In addition to these two glare categories, there is *direct* and *indirect* glare. Direct glare is caused when a person views the source of illumination. Indirect glare results from light being reflected off surfaces.

Like the strain associated with glare, the eye has a difficult time adapting to high *brightness ratios* between differently illuminated tasks within one's field of view. Because brightness is a function of reflectance and illumination, the brightness ratio is controllable through good design. Anatomically, the eye is more sensitive in brightness ratios at the center of the field of vision, but brightness ratios in the periphery nevertheless invoke a reflex to center the eye on the brightness difference. Thus, changes in brightness ratios due to daylighting or artificial lighting need to be kept low over large areas of an occupant's field of view in a space. By keeping the reflectance of wall surfaces within the levels shown in Figure 2-38, excessive brightness ratios can be minimized. Direct sun also must be controllable. The

*Figure 2-38: Recommended surface reflectance and brightness ratios*

| Area | Minimum Reflectance |
|---|---|
| Ceilings | 70 |
| Vertical surfaces | 40 |
| Work surfaces | 50 |
| Floors | 20 |

Illuminating Engineering Society (IES) recommends that small patches of sunlight be controlled to less than 79 candelas per square foot.

To provide a general indication of the potential glare problem with different windows, the DOE-2.1E program calculates a *daylight glare index* at a specified location and orientation of a viewer within the space. This glare index is based on a subjective response to brightness within one's field of view. In this analysis, the average annual glare index is computed for a person facing one of the side walls sitting 5 feet from the window. A glare index of 10 is the threshold for *just perceptible* glare, while a glare index of 16 is the threshold where glare is *just acceptable*. The threshold for *just uncomfortable* glare and the maximum value recommended for general office tasks is 22. Figure 2-39 shows the average glare index in a south-facing perimeter office in Chicago. The lowest glare index occurs with Window D, which has a very low VT of 0.10. None of the windows has an average glare index over 10 even though the window is unshaded.

Similar to daylighting, the average annual glare index does not reveal severe glare problems that may occur infrequently over the

*Figure 2-39. Average annual glare index*
Average glare index is calculated at a point 5 feet from the window for a person facing the side wall. A lower index is better. All cases are south-facing with no shading and a window-to-wall ratio of 0.30. Results were computed using DOE-2.1E for a typical office building in Chicago, Illinois (Appendix A).

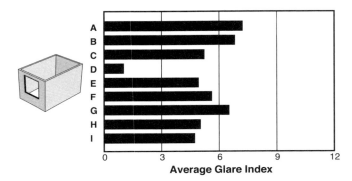

*Figure 2-40. Weighted glare index*
Weighted glare index is calculated at a point 5 feet from the window for a person facing the side wall. A lower index is better. All cases are south-facing with no shading and a window-to-wall ratio of 0.30. Results were computed for a typical office building in Chicago, Illinois (Appendix A).

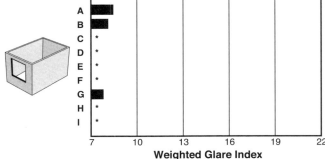

year. Because an annual average may be misleading, a weighted glare index was developed to emphasize the fairly infrequent periods of perceptible or uncomfortable glare that occur (see Appendix A). Figure 2-40 shows the weighted glare index for nine glazings in a south-facing office in Chicago with moderately sized windows (WWR=0.30). As shown in Chapters 5 and 6, the weighted glare index varies considerably depending on orientation, the presence of shading devices, and other window properties and design conditions. The weighted glare index is used as the basis to compare windows on a 0–10 scale in later chapters.

## VIEW

View is the most subjective of the attributes in this analysis. Nevertheless, it deserves attention since it is a desirable characteristic in workplaces and is clearly influenced by window design and selection. Research has shown that window size, shape, proportion, and view content greatly influence human perceptions such as spaciousness as well as the attractiveness and acceptability of the window (Al-Sahhaf 1987). In this analysis, the focus is on the attributes of the window itself—shape and content issues are left to the designer.

The *view index* devised for this analysis results from multiplying the following factors: window area, the visible transmittance of the glass, the fraction of window area not obstructed by permanent exterior shading devices (overhangs and fins), and the percentage time that interior shades do not obstruct the view. A final factor is designed to lower the view index for windows that cause interior reflections when interior light levels are low. With the resulting index

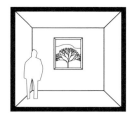

WWR=0.15
No Shading

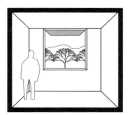

WWR=0.30
Overhang

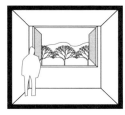

WWR=0.45
Vertical Fins

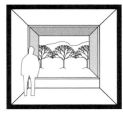

WWR=0.60
Deep Overhang + Fins

*Figure 2-41. View index*

View index is calculated at a point 10 feet from the window. A higher index is better. All cases are south-facing with no shading and a window-to-wall ratio of 0.30. Results were computed for a typical office building in Chicago, Illinois (Appendix A).

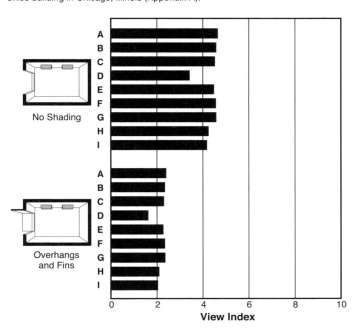

*Figure 2-42. View factor is affected by the window area, the visible transmittance of the glass, and the degree that shading devices obstruct the view*

factor, a higher number is better. The view index does not take into consideration the potentially significant effects of the shape of the window, or that *view blockage* through artfully subdividing or intersecting a window by a building structural element may actually enhance the window's appeal to the viewer. Nor does the view index take glass color into account, although research suggests that the more strongly monochromatic transmitted window light becomes, the less acceptable it is in rendering the interior (Cuttle 1979).

Figure 2-41 indicates the view index for nine window types under different shading conditions. With no exterior shading devices and a constant window area, the window visible transmittance (VT) has the strongest influence on the view index. Window D with a very low VT has the lowest view index. With exterior shading devices, all view indices are reduced substantially. Figure 2-42 illustrates the view for four window designs. Obstructions from exterior shading devices are overlaid on the images to show view reduction.

## THERMAL COMFORT

Thermal comfort is determined by air temperature, relative humidity, air movement, mean radiant temperature, the presence of direct solar radiation (insolation), and occupants' clothing and activity levels. Windows affect human comfort in several ways. During cold periods, exterior temperatures drive interior glass surface temperatures down below the room air temperature; how low the glass temperature drops depends on the window's insulating quality. If people are exposed to the effects of a cold surface, they can experience significant radiant heat loss to that cold surface and they feel uncomfortable, even if the room air temperature is comfortable (Figure 2-43). The closer they are to a window, the more they will feel its influence. The fact that this heat loss occurs on one side of the body more than the other is called radiant asymmetry, and this leads to further discom-

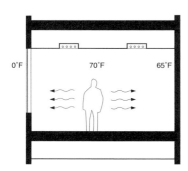

*Figure 2-43. Radiation from a warmer body to the colder glass causes discomfort because the two sides of the body have very different rates of radiant heat loss*

*Figure 2-44. Comparison of inside glass surface temperature for different glazing types at 20°F and 0°F outside temperatures and 0°F interior air temperature*

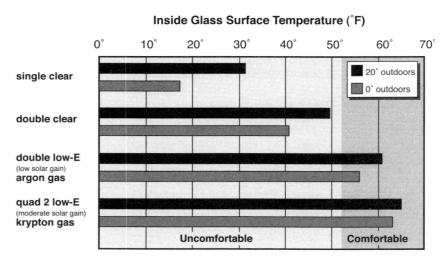

*Basic Issues in Window Selection and Design*

fort. A familiar example of *radiant asymmetry* is the experience of sitting around a campfire on a winter night. The side of the body facing the fire is hot, while the side facing away is cold. In the case of a cold window, a person may be cold in warm clothes in a 70 degrees Fahrenheit room air temperature if part of the body is losing heat to a cold window.

Figure 2-44 shows interior glass surface temperatures for several types of windows with outside temperatures of 20 degrees Fahrenheit and 0 degrees Fahrenheit. When it's cold outside, the window interior surface temperature drops. How far it drops depends on the window's insulating value. The surface temperature of single glazing, for example, is only 10–15 degrees Fahrenheit greater than outdoor temperatures. The interior surface temperature of clear double glazing is warmer but still significantly lower than room air temperature. The double-glazed window with a low-emissivity (low-E) coating and argon gas fill has an interior surface temperature that is warmer still. The window with three to four glazing layers, multiple low-E coatings, and gas fills has interior glass surface temperatures very close to the indoor air temperature. The two high-performance windows in Figure 2-44 provide glass temperatures in the comfort range, while clear single and clear double-glazed windows do not. Frames, which can make up 10–30 percent of the area of a typical window, also have noticeable effects; surface temperatures of windows with insulating frames will be much warmer than those with highly conductive frames.

Drafts near windows are the second major source of winter discomfort. Many people mistakenly attribute drafts to leaky windows when in fact they are the result of cold air patterns initiated by cold window surfaces. Air next to the window is cooled and drops to the floor. It is then replaced by warmer air from the ceiling, which in turn is cooled. This sets up an air movement pattern that feels drafty and accelerates heat loss (Figure 2-45). Cold-temperature-induced drafts occur at the same time as radiant discomfort. This emphasizes the need for insulating windows that maximize interior glass surface temperatures under cold environmental conditions.

Drafts can also be caused by windows with significant air leakage. These leaks can be a result of poor installation and/or ineffective weatherstripping. Such drafts correlate directly to air infiltration levels (see energy-related issues in this chapter). Radiant heat loss, convective currents from cold window surfaces, and drafts from air infiltration leaks all cause people to turn up thermostats during cold periods. Because this action may have little effect on increasing comfort levels, it can be wasteful and costly.

Direct sun has fairly obvious impacts on thermal comfort as well. During cold periods, solar radiation (within limits) can be a pleasant sensation. During warm weather, however, it invariably causes discomfort (Figure 2-46). People often close shades or blinds to block sunlight even though this means they can no longer enjoy the view. Just as people turn up the heat to compensate for cold windows in winter, they may use air-conditioning to counter the effects of warm window surfaces and sunlight in summer. If air conditioners are not sized or installed properly, some areas of a room may become comfortable while others are not, causing significant waste of energy.

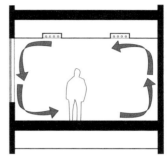

*Figure 2-45. Cold glass temperatures can cause air near the window to fall, setting up uncomfortable air movement in a convective loop*

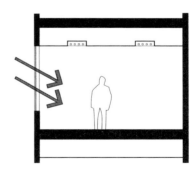

*Figure 2-46. Direct solar radiation through windows can cause discomfort*

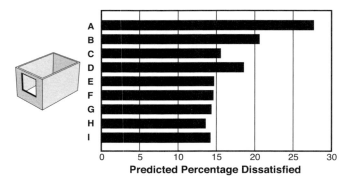

*Figure 2-47. Thermal comfort*
Thermal comfort is calculated at a point 5 feet from the window. A lower PPD is better. All cases are south-facing with no shading and a window-to-wall ratio of 0.30. Results were computed using DOE-2.1E for a typical office building in Chicago, Illinois (Appendix A).

The glazing surface temperature increase due to solar radiation depends on the absorptance of the glass and environmental conditions. Typical clear glass windows do not absorb enough solar radiation to cause a significant difference in surface temperature. With tinted glass, surface temperature increases can be significant. While poorly insulated tinted glass may actually feel quite comfortable on a cold sunny day, this practice is not recommended—the comfort consequences on hot summer days can be disastrous. During warm periods, the interior surface temperatures of poorly insulated tinted glass and clear glass with tinted film can get hot, as high as 140 degrees Fahrenheit. These surfaces radiate heat to building occupants and can also create uncomfortable convection currents of warm air.

In this analysis, it is assumed that the two major effects of windows on local thermal discomfort are asymmetric radiation from hot and cold window surfaces and from direct sunlight. Hourly values of *predicted percentage dissatisfied* (PPD) were computed based on the mean radiant temperature given these two effects, room air temperature, humidity, air speed, and ASHRAE Standard 55-92 values for clothing and activity levels. This definition of PPD is more stringent than that defined for ASHRAE 55-92 because of the inclusion of direct sun effects on local discomfort. Nevertheless, it is assumed in this book that the PPD must be less than 20 percent to comply with the Standard.

Figure 2-47 illustrates the impact of window type on thermal comfort in Chicago. Only Windows A and B exceed the 20 PPD level. Since there can be thermal discomfort during both heating and cooling periods, the PPD is influenced by climate and window properties such as U-factor and SHGC, as well as window orientation, size, and shading conditions.

Operable windows can contribute to improved thermal comfort. People have the opportunity to regulate their own thermal environment and use air movement from natural ventilation to feel cooler at higher temperatures. Even though operable windows may not save significant amounts of energy, the fresh air and sense of control they provide contributes to occupant satisfaction.

*Basic Issues in Window Selection and Design*

# Technical Issues

In addition to energy and human factor concerns, windows are influenced by other requirements that at times limit the ability to achieve energy efficiencies within acceptable cost parameters. These technical issues include acoustical performance, structural design, water and weather tightness, condensation resistance, durability, fire protection, and blast resistance.

## ACOUSTIC PERFORMANCE

With noise concerns mounting in both urban and suburban environments, commercial building windows must increasingly address sound transmission. Fortunately, typical strategies for making an energy-efficient window also contribute to its acoustic efficiency; notably, a window that is tightly sealed to arrest unwanted heat or cold will likely minimize unwanted sound. Triple-pane windows and even double-envelope facade systems have acoustic benefits in addition to superior energy performance. However, some acoustic design strategies, such as the use of mass, affect a window's structural and thermal performance, and may adversely impact cost and operability.

This section covers the main issues associated with window system acoustics and design, and the relationships between acoustic design and optimum thermal and structural characteristics. For additional information on acoustics and windows, several references are available (Harris 1997, Bell 1982, Kopec 1997, AAMA TIR A1-02).

### Basic Concepts of Sound

Sound can be compared to waves on a body of water. When the surface of the water is disturbed—for example, when a stone is dropped into a pond—a series of waves spread out concentrically on the water's surface from the point of disturbance. Sound moves through air in roughly the same way; spreading sound waves travel as a series of pressure pulses. Each pulse has a point of maximum pressure followed by a period of lower pressure. The distance between two points of maximum pressure defines the wavelength of the sound. The number of wavelength *periods* that occur in one second determines the frequency of the sound (AAMA TIR A1-02).

Frequency, expressed as Hertz (Hz), is detected by the ear as the pitch of a sound. The higher the frequency, the higher the pitch. An average, healthy human ear can detect a frequency range of 20 to 20,000 Hz. Amplitude is the difference between the maximum and minimum pressures of a sound wave. Amplitude is represented as a Sound Pressure Level (SPL) and is perceived by the ear as the "loudness" of a sound. Figure 2-48 illustrates the comparison between sound waves and waves on water and the relationship of wavelength, frequency, and amplitude.

When sound waves encounter a building component such as a wall, window, or door, the energy of the waves dissipates by reflection, absorption, and/or transmission through the wall. Reflected sound can be perceived as noise—unwanted sound—in adjacent buildings although it may not cause concern in the building from

*Figure 2-48. Sound waves*
Courtesy of AAMA, used with permission.

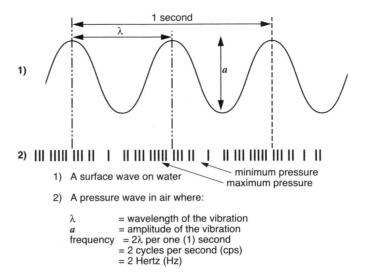

1) A surface wave on water
2) A pressure wave in air where:

$\lambda$ = wavelength of the vibration
$a$ = amplitude of the vibration
frequency = $2\lambda$ per one (1) second
= 2 cycles per second (cps)
= 2 Hertz (Hz)

which it originated. Absorbed sound dissipates as heat and is of little consequence at audible frequencies. Transmitted sound is of concern if it is unwanted and therefore defined as noise within the building that it enters (Figure 2-49).

Sound can be transmitted through fenestration in two ways: a sound wave can pass through the window or door, or cause the window or door to vibrate and act as a secondary sound source. The process of sound passing through a window or door is known as *flanking* (see Figure 2-50).

### Reducing Sound Transmission

Designing acoustically efficient fenestration means maximizing Sound Transmission Loss (STL). Techniques for maximizing STL include absorbing sound or introducing barriers to its transmission. Absorption is most effective at the location of a sound's source (Harris 1997). If unwanted sound cannot be absorbed at its source, a barrier (i.e., a sound-attenuating window in this case) is required. Barriers rely on a combination of reflection and absorption.

Windows and doors that are susceptible to water penetration and air leakage are also susceptible to flanking, so improving the structural and energy performance of a fenestration product will also improve its acoustic performance. Acoustically efficient windows or doors often have multiple rows of gaskets at operating joints. Gaskets or weatherstrips must seal tightly, and their corners must be sealed without increasing the force necessary to open or close the window. Relying on multiple layers rather than a single, super-compressed layer of weatherstripping or gaskets can help keep operational force at an acceptable level. Sealants that are used as barriers to both weather and sound must be applied using proper techniques and must exhibit long service life. A crack in a sealant is an acoustic failure point. As with gaskets and weatherstripping, two lines of sealant,

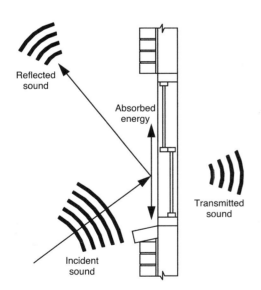

*Figure 2-49. Transmitted sound*
Courtesy of AAMA, used with permission.

preferably with the second one not directly exposed to weather, are more effective in reducing sound transmission than a single sealant.

To reduce the impact of secondary sound transmission—which occurs when a sound wave causes a window or door to vibrate and become a secondary sound source—designers can select components that take maximum advantage of the Mass Law. The Mass Law states that the denser a material (i.e., the greater its mass), the less sound will be transmitted through it (i.e., the molecules of the material are less affected by the energy of the sound wave). The higher the frequency of a sound wave and the greater the decibel level, the more it can cause materials to vibrate. When a sound wave causes the material on the outside of a window or door to vibrate, the material on the opposite side of the fenestration from the incident sound wave is excited, propagating the sound wave. Some sound energy is absorbed by the material, whose natural resonance may also affect the frequency of the transmitted sound.

Fenestration designers and engineers can take advantage of the Mass Law by specifying combinations of materials that vibrate at different frequencies—i.e., have different natural resonances—and thus attenuate the sound energy that is transmitted. Although this design principle can be applied to all window components, including the sash and frame, applying it to glazing most readily and inexpensively produces the desired results. Use of laminated glass is very effective, especially if the glass layers are of different thicknesses. Each layer will have a different mass, resulting in a reasonably predictable STL. The plastic interlayer between glass layers will have a very different mass from the glass and will act as an elastic damper, considerably reducing sound transfer. If an insulating glass unit (IGU) is used, the gas between the lights can also have a beneficial effect if it is heavier than air. An exterior laminated glass pane that combines dissimilar glass thicknesses in an IGU with a heavy gas fill can significantly reduce sound transmission. Increasing the cavity thickness between the inner and outer panes will also change the resonant point of the inner pane, adding to the sound attenuation.

Similar techniques can be used in the design of the sash and frame. An aluminum frame or sash can incorporate a thermal barrier, that also reduces sound transmission. The thermal barrier material acts much like the polyvinyl butyral (PVB) interlayer in laminated glass to create STL. Its elastic properties dampen sound, and the difference in mass between the aluminum and the barrier material behaves according to the Mass Law. Similarly, some acoustically superior frame and sash designs incorporate differing materials in the same cross section. For example, a wood frame may incorporate aluminum cladding on the exterior, or even a significant aluminum frame section joined to the wood, to create a composite frame. This arrangement will produce a measurable STL and appreciably increase the frame's weather resistance while reducing required maintenance. Similar composites have been made from wood and polyvinyl chloride (PVC) or PVC and aluminum.

When techniques such as custom glass or insulating glass and modified frames are used, it is imperative that there are no air leaks or cracks around the window. The positive impact of these expensive physical solutions can be drastically reduced through poor quality control or installation.

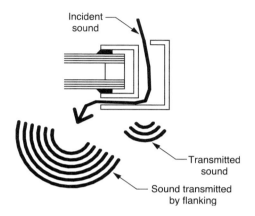

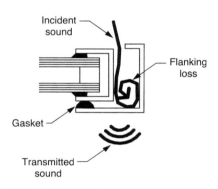

*Figure 2-50. Flanking*
Courtesy of AAMA, used with permission.

## Standards for Assessing Acoustic Performance

The range of human hearing is remarkably large. For example, loud street noise is several hundred times greater than normal breathing, yet both fall within the normal hearing range. Perceptions of variation in the pitch and loudness of sounds are also highly subjective, requiring a widely understood and accepted standard. Figure 2-51 illustrates the range of sounds audible to the human ear.

ASTM Standard E 413, developed in 1970 as a method for determining a Sound Transmission Class (STC) for products, dramatically simplified the process of comparing the acoustic performance of different products. Although the numerical values in this standard "correlate in a general way with subjective impressions of sound transmission for speech, radio, television and similar sources of noise in offices and buildings," they are not appropriate for other sources such as machinery, industrial processes, and transportation (motor vehicles, aircraft, trains, etc.). Specifically, the STC system is not accurate for incident sound that is dominated by low-frequency energy (125 Hz and below), which is characteristic of "railways, airport and highway noise" (AAMA TIR A1-02).

ASTM Standard E 1332 was developed in the late 1980s for comparing product performance for lower-frequency sound sources—80 to 4,000 Hz, with particular attention to the 80 to 100 Hz range that is typically the objectionable portion of the sound emanating from aircraft, trains, and traffic. This standard determines the Outdoor-Indoor Transmission Class (OITC) of a product. Many existing products rated for STC exhibit better performance against mid- and high-frequency incident sound; an OITC rating for the same products may be 5 to 10 points lower if low-frequency sound is a dominant concern in the product's performance. Figure 2-52 compares the STC and OITC ratings for various glazing configurations. Given the differences in STC and OITC ratings, architects or specifiers would be wise to require products with an OITC rating for installations that are near transportation noise sources.

*Figure 2-51. Range of sounds audible to the human ear*
Courtesy of AAMA, used with permission.

| Sound Intensity (W/m²) | Relative Pressure | SPL (dB) | Relative Loudness | Typical Sound |
|---|---|---|---|---|
| 1,000,000,000,000 | 1,000,000 | 120 | 4096 | Thunder clap |
| 100,000,000,000 | 316,228 | 110 | 2048 | Nearby river |
| 1,000,000,000 | 31,623 | 90 | 512 | Loud street noise |
| 100,000,000 | 10,000 | 80 | 256 | Noisy office |
| 10,000,000 | 3,162 | 70 | 128 | Average street noise |
| 1,000,000 | 1,000 | 60 | 64 | Average office |
| 100,000 | 316 | 50 | 32 | Restaurant chatter |
| 10,000 | 100 | 40 | 16 | Private office |
| 1,000 | 32 | 30 | 8 | Bedroom |
| 100 | 10 | 20 | 4 | Whisper |
| 10 | 3 | 10 | 2 | Normal breathing |
| 1 | 1 | 0 | 1 | Audibility threshold |

*Figure 2-52. Sound transmission loss of various glass configurations*
Courtesy of AAMA, used with permission.

| Nominal Thickness | Configuration | STC | OITC |
|---|---|---|---|
| ¼" | Monolithic | 31 | 26 |
| ½" | Monolithic | 36 | 33 |
| ⅜" | ¼" – 0.030 – ⅛" Laminated | 36 | 33 |
| 1" | ¼" – 1/2" air space – ¼" IGU | 35 | 28 |
| 1" | ⅛" – 0.030 – ⅛" Lami – ½" air space – ¼" IGU | 39 | 31 |
| 1 ⅛" | ⅛" – 0.030 – ¼" Lami – ½" air space – ¼" IGU | 40 | 31 |
| 1 1/16" | ⅛" – 0.030 – ⅛" Lami – ½" air space – ⅛" – 0.030 – ⅛" Lami IGU | 42 | 33 |
| 2 5/16" | ⅛" – 0.030 – ⅛" Lami – ½" air space – ⅛" – 0.030 – ⅛" Lami – ½" air space – ⅛" – 0.030 – ⅛" Lami IGU | 49 | 39 |

## Design Strategy for Maximizing Acoustical Performance

Architects and engineers of buildings where noise is a problem must use a systematic approach to select appropriate fenestration products. This approach should consider not only the project's acoustic demands but also other performance requirements, including structural and thermal considerations. The approach described below has been used successfully by many designers:

• *Determine the extent of the problem.*

Determining the frequency and amplitude of the sounds incident on a building requires a survey of the building site as a function of season and time of day. It is recommended that a professional acoustic engineer conduct the survey (*see* Harris 1997).

• *Identify products that can provide the required attenuation.*

After determining the sound transmission rating required for the products to be used, based on the survey of noise sources at the site and the intended use of the building, the specifier can solicit manufacturers for products that provide the necessary STL (standard ratings are Sound Transmission Class (STC) or Outdoor-Indoor Transmission Class (OITC), as explained in the prior subsection). Many manufacturers offer acoustically improved versions of their standard products. The inclusion of features like laminated glass and secondary gaskets or weatherstrips may be adequate to address acoustic needs for low- and mid-range noise. For higher acoustic requirements, the product design will need to be customized and may include up to 4-inch air cavities and dual sash configurations. Triple-pane windows and double-envelope facade systems can be designed to have good acoustic performance.

• *Determine structural and operational adequacy.*

Standard products with added acoustic features, such as laminated glass, may or may not exhibit enhanced structural performance. The weight of acoustic glazing must also be considered. Highly customized, acoustically enhanced windows and doors may contain glazing options that reduce the products' ability to survive sustained winds; this is most likely in a dual window configuration where the exterior glazing is monolithic rather than an IGU. For operable windows, the added glass weight may dictate the need to use heavy-duty operating mechanisms.

- *Determine thermal impact.*

  The thermal performance of fenestration products is highly dependent on glazing. Revisions to the glazing requirements necessitated by the project's acoustic requirements may adversely affect a product's thermal efficiency by changing the space available for a gap and/or the gas fill used. If glazing changes are contemplated, the thermal performance of these altered configurations should be simulated using the procedures developed by the National Fenestration Rating Council (NFRC). The glazing choice that will produce optimum thermal performance may not meet the project's structural wind-load requirements, and the glazing that will give the best acoustic performance may affect the product's structural design—e.g., the product might have to be redesigned with heavy-duty balances or a second set of balances. This structural change could, in turn, cause revisions in the cross section design of the frame and sash members, which could compromise the optimum thermal design. Excessive air gaps for sound attenuation might affect condensation resistance. The specifier must meet all project requirements, which will dictate the glazing options.

- *Review aesthetic and cost considerations.*

  All of the issues discussed above may limit the ability of the acoustically enhanced product to satisfy the aesthetic requirements within the available budget. Larger-than-conventional frame and sash dimensions may be required to provide room for acoustically efficient glazing and additional hardware. Very large air gaps may introduce a small amount of distortion not found in conventional IGUs. Design features such as internal grids may not be possible in acoustic glazing without compromising noise transmission capability. Exactly matching historical profiles, such as true divided lights, is very difficult when a product must also significantly reduce sound transmission. Therefore, the architect is encouraged to explore design possibilities carefully with several manufacturers before deciding on the final appearance of windows and doors.

### Retrofitting to Improve Acoustic Performance

Retrofitting existing windows to improve acoustic performance is not usually feasible. The types of glazing required for acoustic efficiency do not normally fit into standard sash pockets. Some improvements are possible, however. Flanking might be reduced by replacing sealants, which will not only enhance acoustic performance but also reduce air leakage and possibly water penetration. It is also possible to replace glazing weatherstrips and add new, aftermarket weatherstrips. Replacement of glazing gaskets poses a challenge because it requires specialized knowledge, commercial sources of proprietary gaskets are lacking, and there are safety issues associated with the handling of glass units during regasketing which should be undertaken only by a professional glazier.

Reducing air leakage is typically the most effective retrofitting strategy; other approaches should not usually be considered if leakage cannot be controlled. Replacement of existing glazing with glazing that includes laminated glass can also improve acoustic performance. In this case, each piece of glass within the laminated glass should be of a different thickness. Improving acoustic performance by increasing the IGU air cavity is normally impossible because existing sashes will not accommodate marked increases in the IGU thickness. Aftermarket storm products, especially those with laminated glass, can offer improved acoustic and thermal performance. They should be installed so that the perimeter joints where they attach to the building or window are as airtight as possible to prevent flanking. The disadvantage of permanently fixing storm products over operable windows is that they effectively render them inoperable.

## STRUCTURAL ISSUES

The primary structural requirement of fenestration products and systems in commercial buildings is a capacity to withstand wind and other structural loads. A fenestration system which has catastrophic structural failures can lead to property damage, can be a potential source of injury, and can lead to increased energy use. Structural issues will thus preempt any energy concerns. Secondary structural failures (cracked or broken glass, loss of air or water resistance, or sealant failures caused by excessive deflection) can compromise the thermal integrity of a building envelope and lead to long-term increases in energy use.

This section highlights issues which must be considered in the design of a fenestration product to meet its structural requirements. The energy implications of these issues are summarized briefly in this section. An explanation of the engineering design of windows for structural performance is outside the scope of this book. For additional information on structural issues in windows, several references are available (AAMA TIR A10-00, TIR A11-96, and GDSG-97).

### Types of Loads

Wind blowing against a structure is not constant in force or direction and does not act in a uniform fashion, although it is often convenient to treat it as a uniformly applied force. Wind gusts change velocity and wind direction changes over short periods of time. The effect of wind on a building or other structure is also variable. On the windward side of the building the wind exerts a positive or inward-acting pressure. At the building corners and on the leeward side, the wind exerts a suction or negative pressure acting outward. Because of the directional changes and gusting velocities characteristic of wind, all sides of the structure are subjected to both positive and negative loads of varying intensities over time. Building structural engineers must design to address these wind-imposed loads.

The primary elements of a building which transfer the force of the wind to the building's main structural elements are known as components and cladding, which can be partially or almost completely comprised of fenestration products. Like the main structural frame, they must be designed to carry the full or design wind load mandated in the building code for the anticipated life of the building. Unlike the mainframe, components and cladding are not required to carry dead loads and live loads imposed by the building structure, the occupants, a snow load, or other long-term loads.

Designers use commonly accepted codes or standards (such as ASCE 7) to determine the required design window loads. Several requirements must be established including the positive and negative design load(s), the area of the building where these loads are to be applied, and the effect of the building configuration in generating special localized loads, if any. Before this set of requirements can be determined, the designer must be able to specify the location of the building on a wind-speed map, the mean roof height of the building, the presence of any ground irregularities such as deep valleys or cliffs, the proximity to large bodies of water, the importance of the building surviving a severe weather event (i.e., buildings where emergency services might be offered after a severe storm) and any other localized conditions that might affect the design pressures.

Subsequent to defining the design requirements, the design engineer must address the ability of both the framing and glazing to meet or exceed the required design loads. In moderate and colder climates, snow loads on sloped glazings must also be considered. Generally, sloped glazing is considered as anything with more than a 15-degree slope off vertical or up from horizontal.

Another concern in the basic design approach for glass is the concept of thermal stress. Thermal breakage of glass is generally caused by the uneven heating of glass by solar radiation and is one of the most common causes of annealed glass breakage in buildings. The classic thermal breakage situation occurs when the edges of a glass plate are shielded by the window frame or another shading condition, thereby causing an uneven buildup of heat (and thus extreme temperature gradients) on the glass. This condition causes tensile stress to develop along certain edges of the glass, and can lead to a higher thermal load than the glass can withstand. If the glass is not properly strengthened to meet the anticipated thermal loading conditions, a thermally induced crack will be introduced.

It is important to have a thermal analysis performed using general information available from the glass manufacturer's guidelines. In very specific cases, the results of a finite element analysis model can be used to determine the thermal stress conditions of a glass product. Other factors that influence thermal stresses include the thermal performance of the glazing system, gaskets and sealants around the glass edge, glass bite or engagement into the framing system, and the edge support conditions of the glass. It is important to conduct a review of the shading conditions from the exterior along with a review of interior shading devices. These devices can cause heat-traps, or give rise to higher glass temperatures if the shading device is not properly installed or ventilated. An ASTM committee is presently developing a thermal stress standard.

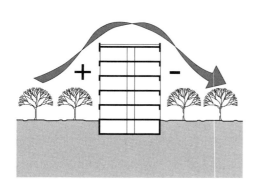

*Figure 2-53. Positive and negative pressures around a building induced by wind*

*Basic Issues in Window Selection and Design*

## Resisting Loads

Structural loads imposed on fenestration products are met by a variety of means including glass and frame materials as well as connections. How these loads are met in the design and construction of a building and its window systems impacts thermal performance, as illustrated below:

### Framing Material

Typically, fenestration products in commercial buildings utilize aluminum or steel as the primary framing material. These materials have the strength and stiffness necessary to resist large structural loads. However, they are much more conductive materials than wood or plastic. This increased conductivity requires that the interior frame be separated from the exterior by a less conductive material such as plastic or rubber. The inclusion of these thermal barriers or thermal breaks allows the use of aluminum or steel framing systems that can meet or exceed condensation and heat loss specifications, from either the architect or a building code. Since the thermal barrier materials do not normally have the same structural capacity as the framing materials, designing for thermal efficiency may compromise maximum structural capacity.

### Span of Framing Elements

Minimizing glass, framing, and sash deflection under structural loading is extremely important to the proper selection of glass and framing elements. Excessive deflections can lead to glass and frame cross-section breakage, as well as air and water infiltration. Allowable deflections depend on the building construction type (less deflection is allowed in masonry buildings) and the type of glass used. Larger and/or more frequent framing cross sections are required to minimize deflections. The implication of larger framing areas is that the window properties are more dependent on the frame properties than the glass properties—generally leading to increased U-factors (more heat is lost through frames) and lower solar heat gain coefficients.

### Anchoring of Framing to Building

Framing for fenestration products must be anchored to the building. There are various methods for doing so, but the most common is for the vertical frames to be anchored at both ends and for the head and sill framing to be anchored to the structure on a relatively continuous basis by fasteners spaced as closely as necessary to achieve the full load-carrying capacity of the fenestration product. This scenario is referred to as *simply supported* or *single-span* loading.

If a thermally broken aluminum or steel frame is used, fasteners may create a thermal short circuit through the thermal break, decreasing its effectiveness in insulating against heat loss and preventing condensation. The more fasteners, the greater the chance of short circuiting. Two-dimensional heat transfer simulations show how stainless steel bolts increase heat transfer through a curtain wall cross section (Figure 2-54). The image on the left shows a curtain wall cross section (with insulating glass on either side), without a bolt. The image on the right includes the effects of bolts spaced at regular intervals. The presence of the bolt reduces the inside surface temperatures (inside on the right of each image) by approximately 4 degrees Fahrenheit, leading to increased energy use, condensation, as well as occupant discomfort. However, bolts are required to keep the curtain wall attached to the building frame. Systems that do not use fasteners spanning the thermal barrier are available and would typically be more thermally efficient but may be more costly to install.

### Type of Glass

In addition to the frame materials and connections, the type of glass affects structural performance as well. While glass has been produced for thousands of years, the float glass process has revolutionized the production of glass over the last 40 years. Standard float or annealed glass starts out as a molten mix and goes through an annealing process in which the glass is slowly cooled by controlled heating and cooling. This is followed by gradually blowing air through a sheet-cooling device to the point where the glass can be cut. The annealing process allows the glass to be cooled so that residual stresses are minimized. The strength of annealed glass can be enhanced to meet higher mechanical and thermal loads by subjecting it to a heat-treatment process. This process locks a residual stress distribution in the glass, and subsequently increases its overall strength. In this heat-strengthening process, annealed glass is heated to a temperature near its softening point and is quickly cooled or quenched, allowing the surface to cool faster than the center. The end result is that residual stresses are locked inside the glass. Depending on the surface compression left in the glass from the heat-strengthening process, the glass is either referred to as "heat-strengthened" or "fully tempered."

*Figure 2-54. Two-dimensional heat transfer simulations show how stainless steel bolts increase heat transfer through a curtain wall cross section*

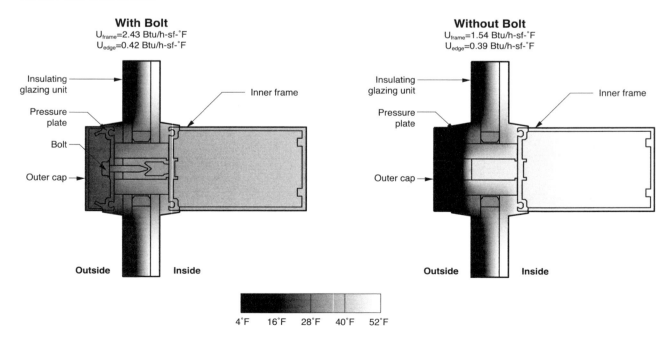

*Basic Issues in Window Selection and Design*

It is conservatively estimated that heat-strengthened glass is twice as strong as annealed glass of the same size and thickness while fully tempered glass is four times as strong.

*Glass Thickness*

Increases in the thickness of glass enhance its ability to resist a given load. The industry is continually developing more specific and accurate means to determine the load resistance of specific glass types, including many combinations of monolithic, insulated, and heat-strengthened glass. Glass thickness typically has its most significant impact on solar gain—a thicker glass of the same type (tint) has a reduced solar transmittance. Thicker glass has an insignificant impact on heat loss rates (U-factor) and reducing condensation as long as the cavity between the panes in an IGU is kept constant. If the glass thickness has to be increased and the overall dimensions of the IGU must remain constant, the cavity will have to be reduced and there will likely be a reduction in the window's insulating value.

## WATER CONTROL AND WEATHERPROOFING

Preventing water transmission and minimizing unwanted air movement are prime requirements of windows and other fenestration products. Commercial building products are designed and built to achieve certain goals in this regard. This section briefly covers the main constraints that water/weatherproofing impose on window design and discusses related thermal impacts. For additional information on this subject, the reader is referred to specific references (AAMA SFM-87, Burt et al 1969, Galitz et al, Rousseau and Quirouette, Lstiburek and Carmody 1994, AAMA CW-RS-1 and CW-RS-2).

### Air Infiltration and Exfiltration

Air infiltration and exfiltration through fenestration products is the uncontrolled movement of air through joints in the product and in the surrounding framing. Infiltration is the movement of air from the outside in, while exfiltration is the movement of air from the inside out. Infiltration and exfiltration are typically unwanted and minimized, although in certain instances, nominal levels of infiltration/exfiltration may be beneficial for addressing air quality issues.

Infiltration and exfiltration occurs due to three factors: poor product design, poor quality control during product manufacturing, and poor construction detailing and/or installation. Test procedures such as ASTM E283 are used widely in the industry to account for product design, and to some extent, quality control. Testing actual products off the production line at random will ensure that quality control is accounted for in infiltration test results. Infiltration due to poor construction detailing and/or installation can only be accounted for in test results if specific mock-ups of the wall section are designed and tested.

Two guide specifications (ANSI/AAMA/NWWDA 101/I.S. 2 and ANSI/AAMA/WDMA 101/I.S. 2/NAFS) were developed for window, door, and skylight performance, including permissible air leakage. These specifications are generally consistent with building codes used throughout the United States. Generally, operable products with an infiltration rate of less than 0.3 cfm/square foot are required. Architectural grade products utilizing a compression seal are required to have an infiltration rate of less than 0.1 cfm/square foot. Nonoperable products are not expected to have a measurable level of infiltration.

Natural ventilation—the practice of operating windows to provide fresh air and cooling—is distinct from the issue of infiltration/exfiltration as it is based on the controlled movement of air through open windows.

## Waterproofing

Water penetration through windows and doors has been a problem since the first holes were poked in the walls of the earliest buildings. Uncontrolled water can destroy window and door framing members, destroy or deteriorate interior furnishings, promote the growth of mold and mildew, and deteriorate the elements of walls and wall cavities found below window- and doorsills. It is absolutely necessary that fenestration products control and weep to the exterior any water that enters the product as a result of rainstorms.

Many recent studies of water penetration in buildings have attempted to relate rain intensity and wind velocity in order to model more accurately the amount of water incident on a wall or fenestration product (Galitz et al, Rousseau and Quirouette). Wind-driven rain impacts different points on a building envelope at different angles, speeds, and volumes. The greatest amounts of incident water are not on the center of the windward wall but at the upper vertical corners and the upper edge of the wall near the roof line. In fact, the center and lower half of the building has much less water volume from wind-driven rain than had been previously expected. After a storm has begun, water cascades down the building from the top, providing a second source for potential penetration (Rousseau and Quirouette). The designer must understand the mechanics of water exposure in order to design wall assemblies properly, including the integration of fenestration products.

The designer must also be aware that the mechanism commonly causing condensation on visible interior glazing surfaces can cause condensation within wall cavities as well. This condensation, which often goes undetected, can lead to the destruction of wall components and building finishes, and may also result in mold and mildew.

Water that appears to be the result of leaking windows and doors is often a result of penetration at another location. The most obvious source is the perimeter sealant between the fenestration product and the building. The vast majority of field calls for water leakage are actually due to poor installation. Fenestration products are often designed with multiple, sometimes redundant, lines of sealant or weatherstripping to prevent water penetration. They may also be designed as rainscreen or pressure-equalized systems for enhanced performance. When tested in the laboratory for high performance levels these products must remain watertight at conditions exceeding Category 5 hurricanes. Therefore it should not be surprising that the majority of water leaks are due to the often-untested installation or its detailing rather than the fenestration product.

Water that appears on window- and doorsills may be an indication of leaks within roof and wall assemblies, not the window itself. Water that enters the building may penetrate at roof parapets, overflowing gutters, balconies, and holes or voids in the weatherproof barrier provided by the wall sheathing. This water flows downward in the wall cavity due to gravity. If it fails to meet an obstruction such as a window or door it may reach the bottom of the wall and weep to the exterior, causing little damage. If it fails to exit at the bottom of the wall, it may cause considerable structural damage to the building. When water flowing in a wall cavity encounters the top or head of a window or door it may be diverted into the framing of the fenestration products. Even then, a well-designed product can capture this water flow and divert it to the wall exterior. If the water is not directed to the exterior, it may appear at the window- or doorsill as visible water. This "leak" is not attributable to the fenestration product, but the uninformed may identify this as poor product performance.

Several test methods that can be used at the building site have been developed to evaluate water penetration. ASTM E 1105 is a method for field testing windows and doors for water penetration. AAMA 502 is a specification for the field testing of windows and doors which guides the testing agency in using E 1105 and provides the architect with a means of requiring quality control testing of large building projects. AAMA 503 provides similar guidance for storefronts and curtain walls. These test methods can be used to evaluate both the fenestration assembly and installation details.

## Product Design Issues

The design of fenestration system framing materials must take into account waterproofing. While most water is stopped at the outer surface of the wall, designers must acknowledge some penetration and develop means to control the penetration of water. Features to minimize water penetration and direct water which penetrates the exterior surface back to the outside are discussed in this section. How such issues are addressed can influence heat transfer through window frames.

### Designing for Drainage

Operating products should be designed to resist as much water as possible but also to acknowledge that some water will penetrate the exterior plane of the product. This water, which will collect at the sill, must be allowed to exit through "weep holes." Weep holes often contain baffles or capping devices that allow water to flow to the exterior but do not permit wind-driven rain to enter through the sweeps. A window or door which does not weep to the exterior will leak to the interior.

### Internal Drain Paths

Internal drain paths should direct water away from internal sealant joints in order to keep sealants from failing and divert water from the edge seals of insulating glass units. Insulating glass units should never be allowed to sit in water at the sill and incidental water in the fenestration assembly should not be allowed to fall on top of an IGU.

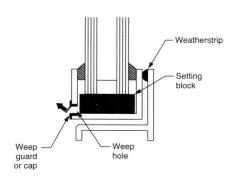

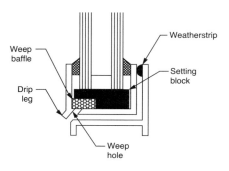

Figure 2-55. Weep holes in windows

## Weep Systems

These devices must be large enough to provide adequate flow of water from the internal cavities of the assembly. For large windows used in commercial buildings, the equivalent of two ⅜-inch diameter holes is generally enough (Figure 2-55).

## Subsills and Flashing

Subsills and flashing provide water protection for the space between the window product and the opening in the wall. Subsills are tracks secured to the bottom of the rough opening in a building to aid in window installation and to provide some redundancy in preventing water from entering building cavities. Flashings are generally fabricated from sheet metal to fit around the corners of the lower portion of the rough opening; they generally provide a vertical leg along the inside of the opening which continues up the vertical sides of the rough opening (Figure 2-56).

## Gaskets and Sealants

Gasket or sealant failure will adversely affect window performance, including lowering resistance to water and air infiltration and reductions in thermal efficiency. Gaskets must remain resilient over the expected service life of the window, and are integral with a window unit. Sealants are typically applied in the field, but they must also be resilient and long-lasting. Both require attention from the designer.

Gaskets—available in a wide variety of shapes, sizes, and designs—cushion the glazing, with gasket compression a prime issue of window and door design. If the gasket is not compressed sufficiently, air and water infiltration will be increased. If the gasket is over

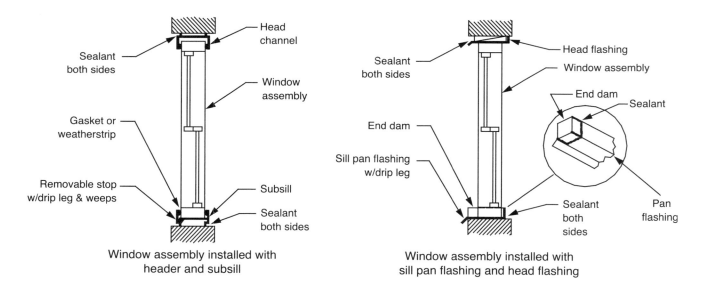

Figure 2-56. Subsills and pan flashing

compressed there may be enough force to either deform the gasket, causing a loss or reduction in its sealing abilities, or in rare cases the gasket may be forced out of the glazing pocket over time.

Sealants must be compatible with the substrates to which they are expected to adhere. It is very important that sealants be properly installed, to guard against adhesive or cohesive failure. A typical installation concern is temperature; most sealants cannot be applied to surfaces colder than 40 degrees Fahrenheit. Sealant manufactures and product literature must be consulted on environmental and other material related factors affecting adhesion.

### Pressure Equalization in Air Chambers

The concept of a pressure-equalized wall has been developed to limit water penetration by minimizing the pressure difference between the interior and exterior. The theory behind such envelope designs is complex and the interested reader is referred to specific references on this subject (Rousseau and Quirouette, Lstiburek and Carmody 1994, AAMA CW-RS-1 and CW-RS-2). However, the use of such a technique requires building interior chambers into the fenestration product design which can build up to the same air pressure as the exterior (Figures 2-57 and 2-58).

## Waterproofing and Thermal Efficiency

The techniques used to develop waterproof products and installation measures necessary to combat water infiltration impacts thermal efficiency. Air flowing in and out of weep holes and pressure equalization chambers reduce energy performance, as do the thermal bridges created by sills and flashing. These thermal compromises are needed, however, as water penetration or sitting water (a thermal

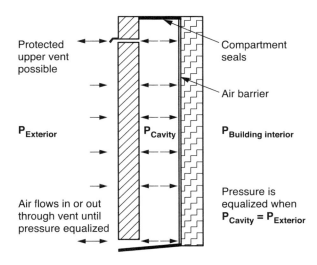

Figure 2-57. Principle of pressure equalization
Courtesy of AAMA, used with permission.

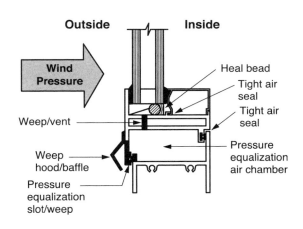

Figure 2-58. Pressure-equalized rain screen system design
Courtesy of AAMA, used with permission.

short circuit) in walls and windows is far more devastating, and leads to increased energy use. Proper window installation, from their initial setting to final sealant application, is critical to maintaining IGU durability and effectiveness.

## CONDENSATION RESISTANCE

Condensation costs building owners millions of dollars a year in repair costs and thermal energy losses. Poorly or moderately insulating windows can contribute significantly to the formation of condensation in interior spaces. Furthermore, when water enters the framing of fenestration, it creates a thermal short circuit that can compromise the insulation value of the sash and framing members and increase heat transfer through the product, reducing the window's energy efficiency.

This section summarizes three issues: the mechanisms by which condensation forms, the relationship between condensation and fenestration design, particularly with regard to windows' thermal efficiency, and standards and computer modeling relevant to condensation issues. For more information about condensation and windows, the reader should consult the Moisture Control Handbook (Lstiburek and Carmody 1994) and other resources (AAMA 1503-98, AAMA SFM-87, Burt et al 1969, NFRC 500 User's Guide).

### How Condensation Forms

Condensation forms when air encounters a surface with a temperature at or below the air's dew point. The dew point is based on the relative humidity of the air; the more moisture is in the air, the higher the temperature at which condensation begins to form. In addressing condensation resistance, designers attempt to keep all surface temperatures above the dew point, taking into account indoor and outdoor temperatures, relative humidity, air movement, and specific elements of the building that affect air movement around fenestration (e.g., use of heavy drapes) and could create local areas of condensation.

#### Indoor Temperature

Although heating, ventilation, and air-conditioning (HVAC) systems are designed to provide a constant indoor temperature, temperatures are not typically uniform throughout a space. Condensation resistance strategies must consider the range of possible temperatures in a space. Condensation is often a result of building design conditions not being maintained at indoor surfaces, particularly next to fenestration products and in wall cavities. An example of this phenomenon is described in the next subsection.

#### Outdoor Temperature

Designers typically determine the coldest outdoor temperature that a building is likely to experience during a 50-year period using a reference such as the ASHRAE Handbook of Fundamentals or the SAMSON or CWEEDS databases.

*Relative Humidity*

Actual indoor relative humidity may vary from that specified by the HVAC design as the result of a number of interior elements and activities, including carpets, synthetic fibers, desktop computers and other electronic devices, humidifiers, plants, smoking, cooking, bathing, and clothes washing and drying.

*Air Movement*

Air movement in commercial buildings can be affected by the configuration (and reconfiguration) of interior walls and movable partitions, tall furniture (e.g., bookcases, filing cabinets), and drapes. When airflow is blocked, significant air temperature variations and stratification of humid air adjacent to cool surfaces can result, which can cause condensation problems.

## Examples of Condensation

The temperature and humidity of indoor air is rarely uniform throughout an occupied building. Consider the example of a warm-air inlet located directly below a window equipped with floor-to-ceiling drapes or other window treatments. The air that exits the ventilator may be at design conditions for temperature and humidity; however, as heated air flows into the room, it will rise and draw cooler air in at the floor from hallways and other rooms, as well as air infiltration through the window and other wall openings. This inflow of cooler air results in vertical temperature differences from floor to ceiling. The degree of vertical stratification will depend on many factors, including the relative airtightness of the building, the conditions in adjacent spaces, and the efficiency of the HVAC system.

Similarly, temperature and humidity are less uniform in the reveals of windows because of turbulent airflow. If the window frame and glazing are relatively flush with the interior walls, the inlet air will experience little turbulence as it passes the window reveal. However, if the reveal is deeper than one or two inches, turbulence will cause air to be trapped in pockets near the corners of the framing or, in severe cases, in a layer that covers a substantial portion of the glazing's interior surface. Figure 2-59 illustrates the trapping of air next to windows.

During daylight hours, the sun heats the air trapped next to the window's interior surface to a temperature higher than that of the room air, increasing the trapped air's capacity to hold water vapor. Excess moisture will be drawn from the room air and concentrated in the trapped air pockets. Although both the room air and the trapped air will have the same relative humidity, the trapped air will have a higher water vapor content because of its higher temperature. After the sun goes down, particularly if drapes or blinds are closed over the window at night, the trapped air cools, and its capacity to hold water drops. At the same time, the window surface temperature drops as solar heating and outdoor air temperatures decrease. The dew point of the trapped air becomes higher than that of the room air, which remains at design levels of temperature and relative humidity. If the window surface temperatures reach the dew point of the trapped air,

*Figure 2-59. Trapping of air next to windows*
Courtesy of AAMA, used with permission.

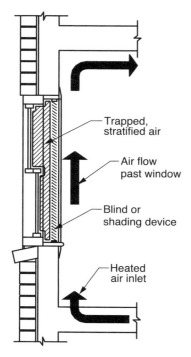

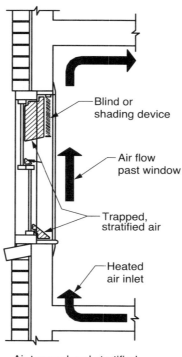

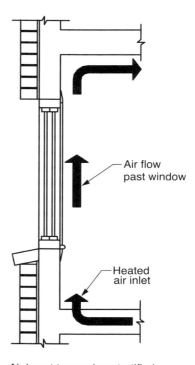

Air trapped and stratified
behind blind or shading device
is isolated from room air

Air trapped and stratified
behind blind or shading device
is isolated from room air

Air is not trapped or stratified
behind blind or shading device
and is not isolated from room air

condensation will result. If the air had not been stratified and trapped by the window, it would have the same properties as the room air, and condensation would likely not occur.

Many condensation problems in buildings have been solved by opening drapes and placing box fans next to windows to direct room air toward the window surfaces. Good design practice can avoid the need for such after-the-fact fixes. The example illustrates the importance of the installed position of a window or door, the use of window coverings, and designs for non-turbulent air movement over window and door surfaces, especially at night, to reduce the likelihood of condensation. If elements that increase the risk of condensation are part of a design, fenestration products that have better than ordinary condensation performance should be used.

It should be noted that temperatures in wall cavities are different from indoor room air and surface temperatures. Moreover, a thermally efficient wall includes a moisture barrier designed to isolate the cavity from the interior in northern climates and the exterior in southern climates (Lstiburek and Carmody 1994).

*Basic Issues in Window Selection and Design*

## Rating Condensation Resistance

Both the National Fenestration Rating Council (NFRC) and the American Architectural Manufacturers Association (AAMA) have developed systems for rating the condensation resistance (CR) of fenestration products.

AAMA 1503, developed in the 1970s, gives a dimensionless rating, the Condensation Resistance Factor (CRF), ranging from 0 to 100; the higher the number, the better a product resists forming condensation. A value of 35 is considered to be a "thermally improved" product. The standard's testing method measures temperatures on the product's interior surfaces to assess the potential for condensation; the rating is based on an algorithm that is heavily weighted toward the four coldest surface temperature measurements. Figure 2-60, which is included in the standard, enables the user to determine the required CRF value for a building location based on the outside design temperature and the design relative humidity for the building interior.

Adopted in 2002, NFRC 500 determines Condensation Resistance (CR) based on computer simulation. The rating value is based on interior surface temperatures at 30 percent, 50 percent, and 70 percent indoor relative humidity for a given outside air temperature of 0 degrees Fahrenheit under 15 mph wind conditions.

## Computer Modeling

Computer simulation can be used to model the expected performance of fenestration in buildings and optimize designs for condensation resistance. *WINDOW 5* and *THERM 5*, developed by the Lawrence

*Figure 2-60. Condensation resistance factor*
Courtesy of AAMA, used with permission.

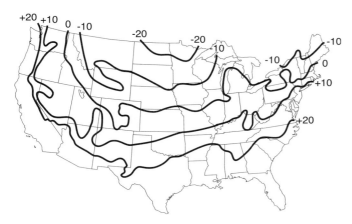

WINTER OUTSIDE DESIGN TEMPERATURE ASHRAE 97.5% BASE*
Temperature data for specific locations are given in Chapter 33, Weather Data and Design Conditions, *ASHRAE Handbook of Fundamentals* published by American Society of Heating, Refrigerating and Air-Conditioning Engineers, Inc.

*97.5% of the time during the months of December, January, and February, the temperature will not be at or below the indicated design temperature.

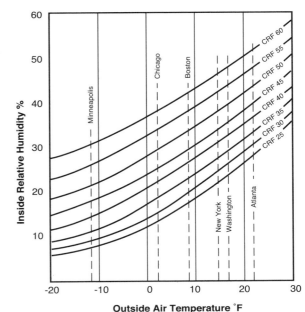

Berkeley National Laboratory for the United States Department of Energy, can simulate U-factors for fenestration products as outlined in NFRC 100. The surface temperatures calculated by the software can also be input to the equations in NFRC 500 to determine the potential CR rating of a proposed design.

### Condensation Resistance and Energy Efficient Design

A design that includes good thermal insulation and solar heat gain control may need to be modified in consideration of condensation resistance. The high inside surface temperatures associated with a low U-factor will reduce the potential for condensation where air movement is maintained and the potential for stratification is minimized. However, as noted above, if a window design includes deep reveals and/or window coverings, increased air infiltration into the reveal area may be needed. This strategy will decrease the overall thermal efficiency of the wall. (However, because cold outside air has a limited capacity to hold water vapor, the drying effect of this air as it infiltrates lowers the apparent relative humidity of the air next to the window's surface, which reduces the likelihood of condensation.)

Condensation can cause the degradation of materials such as insulation and thermal barriers, decreasing their thermal efficiency. Water in window, door, or wall cavities can also cause sealants to lose adhesion, resulting in increased air infiltration. Window, door, and wall systems that are not appropriate to a building's climate can result in lower-than-desirable interior surface temperatures, which increase the probability of condensation.

To address both thermal efficiency and condensation, an architect can begin by selecting the required thermal transmittance (U-factor) and solar heat gain coefficient (SHGC) for fenestration. Having established energy performance objectives consistent with the project budget and aesthetic goals, the designer should then specify the minimum CR/CRF for the interior surfaces temperatures and room conditions.

## DURABILITY

The durability of a fenestration product directly affects its energy performance. If, for example, insulating glass seals or low-emissivity coatings fail, a product's thermal performance will be seriously compromised. Durability denotes a product's ability to perform as designed over a period of time. Important elements of a fenestration product's durability include the ability to resist condensation and air and water infiltration while maintaining thermal and structural performance as well as aesthetic features.

A durable fenestration system must address climate, including exposure to extreme weather, as well as particular site microclimate conditions. Regular maintenance is important to maintain product durability; degradation of structural and material components will negatively affect durability and energy performance.

This section briefly summarizes some of the major influences on the durability of fenestration systems, the general impact of compromised durability on energy performance, and standards relevant to testing the durability of products.

## Designing for Durability

Key fenestration components affecting durability that should be carefully considered during design include: framing components, glazing compounds, gasket and sealant materials, gas infill materials, and hardware and mechanical devices used to operate system elements. Designers should take into account the sensitivity of products to heat, ultraviolet radiation, and moisture. Solar control and low-emissivity coatings in particular may be sensitive to other environmental conditions, including exposure to salts and corrosive materials. Controlling moisture penetration and exposure of an insulating glass unit's edge seals to water is of great importance in any commercial building fenestration design.

The durability of a proposed fenestration design can best be assessed in accelerated weathering tests as well as field studies. These tests, typically conducted over extended time periods, determine whether a window system can meet the demands of weather and temperature differences that it will likely encounter during its lifetime. Window systems rather than individual components are typically tested. Suppliers and manufacturers also examine the durability of materials, components, and assemblies with positive and negative pressure cycling tests, temperature cycling, and motion testing.

## Impact of Durability Issues on Energy Performance

A durable window system will meet its energy performance criteria—U-factor, solar heat gain coefficient, and air infiltration parameters—over time. Failure of components such as sealants and gaskets will degrade thermal performance and may lead to loss of insulating gas in units with gas infill, in addition to permitting air and water to penetrate the glazing system and the building. The National Fenestration Rating Council is in the process of developing long-term durability test procedures aimed at determining the effects of individual physical weathering and durability impacts on specific product U-factors, solar heat gain coefficients, air-infiltration rates, and condensation resistance.

The durability of insulating glass units is critical to maintaining the energy performance of window and door assemblies. Minimum performance levels have been established in the United States and Canada requiring that insulating glass units conform to ASTM E 774, Level A, CGSB 12.8, or ASTM E 2190. Proof of compliance may be by a test report from an independent accredited laboratory or by certification of the IGU by IGMA, IGCC, ALI or another certifying agency acceptable to the specifier. These certification programs require compliance with the performance standards and the establishment of a reliable quality control program at the manufacturing plant. The IGMA technical manual, TM-4000-02 "Insulating Glass Manufacturing Quality Procedure Manual", and IGU certification represents a significant increase in quality control requirements for the manufacture of insulating glass.

The IGMA quality control provisions, or equivalent, should be the minimum level of quality control acceptable for IGU production. However, there are a number of quality control provisions that are referenced in EN 1279—which should be considered by the manufacturer. Standards related to durability and durability testing are listed in the references. Most of these standards relate to the durability of individual components (such as IGU sealants) or impacts from specific conditions (such as seismic and wind).

## FIRE PROTECTION

In the past, the only option for architects and engineers designing fire-resistant buildings was solid walls with no fenestration; today, however, a number of window and door options are available that are both fire resistant and also energy efficient.

This section summarizes the key concepts related to fire protection and fenestration, the relationship between fire-resistant and energy-efficient fenestration designs, and relevant standards.

### Key Concepts of Fire Protection and Fenestration Design

The key fire protection issues for a fenestration product are the ability of the frame and glazing to resist heat, flames, and smoke. Extremely high temperatures can transfer through glass; fire-rated glass products must be able to meet the same standards as fire-rated barrier walls.

Door and window frames are available with fire ratings ranging from 20 minutes to three hours. Fire-resistant glazing materials include: wire glass, ceramic products, glass ceramics combined with insulating glass, and multiple transparent glass layers with an intumescent material. The whole window unit—glazing, frame, and sealants—must meet the required fire rating.

Materials and components needed for a fire-rated fenestration product may not be available in all sizes, so designers should verify the availability of materials before finalizing a design. Impact safety ratings should also be considered when choosing materials. In addition, the location of building sprinklers should be taken into account because hot glass may shatter when struck by sprinkler water.

### Fire Protection and Energy Efficiency

Designers can incorporate insulating glass into a fire-rated window by using a glass light with a fire-rated, fire-resistant material on one side of the IGU and a tempered or annealed light on the other side. Fire-rated glazing material can also be used in combination with some low-emissivity glass, solar control coatings, applied films, and laminated glass constructions to meet energy-performance requirements. Fire-rated glazing systems can also meet sound reduction, blast resistance, and hurricane resistance requirements. ASTM standards, noted in the references, have been developed to evaluate product performance.

## BLAST RESISTANCE

Fenestration design for commercial buildings must address the vulnerability of window glass to storms and other natural forces as well as man-made threats such as bomb blasts.

This section summarizes the major considerations in designing fenestration to withstand the force of major storms, bomb explosions, and similar conditions. It also considers the relationship between blast-resistant and energy-efficient fenestration design, and the standards relevant to blast resistance.

## Key Concepts of Blast Resistance

The primary purpose of blast-resistant glazing is to protect building occupants, bystanders, and building contents from shattering and flying glass. Blast-resistant glazing is designed to maintain its integrity under major air pressure loads; it should either remain in the frame to protect the building interior and occupants without creating hazardous falling debris or, if it fails, should exhibit predictable fragmentation characteristics, minimizing risk to people and property. In addition to the glazing, other structural elements of a window system—such as the frame—must also be designed to resist air pressure loads from blasts and storms.

Blast-resistant fenestration products available today use monolithic glass, laminated glass, glass-clad polycarbonates, or insulating glass. Laminated glass generally consists of two or more plies of a monolithic glass adhered with an interlayer of polyvinyl butryl (PVB). The glass in a blast-resistant laminated product can be annealed, heat-strengthened, fully tempered, or chemically tempered. Glass-clad polycarbonate products consist of two glass plies with a thin polycarbonate interlayer that provides blast resistance. Two lights of insulating glass with a sealed air space between them can be considered blast resistant if one light is monolithic, laminated, glass-clad polycarbonate, or a combination of these.

Special safety films can be retrofitted to create blast resistant windows. For instance, window films of polyethylene terephthalate (PET) can be adhered to inside lights of existing windows. The security provided by these films hinges on their thickness and how they are attached to the glass. Different edge conditions are considered with the security window film application, which could consist of daylight on the window, edge to edge, a wet-glazed technique, or mechanically attached.

## Blast-Resistant Design Strategy

Architects and engineers typically consult specialists for assistance with blast designs. The key elements of the design process are to assess the peak increase in pressure (over atmospheric) for which a product needs to be designed, the duration of the overpressure (in milliseconds), and the peak pressure in pounds per square inch. As shown in Figures 2-61 and 2-62, the Government Services Administration GSA identifies five performance conditions, representing different protection levels. In many instances, a specific test will be required to verify a fenestration product's actual load resistance and fragmentation pattern. The design is sometimes limited by the test facility. For hurricane-resistant products, specific test protocols assess the impact of small projectiles fired at the glass, as well as larger projectiles, such as a two-by-four.

*Figure 2-62. Levels of blast resistance*

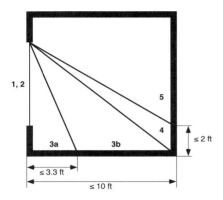

*Figure 2-61. Performance requirements for distribution of glass fragments illustrated in a typical space*

| Performance Condition | Protection Level | Hazard Level | Description of Window Glazing Response |
|---|---|---|---|
| 1 | Safe | None | Glass does not break. No visible damage to glazing or frame. |
| 2 | Very High | None | Glass cracks but is retained by the frame. Dusting or very small fragments near sill or on floor acceptable. |
| 3a | High | Very Low | Glass cracks. Fragments enter space and land on floor no further than 3.3 feet from the window. |
| 3b | High | Low | Glass cracks. Fragments enter space and land on floor no further than 10 feet from the window. |
| 4 | Medium | Medium | Glass cracks. Fragments enter space and land on floor and impact a vertical witness panel at a distance of no more than 10 feet from the window at a height no greater than 2 feet above the floor. |
| 5 | Low | High | Glass cracks and window system fails catastrophically. Fragments enter space impacting a vertical witness panel at a distance of no more than 10 feet from the window at a height greater than 2 feet above the floor. |

## Blast-Resistance and Energy-Efficient Design

Generally, the components used in blast-resistant and security glazing are combinations of known glazing products. Energy-performance criteria can often be incorporated into blast-resistant designs. In particular, solar-control or low-emissivity coatings and combinations of insulating glass products can be used and, as noted above, insulating glass can be used in laminated blast-resistant products. However, because many of these products are still considered specialty products at the time of this writing, cost increases can be significant and product choice can be limited.

*Basic Issues in Window Selection and Design*

# CHAPTER 3

# Window Materials and Assemblies

## Introduction

Designers of commercial buildings must choose from a wide range of possible window materials and assemblies. This chapter provides an introduction to these components, beginning with simple glazing materials and leading to complex facade systems. Conventional glazing materials and emerging glazing technologies are presented in the first two sections, which is followed by descriptions of frame materials and types of facade construction. In addition to the glazing and frame materials, the window is often integrated with various attachments and components that provide sun control and daylight redirection. The window and sun control devices may also be integrated with other building systems (such as ventilation) into more complex, double-envelope facade systems. The last section of the chapter addresses skylights, atriums, and other means of providing daylight from above.

*Figure 3-1: BRE Environmental Building in Garston, UK. To make maximum use of available daylight the building has extensive glazing on the south facade, optimized to provide high light levels with low heat losses and solar gain. Motorized glass louvers (left) prevent excessive heating and glare. Each louver has a translucent ceramic coating on the underside which obscures direct sunshine while allowing diffuse light through. During the day the angle of the louvers changes according to sun position. At times when direct sunshine is not a problem the louvers are angled to act as "light shelves"—reflecting light onto the office ceilings. Architect: Feilden Clegg; Photo: Colt International*

# Glazing Materials

## BACKGROUND

Architectural glass is common today. Traditionally, however, the alchemy by which sand, limestone, soda ash, and other ingredients transform by heat into a brittle, transparent, supercooled liquid was so labor- and energy-intensive as to render glass rare. The transparency and other qualities of glass define modernism, which is surprising for an ancient material not utilized in architecture for most of its history.

As early as 6000 to 5000 B.C., Egyptians fabricated glass jewelry of fine workmanship and beauty. Other civilizations followed in the cultivation of glass arts, most notably the Romans, whose use of the material nearly rivals that of the twentieth century. For all the Romans' glass prowess, however, it was not a key architectural component. Cast or blown glass was only one of many options for enclosing apertures—competing with shutters, parchment, or thin, translucent alabaster slabs.

It was not until the twelfth century that glass and architecture first fused in the design of cathedrals. Yet the cathedrals' fixed, stained glass windows were an anomaly. Window literally means "wind eye," and ventilation has traditionally been the prime window function, with glazing only an afterthought. As late as the fifteenth century in England, casements usually belonged to the tenant, not the landlord—if the tenant moved, the window sash went too. Some castles' glazing was only in place when the lord was present, and stored when he was away.

Throughout European history, linen or paper remained the prime means of controlling window openings, with glass only one alternative. The conception that glass was a luxury good is evident in the 1690 English window tax; assessments were based on the number of glazed windows. Form followed finance: many of the era's new buildings had bricked-up recesses, awaiting the abolition

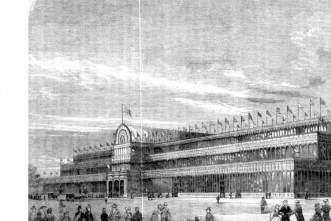

*Figure 3-2. The Crystal Palace covered approximately 18 acres of London's Hyde Park. With 900,000 square feet of glass, it was the largest glass order that had ever been filled by a manufacturer. Source: Edward Walford,* Old and New London, *Volume 5*

of the tax or increased owner wealth. The window tax was repealed only in 1851, not surprising with the increased availability of glass during the Industrial Revolution.

Advances in furnaces and mechanization in the Industrial Revolution yielded relatively large sheets of moderately priced glass. William Paxton's famous Crystal Place rose in London the same year the window tax was eliminated (Figure 3-2). It was the first great iron and glass exposition space, where literal transparency became architecturally possible, transforming architecture's traditional opaqueness. Iron and steel developments, of course, ran parallel to glass, with metal framing technology giving structure to glass expanses. Glass quickly evolved from a luxury product to one inseparable from modern architecture.

## Traditional Glass Production

The Industrial Revolution marks a turning point in glass making, yet the actual glass production principles remained much the same. The primary innovation occurred in late-seventeenth-century France, when cast plate glass fabrication yielded larger, thicker sheets. Romans may have cast glass into shallow molds or onto smooth pieces of stone, but for centuries window glass production involved one of two methods: blowing a glass sphere and shaping it into a disc, or blowing a glass cylinder, and slitting and flattening it to yield glass sheets. The former process yielded crown glass, the latter, cylinder glass.

Essentially, creating traditional window glass involved blowing a vessel, which was altered to sheet form while still hot. Crown glass was at most two by three feet, with most pieces much smaller; cylinder glass could reach three by four feet. Both these fabrication methods produced glass of limited dimensions, and significant waste resulting as rectilinear panes were cut from curvilinear glass sheets. The small-paned windows with wood or lead mullions that define much traditional architecture stemmed from the limited glass size available from these production techniques.

Glass unearthed in Pompeii—about one meter square—is the largest piece of Roman glass found and is undoubtedly cast glass. Crown and cylinder glass production techniques limited glass size to similar dimensions. And both processes were labor-intensive, involving not only blowing and forming, but tending fire and performing other supporting tasks. More modern cast glass methods of the seventeenth century—taking molten glass and passing it through slots and rollers to form a plate which was later ground and polished—was less labor-intensive, and offered new architectural possibilities.

The window evolved in turn. Compared to the small-paned windows possible with crown or cylinder glass, the great glass and mirror expanses at Versailles capture the breakthrough. The possibilities of glazing perhaps reached their pinnacle in the greenhouses and conservatories of the 1800s. Because of the window tax, it is estimated that English houses had half as many windows as their counterparts elsewhere in Europe. Certainly, the Victorian greenhouse responded to a repressed demand for the light and lightness offered by windows and glazing—and utilized the great quantities of glass available during the Industrial Revolution.

*Figure 3-3. Engravings illustrating the production of plate glass by casting. A copper roller is ready to spread glass poured on the casting table* (Top). *After the glass hardens, the table is rolled into the annealing oven. Glass being removed from the oven* (Bottom). *Cast plate glass enjoyed several advantages over blown glass: cast glass sheets are both larger and thicker, the casting process took half the time, required less workers, and cast glass replaced skilled glass blowers with unskilled workers at less than half their wages. Source: Denis Diderot,* Encyclopédie, *"Glaces," plates 25 and 26*

## Modern Glass Production

Although the nineteenth century saw increases in size and volume of glass production, it was innovation in the twentieth century that produced glass of better optical quality at even lower costs. The glass production processes developed in the 1900s, Fourcault's innovations drawing glass in the 1910s, and Pilkington's float glass techniques of the 1950s were technological breakthroughs.

The technique of producing float glass (molten glass "floats" over a tank of molten tin) provides extremely flat surfaces, uniform thicknesses, and few if any visual distortions. Float glass is now used in virtually all commercial windows. This was a key breakthrough that has become important decades later because the high-quality surface of float glass is required for the application of thin coatings that are commonly used in windows today.

Currently glass is one of the most ubiquitous building materials. With ready availability, and at cheaper prices, glass today is not simply employed for its transparent qualities. Rather, it is also used as cladding in curtain walls, where light transmission capabilities are not necessarily an issue. In a curtain wall spandrel, the glass offers no light.

While the qualities of light and view are desirable, they have been moderated by energy conservation and comfort concerns since the 1970s. In commercial buildings dominated by internal loads, it is necessary to guard against solar gains that increase cooling loads. Fortunately, new technologies have made glazing much less of a negative factor in energy conservation. In fact, with proper design and glazing selection, glazing area is less of a concern than it once was.

In all building types, the architect and client must balance the great advantages of natural light in reducing artificial light demands and providing indoor environmental benefits against glazing's thermal drawbacks. As phototropic beings with vision our most developed sense and light the main means of perceiving the world, windows define much of architecture.

## Technological Advances

Although float glass is by far the most common type, glass is made into various architectural products by a variety of specialized processes. These include drawn, patterned and rolled sheets, polished wired glass, channel-shaped units, and glass blocks.

A number of innovations in recent decades have given glass enhanced properties as well as a wide range of color and appearance options. Insulating glass with two or more layers provides improved thermal performance. Tinted glazing reduces heat gain and glare, while coatings can be formulated to serve a variety of functions. Reflective coatings can almost completely reject heat and light, while low-E coatings may be designed to reject solar heat gain but transmit daylight. Surface coatings or treatments such as frit, acid etching, and sandblasting can also reject heat and diffuse light while creating unique aesthetic possibilities. Glass can be heat-strengthened and tempered or treated to give it other properties. Laminated glass provides strength, impact resistance and improved sound control. In practice, many of these technologies are

*Figure 3-4. Curtain wall of the IDS Center in Minneapolis, MN. The advent of the glass curtain wall posed new challenges. With their great glass expanses, glare and heat gains became prime concerns. Tinted glass and reflective coatings were developed to address these issues. The explosion in glass production and use created demand to combat—through innovation and technology—the material's shortcomings. Photo: CALA Visual Resources Collection*

combined to create very high-performance windows for commercial buildings. Of course, rigid plastic layers are substituted for glass in certain cases to provide even greater impact resistance, although plastics can have drawbacks such as durability and cost. Suspended plastic films are used within insulated glazing units where they are not exposed to abuse or weather conditions.

Several new technologies are emerging that further enhance the properties of windows. These include using various insulating materials between glazing layers to further improve thermal performance. In addition, a range of switchable glazings with dynamically changing properties are under development and have begun to appear in the market. Finally, windows are becoming energy generators by incorporating photovoltaic systems into glazing and facade systems. The remainder of this section discusses both current and emerging technologies.

## INSULATED GLAZING

One of the shortcomings of glass is its relatively poor insulating qualities. Multiple panes of glass with air spaces in between improve the insulating value considerably. Figure 3-5 illustrates the performance of single glazing with clear glass. Relative to all other glazing options, clear single glazing allows the highest transfer of solar energy while permitting the highest daylight transmission.

Figure 3-6 illustrates the performance of a typical double-glazed unit with two panes of clear glass. The inner and outer panes of glass are both clear, and they are separated by an air gap. Double glazing reduces heat loss (as reflected by the U-factor) by more than 50 percent in comparison to single glazing. Although U-factor is reduced significantly, the VT and SHGC for a double-glazed unit with clear glass remain relatively high.

### Edge Spacers

The panes of glass in an insulating unit must be held apart at the appropriate distance by spacers. In addition to keeping the glass units separated, the spacer system must serve a number of functions:

- accommodating stress induced by thermal expansion and pressure differences;

- providing a moisture barrier that prevents passage of water or water vapor that would fog the unit;

- providing a gas-tight seal that prevents the loss of any special low-conductance gas in the air space;

- creating an insulating barrier that reduces the formation of interior condensation at the edge.

Early glass units were often fabricated with an integral welded glass-to-glass seal. These units did not leak but were difficult and costly to fabricate, and typically had a less-than-optimal narrow spacing. The standard solution today for insulating glass units (IGUs) is the use of metal spacers and sealants. These spacers, typically aluminum, also contain a desiccant that absorbs residual moisture. The spacer is sealed to the two glass layers with organic

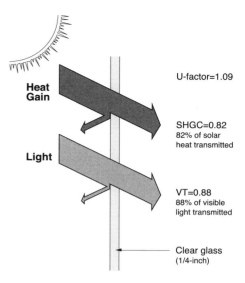

*Figure 3-5. Clear single glazing*

All values are for the glazing alone (center-of-glass). Values for the total window will vary with frame type.
U-factor is in Btu/hr-sf-°F
SHGC=solar heat gain coefficient
VT=visible transmittance

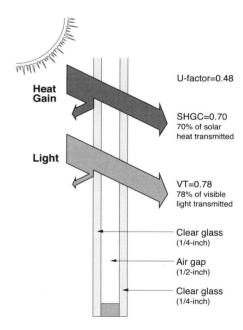

*Figure 3-6. Clear double glazing*

All values are for the glazing alone (center-of-glass). Values for the total window will vary with frame type.
U-factor is in Btu/hr-sf-°F
SHGC=solar heat gain coefficient
VT=visible transmittance

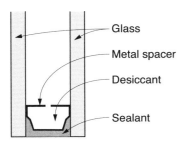

*Figure 3-7. Single-seal with metal spacer*

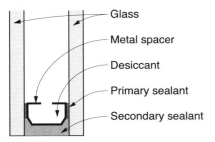

*Figure 3-8. Double-seal with metal spacer*

sealants that provide structural support and act as a moisture barrier. There are two generic systems for such IGUs: a single-seal spacer and a double-seal system (Figures 3-7 and 3-8).

In the single-seal system, an organic sealant, typically a butyl material, is applied behind the spacer and serves to hold the unit together and prevent moisture intrusion. These seals are normally not adequate to contain special low-conductance gases.

In a double-seal system, a primary sealant, typically butyl, seals the spacer to the glass to prevent moisture migration and gas loss, and a secondary backing sealant, often silicone, provides structural strength. When sputtered low-E coatings are used with double-seal systems, the coating must be removed from the edge first (*edge deletion*) to provide a better edge seal.

Since aluminum is an excellent heat conductor, the aluminum spacer used in most standard edge systems represents a significant thermal "short circuit" at the IGU edge, reducing the benefits of improved glazings. Window manufacturers have developed a series of innovative edge systems to address this problem, including solutions that depend on material substitutions as well as radical new designs. One approach to reducing heat loss replaces the aluminum spacer with a less conductive metal, e.g., stainless steel, and changing the cross-sectional shape of the spacer.

Another approach is to replace the metal with a design that uses better insulating materials. An example is an insulating silicone foam spacer that incorporates a desiccant and has a high-strength adhesive at its edges to bond to glass. The foam is backed with a secondary sealant. Both extruded vinyl and pultruded fiberglass spacers have also been used in place of metal designs.

*Warm edge spacers* have become increasingly important as manufacturers switch from conventional double glazing to higher-performance glazing. For purposes of determining the overall window U-factor, the edge spacer has a thermal effect that extends beyond the physical size of the spacer to a band about 2-½ inches wide. The contribution of this 2-½-inch-wide "edge of glass" to the total window U-factor depends on the size of the window. For instance, edge of glass effects are more important for smaller windows, which have a proportionately larger glass edge area.

A more significant benefit may be the rise in interior surface temperature at the bottom edge of the window, which is most subject to condensation. With an outside temperature of 0 degrees Fahrenheit, a thermally improved spacer could result in temperature increases of 6–8 degrees Fahrenheit at the window sightline or 4–6 degrees Fahrenheit at a point one inch in from the sightline, which is an important improvement. As new highly insulating multiple layer windows are developed, the improved edge spacer becomes an even more important element.

### Gas Fills and Gap Width in Multiple-Glazed Units

Another improvement to the thermal performance of insulating glazing units involves reducing the conductance of the air space between the layers. Originally, the space was filled with air or flushed with dry nitrogen just prior to sealing. In a sealed-glass insulating unit, air currents between the two panes of glazing carry heat to the top of the unit along the inner pane and settle down the outer pane into cold pools at the bottom. Filling the space with a less conductive, more viscous, or slow-moving gas minimizes the convection currents within the space, reducing conduction through the gas and the overall heat transfer between the interior and exterior.

Manufacturers generally use argon or krypton gas fills, with measurable improvement in thermal performance. Both gases are inert, nontoxic, nonreactive, clear, and odorless. Krypton has better thermal performance than argon and is more expensive to produce. The optimal spacing for an argon-filled unit is the same as for air, about ½ inch. Krypton is particularly useful when the space between glazings must be thinner than normally desired, for example, ¼ inch. A mixture of krypton and argon gases is also used as a compromise between thermal performance and cost (Figure 3-9).

Argon and krypton occur naturally in the atmosphere, but maintaining long-term thermal performance is certainly an issue. Studies have shown less than 0.5 percent leakage per year in a well-designed and well-fabricated unit, or a 10 percent loss in total gas over a twenty-year period. The effect of a 10 percent gas loss would only be a few percent change in U-factor on an overall product basis. Keeping the gas within the glazing unit depends largely upon the quality of the design, materials, and, most important, assembly of the glazing unit seals.

The use of low-conductance gas fills is far less common in commercial glazing than it is in residential windows. This results from the fact that solar control technologies are more important in typical commercial buildings than techniques for reducing heat transfer by conduction. However, as higher performance facades are developed, gas fills may become more common in commercial building windows as well.

*Figure 3-9. U-factor as a function of air-space thickness and emittance* (e)

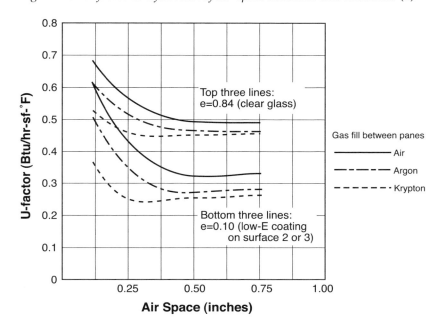

## Multiple Panes and Suspended Plastic Films

By adding a second pane, the insulating value of the window glass alone is doubled (the U-factor is reduced by half). As expected, adding a third or fourth pane of glass further increases the insulating value of the window, but with diminishing effect.

Triple- and quadruple-glazed windows became commercially available in the 1980s as a response to the desire for more energy-efficient windows (Figure 3-10). As each additional pane of glass adds to the insulating value of the assembly, it also reduces the visible light transmission and the solar heat gain coefficient. Additional panes of glass increase the weight and thickness of the unit, which makes mounting and handling more difficult and transportation more expensive. Prototype windows using very thin layers of glass (0.5–1.0 mm) have been fabricated but are not in commercial production.

It is apparent that there are physical and economic limits to the number of glass panes that can be added to a window assembly. However, multiple-pane units are not limited to glass assemblies. One innovation is based on substituting an inner plastic film for the middle layer of glass. The light weight of plastic film is advantageous, and because it is very thin, does not increase the unit thickness. As with triple- or quadruple-glazed windows, windows using plastic films decrease the U-factor of the unit assembly by dividing the inner air space into multiple chambers.

When protected by glass panes from scratching, wear, weathering, and visual distortions caused by wind, the limited strength and

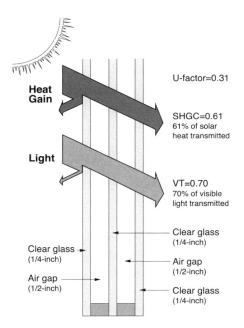

*Figure 3-10. Clear triple glazing*
All values are for the glazing alone (center-of-glass).
Values for the total window will vary with frame type.
U-factor is in Btu/hr-sf-˚F
SHGC=solar heat gain coefficient
VT=visible transmittance

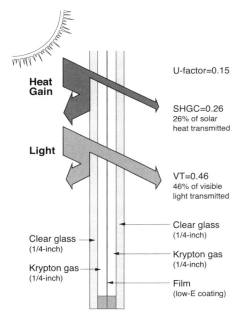

*Figure 3-11. Triple glazing with clear glass and a low-E coating on plastic film*
All values are for the glazing alone (center-of-glass).
Values for the total window will vary with frame type.
U-factor is in Btu/hr-sf-˚F
SHGC=solar heat gain coefficient
VT=visible transmittance

*Window Materials and Assemblies*

durability of the plastic film is overcome. The plastic films are specially treated to resist UV degradation and are heat shrunk so they remain taut and flat. Like glass, a low-E coating can be bonded to the plastic film to lower the assembly U-factor. The plastic film can also be treated with spectrally selective coatings to reduce solar gain in hot climates without significant loss of visible transmittance.

Figure 3-11 illustrates a triple-glazed window with a very low heat flow rate (low U-factor) as well as low-solar-heat-gain properties. There are three glazing layers and one low-E coating with ¼-inch krypton gas fill in the cavities, and low-conductance edge spacers. In this case, the middle glazing layer is a suspended plastic film. The low-E coatings can be applied to the glass or plastic. Figure 3-12 illustrates a window with four glazing layers (two glass panes and two suspended plastic films). The combination of multiple glass panes and plastic films with low-E coatings and gas fills achieves very low center-of-glass U-factors. In this example, both low-E coatings have low-solar-gain properties in order to reduce cooling loads. The combination of multiple glass and plastic film layers with low-E coatings and gas fills has been used to achieve center-of-glass U-factors as low as 0.08. The properties of low-E coatings and tints are discussed in the following sections.

## TINTED GLAZING

Glass is available in a number of tints which absorb a portion of the solar heat and block daylight. Tinting changes the color of the window and can increase visual privacy. The primary uses for tinted glass are reducing glare from the bright outdoors and reducing the amount of solar energy transmitted through the glass.

Tinted glazings retain their transparency from the inside, although the brightness of the outward view is reduced and the color is changed. The most common colors are neutral gray, bronze, and blue-green, which do not greatly alter the perceived color of the view and tend to blend well with other architectural colors (Figure 3-13).

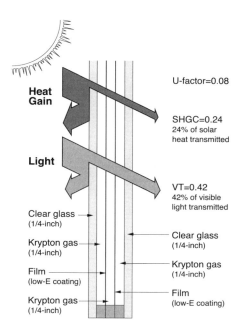

*Figure 3-12. Quadruple glazing with clear glass and low-E coatings applied to two suspended plastic films*

All values are for the glazing alone (center-of-glass). Values for the total window will vary with frame type.
U-factor is in Btu/hr-sf-°F
SHGC=solar heat gain coefficient
VT=visible transmittance

*Figure 3-13. Typical properties of tinted glass*

All cases are center-of-glass values for ¼-inch thick glass. The double-glazed unit has ¼-inch tinted glass on the outside with ¼-inch clear glass on the inside and a ½-inch air space in between. U-factor is in Btu/hr-sf-°F, SHGC=solar heat gain coefficient, VT=visible transmittance

| Tint | Single | | | Double | | |
|------|--------|------|------|--------|------|------|
| | U-factor | SHGC | VT | U-factor | SHGC | VT |
| Clear | 1.09 | 0.81 | 0.88 | 0.48 | 0.70 | 0.78 |
| Green | 1.09 | 0.58 | 0.74 | 0.48 | 0.47 | 0.66 |
| Gray | 1.09 | 0.57 | 0.44 | 0.48 | 0.45 | 0.39 |
| Bronze | 1.09 | 0.62 | 0.54 | 0.48 | 0.50 | 0.48 |
| Blue | 1.09 | 0.58 | 0.55 | 0.48 | 0.46 | 0.49 |
| Blue-Green | 1.09 | 0.62 | 0.75 | 0.48 | 0.50 | 0.67 |
| Spectrally Selective Blue | 1.09 | 0.50 | 0.68 | 0.48 | 0.38 | 0.60 |
| Spectrally Selective Green | 1.09 | 0.51 | 0.66 | 0.48 | 0.39 | 0.59 |

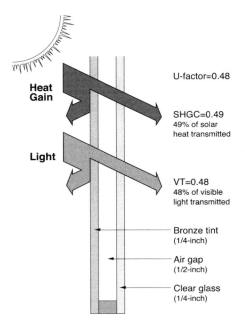

*Figure 3-14. Double glazing with bronze-tinted glass on the outside layer*

All values are for the glazing alone (center-of-glass).
Values for the total window will vary with frame type.
U-factor is in Btu/hr-sf-°F
SHGC=solar heat gain coefficient
VT=visible transmittance

U-factor=0.48

SHGC=0.49
49% of solar
heat transmitted

VT=0.48
48% of visible
light transmitted

Bronze tint
(1/4-inch)

Air gap
(1/2-inch)

Clear glass
(1/4-inch)

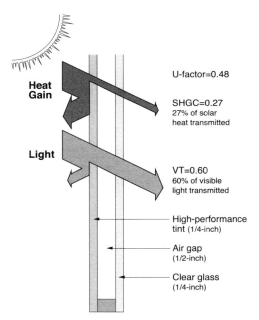

*Figure 3-15. Double glazing with high-performance tint on the outside layer*

All values are for the glazing alone (center-of-glass).
Values for the total window will vary with frame type.
U-factor is in Btu/hr-sf-°F
SHGC=solar heat gain coefficient
VT=visible transmittance

U-factor=0.48

SHGC=0.27
27% of solar
heat transmitted

VT=0.60
60% of visible
light transmitted

High-performance
tint (1/4-inch)

Air gap
(1/2-inch)

Clear glass
(1/4-inch)

Tinted glass is made by altering the chemical formulation of the glass with special inorganic additives. The color is durable and does not change over time. Its color and density changes with the thickness of the glass. Coatings can also be applied after manufacture. Every change in color or combination of different glass types affects transmittance, solar heat gain coefficient, reflectivity, and other properties. Glass manufacturers list these properties for every color, thickness, and assembly of glass type they produce (see NFRC database in Appendix C).

Tinted glazings are specially formulated to maximize their absorption across some or all of the solar spectrum and are often referred to as *heat-absorbing*. All of the absorbed solar energy is initially transformed into heat within the glass, thus raising the glass temperature. Depending upon climatic conditions, up to 50 percent of the heat absorbed in a single pane of tinted glass may then be transferred to the inside via radiation and convection. Thus, there may be only a modest reduction in overall solar heat gain compared to other glazings. This heat gain from absorption that is transmitted to the room leads to discomfort near tinted windows as well. Heat-absorbing glass provides more effective sun control when used as the outer layer of a double-pane window.

Traditional tinted glazing, bronze and gray, often force a trade-off between visible light and solar gain. There is a greater reduction in visible transmittance than in solar heat gain coefficient (Figure 3-14). This can decrease glare by reducing the apparent brightness of the glass surface, but it also diminishes the amount of daylight entering the room. For windows where daylighting is desirable, it may be more satisfactory to use a high-performance tint or coating along with other means of controlling glare. Tinted glazings can provide a measure of visual privacy during the day, when they reduce visibility from the outdoors. However, at night the effect is reversed and it is more difficult to see outdoors from the inside, especially if the tint is combined with a reflective coating.

To address the problem of reducing daylight with traditional tinted glazing, glass manufacturers have developed high-performance tinted glass that is sometimes referred to as *spectrally selective* (Figure 3-15). This glass preferentially transmits the daylight portion of the solar spectrum but absorbs the near-infrared part of sunlight (Figure 3-16). This is accomplished with special additives during the float glass process. Like other tinted glass, it is durable and can be used in both monolithic and multiple-glazed window applications.

Spectrally selective glazings have a light blue or light green tint and have higher visible transmittance values than traditional bronze- or gray-tinted glass, but have lower solar heat gain coefficients. Because they are absorptive, they are best used as the outside glazing in a double-glazed unit. They can also be combined with low-E coatings to enhance their performance further. High-performance tinted glazings provide a substantial improvement over conventional clear, bronze, and gray glass, and a modest improvement over the existing green and blue-green color-tinted glasses that already have some selectivity.

Tinted glazing is more common in commercial windows than in residential windows. In retrofit situations, when windows are not being replaced, tinted plastic film may be applied to the inside

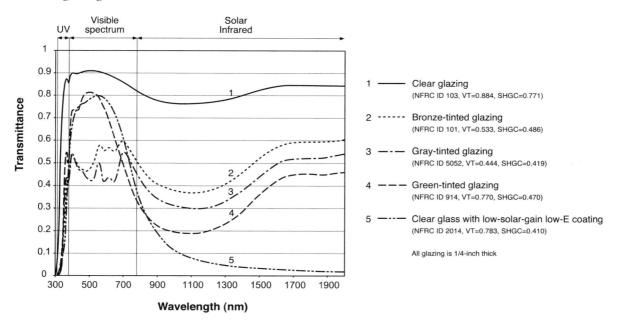

*Figure 3-16. Spectral transmittance curves for common tinted and spectrally selective glazings*

1 ——— Clear glazing
(NFRC ID 103, VT=0.884, SHGC=0.771)

2 ----- Bronze-tinted glazing
(NFRC ID 101, VT=0.533, SHGC=0.486)

3 —·—·— Gray-tinted glazing
(NFRC ID 5052, VT=0.444, SHGC=0.419)

4 — — — Green-tinted glazing
(NFRC ID 914, VT=0.770, SHGC=0.470)

5 —··—··— Clear glass with low-solar-gain low-E coating
(NFRC ID 2014, VT=0.783, SHGC=0.410)

All glazing is 1/4-inch thick

surface of the glazing. The applied tinted films provide some reduction in solar gain compared to clear glass but are not as effective as spectrally selective films or reflective glue-on films, and are not as durable as tinted glass.

## REFLECTIVE COATINGS

As the SHGC falls in single-pane tinted glazings, the daylight transmission (VT) drops even faster, and there are practical limits on how low the SHGC can be made using tints. If larger reductions are desired, a reflective coating can be used to lower the solar heat gain coefficient by increasing the surface reflectivity of the material. These coatings usually consist of thin metallic or metal oxide layers. The reflective coatings come in various metallic colors—silver, gold, bronze—and they can be applied to clear or tinted glazing. The solar heat gain coefficient can be reduced by varying degrees, depending on the thickness and reflectivity of the coating, and its location in the glazing system. Some reflective coatings are durable and can be applied to exposed surfaces; others must be protected in sealed insulating glass units.

Figure 3-17 illustrates a highly reflective coating placed over a bronze-tinted, double-glazed unit. Figure 3-18 shows the range of typical reflective coatings applied to clear and tinted glazings. The emittance of the coating creates modest changes in the U-factor.

Similar to tinted films in retrofit situations, reflective coatings may be applied to the inner glass surface of an existing window by means of an adhesive-bonded, metallic-coated plastic film. The applied films are effective at reducing solar gains but are not as durable as some types of coated glass.

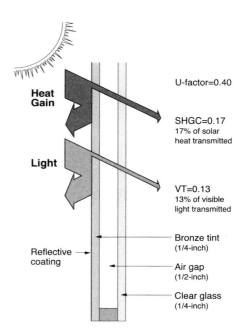

*Figure 3-17. Double glazing with bronze tint and a highly reflective coating*

All values are for the glazing alone (center-of-glass). Values for the total window will vary with frame type.
U-factor is in Btu/hr-sf-°F
SHGC=solar heat gain coefficient
VT=visible transmittance

*Figure 3-18. Typical properties of glass with reflective coatings*

All cases are center-of-glass values for ¼-inch thick glass. The double-glazed unit has ¼-inch glass on the outside (either clear or tinted as noted) with ¼-inch clear glass on the inside and a ½-inch air space in between. U-factor is in Btu/hr-sf-°F, SHGC=solar heat gain coefficient, VT=visible transmittance

| Outer Glazing | Coating Type (SHGC and VT) | Single-glazed | | | Double-glazed | | |
|---|---|---|---|---|---|---|---|
| | | U-factor | SHGC | VT | U-factor | SHGC | VT |
| Clear | Low | 0.84 | 0.06 | 0.08 | 0.39 | 0.05 | 0.08 |
| Clear | Moderate | 0.93 | 0.15 | 0.20 | 0.43 | 0.12 | 0.18 |
| Clear | High | 1.03 | 0.32 | 0.40 | 0.46 | 0.26 | 0.36 |
| Bronze | Low | 0.84 | 0.04 | 0.05 | 0.39 | 0.03 | 0.04 |
| Bronze | Moderate | 0.93 | 0.09 | 0.12 | 0.43 | 0.08 | 0.11 |
| Bronze | High | 1.03 | 0.20 | 0.24 | 0.46 | 0.16 | 0.22 |
| Spectrally Selective Tint | Low | 0.84 | 0.03 | 0.06 | 0.39 | 0.02 | 0.06 |
| Spectrally Selective Tint | Moderate | 0.93 | 0.07 | 0.15 | 0.43 | 0.06 | 0.13 |
| Spectrally Selective Tint | High | 1.03 | 0.14 | 0.30 | 0.46 | 0.12 | 0.27 |

As with tinted glazing, the visible transmittance of a reflective glazing usually declines more than the solar heat gain coefficient. Reflective glazings are usually used in commercial buildings for large windows, for hot climates, or for windows with substantial solar heat gains. Reflective glazing is also used by many architects because of its glare control and uniform, exterior appearance.

Special consideration should always be given to the effect of the reflective glazing on the outside. Acting like a mirror, the reflective glass intensifies the sun's effects, and should be avoided (or is not permitted by local zoning regulations) in some locations because of its impact on adjacent buildings. It is also important to remember that reflective glass acts like a mirror on the side facing the light. Thus, a reflective window that acts like a mirror to the outside during the day will look like a mirror on the inside during the night. These coatings will not provide visual privacy at night if interior lights are on.

## LOW-E COATINGS

When heat or light energy is absorbed by glass, it is either convected away by moving air or reradiated by the glass surface. The ability of a material to radiate energy is called its *emissivity*. All materials, including windows, emit (or radiate) heat in the form of long-wave, far-infrared energy depending on their temperature (see Chapter 2). This emission of radiant heat is one of the important components of heat transfer for a window. Thus reducing the window's emittance can greatly improve its insulating properties.

Standard clear glass has an emittance of 0.84 over the long-wave portion of the spectrum, meaning that it emits 84 percent of the energy possible for an object at its temperature. It also means that 84 percent of the long-wave radiation striking the surface of the glass is absorbed and only 16 percent is reflected (see Chapter 2 for solar spectrum discussion). By comparison, low-E glass coatings can have an emittance as low as 0.04. Such glazing would emit only 4 percent of the energy possible at its temperature, and thus reflect

96 percent of the incident long-wave, infrared radiation. Window manufacturers' product information may not list emittance ratings. Rather, the effect of the low-E coating is incorporated into the U-factor for the unit or glazing assembly.

The solar reflectance of low-E coatings can be manipulated to include specific parts of the visible and infrared spectrum. This is the origin of the term *spectrally selective coatings*, which selects specific portions of the energy spectrum, so that desirable wavelengths of energy are transmitted and others specifically reflected. A glazing material can then be designed to optimize energy flows for solar heating, daylighting, and cooling.

With conventional clear glazing, a significant amount of solar radiation passes through the window, and heat from objects within the space is reradiated back into the glass, then from the glass to the outside of the window. A glazing design for maximizing energy efficiency during underheated periods would ideally allow all of the solar spectrum to pass through, but would block the reradiation of heat from the inside of the space. The first low-E coatings, intended mainly for residential applications, were designed to have a high solar heat gain coefficient and a high visible transmittance to allow the maximum amount of sunlight into the interior while reducing the U-factor significantly.

A glazing designed to minimize summer heat gains, but allow for some daylighting, would allow most visible light through, but would block all other portions of the solar spectrum, including ultraviolet and near-infrared radiation, as well as long-wave heat radiated from outside objects, such as pavement and adjacent buildings. These second-generation low-E coatings still maintain a low U-factor, but are designed to reflect the solar near-infrared radiation, thus reducing the total SHGC while providing high levels of daylight transmission (Figure 3-19).

Low-solar-gain coatings reduce the beneficial solar gain that could be used to offset heating loads, but in most commercial buildings this is significantly outweighed by the solar control benefits. In commercial buildings, it is common to apply low-E coatings to both tinted and clear glass. While the tint lowers the visible transmittance somewhat, it contributes to solar heat gain reduction and glare control. Figure 3-20 illustrates a low-solar-gain low-E coating on a bronze-tinted, double-glazed unit. Figure 3-21 shows the same coating on spectrally selective tinted glass. Low-E coatings can be formulated to have a broad range of solar control characteristics while maintaining a low U-factor (Figure 3-22).

There are two basic processes for making low-E coatings—sputtered and pyrolytic. A sputtered coating is multilayered (typically, three primary layers with at least one layer of metal) and is deposited on glass or plastic film in a vacuum chamber. The total thickness of a sputtered coating is only one ten thousandth the thickness of a human hair. Sputtered coatings often use a silver layer and must be protected from humidity and physical contact. For this reason they are sometimes referred to as *soft coats*. Since sputtering is a low-temperature process, these coatings can be deposited on flat sheets of glass as well as thin plastic films. While sputtered coatings are not durable in themselves, when located within a sealed double- or triple-glazed assembly they should last

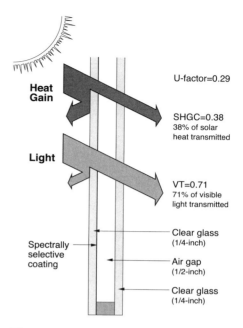

U-factor=0.29

SHGC=0.38
38% of solar heat transmitted

VT=0.71
71% of visible light transmitted

Clear glass (1/4-inch)

Air gap (1/2-inch)

Clear glass (1/4-inch)

*Figure 3-19. Double glazing with clear glass and low-solar-gain low-E coating*

All values are for the glazing alone (center-of-glass). Values for the total window will vary with frame type.

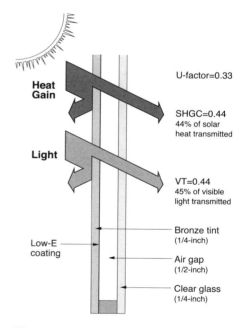

U-factor=0.33

SHGC=0.44
44% of solar heat transmitted

VT=0.44
45% of visible light transmitted

Bronze tint (1/4-inch)

Air gap (1/2-inch)

Clear glass (1/4-inch)

*Figure 3-20. Double glazing with bronze tinted glass and low-solar-gain low-E coating*

All values are for the glazing alone (center-of-glass). Values for the total window will vary with frame type.
U-factor is in Btu/hr-sf-°F
SHGC=solar heat gain coefficient
VT=visible transmittance

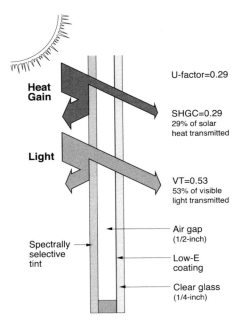

U-factor=0.29

SHGC=0.29
29% of solar
heat transmitted

**Heat Gain**

**Light**

VT=0.53
53% of visible
light transmitted

Air gap
(1/2-inch)

Low-E
coating

Clear glass
(1/4-inch)

Spectrally
selective
tint

*Figure 3-21. Double glazing with low-solar-gain low-E coating on spectrally selective tinted glass*

All values are for the glazing alone (center-of-glass).
Values for the total window will vary with frame type.
U-factor is in Btu/hr-sf-°F
SHGC=solar heat gain coefficient
VT=visible transmittance

as long as the sealed glass unit. Sputtered coatings have emittances as low as 0.04 which are typically lower than those for pyrolytic coatings.

A typical pyrolytic coating is a metallic oxide, most commonly tin oxide with some additives, which is deposited directly onto a glass surface while it is still hot. The result is a baked-on surface layer that is quite hard and thus very durable, which is why this is sometimes referred to as a *hard coat*. A pyrolytic coating can be ten to twenty times thicker than a sputtered coating but is still extremely thin. Pyrolytic coatings can be exposed to air, cleaned with appropriate products, and subjected to general wear and tear without losing their low-E properties.

Because of their greater durability, pyrolytic coatings are available on single-pane glass, but not on plastics, since they require a high-temperature process. In general, though, pyrolytic coatings are used in sealed, double-glazed units with the low-E surface inside the sealed air space. They can also be readily used in multiple-layer window systems where there is air flow between the glazings as well as with nonsealed multiple-glazed units.

Low-solar-gain low-E coatings on plastic films can also be applied to existing glass as a retrofit measure, thus reducing the SHGC of an existing clear glass considerably while maintaining a high visible transmittance and lower U-factor. Other conventional tinted and reflective films will also reduce the SHGC but at the cost of lower visible transmittance. Reflective mirror-like metallic films can also decrease the U-factor, since the surface facing the room has a lower emittance than uncoated glass.

## SURFACE TREATMENTS

### Frit Glass

Silk-screening ceramic frit onto glass enables the designer to use color and patterns on architectural glazing. Combined with clear or tinted glass substrates, as well as high-performance coatings, fritted

*Figure 3-22. Typical properties of glass with low-E coatings*

All cases are center-of-glass values for ¼-inch thick glass. The double-glazed unit has ¼-inch glass on the outside (either clear or tinted as noted) with ¼-inch clear glass on the inside and a ½-inch air space in between. U-factor is in Btu/hr-sf-°F, SHGC=solar heat gain coefficient, VT=visible transmittance

| Glazing | Coating Type (SHGC) | Double-glazed | | |
|---|---|---|---|---|
| | | U-factor | SHGC | VT |
| Clear | High | 0.31 | 0.46 | 0.26 |
| Clear | Moderate | 0.32 | 0.32 | 0.49 |
| Clear | Low | 0.31 | 0.20 | 0.36 |
| Bronze | High | 0.31 | 0.28 | 0.45 |
| Bronze | Moderate | 0.32 | 0.19 | 0.30 |
| Bronze | Low | 0.31 | 0.13 | 0.22 |
| Spectrally Selective Tint | High | 0.31 | 0.24 | 0.57 |
| Spectrally Selective Tint | Moderate | 0.32 | 0.16 | 0.37 |
| Spectrally Selective Tint | Low | 0.31 | 0.11 | 0.28 |

glazing can help reduce solar heat gain. An opaque frit pattern can help control glare but translucent frit patterns may provide diffuse light that increases glare.

Ceramic frit paint is comprised of minute glass particles, pigment, and a medium to mix the glass and pigment together. The paint is applied to one side of the glass—either heat-strengthened or fully tempered to prevent glass breakage due to thermal stresses under sunlit applications—and is fired in a tempering furnace to create a permanent coating. For an insulating glass unit, the silk screen pattern is ideally located within the sealed cavity for protection. Frit can also be applied to laminated glass units. A low-E coating can be placed on top of the frit. To reduce long-wave radiative heat gains, it is best to use the fritted layer on the interior surface of the exterior pane of an insulating glass unit.

White ceramic frit has been the predominant color, however, dark ceramic frits, such as neutral gray, black, and silver metallic are increasingly utilized. These colors also help reduce reflection and offer alternative design options without adversely affecting performance. Frit location—or multiple frit combinations—within a glazing assembly affect such factors as solar absorption, shading coefficient, and appearance.

The design flexibility—in terms of pattern and color—of fritted glass is appealing, but many manufacturers also offer standard patterns, such as dots, lines, and holes. Pattern coverage is specified, most often in the 40 to 60 percent range, with density naturally impacting glass performance characteristics and vision area. Figure 3-24 indicates the properties of typical frit glazings. In practice, the SHGC of a frit coating is affected by its color and location in the window assembly. An example of an architectural application of frit glazing is found in the atrium of the Debis Tower project (Chapter 8).

## Acid-Etched and Sandblasted Glass

Acid etching gives a matte finish to glass panes, with the degree of finish being determined by the length of time the acid is in contact with the surface. By masking, patterns and pictures can be etched into the glass to give the architect design flexibility. An intense

*Figure 3-23. Detail view of frit glazing, of custom color and design, on Blue Cross/Blue Shield building. See Figure 5-1 for general view. Architect: Lohan & Associates; Photo courtesy of Viracon; Photo: Wes Thompson*

*Figure 3-24. Typical properties of glass with ceramic frit treatment*

All cases are center-of-glass values for ¼-inch thick glass. The double-glazed unit has ¼-inch clear glass on the outside with ¼-inch clear glass on the inside and a ½-inch air space in between. U-factor is in Btu/hr-sf-˚F, SHGC=solar heat gain coefficient, VT=visible transmittance

| Frit | Single | | | Double | | |
|------|--------|------|------|--------|------|------|
| | U-factor | SHGC | VT | U-factor | SHGC | VT |
| None 0% | 1.09 | 0.81 | 0.88 | 0.48 | 0.70 | 0.78 |
| Dots 40% | 1.09 | 0.64 | 0.63 | 0.48 | 0.54 | 0.57 |
| Lines 50% | 1.09 | 0.59 | 0.56 | 0.48 | 0.49 | 0.51 |
| Holes 60% | 1.09 | 0.54 | 0.49 | 0.48 | 0.44 | 0.45 |

*Dots*  *Lines*  *Holes*

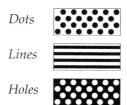

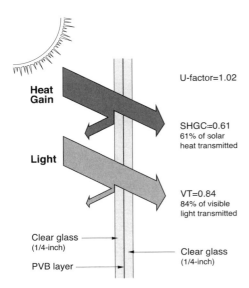

**Figure 3-25. Clear laminated glazing**

Heat Gain

Light

U-factor=1.02

SHGC=0.61
61% of solar
heat transmitted

VT=0.84
84% of visible
light transmitted

Clear glass (1/4-inch)

Clear glass (1/4-inch)

PVB layer

All values are for the glazing alone (center-of-glass).
Values for the total window will vary with frame type.
U-factor is in Btu/hr-sf-°F
SHGC=solar heat gain coefficient
VT=visible transmittance

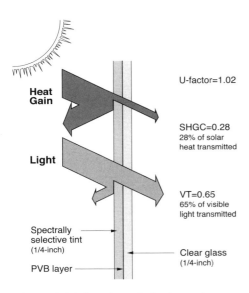

**Figure 3-26. Laminated glazing using a spectrally selective tint**

Heat Gain

Light

U-factor=1.02

SHGC=0.28
28% of solar
heat transmitted

VT=0.65
65% of visible
light transmitted

Spectrally selective tint (1/4-inch)

Clear glass (1/4-inch)

PVB layer

All values are for the glazing alone (center-of-glass).
Values for the total window will vary with frame type.
U-factor is in Btu/hr-sf-°F
SHGC=solar heat gain coefficient
VT=visible transmittance

etching process roughens the glass surface, which diminishes transparency. Light passing through the glass is scattered to obscure view and diffuse light. Designers on the Hoffmann-La Roche Ltd. Office Building (Chapter 8) utilized acid-etched glass to achieve this effect, as they found light coming through transom windows to be too bright and directional. Glass can also be sand-blasted to give a similar matte finish. It should be noted that diffusing glass can sometimes increase glare since surface brightness is increased.

## LAMINATED GLASS

Laminated glass consists of a tough plastic interlayer made of polyvinyl butyral (PVB) bonded between two panes of glass under heat and pressure. Once sealed, the glass sandwich behaves as a single unit and looks like normal glass. Laminated glass provides durability, high performance, and multifunctional benefits while preserving aesthetic appearance.

Similar to car windshield glass, laminated glass may crack upon impact, but the glass fragments tend to adhere to the plastic interlayer rather than falling free and potentially causing injury. Laminated glass resolves many design problems, offering increased protection from the effects of disasters such as hurricanes, earthquakes, and bomb blasts.

Annealed, heat-strengthened, or tempered glass can be used to produce laminated glass; the glass layers may be of equal or unequal thickness. With respect to solar control, laminated glass retains the characteristics of the glass making up the assembly (Figures 3-25 and 3-26). Reflective coatings and frit patterns may also be applied within a laminated glass sandwich. Laminated glass can also be used as a component of an insulated glazing unit.

Single-pane laminated glass with a spectrally selective low-E sputtered coating on plastic film sandwiched between two panes of glass offers the energy performance of single-pane, spectrally selective glass and the safety protection of laminated glass. However, in this configuration, since the low-E surface is not exposed to an air space, the lower emittance has no effect on the glazing U-factor and SHGC. With double-pane laminated glass, the full benefit of the low-E coating can be realized by placing the coating on one of the glass surfaces facing the air space.

Glass has inherently poor acoustic properties, but laminated glass, alone or combined with additional glass plies to form a sealed, insulating glass unit, outperforms other glazing assemblies. Laminated glass reduces noise transmission due to the PVB layer's sound-dampening characteristics (see Chapter 2 for acoustics discussion).

# Emerging Glazing Technologies

Most of the emerging glazing technologies presented in this section are available or nearly on the market. These include insulation-filled and evacuated glazings to improve heat transfer by lowering U-factors. Switchable glazings such as electrochromics change properties dynamically to control solar heat gain, daylight, glare, and view. Building-integrated photovoltaic solar collectors involving window systems not only generate energy but also form part of the building envelope.

## INSULATION-FILLED GLAZINGS

There are several options for highly insulating windows with aerogel, honeycombs, and capillary tubes located between glazing panes. These materials provide diffuse light, not a clear view. Some of these materials are used in Europe for passive solar applications.

Aerogel is a silica-based, open-cell, foam-like material composed of about 4 percent silica and 96 percent air. The microscopic cells of the foam entrap air (or another gas if gas-filled), thereby preventing convection while still allowing light to pass. The cell sizes are smaller than the mean free path of air/gas molecules, thus reducing conduction to values below those of pure conduction for the air/gas. Long-wave thermal radiation is virtually eliminated due to the multiple cell walls through which long-wave infrared radiation must be absorbed and reradiated. The particles that make up the thin cell walls slightly diffuse the light passing through, creating a bluish haze similar to that of the sky.

Aerogel has received research attention for its ability to be both highly transparent and insulating, making it one of a number of materials that are generically referred to as transparent insulation. It should be technically possible to produce windows made of aerogel with a center-of-glass U-factor as low as 0.05. However, aerogel has only been produced in small quantities and sizes, so only tile-sized samples have been used as windows for research purposes. European manufacturers have produced double-glazed windows filled with small beads of aerogel and while the units have good insulating values, they are diffusing and do not provide a view. Aerogel might find a future application as a component of a larger window system, such as spacers between insulating panes of glass, or in skylights or glass blocks.

## EVACUATED WINDOWS

The most thermally efficient gas fill would be no gas at all—a vacuum. A number of researchers around the world have been pursuing the development of insulating window units in which the space between the panes is evacuated. If the vacuum pressure is low enough, there would be no conductive or convective heat exchange between the panes of glass, thus lowering the U-factor. A vacuum glazing must have a good low-E coating to reduce radiative heat transfer—the vacuum effect alone is not adequate. This principle has been used in the fabrication of thermos bottles for many years, with the silver coating serving as the low-emittance surface.

*Figure 3-27. Exterior view of Rapson Hall at the University of Minnesota using channel glass with translucent insulation. Architect: Steven Holl Architects; Photo: Warren Bruland*

*Figure 3-28. Interior view of Rapson Hall using channel glass with translucent insulation. Channel glass is used as a linear glazing system, with translucent insulation sandwiched between interlocking pieces of glass. The channel glass itself has a U-factor of 0.53, SHGC of 0.69, and VT of 0.75. The insulation improves the assembly U-factor to 0.29 and SHGC to 0.36. VT falls to 0.38. Photo: Warren Bruland*

Evacuated window assemblies present a number of engineering problems, however. One major issue is the structural requirement to resist normal air pressure and variable pressures caused by wind and vibration. There can be large thermal stresses between large, window-sized panes of glass. A thermos bottle resists these forces easily because of its strong curved shape, but the large, flat surfaces of a window tend to bow and flex with changing pressures. In prototypes, minute glass pillars or spheres have been used to maintain the separation between the panes. The pillars are very small but are somewhat visible, reducing the window clarity.

Another issue is the maintenance of an airtight seal around the unit edge. The seal must be maintained to eliminate gaseous conduction by keeping the air density within the unit to less than one millionth of normal atmospheric pressure; an air density of only ten times this amount is sufficient to re-establish conduction to its normal value. This vacuum seal must remain intact for the life of the window, through manufacture, transportation, installation, and normal operation, wear, and weathering. Special solder glass seals have been used successfully by Australian researchers in the development of large prototypes. Center-of-glass U-factors of 0.2 have been achieved to date, with the possibility of reaching 0.12, while maintaining a high SHGC. This unit also has the advantage of being thin and thus suitable for many glazing retrofits. However, edge condition losses are larger than for conventional IGU designs, although these can be compensated for in the frame design. A major glass company now offers this technology as a commercially available product in Japan.

## SMART WINDOWS

The emerging concept for the window of the future is more as a multifunctional "appliance-in-the-wall" rather than simply a static piece of coated glass. These facade systems include switchable windows and shading systems such as motorized shades, switchable electrochromic or gasochromic window coatings, and double-envelope window-wall systems that have variable optical and thermal properties that can be changed in response to climate, occupant preferences and building system requirements. By actively managing lighting and cooling, smart windows could reduce peak electric loads by 20–30 percent in many commercial buildings, increase daylighting benefits throughout the United States, improve comfort, and potentially enhance productivity in homes and offices. These technologies can provide maximum flexibility in aggressively managing demand and energy use in buildings in the emerging deregulated utility environment. They can also move the building community towards a goal of producing advanced buildings with minimal impact on the nation's energy resources.

The ideal window would be one with optical properties that could readily adapt in response to changing climatic conditions or occupant preferences. Researchers have been hard at work on new glazing technologies for the next generation of smart windows. After many years of development, various switchable window technologies are now in prototype testing phases and should be commercially available in the near future. As with other window technologies, the architect will need to understand these new systems in order to specify them properly.

There are two basic types of switchable windows—passive devices that respond directly to a single environmental variable such as light level or temperature, and active devices that can be directly controlled in response to any variable such as occupant preferences or heating and cooling system requirements. The main passive devices are photochromics and thermochromics; active devices include liquid crystal, suspended particle, and electrochromics.

## Photochromics

Photochromic materials change their transparency in response to light intensity. Photochromic materials have been used in eye-glasses that change from clear in the dim indoor light to dark in the bright outdoors. Photochromics may be useful in conjunction with daylighting, allowing just enough light through for lighting pur-poses, while cutting out excess sunlight that creates glare and overloads the cooling system. Although small units have been produced in volume as a consumer product, cost-effective, large, durable glazings for windows are not yet commercially available.

## Thermochromics

Thermochromics change transparency in response to temperature. The materials currently under development are gels sandwiched between glass and plastic that switch from a clear state when cold to a more diffuse, white, reflective state when hot. In their switched-on state, the view through the glazing is lost. Such win-dows could, in effect, turn off the sunlight when the cooling loads become too high. Thermochromics could be very useful to control overheating for passive solar heating applications. The temperature of the glass, which is a function of solar intensity and outdoor and indoor temperature, would regulate the amount of sunlight reach-ing the thermal storage element. Thermochromics would be par-ticularly appropriate for skylights because the obscured state would not interfere with views as much as with a typical vision window. Such units would come with a preset switching tempera-ture, which would have to be selected carefully for the specific application. A thermochromic window can also be activated by a heating element in the window, making it operate like other swit-chable glazings, but this tends to be less energy efficient. Prototype glazings have been tested but are not yet commercially available.

## Liquid Crystal Device Windows

A variant of the liquid crystal display technology used in wrist-watches is now serving as privacy glazing for new windows. A very thin layer of liquid crystals is sandwiched between two transparent electrical conductors on thin plastic films and the entire emulsion or package (called a PDLC or polymer dispersed liquid crystal device) is laminated between two layers of glass. When the power is off, the liquid crystals are in a random and unaligned state. They scatter light and the glass appears as a translucent layer, which obscures direct view and provides privacy. The material transmits most of the incident sunlight in a diffuse mode, thus its solar heat gain coefficient remains high.

When power is applied, the electric field in the device aligns the liquid crystals and the glazing becomes transparent in a fraction of a second, permitting view in both directions. Most such devices have only two states, clear and diffusing, and the power (about 0.5 W/sf, operating between 24 and 100 volts AC) must be continuously applied for the glazing to remain in the clear state. The visible transmittance range is typically 50–80 percent and the SHGC is 0.55–0.69, although dyes can be added to darken the device in the off state. Some manufacturers offer products in a variety of colors and for curved and flat-shaped glass. Glazings can be fabricated up to 3-by-7.5-foot sheets. Ultraviolet (UV)-stable formulations now permit exterior applications but UV stability and cost remain as issues.

## Suspended Particle Device (SPD) Windows

This electrically controlled film utilizes a thin, liquid-like layer in which numerous microscopic particles are suspended. In its unpowered state the particles are randomly oriented and partially block sunlight transmission and view. Transparent electrical conductors allow an electric field to be applied to the dispersed particle film, aligning the particles and raising the transmittance. Typical visible transmittance (VT) and solar heat gain coefficient (SHGC) ranges for the film alone are VT=0.22–0.005 or 0.57–0.12 and SHGC=0.56–0.41 or 0.70–0.50, respectively, with near instant switching times (less than one second). The SHGC switching range is more limited than electrochromic windows (see below). The device requires about 100 volts AC to operate from the off state (colored) to the on state (near transparent) and can be modulated to any intermediate state. Power requirements are 0.5 W/sf for switching and 0.05 W/sf to maintain a constant transmission state if not off (the most colored, cobalt blue state). With research, the operating voltages could get down to about 35 volts AC. New suspensions are also under development to achieve several different colors (green, red, and purple) and to affect up to a 50 percent change in solar transmittance. Manufacturers state that these laminated glazings can be fabricated in up to 4-by-8-foot sheets and can be offered in both curved and flat shapes. Long-term durability and solar-optical properties have not been independently verified. Products are now entering the market, but cost remains an issue.

## Electrochromic Windows

The most promising switchable window technology today is electrochromic (EC) windows. An electrochromic coating is typically five layers, about one micron thick, and is deposited on a glass substrate. The electrochromic stack consists of thin metallic coatings of nickel or tungsten oxide sandwiched between two transparent electrical conductors. When a voltage is applied between the transparent electrical conductors, a distributed electrical field is set up. This field moves various coloration ions (most commonly lithium or hydrogen) reversibly between the ion storage film through the ion conductor (electrolyte) and into the electrochromic film. The effect is that the glazing switches between a clear and transparent prussian blue-tinted state with no degradation in view, similar in appearance to photochromic sunglasses.

The main advantages of EC windows is that they typically only require low-voltage power (0–10 volts DC), remain transparent across its switching range, and can be modulated to any intermediate state between clear and fully colored. Switching occurs through absorption (similar to tinted glass), although some switchable reflective devices are now in research and development. Low-emittance coatings and an insulating glass unit configuration can be used to reduce heat transfer from this absorptive glazing layer to the interior. Typical EC windows have an upper visible transmittance range of 0.50–0.70 and a lower range of 0.02–0.25. The SHGC ranges from 0.10–0.50. A low transmission is desirable for privacy and for control of direct sun and glare, potentially eliminating the need for interior shading. A high transmission is desirable for admitting daylight during overcast periods. Therefore, the greater the range in transmission, the more able the window is to satisfy a wide range of environmental requirements.

For some EC types (polymer laminate), the device is switched to its desired state and then no power is needed to maintain this desired state. This type of device has a long memory once switched (power is not required for three to five days to maintain a given switched state). Another EC type (all-solid-state) requires minimal low-voltage power to both change and maintain a given state (0.02 W/sf). When powered off, the EC goes to clear. The advantage of this type of EC is that it can switch faster than its long-memory counterpart. This second type has also been shown through independent tests to be extremely durable under hot and

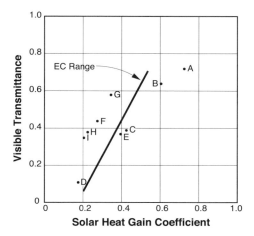

*Figure 3-29. SHGC and VT range for electrochromic glazing*
See Figure 3-32 for glazing properties of A–H.

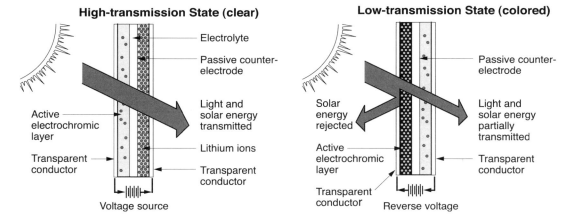

*Figure 3-30. Schematic diagram of a five-layer electrochromic coating (not to scale—the actual thickness is 4 microns or 1/50th of a human hair). A reversible low-voltage source moves ions back and forth between an active electrochromic layer and a passive counterelectrode. When the lithium ions migrate into the active electrochromic layer, an electrochemical reaction causes that layer to darken. When the voltage is reversed and the ions are removed, the electrochromic layer returns to its clear state.*

cold conditions and under intense sun. These devices have been cycled (from clear to colored and then back again) numerous times under realistic conditions so that one can expect long-term sustained performance over the typical 20–30 year life of the installation.

Switching speed is tied to the size and temperature of the window. Coloring typically takes longer than bleaching. A 3-by-6-foot window can take 10–15 minutes to switch across its full range if warm and up to 25 minutes if cold. If the conditions are adverse (too hot, too cold, ice, thermal shock), the window may be prevented from switching. Typical operating temperatures are between –20 and 190 degrees Fahrenheit.

Electrochromic glazings are fabricated as insulated glass units using standard or laminated glazing. Wire leads extending from one edge are tied into the building's electrical system. The window can also be powered using photovoltaic cells to avoid the cost of wiring to the building. Once installed, the window or skylight can be operated by a manual switch or remote controller, a simple stand-alone automatic system, or a sophisticated central energy management system that integrates its operation with other building systems, such as the electric lighting and mechanical system.

Controlling and modulating incoming light and solar heat gains leads to lower energy bills and increased occupant comfort. The higher initial price of electrochromic glazing can be partially offset by these and other factors, such as reduction in HVAC equipment size and window treatment. Electrochromic windows give building owners the ability to modulate heat gain through the window, reducing cycling stress on HVAC motors and other equipment. Additional operating costs for the static glazings— shade replacement and cleaning, UV fading of textiles and fabrics, increased HVAC maintenance, and reduced life of the HVAC system—can also buy down electrochromic glazing's higher initial cost. Electrochromic glazing provides functionality that other types of shading do not—for example, in darker states, it is still possible to provide view rather than blocking it completely with drawn shades or blinds.

Electrochromic technology has been actively researched throughout the world for over thirty years, and promising laboratory results have led to prototype window development and demonstration. Examples of electrochromic window prototypes have been demonstrated in a number of buildings in Japan and more recently in Europe and the United States. Millions of small electrochromic mirrors have been sold for use as rearview mirrors in automobiles and trucks. Electrochromic glazings have also been installed as prototype sunroofs in cars.

Electrochromic glazings are nearing commercial readiness. Currently, flat durable window and skylight products are emerging on the market in sizes of 18-by-36 inches, although larger sizes are expected in the next three to five years. A full-scale field test is now underway at the Lawrence Berkeley National Laboratory (LBNL). An additional field test in a home in Houston, conducted by the National Renewable Energy Laboratory, is scheduled to begin in winter 2003. For the LBNL test, 10-by-15-foot-deep private offices have been fitted with a large 10-by-9-foot window wall of EC glass. Each EC window can be switched independently to control local sources of glare and to admit daylight. The windows are linked electronically to light sensors and dimmable fluorescent office lighting. The glazings are operated so that they admit maximum daylight under dark, overcast conditions and minimum solar heat when sunny skies prevail. Occupants in the offices can override the automated controls if they desire. Overall, this building-scale field test reinforces the capability of switchable windows to provide energy savings while improving comfort and amenity in an office environment.

Figure 3-32 illustrates the simulated energy and peak demand performance for electrochromic glazing (EC) in south-facing offices located in Chicago and Houston. In both climates, the electrochromic glazing results in the lowest energy use and peak demand if the windows are controlled to maintain a daylight workplane illuminance of 50 fc and the lights are dimmed.

Figure 3-31. Field test of electrochromic windows at LBNL. (Left) Interior view of EC window with the lefthand window column set to fully bleached or clear and the righthand window column set to fully colored. The middle window column is set to a transmission level halfway between the two extreme states. (Right) Exterior view of EC window. Photo: Courtesy of LBNL; Photo: Roy Kaltschmidt

*Figure 3-32. Energy use and peak demand comparison of electrochromic (EC) and other windows*

All cases are south-facing with a 0.60 window-to-wall ratio and no shading. Numbers are expressed per square foot within a 15-foot-deep perimeter zone. Results were computed using DOE-2.1E for typical office buildings in Chicago, Illinois and Houston, Texas (see Appendix A).

## Chicago

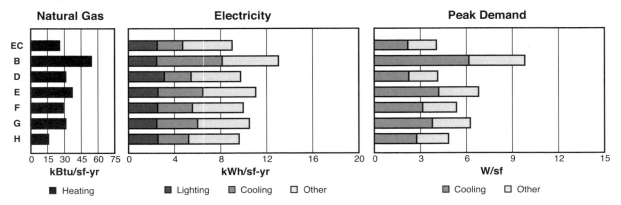

## Houston

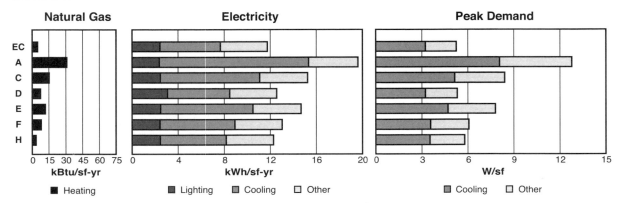

**Window A**
single glazing
clear
U=1.07
SHGC=0.69
VT=0.71

**Window B**
double glazing
clear
U=0.60
SHGC=0.62
VT=0.63

**Window C**
double glazing
bronze tint
U=0.60
SHGC=0.42
VT=0.38

**Window D**
double glazing
reflective coating
U=0.54
SHGC=0.17
VT=0.10

**Window E**
double glazing
low-E, bronze tint
U=0.49
SHGC=0.39
VT=0.36

**Window F**
double glazing
spectrally selective low-E
tint
U=0.46
SHGC=0.27
VT=0.43

**Window G**
double glazing
spectrally selective low-E
clear
U=0.46
SHGC=0.34
VT=0.57

**Window H**
triple glazing
1 low-E layer, clear
U=0.20
SHGC=0.23
VT=0.37

## Gasochromic Windows

Gasochromic windows produce a similar effect to electrochromic windows, but in order to color the window, diluted hydrogen (below the combustion limit of 3 percent) is introduced into the cavity in an insulated glass unit. Exposure to oxygen returns the window to its original transparent state. To maintain a particular state, the gap is simply isolated from further changes in gas content. The optically active component is a porous, columnar film of tungsten oxide, less than 1 micron thick. This eliminates the need for transparent electrodes or an ion-conducting layer. Variations in film thickness and hydrogen concentration can affect the depth and rate of coloration.

Visible transmittance can vary between 0.10–0.59 with a SHGC range of 0.12–0.46. Transmittance levels of less than 0.01 for privacy or glare control are possible. An improved U-value can be obtained with a triple-pane, low-E system (since one gap is used to activate the gasochromic). Switching speeds are 20 seconds to color and less than a minute to bleach. The gas can be generated at the window wall with an electrolyser and a distribution system integrated into

*Window Materials and Assemblies*

the facade. Gasochromic windows with an area of 2-by-3.5 feet are now undergoing accelerated durability tests and full-scale field tests and are expected to reach the market in the near future.

## Motorized Shading

Motorized roller shades, drapes, blinds, exterior awnings and louvers are commercially available systems analogous to switchable windows. These systems have been used over the past thirty years in numerous buildings and so do not fall into the category of emerging technologies—they are discussed in the following section on sun-control devices.

## BUILDING INTEGRATED PHOTOVOLTAICS (BIPV)

Photovoltaics (PV) are solid-state, semiconductor type devices that produce electricity when exposed to light. Electrons in the photovoltaic material are knocked free by light to flow out of the device as an electric current. The more intense the sunlight, the stronger the electric current.

*Figure 3-33. Photovoltaics integrated with glazing. In this type of application, the solar cells provide shading and generate electricity. Photo courtesy of DOE/NREL; Photo: Paul Maycock*

This phenomenon was discovered in the mid-1800s, yet important applications followed much later—for satellites and applications where extending the electric grid is cost prohibitive. Architectural applications have only recently become prominent. With Building Integrated Photovoltaics (BIPV), for instance, photovoltaics are integral to the building skin: the walls, roof, and vision glass. The envelope produces electricity, which flows through power conversion equipment and into the building's electrical system.

Photovoltaic vision glass integrates a thin-film, semitransparent photovoltaic panel with an exterior glass panel in an otherwise traditional double-pane window or skylight. All the PV types can be integrated and/or laminated in glass, but only thin-film photovoltaics will be translucent. Electric wires extend from the sides of each glass unit and are connected to wires from other windows, linking up the entire system. If the PV cells are part of the vision glass, various degrees of transparency are possible—as in frit glass—since the PV cells offer shade and produce electricity (Figure 3-33). In some cases, the PV panels are placed in spandrel panels, rather than the vision glass. Smaller PV systems can be used to power facade equipment directly instead of being connected to the electrical grid in the building. Vertically oriented PV panels are optimally not positioned toward the sun. One approach to position the PV panels more perpendicular to the sun is to place them into fixed shading devices on the facade or on movable shading panels, using the generated power to track the shades to the optimal solar angle (Figure 3-34).

*Figure 3-34. Photo of PV panels integrated into sun-shading system. Photo courtesy of Kawneer Company; Photo: Gordon Schenck, Jr.*

Current PV production technologies, pricing structure, and energy rates limit BIPV use to prominent, prestige buildings (although PV-integrated cladding costs are comparable to marble). Of course, as these factors are in constant flux, BIPVs are receiving increased attention that is justified by the promise of a building envelope that can generate energy in addition to providing shelter.

# Window Assemblies and Frame Materials

Window assemblies in commercial buildings fall into two basic categories—manufactured window units that are delivered to the site and field-assembled systems that include curtain walls and storefronts. In some cases, curtain walls are unitized so that whole sections of glazing and frame are produced in a factory and assembled on site.

## MANUFACTURED WINDOW UNITS

Residential construction uses manufactured window and skylight units (glazing and frame) almost exclusively, but there are many commercial buildings with punched openings that use either standard or custom-manufactured units as well. A series of units can be placed together with intervening mullions to create a window wall with a larger expanse of glazing more commonly associated with curtain walls and storefronts. Manufactured units can be made with many frame materials, including aluminum, wood, vinyl, fiberglass or other composites. Aluminum is the most widely used frame type in the commercial window market.

The material used to manufacture the frame governs the physical characteristics of the window, such as frame thickness, structural concerns, weight, and durability, but it also has an impact on the thermal characteristics of the window. Manufacturers are beginning to produce hybrid or composite sash and frame units, in which multiple materials are selected and combined to best meet the overall required performance parameters.

While it is useful to understand the role that frame type plays in window thermal performance, the frame U-factor is not normally reported by manufacturers. The window U-factor, as given on an NFRC certified rating or label, incorporates the thermal properties of both the frame and the glazing. The remainder of this section describes aluminum, wood, and vinyl frames, and introduces some new frame materials that are commercially available.

### Aluminum Frames

Light, strong, durable, noncorrosive, and easily extruded into the complex shapes required for window parts, aluminum can be fabricated to extremely close tolerances to create special forms for the insertion of glazing, weatherstripping, and thermal breaks. Aluminum frames are available in anodized and factory-applied high-performance painted finishes that are extremely durable and low-maintenance (Figure 3-35).

The biggest disadvantage of aluminum as a window frame material is its high thermal conductance, which raises the overall U-factor of a window unit. Because of this, the thermal resistance of an aluminum frame is determined more by the surface area of the frame than by the thickness or projected area, as with other frame materials. Thus, an aluminum frame profile with a simple, compact shape will perform better than a profile with many fins and undulations.

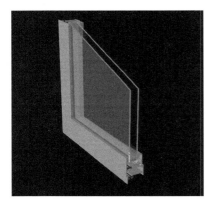

*Figure 3-35. Aluminum frame with thermal break*

In cold climates, a non-thermally broken aluminum frame can easily become cold enough to condense moisture or frost on the inside surfaces of window frames. Even more than the issue of heat loss, condensation problems have spurred development of better insulating aluminum frames. The most common solution to the heat conduction and condensation problem of aluminum frames is to provide a *thermal break* by splitting the frame components into interior and exterior pieces, which are joined by a less conductive material. There are many designs available for thermally broken aluminum frames.

Current technology with standard thermal breaks has improved aluminum frame U-factors from roughly 2.0 to about 1.0. Innovative new thermal break designs have been combined with changes in frame design to achieve U-factors lower than 0.5, but at a higher cost than current thermally broken frames. In commercial buildings where controlling solar gain is often more important than reducing conductive heat transfer, improving the insulating value of the frame is less important than using a solar control glazing system.

*Figure 3-36. Wood or wood-clad frame*

## Wood Frames

Wood is a traditional window frame material because it is widely available and easy to mill into the complex shapes required to make windows (Figure 3-36). Wood is not intrinsically the most durable window frame material because of its susceptibility to rot and its high maintenance requirements, but well-built and well-maintained wood windows can have a very long life. Cladding the exterior face of a wood frame with either vinyl or aluminum creates a permanent weather-resistant surface. Clad frames thus have lower maintenance requirements, but retain the attractive wood finish on the interior.

From a thermal point of view, wood-framed windows perform well, with frame U-factors in the range of 0.3 to 0.5 Btu/hr-sq ft-°F. The thicker the wood frame, the more insulation it provides. However, metal cladding, metal hardware, or the metal reinforcing often used at corner joints can lower the thermal performance of wood frames.

## Vinyl Frames

Vinyl, also known as polyvinyl chloride (PVC), is a very versatile plastic with good insulating value, high impact resistance, and good resistance to abrasion (Figure 3-37). Because its color runs all the way through the material, there is no finish coat that can be damaged or deteriorate over time. Recent advances have improved PVC's dimensional stability and resistance to degradation from sunlight and temperature extremes.

Similar to aluminum windows, vinyl windows are fabricated by cutting standard lineal extrusions to size and assembling the pieces into complete sash and frame elements. Vinyl window frames require very little maintenance, do not require painting, and have good moisture resistance. To provide the required structural performance, vinyl sections are often larger than aluminum win-

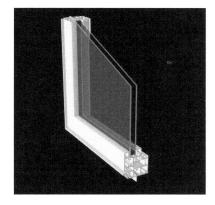

*Figure 3-37. Vinyl frame*

dow sections, with sizes closer to the dimensions of wood frame sections. Larger vinyl units will often need to incorporate metal or wood stiffeners.

Since vinyl has a higher coefficient of expansion than either wood or aluminum, vinyl window frame profiles should be designed and assembled to eliminate excessive movement caused by thermal cycles. In terms of thermal performance, most vinyl frames are comparable to wood. Large hollow chambers within the frame can allow unwanted heat transfer through convection currents. Creating smaller cells within the frame reduces this convection exchange. Vinyl frames can also be insulated—the hollow cavities of the frame filled with insulation—making them thermally superior to standard vinyl and wood frames.

## Hybrid Frames

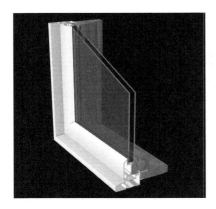

*Figure 3-38. Hybrid wood and vinyl frame*

Manufacturers have begun marketing hybrid frame designs that use two or more of the frame materials described above to produce a complete window frame system. The wood industry has long built vinyl- and aluminum-clad windows to reduce exterior maintenance needs. Vinyl manufacturers offer interior wood veneers to produce the appearance of wood, and split-sash designs may have an interior wood element with an exterior vinyl or fiberglass element (Figure 3-38).

## Wood/Polymer Composites

Most people are familiar with composite wood products, such as particle board and laminated strand lumber, in which wood particles and resins are compressed to form a strong composite material. The window industry has taken this technology a step further by creating a new generation of wood/polymer composites that are extruded into a series of lineal shapes for window frame and sash members. These composites are very stable, and are comparable to or exceed the structural and thermal properties of conventional wood, with better moisture resistance and more decay resistance.

## Fiberglass Pultrusions

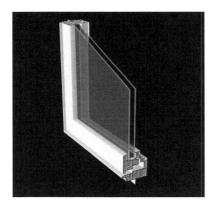

*Figure 3-39. Insulated fiberglass frame*

Window frames can be made of either glass-fiber-reinforced polyester or fiberglass, which is pultruded into lineal forms and then assembled into windows (Figure 3-39). Such frames are dimensionally stable and achieve good insulating value by incorporating air cavities (similar to vinyl). Like vinyl, the cavities can be filled with insulation for higher thermal performance. The strength of fiberglass allows manufacturers to maintain the same sight lines as aluminum windows while achieving significantly lower U-factors. The low coefficient of thermal expansion maintains seal integrity and minimizes warpage or leakage in high inside/outside temperature differentials. Fiberglass pultrusions have a higher heat deflection temperature than vinyl, permitting the use of dark colors unlike other thermoplastic extrusions. They can be painted, powder coated, or finished with coextruded acrylic resin.

## Engineered Thermoplastics

Another alternative to vinyl is extruded engineered thermoplastics, a family of plastics used extensively in automobiles and appliances. Like fiberglass, they have some structural and other advantages over vinyl but are also more expensive and have not yet captured a large market share.

## Performance Comparison of Different Frame Types

While the overall window performance is often dominated by the glazing type, there are some differences in thermal performance between frame materials. Figure 3-40 illustrates the impact of frame type alone on energy and peak demand performance for south-facing office spaces in Chicago, Illinois, and Houston, Texas.

In both cities, the worst performance is attributed to the case with aluminum frame windows with no thermal break. There is some reduction in energy use when substituting a thermally broken aluminum frame. Exterior flush glazing represents further improvement while wood, vinyl, or fiberglass frames result in the lowest energy costs. In Chicago, improving the frame primarily

*Figure 3-40. Energy use comparison of different window frame types*

All cases are south-facing with a 0.30 window-to-wall ratio and no shading. Numbers are expressed per square foot within a 15-foot-deep perimeter zone. Results were computed using DOE-2.1E for typical office buildings in Chicago, Illinois and Houston, Texas (see Appendix A).

### Chicago

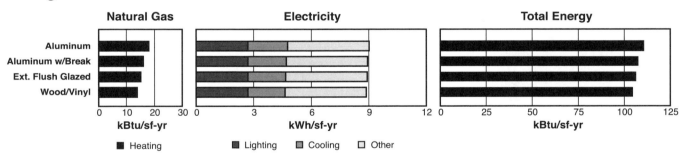

### Houston

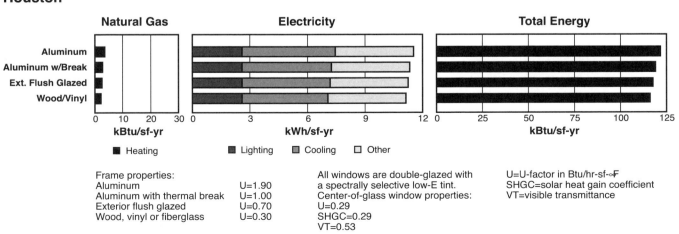

| Frame properties: | | All windows are double-glazed with | U=U-factor in Btu/hr-sf-°F |
| Aluminum | U=1.90 | a spectrally selective low-E tint. | SHGC=solar heat gain coefficient |
| Aluminum with thermal break | U=1.00 | Center-of-glass window properties: | VT=visible transmittance |
| Exterior flush glazed | U=0.70 | U=0.29 | |
| Wood, vinyl or fiberglass | U=0.30 | SHGC=0.29 | |
| | | VT=0.53 | |

reduces the heating energy use, with small reductions in electricity use. In Houston, with a significant cooling load and smaller heating requirements, the frame material has less effect, but U-factor plays a role in both heating and cooling. In commercial buildings, strength and durability often outweigh energy performance, leading to predominant selection of thermally broken aluminum frames.

## CURTAIN WALLS AND STOREFRONTS

A curtain wall is an external, nonbearing wall that is intended to separate the exterior and interior environments. Unlike manufactured windows or skylights placed into a wall or roof opening, curtain walls can compose the entire outer skin of the building. They consist of vision glazing as well as opaque spandrel panels.

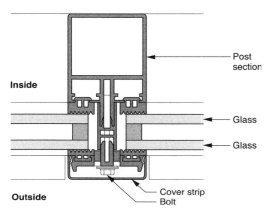

*Figure 3-41. Pressure plate detail*

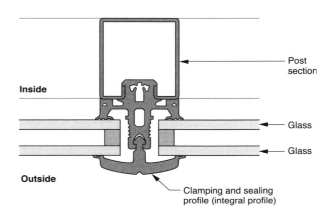

*Figure 3-42. Synthetic rubber profile*

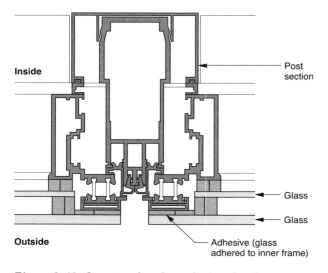

*Figure 3-43. Structural sealant glazing detail*

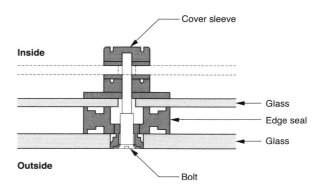

*Figure 3-44. Point-fixing connection*

The spandrel panels may be glass as well, forming an exterior envelope made completely of glass and framing materials.

Similar to a glass curtain wall, a storefront is a system of doors and windows mulled together as a composite structure. Storefronts are typically designed for high use and strength. A storefront system is usually installed between floor and ceiling on the street level of a building.

Aluminum is used almost exclusively as the frame material in both curtain walls and storefronts. Some steel is used as well, but is often clad on the exterior with aluminum or stainless steel caps. For larger glazing areas, the structural strength and durability of aluminum and steel cannot be equalled by other materials.

## Types of Curtain Wall Systems

One basic method of designing the glazing and frame connection in a curtain wall is to use pressure plates (Figure 3-41). The glass is held in place by a metal pressure plate on the outside which is attached to the metal framing members on the interior. Synthetic rubber profiles can also be used to hold glazing units in place (Figure 3-42). As a means of minimizing the exterior portion of the frame for aesthetic reasons, structural sealant glazing was developed (Figure 3-43). Silicone adhesives permit the glass to be structurally adhered directly to the interior frame. The silicone carries some of the weight of the glass itself and transfers wind pressure to the frame. All that appears on the outside are the glazing panes with narrow, sealed joints in between.

Another innovation in curtain wall construction is the use of suspended glazing with patch fittings (Figure 3-45). One of the early innovative examples of this type of system is the Willis Faber and Dumas Headquarters in Ipswich, UK, where multiple panes of glass are hung from the roof slab, resulting in a frameless appearance. Point-fixing is an evolution of this curtain wall concept, with various systems developed (Figure 3-44). Typically, holes are drilled through the glass and bolts or screws attach the glass to the interior frame structure. Unlike patch fittings, which project beyond the glazing plane and clamp adjacent panes together, point fittings are held within the plane of the glazing itself.

To stiffen glass curtain walls while maintaining the light appearance of the structure, glass fins or networks of truss cables are used. Cable net structures can be used to cover atrium spaces with minimal structure.

## Thermal Issues

The metal frames in a curtain wall design represent a potential path for heat transfer that can result in increased energy use, discomfort and condensation. Thermal breaks in the aluminum frames are designed to address these problems. However, it is still possible to defeat the thermal break with bolts and other connections. In addition to careful design of details to prevent thermal bridges, minimizing or eliminating metal frames on the exterior of the glazing is another solution. Chapter 2 discusses these issues in greater detail.

*Figure 3-45. The Willis Faber and Dumas Headquarters in Ipswich, UK, envelope is a curtain wall suspended from the roof, with internal glass fins hung from floor slabs to stiffen the facade. Patch fittings are utilized to clamp adjacent glass panes together. Architect: Foster & Associates; Photo: CALA Visual Resources Collection.*

## Sun- and Light-control Elements

The modern glass types discussed in the previous sections begin to address—within the glass structure or surface itself—issues of solar gain and heat loss, but it is a modern notion that glass has this capacity. The history of architecture, as often noted, is traceable through windows, whose size, shape, and interface with the building envelope define architectural styles. In the broadest sense, windows not only encompass the glazing proper, but also external or internal shading and light control elements—like overhangs, louvers, shades and blinds, light shelves, or brise soleil.

Any discussion of windows is incomplete without considering the means to temper and control light in an integrated manner. Window design is not just glazing selection, but the use of related architectural elements and the design of the space itself—room height and depth, partitions, colors—all elements that impact the luminous environment. In short, windows and glazing must be considered in the context of the total design. In this and the subsequent section, sun- and light-control elements are described, from simple shades and overhangs, used throughout history, to the more recently developed light redirection technologies.

### BACKGROUND

Humans are phototropic, with natural light necessary for well being. Natural light is associated with greater productivity and health benefits in the workplace. The importance of daylight has

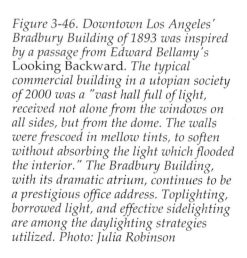

*Figure 3-46. Downtown Los Angeles' Bradbury Building of 1893 was inspired by a passage from Edward Bellamy's* Looking Backward. *The typical commercial building in a utopian society of 2000 was a "vast hall full of light, received not alone from the windows on all sides, but from the dome. The walls were frescoed in mellow tints, to soften without absorbing the light which flooded the interior." The Bradbury Building, with its dramatic atrium, continues to be a prestigious office address. Toplighting, borrowed light, and effective sidelighting are among the daylighting strategies utilized. Photo: Julia Robinson*

*Window Materials and Assemblies*

long been reflected in law. From the first century A.D. until the fall of Rome, laws established solar rights. British legislation, dating from 1189 and embodied in an 1832 statute, guarantees that if a window has twenty years of uninterrupted access to daylight, that access becomes permanent. Planning principles adopted in Boston and New York in 1905 and 1916 combated the dark street canyons emerging in urban centers. Today, Japanese building codes dictate that apartments receive four hours of direct sunlight per day, while German codes mandate that every workstation in new commercial buildings has direct contact with natural light—no more than twenty-five feet from a window (see the Debis Tower in Chapter 8).

Daylight is critical to people, as demonstrated by legislation, but it must be controlled effectively. Window design has developed in parallel with the means to shape light. Islamic latticework in window apertures shade occupants from the desert sun, Gothic expanses of stained glass diffuse direct sunbeams, and other examples illustrate that the combination of both providing and tempering daylight is a defining influence upon architectural design.

Many of the best solutions reflect their specific climate. Windows in the desert climate are small and shielded by lattices of wood or other material; passages in the Koran celebrate the luxury of dense shade in a desert climate. On the other hand, in the cloudy climate where Gothic forms evolved, huge stained glass windows let filtered light in to illuminate Biblical stories. Both window design approaches recognize their climatic context.

The noted landscape architect Michael Van Valkenburgh muses that "the wonderful thing about designing with plants is that they grow, change color, and eventually die. The most frustrating thing about designing with plants is that they grow, change color, and eventually die." A similar statement could be made about designing with daylight. The sun's varying path through the course of a day and year, changing sky conditions, and building orientation are just some of the factors influencing daylight design. Daylight's delight, however, is that it is never constant or static, and connects the building occupant to the outdoors' rich variability.

Of course, this variability is why daylighting design is a challenge. With overcast skies providing over 1,000 footcandles, and clear-sky conditions yielding thousands more, most regions have abundant daylight. Even with exacting tasks requiring 100 footcandles, lighting is rarely a question of quantity. After all, one can read by moonlight, which is less than one footcandle. The real challenge is to harness and tame daylight, to "drink from the fire hose," finding quality within the great quantity of light available.

Some of the very best architecture uses daylight and light control to create a quality luminous environment. Glare, veiling reflectance, and other critical factors all shape the comfort and usability of a room. Light levels required in a space—based on occupant needs, space usage, and the tasks performed in it—impact window and light-control direction. How daylighting integrates with electric lighting and the HVAC system and controls (including provisions for natural ventilation) as well as computer screens—another light source in many spaces—informs and impacts daylight strategies.

*Figure 3-47. Sun screen in the Alhambra, in Granada, Spain. Lattice screens of stone, wood, and stucco are integral parts of Islamic architecture. Photo: Todd Willmert*

*Figure 3-48. Computer rendering of "plant wall" at the National Wildlife Federation headquarters. Image: Manual Sanchez, HOK*

## SUN CONTROL BASICS

Sun control is fundamental for preventing overheating and diffusing bright sunlight. Yet while windows and sun-control devices are significant parts of the history of architecture, in the twentieth century there was a shift away from the sun-control and shading considerations with the advent of mechanical systems and the availability of inexpensive energy. A renewed interest in daylighting for energy as well as human benefits—as evident in the work of many architects today—recaptures the rich idea that windows and sun control are inextricably linked.

### Shading with Vegetation

Designing for sun control provides architects with a wide range of options, with foliage the most elemental material associated with shading. Deciduous vines and trees provide shade in summer, when it is needed. In winter, they allow more direct light and solar gains to enter the building. Other types of plants provide shade year-round. That an architectural element, like trellises, or architectural forms, like pergolas, evolved to support plants illustrates their importance. The green trellis at the National Wildlife Federation headquarters in Virginia is a modern manifestation of this idea (Figure 3-48).

### Shading with Fabric

Similarly, fabric awnings have long provided shade. The Roman word still used today "velarium," a large awning, especially one suspended over a Roman theatre or amphitheater—just hints at the ancient history behind this concept. The masonry of many of these Roman buildings is still with us, but the fabric has long vanished. Both of these materials must be visualized to understand the

*Figure 3-49. Traditional awnings on the Hamm Building in St. Paul, MN. The fabric and prismatic glazing in the ground floor clerestory windows offer sun control. Photo: Todd Willmert*

*Window Materials and Assemblies*

creation of climate-responsive habitable space. In our era, Main Street storefronts traditionally had simple, retractable cloth awnings (Figure 3-49). "Sails" on the Phoenix Central Library reinterpret the use of fabric in a modern manner (see Chapter 8).

## Fixed Exterior Shading Devices

If fabric and foliage are the most elemental materials for sun control, surely simple overhangs and porticoes follow. In Mediterranean and Arab cities, with their tight mazes of streets, buildings are so close that they shade each other. In other architectural traditions, porticoes and overhangs offer similar protection. The cantilevered overhangs in Prairie Style architecture were often calculated to reject summer sun, yet allow the winter sun to penetrate. The overhangs in the Cambria and Xilinx buildings function similarly, as shown in the Chapter 8 case studies.

The sun's seasonal altitude and orientation impact shading device design. Horizontal shading or light-control elements perform best on south facades, due to the high sun angles at those orientations. Vertical elements, in contrast, perform better on east or west facades—overhangs on the east and west are not effective in blocking the very low rising and setting sun. Overhangs on the east and west do provide shade, however, when the sun is higher in the sky.

The classic shading solution for east and west orientations is vertical fins, however, egg crate, brise soleil, or other architectural expression can be even more effective in blocking the low sun that impacts these facades (Figure 3-50). The inherent difficulty of fully addressing sun shading on the east and west is illustrated by the design of the Phoenix Central Library, where windows are avoided completely on those orientations (see Chapter 8). The building only opens up to the north and south, where sunlight can be more easily tempered.

*Figure 3-50. Brise soleil in India— Le Corbusier's shading approach to east- or west-facing facades. Photo: Leon Satkowski*

## Interior Shades and Blinds

A building is a fixed, static object, but the sun and sky conditions are dynamic. While passive controls such as overhangs are fixed, other controls allow for adjustment or change. Plants that shed their leaves in the fall, permitting sun penetration in winter, change on a seasonal basis. Blinds, drapes, and awnings can allow the user to more readily tune light levels at any time. The effectiveness of sun-control elements is increased when they are adjustable, to better account for the inherent daily and seasonal variability of the sun and sky.

Variability of space use also requires that occupants have the ability to adjust natural light. For instance, in many rooms daylight is usually a welcome feature, but a room might need to be dark at times for audiovisual presentations. In addition, shades may be necessary to filter the sun at certain times of the day or in certain seasons. Interior shades often complement daylighting strategies. In case studies like the Seattle Justice Center and the Hoffmann-La Roche Ltd. Office Building, interior shades are only one of the daylighting features integral in creating a comfortable, controllable luminous environment (see Chapter 8).

Interior shade options range from the traditional roller shades, venetian blinds, drapes, and blackout screens to blinds located between the panes of an insulated glazing unit. The finish options are similarly diverse. For instance, interior sun screens can be specified with different openness factors ranging from 0 to 18 percent (the lower end of the range for full blackout screens). Appropriate shadecloth densities, when matched to a glazing's visible light transmittance, can combine to control excess brightness and glare while maintaining a view to the outside.

One variable to consider when selecting shadecloth properties is orientation. For instance, north-facing windows can receive fabrics with a higher openness factor than windows facing east. Fabric backing is also important. Selecting a fabric with a white backing, to help reject solar heat, might be critical if there are no other means to control solar gains.

## Motorized Shading

There has been increasing interest in motorized shading systems due to the recent trend toward all-glass, fully-transparent facades. Landmark buildings in Europe often use motorized shades installed within a ventilated, double-layer glazed cavity to work as part of a heat extraction system (described later in the chapter). In the United States, energy economics differ from Europe. Due to this and other practical considerations, most motorized shading systems are usually interior installations—wind loads typically limit use of exterior shades to buildings that are no more than ten stories high.

Motorized shades typically rely on tubular motors mounted in the roller tube or head rail of the shade. The motor is either AC or DC powered (AC being much more prevalent), depending on the size and desired operation of the window shade. Usually, AC motors are used to raise or lower large, heavy shades or large groups of shades to preassigned heights. DC low-voltage motors, normally quieter than AC motors, are used with lower smaller

*Figure 3-51. Interior shades in the First Hawaiian Center. Even though the glazing has a low visible light transmittance of 24 percent, the bright Honolulu skies also require shading attention. Approximately 2000 internal sunscreens provide additional light control on the 30-story facility. North elevation shades have an openness factor of 10 percent, while the other three elevations, which receive more sunlight, have an openness factor of 5 percent. In this project, orientation impacted shade selection. In meeting and training rooms, blackout shades optimize conditions for audiovisual presentations. Architect: Kohn Pederson Fox; Interior Architects: Gensler and Associates; Photo: Courtesy of MechoShade; Photo: Augie Salbosa*

shades (although DC motors can be designed to lift large loads like AC motors). DC motors can also be used to make fine slat angle adjustments quietly and smoothly if venetian blinds are desired. Tubular AC motor life is claimed to be 20–30 years by some manufacturers. For interior shades, motor noise can be dampened by locating the motor in the ceiling plenum and providing appropriate sound insulation. Manufacturers can also design motor and control systems that ensure quiet, non-jerky operations, and bottom-edge alignment or slat alignment across a window wall.

The shade material and location of the shade in the window wall dictates the degree of daylight transmission and solar heat gain rejection. Exterior shades reject more heat than interior shades. Between-pane shades perform somewhere between exterior and interior shades depending on the size of the glazing cavity and whether it is ventilated. For roller shades, daylight, solar heat gain transmission, view, and privacy can be controlled by the perforation of the shade, shade weave, changes in material over the height of the shade, and differences in shade material on the front and back surfaces. View is possible through a roller shade with an openness factor as low as 2 percent. The venetian blind has a second option for movement—tilt angle—that enables it to control daylight and allow partial view while fully blocking direct sun. Automated roller shades have been the primary shade type for large-scale commercial window applications in the United States.

Automatically controlled systems can be quite sophisticated. Long-running examples of automated shades include the State of California Gregory Bateson Building in Sacramento and JC Penney's Corporate Headquarters in Plano, Texas. Today's systems often have wall switches or hand-held remote controllers so that individual shades can be controlled. Automated controls feature scheduling, direct sun control or depth of sun penetration, solar heating, glare control, daylighting, occupancy, response to HVAC operations, and limits on exterior shade operations, in the case of high winds, snow, or ice. Most systems use dry contact inputs or a programmable control bus to set the position of the window shades. Typically, the programmable control bus interface uses proprietary networking protocols, but a few manufacturers have built products that comply with open protocol standards so that the shades can "plug and play" with other building systems using the same protocols.

Individually addressed and controlled shades enable the building owner to attain complete flexibility in layout, reconfiguration, and operations over the life of the building without rewiring because the control grouping can be reconfigured in software. However, shades are often zoned or grouped so that a practical compromise can be reached between functionality and capital costs. For example, north-facing windows can be controlled as zones or controlled as an elevation. If automated, the zoning needs to be properly planned to ensure the best match between energy management needs, individual personal comfort, and functional task needs across the building's floor plan (if it is an open-plan office). Some products offer control flexibility that enables partial user control for comfort and satisfaction and facility manager control with the capability of overriding local user control during critical periods (peak electricity demand or high energy costs) or for other special needs.

*Figure 3-52. Motorized interior shades on the SABRE Holdings Campus in Southlake, TX, which earned a LEED™ Silver Rating. The interior shades are programmed to adjust in accordance with sun angles, Btu load on the glazing, and microclimatic conditions. Incremental shade movements maximize energy efficiency, daylighting, and view while reducing solar gain. The glazing's visible transmittance of 46 percent is combined with sunshades of 10–12 percent openness for heat and glare control. A darker value screen cloth was selected to enhance view through the shade cloth and to reduce the surface brightness of the sunlit screen cloth. Architect: HKS, Inc.; Photo: Courtesy of MechoShade; Photo: Ed LaCasse*

No Shading

Interior Shades

1-Foot Setback

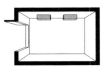

Shallow Overhang

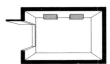

Deep Overhang

Vertical Fins

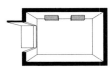

Overhang and Fins

Automated shading systems have significant potential to reduce energy use and improve environmental quality. Performance benefits are quantified in Chapters 5 and 6 for an interior shade that is "reliably" deployed in real-time to control direct sun or glare (see Appendix A for a description of this shade). For buildings with low-performance glass (e.g., single-pane clear), automated (and manual) shades can also increase thermal comfort by raising or lowering the effective surface temperature of the window wall during the winter or summer, respectively (see Chapter 2). The higher initial price of automated shades can be partially offset by these performance benefits as well as the reductions in HVAC installed capacity and ongoing HVAC maintenance costs, and decreased cost for furnishings replacement due to UV fading and degradation.

## PERFORMANCE OF CONVENTIONAL SHADING

Facade orientation has often influenced the form of shading elements in traditional shading strategies. Given the sun path, horizontal shading elements function most effectively on south-facing facades. Sun angles on eastern or western orientations dictated vertical or egg crate elements. Many building of the 1970s, and earlier, explored the interplay of shading devices, developing a shading vocabulary dependent on orientation. A more recent project, the Phoenix Central Library, was similarly developed, mindful of orientation, the sun path, and solar angles (see Chapter 8).

While this traditional attitude toward shading was an ideal solution with poorly performing glazings in the past, recent technical advances in glazing raise questions about these assumptions. New tints, coatings, and films in multipane glazing assemblies can provide effective shading within the glazing unit itself.

Figure 3-53 shows the impact of several shading conditions on energy performance for a south-facing office perimeter zone in Chicago. Shading impacts performance differently depending on the glazing type. In general, shades have the largest impact with high-VT, high-SHGC clear glazing (Window B) and the least with low-VT, low-SHGC reflective glazing (Window D). Shading has some impact on energy use with Window G and less with Window H. In situations where shading has an impact (Windows B and G), vertical fins alone are not a solution on a south-facing facade. Interior shades are an improvement, but deep overhangs and deep overhangs with fins result in the lowest total energy use for these cases.

Figure 3-54 shows the peak demand performance with different shading conditions. Similar to energy use, peak demand is affected significantly when shading Windows B and G with their higher VT and SHGC. This impact is diminished with Window H, which has a lower VT and SHGC, and there is almost no impact with Window D. A more extensive analysis of shading impacts for all orientations and window areas appears in Chapter 5 for a cold climate (Chicago) and Chapter 6 for a warm climate (Houston).

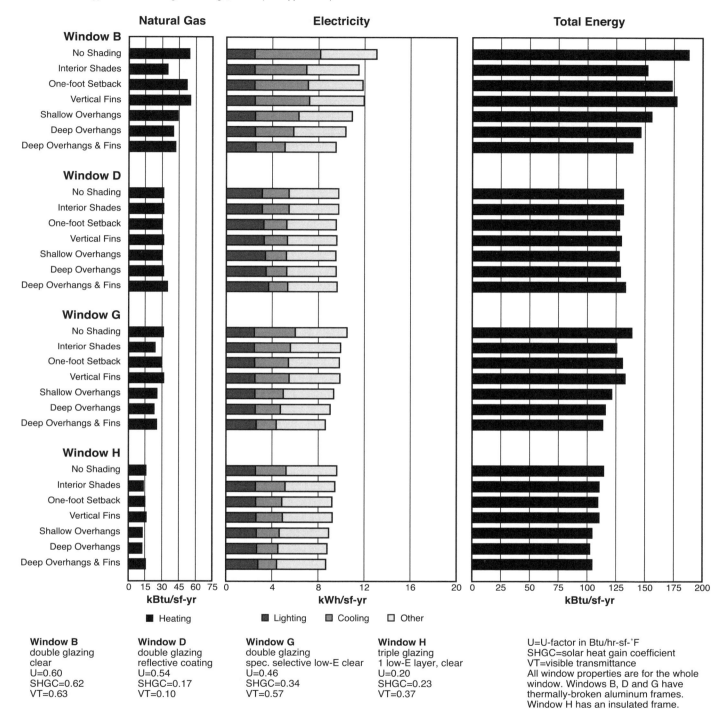

Figure 3-53. Energy use comparison of different shading conditions
All cases are south-facing with a 0.30 window-to-wall ratio and have daylighting controls. Numbers are expressed per square foot within a 15-foot-deep perimeter zone. Results were computed using DOE-2.1E for typical office buildings in Chicago, Illinois (see Appendix A).

**Natural Gas**
**Electricity**
**Total Energy**

**Window B**
No Shading
Interior Shades
One-foot Setback
Vertical Fins
Shallow Overhangs
Deep Overhangs
Deep Overhangs & Fins

**Window D**
No Shading
Interior Shades
One-foot Setback
Vertical Fins
Shallow Overhangs
Deep Overhangs
Deep Overhangs & Fins

**Window G**
No Shading
Interior Shades
One-foot Setback
Vertical Fins
Shallow Overhangs
Deep Overhangs
Deep Overhangs & Fins

**Window H**
No Shading
Interior Shades
One-foot Setback
Vertical Fins
Shallow Overhangs
Deep Overhangs
Deep Overhangs & Fins

0  15  30  45  60  75
**kBtu/sf-yr**

0  4  8  12  16  20
**kWh/sf-yr**

0  25  50  75  100  125  150  175  200
**kBtu/sf-yr**

■ Heating    ■ Lighting    ■ Cooling    □ Other

**Window B**
double glazing
clear
U=0.60
SHGC=0.62
VT=0.63

**Window D**
double glazing
reflective coating
U=0.54
SHGC=0.17
VT=0.10

**Window G**
double glazing
spec. selective low-E clear
U=0.46
SHGC=0.34
VT=0.57

**Window H**
triple glazing
1 low-E layer, clear
U=0.20
SHGC=0.23
VT=0.37

U=U-factor in Btu/hr-sf-°F
SHGC=solar heat gain coefficient
VT=visible transmittance
All window properties are for the whole window. Windows B, D and G have thermally-broken aluminum frames. Window H has an insulated frame.

*Sun- and Light-control Elements*

115

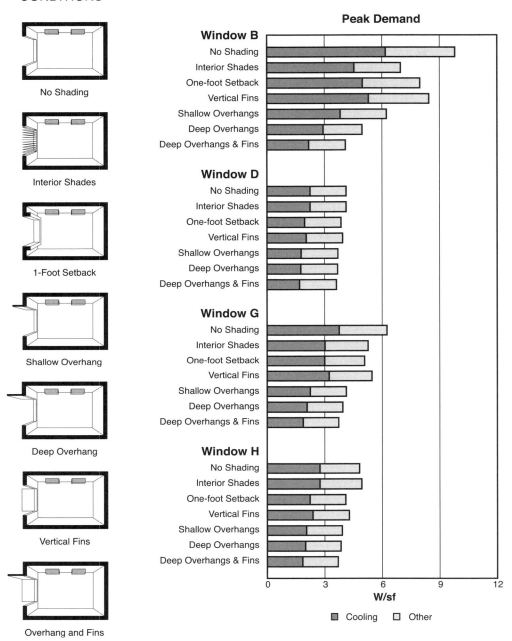

## SHADING CONDITIONS

No Shading

Interior Shades

1-Foot Setback

Shallow Overhang

Deep Overhang

Vertical Fins

Overhang and Fins

*Figure 3-54. Peak demand comparison of different shading conditions*

All cases are south-facing with a 0.30 window-to-wall ratio and have daylighting controls. Numbers are expressed per square foot within a 15-foot-deep perimeter zone. Results were computed using DOE-2.1E for typical office buildings in Chicago, Illinois (see Appendix A).

**Peak Demand**

**Window B**
- No Shading
- Interior Shades
- One-foot Setback
- Vertical Fins
- Shallow Overhangs
- Deep Overhangs
- Deep Overhangs & Fins

**Window D**
- No Shading
- Interior Shades
- One-foot Setback
- Vertical Fins
- Shallow Overhangs
- Deep Overhangs
- Deep Overhangs & Fins

**Window G**
- No Shading
- Interior Shades
- One-foot Setback
- Vertical Fins
- Shallow Overhangs
- Deep Overhangs
- Deep Overhangs & Fins

**Window H**
- No Shading
- Interior Shades
- One-foot Setback
- Vertical Fins
- Shallow Overhangs
- Deep Overhangs
- Deep Overhangs & Fins

0   3   6   9   12

**W/sf**

■ Cooling   □ Other

**Window D**
double glazing
reflective coating
U=0.54
SHGC=0.17
VT=0.10

**Window G**
double glazing
spec. selective low-E clear
U=0.46
SHGC=0.34
VT=0.57

**Window H**
triple glazing
1 low-E layer, clear
U=0.20
SHGC=0.23
VT=0.37

U=U-factor in Btu/hr-sf-°F
SHGC=solar heat gain coefficient
VT=visible transmittance
All window properties are for the whole window.

## Advanced Sun Control Elements

In addition to fixed and manually operable sun controls are those that automatically track the sun or respond to solar heat gain and light levels. Such sun-control technologies have been raised to an art form in recent projects. Consider the south wall of Jean Nouvel's L'Institut du Monde Arabe, Paris (Figure 3-55). Exquisite metal irises sandwiched between sheets of glass in the guise of traditional Islamic patterns open and close like the aperture of a camera to control the level and intensity of daylight entering the building. In the Siemens Pavilion in Seville, Spain, a sun screen—made of prismatic louvers—moves around the circular building. The louvers themselves are adjusted seasonally, but the screen itself follows the sun as it courses across the sky (Figures 3-56 and 3-57).

In both these emblematic, prestigious projects—one in cloudy, northern France and one in scorching, southern Spain—sun control becomes a featured building design element. The Institut Arabe and Siemens Pavilion showcase technological solutions, but their adjustable sun-control features have the same effect as manually operated devices like operable awnings or blinds. The advantages of automated systems are their ability to optimize energy use and to control interior conditions without relying on occupants.

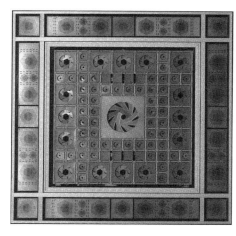

*Figure 3-55. Detail of sun screen on the south facade of L'Institut du Monde Arabe in Paris, France. The diaphragms open or close according to light levels. Photo: Todd Willmert*

*Figure 3-56. Overall view of the Siemens Pavilion in Seville, Spain. The louvers track the sun over the course of the day. Photo: Peter Bartenbach*

*Figure 3-57. Detail of sun screen at the Siemens Pavilion in Seville, Spain. The prismatic louvers track the sun around the circular building and can be pivoted for seasonal adjustment. Photo: Todd Willmert*

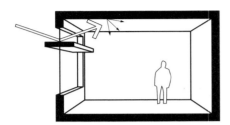

*Figure 3-58. Composite light shelf—both exterior and interior components*

*Figure 3-59. Curved exterior light shelves on the Hoffmann-La Roche Ltd. Office Building in Nutley, NJ, with prismatic transom windows above the shelves. Photo: Philippe Dordai*

# COMBINING DAYLIGHT REDIRECTION WITH SUN CONTROL

Shading devices control light and heat gain, yet they also can reduce the amount of light in a space, increasing electric lighting loads. Cooling loads are often highest on summer afternoons when there is abundant sunlight. Shades can be drawn to block the sun, but if electric lights need to be turned on, cooling and lighting energy use rises. It is possible, however, for sun control and daylighting to be addressed in tandem. For instance, an element like a light shelf can both shade and reduce glare, while allowing daylight to better penetrate the space. Sun control solutions should offer shading of direct sun and reduce glare from sky brightness. The most innovative approaches also improve daylight illuminance distribution and increase illuminance levels deeper into the space.

Daylight typically penetrates a room by about 1.5–2 times the window head height. Courtyards and notched floor plans are direct consequences of this rule of thumb, which has guided architectural development through the centuries. Daylight and ventilation requirements—in eras without air-conditioning or electric lights—meant that window design governed building depth until well into the 1900s.

A problem with providing daylight is that there is often too much light and glare near the window, and not enough light further back. Light shelves and prismatic glazing, as well as holographic films and innovative blind systems, address glare while facilitating daylighting. There is widespread interest in increasing the floor area that can be effectively daylit from a window.

Advanced light control elements and systems are based on physical phenomenon such as reflection with light shelves, refraction with prisms, and diffraction with holographic elements. These alternatives, connected with the window glazing or immediately adjacent to it, are not all in widespread use, but are worth consideration, both as expressive opportunities and effective light control measures.

## Reflectivity and Light Shelves

Architects have long harnessed the principle behind light shelves—reflectivity. Reflecting pools have the capacity to capture the play of light and bounce it into buildings. In Scandinavia, the reflectivity of white snowfields in winter plays a similar role. Water and snow can be considered as light shelves that extend well beyond the immediate building envelope, but they can also be sources of unwanted glare and light.

At the building scale, light shelves are typically flat or curved elements in the window facade that reflect incoming light. The elements typically divide the window aperture into a view window below the shelf, with a clerestory above. The lower window provides view for the occupants, while the upper transmits daylight.

Light shelves improve the quantity and quality of light in a space, and should be designed specifically for each window orientation, room configuration, building latitude, and climate. They are most appropriate for clear sky climates, particularly on south building elevations. Light shelves are less effective on eastern and western orientations and in overcast climates. There are significant light shelf nuances and variations, be they interior, exterior, or composite (Figure 3-58 and Figure 3–59).

Exterior light shelves are most effective with mirrored finishes, with their angle impacting performance. As the light shelf reflects light up and back in a space, ceiling reflectivity is critical—white ceilings are most effective. Higher ceilings will also positively impact light shelf effectiveness. Exterior light shelves, or exterior components of a composite light shelf, mainly contribute to higher light level in the space; their interior counterparts mainly address the glare issue.

Exterior light shelves, as with other shading and light control elements located outside the glazing, have the advantage of reducing thermal gains as well as helping control light. By contrast, interior light shelves and shading devices absorb heat that is retained in the space. This type of issue must be balanced against factors such as visual and thermal comfort, energy costs, initial and long-term costs—elements outside the building envelope generally being more costly and requiring more to maintain—in developing a building envelope.

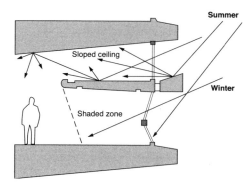

Figure 3-60. Section of Lockheed Building 157

There is wide variety of light shelf designs as shown by the Chapter 8 case studies—over half have light shelves. Another notable example, Lockheed Building 157, has light shelves over ten feet deep—much greater than any of the case studies. Building 157 illustrates the full impact light shelves can have on building development and final form. Composite light shelves on the facility's north and south facades, along with other daylighting strategies—such as 18-foot floor-to-floor heights and internal atriums, called *litriums*, all contribute to Building 157 being celebrated for its lighting design (Figure 3-60).

A number of innovative blind and louver systems have been developed employing the light shelf concept. The mini optical light shelf system (MOLS) in the Xilinx Building (Chapter 8) or the system of reflective blinds within an IGU shown in Figure 3-61, function as light shelves—helping to redirect light and temper sunlight.

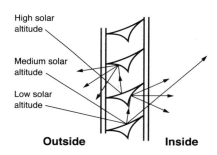

Figure 3-61. Blinds used as miniature light shelves

## Refraction and Prismatic Glazing

Heralded by *Inland Architect* magazine as the "century's triumph in lighting" when introduced in the early 1900s, prismatic glazing remains a surprisingly simple concept—horizontal prism ribs redirect light through refraction, sending it more deeply into a room (Figure 3-62). Prismatic glazing thus allowed deeper floor plates in office buildings. Another prominent use was as storefront transom windows—above the clear glazing used to display goods—to reduce glare and to introduce light back in the store (Figure 3–49).

Sullivan, Wright, and Loos were among the noted architects using prismatic glazing. Despite its popularity, a number of factors, including the increasing availability of cheap electric light and cleaning issues associated with the prismatic ribs, caused the glazing to fall from favor by the 1920s. The same factors causing the original interest in prismatic systems, energy conservation and providing naturally lit spaces, is fostering a resurgence. Recent applications on a variety of building types in different climates are promising.

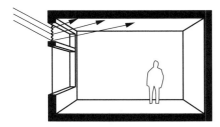

*Figure 3-62. Prismatic glazing redirects light upward and deeper into the space*

*Figure 3-63. SBV Biel facility in Switzerland, with prismatic louvers on the south facade. Photo: Croci + Du Fresne*

At SBV Biel in Switzerland, for example, prismatic elements placed high in the window bays reduce glare and veiling reflectance while preserving views out of the lower, clear glazing (Figure 3-63). Even though window height is only 10.5 feet, prismatic components redirect light 52 feet into the space—effectively extending the daylit zone.

The Siemens Pavilion, from the 1992 Expo in Seville, Spain, illustrates prismatic glazing's applicability in a different climate (Figures 3-56 and 3-57). The pavilion's movable prismatic panels, operable for seasonal adjustment, track the sun around the building's cantilevered walkways and stairs, a circular form driven by program. During Expo, visitors would progress up the exterior walks, waiting to enter exhibitions in the pavilion's upper floors; after Expo, Siemens planned to enclose the walkways, converting them to office space. In the new configuration, prismatic elements facilitate light penetration while still offering sun protection.

The cost of prismatic elements limits their use to prestigious, emblematic buildings, such as the pavilion. These costs are partially offset by energy savings for lighting and air-conditioning, as well as reductions in luminaries and HVAC capacity. It is this potential that is spurring further development. In the Hoffmann-La Roche Ltd. Office Building in Nutley, New Jersey, for example, the transom windows are acrylic prisms sandwiched between glass (Figure 3–59 and Chapter 8). The prism elements redirect light to the ceiling—which functions as a light reflector—a goal augmented by the sun catching light shelves directly below the transom. Both elements, the shelf and the prism panels, help control sun and reduce glare, with the prisms filtering UV rays.

The refinement of these innovative systems and the proven range of works in divergent climates show promise in the architectural application of prismatic components—offering both daylighting advantages and solar protection. The allure of prisms attracted notable early modern architectural designers at the beginning of the twentieth century. Prismatic glazing became an expressive element that forged an alternative daylighting approach, which is being rediscovered a century later.

## Diffraction and Holographic Elements

Holographic optical elements (HOE) bend light by diffraction. The technology's principle—with regard to glazing—is that a window is coated with a transparent layer in which an invisible diffraction pattern is printed by a holographic technique. The window will then deflect direct and diffuse solar radiation over a defined angle, a function of the holographic pattern, deep into a building.

Holographic elements do not have 100 years of application like prismatic glazing, but they are receiving more attention. Like prismatic elements, HOEs can address several functions at an aperture—redirecting light, sunshading, and offering passive control of energy consumption. Because they are integral with the glazing, HOEs can be used with insulating, security, and other glazing types and assemblies.

*Window Materials and Assemblies*

# Double-envelope Facades

Double-envelope building systems have gained increased attention over the past two decades, with technological advances allowing a fuller realization of a concept that has existed for over two millennia. For instance, hypocaust heating, circulating a fire's smoke within wall and floor cavities to temper space, was integral to the design of Roman baths. The bath wall itself became a source of radiant heat, resulting in the integration of the building envelope and heating system.

The early modernists recognized the potential of glass as a building envelope material, but it was one not easily or readily integrated with a building's HVAC system. Paul Scheerbart's visionary writings explored the new architecture stemming from the increasing availability of glass. His comments, written in 1914, touched on the thermal limitations of glass, suggesting a double layer of glazing was to prevent excessive heat loss—"Since air is one of the worst conductors of heat, all glass architecture needs this double wall. The two glass skins can be a meter, or even farther, apart" (Banham 1984).

Scheerbart's writings are prescient, yet they did not consider a glass facade's compatibility with an HVAC system. "Convectors and radiators should not be put between the two skins because too much of their output will be lost to the outside air." His contemporaries, such as Le Corbusier, challenged this conception with innovations including the development of the *mur neutralisant*—the neutralizing wall—where mechanical systems are integral with the envelope. Consider Le Corbusier's 1916 Villa Schwob, where brick walls and double-glazed windows serve as both enclosures and radiant fields, with heating pipes placed in their cavities. "The walls of former days, thick and cumbrous, have been replaced by insulating membranes with cushions of air that are thin as a shell. Large air conditioners with double partitions of eleven centimeters and an air space between these partitions have been constructed" (Caron 1979). This work suggests a distinct attitude about the integration of wall, window, and mechanical system.

Le Corbusier strove to incorporate double envelopes in subsequent, larger projects, like his Salvation Army complex in Paris, but the integration of double envelope with mechanical system was never realized. In fact, his ideas were ahead of the era's mechanical technology. Today there is a reevaluation of the basic concepts he was exploring.

## RECENT DEVELOPMENTS

Most current examples of double-envelope buildings are located in Europe, yet ironically one of the first noteworthy double-envelope buildings of the modern era in is the United States—the Occidental Chemical Corporate Office Building in Niagara Falls, New York (Figures 3-64 and 3-65). This 1980 design outwardly appears to be a conventional curtain wall building. Up close, two perimeter curtain walls can be seen which are 4 feet apart. The cavity has operable, white, horizontal shading devices that can be adjusted in response to sun position—they help to distribute daylight evenly and provide

Figure 3-64. Exterior of Occidental Chemical Corporation in Niagra Fall, NY, one of the first double-envelope buildings. Photo: Cannon Design

Figure 3-65. Interstitial space within double envelope of Occidental Chemical Corporation. Note interior louvers and vents between floor levels. Photo: Cannon Design

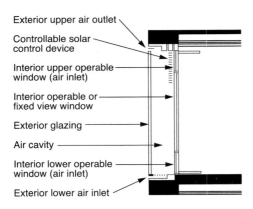

Exterior upper air outlet

Controllable solar control device

Interior upper operable window (air inlet)

Interior operable or fixed view window

Exterior glazing

Air cavity

Interior lower operable window (air inlet)

Exterior lower air inlet

*Figure 3-66. Basic components of a double-envelope system*

some night insulation. The ample cavity allows for maintenance walkways and, with its dampers at the top and bottom, natural ventilation by the stack effect. The Seattle Justice Center is a more recent project, but there are few other examples of double-envelope buildings in the United States (see Chapter 8).

Typically, these assemblies are composed of a single-pane of glass paired with double-glazed windows, with both assemblies separated by an air space. The glass types may be dissimilar, with the single pane on the interior or exterior, and other factors keyed to specific site, climate, and space requirements. While there is great variability within double-envelope construction, all double envelopes can help provide the following: thermal buffer and insulation, wind and weather protection for sunshades, and acoustic attenuation.

The cavity can be closed or heated to create a warm buffer that insulates in winter, or otherwise developed to reduce heat gains, functioning as a thermal chimney to vent out excess heat. Additionally, operable louvers or other shading devices are commonly installed in the cavity to control solar gains and light levels. Locating shading devices within the cavity protects them from the elements and their location outside the occupied spaces helps limit solar gains.

One of the greatest driving forces behind recent interest in double-envelope systems is the aesthetic desire to create transparent all-glass buildings that perform well. The potential energy savings, as well as the noise attenuation and greater occupant comfort they offer, are advantages that help justify the system. A second skin of glass placed in front of a conventional facade reduces sound levels at particularly loud locations, such as airports or high-traffic urban areas. A double-envelope system is also a natural solution to the requirement for operating windows in some European office towers. Operating windows in the upper floors of single-skin buildings must contend with high wind pressures and wind-driven rain. A double-envelope system provides a wind and rain screen on the outside and natural ventilation through the operating windows connected to the cavity. The basic components of a single-story double-envelope system are shown in Figure 3-66.

## DOUBLE-ENVELOPE OPERATION

A common feature of most double-envelope systems is the ability to ventilate the cavity between the glazing skins. The ventilation can operate in two modes—heat extraction and heat recovery (Figures 3-67 and 3-68). Heat extraction double-skin facades rely on sun shading located in the intermediate or interstitial space between the exterior glass facade and interior facade to control solar loads. The concept is similar to exterior shading systems in that solar radiation loads are blocked before entering the building, except that heat absorbed by the between-pane shading system is released within the intermediate space, then drawn off through the exterior skin by natural or mechanical ventilation. Cooling load demands on the mechanical plant are diminished with this strategy.

This concept is manifested with a single exterior layer of heat-strengthened safety glass or laminated safety glass, with exterior air inlet and outlet openings controlled with manual or automatic throttling flaps. The second interior facade layer consists of fixed or operable, double- or single-pane, casement or hopper windows. Within the intermediate space are retractable or fixed venetian blinds, whose operation can be manual or automated.

During cooling conditions, the venetian blinds cover the full height of the facade and are tilted to block direct sun. Absorbed solar radiation is either convected within the intermediate space or re-radiated to the interior or exterior. Low-emittance coatings on the interior glass facade reduce radiative heat gains to the interior. If operable, the interior windows are closed. Convection within the intermediate cavity occurs either through thermal buoyancy or is wind driven. In some cases, mechanical ventilation is used to extract heat. Heat recovery strategies can be implemented using the same construction to reduce heating load requirements during the winter.

Another design variable in double-envelope buildings is whether the inner or outer skin is sealed or operable. In the Occidental Chemical Building and the Seattle Justice Center (Chapter 8), the inside facade envelope is sealed with vents and baffles at the top and base of the cavity flue to allow outside air to be drawn through the cavity. With both skins operable, a single-story-high cavity can be utilized, as in the Debis Tower (Chapter 8). The outer envelope of glass louvers is open in summer and closed in winter. Interior double-glazed windows can be opened by individual occupants. Another variation employs a full-building-height cavity. Dampers at the head and base of the double-envelope cavity are used in combination with operable inner-skin double-glazed windows.

Of course, each of the permutations has particular advantages. For instance, sealing the outer skin creates better noise attenuation if traffic or other sounds are a prime concern. The Debis Tower's skin offers a high degree of occupant control, something not possible at the Seattle Justice Center. Designers and clients have to weigh the merits of each system and other constraints of their particular project.

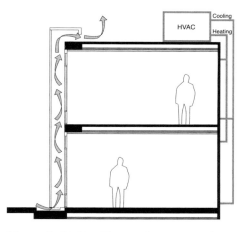

Figure 3-67. Double-envelope system in heat extraction mode where ventilated cavity air is exhausted to the outside

## COSTS AND BENEFITS

While the double-skin facade presents some advantages over the conventional single-skin facade, the costs and benefits can vary. Research in the United Kingdom shows that double-skin buildings are able to reduce energy consumption by 65 percent, running costs by 65 percent, and cut $CO_2$ emissions by 50 percent in England's cold to temperate climate when compared to advanced single-skin buildings (Wigginton et al 2000). However, other energy evaluations show that compared against a simple, energy-efficient glazed facade, a double envelope acting as a simple thermal buffer does not contribute much to energy savings. In fact, it is difficult to ascertain how well many existing systems are actually operating.

The benefits of double-envelope facades in terms of energy savings might be questionable, but the acoustic isolation and thermal comfort they offer is widely recognized. Many double-envelope systems are utilized in high traffic areas. In winter, the increased surface temperature of the inner glazing layer in winter improves comfort and reduces condensation. Proper venting of the interstitial space is essential in summer to dissipate solar gains, an issue remedied with louvers or other means.

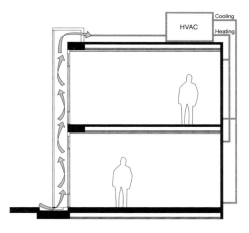

Figure 3-68. Double-envelope system in heat recovery mode where ventilated cavity air is recirculated to the building

The widespread acceptance of double-envelope curtain walls is perhaps best reflected in the fact that manufacturers are now marketing complete systems. There are double-envelope systems that can be assembled from prefabricated components on site that include glazing and enclosures that provide window and facade ventilation. More complex systems actually integrate the cavity of the double-skin facade as a mechanical system air duct—echoing Le Corbusier's early explorations. The savings in ductwork—in terms of reduced height necessary on each floor—can be substantial. Transferring the supply and exhaust ducts to the cavity in one 30-story double-envelope facade gained 30 percent more rentable space (Schittich et al 1999).

In Europe, twin-face facades are between 25 and 100 percent more costly than a conventional curtain wall, while in the United States they may be four to five times more expensive. Double-envelope projects, like the Debis Tower, are built with more frequency in Europe. A factor driving high costs in the United States is the relative scarcity of design tools. In spite of these cost barriers, double-envelope and other advanced facade concepts are a source of innovation and their potential must be explored as part of the transition to much higher performance buildings in the future.

## Toplighting

Providing daylight with vertical windows can mean overlighting the area near the windows to get sufficient light to areas deeper in the building. Toplighting with skylights, clerestory windows, or atriums can bring daylight deeper into buildings. The main objective is to provide light, with issues such as view and thermal comfort being less relevant.

Toplighting enjoys basic advantages over sidelighting in that illumination can be evenly distributed with minimal glazing, resulting in a high ratio of daylight illumination to heat loss and gain through the glazing. Skylights can require 5 percent or less of the total roof area to provide 50 footcandles of illumination. Toplighting also enables more design flexibility—it is less subject to interference from surrounding buildings and skylights are not affected by orientation as much as vertical windows. Of course, other issues come to the fore with toplighting. The strategy is less applicable to tall, multistory buildings, and when views are desirable, sidelighting is often a more appropriate lighting strategy as long as building floor plates are narrow.

Before air-conditioning and artificial lighting made large floor areas feasible, the art of toplighting was critical. Glazed skylight atriums and clerestories were necessary for daylighting and ventilation. Toplighting remains the most relevant daylighting strategy for several building types, such as factories, warehouses, museums, or large retail spaces. But it is also important in office buildings and schools as a complement to sidelighting. When toplighting and sidelighting are used together, light comes from two directions, providing more balanced light levels that reduce glare problems.

Toplighting is used in six of the seven case studies in Chapter 8. A major skylight atrium graces the lower floors of the Debis Tower,

*Figure 3-69. Atrium of the Old Post Office Pavilion, a restored former U.S. Postal Service headquarters in Washington, D.C. Finished in 1899—before reliable electric lighting or extensive mechanical systems—the atrium gives borrowed light and ventilates adjoining offices. Photo: CALA Visual Resources Collection*

with minor skylit spaces in the Hoffmann-La Roche Ltd. Office Building and the Phoenix Central Library. Small round and linear skylights animate the fifth-floor reading room in the Phoenix Central Library. Clerestories in Cambria and Xilinx provide essential daylight in interior spaces, as do the roof monitors in the Florida Solar Energy Center. In clerestory applications, the same conventional vertical windows serve for both sidelighting and toplighting.

Although toplighting and sidelighting can be complementary, there are profound differences. In La Tourette, for instance, Le Corbusier explored how toplighting and sidelighting diverged aesthetically. Toplighting is the mysterious light from above, reserved for sacred spaces, its source most often concealed by baffling or filtering. The secular spaces, dormitory rooms and communal halls, are more simply sidelit. Lighting within the everyday realm is distinct from that in the spiritual realm.

There are profound perceptual differences between sidelighting and toplighting, however both pose challenges. As with sidelighting, the best toplighting solutions reflect a particular program, climate, latitude or other variables inherent within a building and its site. It is beyond the scope of this book to fully address toplighting, but since it is commonly employed in conjunction with sidelighting, the topic is briefly addressed in this section.

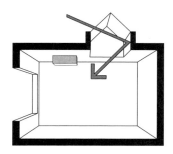

*Figure 3-70. Typical skylight*

## Skylights

Skylights range from the mass-produced versions with standard sizes and curb details, to major custom-designed sloped glazing installations. The difference between the prefabricated skylight punched into a warehouse roof and I. M. Pei's grand glass pyramid skylight at the renovated Louvre are obviously profound.

Smaller prefabricated skylights do not require great structural changes and can be specified in a project during construction or occupation with little architectural impact. They can maintain a low profile and cost less that custom-designed systems. A flat skylight is likely to cost less than constructing a roof monitor with a vertical clerestory window. With a major skylight form like the Louvre pyramid, significant design and engineering are required. Pei's pyramidal skylight is highly visible, and has become an icon for the museum. Its architectural impact is considerable.

The range of skylight designs and products is tremendous, but in general only a relatively small glazing area, appropriately placed, is required to illuminate. Though codes relevant to horizontal glazing, like specification of wire or laminated glass, must be heeded and problems pertaining to horizontal glass, such as leakage, must be addressed, skylights remain a low first cost daylighting option.

Horizontal skylights provide light from above. As such, skylights are very effective in equatorial locations. If properly designed for sunny conditions, a small glazing area—about 2 percent of the floor area—can illuminate effectively, without additional cooling requirements that offset the savings from reduced electric lighting. Overcast climates with a uniformly bright sky vault are also good candidates for skylight applications.

*Figure 3-71. Prefabricated skylight units are often used in a "generic" manner. In this "specific" application, skylights are integrated with the truss system. Photo: Velux America*

*Figure 3-72. Iconic skylight of the Louvre in Paris, France. Photo: Courtesty of Pei Cobb Freed & Partners; Photo: Koji Horiuchi*

In contrast, low sun angles in more northerly latitudes limit the effectiveness of horizontal skylights. For instance, during winter—when you want to maximize light and warmth of the sun—there is little sun penetration. To address this drawback, skylights can be tilted to maximize efficacy. For instance, at 40 degrees North latitude, a south-facing skylight at a 45-degree slope improves the ratio of summer heat admitted to winter light admitted from 5:1 to 2:1. At a 60-degree slope, noon illumination in both summer and winter would be the same (Lam 1986).

Other skylight issues include room height, color, and other details involving the integration of the ceiling plane and skylight. As with conventional windows, skylight development can include shades and louvers. The Phoenix Central Library illustrates one approach to skylight design in a hot climate (see Chapter 8). The round, fifth-floor skylights that hover above the column heads are over 3 feet in diameter, but their deep light wells with translucent glazing at the base primarily provide indirect, filtered light. Direct light only enters through a small hole on the glazing at noon on the solar solstice.

In contrast to the Phoenix Library's small skylights, a whole roof might be luminous. The Crystal Palace can be considered one large skylight. As a temporary exhibit hall, the Crystal Palace did not have burdensome environmental control concerns, especially in the cloudy, temperate London climate. In many cases today, luminous roofs face rigorous standards. At Bonn's German History Museum, prismatic glazing forms a glass sandwich approximately 3 inches thick, with two prism layers (Figure 3-73). The outer layer is mirrored to offer sun protection; solar radiation is minimized, with diffuse light passing through. The inner layer is non-reflective, serving to limit horizontal glare. The prismatic elements, along with other components, create a compact, panel system for sun protection, providing a diffuse daylight spectrum optimized for the museum's requirements. It accomplishes this while yielding daylight factors from 5 to 8 percent in the main exhibit hall. These innovations are furthered in the toplighting approach in the former German Parliament in Bonn, where adjustable prism banks redirect light for the main hall. The prism panels help attain excellent illumination—enough light during the day to operate without electric lights—all without glare.

*Figure 3-73. Luminous roof of German History Museum in Bonn. Prismatic panels form one large skylight. Photo: Peter Bartenbach*

In addition to these highly specific skylight applications, there are many standardized components and systems available in the marketplace. Light pipes, standard skylight-tubes utilized in big box retail facilities, warehouses and work spaces, are unitized elements. Skylights also come as manufactured units, to be used individually or ganged together. Sloped glazing systems are similar to curtain wall construction and can be custom-designed for specific situations. Sun-tracking heliostats, to increase light entering a skylight, are available, as are skylights with integral blinds.

## Clerestories

Skylights are often inconspicuous elements, but clerestory monitors that poke up from the roof can have a more noticeable impact on exterior architectural form (Figures 3-74). With their vertical glazing, clerestory windows easily capture low angle sun, in contrast to skylights. Clerestory windows' orientation impacts their thermal performance and nomenclature. Roof monitors oriented toward the sun are called *sunscoops*, while monitors that face away from the sun are called *lightscoops*. Shading strategies for conventional windows such as overhangs and louvers work with clerestories as well. As with windows, orientation impacts shading approaches. The Florida Solar Energy Center roof monitors are lightscoops that face north and essentially require no shading even in such a sunny climate (Chapter 8).

Scoops can easily be baffled with the reflected, indirect light entering the space. Thus clerestories can provide glare-free light more easily than conventional windows. Their wide application in museums and work spaces, where even light is appreciated or necessary, can be traced to these characteristics. As with sidelighting, clerestory windows should be developed mindful of reflected light sources. Utilizing the roof as a reflecting surface can positively impact the amount of light a clerestory can capture.

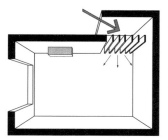

*Figure 3-74. Clerestory raised above the roof line brings light to the rear of the space; baffles diffuse direct sunlight*

Clerestories such as those located in the center court of 3M's Austin Center in Texas, illustrate their applicability in a commercial office building (Figure 3-75). North-facing, prismatic films and reflecting devices on daylighting panels bounce light through the clerestory windows to provide even light 80 feet deep throughout the 54,000-square-foot space. This passive system has less glazed area than conventional skylights while simultaneously giving better light distribution and reducing its glare—critical with Texas's clear skies. Prismatic films can also be effective in gathering light in more overcast conditions.

Another clerestory application is a simple band of windows high in the wall plane. For instance, the first-floor map room at Cambria is lit by clerestory windows (Chapter 8). These high windows free up wall space, and their height means that light can penetrate through the glass in the center table to toplight the lobby below. The open office space on the first floor is also lit by clerestory windows. The space's depth could not adequately be sidelit alone, requiring toplighting in some form.

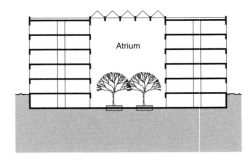

Figure 3-75. Atrium

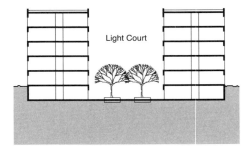

Figure 3-76. Light court

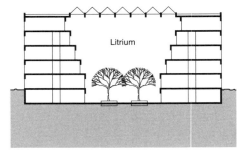

Figure 3-77. Litrium

## Atriums

A traditional courtyard, defined by buildings or walls, is an outdoor room open to the sky. An atrium, which is a covered courtyard, evolved from this archetypal form. Skylights and clerestories are utilized in atriums to provide light from above. Multistory atriums are relatively common in commercial buildings, providing a central focus to a facility and as a source of borrowed light to adjacent rooms.

Variations of courts and atriums merit attention. For instance, a *light court* is a court designed specifically to enhance lighting, with highly reflective surfaces or other strategies utilized to increase light penetration to adjacent spaces. A *litrium* is an atrium designed to optimize daylighting within its adjacent spaces. Special tracking mirrors and light shelves within the litrium at Lockheed Building 157, augments its effectiveness as a source of natural daylight. An atrium that steps back as its opens to the sky might also be called a litrium, the geometry increasing its capacity to provide daylight.

In Chapters 4–7, design guidance is given for exterior windows in offices and schools. Selecting windows for spaces facing atriums can involve the same issues as selecting exterior windows. These include the concern for daylight, view, and glare control as they affect people as well as energy use and peak demand reduction related to electric lighting. Thermal comfort and energy use related to heat loss and gain are of less concern in these interior glazed walls. All these issues are of concern for the design and glazing selection related to skylights and clerestories at the top of the atrium.

Figure 3-78. Atrium with clerestory toplighting in 3M Austin Center in Texas. Photo: 3M Company

*Window Materials and Assemblies*

# CHAPTER 4

# A Decision-making Process for Window Design

## Introduction

The previous chapters have described a number of window design and selection issues as well as a wide range of window technologies. With all these variables and possibilities, making a design decision can be overwhelming. It would be easy if there were a simple sequence of steps leading to the right solution based on a few well-defined criteria. Unfortunately, it is not so simple—making design decisions involves a web of interdependent variables.

This chapter attempts to provide information and methods for thinking through these decisions, although it must be recognized that the process is really shaped by the questions the designer is trying to answer. For example, one architect may ask what is the optimal way to design windows in terms of orientation and size to meet multiple criteria of energy, appearance, and cost. Another may simply ask whether shading devices are justified or what is the best glazing for peak demand reduction. This chapter provides an approach to aid in this decision-making process.

In the following section, a method is presented that leads the designer from large-scale decisions such as building orientation down to the glazing selection itself. This is the framework for Chapters 5, 6, and 7 where extensive, comparative performance information is outlined for offices and schools in two climates. This chapter concludes with a section on the impact of climate on window decision making, and finally, a section which addresses how building type (offices versus schools) affects window design decisions.

*Figure 4-1. WMEP Interdistrict Downtown School in Minneapolis, MN. Architect: Cuningham Group; Photo: Peter Kerze*

# A Method of Decision Making

## DECISIONS WITHIN THE DESIGN PROCESS

An architect makes decisions at several scales in the building design process. The larger scale issues of placement on the site, building configuration, and overall layout come first. Even in these early stages, the orientation, size, and shape of individual spaces and whether they have windows are being established. The refinement of individual spaces and systems follows, which involves window size and shape as well as the use of shading devices and daylight control systems. Finally, glazing and frame type are specified with the desired properties.

As a designer proceeds from larger to smaller scale decisions, however, discoveries are made at the later stage that may raise questions about earlier assumptions. In fact, this dialogue between scales is a normal part of the design process that ensures building design and performance goals are achieved. The challenge is that decisions made at different scales are interdependent so it becomes difficult to draw simple conclusions based on rules of thumb.

What's worse is that experienced designers may use old rules of thumb that are no longer applicable given new window technologies. For example, many designers assume that window orientation affects energy use a great deal in commercial buildings. This is certainly true in some cases when using conventionally performing windows with no shading. However, there can be little difference in energy performance between orientations if windows are properly shaded or if high-performance windows are used.

This example illustrates that assumptions made in site planning about orientation affecting energy use may be questionable when performance is understood at the detailed level of window properties. This is not to say that orientation is not a critical issue in terms of the amount and direction of daylight and the ability to control glare. Because of this interdependent set of design parameters, decisions must be made within a given context—there is no absolute right answer.

The purpose of this book is to provide designers with information they need to make informed choices about windows—particularly how to optimize for energy efficiency and human factors issues. To do this, performance information is organized around a series of questions the designer might ask at different times and different levels of detail within the process. This process is illustrated in Figure 4-2. There are two given conditions in any design—the climate and the building type (or space types within a building). Once these are established, questions about window orientation, daylight controls, window size, shading systems, and window type can be addressed. The decision to use daylight controls appears early in the process since it is nearly always recommended and affects other decisions that follow.

In some cases, the designer may be able to control all these variables; in others, they may be predetermined. For example, the designer of a building in a suburban office park may be able to manipulate the variables of orientation and solar exposure to optimize energy use and other design goals. On the other hand, the

*Figure 4-2. A decision-making process for window design and selection*

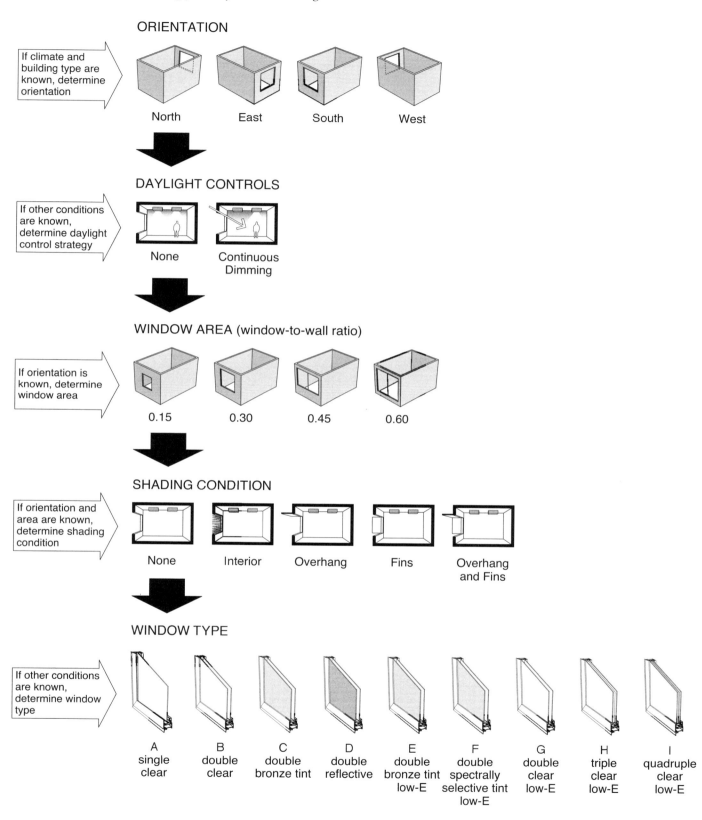

ORIENTATION

If climate and building type are known, determine orientation

North    East    South    West

DAYLIGHT CONTROLS

If other conditions are known, determine daylight control strategy

None    Continuous Dimming

WINDOW AREA (window-to-wall ratio)

If orientation is known, determine window area

0.15    0.30    0.45    0.60

SHADING CONDITION

If orientation and area are known, determine shading condition

None    Interior    Overhang    Fins    Overhang and Fins

WINDOW TYPE

If other conditions are known, determine window type

A
single clear

B
double clear

C
double bronze tint

D
double reflective

E
double bronze tint low-E

F
double spectrally selective tint low-E

G
double clear low-E

H
triple clear low-E

I
quadruple clear low-E

architect for a downtown office building may be presented with a site dictating form and orientation, while surrounding buildings completely block solar access. Sometimes the building type shapes variables. For example, storefront glazing on a strip mall development may always be under a covered walkway, thus having no direct solar exposure and limited opportunity for daylight.

The approach illustrated in Figure 4-2 and used in Chapters 5–7 is applied at the scale of a single perimeter zone with windows. For an office building, the zone is a series of 10-by-15-foot enclosed offices, and for a school it is a series of 30-by-30-foot classrooms. This zone can have different orientations, window areas, shading devices, lighting control systems, and glazing types. Energy and peak demand data are expressed per square foot of floor area.

The impacts of all these design parameters working in an integrated fashion can be analyzed with computer simulations at the scale of a perimeter zone. The building is made up of these perimeter zones combined with other internal zones. The ratio of perimeter to internal zones is not of concern in this analysis, nor is the exact distribution of perimeter zones facing different orientations. These impacts must be modeled at the scale of the whole building. However, the lessons from analyzing the individual perimeter zones can be applied to issues of site and whole building design.

While the process outlined in Figure 4-2 suggests moving from larger to smaller scale decisions, designers can enter at any level to make a decision within a given context. For example, the site may dictate that windows can only be oriented to the west, so the designer can assess the optimal window area and other choices within the context of west-facing windows. In another case, costs or aesthetics may rule out external shading devices, so the designer can determine the best glazing type for the unshaded condition. This diagram represents the basic organization of information in Chapters 5–7.

The book does not provide performance information for more advanced daylighting techniques such as light redirection and toplighting, or more advanced facade designs using double envelopes with integrated ventilation systems. These advanced strategies would obviously influence the energy and human factors performance of the perimeter zones and will be the subject of future comparative evaluations.

## CRITERIA USED IN DECISION MAKING

In making decisions about window selection and related systems (i.e., shading, daylighting controls), there are many factors leading to long lists of decision-making criteria. The fundamental criteria relate to the original purpose of having windows in a building—providing daylight, view, and fresh air. Of course, fresh air is commonly provided by mechanical means in commercial buildings, but if daylight and view are desired, windows should be evaluated in terms of how well they are provided.

In addition to these basic functions, architects often utilize windows as a key part of the aesthetic expression of a building. The color, transparency, reflectance, and other visual qualities of glass are highly valued as a material in architecture. In the future, there may be another fundamental purpose of windows—to generate energy using

## Figure 4-3. *Energy and human factors criteria used in decision-making process*

All cases are south-facing with a 0.60 window-to-wall ratio, no shading, and includes daylighting controls for a typical office building in Chicago, Illinois (Appendix A). All window properties are for the whole window. Windows B–H have thermally broken aluminum frames. Window H has an insulated frame. U=U-factor in Btu/hr-sf-°F, SHGC=solar heat gain coefficient, VT=visible transmittance

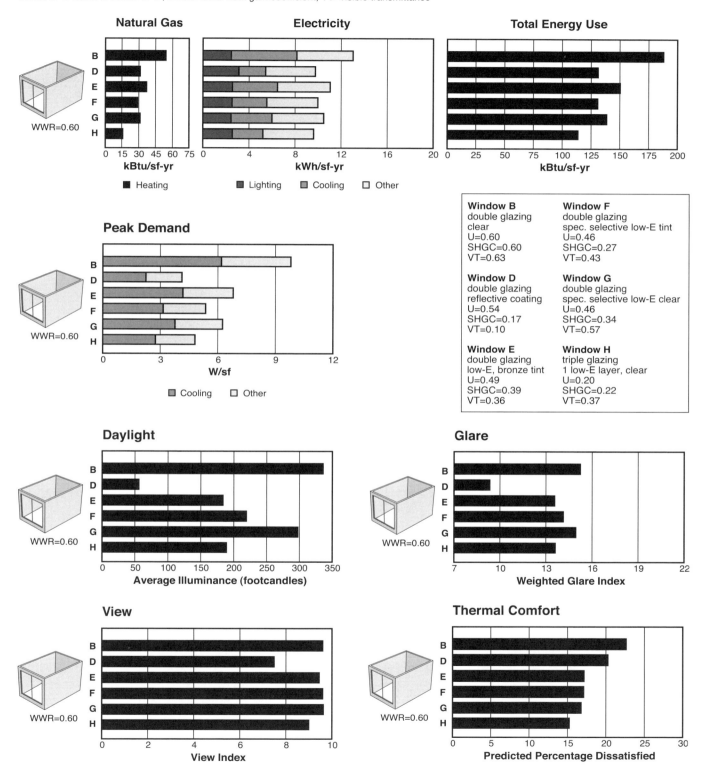

**Window B**
double glazing
clear
U=0.60
SHGC=0.60
VT=0.63

**Window D**
double glazing
reflective coating
U=0.54
SHGC=0.17
VT=0.10

**Window E**
double glazing
low-E, bronze tint
U=0.49
SHGC=0.39
VT=0.36

**Window F**
double glazing
spec. selective low-E tint
U=0.46
SHGC=0.27
VT=0.43

**Window G**
double glazing
spec. selective low-E clear
U=0.46
SHGC=0.34
VT=0.57

**Window H**
triple glazing
1 low-E layer, clear
U=0.20
SHGC=0.22
VT=0.37

photovoltaic films embedded into the glazing unit. This will only become a basic reason for installing these types of windows when emerging technologies begin to be cost effective.

There is a second set of criteria that do not relate to the fundamental purpose of having windows in buildings, but are limiting factors none the less. This group includes cost, energy performance, glare control, thermal comfort, acoustic control, and requirements for structure, water protection, safety, and security. An emerging criterion is the life cycle environmental impact of the window materials themselves. Many of these criteria are discussed in Chapter 2. It is beyond the scope of this analysis to evaluate costs, aesthetics, and other issues.

The focus of this book analysis is six criteria related to energy performance and human factors—annual energy use, peak electricity demand, daylight, glare, view, and thermal comfort. These parameters are defined in Chapter 2 and in Appendix A. The designers must integrate these criteria into a broader set of design issues and values while understanding the long-term implications of their decisions. Examples of these six criteria are shown in Figure 4-3 for a south-facing perimeter office zone in Chicago.

## PUTTING ENERGY USE INTO PERSPECTIVE

Figure 4-4 shows the total energy performance of six window options in office perimeter zones with different orientations in Chicago, Illinois. The top edge of the gray tone represents the maximum energy budget for such a perimeter zone using the ASHRAE 90.1-99 method of calculation (see Appendix A). On north-facing orientations, all window types fall below the ASHRAE budget at all window areas (except Window D at WWR=0.60). For south-, east-, and west-facing zones, all windows meet the ASHRAE budget up to WWR=0.30, but above that Windows B exceeds the limit. Window E exceeds the budget at WWR=0.45 and above, while Window G exceeds the budget at about WWR=0.55. Figure 4-5 illustrates similar patterns for peak demand in Chicago.

Figure 4-6 shows the total energy performance of six window options in office perimeter zones in Houston, Texas. The set of six windows is different for Houston in order to include options more representative of hot climate choices. Single-pane clear Window A is the base case for comparison since this type of glazing is still common on some existing buildings. With a north-facing orientation, all windows at all window areas fall below the ASHRAE budget except for Window A above WWR=0.50. For south-, east-, and west-facing zones, Window A exceeds the budget at WWR=0.20, and Windows C and E exceed it in the WWR=0.40–0.45 range. Figure 4-7 shows peak demand compared to the ASHRAE budget in Houston. All windows meet the budget with north-facing orientation at any window area except Window A above WWR=0.45. For south-, east-, and west-facing zones, the peak demand budget can never be met with Window A and can only be met below WWR=0.30 for Windows C and E. Only Window D meets the budget at any window area.

## Figure 4-4. Total annual energy use comparison in a cold climate

All cases have and no shading and include daylighting controls. Numbers are expressed per square foot within a 15-foot-deep perimeter zone. Percentage difference compared to an opaque wall is given on the 2nd y-axis. Results were computed using DOE-2.1E for a typical office building in Chicago, Illinois (Appendix A). Total annual energy use is calculated by multiplying electricity use by 3 and adding heating energy use. This reflects the 3:1 ratio of primary to end use energy for electricity. Shaded area indicates the ASHRAE 90.1-99 budget.

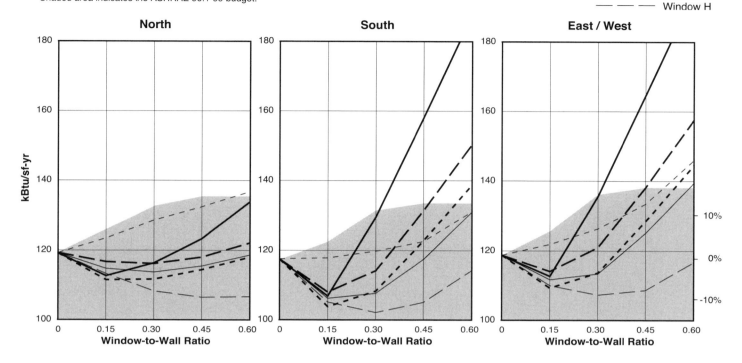

## Figure 4-5. Peak demand comparison in a cold climate

All cases have and no shading and include daylighting controls. Numbers are expressed per square foot within a 15-foot-deep perimeter zone. Percentage difference compared to an opaque wall is given on the 2nd y-axis. Results were computed using DOE-2.1E for a typical office building in Chicago, Illinois (Appendix A). Shaded area indicates the ASHRAE 90.1-99 budget.

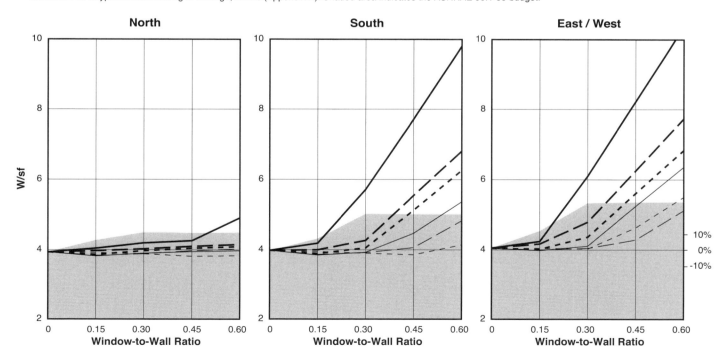

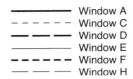

*Figure 4-6. Total annual energy use comparison in a hot climate*
All cases have and no shading and include daylighting controls. Numbers are expressed per square foot within a 15-foot-deep perimeter zone. Percentage difference compared to an opaque wall is given on the 2nd y-axis. Results were computed using DOE-2.1E for a typical office building in Houston, Texas (Appendix A). Total annual energy use is calculated by multiplying electricity use by 3 and adding heating energy use. This reflects the 3:1 ratio of primary to end use energy for electricity. Shaded area indicates the ASHRAE 90.1-99 budget.

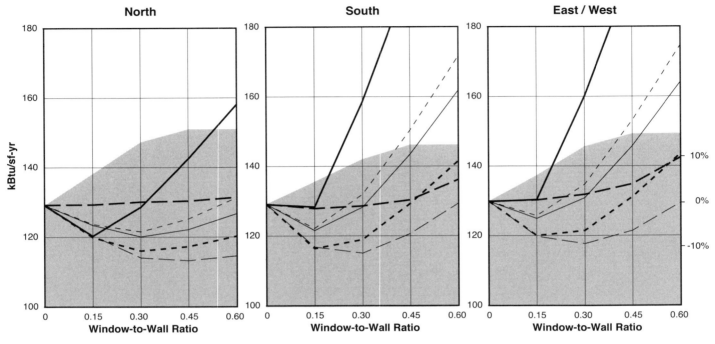

*Figure 4-7. Peak demand comparison in a hot climate*
All cases have and no shading and include daylighting controls. Numbers are expressed per square foot within a 15-foot-deep perimeter zone. Percentage difference compared to an opaque wall is given on the 2nd y-axis. Results were computed using DOE-2.1E for a typical office building in Houston, Texas (Appendix A). Shaded area indicates the ASHRAE 90.1-99 budget.

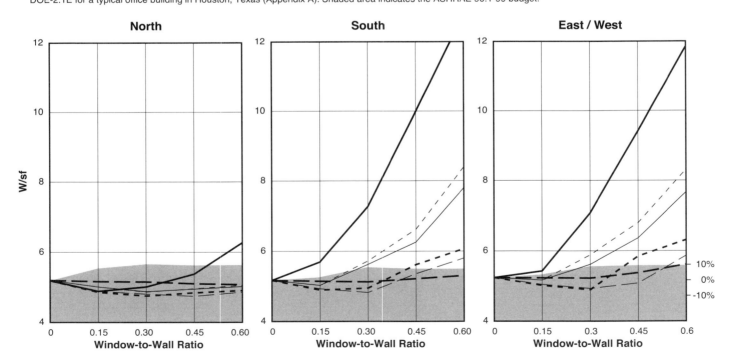

*A Decision-making Process for Window Design*

For a designer deciding on the basis of energy use and peak demand, the concept of an energy unit must be understood. What is the significance of the various units? For energy and peak demand, it may help to have several reference points:

- Most sustainable building designers claim that they can easily beat ASHRAE 90.1 by 10-15 percent. Reducing total annual energy use by 20 kBtu/sf-yr is equivalent to beating ASHRAE 90.1 by 15 percent for a south-facing perimeter zone with large-area windows (WWR=0.45-0.60) in Chicago.

- For a typical U.S. office building (all old and new building stock in the United States), 20 kBtu/sf-yr represents 10 percent of the total annual energy use of the entire building (EIA CBECS 1995—see graph in Chapter 2). For a typical U.S. warehouse, 20 kBtu/sf-yr represents 30 percent of the total annual energy use (its energy use intensity is much less than an office). For a typical U.S. hospital, 20 kBtu/sf-yr represents 5 percent of the total annual energy use of the entire building (energy use intensity is much greater than an office).

- Reducing peak demand by 1 W/sf is the equivalent of eliminating all equipment energy use (from computers, task lights, copiers, fans, etc.) in a building during that peak hour.

- Reducing peak demand by 1 W/sf of all new commercial buildings built between 2000–2010 prevents the construction of 22 new 600 MW nuclear power plants or 81 new 160 MW diesel generators. It also eliminates the environmental impact on the nation's resources and air quality that result from these power plants.

## WEIGHING MULTIPLE CRITERIA

Comparing design options based on multiple criteria, and presenting them to designers in a straightforward, useful manner is a challenge. Figure 4-8 illustrates a graphical method for comparing six windows across the six energy and indoor environment attributes used in this analysis. There is a column of shaded dots for each of these characteristics—energy use, peak demand, daylight, glare, view, and thermal comfort. Each attribute is converted to a 0-to-10 scale with 10 being the most positive condition (lowest energy, least glare, most daylight, best view). The lighter the shaded area, the better the window performance for a given criterion.

While some windows may be superior in one or two attributes, such as energy performance and peak demand reduction, they may be deficient in other areas, such as providing daylight and view. For example, clear, double-glazed Window B performs well in terms of daylight and view but poorly in terms of energy and peak demand. Window D with the reflective coating is almost the opposite—it performs better than Window B on energy, peak demand, and glare control but worse on daylight and view. The most balanced performance is found with the triple-glazed, low-E Window H which rates relatively highly in terms of all the attributes except glare control (which can be managed with shading).

*Figure 4-8. Comparison of multiple attributes by shading condition*

All cases are south-facing with no shading and a window-to-wall ratio of 0.60 and daylighting controls for an office in Chicago, Illinois.

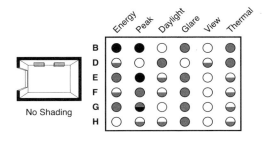

To compare different window conditions across all attributes, the six measures of window performance are placed on a 0-to-10 scale. See Appendix A for the methodology.

○ 8–10 Best
◑ 6–8
◕ 4–6
◕ 2–4
● 0–2 Worst

Using the style of graph shown in Figure 4-8 for decision making requires an understanding that all of these attributes may not be valued equally. Users may place their own priorities on the six factors and weight each column to reflect their value system. For example, maintaining a low interior light level with glare control may be a higher priority than maximizing daylight and view for some applications.

Unfortunately, these six attributes can not easily be converted to a common measure that is meaningful (i.e., dollars). It is misleading to combine the points into a single number for each window—positive and negative attributes would cancel each other out and very different windows may end up with similar total performance. For this reason, window performance is left in this matrix format so designers can perceive strengths and weaknesses of different options and make their own trade-offs.

## Impact of Climate on Window Design Decisions

Because of climatic differences, the impact of windows on energy use and peak demand in perimeter spaces can vary considerably with location. In Chapters 5–7, detailed data are given only for Chicago and Houston. To put these two cities into context, Figure 4-9 illustrates the annual energy performance of six window types in six North American cities. In all cases, the windows are in south-facing office perimeter zones with daylighting controls and no shading.

One obvious difference between climates is that heating energy use matters a great deal more in colder cities (Minneapolis, Chicago, and even Washington, DC), than in warmer cities (Los Angeles, Houston, and Phoenix). In all climates, electricity for cooling and lighting is a more dominant energy use in perimeter office spaces than gas for heating.

In Figure 4-9 heating and electricity use are combined into total energy use by converting them into source energy (a 3 to 1 fuel ratio of electricity to natural gas) Electricity use is multiplied by three to account for inefficiencies in production and transmission. The factor of three is also the approximate cost difference between the two types of energy. The actual cost differences vary by region, but 3 to 1 is a national average.

In spite of the differences in results between climates, the ranking of windows remains generally the same between window types across all window areas for unshaded windows. With exterior shades, the ranking is nearly the same but there are variations due to the fact that solar angles vary by latitude.

Clear, single- and double-glazed windows (A and B) always perform the worst, as expected, in all cities. The conventional bronze tints and reflective coatings in the middle group (Windows C–E) are an improvement. The high-performance group (Windows F–I) tend to have the lowest electricity and heating use in all climates. There are some exceptions, however. For example, in colder climates, Window E performs nearly as well as the high-performance group (Windows F–I). Because of its moderate SHGC, which offsets heating needs, Window E is not penalized as it is in warmer climates. On the other hand,

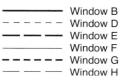

*Figure 4-9. Annual energy use comparison for six window types in six North American climates*

All cases are south-facing with no shading and include daylighting controls. Numbers are expressed per square foot within a 15-foot-deep perimeter zone. Results were computed using DOE-2.1E for a typical office building (Appendix A). HDD=heating degree days base 65. CDD=cooling degree days base 50.

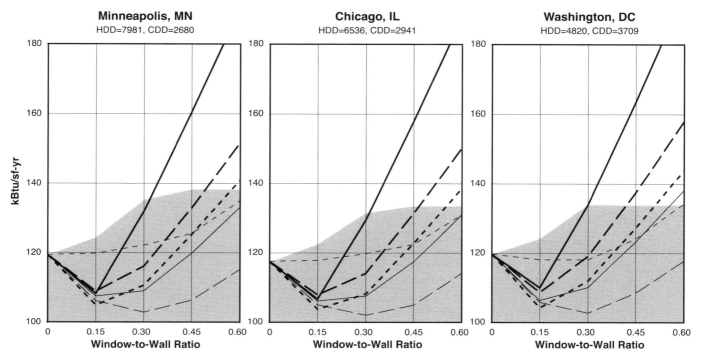

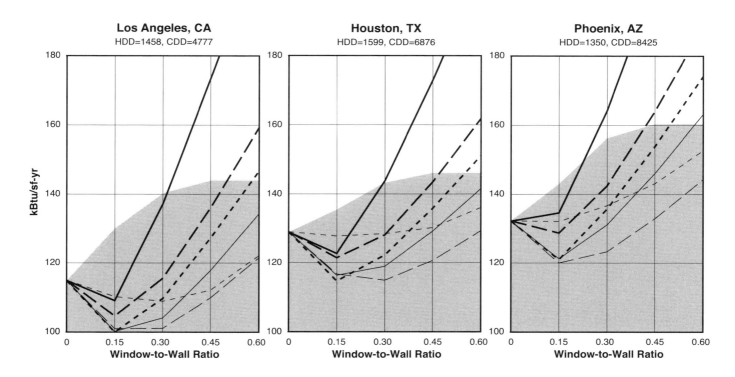

*Figure 4-10. Peak demand comparison for six window types in six North American climates*

All cases are south-facing with no shading and include daylighting controls. Numbers are expressed per square foot within a 15-foot-deep perimeter zone. Results were computed using DOE-2.1E for a typical office building (Appendix A). HDD=heating degree days base 65. CDD=cooling degree days base 50.

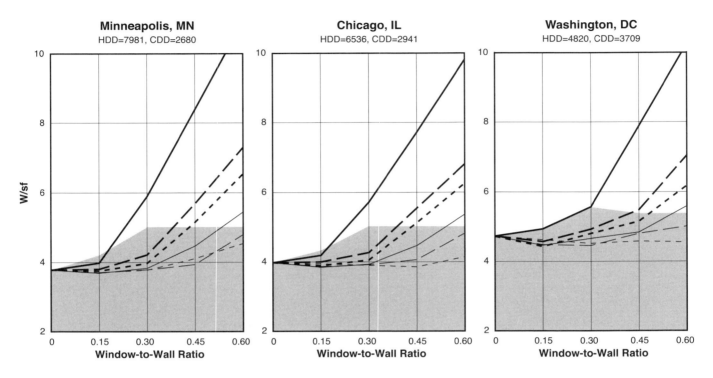

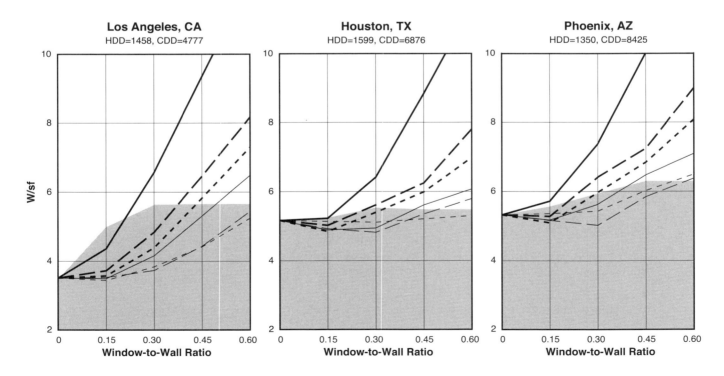

*A Decision-making Process for Window Design*

Window G, which is one of the higher performing windows in cold climates, ranks lower in warm climates because it does not have a lower SHGC, which is more important than a high VT for daylighting.

These differences in annual energy use mean that there will be different relative energy savings and, thus, different economic consequences when comparing window choices. For more extreme climates like Minneapolis or Phoenix, energy performance differences are amplified from those observed for Chicago and Houston illustrated climates in Chapters 5 and 6. For milder climates such as Washington, DC and Los Angeles, the differences are reduced and window design options increase.

Figure 4-10 shows the peak electricity demand for the same six windows in six North American cities. While there are some differences between cities, peak demand falls in a similar range of 4–6 W/sf for most moderately sized windows (except Window A) in most locations. Peak demand is primarily dictated by outdoor air temperature and/or solar radiation levels (which are determined by solar angle and cloudiness). For example, peak demand may occur during the winter for southern zones despite cooler temperatures. The day and time when the peak occurs may differ between climates. For the same window condition, the peak condition may even occur at a different day and time between window types. Therefore, the ranking and savings in peak demand between window designs vary with climate.

Figure 4-11 illustrates five basic climate zones in the United States, based on heating and cooling degree days. At least one of the cities shown in Figures 4-9 and 4-10 appears in each zone.

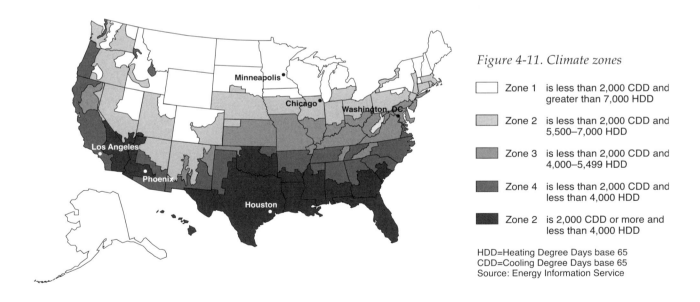

*Figure 4-11. Climate zones*

| | Zone 1 | is less than 2,000 CDD and greater than 7,000 HDD |
| Zone 2 | is less than 2,000 CDD and 5,500–7,000 HDD |
| Zone 3 | is less than 2,000 CDD and 4,000–5,499 HDD |
| Zone 4 | is less than 2,000 CDD and less than 4,000 HDD |
| Zone 2 | is 2,000 CDD or more and less than 4,000 HDD |

HDD=Heating Degree Days base 65
CDD=Cooling Degree Days base 65
Source: Energy Information Service

# Impact of Building Type on Window Design Decisions

Just as climate affects the impact of windows on energy use and peak demand, building type has an important effect as well. Different commercial building types (i.e. offices, schools, libraries, retail) have varying hours of operation and different internal requirements. Because of these differences, lighting and mechanical system designs vary, resulting in different energy use profiles. Placing windows into these different building types may lead to different conclusions about the best window option and whether it is cost effective.

Offices are one of the most commonly built types of commercial space. Perimeter office spaces are extensively analyzed in Chapters 5 and 6 for a colder climate (Chicago, Illinois) and a hotter climate (Houston, Texas). To better understand how building type influences window performance, a more limited set of conditions and criteria are analyzed for school classrooms in Chapter 7 for the same two locations.

## Comparing Offices and Schools in a Colder Climate

Figure 4-12 compares annual energy use for a perimeter office space and school classroom with six window types in Chicago. Although the perimeter spaces have different depths (15 feet for the office and 30 feet for the classroom), results are shown per square foot to provide a meaningful comparison. In both cases, the windows are south-facing and cover 30 percent of the wall area. It should be noted that in this set of comparisons, it is assumed that interior shades are operated in response to certain thresholds for direct sun and glare. Previous examples in this chapter have shown unshaded conditions. In both cases, the buildings are operated twelve months per year.

The most notable difference between office and school energy performance in Chicago is the greater amount of heating and lower amount of electricity use for the school cases. This occurs because offices have more computers and other plug loads that generate heat. Consequently, the requirement for additional heat is less for offices, but the requirement for electricity is higher. When heating and electricity are combined, offices still use more energy per square foot, but the difference between the building types is not large.

Total energy use shown in Figure 4-12 reveals the same ranking between windows for both offices and schools in Chicago. Triple-glazed Window H performs best and reflective Window D performs worst in both cases. The poor performance of Window D occurs because even though it has a very low SHGC to reduce cooling, its low VT reduces daylighting, causing an even greater amount of energy spent for electric lighting. The absolute difference between double-glazed, clear Window B and any of the higher performance alternatives (Windows E–H) is very similar for both offices and schools.

Comparing peak electricity demand for office and school perimeter zones does reveal some differences between building types (Figure 4-13). While the total peak demand is in a similar range for offices and schools, the portion attributed to cooling is higher in the school case. For both building types, triple-glazed Window H per-

## Figure 4-12. *Annual energy use comparison for office and school perimeter zones in a cold climate*

All cases are south-facing with 0.30 window-to-wall ratio, include daylighting controls and interior shades for perimeter zones in Chicago, Illinois. The energy is expressed per square foot within a 15-foot-deep perimeter zone for offices and a 30-foot-deep perimeter zone for schools. Both offices and schools are operated twelve months per year. Results were computed using DOE-2.1E. Total annual energy use is calculated by multiplying electricity use by 3 and adding heating energy use. This reflects the 3:1 ratio of primary to end use energy for electricity.

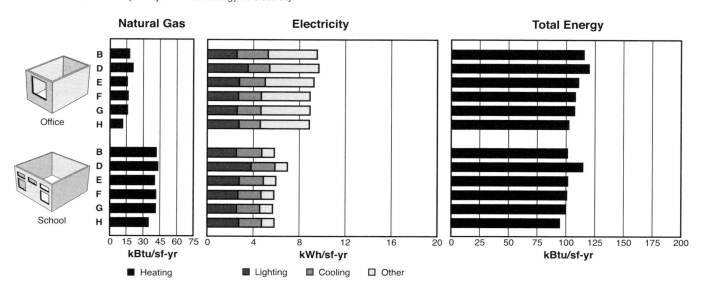

## Figure 4-13. *Peak electricity demand comparison for office and school perimeter zones in a cold climate*

All cases are south-facing with 0.30 window-to-wall ratio, include daylighting controls and interior shades for perimeter zones in Chicago, Illinois. The peak demand is expressed per square foot within a 15-foot-deep perimeter zone for offices and a 30-foot-deep perimeter zone for schools. Results were computed using DOE-2.1E.

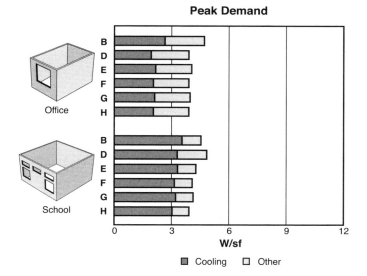

**Window B**
double glazing
clear
U=0.60
SHGC=0.60
VT=0.63

**Window D**
double glazing
reflective coating
U=0.54
SHGC=0.17
VT=0.10

**Window E**
double glazing
low-E, bronze tint
U=0.49
SHGC=0.39
VT=0.36

**Window F**
double glazing
spec. selective low-E tint
U=0.46
SHGC=0.27
VT=0.43

**Window G**
double glazing
spec. selective low-E clear
U=0.46
SHGC=0.34
VT=0.57

**Window H**
triple glazing
1 low-E layer, clear
U=0.20
SHGC=0.22
VT=0.37

U=U-factor in Btu/hr-sf-˚F
SHGC=solar heat gain coefficient
VT=visible transmittance
All window properties are for the whole window.
Windows B–H have thermally broken aluminum frames. Window H has an insulated frame.

*Impact of Building Type on Window Design Decisions*

forms best in terms of peak demand while other high-performance options (Windows E, F, and G) perform nearly as well. The worst performing cases are different for the two building types—Window B performs worst for offices and Window D is worst for schools. In both building types, the high SHGC of Window B increases peak demand for cooling, while the low VT of Window D reduces daylight and causes greater peak demand for electric lighting loads. In the relatively shallow office zone (15 feet), the cooling issue predominates and in the deeper (30 feet) classroom zone, lighting is a bigger factor.

## Comparing Offices and Schools in a Warmer Climate

Figure 4-14 compares annual energy use for a perimeter office space and school classroom in a warmer climate—Houston, Texas. The six windows used in this comparison differ from those used in the previous comparisons for Chicago. This window set includes a clear, single-glazed window (Window A) as a base case representing some existing buildings in warmer climates, and a bronze-tinted, double-glazed window (Window C) to reflect a conventional approach to solar gain control in this region.

Similar to the colder climate examples, electricity use for computers and other plug loads are less in the school classroom than the office. Consequently, electricity use is lower in schools and heating is higher compared to offices. With the lower heating requirement in warmer climates, electricity becomes even more dominant in calculating total energy use.

Total energy use shown in Figure 4-14 for Houston reveals the same ranking between most windows for both offices and schools. Triple-glazed Window H performs best, with Window F a close second for both building types. However, Window A performs worse in the office while Window D is the worst case for schools. In both building types, the high SHGC of Window A increases annual energy use for cooling, while the low VT of Window D reduces daylight and causes greater annual energy use for electric lighting. In the relatively shallow office zone (15 feet), the cooling issue predominates and in the deeper (30 feet) classroom zone, lighting is a bigger factor.

Peak electricity demand for office and school perimeter zones in Houston follows the same pattern as energy use (Figure 4-15). For both building types, triple-glazed Window H performs best in terms of peak demand, while other high-performance options (Windows E and F) perform nearly as well. Window A has the highest peak demand for offices and Window D has the highest for schools. As explained above, this reflects differences in the depths of the zones and load profiles. As in the colder climate, the portion of peak demand attributed to cooling is much higher in the school case.

## Conclusion

Considering all the envelope, internal, and infiltration loads that contribute to the need for heating and cooling, window loads from conduction and solar radiation constitute 74 percent of the total heating load and 38 percent of the total cooling load in a typical large office building in the United States. Windows need full, thorough consideration.

## Figure 4-14. Annual energy use comparison for office and school perimeter zones in a warm climate

All cases are south-facing with 0.30 window-to-wall ratio, include daylighting controls and interior shades for perimeter zones in Houston, Texas. The energy is expressed per square foot within a 15-foot-deep perimeter zone for offices and a 30-foot-deep perimeter zone for schools. Both offices and schools are operated twelve months per year. Results were computed using DOE-2.1E. Total annual energy use is calculated by multiplying electricity use by 3 and adding heating energy use. This reflects the 3:1 ratio of primary to end use energy for electricity.

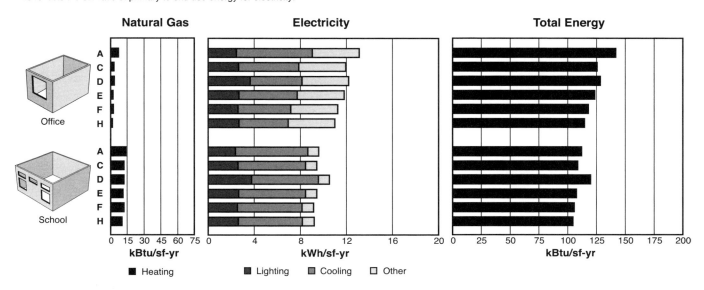

## Figure 4-15. Peak electricity demand comparison for office and school perimeter zones in a warm climate

All cases are south-facing with 0.30 window-to-wall ratio, include daylighting controls and interior shades for perimeter zones in Houston, Texas. The peak demand is expressed per square foot within a 15-foot-deep perimeter zone for offices and a 30-foot-deep perimeter zone for schools. Results were computed using DOE-2.1E.

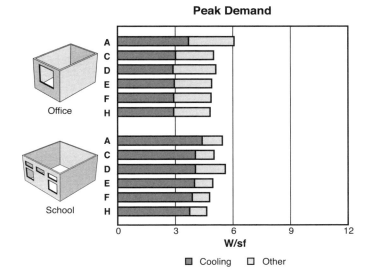

**Window A**
single glazing
clear
U=1.25
SHGC=0.72
VT=0.71

**Window C**
double glazing
bronze tint
U=0.60
SHGC=0.42
VT=0.38

**Window D**
double glazing
reflective coating
U=0.54
SHGC=0.17
VT=0.10

**Window E**
double glazing
low-E, bronze tint
U=0.49
SHGC=0.39
VT=0.36

**Window F**
double glazing
spec. selective low-E tint
U=0.46
SHGC=0.27
VT=0.43

**Window H**
triple glazing
1 low-E layer, clear
U=0.20
SHGC=0.22
VT=0.37

U=U-factor in Btu/hr-sf-°F
SHGC=solar heat gain coefficient
VT=visible transmittance
All window properties are for the whole window.
Windows C–H have thermally broken aluminum frames. Window A has an aluminum frame.

This book focuses mainly on offices, the most prominent commercial building type, with some additional analysis for schools. Among the many other commercial building types, windows can have higher or lower impacts on energy, peak demand, and human factors, depending on the building type and application. When considering building types other than those presented in this book, the technologies and principles presented still apply. A wide variety of windows are available to offer the right balance of heat loss (U-factor), solar heat gain control (SHGC), and visible light transmittance (VT).

A detailed building energy simulation is the only certain way to estimate projected building performance. Trends seen in office windows may or may not be similar. To put this in perspective, Figure 4-16 shows the percentage of heating and cooling loads that can be attributed to windows, for different building types. These numbers are averages encompassing many variables, but they do point out how windows are important from an energy perspective in some building types, less important in others. Overall, the data indicates the huge impact windows have on energy use.

In studying these numbers, it should be emphasized that the percentages shown in Figure 4-16 are based on theoretical thermodynamic building loads. The actual energy requirements of the HVAC system can often be several times larger due to inefficiencies and losses in the air-heating system, heating and cooling equipment, and central plant. In short, the impact of windows is even higher than the numbers indicate. Windows provide both challenges and opportunities as designers make inroads into creating more sustainable, high performance buildings.

*Figure 4-16. Percentage of total heating and cooling loads attributed to windows for different buildings. The analysis considered buildings of varying types and ages in a range of climates.*

| Building Type | Percent of Total System Heating Load | Percent of Total System Cooling Load |
|---|---|---|
| Large Office | 74 | 38 |
| Small Office | 34 | 47 |
| Large Retail | 33 | 42 |
| Small Retail | 27 | 39 |
| Large Hotel | 48 | 40 |
| Small Hotel | 18 | 63 |
| Fast Food Restaurant | 12 | 32 |
| Sit Down Restaurant | 6 | 11 |
| Hospital | 45 | 10 |
| School | 5 | 41 |
| Supermarket | 17 | 13 |
| Warehouse | 1 | 34 |

Source: Huang, Joe, and Ellen Franconi. *Commercial Heating and Cooling Loads Component Analysis.* November 1999. Lawrence Berkeley National Laboratory, Berkeley CA 94720. LBNL-37208

*A Decision-making Process for Window Design*

# CHAPTER 5

# Window Design for Offices in a Cold Climate

## Introduction

The analysis in this chapter will guide the designer in making decisions about windows for an office building in Chicago, Illinois, a representative cold-climate city. The focus is on energy and indoor environmental factors. This information can be placed into a larger decision-making framework that includes appearance, cost, technical requirements, and environmental issues. In a predominantly cold climate, window design and selection must address solar heat gain control, daylight, and heat loss during cold periods.

The sections in this chapter questions beginning with large-scale issues progressing down to individual zone design. The impact of window orientation is considered, followed by analysis and design guidance for north-, south-, and east-/west-facing zones. Within each of these sections, the effects of daylighting controls, window size and shading are studied. Window design and selection guidelines for offices in Chicago are summarized in the final section.

Throughout this chapter, a set of six representative window types is used for comparison purposes. A double-pane clear window is used as a base case for the climate. Window types are discussed in detail in Chapter 3. Annual energy use and peak demand per square foot of perimeter floor area are shown for each set of conditions being compared. This is followed by a comparison of performance measures for daylight, glare, view, and thermal comfort.

This analysis pertains only to office space perimeter zones (the area of a building within 15 feet of the exterior facade). The degree to which these perimeter zones contribute to overall building energy use and peak demand depends on the size, shape, and use of the whole building. Chapter 7 includes an analysis of a school in this climate.

The six components of energy and interior environment that are part of this analysis are described in Chapter 2 (additional details of the methodology are given in Appendix A). All parameters were computed using DOE-2.1E, a building energy simulation program, for a typical office building in Chicago, Illinois.

*Figure 5-1. Blue Cross/Blue Shield Building in Chicago, IL. Architect: Lohan & Associates; Photo courtesy of Viracon; Photo: Wes Thompson*

# Orientation

This section addresses the question of how window orientation impacts energy and indoor environmental performance in a cold-climate city like Chicago.

## Effect of Orientation on Energy Use

In Chicago, differences in annual electricity use between orientations are driven by solar gain affecting cooling and daylight affecting electric lighting. Figure 5-2 clearly illustrates that in the unshaded condition, a northern orientation performs best with regard to electricity use for some window types (B and E). On the other hand, as SHGC falls, there is less variation between orientations (Windows F–H). With very low-SHGC Window D, there is virtually no variation. With moderate window sizes, in short, there is relatively little variation in annual electricity use between the south-, east-, and west-facing perimeter zones (Figure 5-2). Although south-, east-, and west-facing windows appear to perform similarly, remember that

*Figure 5-2. Annual electricity and heating use comparison by orientation with no shading*

All cases have a 0.30 window-to-wall ratio and include daylighting controls. Numbers are expressed per square foot within a 15-foot-deep perimeter zone. Results were computed using DOE-2.1E for a typical office building in Chicago, Illinois (Appendix A).

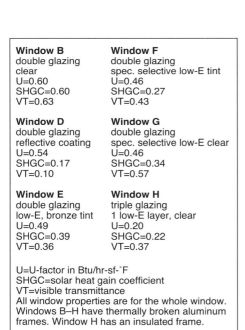

**Window B**
double glazing
clear
U=0.60
SHGC=0.60
VT=0.63

**Window D**
double glazing
reflective coating
U=0.54
SHGC=0.17
VT=0.10

**Window E**
double glazing
low-E, bronze tint
U=0.49
SHGC=0.39
VT=0.36

**Window F**
double glazing
spec. selective low-E tint
U=0.46
SHGC=0.27
VT=0.43

**Window G**
double glazing
spec. selective low-E clear
U=0.46
SHGC=0.34
VT=0.57

**Window H**
triple glazing
1 low-E layer, clear
U=0.20
SHGC=0.22
VT=0.37

U=U-factor in Btu/hr-sf-°F
SHGC=solar heat gain coefficient
VT=visible transmittance
All window properties are for the whole window.
Windows B–H have thermally broken aluminum frames. Window H has an insulated frame.

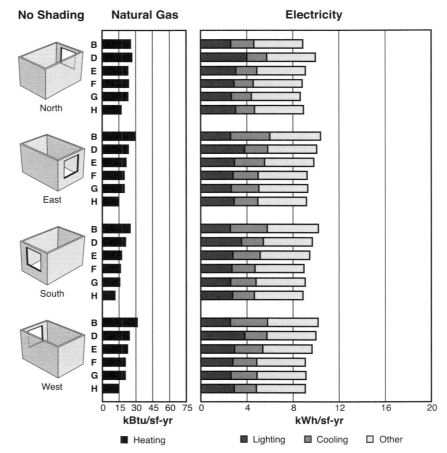

*Window Design for Offices in a Cold Climate*

south-facing windows are easier to shade with exterior attachments (e.g., overhangs). When effective exterior shading is used on moderately sized windows (WWR=0.30), there is virtually no difference in electricity use between orientations (Figure 5-3).

Windows properties impact heating energy use in three ways—a lower U-factor results in less heat loss, a higher SHGC provides more solar heat gain, and a higher VT allows more daylight to reduce electric lighting loads (which results in less heat gain from lights, which in turn increases heating loads). When these three factors combine, unshaded south-facing zones will usually have lower annual heating energy compared to other orientations with a moderate window area (Figure 5-2). When effective exterior shading devices are used on moderate window areas, there are slight increases in heating energy use in most cases but the same patterns hold true (Figure 5-3).

Figure 5-4 shows the total annual energy use (combined heating and electricity use) for each window type over a range of window sizes. In the unshaded condition, differences between orientations

*Figure 5-3. Annual electricity and heating use comparison by orientation with exterior shading*

All cases have a 0.30 window-to-wall ratio and include daylighting controls. Numbers are expressed per square foot within a 15-foot-deep perimeter zone. Results were computed using DOE-2.1E for a typical office building in Chicago, Illinois (Appendix A).

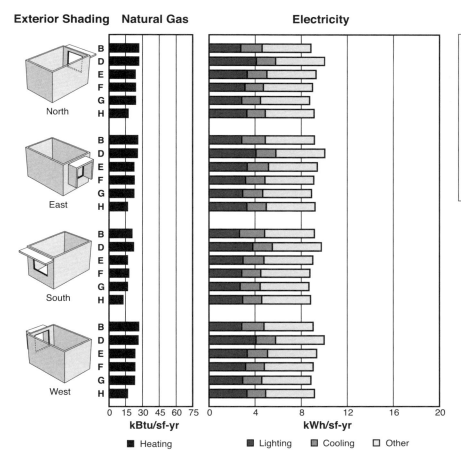

**Shading Conditions**
Figures 5-2 through 5-13
All cases have WWR=0.30.
(6 feet wide x 6 feet high)
See Appendix A for details.

| North | 2.8-foot-deep overhang |
| East | 4.2-foot-deep overhang<br>3.0-foot-deep vertical fins |
| South | 2.8-foot-deep overhang |
| West | 4.2-foot-deep overhang<br>3.0-foot-deep vertical fins |

## Figure 5-4. Total annual energy use comparison by orientation

All cases have no shading and include daylight controls. Numbers are expressed per square foot within a 15-foot-deep perimeter zone. Results were computed using DOE-2.1E for a typical office building in Chicago, Illinois (Appendix A). Total annual energy use is calculated by multiplying electricity use by 3 and adding heating energy use. This reflects the 3:1 ratio of primary to end use energy for electricity. All window properties are for the whole window. Windows B–H have thermally broken aluminum frames. Window H has an insulated frame. U=U-factor in Btu/hr-sf-˚F, SHGC=solar heat gain coefficient, VT=visible transmittance

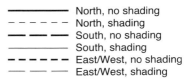

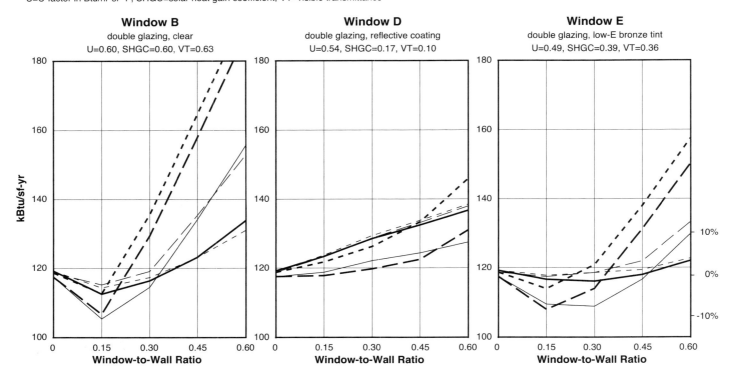

### Window B
double glazing, clear
U=0.60, SHGC=0.60, VT=0.63

### Window D
double glazing, reflective coating
U=0.54, SHGC=0.17, VT=0.10

### Window E
double glazing, low-E bronze tint
U=0.49, SHGC=0.39, VT=0.36

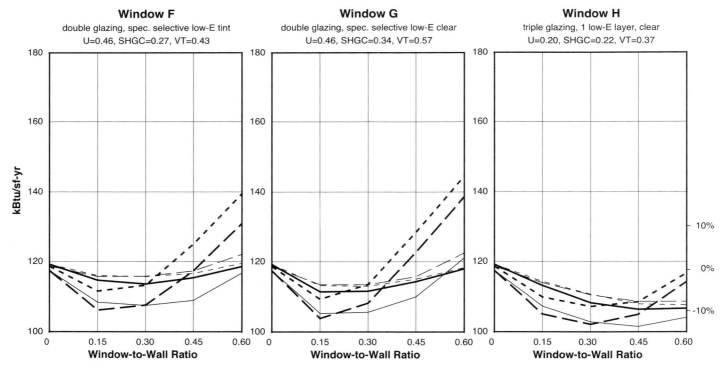

### Window F
double glazing, spec. selective low-E tint
U=0.46, SHGC=0.27, VT=0.43

### Window G
double glazing, spec. selective low-E clear
U=0.46, SHGC=0.34, VT=0.57

### Window H
triple glazing, 1 low-E layer, clear
U=0.20, SHGC=0.22, VT=0.37

*Window Design for Offices in a Cold Climate*

increase with greater window area. The orientation with the lowest annual energy use changes as area increases. At a moderate window area (WWR=0.30), a south-facing orientation is best for all cases except Window B, where a northern orientation has the lowest use. At a larger window area (WWR=0.60), the north side has the lowest annual energy use in all cases.

With exterior shading, total annual energy use also increases with window area but to a lesser degree than the unshaded case. For a moderate window area (WWR=0.30), a shaded, south-facing window performs best with any glazing (except Window D). For a larger window area (WWR=0.60) with exterior shading, the best orientation for energy performance varies with window type—southern orientation has the lowest total annual energy use for Windows D, F, and H while northern is lower for the rest.

### Effect of Orientation on Peak Demand

The effect of orientation on peak electricity demand depends on the window type. As shown in Figure 5-5 for moderately sized unshaded windows, a north-facing orientation offers the lowest peak demand

| Window B | Window F |
|---|---|
| double glazing | double glazing |
| clear | spec. selective low-E tint |
| U=0.60 | U=0.46 |
| SHGC=0.60 | SHGC=0.27 |
| VT=0.63 | VT=0.43 |
| **Window D** | **Window G** |
| double glazing | double glazing |
| reflective coating | spec. selective low-E clear |
| U=0.54 | U=0.46 |
| SHGC=0.17 | SHGC=0.34 |
| VT=0.10 | VT=0.57 |
| **Window E** | **Window H** |
| double glazing | triple glazing |
| low-E, bronze tint | 1 low-E layer, clear |
| U=0.49 | U=0.20 |
| SHGC=0.39 | SHGC=0.22 |
| VT=0.36 | VT=0.37 |

U=U-factor in Btu/hr-sf-°F
SHGC=solar heat gain coefficient
VT=visible transmittance
All window properties are for the whole window. Windows B–H have thermally broken aluminum frames. Window H has an insulated frame.

*Figure 5-5. Peak demand comparison by orientation*

All cases have a 0.30 window-to-wall ratio and include daylighting controls. Numbers are expressed per square foot within a 15-foot-deep perimeter zone. Results were computed using DOE-2.1E for a typical office building in Chicago, Illinois (Appendix A).

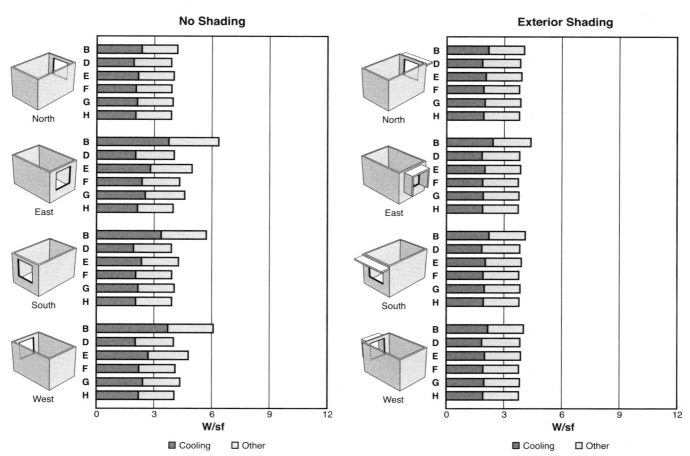

*Figure 5-6. Peak demand for different orientations*

All cases have no shading and include daylight controls. Numbers are expressed in Watts per square foot within a 15-foot-deep perimeter zone. Results were computed using DOE-2.1E for a typical office building in Chicago, Illinois (Appendix A). All window properties are for the whole window. Windows B–H have thermally broken aluminum frames. Window H has an insulated frame. U=U-factor in Btu/hr-sf-°F, SHGC=solar heat gain coefficient, VT=visible transmittance

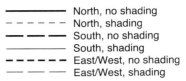

North, no shading
North, shading
South, no shading
South, shading
East/West, no shading
East/West, shading

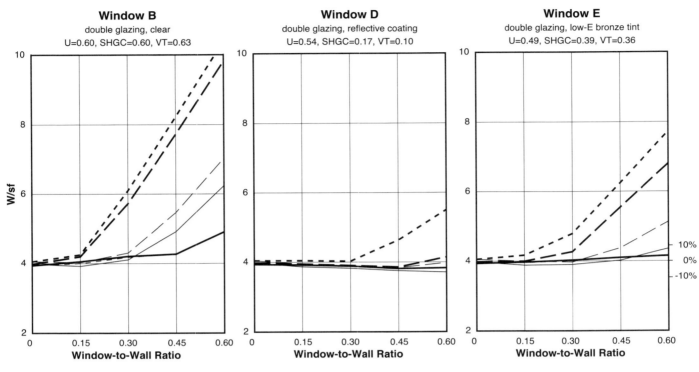

**Window B**
double glazing, clear
U=0.60, SHGC=0.60, VT=0.63

**Window D**
double glazing, reflective coating
U=0.54, SHGC=0.17, VT=0.10

**Window E**
double glazing, low-E bronze tint
U=0.49, SHGC=0.39, VT=0.36

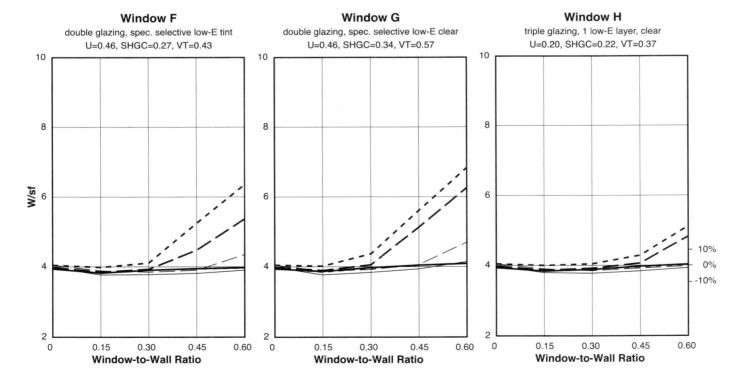

**Window F**
double glazing, spec. selective low-E tint
U=0.46, SHGC=0.27, VT=0.43

**Window G**
double glazing, spec. selective low-E clear
U=0.46, SHGC=0.34, VT=0.57

**Window H**
triple glazing, 1 low-E layer, clear
U=0.20, SHGC=0.22, VT=0.37

*Window Design for Offices in a Cold Climate*

for most types of unshaded windows, followed by a south orientation. East- or west-facing windows have the highest peak demand. The variations between orientations are greatest with Window B and least with Windows D and H. For unshaded windows, the difference in peak demand between orientations increases significantly with window size (Figure 5-6). With exterior shading, greater window area has much less impact on peak demand for all orientations.

Utility rates (based on time of use) usually penalize high-demand use from south- and west-facing zones during mid- to late-afternoon summer hours. Peak demand charges can result in electricity costs that are three to five times greater that off-peak periods, so it is worthwhile to consider rate schedules and design affected facades accordingly. It is also noteworthy that peak demand is in direct proportion to the cooling capacity of the building's mechanical system, which impacts capital costs.

## Effect of Orientation on Daylight

Daylight and sunlight are often cherished by building occupants during the winter, when shortened days, low light levels, cloud cover, rain, or snowfall dull one's sense of diurnal patterns. For increased

| Window B | Window F |
|---|---|
| double glazing | double glazing |
| clear | spec. selective low-E tint |
| U=0.60 | U=0.46 |
| SHGC=0.60 | SHGC=0.27 |
| VT=0.63 | VT=0.43 |
| **Window D** | **Window G** |
| double glazing | double glazing |
| reflective coating | spec. selective low-E clear |
| U=0.54 | U=0.46 |
| SHGC=0.17 | SHGC=0.34 |
| VT=0.10 | VT=0.57 |
| **Window E** | **Window H** |
| double glazing | triple glazing |
| low-E, bronze tint | 1 low-E layer, clear |
| U=0.49 | U=0.20 |
| SHGC=0.39 | SHGC=0.22 |
| VT=0.36 | VT=0.37 |

U=U-factor in Btu/hr-sf-°F
SHGC=solar heat gain coefficient
VT=visible transmittance
All window properties are for the whole window. Windows B–H have thermally broken aluminum frames. Window H has an insulated frame.

*Figure 5-7. Average annual daylight illuminance comparison by orientation*

Average daylight illuminance is calculated at a point 10 feet from the window. All cases have a moderate window area (WWR=0.30). Results were computed using DOE-2.1E for a typical office building in Chicago, Illinois (Appendix A).

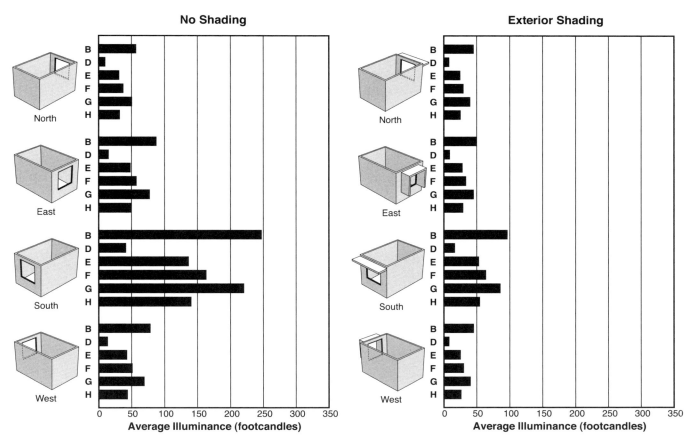

daylight (without interior shades), north-facing windows may be preferred. For the perceived warmth and brightness of direct sunlight, south-facing windows may be preferred.

Orientation has a significant effect on daylight illuminance levels in a perimeter space. Generally, south-oriented perimeter spaces have noticeably more daylight on average than any of the other orientations in an unshaded condition due to direct sun (Figure 5-7). North-facing zones have a slightly lower average annual illuminance than those facing east and west, but all orientations provide at least 30 footcandles on average for most window types at a point 10 feet from the window. The exception is Window D with much lower daylight levels due to a very low VT. With exterior shading, average annual daylight illuminance is diminished in all cases (Figure 5-7). The effect of other shading options is shown later in the chapter.

### Effect of Orientation on Glare

Figure 5-8 illustrates that there is a low weighted glare index for all window types in the north-facing perimeter zones with moderate window area. The indices are also very low for all windows in south-

---

**GLARE INDEX**

| | |
|---|---|
| * | = less than 7 |
| 7 | = imperceptible glare |
| 10 | = just perceptible glare |
| 16 | = just acceptable glare |
| 22 | = just uncomfortable glare |

---

*Figure 5-8. Weighted glare index comparison by orientation*

The weighted glare index is calculated at a point 5 feet from the window for a person facing the side wall. A lower index is better. All cases have a moderate window area (WWR=0.30). Results were computed using DOE-2.1E for a typical office building in Chicago, Illinois (Appendix A).

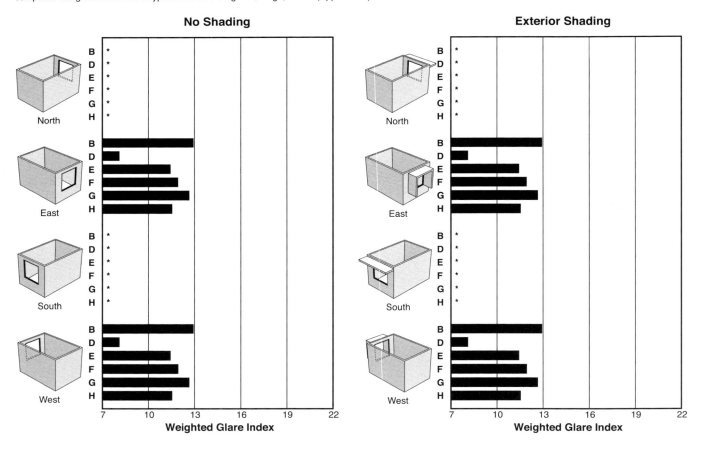

facing zones. Glare for most windows in the east- and west-facing zones is higher than that for the north and south because the former zones receive low angle sun for extended periods in the early morning and late afternoon. When exterior shading is added to the east and west, the weighted glare index does not decline significantly because low angle sun still penetrates. In general, moderately sized windows (WWR=0.30) result in a relatively low weighted glare index. Glare for the darker, reflective Window D remains low in all cases because of its very low visible transmittance.

### Effect of Orientation on View

Orientation does not impact view (Figure 5-9). The appropriate shading for each orientation, however, does impact view. Exterior shading devices such as overhangs reduce view slightly in the north- and south-facing cases. The deeper overhangs and vertical fins on the east- and west-facing cases have a greater effect on view.

| Window B | Window F |
|---|---|
| double glazing | double glazing |
| clear | spec. selective low-E tint |
| U=0.60 | U=0.46 |
| SHGC=0.60 | SHGC=0.27 |
| VT=0.63 | VT=0.43 |
| **Window D** | **Window G** |
| double glazing | double glazing |
| reflective coating | spec. selective low-E clear |
| U=0.54 | U=0.46 |
| SHGC=0.17 | SHGC=0.34 |
| VT=0.10 | VT=0.57 |
| **Window E** | **Window H** |
| double glazing | triple glazing |
| low-E, bronze tint | 1 low-E layer, clear |
| U=0.49 | U=0.20 |
| SHGC=0.39 | SHGC=0.22 |
| VT=0.36 | VT=0.37 |

U=U-factor in Btu/hr-sf-°F
SHGC=solar heat gain coefficient
VT=visible transmittance
All window properties are for the whole window.
Windows B–H have thermally broken aluminum frames. Window H has an insulated frame.

*Figure 5-9. View index comparison by orientation*

View index is calculated at a point 10 feet from the window. A higher index is better. All cases have a moderate window area (WWR=0.30). Results were computed using DOE-2.1E for a typical office building in Chicago, Illinois (Appendix A).

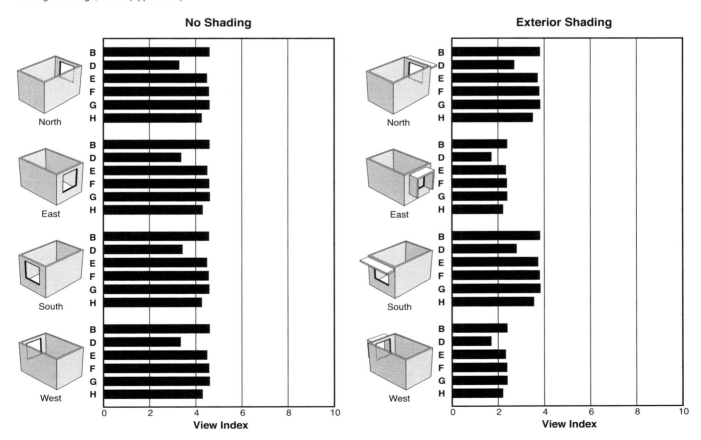

**Window B**
double glazing
clear
U=0.60
SHGC=0.60
VT=0.63

**Window F**
double glazing
spec. selective low-E tint
U=0.46
SHGC=0.27
VT=0.43

**Window D**
double glazing
reflective coating
U=0.54
SHGC=0.17
VT=0.10

**Window G**
double glazing
spec. selective low-E clear
U=0.46
SHGC=0.34
VT=0.57

**Window E**
double glazing
low-E, bronze tint
U=0.49
SHGC=0.39
VT=0.36

**Window H**
triple glazing
1 low-E layer, clear
U=0.20
SHGC=0.22
VT=0.37

U=U-factor in Btu/hr-sf-°F
SHGC=solar heat gain coefficient
VT=visible transmittance
All window properties are for the whole window.
Windows B–H have thermally broken aluminum
frames. Window H has an insulated frame.

## Effect of Orientation on Thermal Comfort

For most windows with a moderate area, south-facing spaces are the most comfortable and north-facing the least in a colder climate such as Chicago (Figure 5-10). In the unshaded condition, the benefits of southern orientation are greatest for Windows E–H and least for Windows B and D. Exterior shading affects thermal comfort by blocking direct sun at times, which has positive or negative impact depending on outdoor conditions. The net effect is that shading can be beneficial with poor glazing (Window B), but it can increase thermal discomfort with other window types. The average thermal comfort index changes by no more than 6–7 PPD due to shading.

## Effect of Orientation on All Attributes Combined

In Figure 5-11, the relative performance of all six attributes for all orientations is shown on a 0-to-10 scale. The window area for all cases in Figure 5-11 is moderate (WWR=0.30). The impact of orientation on each of the individual performance measures is summarized below.

*Energy:* For Windows B and G, both north- and south-facing orientations use less total annual energy than the others. Orientation has

*Figure 5-10. Thermal comfort comparison by orientation*

Thermal comfort is calculated at a point 5 feet from the window. A lower PPD is better. All cases have a moderate window area (WWR=0.30). Results were computed using DOE-2.1E for a typical office building in Chicago, Illinois (Appendix A).

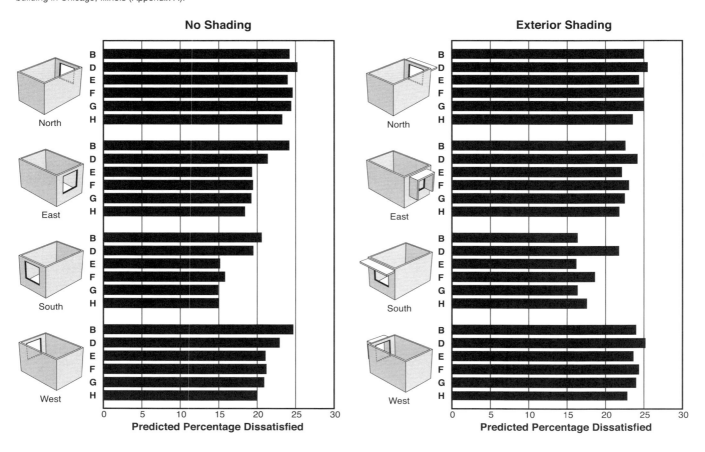

*Window Design for Offices in a Cold Climate*

little effect on energy use with Windows D, E, F, and H at moderate window areas (WWR=0.30) but some effect at larger areas. Exterior shading reduces energy use variation between orientations for Windows B and G. Shading has very little impact on energy use with Windows D, F, and H at moderate window areas. Energy indices are in the higher range (6–10) in most cases in Figure 5-11 because of the moderate window area.

*Peak Demand:* For Windows B and E, north-facing orientations outperform the others, and east- or west-facing orientations perform worst. Orientation has less impact on peak demand with all other windows at a moderate window area (WWR=0.30), but it increases with higher areas. In most cases, exterior shading reduces peak demand variation between orientations. Windows D and H perform best in all cases. The moderate window area keeps the peak demand index in Figure 5-11 in the higher range for most of the cases.

*Figure 5-11. Comparison of multiple attributes by orientation*

All cases have a moderate window area (WWR=0.30) and include daylighting controls. Results are for a typical office building in Chicago, Illinois. To compare different window conditions across all attributes, the six measures of window performance are placed on a 0-to-10 scale. See Appendix A for the methodology.

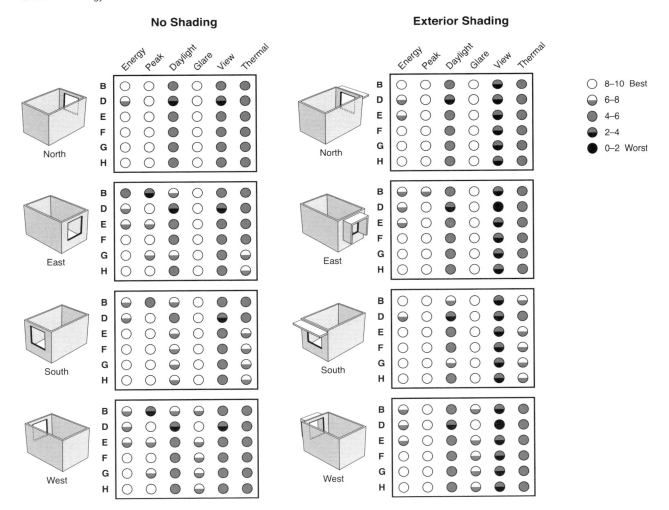

*Daylight:* South-facing zones have greater average interior daylight illuminance levels over the year than other orientations due to direct sun; north-facing orientations have the least. The impact of orientation on daylight is most with high-VT windows (Windows B and G) and least with low-VT windows. In reality, north-facing zones will probably capture more useful daylight than other orientations since there is less need to deploy interior shades to control glare and direct sun. Exterior shading reduces daylight—the index in Figure 5-11 remains in the middle range (4–6) for most cases because of the moderate window area.

*Glare:* For a moderate window area, discomfort glare for north- and south-facing orientations is not of great concern. East and west orientations are much worse, given the low sun angles they experience. Exterior shading reduces glare problems to some extent, as does a low-VT glazing like Window D.

*View:* Overhangs and vertical fins reduce the view index and Window D has the lowest index because of its low VT. Most view indices shown in Figure 5-11 are in the middle range because of the moderate window area.

*Thermal comfort:* For all windows, south-facing orientations perform best thermally. East- and west-facing windows are next best while north-facing windows perform worst.

These results reveal that south-facing perimeter zones generally perform better when compared to other orientations in a colder climate like Chicago, although in many cases the differences are not significant. With proper design and window selection, a space may be oriented in any direction without significant energy penalty.

Shading is one of the design strategies contributing to this possibility. Figure 5-11 shows the overall effect of adding external shading devices—overhangs on the north and south, and deeper overhangs combined with vertical fins on the east and west. While many attributes are unaffected by shading, peak demand improves. With shading, orientation has no impact on peak demand. In addition, the energy performance of Window B improves with shading on the south-, east-, and west- facing orientations, making it equivalent to an unshaded north window in terms of energy use.

While shading can limit or reduce the energy penalty of orientation, the advantages of southern orientation in Chicago generally hold true for any window area. There are, however, a few exceptions. For example, the orientation with the lowest total annual energy use changes from south at WWR=0.30 to north for WWR=0.60. With the larger window area, unwanted solar gains during the cooling season outweigh desired solar gains during the heating season. For most performance attributes, there is a more noticeable difference between orientations with larger window areas, as illustrated in later sections.

# North-facing Perimeter Zones

Once the decision has been made to orient perimeter zones to the north, the designer must examine more detailed issues related to window design and selection. The following sections address how lighting controls, window area, and shading affect performance.

## The Effect of Lighting Controls on Annual Energy Use and Peak Demand in a North-facing Perimeter Zone

North-facing zones offer good potential for daylighting controls because of the quality of daylight and lower potential use of interior shades that reduce daylight admission. In a cold climate like Chicago, annual electricity use is cut significantly by installing dimmable light fixtures and controls that reduce electric lighting when there is sufficient daylight (Figure 5-12). The lighting load decline leads to a cooling load reduction because heat gain from the lights decrease. The heating load rises slightly because of this heat gain reduction.

Figure 5-13 illustrates that without daylighting controls in a space, total annual energy use increases with window area in proportion to admitted solar heat gains, rising at a faster rate with higher SHGC and U-factor windows. With daylighting controls, total annual energy use is actually lower than an opaque wall (WWR=0) for even very large window areas (WWR=0.60) for most glazing types.

Daylighting controls also reduce peak electricity demand for all window types (Figure 5-12). Without daylighting controls, Window D, with the lowest SHGC, has the lowest peak demand. With daylighting controls, Window D has the highest peak demand at a moderate window area (WWR=0.30). Figure 5-14 illustrates that without daylight controls, peak demand rises with greater window

| Window B | Window F |
|---|---|
| double glazing | double glazing |
| clear | spec. selective low-E tint |
| U=0.60 | U=0.46 |
| SHGC=0.60 | SHGC=0.27 |
| VT=0.63 | VT=0.43 |
| **Window D** | **Window G** |
| double glazing | double glazing |
| reflective coating | spec. selective low-E clear |
| U=0.54 | U=0.46 |
| SHGC=0.17 | SHGC=0.34 |
| VT=0.10 | VT=0.57 |
| **Window E** | **Window H** |
| double glazing | triple glazing |
| low-E, bronze tint | 1 low-E layer, clear |
| U=0.49 | U=0.20 |
| SHGC=0.39 | SHGC=0.22 |
| VT=0.36 | VT=0.37 |

U=U-factor in Btu/hr-sf-°F
SHGC=solar heat gain coefficient
VT=visible transmittance
All window properties are for the whole window.
Windows B–H have thermally broken aluminum frames. Window H has an insulated frame.

*Figure 5-12. Annual energy use and peak demand comparison by lighting system*

All cases are north-facing with a 0.30 window-to-wall ratio and no shading. Numbers are expressed per square foot within a 15-foot-deep perimeter zone. Results were computed using DOE-2.1E for a typical office building in Chicago, Illinois (Appendix A).

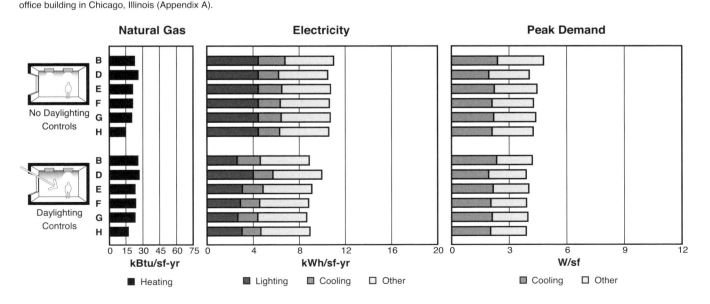

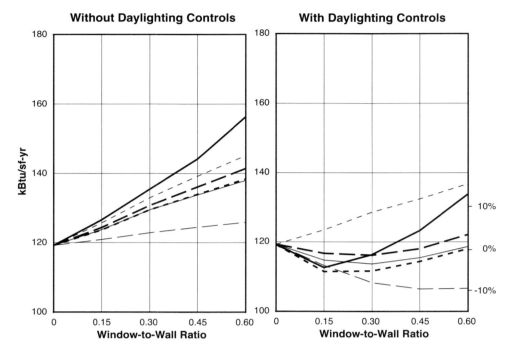

### Figure 5-13. *Total annual energy use comparison by lighting system*

All cases have no shading. Numbers are expressed per square foot within a 15-foot-deep perimeter zone. Results were computed using DOE-2.1E for a typical office building in Chicago, Illinois (Appendix A).

Window B
Window D
Window E
Window F
Window G
Window H

Total annual energy use is calculated by multiplying electricity use by 3 and adding to heating energy use. This reflects the 3:1 ratio of primary to end use energy for electricity compared to natural gas.

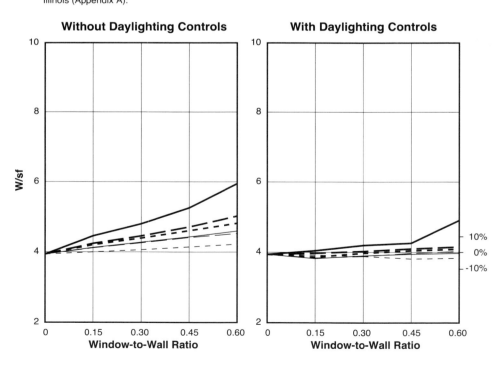

### Figure 5-14. *Peak demand comparison by lighting system*

All cases have no shading. Numbers are expressed in Watts per square foot within a 15-foot-deep perimeter zone. Results were computed using DOE-2.1E for a typical office building in Chicago, Illinois (Appendix A).

*Window Design for Offices in a Cold Climate*

area. However, with controls, peak demand shows little increase with greater window area, except for Window B. Although the north-facing zone has lower peak demand than other orientations, it is important to remember that the late afternoon summer sun (the low-angle direct sun from the sky's northwest quadrant) can escalate total building peak demand.

While all the energy use comparisons in this section show significant savings by using daylighting controls, there is a range of possible performance (see Chapter 2). Lighting controls do not affect daylight, view, glare, and thermal comfort.

### The Effect of Window Area in a North-facing Zone

This section addresses the question of the optimal window area on a north-facing perimeter zone. Only the unshaded condition is examined here. The following sections discuss how shading conditions can mitigate the negative impacts of larger window areas.

| Window B | Window F |
|---|---|
| double glazing clear U=0.60 SHGC=0.60 VT=0.63 | double glazing spec. selective low-E tint U=0.46 SHGC=0.27 VT=0.43 |
| **Window D** double glazing reflective coating U=0.54 SHGC=0.17 VT=0.10 | **Window G** double glazing spec. selective low-E clear U=0.46 SHGC=0.34 VT=0.57 |
| **Window E** double glazing low-E, bronze tint U=0.49 SHGC=0.39 VT=0.36 | **Window H** triple glazing 1 low-E layer, clear U=0.20 SHGC=0.22 VT=0.37 |

U=U-factor in Btu/hr-sf-°F
SHGC=solar heat gain coefficient
VT=visible transmittance
All window properties are for the whole window.
Windows B–H have thermally broken aluminum frames. Window H has an insulated frame.

*Figure 5-15. Annual energy use and peak demand comparison by window area*

All cases are north-facing with no shading and include daylighting controls. Numbers are expressed per square foot within a 15-foot-deep perimeter zone. Results were computed using DOE-2.1E for a typical office building in Chicago, Illinois (Appendix A).

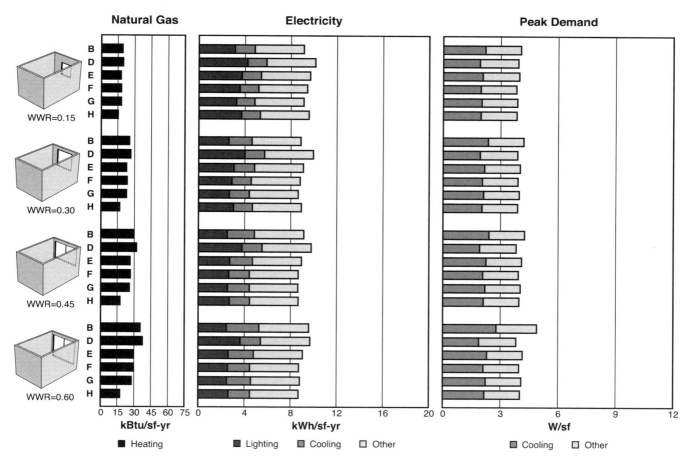

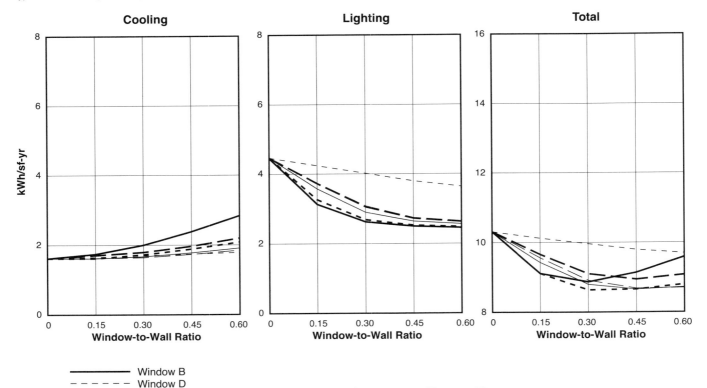

*Figure 5-16. Annual electricity use*

All cases are north-facing with no shading and include daylighting controls. Numbers are expressed per square foot within a 15-foot-deep perimeter zone. Results were computed using DOE-2.1E for a typical office building in Chicago, Illinois (Appendix A).

——————— Window B
— — — — — Window D
— ▬ — ▬ — Window E
——————— Window F
— ▬ ▬ ▬ — Window G
— — — — Window H

| Window B | Window F |
|---|---|
| double glazing | double glazing |
| clear | spec. selective low-E tint |
| U=0.60 | U=0.46 |
| SHGC=0.60 | SHGC=0.27 |
| VT=0.63 | VT=0.43 |
| **Window D** | **Window G** |
| double glazing | double glazing |
| reflective coating | spec. selective low-E clear |
| U=0.54 | U=0.46 |
| SHGC=0.17 | SHGC=0.34 |
| VT=0.10 | VT=0.57 |
| **Window E** | **Window H** |
| double glazing | triple glazing |
| low-E, bronze tint | 1 low-E layer, clear |
| U=0.49 | U=0.20 |
| SHGC=0.39 | SHGC=0.22 |
| VT=0.36 | VT=0.37 |

U=U-factor in Btu/hr-sf-°F
SHGC=solar heat gain coefficient
VT=visible transmittance
All window properties are for the whole window.
Windows B–H have thermally broken aluminum
frames. Window H has an insulated frame.

## Effect of Window Area on Energy Use

In north-facing perimeter zones in a cold climate like Chicago, energy use does not necessarily increase substantially with greater window area. The relationship between window area and energy use depends on several factors. Heating energy use in a north-facing space always increases with window area (Figure 5-15). However, there is not a simple linear relationship between window area and electricity use when daylighting controls are used. Figure 5-16 illustrates that cooling energy use rises with window area, but the electric lighting energy falls with greater window area as more daylight enters. When cooling and lighting are combined into total annual electricity use, each window type has a different optimal area (as represented by the low point on the curve in Figure 5-16).

For the combined electricity and heating energy use (assuming a fuel ratio of 3:1), the optimal window area is dependent on window type (Figure 5-13). There is a point where the energy-saving benefits of daylight controls are realized and increasing the window area produces little additional lighting energy savings while cooling and heating energy use continue to rise. For example, the lowest total annual energy use with Window H (high VT, low SHGC, and low U-factor) occurs at a window-to-wall ratio (WWR) of 0.45–0.60. For Windows B and G, the lowest occurs at WWR=0.15, while for Windows E and F, it occurs at WWR=0.30. For Window D, the lowest occurs at WWR=0 (no windows).

## Effect of Window Area on Peak Demand

With north-facing Windows E–H, peak demand increases by no more than 0.2 W/sf as window area rises from a 0 to 0.60 window-to-wall ratio. The rate of increase is relatively low compared to other orientations since there is almost no direct solar heat gain on the north. As shown in Figures 5-14 and 5-15, peak demand does climb significantly (about 1 W/sf) with greater window area for clear double-pane windows (Window B), while it decreases by 0.1 W/sf with reflective windows (Window D).

## Effect of Window Area on Daylight

For all window types, greater window area yields more daylight illuminance in north-facing perimeter zones (Figure 5-17). When the window-to-wall ratio is equal to or exceeds 0.30, the average annual daylight illuminance is at least 30 footcandles for all cases except Window D (VT=0.10), which provides little daylight at any size. Compared to other orientations, daylight from north-facing windows is less compromised by shades, due to infrequent direct sun, than other orientations.

*Figure 5-17. Average annual daylight illuminance*

Average daylight illuminance is calculated at a point 10 feet from the window. All cases are north-facing with no shading. Results were computed using DOE-2.1E for a typical office building in Chicago, Illinois (Appendix A).

*Figure 5-18. Weighted glare index*

Glare index is calculated at a point 5 feet from the window for a person facing the side wall. A lower index is better. All cases are north-facing with no shading. Results were computed using DOE-2.1E for a typical office building in Chicago, Illinois (Appendix A).

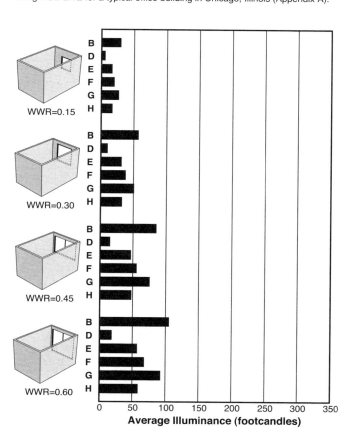

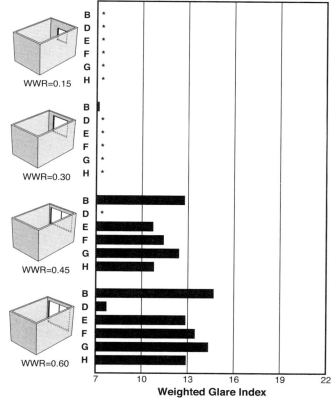

**Window B**
double glazing
clear
U=0.60
SHGC=0.60
VT=0.63

**Window F**
double glazing
spec. selective low-E tint
U=0.46
SHGC=0.27
VT=0.43

**Window D**
double glazing
reflective coating
U=0.54
SHGC=0.17
VT=0.10

**Window G**
double glazing
spec. selective low-E clear
U=0.46
SHGC=0.34
VT=0.57

**Window E**
double glazing
low-E, bronze tint
U=0.49
SHGC=0.39
VT=0.36

**Window H**
triple glazing
1 low-E layer, clear
U=0.20
SHGC=0.22
VT=0.37

U=U-factor in Btu/hr-sf-°F
SHGC=solar heat gain coefficient
VT=visible transmittance
All window properties are for the whole window.
Windows B–H have thermally broken aluminum
frames. Window H has an insulated frame.

## Effect of Window Area on Glare

Figure 5-18 illustrates that there is a low weighted glare index for all window types in north-facing perimeter zones with a small to moderate window area (WWR=0.15–0.30). For most window types, glare increases significantly as the window area rises above WWR=0.30. With larger windows, glare can be a significant problem in an unshaded condition even in north-facing zones. Interior shades can address this problem. The weighted glare index for the darker, reflective Window D remains low at greater window areas because of its very low VT.

## Effect of Window Area on View

As the window area increases, the view improves because a main component of the view index in this analysis is window size (Figure 5-19). Other factors such as visible transmittance, and the amount of time interior shades obstruct the view, do not vary with window area. The lower view index from the reflective glass (Window D) is due to its low VT and the greater frequency of reflected images which obscure the view out of the window during periods of low exterior daylight levels (i.e., winter, early morning, late afternoon).

*Figure 5-19. View index*

View index is calculated at a point 10 feet from the window. A higher index is better. All cases are north-facing with no shading. Results were computed using DOE-2.1E for a typical office building in Chicago, Illinois (Appendix A).

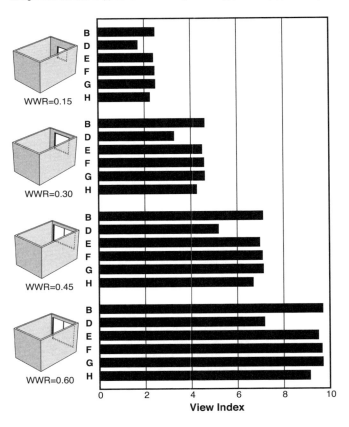

*Figure 5-20. Thermal comfort*

Thermal comfort is calculated at a point 5 feet from the window. A lower PPD is better. All cases are north-facing with no shading. Results were computed using DOE-2.1E for a typical office building in Chicago, Illinois (Appendix A).

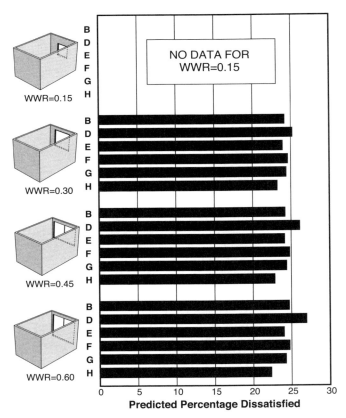

## Effect of Window Area on Thermal Comfort

The effect of window area on thermal comfort in unshaded north-facing zones in Chicago is minor in most cases. Figure 5-20 compares thermal comfort in terms of predicted percentage dissatisfied (PPD) for three different window areas at a point 5 feet from the window. For Windows B and D, thermal discomfort rises slightly with greater window area. For triple-glazed Window H, thermal comfort improves slightly with greater window area. Note that none of the window types achieve the ASHRAE Standard 55 specifying less than 20 PPD (although Window H, without daylight controls, nearly meets it).

## Effect of Window Area on All Attributes Combined

In Figure 5-21, the relative performance of all six attributes for a range of window areas is shown on a 0-to-10 scale. All cases have daylighting controls and no exterior or interior shading devices. The impact of window area on each of the individual performance measures is summarized below.

*Energy:* Because annual heating energy rises with window area but annual electricity use generally falls because of daylighting benefits, the optimal window area for total energy use varies depending on the window type. For Window D, greater window area significantly increases total energy use; for Window H, greater window area significantly decreases total energy use. The optimal window area for Windows E–G is small to moderate (WWR=0.15–0.30).

*Peak Demand:* Peak demand changes by less than 0.2 W/sf with greater window area on the north (except for Window B). Peak demand indices in Figure 5-21 are in the high range for most cases because of the northern orientation.

*Daylight:* For most window types, daylight and brightness improve with greater window area. The average daylight illuminance rises by 30–50 footcandles going from moderate- to large-area windows. Most daylight indices in Figure 5-21 remain in the middle range because of the northern orientation.

*Glare:* For most window types, glare becomes significant when the window size exceeds a window-to-wall ratio of 0.30. Yet, greater window area has little impact on the weighted glare index of Window D.

*View:* For all window types, the view index improves with greater window area.

*Thermal comfort:* For most window types, there is little difference in thermal comfort with greater window area.

For north-facing perimeter zones in a colder climate like Chicago, Window H performs well on all measures, except glare, with a large window area (WWR-0.60). This window yields the least total annual energy use, least peak demand, good illuminance levels, and best thermal comfort of all window types. On glare, Window H outperforms all other types except for Window D, and Window G provides the next best performance at WWR=0.30–0.45, although total annual energy use is 7 percent greater. For small windows (WWR=0.15), the

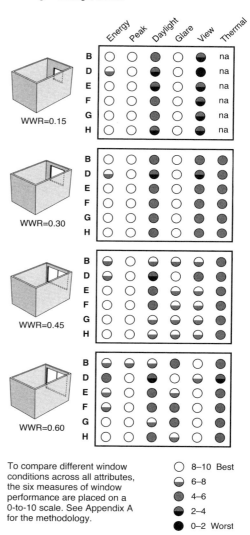

*Figure 5-21. Comparison of multiple attributes by window area*

All cases are north-facing with no shading and include daylighting controls. Results are for a typical office building in Chicago, Illinois.

To compare different window conditions across all attributes, the six measures of window performance are placed on a 0-to-10 scale. See Appendix A for the methodology.

- ○ 8–10 Best
- ◔ 6–8
- ◑ 4–6
- ◕ 2–4
- ● 0–2 Worst

total annual energy use of Window B is lower than Window E and it provides equal performance on the remaining attributes to Windows E and F. Based on these results, increased window area in north-facing perimeter zones does not have to negatively affect performance in a mostly cold climate like Chicago.

### The Effects of Shading Conditions in a North-facing Perimeter Zone with Moderate Window Area

This section addresses design decisions about shading once a moderate window area (WWR=0.30) has been chosen.

#### Effect of Shading Conditions on Energy Use

Generally, shading affects energy use in three ways: cooling energy declines with control of solar heat gains, lighting energy rises if the shading blocks daylight, and heating energy climbs with less solar gains. Figure 5-22 illustrates electricity and heating energy performance for various shading conditions on a north-facing zone with moderate window area (WWR=0.30) in Chicago. Shading cuts annual electricity use by up to 0.2 kWh/sf-yr (3 percent) and raises annual heating energy by up to 1.7 kWh/sf-yr (18 percent). As shown in Figure 5-23, total annual energy use (combined heating and electricity use) rises a small amount (3–5 percent) in most cases. The impact of shading is similar on any window size.

Based on these results, there is no reason to consider an exterior shading device on the north side to save energy. For north-facing windows, the effect of interior shades is not shown since they are never deployed, given the direct sun and glare thresholds defined in the DOE-2 building energy simulation model. The energy use impact of shading conditions for large windows is discussed in the following section.

#### Effect of Shading Conditions on Peak Demand

Shading can significantly decrease peak demand (Figures 5-22 and 5-24). For all window types except Window D, peak demand declines by up to 8–12 percent or 0.3–0.5 W/sf with shading for moderate window areas. The most effective shading is a high-rise obstruction, which blocks solar heat gains from low-angle sun in the late afternoon.

#### Effect of Shading Conditions on Daylight

North-facing zones rely primarily on indirect light from the sky to illuminate interiors. Although shading reduces interior daylight levels, the impact is minor. Exterior obstructions perform better than other shade types (Figure 5-25).

Daylight illuminance and interior brightness is more dependent on the visible transmittance of the window. For moderately sized windows with overhangs, the average annual daylight illuminance declines by 6–12 footcandles (20 percent) compared to the unshaded case for all window types except Window D.

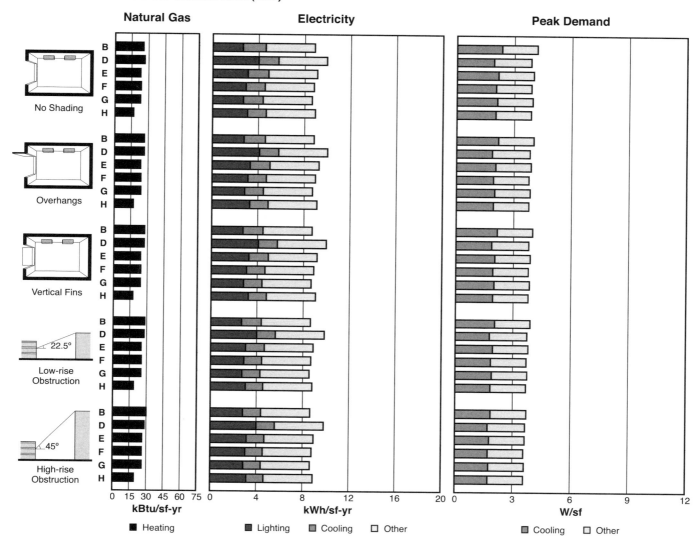

*Figure 5-22. Annual energy use and peak demand comparison by shading type*

All cases are north-facing and include daylighting controls. Numbers are expressed per square foot within a 15-foot-deep perimeter zone. Results were computed using DOE-2.1E for a typical office building in Chicago, Illinois (Appendix A).

**Moderate Window Area (0.30)**

| Natural Gas | Electricity | Peak Demand |

■ Heating    ■ Lighting    ■ Cooling    □ Other        ■ Cooling    □ Other

**Shading Conditions**
Figures 5-22 through 5-29
All cases have WWR=0.30.
(6 feet wide x 6 feet high)
See Appendix A for details.

Overhang: 2.8-foot-deep
Vertical fins: 3.0-foot-deep
Low-rise obstruction: Opposing buildings with a
  vertical angle of 22.5 degrees.
High-rise obstruction: Opposing buildings with a
  vertical angle of 45 degrees.

*Figure 5-23. Total annual energy use for different shading conditions*

All cases are north-facing and include daylighting controls. Numbers are expressed per square foot within a 15-foot-deep perimeter zone. Results were computed using DOE-2.1E for a typical office building in Chicago, Illinois (Appendix A). Total annual energy use is calculated by multiplying electricity use by 3 and adding heating energy use. This reflects the 3:1 ratio of primary to end use energy for electricity. All window properties are for the whole window. Windows B–H have thermally broken aluminum frames. Window H has an insulated frame. U=U-factor in Btu/hr-sf-°F, SHGC=solar heat gain coefficient, VT=visible transmittance

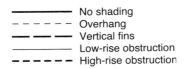

No shading
Overhang
Vertical fins
Low-rise obstruction
High-rise obstruction

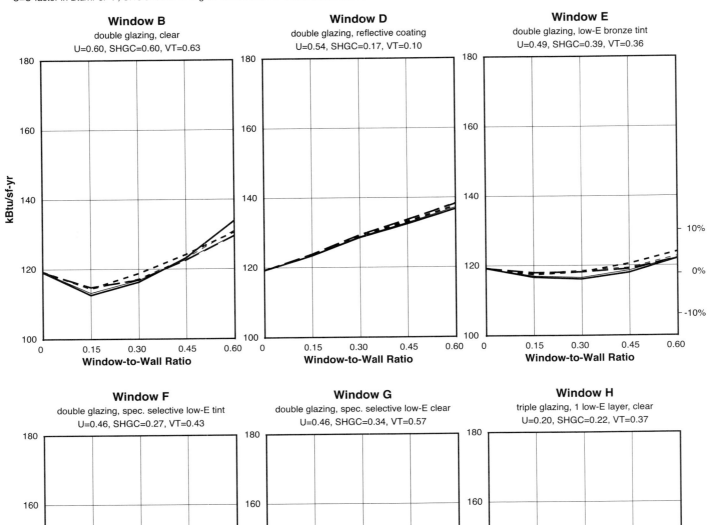

**Window B**
double glazing, clear
U=0.60, SHGC=0.60, VT=0.63

**Window D**
double glazing, reflective coating
U=0.54, SHGC=0.17, VT=0.10

**Window E**
double glazing, low-E bronze tint
U=0.49, SHGC=0.39, VT=0.36

**Window F**
double glazing, spec. selective low-E tint
U=0.46, SHGC=0.27, VT=0.43

**Window G**
double glazing, spec. selective low-E clear
U=0.46, SHGC=0.34, VT=0.57

**Window H**
triple glazing, 1 low-E layer, clear
U=0.20, SHGC=0.22, VT=0.37

*Window Design for Offices in a Cold Climate*

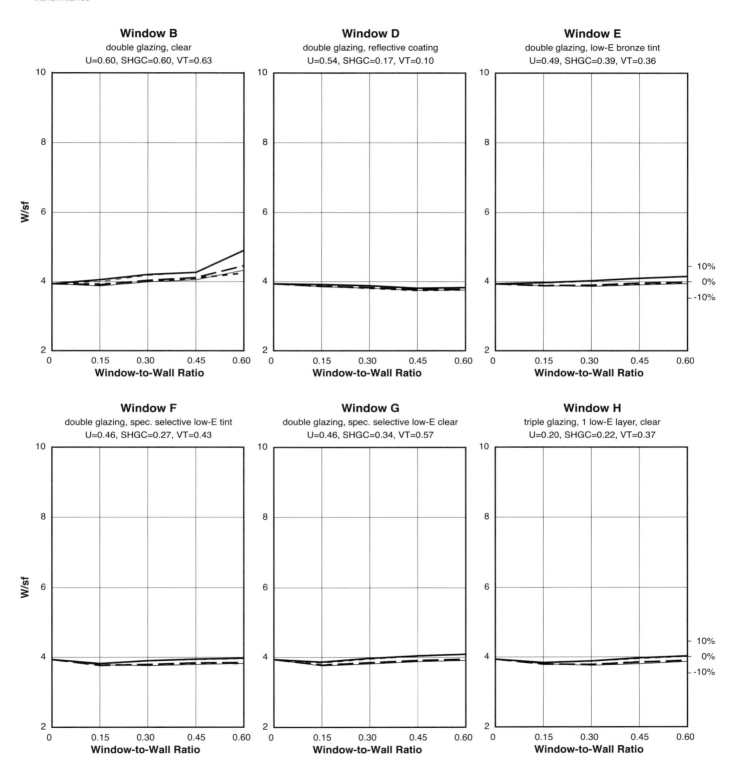

*Figure 5-24. Peak demand for different shading conditions*

All cases are north-facing and include daylighting controls. Numbers are expressed in Watts per square foot within a 15-foot-deep perimeter zone. Results were computed using DOE-2.1E for a typical office building in Chicago, Illinois (Appendix A). All window properties are for the whole window. Windows B–H have thermally broken aluminum frames. Window H has an insulated frame. U=U-factor in Btu/hr-sf-°F, SHGC=solar heat gain coefficient, VT=visible transmittance

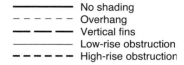

———— No shading
– – – – – Overhang
━ ━ ━ Vertical fins
———— Low-rise obstruction
– ━ – ━ – High-rise obstruction

**Window B**
double glazing, clear
U=0.60, SHGC=0.60, VT=0.63

**Window D**
double glazing, reflective coating
U=0.54, SHGC=0.17, VT=0.10

**Window E**
double glazing, low-E bronze tint
U=0.49, SHGC=0.39, VT=0.36

**Window F**
double glazing, spec. selective low-E tint
U=0.46, SHGC=0.27, VT=0.43

**Window G**
double glazing, spec. selective low-E clear
U=0.46, SHGC=0.34, VT=0.57

**Window H**
triple glazing, 1 low-E layer, clear
U=0.20, SHGC=0.22, VT=0.37

## Effect of Shading Conditions on Glare

The northern orientation experiences little direct sun. That fact, combined with a moderate window area (WWR=0.30) translates into a low weighted glare index, with or without shading (Figure 5-26). Shading has a greater impact on glare with larger window areas as shown in the next section.

## Effect of Shading Conditions on View

Exterior shading devices, such as overhangs and fins, reduce view out north-facing windows (Figure 5-27). For moderately sized windows, the view index drops up to 28 percent with vertical fins. Obstructions such as mountains, trees, and buildings are considered part of the view and therefore do not impact the index. Window D, with a low VT, offers the poorest view index.

**GLARE INDEX**

| | |
|---|---|
| * | = less than 7 |
| 7 | = imperceptible glare |
| 10 | = just perceptible glare |
| 16 | = just acceptable glare |
| 22 | = just uncomfortable glare |

*Figure 5-25. Average annual daylight illuminance*

Average daylight illuminance is calculated at a point 10 feet from the window. All cases are north-facing. Results were computed using DOE-2.1E for a typical office building in Chicago, Illinois (Appendix A).

*Figure 5-26. Weighted glare index*

Glare index is calculated at a point 5 feet from the window for a person facing the side wall. A lower index is better. All cases are north-facing with no shading. Results were computed using DOE-2.1E for a typical office building in Chicago, Illinois (Appendix A).

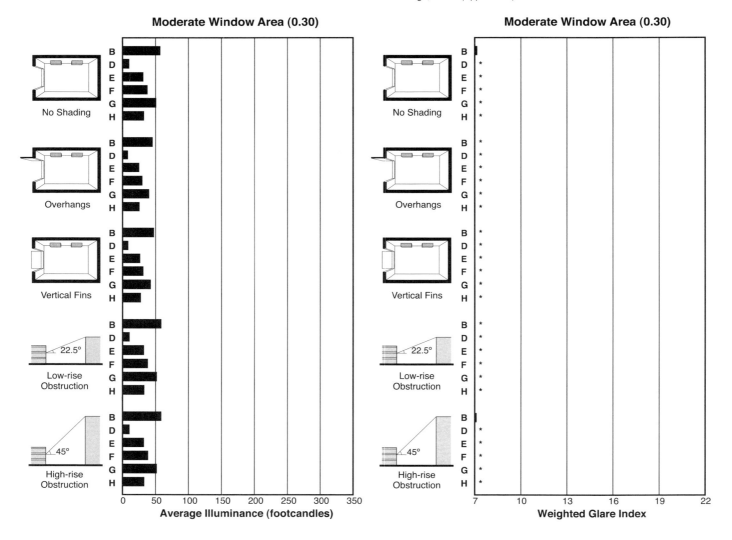

*Window Design for Offices in a Cold Climate*

## Effect of Shading Conditions on Thermal Comfort

Figure 5-28 compares the thermal comfort with and without shading in terms of predicted percentage dissatisfied (PPD) at a point 5 feet from the window. Two key factors in this analysis that influence thermal comfort are hot or cold window surface temperatures, as well as direct sun.

For most window types, thermal comfort is minimally affected by exterior shading. In all cases, the PPD is more than 20 (ASHRAE 55 specifies a thermal environment less than 20 PPD). Even triple-pane Window H does not meet the standard, although it does outperform the others.

*Figure 5-27. View index*

View index is calculated at a point 10 feet from the window. A higher index is better. All cases are north-facing with no shading. Results were computed using DOE-2.1E for a typical office building in Chicago, Illinois (Appendix A).

*Figure 5-28. Thermal comfort*

Thermal comfort is calculated at a point 5 feet from the window. A lower PPD is better. All cases are north-facing with no shading. Results were computed using DOE-2.1E for a typical office building in Chicago, Illinois (Appendix A).

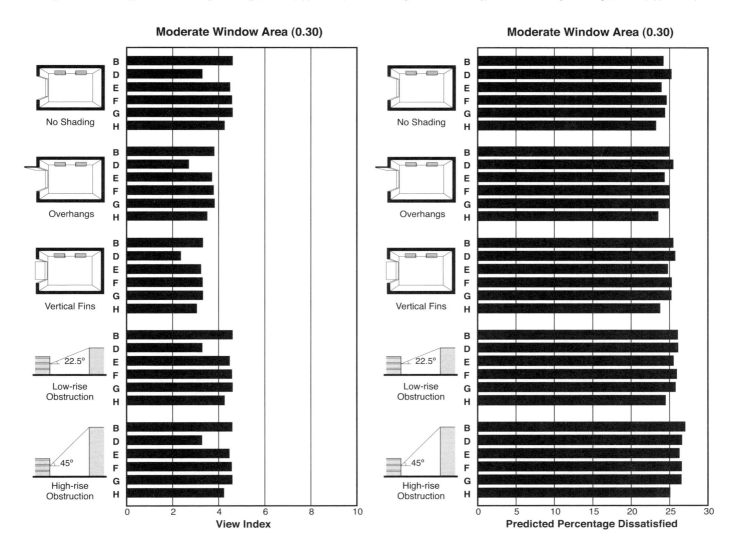

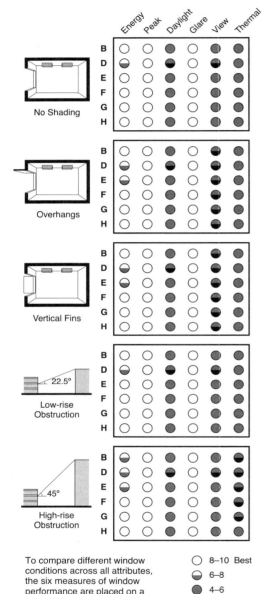

No Shading

Overhangs

Vertical Fins

22.5°
Low-rise Obstruction

45°
High-rise Obstruction

To compare different window conditions across all attributes, the six measures of window performance are placed on a 0-to-10 scale. See Appendix A for the methodology.

○ 8–10 Best
◔ 6–8
◑ 4–6
◕ 2–4
● 0–2 Worst

## Effect of Shading Conditions on All Attributes Combined

In Figure 5-29, the relative performance of all six attributes for a range of window shading conditions is shown on a 0-to-10 scale. All cases have daylighting controls and a window-to-wall ratio of 0.30. The impact of shading conditions on the individual performance measures is summarized below.

*Energy:* For most types of moderately sized windows, exterior shading does not significantly affect annual energy use on a northern orientation. Shading increases total annual energy use by 3–5 percent in most cases.

*Peak Demand:* Shading can reduce peak demand on the north side. The most effective shading is a high-rise obstruction which blocks solar heat gains from low-angle sun in the late afternoon.

*Daylight:* Shading reduces average annual daylight illuminance by 20 percent, further reducing interior brightness on the north side during the cold winter season.

*Glare:* Glare is not a problem on the north side with moderate window area. There is no difference in the weighted glare index with or without shading.

*View:* Shading reduces view. For all window types, view declines in proportion to the shading device obstruction.

*Thermal comfort:* Shading slightly increases thermal discomfort on the north side. All windows perform similarly, with or without shading.

Generally, exterior shading on a north-facing zone has little positive impact and is not recommended for moderate window areas (WWR=0.30). Although this analysis indicates that interior shades would never be deployed on the north side, they may be desirable for occasional glare control even though they have minimal energy-related benefit.

## The Effects of Shading Conditions in a North-facing Perimeter Zone with Large Window Area

This section addresses design decisions about shading once a large window area (WWR=0.60) has been chosen.

### Effect of Shading Conditions on Energy Use

Shading a north elevation with a large window area in Chicago can slightly increase or decrease total annual energy use depending on the specific glazing and shading type. While shading lowers electricity use, this is offset by greater heating energy use (Figure 5-30). Exterior shading decreases annual electricity use by 0.9 kWh/sf-yr (9 percent) if Window B is used. For all other window types, shading reduces electricity use by 0.2–0.4 kWh/sf-yr (2–4 percent). Shading raises annual heating energy use by no more than 6.1 kBtu/sf-yr (17 percent). With shading, total annual energy use (electricity and heating loads combined) declines by 3 percent with Window B and rises by 1–2 percent for all other window types.

## Effect of Shading Conditions on Peak Demand

Shading large north-facing glazing areas decreases peak demand by 1.15 W/sf (23 percent) with Window B or by 0.25–0.50 W/sf (7–12 percent) with all other window types. The most effective shading is a high-rise exterior obstruction, which blocks solar heat gains from low-angle sun in the late afternoon but still allows sufficient daylight.

## Effect of Shading Conditions on Daylight

Exterior shading reduces interior daylight levels. Low- and high-rise obstructions outside the building have little to no effect on average annual daylight illuminance. Overhangs and vertical fins, which block part of the view, cut daylight penetration (Figure 5-31).

*Figure 5-30. Annual energy use and peak demand comparison by shading type*

All cases are north-facing and include daylighting controls. Numbers are expressed per square foot within a 15-foot-deep perimeter zone. Results were computed using DOE-2.1E for a typical office building in Chicago, Illinois (Appendix A).

> **Shading Conditions**
> Figures 5-30 through 5-35
> All cases have WWR=0.60
> (10 feet wide x 7.2 feet high)
> See Appendix A for details.
>
> Overhang: 3.4 feet deep
> Vertical fins: 2.5 feet deep (every 5 feet)
> Low-rise obstruction: Opposing buildings with a vertical angle of 22.5 degrees.
> High-rise obstruction: Opposing buildings with a vertical angle of 45 degrees.

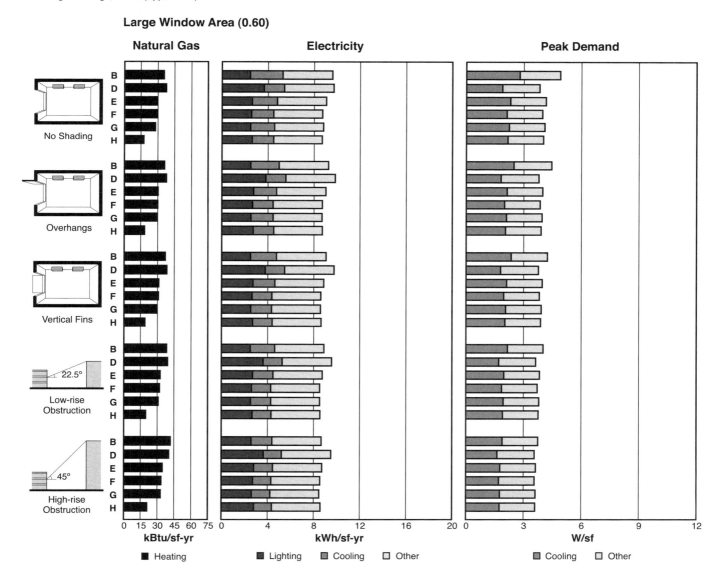

**Large Window Area (0.60)**

Aside from shading, daylight illuminance levels also depend on a window's visible transmittance. Average annual daylight illuminance remains above 45 footcandles under all shaded conditions with any window except Window D.

## Effect of Shading Conditions on Glare

Glare can be a problem with large north-facing windows. Overhangs and vertical fins reduce glare but exterior obstructions do not (Figure 5-32). Overhangs or vertical fins reduce the weighted glare index by 15 to 18 percent for all window types except Window D, which provides good glare control without shading. Exterior building obstructions do not significantly affect glare from the sky.

```
GLARE INDEX
 *  = less than 7
 7  = imperceptible glare
10  = just perceptible glare
16  = just acceptable glare
22  = just uncomfortable glare
```

*Figure 5-31. Average annual daylight illuminance*
Average daylight illuminance is calculated at a point 10 feet from the window. All cases are north-facing. Results were computed using DOE-2.1E for a typical office building in Chicago, Illinois (Appendix A).

*Figure 5-32. Weighted glare index*
Glare index is calculated at a point 5 feet from the window for a person facing the side wall. A lower index is better. All cases are north-facing with no shading. Results were computed using DOE-2.1E for a typical office building in Chicago, Illinois (Appendix A).

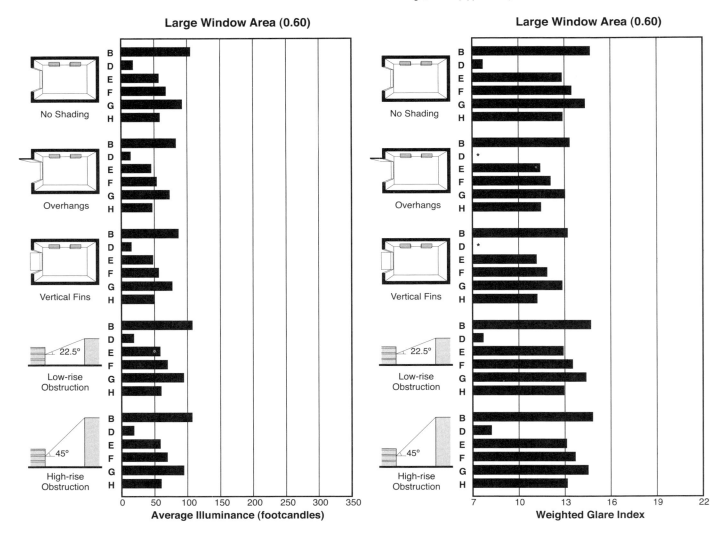

*Window Design for Offices in a Cold Climate*

## Effect of Shading Conditions on View

Both overhangs and vertical fins limit the view out north-facing windows (Figure 5-33). For large-area windows, the view index with vertical fins drops 21 percent and by about 15 percent with overhangs. Window D has the poorest view index because of a low VT. Obstructions such as mountains, trees, and buildings are regarded as part of the view and therefore do not reduce the view index.

## Effect of Shading Conditions on Thermal Comfort

Figure 5-34 compares the thermal comfort with and without shading in terms of predicted percentage dissatisfied (PPD) at a point 5 feet from the window. Two key factors used in this analysis that influence thermal comfort are direct sun and the window's surface temperature.

*Figure 5-33. View index*

View index is calculated at a point 10 feet from the window. A higher index is better. All cases are north-facing with no shading. Results were computed using DOE-2.1E for a typical office building in Chicago, Illinois (Appendix A).

*Figure 5-34. Thermal comfort*

Thermal comfort is calculated at a point 5 feet from the window. A lower PPD is better. All cases are north-facing with no shading. Results were computed using DOE-2.1E for a typical office building in Chicago, Illinois (Appendix A).

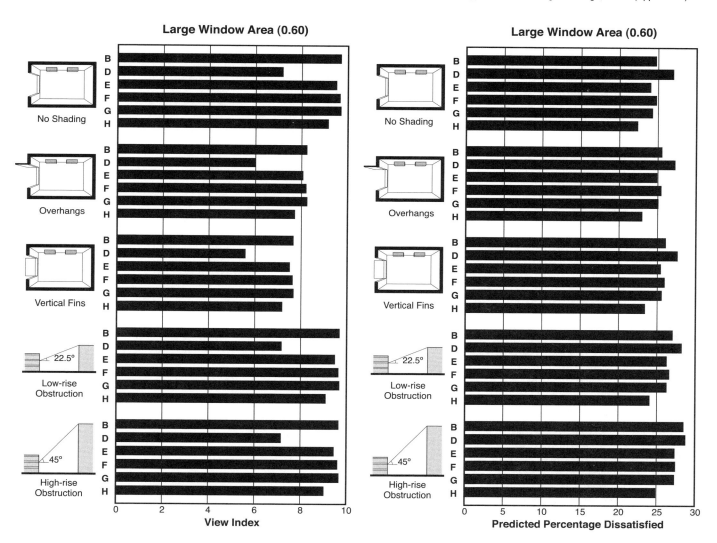

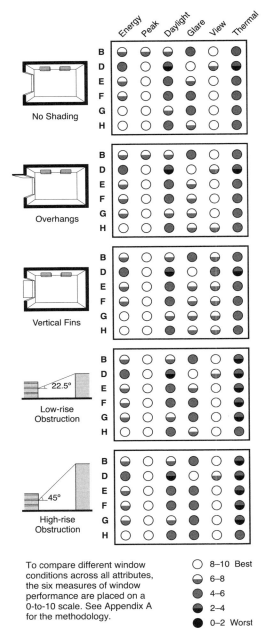

*Figure 5-35. Comparison of multiple attributes by shading condition for large window areas*

All cases are north-facing and have WWR=0.60 and include daylighting controls. Results are for a typical office building in Chicago, Illinois.

No Shading

Overhangs

Vertical Fins

22.5°
Low-rise
Obstruction

45°
High-rise
Obstruction

To compare different window conditions across all attributes, the six measures of window performance are placed on a 0-to-10 scale. See Appendix A for the methodology.

○ 8–10 Best
◔ 6–8
◑ 4–6
◕ 2–4
● 0–2 Worst

Thermal discomfort rises by about 2–4 PPD with exterior shading. In all cases, the percentage dissatisfied is more than 20 (ASHRAE 55 specifies a thermal environment that is less than 20 PPD). Triple-pane Window H with a low U-factor yields the best performance in terms of thermal comfort.

### Effect of Shading Conditions on All Attributes Combined

In Figure 5-35, the relative performance of all six attributes for a range of window shading conditions is shown on a 0-to-10 scale. All cases have daylighting controls and a window-to-wall ratio of 0.60. The impact of shading conditions on the individual performance measures is summarized below.

*Energy:* For most windows, exterior shading increases total annual energy use by less than 5 percent for north-facing windows. There is some improvement when Window B is shaded.

*Peak Demand:* High-rise obstructions have the greatest impact on peak demand reduction. Overhangs or fins also cut demand, by 3–9 percent, depending on window type.

*Daylight:* Average annual daylight illuminance declines by up to 20 percent on the north side with attached exterior shading. High-rise obstructions have little effect on daylight levels.

*Glare:* Overhangs and vertical fins can reduce glare on the north, by 15–18 percent, for all window types except Window D. High-rise obstructions have no effect on glare.

*View:* For all window types, overhangs and vertical fins reduce view.

*Thermal comfort:* Shading increases thermal discomfort slightly on the north side.

Exterior shading devices such as overhangs and vertical fins are not recommended for large-area north-facing windows in Chicago. Shading can significantly limit glare, but the improvement results in negative impacts on daylight, view, and thermal comfort. Exterior obstructions such as mountains, trees, or buildings are most effective at controlling peak demand associated with solar heat gains, while minimally impacting daylight and view.

For a large north-facing window area, Figure 5-35 reveals that triple-pane Window H performs well across all attributes and does not require shading unless it is for glare control—effective interior shades are likely to provide the best control. Window D is most effective at glare control at the expense of energy, daylight, and view.

*Window Design for Offices in a Cold Climate*

# South-facing Perimeter Zones

Once the decision has been made to orient perimeter zones to the south, the designer must examine more detailed issues related to window design and selection. The following sections address how lighting controls, window area, and shading affect performance.

## The Effect of Lighting Controls on Annual Energy Use and Peak Demand in a South-facing Perimeter Zone

Annual electricity use always declines by installing controls that dim or turn off electric lighting when there is sufficient daylight. With such daylighting controls, for all window types except Window D there is an average reduction of 2.0–2.4 kWh/sf yr (15–20 percent) compared to a zone without them (Figure 5-36). Lighting energy use associated with low-VT Window D does not decline significantly; little light enters Window D, giving little opportunity to dim lights and save energy. With the other window cases, however, the higher the VT, the greater the lighting load reduction.

Daylighting controls also translate into reduced cooling loads because of the diminished heat gain from the lights. Therefore, annual heating energy use increases by 0.2–0.6 kWh/sf-yr in zones with daylighting controls, as opposed to zones without them. Heating loads rise in proportion to reduced heat gains. For Chicago's cold climate, heating energy represents about 20 percent of the total annual energy use for moderately sized windows and 30 percent for large-area windows (assuming an electricity-to-gas fuel ratio of 3:1) so this increase can produce a significant effect on the total perimeter zone performance.

Without daylighting controls, annual electric use rises rapidly with greater window area, as well as higher SHGC and U-factor, in

| Window B | Window F |
|---|---|
| double glazing | double glazing |
| clear | spec. selective low-E tint |
| U=0.60 | U=0.46 |
| SHGC=0.60 | SHGC=0.27 |
| VT=0.63 | VT=0.43 |
| **Window D** | **Window G** |
| double glazing | double glazing |
| reflective coating | spec. selective low-E clear |
| U=0.54 | U=0.46 |
| SHGC=0.17 | SHGC=0.34 |
| VT=0.10 | VT=0.57 |
| **Window E** | **Window H** |
| double glazing | triple glazing |
| low-E, bronze tint | 1 low-E layer, clear |
| U=0.49 | U=0.20 |
| SHGC=0.39 | SHGC=0.22 |
| VT=0.36 | VT=0.37 |

U=U-factor in Btu/hr-sf-°F
SHGC=solar heat gain coefficient
VT=visible transmittance
All window properties are for the whole window.
Windows B–H have thermally broken aluminum frames. Window H has an insulated frame.

*Figure 5-36. Annual energy use and peak demand comparison by lighting system*

All cases are south-facing with a 0.30 window-to-wall ratio and no shading. Numbers are expressed per square foot within a 15-foot-deep perimeter zone. Results were computed using DOE-2.1E for a typical office building in Chicago, Illinois (Appendix A).

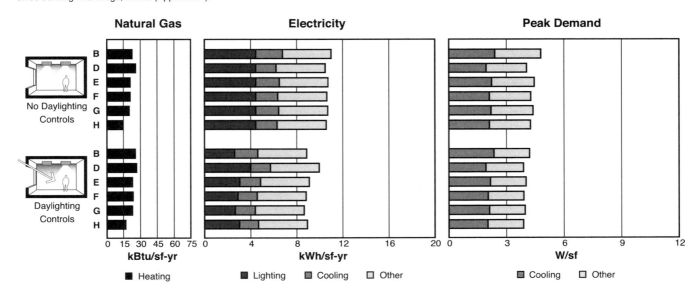

## Figure 5-37. Total annual energy use comparison by lighting system

All cases are south-facing and have no shading. Numbers are expressed per square foot within a 15-foot-deep perimeter zone. Results were computed using DOE-2.1E for a typical office building in Chicago, Illinois (Appendix A).

Window B
Window D
Window E
Window F
Window G
Window H

Total annual energy use is calculated by multiplying electricity use by 3 and adding to heating energy use. This reflects the 3:1 ratio of primary to end use energy for electricity.

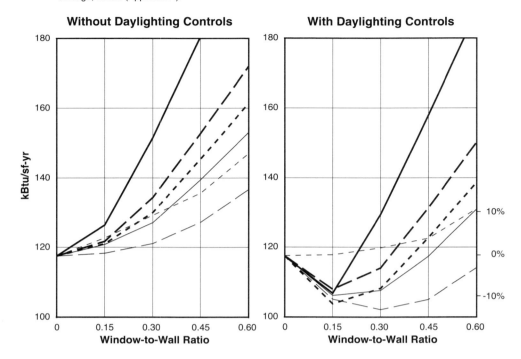

## Figure 5-38. Peak demand comparison by lighting system

All cases are south-facing and have no shading. Numbers are expressed in Watts per square foot within a 15-foot-deep perimeter zone. Results were computed using DOE-2.1E for a typical office building in Chicago, Illinois (Appendix A).

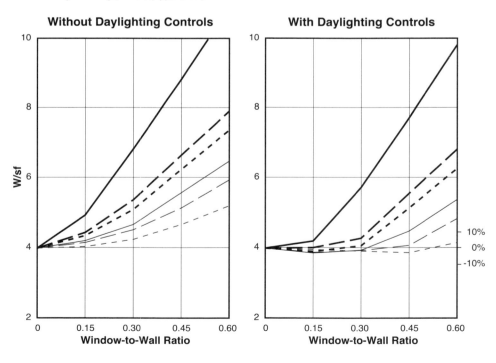

*Window Design for Offices in a Cold Climate*

proportion to admitted solar heat gains (Figure 5-37). Daylighting controls reduce lighting and cooling loads, to offset electricity use. The exact energy use profile depends on the window properties. Window types with a very low SHGC and U-factor and a moderate VT perform best. For example, a spectrally selective, low-E triple-pane window (Window H) has the least total annual energy use for windows above WWR=0.30. A spectrally selective, tinted double-pane window (Window F) outperforms conventional reflective glass (Window D) for all window sizes.

Daylight controls significantly reduce peak electricity demand in south-facing perimeter zones (Figure 5-38). With daylighting controls and a moderate window area, peak demand falls by 0.6–1.1 W/sf (13–20 percent) for all window types except Window D. With a large window area, peak demand is cut by 1.0 W/sf (10–20 percent) for all window types.

While all the energy use comparisons in this section show significant savings with daylighting controls, there is a range of possible performance (see Chapter 2). Lighting controls do not affect daylight, view, glare, and thermal comfort.

## The Effect of Window Area in a South-facing Perimeter Zone

This section is intended to address the question of the optimal window area for a south-facing perimeter zone. Only the unshaded condition is examined here. The following sections discuss how shading conditions can mitigate the negative impacts of larger window areas.

### *Effect of Window Area on Energy Use*

In south-facing perimeter zones with no shading, annual electricity use rises with window area, SHGC, and U-factor in a cold climate like Chicago (Figure 5-39). As window area increases from an opaque wall to a large-area window (WWR=0–0.60), annual electricity use climbs by 2.5 kWh/sf-yr (20 percent) on average for all window types. It rises at the greatest rate for Window B and the least for Windows D and H.

Figure 5-40 illustrates that cooling energy use rises with greater window area. With daylighting controls, electric lighting energy use declines with greater window area to a point where additional daylight produces no significant reductions in lighting energy. When cooling and lighting are combined with other end uses into total electricity use, the optimal window area for most window types (as represented by the low point on the curve in Figure 5-40) is small to moderate (WWR=0.15–0.30) depending on window type. The exception is Window D where the optimal area is WWR=0.45. Increasing window area beyond this point produces little additional lighting energy savings, while cooling energy use continues to climb.

Heating energy use also rises significantly with window area for all window types, on average 22.2 kBtu/sf-yr (190 percent). Yet there are variations—the increase with Window B (high U-factor) is great compared to Window H (very low U-factor). When heating and electricity use are combined (Figure 5-37), the optimal window is small (WWR=0.15) for all window types except Window H, where WWR=0.30 is optimal. Spectrally selective, low-E triple-glazed Window H yields the least combined annual electricity and heating energy use of all window types modeled for moderate- to large-area windows. In fact, a large-area Window H uses 13 percent less total annual energy than its two closest counterparts: Window D (a conventional reflective window with poor daylight transmission) and Window F (a spectrally selective, low-E tinted window).

Advances in window technology allow architects to design larger windows in cold climates with superior energy efficiency and improved connection to the outdoors. Exterior shading also enables architects to use large windows in cold climates without a significant energy penalty.

### Effect of Window Area on Peak Demand

With unshaded south-facing windows, as WWR increases from 0 to 0.60, peak electricity demand rises significantly with window area: by 3.5 W/sf (87 percent) without daylighting controls and by 2.4 W/sf (60 percent) with daylighting controls (Figures 5-38 and 5-39). The rate of increase depends on window type; it is greatest for Windows B and E and least for Windows D, F, and H. A small to moderate area (WWR=0.15–0.30) is optimal for most windows, while

*Figure 5-39. Annual energy use and peak demand comparison by window area*

All cases are south-facing with no shading and include daylighting controls. Numbers are expressed per square foot within a 15-foot-deep perimeter zone. Results were computed using DOE-2.1E for a typical office building in Chicago, Illinois (Appendix A).

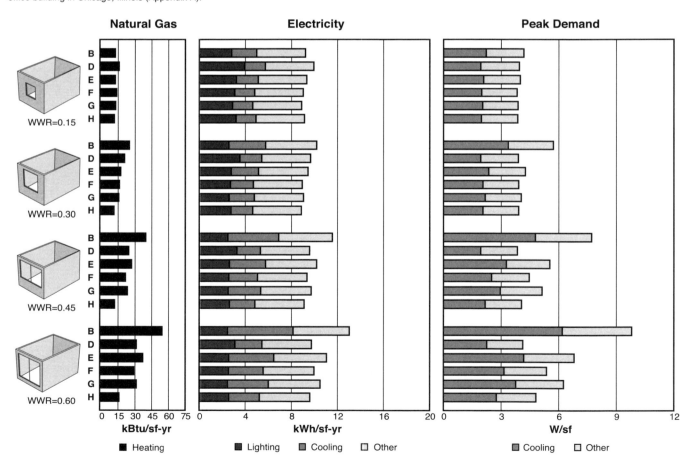

*Figure 5-40. Annual electricity energy use*

All cases are south-facing with no shading and include daylighting controls. Numbers are expressed per square foot within a 15-foot-deep perimeter zone. Results were computed using DOE-2.1E for a typical office building in Chicago, Illinois (Appendix A).

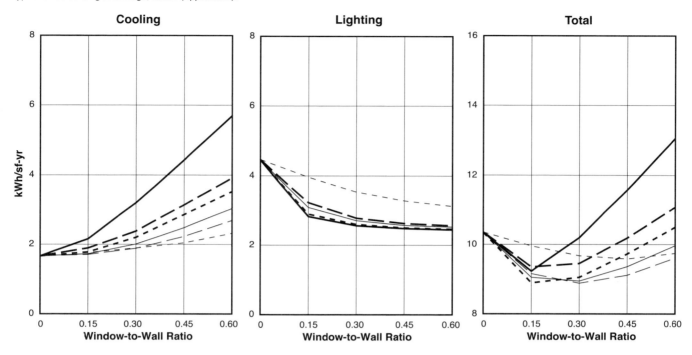

Window D area has little impact on peak demand. Interior and exterior shading can limit the negative impacts of greater window area (see following sections).

Peak demand typically occurs during mid- to late summer. For locations where peak summer demand rates are significantly higher than off-peak hours, reliable control of peak demand can significantly reduce operating costs over the long term.

### Effect of Window Area on Daylight

For all window types, greater window area yields more daylight illuminance in south-facing perimeter zones (Figure 5-41). An average annual daylight illuminance of 40 footcandles is attained with small-area windows (WWR=0.15) of all types except Window D. When the window-to-wall ratio is equal to or exceeds 0.30, the average annual daylight illuminance is at least 100 footcandles for all cases except Window D (VT=0.10), which provides the least daylight at any size.

For lighting designers, it is useful to note that daylight illuminance rises linearly with increased window area and visible transmittance (Figure 5-41), where the product of VT and WWR is known as the effective aperture (EA=VT*WWR). The exact nature of this linear relationship is dependent on latitude and climatic variables, such as frequency and degree of cloud cover.

## Effect of Window Area on Glare

Figure 5-42 illustrates a low weighted glare index for all window types in south-facing perimeter zones with a small to moderate window area (WWR=0.15–0.30). The weighted glare index for all windows except Window D rises significantly (discomfort glare is more frequent) as the window area increases above WWR=0.30. With larger window areas, glare can be a significant problem in an unshaded condition, however, effective exterior shading can address this problem. The weighted glare index for the darker, reflective Window D remains low even with large window areas because of its very low visible transmittance (VT).

## Effect of Window Area on View

As the window area increases, view improves significantly (Figure 5-43). This occurs simply because a major component of the view index in this analysis is window size. Window D, with a very low visible transmittance (VT) and high visible surface reflectance, performs worst with respect to view.

---

**GLARE INDEX**

  * = less than 7
  7 = imperceptible glare
 10 = just perceptible glare
 16 = just acceptable glare
 22 = just uncomfortable glare

---

*Figure 5-41. Average daylight illuminance*

Average daylight illuminance is calculated at a point 10 feet from the window. All cases are south-facing with no shading. Results were computed using DOE-2.1E for a typical office building in Chicago, Illinois (Appendix A).

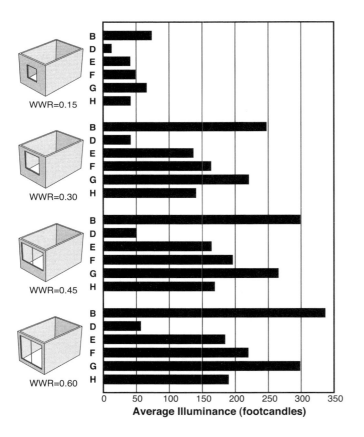

**Average Illuminance (footcandles)**

*Figure 5-42. Weighted glare index*

Glare index is calculated at a point 5 feet from the window for a person facing the side wall. A lower index is better. All cases are south-facing with no shading. Results were computed using DOE-2.1E for a typical office building in Chicago, Illinois (Appendix A).

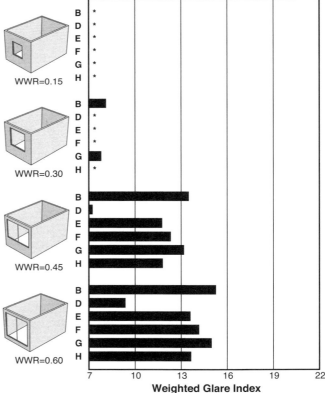

**Weighted Glare Index**

*Window Design for Offices in a Cold Climate*

## Effect of Window Area on Thermal Comfort

Thermal discomfort for unshaded south-facing offices in Chicago rises on average by 1.6 PPD with greater window area (WWR=0.30–0.60) for Windows B–H (Figure 5-44). For all window types except Windows B and D, thermal comfort remains acceptable (below 20 PPD) even with large windows. Triple-pane Window H performs best at higher window areas while Windows B and D are worst.

## Effect of Window Area on All Attributes Combined

In Figure 5-45, the relative performance of all six attributes for a range of window areas is shown on a 0-to-10 scale. All cases have daylighting controls and no exterior or interior shading devices. The impact of window area on the individual performance measures is summarized below.

*Energy:* For most window types with daylighting controls, the lowest total annual energy use occurs with a WWR of 0.15 to 0.30. Larger unshaded windows increase energy use significantly.

| Window B | Window F |
|---|---|
| double glazing | double glazing |
| clear | spec. selective low-E tint |
| U=0.60 | U=0.46 |
| SHGC=0.60 | SHGC=0.27 |
| VT=0.63 | VT=0.43 |
| **Window D** | **Window G** |
| double glazing | double glazing |
| reflective coating | spec. selective low-E clear |
| U=0.54 | U=0.46 |
| SHGC=0.17 | SHGC=0.34 |
| VT=0.10 | VT=0.57 |
| **Window E** | **Window H** |
| double glazing | triple glazing |
| low-E, bronze tint | 1 low-E layer, clear |
| U=0.49 | U=0.20 |
| SHGC=0.39 | SHGC=0.22 |
| VT=0.36 | VT=0.37 |

U=U-factor in Btu/hr-sf-°F
SHGC=solar heat gain coefficient
VT=visible transmittance
All window properties are for the whole window.
Windows B–H have thermally broken aluminum frames. Window H has an insulated frame.

*Figure 5-43. View index*

View index is calculated at a point 10 feet from the window. A higher index is better. All cases are south-facing with no shading. Results were computed using DOE-2.1E for a typical office building in Chicago, Illinois (Appendix A).

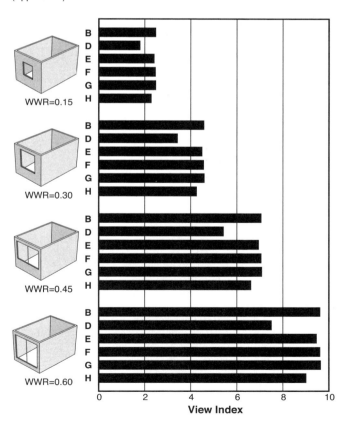

*Figure 5-44. Thermal comfort*

Thermal comfort is calculated at a point 5 feet from the window. A lower PPD is better. All cases are south-facing with no shading. Results were computed using DOE-2.1E for a typical office building in Chicago, Illinois (Appendix A).

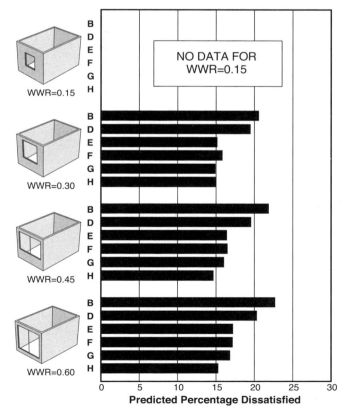

*Peak Demand:* For most window types, lowest peak electricity demand lies between WWR 0.15–0.30. Larger windows increase peak demand significantly for most window types. Window D is least affected by increases in area.

*Daylight:* Daylight levels rise significantly on the south side with greater window area. Even with a small window (WWR=0.15), all except Window D provide 40 footcandles or more average daylight illuminance. With moderate window areas (WWR=0.30), over 100 footcandles is provided.

*Glare:* For all window types except Window D, the weighted glare index increases significantly (discomfort glare is more frequent) as window area rises above WWR=0.30. Greater window area has less impact on the weighted glare index with Window D.

*View:* For all window types, the view index improves with greater window area.

*Thermal comfort:* The thermal discomfort rises slightly with greater window area except for Window H, which remains constant. Windows E–H all perform well thermally at any size.

For south-facing perimeter zones in Chicago, the impact of window area on the performance measures varies by window type. In terms of energy, peak demand, and glare, the optimal size of an unshaded window is small to moderate (WWR=0.15–0.30) for all window types except Window H. Triple-pane spectrally selective windows (Window H) achieves optimal energy efficiency and peak demand at a moderate window size (WWR=0.30–0.45) with good access to view and daylight. For large-area windows (WWR=0.60), triple-pane Window H outperforms double-pane reflective Window D in terms of energy use with significantly better view, daylight, interior brightness, and thermal comfort. However, Window D yields better peak demand performance and glare control.

Attached exterior shading on large-area, south-facing windows improves some of the window types, raising their performance to that of unshaded Window H. The subsequent section on shading will demonstrate how all attributes can be brought into balance through the design and integration of shading devices with glazing.

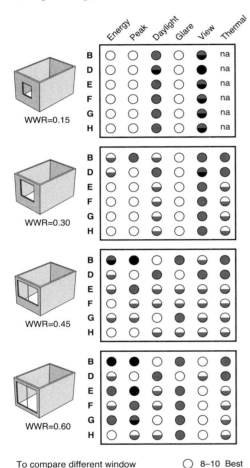

*Figure 5-45. Comparison of multiple attributes by window area*

All cases are south-facing with no shading and include daylighting controls. Results are for a typical office building in Chicago, Illinois.

To compare different window conditions across all attributes, the six measures of window performance are placed on a 0-to-10 scale. See Appendix A for the methodology.

○ 8–10 Best
◔ 6–8
◕ 4–6
◑ 2–4
● 0–2 Worst

*Window Design for Offices in a Cold Climate*

# The Effects of Shading Conditions in a South-facing Perimeter Zone with Moderate Window Area

This section addresses design decisions about shading once a moderate window area (WWR=0.30) has been chosen.

## Effect of Shading Conditions on Energy Use

With moderately sized windows (WWR=0.30), shading affects energy use in south-facing zones in three ways: cooling energy use declines due to control of solar heat gains, lighting energy use increases if daylight availability is reduced, and heating requirements rise due to reduced solar heat gains.

> **Shading Conditions**
> Figures 5-46 through 5-53
> All cases have WWR=0.30.
> (6 feet wide x 6 feet high)
> See Appendix A for details.
>
> Overhang only: 2.8-foot-deep
> Overhang + Vertical fins:
>     4.2-foot-deep overhang + 3.0-foot-deep fins
> High-rise obstruction: Opposing buildings with a
>     vertical angle of 45 degrees.

*Figure 5-46. Annual energy use and peak demand comparison by shading type*

All cases are south-facing and include daylighting controls. Numbers are expressed per square foot within a 15-foot-deep perimeter zone. Results were computed using DOE-2.1E for a typical office building in Chicago, Illinois (Appendix A).

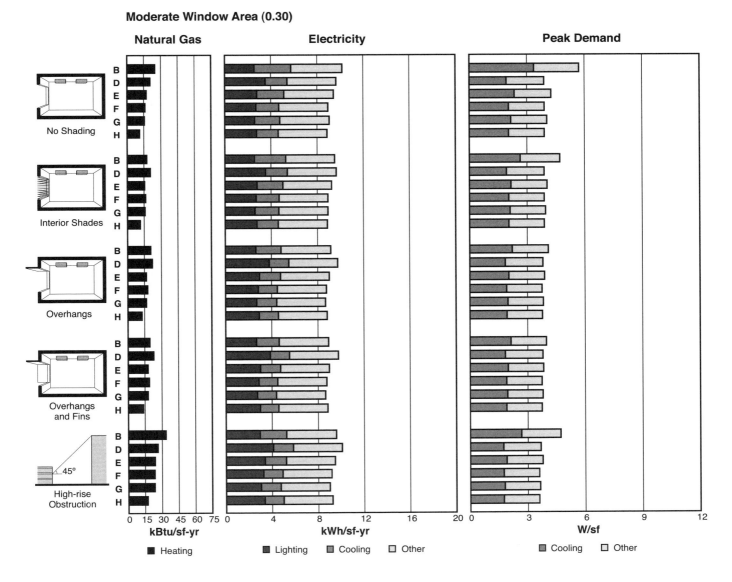

For all window types except B , interior or exterior shades reduce maximum annual electricity use by 0.1–0.6 kWh/sf-yr (1–5 percent) (Figure 5-46). For Window B with high SHGC and U-factor, shading reduces electricity use up to a 1.5 kWh/sf-yr (18 percent). Windows F, G, and H minimize the differences in electricity use between the various shading types. Overhangs and deep overhangs with vertical fins perform similarly with regard to electricity use, as do interior shades—if they are reliably deployed to control direct sun and admit daylight when available. High-rise obstructions increase annual electricity use compared to unshaded windows because they limit daylight while still allowing solar heat gains to penetrate when the sun is high in the sky.

Generally, shading blocks solar heat gains during the winter and increases heating requirements. However, Figure 5-46 shows that attached shading can slightly raise or lower heating energy use. This counterintuitive effect occurs because the mechanical system requires more heating energy for reheating chilled air during cooling periods in the unshaded condition. Deep overhangs plus fins increase heating energy by 3.1–5.1 kBtu/sf-yr (18–36 percent) with all window types except B. Overhangs and interior shades have a minimal effect on heating energy use (less than 3 percent, 0.3 kBtu/sf-yr) with all window types except B and E. High-rise obstructions increase heating energy by 5.8–8.5 kBtu/sf-yr (28–53 percent) across all window types.

For cold climates, a balance between daylight admission and solar heat gain control is needed to attain the least total annual energy use in a commercial building. An unshaded, south-facing, moderately sized window has approximately the same total annual energy use as a window with attached shading for all window types except B and E. Overhangs significantly reduce total energy use with Window B. High-rise obstructions increase total energy use significantly for all window types.

Figure 5-47 shows the total annual energy use (heating and cooling combined) for a range of window areas. It is apparent that the magnitude of energy savings from shading devices increases with window area as illustrated in the following section for large windows.

### Effect of Shading Conditions on Peak Demand

For moderately sized windows (WWR=0.30), attached shading and high-rise obstructions yield maximum peak demand reductions of 0.2–0.5 W/sf (5–12 percent) with Windows D–H. Shading has a greater impact on peak demand if the SHGC and U-factor of the window are high. For example, shading can reduce peak demand by 1.9 W/sf (33 percent) with Window B.

Shading will be most cost effective where peak demand is penalized with significantly higher rates. Reductions in HVAC capacity can offset initial capital costs. Figure 5-48 illustrates that the magnitude of peak demand reduction from shading devices rises with window area (see the following section for large window area results). The increase is less with interior shades: an average 1.7 W/sf (15 percent). Exterior shading will further reduce the impact of greater window area and provide more reliable solar control than manually deployed interior shades.

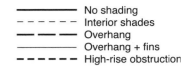

## Figure 5-47. *Total annual energy use for different shading conditions*

All cases are south-facing and include daylighting controls. Numbers are expressed per square foot within a 15-foot-deep perimeter zone. Results were computed using DOE-2.1E for a typical office building in Chicago, Illinois (Appendix A). Total annual energy use is calculated by multiplying electricity use by 3 and adding heating energy use. This reflects the 3:1 ratio of primary to end use energy for electricity. All window properties are for the whole window. Windows B–H have thermally broken aluminum frames. Window H has an insulated frame. U=U-factor in Btu/hr-sf-°F, SHGC=solar heat gain coefficient, VT=visible transmittance

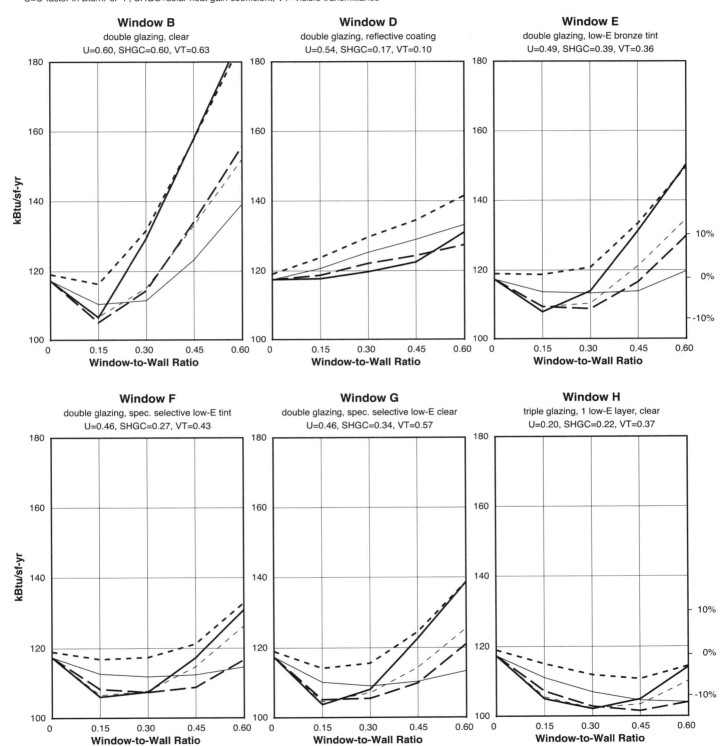

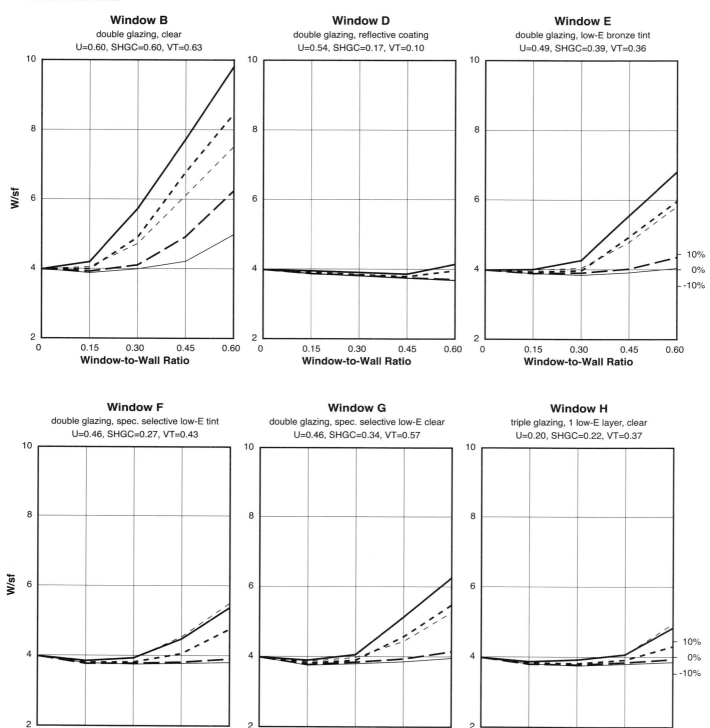

*Figure 5-48. Peak demand for different shading conditions*

All cases are south-facing and include daylighting controls. Numbers are expressed in Watts per square foot within a 15-foot-deep perimeter zone. Results were computed using DOE-2.1E for a typical office building in Chicago, Illinois (Appendix A). All window properties are for the whole window. Windows B–H have thermally broken aluminum frames. Window H has an insulated frame. U=U-factor in Btu/hr-sf-°F, SHGC=solar heat gain coefficient, VT=visible transmittance

——————— No shading
– – – – – – Interior shades
━━━━━ Overhang
——————— Overhang + fins
– ━ – ━ – High-rise obstruction

**Window B**
double glazing, clear
U=0.60, SHGC=0.60, VT=0.63

**Window D**
double glazing, reflective coating
U=0.54, SHGC=0.17, VT=0.10

**Window E**
double glazing, low-E bronze tint
U=0.49, SHGC=0.39, VT=0.36

**Window F**
double glazing, spec. selective low-E tint
U=0.46, SHGC=0.27, VT=0.43

**Window G**
double glazing, spec. selective low-E clear
U=0.46, SHGC=0.34, VT=0.57

**Window H**
triple glazing, 1 low-E layer, clear
U=0.20, SHGC=0.22, VT=0.37

*Window Design for Offices in a Cold Climate*

## Effect of Shading Conditions on Daylight

All types of shading reduce the average annual daylight illuminance on the south side (Figure 5-49). In order of least to greatest impact: interior shades, overhangs, deep overhangs combined with fins, and high-rise obstructions. An average annual daylight illuminance of 50 footcandles at a point 10 feet in from the window is provided by all interior and exterior shades for all window types except Window D. The high-rise obstruction results in less than 50 footcandles in all cases.

## Effect of Shading Conditions on Glare

For small- to moderately sized windows (WWR=0.30 or less), the weighted glare index is low for both unshaded and shaded conditions

<table>
<tr><td colspan="2">GLARE INDEX</td></tr>
<tr><td>*</td><td>= less than 7</td></tr>
<tr><td>7</td><td>= imperceptible glare</td></tr>
<tr><td>10</td><td>= just perceptible glare</td></tr>
<tr><td>16</td><td>= just acceptable glare</td></tr>
<tr><td>22</td><td>= just uncomfortable glare</td></tr>
</table>

*Figure 5-49. Average annual daylight illuminance*

Average daylight illuminance is calculated at a point 10 feet from the window. All cases are south-facing. Results were computed using DOE-2.1E for a typical office building in Chicago, Illinois (Appendix A).

*Figure 5-50. Weighted glare index*

Glare index is calculated at a point 5 feet from the window for a person facing the side wall. A lower index is better. All cases are south-facing. Results were computed using DOE-2.1E for a typical office building in Chicago, Illinois (Appendix A).

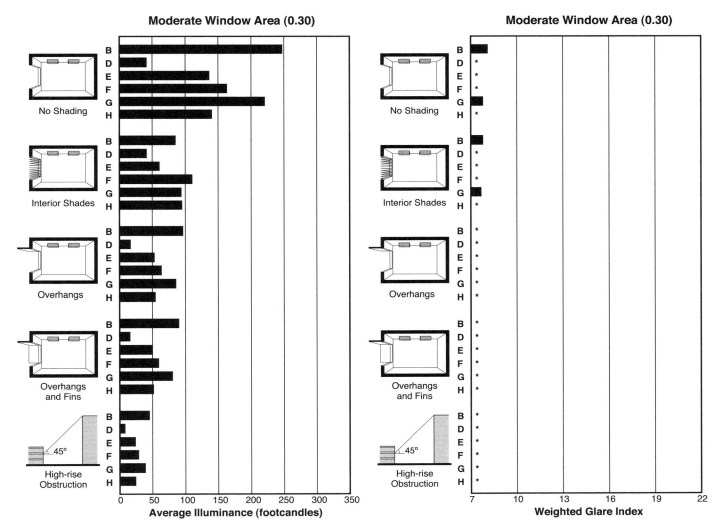

for all window types (Figure 5-50). Glare is minimally affected by shades because the area of the glare source (the window) is small.

### Effect of Shading Conditions on View

In this analysis, view is completely blocked by interior shades when deployed, diminished by exterior overhangs and/or fins, or obstructed by reflections in the window during periods when exterior light levels are low and the interior glass surface reflectance is relatively high.

For a south-facing window with no exterior shading, the frequency of interior shade use to control direct sun and glare is dictated by window type. High-performance windows with a low SHGC and U-factor can control solar loads for thermal comfort, limiting the need to use interior shades to control heat from direct sun. Low-VT win-

*Figure 5-51. View index*

View index is calculated at a point 5 feet from the window. A higher index is better. All cases are south-facing. Results were computed using DOE-2.1E for a typical office building in Chicago, Illinois (Appendix A).

*Figure 5-52. Thermal comfort*

Thermal comfort is calculated at a point 5 feet from the window. A lower PPD is better. All cases are north-facing. Results were computed using DOE-2.1E for a typical office building in Chicago, Illinois (Appendix A).

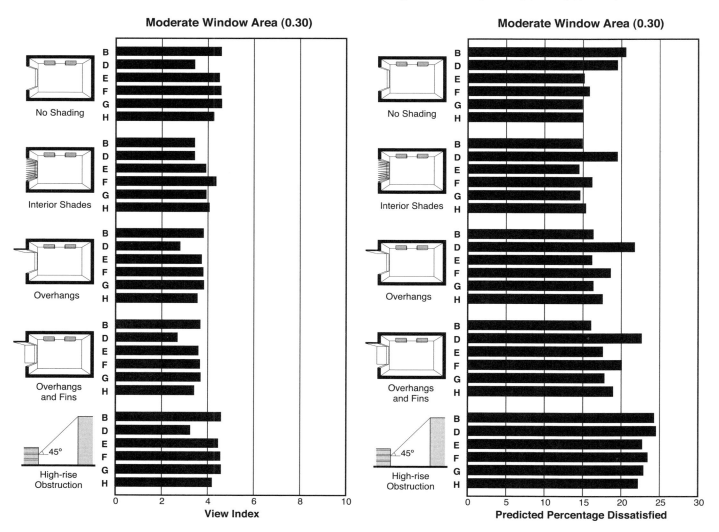

*Window Design for Offices in a Cold Climate*

dows such as Window D can control glare, reducing the need for shade operation. For Window B, view is blocked by interior shades for 19 percent of annual daylit hours, while Windows D, F, and H require interior shades for less than 4 percent of daylit hours. The remaining window types (E and G) require shades for 10–11 percent of daylit hours (Figure 5-51).

View is also partially blocked by exterior overhangs and/or fins, or obstructed by reflections in the window during periods when exterior light levels are low and the interior glass surface reflectance is relatively high. Overhangs reduce the unshaded view index by about 1 point for moderate-area windows across all window types (Figure 5-51). Overhangs combined with fins reduce the index by about 1.5 points.

All window types except Window D have nearly the same view index (within 0.2 points) for any given shade condition except interior shades. The high-rise obstruction is considered part of the view and does not affect the view index. All view indices in Figure 5-51 are in the low to moderate range because of the window area.

### Effect of Shading Conditions on Thermal Comfort

Exterior shading increases thermal discomfort for all windows except Window B (Figure 5-52). Interior shades have little effect on thermal comfort except with Window B where it is improved significantly. For Windows E–H, the ASHRAE 55 standard of less than 20 PPD is attained even with overhangs or interior shades. With Window D, only interior shades can be used and still attain the standard. High-rise obstructions raise discomfort, exceeding 20 PPD with all windows.

### Effect of Shading Conditions on All Attributes Combined

In Figure 5-53, the relative performance of all six attributes for a range of window shading conditions is shown on a 0-to-10 scale. All cases have daylighting controls and a window-to-wall ratio of 0.30. The impact of window area on the individual performance measures is summarized below.

*Energy:* For all window types except Window B, interior or exterior shades produce small reductions in annual electricity use (1–5 percent). Shades produce a mixed effect on heating energy use and cause an insignificant decrease in total annual energy use (but overhangs and interior shades do not significantly raise total energy use). High-rise obstructions increase total energy use significantly for all window types except Window B. For retrofit of existing buildings which have double-pane clear windows (Window B), overhangs or reliably deployed interior shades can significantly reduce total annual energy use.

*Peak Demand:* Exterior shading significantly reduces peak demand for windows with higher SHGC and U-factors (Windows B and E). Shading has a smaller effect on peak demand reduction with other windows.

*Daylight:* Interior daylight illuminance and brightness levels decline with all types of shading, but daylight remains at sufficient levels. For all shading types and window types except Window D, the

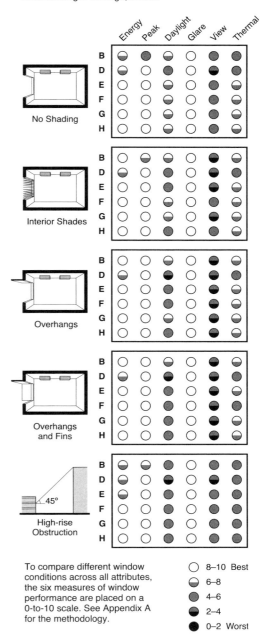

*Figure 5-53. Comparison of multiple attributes by shading condition for moderate window area*

All cases are south-facing and have WWR=0.30 and include daylighting controls. Results are for a typical office building in Chicago, Illinois.

To compare different window conditions across all attributes, the six measures of window performance are placed on a 0-to-10 scale. See Appendix A for the methodology.

○ 8–10 Best
◔ 6–8
◑ 4–6
◕ 2–4
● 0–2 Worst

average annual daylight illuminance remains above 50 foot-candles. It drops below 50 footcandles with high-rise obstructions.

*Glare:* Discomfort glare is infrequent with moderate window areas for any window type, but interior shades are helpful for glare control in those isolated instances when it is problematic.

*View:* All shading systems reduce view. For a moderately sized window, shallow overhangs reduce the view index by about 1 point, while deep overhangs combined with fins reduce it by 1.5 points. The index is in the low- to middle range because of the moderate window area.

*Thermal comfort:* Exterior shading increases thermal discomfort for all windows, except Window B.

For small- to moderately sized high-performance windows (particularly Windows F–H), exterior shading devices such as overhangs or overhangs combined with fins provide little benefit in a cold climate like Chicago. High-performance windows combined with interior shades and daylighting controls result in low total annual energy use, controlled peak demand, adequate interior daylight and brightness levels, low levels of discomfort glare, and acceptable thermal comfort. The triple-pane spectrally selective Window H performs best in this climate.

For moderately sized, south-facing windows, exterior shading is recommended in some cases. Overhangs improve the performance of Windows B and E. On the other hand, Window D is unaffected by shading and is not recommended in any case because of its poor performance in energy, daylight, and view.

### The Effects of Shading Conditions in a South-facing Perimeter Zone with Large Window Area

This section addresses design decisions about shading once a large window area (WWR=0.60) has been chosen.

*Effect of Shading Conditions on Energy Use*

With large-area windows (WWR=0.60), shading can significantly reduce annual electricity use up to 2.3–2.4 kWh/sf-yr (15–19 percent) for all window types except Window D (Figure 5-54). Shading does little to improve its performance. For all other windows, 5-foot-deep overhangs combined with 2.5-foot-deep fins (every 5 feet) result in the least annual electricity use of all shading types. High-performance Windows F and H are less dependent on exterior shades to control solar gains: smaller overhangs are almost as effective (within 0.4 kWh/sf-yr or 3–4 percent) as deep overhangs combined with fins. High-rise obstructions block the sun and reduce electricity use for cooling in summer; they are less effective than overhangs but can eliminate the need for interior shades to save energy.

In Figure 5-54, attached shading diminishes heating energy use even though the beneficial solar heat gain is reduced in colder periods. This counterintuitive effect occurs because the mechanical system requires more heating energy for reheating chilled air during cooling periods in the unshaded condition. High-rise obstructions increase heating energy use significantly. Since heating energy use represents 11–38 percent of total annual energy use (assuming an electricity-to-

**Window B**
double glazing
clear
U=0.60
SHGC=0.60
VT=0.63

**Window F**
double glazing
spec. selective low-E tint
U=0.46
SHGC=0.27
VT=0.43

**Window D**
double glazing
reflective coating
U=0.54
SHGC=0.17
VT=0.10

**Window G**
double glazing
spec. selective low-E clear
U=0.46
SHGC=0.34
VT=0.57

**Window E**
double glazing
low-E, bronze tint
U=0.49
SHGC=0.39
VT=0.36

**Window H**
triple glazing
1 low-E layer, clear
U=0.20
SHGC=0.22
VT=0.37

U=U-factor in Btu/hr-sf-°F
SHGC=solar heat gain coefficient
VT=visible transmittance
All window properties are for the whole window.
Windows B–H have thermally broken aluminum frames. Window H has an insulated frame.

*Window Design for Offices in a Cold Climate*

fuel ratio of 3:1), the decision on whether to use shading and what type to use should be based on total annual energy use (see Figure 5-47 in the previous section).

Exterior shades are highly recommended for large-area, south-facing windows, even in a cold climate like Chicago. Window H combined with overhangs performs best. Its total annual energy use is 3.1 kWh/sf-yr (9 percent) less than the next best alternatives, which are Window F or G with overhangs plus fins. These combinations all perform better than an opaque insulated wall (insulated to ASHRAE 90.1-1999 levels). Overall, deep overhangs with fins result in the least total energy use, but for some window types, the total is nearly equal

<table>
<tr><td>

**Shading Conditions In Section 5.4.4**
Figures 5-54 through 5-59
All cases have WWR=0.60
(10 feet wide x 7.2 feet high)
See Appendix A for details.

Overhang only: 3.4-foot-deep
Overhang + Vertical fins:
   5.0-foot-deep overhang + 2.5 feet deep fins
   (every 5 feet)
High-rise obstruction: Infinitely long vertical plane
   101 feet high at a distance of 80 feet from
   building (45° angle from top of window).
</td></tr>
</table>

Figure 5-54. *Annual energy use and peak demand comparison by shading type*
All cases are south-facing and include daylighting controls. Numbers are expressed per square foot within a 15-foot-deep perimeter zone. Results were computed using DOE-2.1E for a typical office building in Chicago, Illinois (Appendix A).

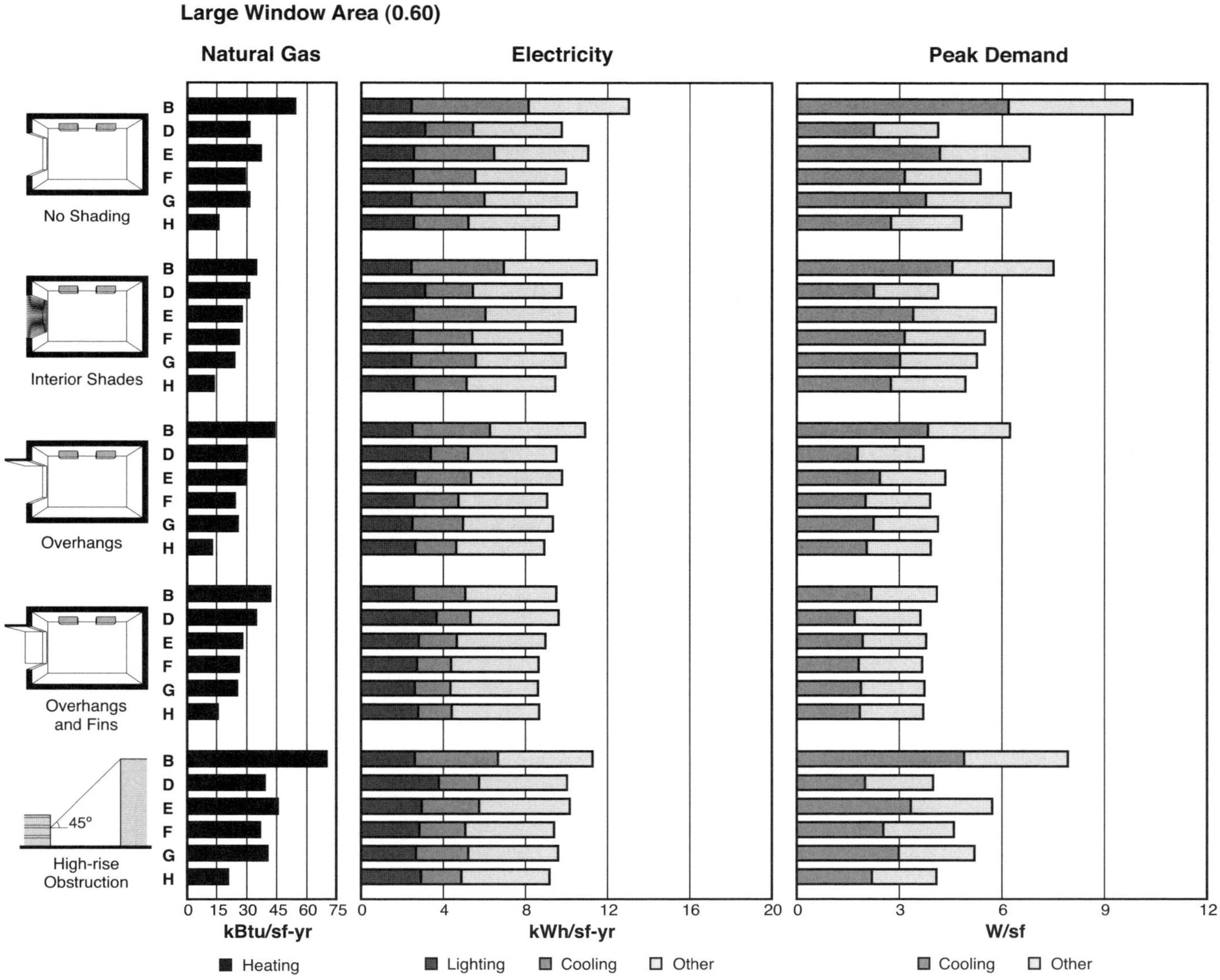

**Large Window Area (0.60)**

South-facing Perimeter Zones

193

to the shallow overhang case. Window D has nearly the same total energy use with and without attached shades; its total energy use is still 25 percent greater than Window H with overhangs. For retrofit conditions, overhangs with fins can reduce the total annual energy use of Window B significantly (26 percent). High-rise obstructions have little effect on total energy use compared to an unshaded window, except for Window D, where obstructions increase total energy use by 8 percent.

## Effect of Shading Conditions on Peak Demand

For large windows (WWR=0.60), shading can significantly reduce peak demand by up to 3.0 W/sf (44 percent) with Windows E–H, and by 5.7 W/sf (58 percent) with Window B (Figure 5-54). Deep over-

| GLARE INDEX | |
|---|---|
| * | = less than 7 |
| 7 | = imperceptible glare |
| 10 | = just perceptible glare |
| 16 | = just acceptable glare |
| 22 | = just uncomfortable glare |

*Figure 5-55. Average annual daylight illuminance*
Average daylight illuminance is calculated at a point 10 feet from the window. All cases are south-facing. Results were computed using DOE-2.1E for a typical office building in Chicago, Illinois (Appendix A).

*Figure 5-56. Weighted glare index*
Glare index is calculated at a point 5 feet from the window for a person facing the side wall. A lower index is better. All cases are south-facing with no shading. Results were computed using DOE-2.1E for a typical office building in Chicago, Illinois (Appendix A).

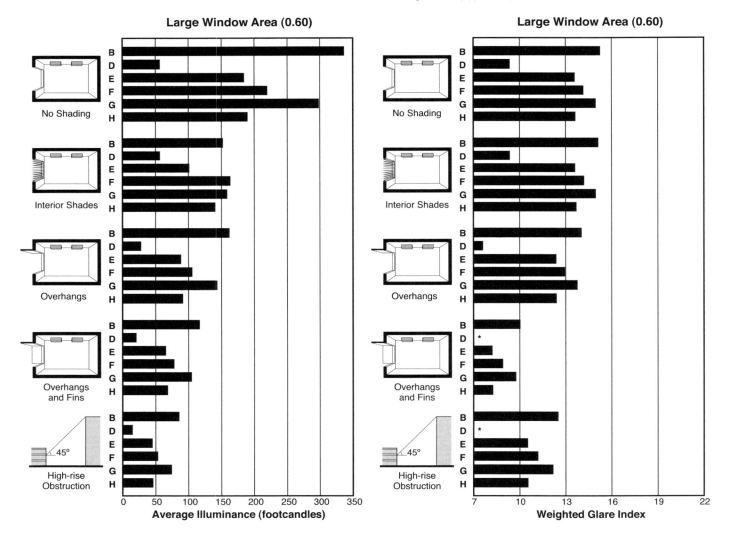

hangs combined with vertical fins result in the lowest peak demand levels and are recommended for Windows B, E, and G. Overhangs are recommended with Windows D, F, and H, since the improvement in demand from using deeper overhangs with fins is marginal. With an unshaded window, high-rise obstructions significantly reduce demand levels by 0.7–1.9 W/sf (14–19 percent) but do not equal the reductions achieved with exterior shading.

The proper combination of window type, size, and shading can significantly cut peak demand, reduce operating costs (particularly in regions where peak demand is penalized with higher rates), and decrease capital costs due to HVAC downsizing. Peak demand levels are greater than 6.5 W/sf for all glazings except Windows D, F, and H; with Window B, peak demand is 9.8 W/sf (compared to a full lighting load of 1.5 W/sf). The best case with shades (Windows D, F, and H with overhangs) brings peak demand to levels of 3.7 W/sf. These reductions can lead to significant savings, in initial capital costs and through more efficient HVAC operations.

### Effect of Shading Conditions on Daylight

All types of shading reduce the average annual daylight illuminance, but it remains relatively high in most cases (Figure 5-55). In order of least to greatest impact, shading alternatives are: interior shades, overhangs, deep overhangs combined with fins, and high-rise obstructions. An average annual daylight illuminance of 50 or more footcandles at a point 10 feet in from the window is provided by all window types with shading except for Window D. Average daylight illuminance drops to levels no less than 45 footcandles with high-rise obstructions (except for Window D).

### Effect of Shading Conditions on Glare

Discomfort glare is dictated mainly by the size of the glare source (the large window). For large windows (WWR=0.45 or above), the weighted glare index is significantly reduced with shading (Figure 5-56). Deep overhangs combined with vertical fins produce the lowest weighted glare index. Smaller overhangs offer some improvement over no shading, but the translucent interior shades used in this analysis are not opaque enough to impact the weighted glare index. High-rise obstructions can reduce the weighted glare index considerably. For Window D, shades provide no benefit since glare is well controlled simply due to its low VT.

### Effect of Shading Conditions on View

For a south-facing window with no exterior shading, window type dictates the frequency of interior shade deployment to control direct sun and glare. High-performance Windows F and H with low SHGC and U-factors can control solar loads for thermal comfort, eliminating the need to use interior shades to control the heat from direct sun. Window D, with a low VT, controls glare well, lessening the need for interior shades. For Window B, view is blocked by interior shades more than any other window type, reducing the view index by about 2 points. With Windows E and G, the view index declines by about 1 point when using interior shades.

Generally, overhangs reduce the unshaded view index by about 1 point for large-area windows across all window types (Figure 5-57). Deep overhangs with fins lower the index by up to 3 points for large-area windows. Window D, with a very low VT, has the lowest view index of all window types.

### Effect of Shading Conditions on Thermal Comfort

Exterior shading affects thermal comfort by blocking direct sun, which has either a positive or negative impact depending on outdoor conditions. If it is cold outside, the direct sun might be welcome, but that same sun might be uncomfortable if hot (Figure 5-58). The predominant factor contributing to increased predicted percentage dissatisfied within a particular thermal environment is the asymmetry of mean radiant temperatures due to hot or cold window surfaces and direct sun on the occupant.

*Figure 5-57. View index*

View index is calculated at a point 10 feet from the window. A higher index is better. All cases are south-facing with no shading. Results were computed using DOE-2.1E for a typical office building in Chicago, Illinois (Appendix A).

*Figure 5-58. Thermal comfort*

Thermal comfort is calculated at a point 5 feet from the window. A lower PPD is better. All cases are south-facing with no shading. Results were computed using DOE-2.1E for a typical office building in Chicago, Illinois (Appendix A).

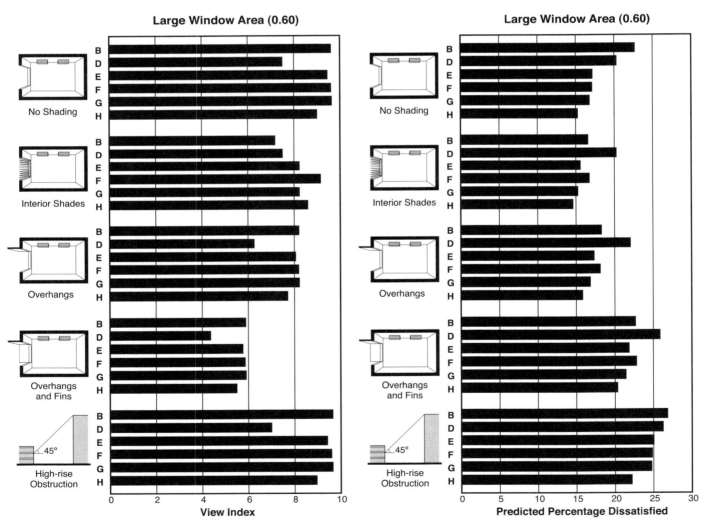

*Window Design for Offices in a Cold Climate*

Interior shades improve thermal comfort for all window types except Window D. With Windows E–H, high-rise obstructions or deep overhangs combined with vertical fins negatively impact thermal comfort—the PPD exceeds the threshold of 20 set by the ASHRAE 55 Standard. Overhangs and interior shades have the biggest positive impact on Window B.

*Effect of Shading Conditions on All Attributes Combined*

In Figure 5-59, the relative performance of all six attributes for a range of window shading conditions is shown on a 0-to-10 scale. All cases have daylighting controls and a window-to-wall ratio of 0.60. The impact of window area on each of the individual performance measures is summarized below.

*Energy:* Exterior shades reduce total energy use for all large, south-facing windows (except Window D). The type of shading that produces the least total annual energy use for each window type varies. High-rise obstructions south of the building do not lower the total annual energy use of an unshaded window.

*Peak Demand:* Exterior shades produce significant reductions in peak demand for all windows types except Window D.

*Daylight:* All types of shade reduce interior daylight illuminance and brightness levels, yet daylight remains at sufficient levels for all window types except Window D.

*Glare:* Shading significantly decreases glare. Overhangs combined with fins produce the largest reduction in the weighted glare index. Shading cuts glare even in a case like Window D with its very low VT.

*View:* All shading systems reduce view. Across all window types and sizes, interior shades and shallow overhangs reduce the view index by about 1 point, while deep overhangs combined with fins lower it by up to 3 points.

*Thermal comfort:* Deep overhangs with vertical fins and high-rise obstructions negatively impact thermal comfort. Shallower overhangs and interior shades have little impact except with Window B, where there is notable improvement.

Window H with simple overhangs achieves the best balance of the six performance measures: total energy use and peak demand are the lowest of all window and shade combinations, while daylight, glare, view, and thermal comfort indices are all acceptable.

If the building designer or owner wants to avoid exterior shading such as overhangs and/or fins yet still wishes to use large-area windows, then an unshaded Window H offers the best balance of the six performance measures. Window D should also be considered, particularly if peak demand rates are high, although performance is not as good in terms of daylight and view.

High-rise obstructions do not affect total annual energy use. They do reduce peak electricity demand and glare in some cases, but negatively impact daylight and thermal comfort.

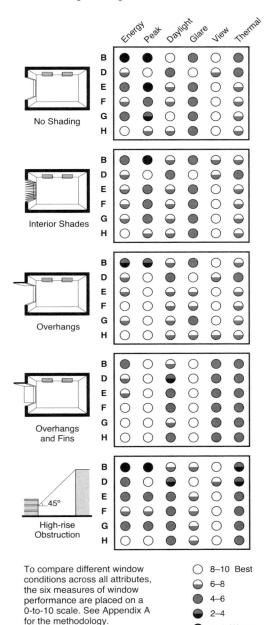

*Figure 5-59. Comparison of multiple attributes by shading condition*

All cases are south-facing and have WWR=0.60 and include daylighting controls. Results are for a typical office building in Chicago, Illinois.

To compare different window conditions across all attributes, the six measures of window performance are placed on a 0-to-10 scale. See Appendix A for the methodology.

○ 8–10 Best
◒ 6–8
◕ 4–6
◑ 2–4
● 0–2 Worst

# East- and West-facing Perimeter Zones

Once the decision has been made to orient perimeter zones to the east or west, the designer must examine more detailed issues related to window design and selection. The following sections address how lighting controls, window area, and shading affect performance. All results shown in this section are for west-facing perimeter zones. In most cases, the results for east-facing zones are very similar.

### Effects of Lighting Controls on Annual Energy Use and Peak Demand in an East- or West-Facing Perimeter Zone

Total annual energy use declines significantly with daylighting controls. Lighting energy use decreases significantly in proportion to increased daylight (higher VT and WWR) and cooling energy use falls slightly because of reduced heat gain from the lights. However, heating energy use rises in proportion to reduced heat gains from the lights (Figure 5-60).

With daylighting controls, for all window types (except Window D) and all sizes, total annual energy use declines by 17–22 kBtu/sf-yr (10–15 percent) compared to an east- or west-facing zone without controls. Figure 5-61 illustrates total energy use (combined heating and electricity) across a range of window areas. Window H yields the least total energy use with or without daylighting controls among all window types and sizes because of its relatively high VT, low SHGC, and low U-factor. For some window types and sizes, total energy use can be lower than an opaque insulated wall (WWR=0).

Daylight controls also significantly reduce peak electricity demand in all cases (Figure 5-62). Peak demand declines by 0.5–1.1 W/sf (8–21 percent) for most window types (except Window D) and sizes

---

| Window B | Window F |
|---|---|
| double glazing | double glazing |
| clear | spec. selective low-E tint |
| U=0.60 | U=0.46 |
| SHGC=0.60 | SHGC=0.27 |
| VT=0.63 | VT=0.43 |
| | |
| **Window D** | **Window G** |
| double glazing | double glazing |
| reflective coating | spec. selective low-E clear |
| U=0.54 | U=0.46 |
| SHGC=0.17 | SHGC=0.34 |
| VT=0.10 | VT=0.57 |
| | |
| **Window E** | **Window H** |
| double glazing | triple glazing |
| low-E, bronze tint | 1 low-E layer, clear |
| U=0.49 | U=0.20 |
| SHGC=0.39 | SHGC=0.22 |
| VT=0.36 | VT=0.37 |

U=U-factor in Btu/hr-sf-°F
SHGC=solar heat gain coefficient
VT=visible transmittance
All window properties are for the whole window.
Windows B–H have thermally broken aluminum frames. Window H has an insulated frame.

---

*Figure 5-60. Annual energy use and peak demand comparison by lighting system*

All cases are west-facing with a 0.30 window-to-wall ratio and no shading. Numbers are expressed per square foot within a 15-foot-deep perimeter zone. Results were computed using DOE-2.1E for a typical office building in Chicago, Illinois (Appendix A).

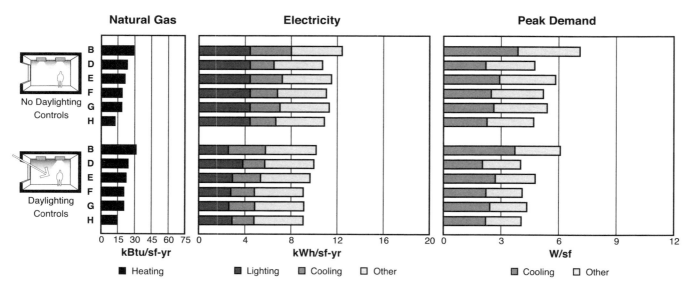

*Window Design for Offices in a Cold Climate*

### Figure 5-61. *Total annual energy use comparison by lighting system*

All cases are west-facing and have no shading. Numbers are expressed per square foot within a 15-foot-deep perimeter zone. Results were computed using DOE-2.1E for a typical office building in Chicago, Illinois (Appendix A).

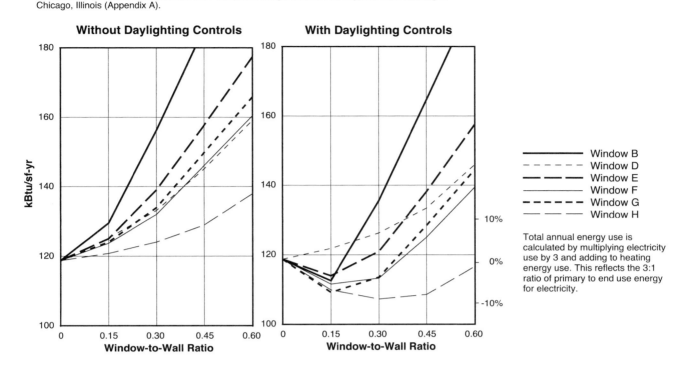

Total annual energy use is calculated by multiplying electricity use by 3 and adding to heating energy use. This reflects the 3:1 ratio of primary to end use energy for electricity.

### Figure 5-62. *Peak demand comparison by lighting system*

All cases are west-facing and have no shading. Numbers are expressed in Watts per square foot within a 15-foot-deep perimeter zone. Results were computed using DOE-2.1E for a typical office building in Chicago, Illinois (Appendix A).

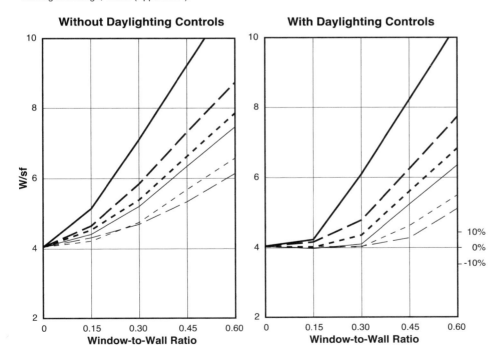

*East- and West-facing Perimeter Zones*

**Window B**
double glazing
clear
U=0.60
SHGC=0.60
VT=0.63

**Window F**
double glazing
spec. selective low-E tint
U=0.46
SHGC=0.27
VT=0.43

**Window D**
double glazing
reflective coating
U=0.54
SHGC=0.17
VT=0.10

**Window G**
double glazing
spec. selective low-E clear
U=0.46
SHGC=0.34
VT=0.57

**Window E**
double glazing
low-E, bronze tint
U=0.49
SHGC=0.39
VT=0.36

**Window H**
triple glazing
1 low-E layer, clear
U=0.20
SHGC=0.22
VT=0.37

U=U-factor in Btu/hr-sf-˚F
SHGC=solar heat gain coefficient
VT=visible transmittance
All window properties are for the whole window.
Windows B–H have thermally broken aluminum
frames. Window H has an insulated frame.

(except WWR=0.15). As with total energy use, peak demand increases with window area and VT.

While all the energy use comparisons in this section show significant savings with lighting controls, there is a range of possible performance (see Chapter 2). Lighting controls do not affect daylight, view, glare, and thermal comfort.

### Effects of Window Area in an East- or West-Facing Perimeter Zone

This section is intended to address the question of the optimal window area on an east- or west-facing perimeter zone. Only the unshaded condition is examined here. The following sections discuss how shading can mitigate the negative impacts of larger window areas.

*Effect of Window Area on Energy Use*

As with south-facing perimeter offices, annual electricity use rises with greater window area, SHGC, and U-factor if no daylighting controls are used (Figure 5-63). With daylighting controls, annual

*Figure 5-63. Annual energy use and peak demand comparison by window area*

All cases are west-facing with no shading and include daylighting controls. Numbers are expressed per square foot within a 15-foot-deep perimeter zone. Results were computed using DOE-2.1E for a typical office building in Chicago, Illinois (Appendix A).

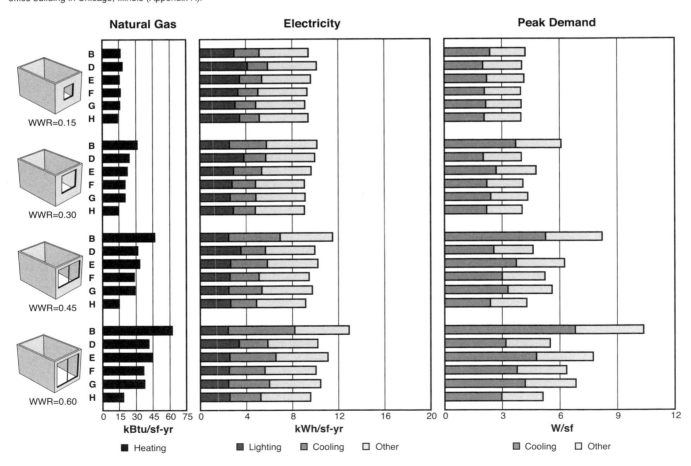

*Window Design for Offices in a Cold Climate*

## Figure 5-64. *Annual electricity energy use*

All cases are west-facing with no shading and include daylighting controls. Numbers are expressed per square foot within a 15-foot-deep perimeter zone. Results were computed using DOE-2.1E for a typical office building in Chicago, Illinois (Appendix A).

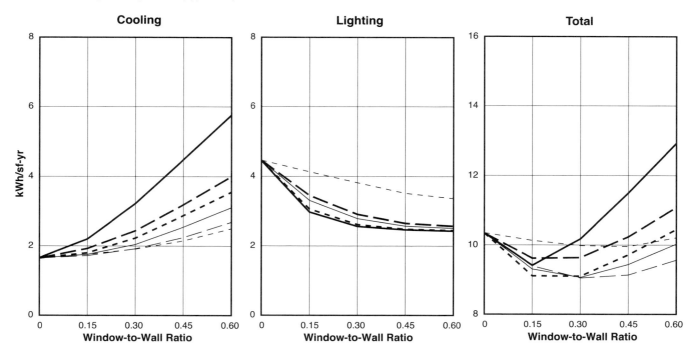

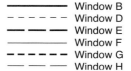

Window B
Window D
Window E
Window F
Window G
Window H

electricity use first falls then rises with window area for all window types. Figure 5-64 illustrates that cooling energy use climbs with greater window area. With daylighting controls, electric lighting energy use decreases with greater window area to a point where additional daylight produces no significant reductions in lighting energy. When cooling and lighting are combined into total electricity use (as well as all other electricity end uses), the optimal window area (as represented by the low point of the curve on Figure 5-64) varies by window type.

Heating energy use also rises with window area for all window types, though there is great variation (Figure 5-63). The increase is great with Window B (high U-factor) compared to very little for Window H (very low U-factor). For total annual energy use (combined electricity and heating energy), the optimal window area is dependent on window type. For all windows except Window D, total annual energy use initially falls then rises significantly (15–65 percent) with window area (Figure 5-61). The optimum window area is small (WWR=0.15) in a cold climate like Chicago. Window H has an optimum window-to-wall ratio of 0.30-0.45 with an annual energy use that is 60 percent (almost half) that of double-pane clear (Window B) at WWR=0.60.

Advances in window technology allow architects to design larger windows in cold climates with superior energy efficiency and improved connection to the outdoors. The triple-glazed window (Window H) consists of a spectrally selective low-E coating on a clear plastic film suspended in between two glass layers (its overall unit thickness is comparable to a double-pane window). Combined with an insulated, thermally broken window frame, this window provides excellent solar heat gain control (SHGC=0.22, U-factor=0.20 Btu/h-sf-°F) with good daylight transmission (VT=0.37).

## Effect of Window Area on Peak Demand

With unshaded windows, as WWR rises from 0 to 0.60, peak electricity demand increases significantly with window area for all window types: by 2.1–7.7 W/sf (53–102 percent) without daylight controls and by 1.1–6.7 W/sf (27–168 percent) with controls (Figures 5-62 and 5-63). The rate of increase is lowest for Windows D and H. For locations where on-peak summer demand rates are significantly greater than off-peak hours, peak demand can significantly raise operating costs.

## Effect of Window Area on Daylight

Greater window area results in increased daylight illuminance in east- and west-facing perimeter zones for all window types (Figure 5-65). When the window-to-wall ratio is equal to or greater than 0.30, the

**GLARE INDEX**
| | |
|---|---|
| * | = less than 7 |
| 7 | = imperceptible glare |
| 10 | = just perceptible glare |
| 16 | = just acceptable glare |
| 22 | = just uncomfortable glare |

*Figure 5-65. Average daylight illuminance*

Average daylight illuminance is calculated at a point 10 feet from the window. All cases are west-facing with no shading. Results were computed using DOE-2.1E for a typical office building in Chicago, Illinois (Appendix A).

*Figure 5-66. Weighted glare index*

Glare index is calculated at a point 5 feet from the window for a person facing the side wall. A lower index is better. All cases are west-facing with no shading. Results were computed using DOE-2.1E for a typical office building in Chicago, Illinois (Appendix A).

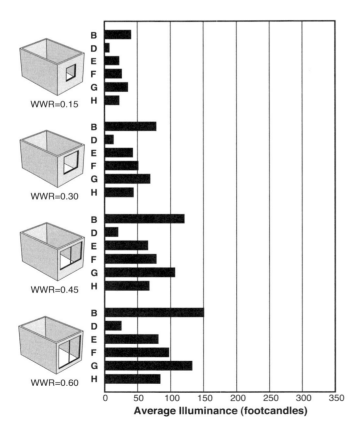

**Average Illuminance (footcandles)**

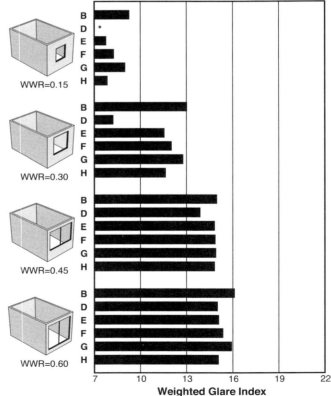

**Weighted Glare Index**

*Window Design for Offices in a Cold Climate*

average annual daylight illuminance is at least 40 footcandles for all cases except Window D (VT=0.10), which provides the least daylight at any size.

For lighting designers, it is useful to note that daylight illuminance rises linearly with increased window area and visible transmittance (Figure 5-65), where the product of VT and WWR is known as the effective aperture (EA=VT*WWR).

## Effect of Window Area on Glare

Figure 5-66 illustrates a low weighted glare index for all window types in east- and west-facing perimeter zones with a small window area (WWR=0.15). Glare is a significant problem for moderate-to large-area unshaded windows (WWR=0.30 and above) of all types due to low-angle sun. The average weighted glare index is 12 for WWR=0.30 for all window types except Window D, and 14 for WWR=0.60. A value of 10 corresponds to "just perceptible" and a value of 16 corresponds to "just acceptable" glare. Even very low-transmission glazing cannot adequately control glare for large-area windows. Interior shading can reduce discomfort glare while allowing some daylight, if deployed properly.

| Window B | Window F |
|---|---|
| double glazing | double glazing |
| clear | spec. selective low-E tint |
| U=0.60 | U=0.46 |
| SHGC=0.60 | SHGC=0.27 |
| VT=0.63 | VT=0.43 |
| | |
| Window D | Window G |
| double glazing | double glazing |
| reflective coating | spec. selective low-E clear |
| U=0.54 | U=0.46 |
| SHGC=0.17 | SHGC=0.34 |
| VT=0.10 | VT=0.57 |
| | |
| Window E | Window H |
| double glazing | triple glazing |
| low-E, bronze tint | 1 low-E layer, clear |
| U=0.49 | U=0.20 |
| SHGC=0.39 | SHGC=0.22 |
| VT=0.36 | VT=0.37 |

U=U-factor in Btu/hr-sf-°F
SHGC=solar heat gain coefficient
VT=visible transmittance
All window properties are for the whole window.
Windows B–H have thermally broken aluminum frames. Window H has an insulated frame.

*Figure 5-67. View index*

View index is calculated at a point 10 feet from the window. A higher index is better. All cases are west-facing with no shading. Results were computed using DOE-2.1E for a typical office building in Chicago, Illinois (Appendix A).

*Figure 5-68. Thermal comfort*

Thermal comfort is calculated at a point 5 feet from the window. A lower PPD is better. All cases are west-facing with no shading. Results were computed using DOE-2.1E for a typical office building in Chicago, Illinois (Appendix A).

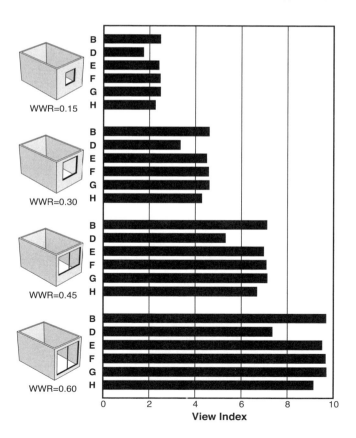

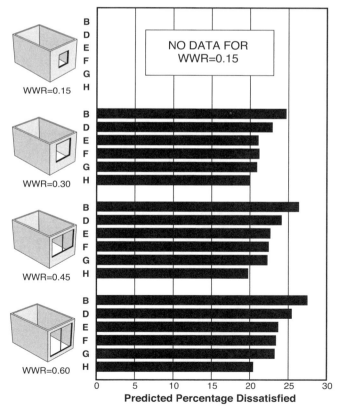

*East- and West-facing Perimeter Zones*

## Effect of Window Area on View

As the window area increases, view improves significantly since a major component of the view index in this analysis is window size (Figure 5-67). Window D, with a very low visible transmittance (VT) and high visible surface reflectance, performs more poorly than all other window types with respect to view.

## Effect of Window Area on Thermal Comfort

Thermal discomfort in unshaded east- and west-facing offices in Chicago increases by 1–3 PPD with greater window area for Windows B–H (Figure 5-68). The ASHRAE 55 maximum PPD of 20 is only met by Window H.

## Effect of Window Area on All Attributes Combined

In Figure 5-69, the relative performance of all six attributes for a range of window areas is shown on a 0-to-10 scale. All cases have daylighting controls and no exterior or interior shading devices. The impact of window area on the individual performance measures is summarized below.

*Energy:* For most window types with daylighting controls, the optimal lowest total annual energy use occurs with a WWR of 0.15–0.30. Larger windows increase total energy use significantly. The optimal area for triple-pane Window H is WWR=0.30.

*Peak Demand:* Larger windows increase peak demand significantly, up to 6.7 W/sf. Opaque walls outperform even the smallest size of Windows B or E. For Windows D and F–H, the lowest peak demand is with WWR=0-0.15.

*Daylight:* Daylight increases as window area and VT rise. Most window types except Window D provide an annual average illumination of 40 footcandles for WWR=0.30 and above.

*Glare:* For all window types except Window D, glare increases significantly as window area climbs above WWR=0.15. At large window areas (WWR=0.45–0.60), the level of discomfort glare is nearly the same for all window types.

*View:* For all window types, the view index improves with greater window area.

*Thermal comfort:* Thermal discomfort increases slightly with greater window area. All windows, except Window H, perform similarly.

For east- and west-facing perimeter zones in a cold climate like Chicago, small unshaded windows (WWR=0.15–0.30) combined with daylighting controls yield the best overall performance—energy use and peak demand are minimized, discomfort glare is controlled, and daylight and interior brightness is adequate. If larger windows are desired, unwanted solar gains during the cooling season outweigh desired solar gains during the heating season. Therefore, among the double-glazed windows, Windows D and F with the lower SHGC perform better, while the triple-pane Window H yields the least energy use (since it significantly reduces heating energy use) while controlling peak demand and providing daylight. To control discomfort glare from low-angle sun, interior shading can be used.

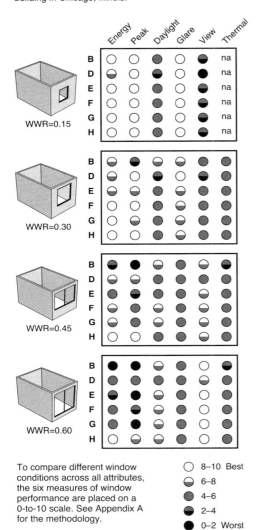

*Figure 5-69. Comparison of multiple attributes by window area*

All cases are west-facing with no shading and include daylighting controls. Results are for a typical office building in Chicago, Illinois.

To compare different window conditions across all attributes, the six measures of window performance are placed on a 0-to-10 scale. See Appendix A for the methodology.

○ 8–10 Best
◔ 6–8
◑ 4–6
◕ 2–4
● 0–2 Worst

## The Effects of Shading Conditions in an East- or West-Facing Perimeter Zone with Moderate Window Area

This section addresses shading design decisions once a moderate window area (WWR=0.30) has been chosen.

### Effect of Shading Conditions on Energy Use

For moderately sized windows (WWR=0.30), shading reduces annual electricity use for Windows B and E. Shading has less effect on Windows D, F, and H (Figure 5-70). Heating energy use increases slightly with exterior shading and decreases slightly with interior shades.

Figure 5-71 shows the total energy use (heating and cooling combined) for a range of window sizes. Interior or exterior shades result in no more than a 4 percent decline in total annual energy use for all window types except Window B. With Window B, overhangs combined with fins cut total annual energy use by 12 percent. High-performance Windows F–H minimize the differences in energy use between shaded and unshaded east- or west-facing windows. Shading has no effect on Window D at a moderate window area. The use of interior shading and vertical fins do not alter the optimal window area from WWR=0.15 for most windows (WWR=0.45 is optimal for Window H).

High-rise obstructions such as mountains, trees, or existing buildings can substantially block low-angle sun on east- and west-facing facades. Similarly, deep overhangs with vertical fins provide the most complete shading. In both cases, however, total annual energy use is affected very little across all window types. Only with Window B does shading substantively impact energy.

While modeling results illustrate limited opportunities for shading moderate window areas, it is apparent that energy savings from shading increase with window area, as illustrated in a later section.

### Effect of Shading Conditions on Peak Demand

For moderately sized windows (WWR=0.30), shading cuts peak demand similar to the energy use trends described above (Figure 5-70). The magnitude of the reductions is dependent on the SHGC and U-factor of the window.

With shades, peak demand declines by 0.7–2.2 W/sf (16–34 percent) for Windows B, E, F, and G. Interior shades result in almost the same demand reduction as overhangs combined with fins and high-rise obstructions. For Windows D and H, shades decrease peak demand by 0.3–0.4 W/sf (8–10 percent).

Shading will be most cost effective where peak demand is penalized with significantly higher time-of-use rates. Reduced peak demand also can lead to reduced mechanical equipment costs. Figure 5-72 illustrates that the magnitude of peak demand reduction from shading devices increases with window area.

### Effect of Shading Conditions on Daylight

All types of shading reduce the average annual daylight illuminance (Figure 5-73). In order of least to greatest impact (nearly identical order for all window types): interior shades, fins, high-rise obstructions, and overhangs combined with fins. Only Windows B, F, and G with their high visible transmittance provide an average annual illuminance of 50 footcandles when unshaded. If shaded with interior shades or fins, only Windows B and G provide 50 footcandles.

## Effect of Shading Conditions on Glare

Even for small- to moderately sized windows (WWR=0.30 or less), there are potential glare problems in east- and west-facing zones (Figure 5-74). For these windows, the weighted glare index falls below "just acceptable" and above "just perceptible" for all window types with and without shades. Interior shades and high-rise obstructions reduce the weighted glare index to below "just perceptible" levels. Windows B, E, and G show the greatest improvement in the weighted

*Figure 5-70. Annual energy use and peak demand comparison by shading type*

All cases are west-facing with a 0.30 window-to-wall ratio and include daylighting controls. Numbers are expressed per square foot within a 15-foot-deep perimeter zone. Results were computed using DOE-2.1E for a typical office building in Chicago, Illinois (Appendix A).

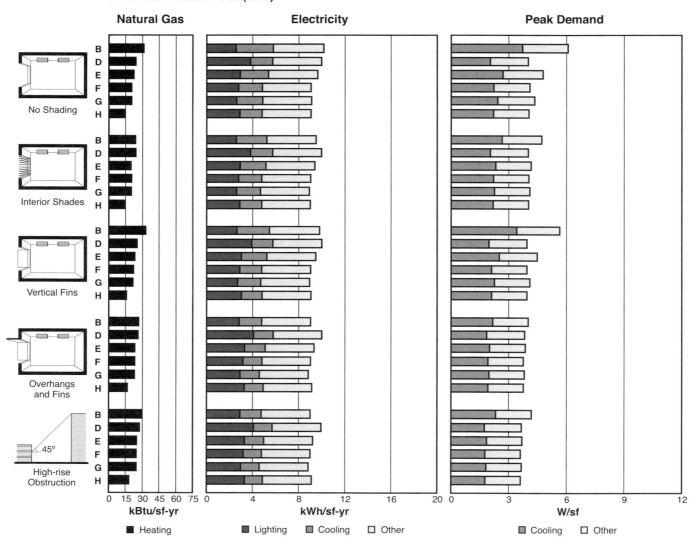

*Window Design for Offices in a Cold Climate*

## Figure 5-71. *Total annual energy use for different shading conditions*

All cases are west-facing and include daylighting controls. Numbers are expressed per square foot within a 15-foot-deep perimeter zone. Results were computed using DOE-2.1E for a typical office building in Chicago, Illinois (Appendix A). Total annual energy use is calculated by multiplying electricity use by 3 and adding heating energy use. This reflects the 3:1 ratio of primary to end use energy for electricity. All window properties are for the whole window. Windows B–H have thermally broken aluminum frames. Window H has an insulated frame. U=U-factor in Btu/hr-sf-°F, SHGC=solar heat gain coefficient, VT=visible transmittance

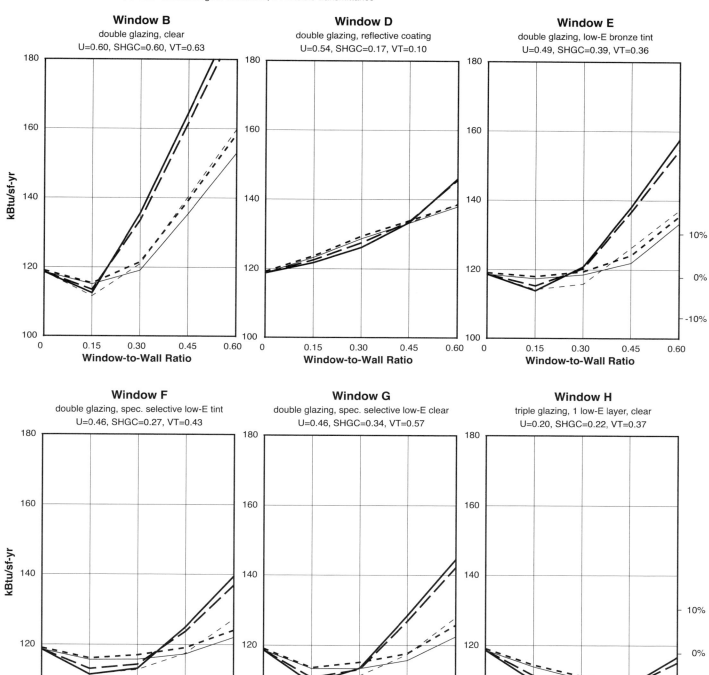

# Figure 5-72. Peak demand for different shading conditions

All cases are west-facing and include daylighting controls. Numbers are expressed in Watts per square foot within a 15-foot-deep perimeter zone. Results were computed using DOE-2.1E for a typical office building in Chicago, Illinois (Appendix A). All window properties are for the whole window. Windows B–H have thermally broken aluminum frames. Window H has an insulated frame. U=U-factor in Btu/hr-sf-°F, SHGC=solar heat gain coefficient, VT=visible transmittance

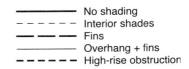

— No shading
− − − − Interior shades
— — Fins
——— Overhang + fins
— — — High-rise obstruction

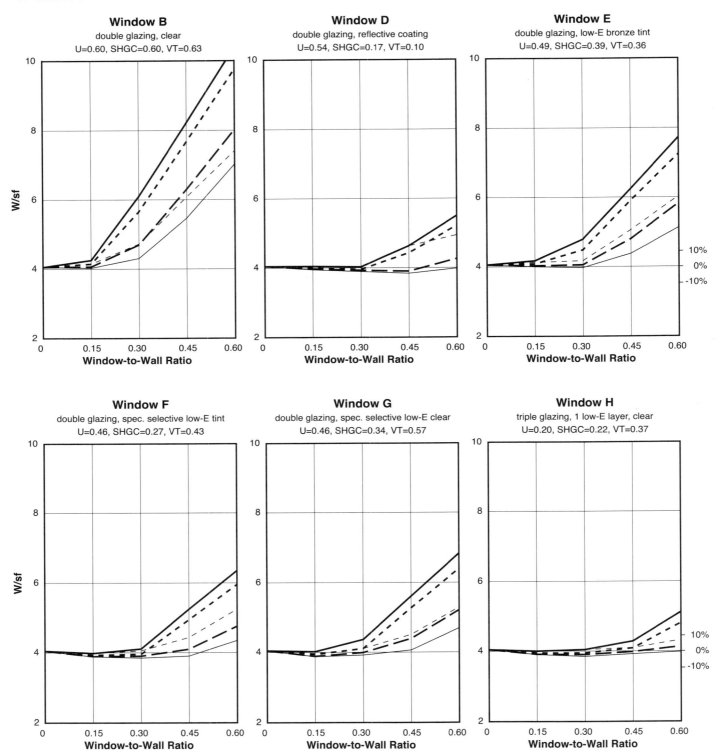

glare index due to interior shades. With these windows, shades are deployed more frequently than for Windows D, F, and H. High-rise obstructions outperform all interior or exterior shades for glare control.

### Effect of Shading Conditions on View

In this analysis, view is completely obscured by interior shades when they are deployed. Interior shade use is dictated by window type, their deployment triggered by a certain level of glare or direct sun. With Windows D, F, and H (WWR=0.30), the view is blocked by interior shades for no more than 2 percent of annual daylit hours. For Windows B, E, and G, view is blocked for 9–16 percent of annual daylit hours (Figure 5-75).

| GLARE INDEX | |
|---|---|
| * | = less than 7 |
| 7 | = imperceptible glare |
| 10 | = just perceptible glare |
| 16 | = just acceptable glare |
| 22 | = just uncomfortable glare |

*Figure 5-73. Average annual daylight illuminance*

Average daylight illuminance is calculated at a point 10 feet from the window. All cases are east-/west-facing. Results were computed using DOE-2.1E for a typical office building in Chicago, Illinois (Appendix A).

*Figure 5-74. Weighted glare index*

Glare index is calculated at a point 5 feet from the window for a person facing the side wall. A lower index is better. All cases are east-/west-facing. Results were computed using DOE-2.1E for a typical office building in Chicago, Illinois (Appendix A).

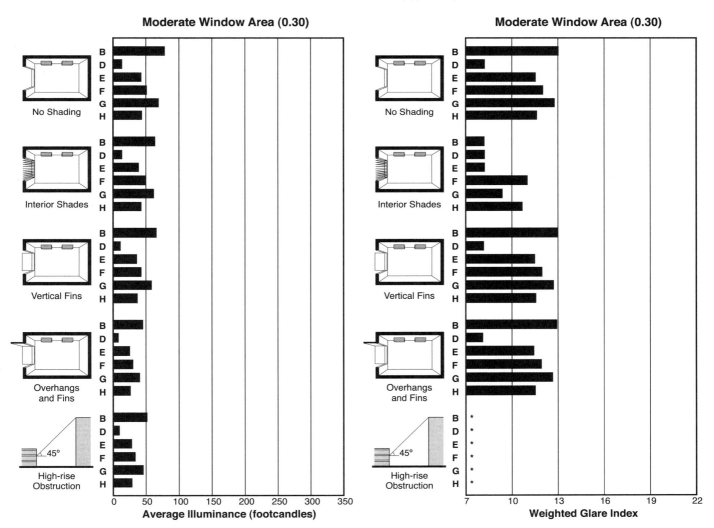

View is also partially obstructed by exterior overhangs and/or fins, or blocked by reflections in the window during periods when exterior light levels are low and the interior glass surface reflectance is relatively high. Vertical fins reduce the unshaded view index by about 1 point for moderate-area windows across all window types (Figure 5-77). Overhangs combined with fins reduce the index by 1.5 points. Window D, given its low VT, has the lowest view index of all window types. All other window types have nearly the same view index (within 0.5 points) for any given shade condition except interior shades. The high-rise obstruction is considered to be part of the view and does not affect the view index. All view indices in Figure 5-75 are in the low to moderate range because of the window area.

*Figure 5-75. View index*

View index is calculated at a point 5 feet from the window. A higher index is better. All cases are east-/west-facing. Results were computed using DOE-2.1E for a typical office building in Chicago, Illinois (Appendix A).

*Figure 5-76. Thermal comfort*

Thermal comfort is calculated at a point 5 feet from the window. A lower PPD is better. All cases are east-/west-facing. Results were computed using DOE-2.1E for a typical office building in Chicago, Illinois (Appendix A).

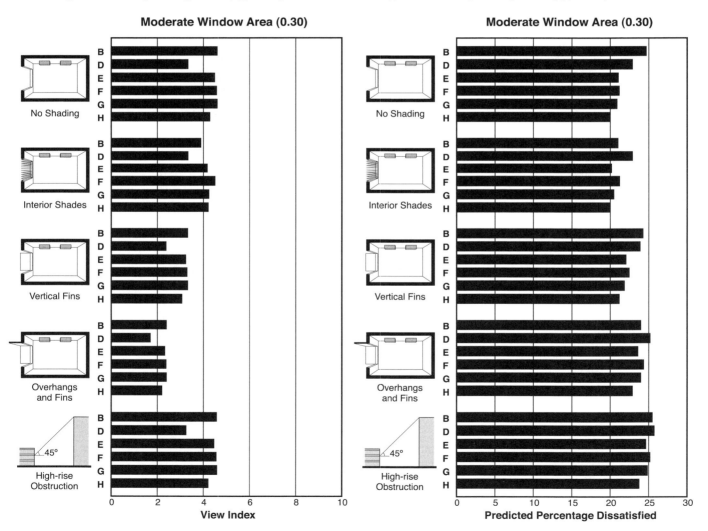

*Window Design for Offices in a Cold Climate*

### Effect of Shading Conditions on Thermal Comfort

Depending on window type, shading can positively or negatively impact thermal comfort (Figures 5-76). Attached exterior shading improves thermal comfort for Window B but discomfort increases with all other windows. Discomfort increases by 3–4 PPD with high-rise obstructions in all cases. For some window types, interior shading improves comfort by 1 PPD. With interior shades or unshaded windows, only Window H attains the 20 PPD criteria of the ASHRAE 55 Standard.

### Effect of Shading Conditions on All Attributes Combined

In Figure 5-77, the relative performance of all six attributes for a range of window shading conditions is shown on a 0-to-10 scale. All cases have daylighting controls and a window-to-wall ratio of 0.30. The impact of window area on the individual performance measures is summarized below.

*Energy:* For all window types except Window B, interior or exterior shades reduce annual energy use slightly (less than 4 percent). For Window B, energy use declines significantly with shades, with overhangs plus fins offering the greatest reduction (12 percent).

*Peak Demand:* Shades significantly reduce peak demand, particularly if the SHGC and U-factor of the window are high (Windows B and E). For low-SHGC windows, there is less effect. For windows facing low- or high-rise obstructions, no shades are recommended.

*Daylight:* All types of shades reduce interior daylight illuminance. Windows B and G provide an average annual illuminance of 50 footcandles if shaded with fins or interior shades.

*Glare:* Glare is of minimal concern with a moderate window size. It can be reduced to below "just perceptible" levels with the use of interior shades.

*View:* All shading systems reduce view. Interior shades minimally impact view. Across all window types, vertical fins lower the view index by about 1 point, while overhangs combines with fins lower it 1.5. All view indices are low because of the moderate window area.

*Thermal comfort:* Thermal discomfort rises with exterior shading except in the case of Window B. Interior shades improve comfort slightly.

For small- to moderately sized high-performance windows (particularly Windows D–H), exterior shading devices such as fins or overhangs combined with fins provide little benefit in a cold climate like Chicago. High-performance Windows F, G, and H combined with interior shades (deployed reliably to control low-angle direct sun and glare) and daylighting controls result in low total annual energy use, controlled peak demand, adequate interior daylight and brightness levels, low levels of discomfort glare, and acceptable thermal comfort. Triple-pane, spectrally selective low-E Window H with interior shades performs best in this climate.

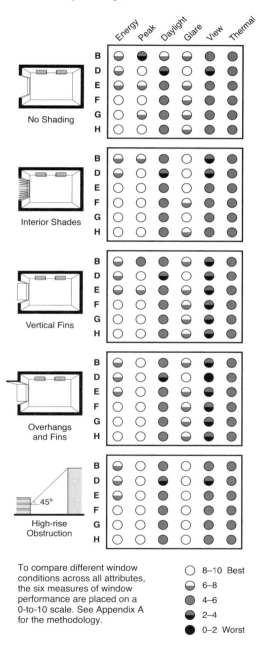

*Figure 5-77. Comparison of multiple attributes by shading condition with moderate window area*
All cases are west-facing and have WWR=0.30 and include daylighting controls. Results are for a typical office building in Chicago, Illinois.

To compare different window conditions across all attributes, the six measures of window performance are placed on a 0-to-10 scale. See Appendix A for the methodology.

○ 8–10 Best
◔ 6–8
◑ 4–6
◕ 2–4
● 0–2 Worst

## The Effects of Shading Conditions in an East- or West-Facing Perimeter Zone with Large Window Area

This section addresses design decisions about shading once a large window area (WWR=0.60) has been chosen.

### Effect of Shading Conditions on Energy Use

Shading diminishes solar heat gains and daylight with the net effect of reducing annual electricity use for large-area windows (WWR=0.60). The greatest reductions occur for Window B, but all windows benefit from shading except Window D.

Shading increases heating energy use in some cases and decreases it in other even though the beneficial solar heat gain is reduced in colder periods (Figure 5-78). This counterintuitive effect occurs because the mechanical system requires more heating energy for reheating chilled air during cooling periods in the unshaded condition. Shading increases annual heating energy use in this cold climate for all shade types except fins.

The net effect on combined electricity and heating energy use is that total annual energy use declines with all shade types compared to an unshaded window (see Figure 5-71 in the previous section). Vertical fins yield the smallest reduction in total energy use (less than 2 percent). Overhangs combined with fins result in the most significant level of reduction (12–15 percent). It should be noted that the vertical fins used in this analysis only extend from the window head to the sill. Continuous vertical fins extending above the window head may perform closer to the deep overhang and fin case, while interior shades perform nearly as well as overhangs with fins (10–11 percent).

If high-rise obstructions are present at the site, shades are not recommended. With a large window area, only Window H achieves total energy use levels that are less than an opaque wall. Windows F and G, with overhangs combined with fins are the next best window choices, yet use 11 percent more total energy per year than Window H with the same shading system. All other shaded window types (Windows B, D and E) result in energy use levels significantly greater than an opaque wall.

### Effect of Shading Conditions on Peak Demand

Shades significantly reduce peak demand for all window types (Figure 5-78). High-rise obstructions result in slightly greater demand levels than a window with overhangs combined with fins, but both of these shade types yield the least peak demand. Therefore, if high-rise obstructions are present, additional attached shades are not recommended, particularly with Window D or H. Otherwise, overhangs combined with fins offer the greatest demand reduction, followed by interior shades (assuming reliable use by occupants). Vertical fins are the least effective. Use of the proper combination of window type, size, and shading can result in significant peak demand reductions, decreased operating costs (particularly in regions where peak demand is penalized with higher rates), and in capital cost savings due to HVAC downsizing.

## Effect of Shading Conditions on Daylight

All types of shading reduce the average annual daylight illuminance (Figure 5-79). Overhangs combined with fins or high-rise obstructions cause the greatest reductions, while vertical fins or interior shades have moderate impact. In all cases, average annual daylight illuminance levels remain near 45 footcandles or above for all window types except Window D.

**Shading Conditions**
Figures 5-78 through 5-83
All cases have WWR=0.60
(10 feet wide x 7.2 feet high)
See Appendix A for details.

Overhang only: 3.4-foot-deep
Overhang + Vertical fins:
   5.0-foot-deep overhang + 2.5 feet deep fins
   (every 5 feet)
High-rise obstruction: Opposing buildings with a
   vertical angle of 45 degrees.

*Figure 5-78. Annual energy use and peak demand comparison by shading type*

All cases are west-facing with a 0.60 window-to-wall ratio and include daylighting controls. Numbers are expressed per square foot within a 15-foot-deep perimeter zone. Results were computed using DOE-2.1E for a typical office building in Chicago, Illinois (Appendix A).

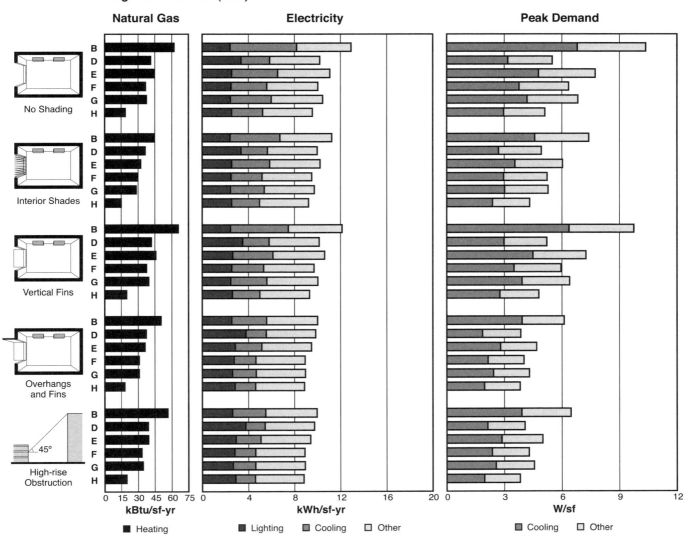

## Effect of Shading Conditions on Glare

For large windows, shades lower the weighted glare index only slightly (Figure 5-80). The translucent interior shades used in this analysis are not sufficient to block the intense glare from low-angle sun. If there are high-rise obstructions, the weighted glare index is significantly improved, particularly for Window D, but for all other window types, the index still remains between "just acceptable" and "just perceptible." The weighted glare index is only nearly "imperceptible" with Window D and a high-rise obstruction.

**GLARE INDEX**

| | |
|---|---|
| * | = less than 7 |
| 7 | = imperceptible glare |
| 10 | = just perceptible glare |
| 16 | = just acceptable glare |
| 22 | = just uncomfortable glare |

*Figure 5-79. Average annual daylight illuminance*

Average daylight illuminance is calculated at a point 10 feet from the window. All cases are east-/west-facing. Results were computed using DOE-2.1E for a typical office building in Chicago, Illinois (Appendix A).

*Figure 5-80. Weighted glare index*

Glare index is calculated at a point 5 feet from the window for a person facing the side wall. A lower index is better. All cases are west-facing with no shading. Results were computed using DOE-2.1E for a typical office building in Chicago, Illinois (Appendix A).

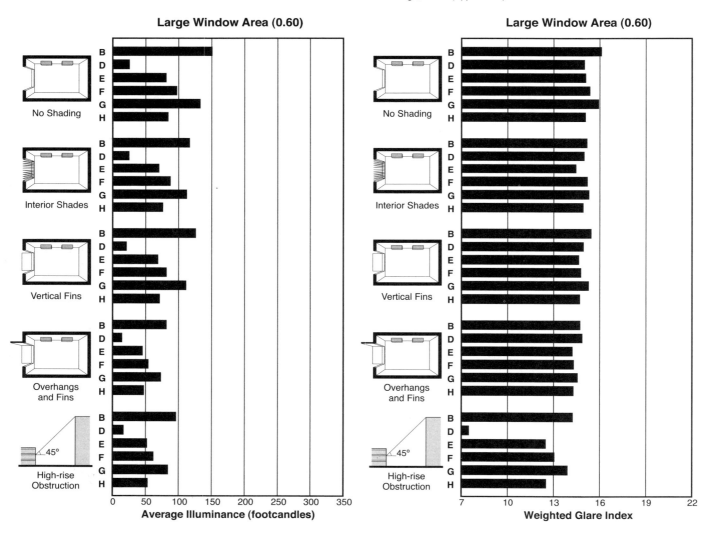

*Window Design for Offices in a Cold Climate*

## Effect of Shading Conditions on View

Of all exterior and interior shading strategies, interior shades provide the least view obstruction if used to control direct sun and glare (particularly for infrequent low-angle sun). The frequency of interior shade use to control direct sun and glare is dictated by window type. High-performance Windows F and H with low SHGC and U-factors can control solar loads for thermal comfort, eliminating the need to use interior shades to control the heat from direct sun. Window D, with a low VT, controls glare well, lessening the need for interior shades. For Window B, view is blocked by interior shades for 17 percent of annual daylit hours, while Windows D, F, and H require interior shades for less than 8 percent of annual daylit hours.

*Figure 5-81. View index*

View index is calculated at a point 10 feet from the window. A higher index is better. All cases are west-facing with no shading. Results were computed using DOE-2.1E for a typical office building in Chicago, Illinois (Appendix A).

*Figure 5-82. Thermal comfort*

Thermal comfort is calculated at a point 5 feet from the window. A lower PPD is better. All cases are west-facing with no shading. Results were computed using DOE-2.1E for a typical office building in Chicago, Illinois (Appendix A).

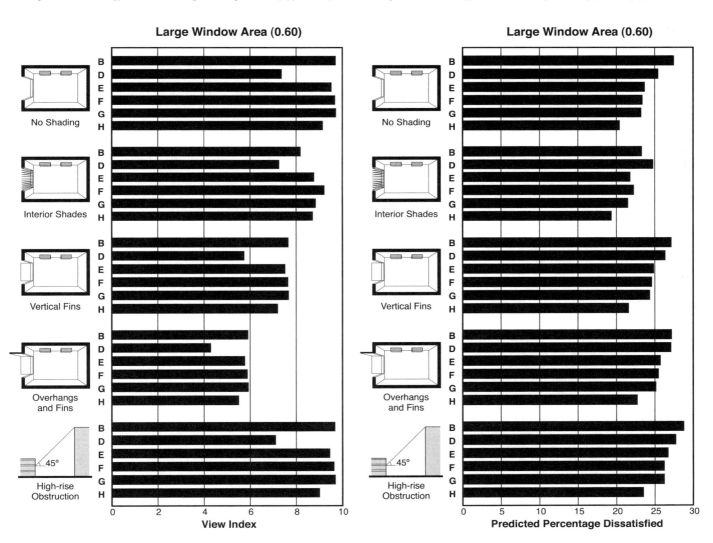

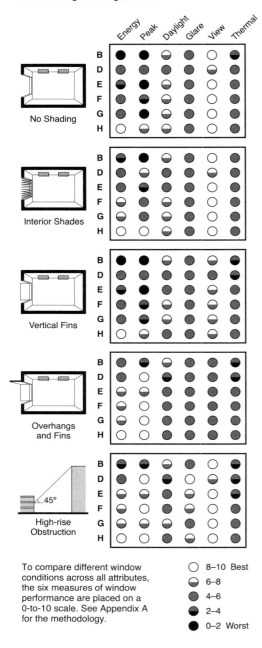

Vertical fins lower the unshaded view index by about 2 points for large-area windows across all window types, while deep overhangs combined with fins lower it by up to 4 points (Figure 5-81). The high-rise obstruction is considered to be part of the view and does not affect the index. Window D with a very low VT has the lowest view index of all window types.

*Effect of Shading Conditions on Thermal Comfort*

Exterior shading affects thermal comfort by blocking direct sun, which has either a positive or negative impact depending on outdoor conditions (Figure 5-82). Vertical fins, overhangs combined with fins, and high-rise obstructions increase thermal discomfort for Windows D–H while interior shades improve thermal comfort. Only Window H with interior shades meets the ASHRAE 55 Standard for PPD less than 20 for this large-area window in cold climates.

*The Effect of Shading Conditions on All Attributes Combined*

In Figure 5-83, the relative performance of all six attributes for a range of window shading conditions is shown on a 0-to-10 scale. All cases have daylighting controls and a window-to-wall ratio of 0.60. The impact of window area on the individual performance measures is summarized below.

*Energy:* With large windows, interior shades are highly recommended if they can be reliably deployed. Otherwise, overhangs combined with fins are recommended. If high-rise obstructions are present, interior or exterior shades will not result in significant energy use reductions.

*Peak Demand:* Shading is recommended to reduce peak demand. Overhangs combined with fins are most effective. If high-rise obstructions are present, shades are not required for peak demand reductions.

*Daylight:* All shade types reduce interior daylight illuminance and brightness levels. Yet, average daylight illuminance remains at sufficient levels (near 50 footcandles) for all window types and shade combinations except Window D.

*Glare:* Shading does not significantly impact glare. Yet high-rise obstructions significantly reduce it. Interior shades, more opaque than the translucent ones used in the analysis, may reduce the weighted glare index to "imperceptible" levels.

*View:* All shading systems result in view reduction. Across all window types and sizes, interior shades reduce the view index by about 1 point, vertical fins alone by 2 points, and overhangs combined with fins reduce the view index by up to 4 points.

*Thermal comfort:* Interior shades improve thermal comfort for most window types. Window H with interior shades performs best thermally.

High-performance Window H with interior shades results in the best balance of the six performance measures—total energy use and peak demand are the lowest of all window and shade combinations, daylight and brightness levels are acceptable, view is not significantly compromised (during periods when the shade is up), and thermal comfort can be addressed. Deep overhangs and fins with Window H provide comparable performance. Windows F and G also perform well with interior shades or deep overhangs and fins on the exterior.

Glare control is not completely achieved with interior or exterior shades for any window type, although it may be better addressed by a more opaque interior shade. However, this may reduce daylight and brightness levels and raise lighting energy use. If there are high-rise obstructions at the site, the unshaded Window H yields the least total annual energy use and peak demand and provides adequate daylight, brightness, and view. Periodic glare and thermal discomfort from low-angle sun can be controlled with interior shades.

# Summary

## Summary of Guidelines for Window Orientation

In a cold climate, south-facing windows perform best in the unshaded condition to reduce energy, peak demand, and glare for moderately sized windows. Orientation has little effect on low-SHGC Windows D and H. With good exterior shading, there is less difference between orientations for all windows, particularly in terms of peak demand.

This section summarizes the window comparisons found in Chapter 5. Guidelines are given for window orientation (Figure 5-84), and then for window type, size and shading within each orientation: north, south, and east/west (Figures 5-85 through 87).

*Figure 5-84. Summary of window performance by orientation*

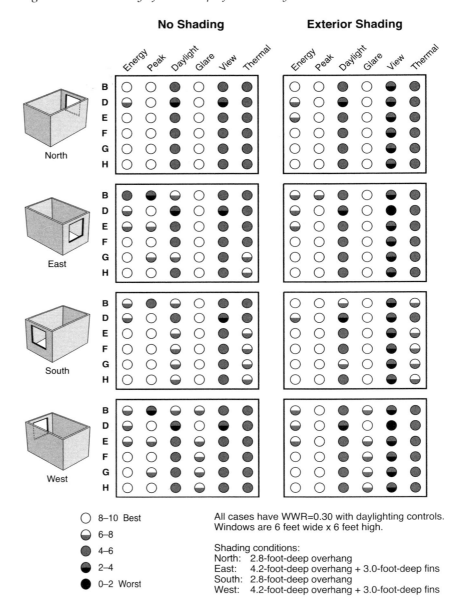

---

**Window B**
double glazing
clear
U=0.60
SHGC=0.60
VT=0.63

**Window F**
double glazing
spec. selective low-E tint
U=0.46
SHGC=0.27
VT=0.43

**Window D**
double glazing
reflective coating
U=0.54
SHGC=0.17
VT=0.10

**Window G**
double glazing
spec. selective low-E clear
U=0.46
SHGC=0.34
VT=0.57

**Window E**
double glazing
low-E, bronze tint
U=0.49
SHGC=0.39
VT=0.36

**Window H**
triple glazing
1 low-E layer, clear
U=0.20
SHGC=0.22
VT=0.37

U=U-factor in Btu/hr-sf-°F
SHGC=solar heat gain coefficient
VT=visible transmittance
All window properties are for the whole window.
Windows B–H have thermally broken aluminum frames. Window H has an insulated frame.

---

○ 8–10 Best
◔ 6–8
◓ 4–6
◕ 2–4
● 0–2 Worst

All cases have WWR=0.30 with daylighting controls. Windows are 6 feet wide x 6 feet high.

Shading conditions:
North: 2.8-foot-deep overhang
East: 4.2-foot-deep overhang + 3.0-foot-deep fins
South: 2.8-foot-deep overhang
West: 4.2-foot-deep overhang + 3.0-foot-deep fins

To compare different window conditions across all attributes, the six measures of window performance are placed on a 0-to-10 scale. See Appendix A for the methodology.

*Figure 5-85. Summary of north-facing window performance*

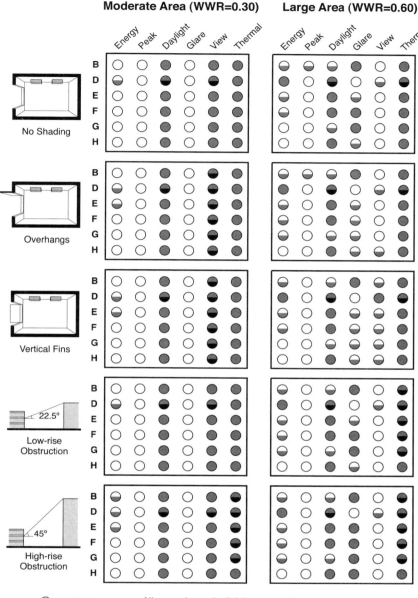

## Summary of Guidelines for North-facing Perimeter Zones

*Daylighting Controls: Recommended.*

Daylighting controls reduce annual electricity use with all window types, although there is less impact with Window D, which has a low visible transmittance (VT). Peak demand also declines with daylighting controls but it is typically small on the north side in any case.

*Window Area: Moderate area recommended.*

Energy use rises with area for all window types, except Window H. Greater window area provides more daylight and view but increases glare problems.

*Shading: No shading recommended.*

Shading has little effect on north-facing perimeter zones with moderate window areas. With larger window areas, glare and peak demand can be improved in some cases with shading. Interior shades may be desirable to control infrequent glare in any case.

*Window Type: Select windows with low U-factor, relatively low SHGC and relatively high VT.*

Triple-pane, low-E Window H performs best across all attributes and window areas. Window G performs nearly as well for moderately sized windows.

## Summary of Guidelines for South-facing Perimeter Zones

*Daylighting Controls: Recommended.*

Daylighting controls reduce total annual energy use and peak demand with all window types, although there is less impact with windows that have a low visible transmittance (VT).

*Window Area: Moderate window area recommended (WWR=0.30 or less).*

Energy use and peak demand rise with window area in an unshaded condition. Greater glazing area provides more daylight and view but increases glare problems.

*Shading for Moderate Window Area: Recommended for some window types.*

Interior and exterior shading devices significantly reduce energy and peak demand for Window B. Shading has less effect on the other windows. High-rise obstructions increase energy use.

*Shading for Large Window Area: Recommended in all cases.*

Overhangs significantly reduce energy and peak demand in all cases. Interior shades also result in a significant improvement in energy use. High-rise obstructions do not offset the need for shading.

*Window Type: Select windows with low U-factor, relatively low SHGC and relatively high VT.*

Triple-pane, low-E Window H performs best across all attributes and window areas. Windows E–G perform nearly as well for moderately sized windows.

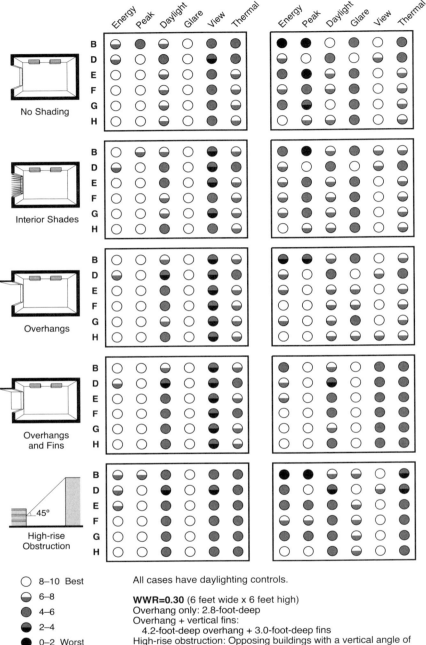

Figure 5-86. Summary of south-facing window performance

○ 8–10 Best
◑ 6–8
◐ 4–6
◕ 2–4
● 0–2 Worst

To compare different window conditions across all attributes, the six measures of window performance are placed on a 0-to-10 scale. See Appendix A for the methodology.

All cases have daylighting controls.

**WWR=0.30** (6 feet wide x 6 feet high)
Overhang only: 2.8-foot-deep
Overhang + vertical fins:
    4.2-foot-deep overhang + 3.0-foot-deep fins
High-rise obstruction: Opposing buildings with a vertical angle of 45 degrees.

**WWR=0.60** (10 feet wide x 7.2 feet high)
Overhang only: 3.4-foot-deep
Overhang + Vertical fins: 5.0-foot-deep overhang + 2.5-foot-deep fins @ 5 feet O.C. or 5.0-foot-deep fins @ 10 feet O.C.
High-rise obstruction: Opposing buildings with a vertical angle of 45 degrees.

*Figure 5-87. Summary of east-/west-facing window performance*

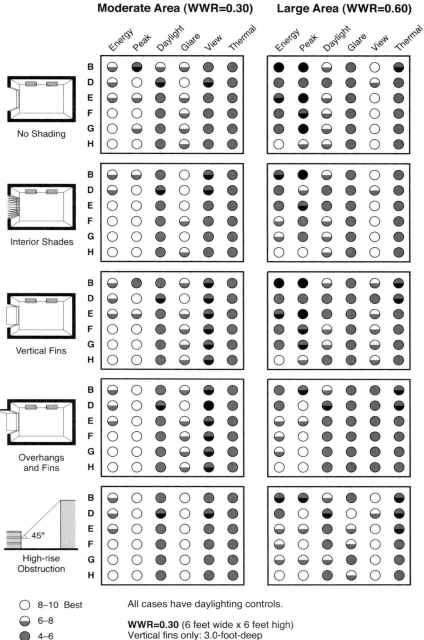

**Moderate Area (WWR=0.30)** **Large Area (WWR=0.60)**

No Shading

Interior Shades

Vertical Fins

Overhangs and Fins

High-rise Obstruction

○ 8–10 Best
◐ 6–8
● 4–6
● 2–4
● 0–2 Worst

To compare different window conditions across all attributes, the six measures of window performance are placed on a 0-to-10 scale. See Appendix A for the methodology.

All cases have daylighting controls.

**WWR=0.30** (6 feet wide x 6 feet high)
Vertical fins only: 3.0-foot-deep
Overhang + vertical fins:
 4.2-foot-deep overhang + 3.0-foot-deep fins
High-rise obstruction: Opposing buildings with a vertical angle of
 45 degrees.

**WWR=0.60** (10 feet wide x 7.2 feet high)
Vertical fins only: 2.5-foot-deep @ 5 feet O.C. or 5.0-foot-deep @
 10 feet O.C.
Overhang + Vertical fins: 5.0-foot-deep overhang + 2.5-foot-deep
 fins @ 5 feet O.C. or 5.0-foot-deep fins @ 10 feet O.C.
High-rise obstruction: Opposing buildings with a vertical angle of
 45 degrees.

## Summary of Guidelines for East- or West-facing Perimeter Zones

*Daylighting Controls: Recommended.*

Daylighting controls reduce annual electrical energy use and peak demand with all window types, although there is less impact with windows that have a low visible transmittance (VT).

*Window Area: Small window area recommended (WWR=0.15 or less).*

Energy use and peak demand rise with window area in an unshaded condition. Greater glazing area provides more daylight and view but increases glare problems.

*Shading for Moderate Window Area: Recommended for some window types.*

Interior and exterior shading devices significantly reduce energy and peak demand for Window B. Interior shades are effective in reducing energy, peak demand, and glare on most windows. Shading has less effect with Windows D, F, and H. High-rise obstructions offset the need for shading for all window types.

*Shading for Large Window Area: Recommended in all cases.*

Interior shades as well as deep overhangs and fins reduce energy and peak demand in all cases. High-rise obstructions offset the need for shading for all window types.

*Window Type: Select windows with low U-factor, relatively low SHGC and relatively high VT.*

Triple-pane, low-E Window H performs best across all attributes and window areas. Windows E–G perform nearly as well for moderately sized windows.

# CHAPTER 6

# Window Design for Offices in a Hot Climate

## Introduction

The analysis in this chapter will guide the designer in making decisions about windows for an office building in Houston, Texas, a representative hot-climate city. The focus is on energy and indoor environmental factors. This information can be placed into a larger decision-making framework that includes appearance, cost, technical requirements, and environmental issues. In a predominantly hot climate, window design and selection must address solar heat gain control and control of plentiful intense daylight.

The sections in the chapter address questions beginning with large-scale issues, later focusing in on space design. Sections initially address the impact of window orientation, with design guidance for north-, south-, and east/west-facing zones. Within each of these sections, the effects of daylighting controls, window size, and shading devices are analyzed. Window design and selection guidelines for offices in Houston are summarized in the final section.

Throughout this chapter, a set of six representative window types is used for comparison purposes. A single-pane clear window is used as a base case in this climate. Window types are discussed in detail in Chapter 3. Annual energy use and peak demand per square foot of perimeter floor area are shown for each set of conditions being compared. This is followed by a comparison of performance measures for daylight, glare, view, and thermal comfort.

This analysis pertains only to office space perimeter zones (the area of a building within 15 feet of the exterior facade). The degree to which these perimeter zones contribute to overall building energy use and peak demand depends on the size, shape, and use of the whole building. See Chapter 7 for an analysis of a school in this climate.

The six components of energy and interior environment that are part of this analysis are described in Chapter 2 (additional details of the methodology are given in Appendix A). All parameters were computed using DOE-2.1E, a building energy simulation program, for a typical office building in Houston, Texas.

*Figure 6-1. 1500 Louisiana in Houston, TX. Architect: Cesar Pelli & Associates; Photo: Courtesy of Viracon; Photo: Wes Thompson*

# Orientation

This section addresses the question of how window orientation impacts energy and indoor environmental performance in a hot climate city like Houston.

## Effect of Orientation on Energy Use

Solar heat gains, which vary by orientation, dominate energy use in a hot climate. When determining perimeter zone orientation in schematic design, conventional rules-of-thumb come to mind—favor north-facing zones, avoid east- and west-facing zones, and shade south-facing zones. Figure 6-2 clearly illustrates that in the unshaded condition, a north orientation performs best with regard to electricity use for some window types (Windows A, C, and E). On the other hand, as SHGC falls, variation between orientations is less (Windows F and H), and with very low-SHGC Window D, there is virtually no variation. Overall, with moderate window sizes there is relatively little difference in annual electricity use between the east-, south-, and west-facing perimeter zones for any window type.

*Figure 6-2. Annual electricity and heating energy use comparison by orientation with no shading*

All cases have a 0.30 window-to-wall ratio and include daylighting controls. Numbers are expressed per square foot within a 15-foot-deep perimeter zone. Results were computed using DOE-2.1E for a typical office building in Houston, Texas (Appendix A).

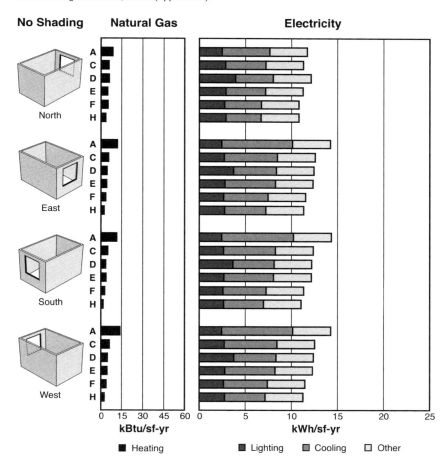

**Window A**
single glazing
clear
U=1.25
SHGC=0.72
VT=0.71

**Window C**
double glazing
bronze tint
U=0.60
SHGC=0.42
VT=0.38

**Window D**
double glazing
reflective coating
U=0.54
SHGC=0.17
VT=0.10

**Window E**
double glazing
low-E tint
U=0.49
SHGC=0.39
VT=0.36

**Window F**
double glazing
spec. selective low-E tint
U=0.46
SHGC=0.27
VT=0.43

**Window H**
triple glazing
1 low-E layer, clear
U=0.20
SHGC=0.22
VT=0.37

U=U-factor in Btu/hr-sf-°F
SHGC=solar heat gain coefficient
VT=visible transmittance
All window properties are for the whole window.
Windows C–H have thermally broken aluminum frames. Window A has an aluminum frame.

In a relatively hot climate like Houston, heating energy use is not a major concern, but a small amount may be required in perimeter zones. Windows influence heating energy use in three ways—a lower U-factor decreases heat loss, a higher SHGC increases solar heat gains, and a higher VT increases daylight, which may reduce electric lighting and associated heat gains, thereby raising heating needs. Figure 6-2 illustrates that when these three factors combine, for a moderate window area (WWR=0.30), orientation has relatively little effect on heating energy use in Houston.

Although south-, east-, and west-facing windows appear to perform similarly, remember that south-facing windows are easier to shade with exterior attachments, like shallow overhangs. If further along in the design process, after window orientation has been determined, differences in energy use due to orientation can be minimized not only by selecting the proper window but by exterior shading as well. Figure 6-3 illustrates that for a moderate window area, exterior shading can nearly eliminate variations, in terms of energy consumption, between orientations.

*Figure 6-3. Annual electricity and heating energy use comparison by orientation with exterior shading*

All cases have a 0.30 window-to-wall ratio and include daylighting controls. Numbers are expressed per square foot within a 15-foot-deep perimeter zone. Results were computed using DOE-2.1E for a typical office building in Houston, Texas (Appendix A).

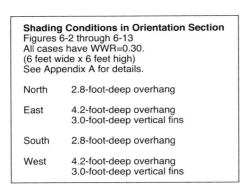

**Shading Conditions in Orientation Section**
Figures 6-2 through 6-13
All cases have WWR=0.30.
(6 feet wide x 6 feet high)
See Appendix A for details.

| | |
|---|---|
| North | 2.8-foot-deep overhang |
| East | 4.2-foot-deep overhang 3.0-foot-deep vertical fins |
| South | 2.8-foot-deep overhang |
| West | 4.2-foot-deep overhang 3.0-foot-deep vertical fins |

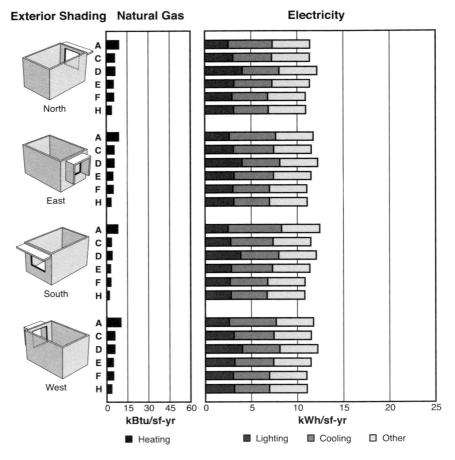

*Window Design for Offices in a Hot Climate*

## Figure 6-4. *Total annual energy use for different orientations*

All cases include daylighting controls. Numbers are expressed per square foot within a 15-foot-deep perimeter zone. Results were computed using DOE-2.1E for a typical office building in Houston, Texas (Appendix A). Total annual energy use is calculated by multiplying electricity use by 3 and adding heating energy use. This reflects the 3:1 ratio of primary to end use energy for electricity. All window properties are for the whole window. Windows C–H have thermally broken aluminum frames. Window H has an insulated frame. U=U-factor in Btu/hr-sf-°F SHGC=solar heat gain coefficient, VT=visible transmittance

North, no shading
North, shading
South, no shading
South, shading
East/West, no shading
East/West, shading

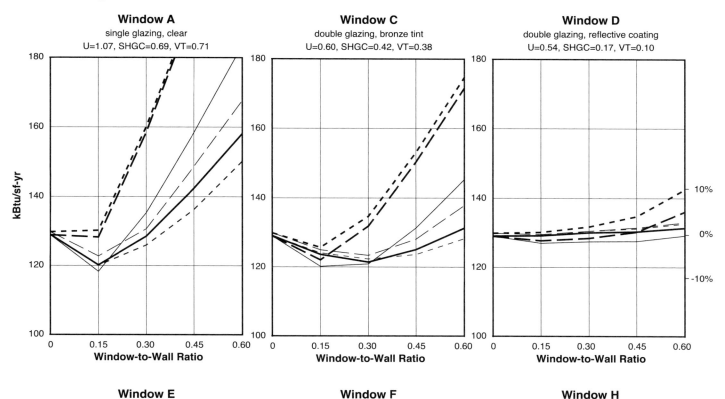

**Window A**
single glazing, clear
U=1.07, SHGC=0.69, VT=0.71

**Window C**
double glazing, bronze tint
U=0.60, SHGC=0.42, VT=0.38

**Window D**
double glazing, reflective coating
U=0.54, SHGC=0.17, VT=0.10

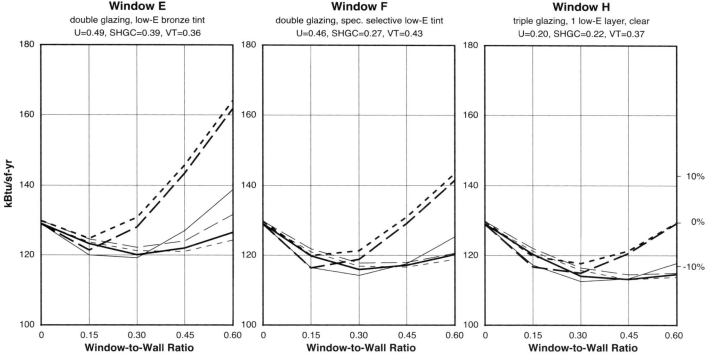

**Window E**
double glazing, low-E bronze tint
U=0.49, SHGC=0.39, VT=0.36

**Window F**
double glazing, spec. selective low-E tint
U=0.46, SHGC=0.27, VT=0.43

**Window H**
triple glazing, 1 low-E layer, clear
U=0.20, SHGC=0.22, VT=0.37

**Window A**
single glazing
clear
U=1.25
SHGC=0.72
VT=0.71

**Window C**
double glazing
bronze tint
U=0.60
SHGC=0.42
VT=0.38

**Window D**
double glazing
reflective coating
U=0.54
SHGC=0.17
VT=0.10

**Window E**
double glazing
low-E tint
U=0.49
SHGC=0.39
VT=0.36

**Window F**
double glazing
spec. selective low-E tint
U=0.46
SHGC=0.27
VT=0.43

**Window H**
triple glazing
1 low-E layer, clear
U=0.20
SHGC=0.22
VT=0.37

U=U-factor in Btu/hr-sf-°F
SHGC=solar heat gain coefficient
VT=visible transmittance
All window properties are for the whole window.
Windows C–H have thermally broken aluminum
frames. Window A has an aluminum frame.

Figure 6-4 shows the total annual energy use (combined heating and electricity) for each of the six window types over a range of window areas. As window area rises, the variation in energy use between orientations increases as well. While orientation makes little difference with Windows D, F, and H at a moderate window area (WWR=0.30), it is more of a factor with larger window areas (WWR=0.60). For example, with spectrally selective tinted Window F, the variation in total annual energy use between north- and south-facing zones with moderately sized windows (WWR=0.30) is 3 percent, while with large windows (WWR=0.60 ) it is 18 percent. With exterior shading, variation declines between orientations. For Windows F and H with large window area (WWR=0.60), annual energy use for a west-facing window with a deep overhang and fins performs similarly to an unshaded, north-facing window.

*Figure 6-5. Peak demand comparison by orientation*

All cases have a 0.30 window-to-wall ratio and include daylighting controls. Numbers are expressed per square foot within a 15-foot-deep perimeter zone. Results were computed using DOE-2.1E for a typical office building in Houston, Texas (Appendix A).

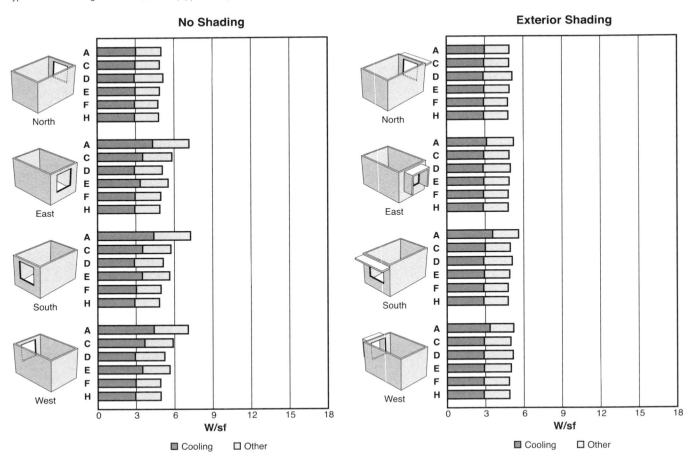

*Window Design for Offices in a Hot Climate*

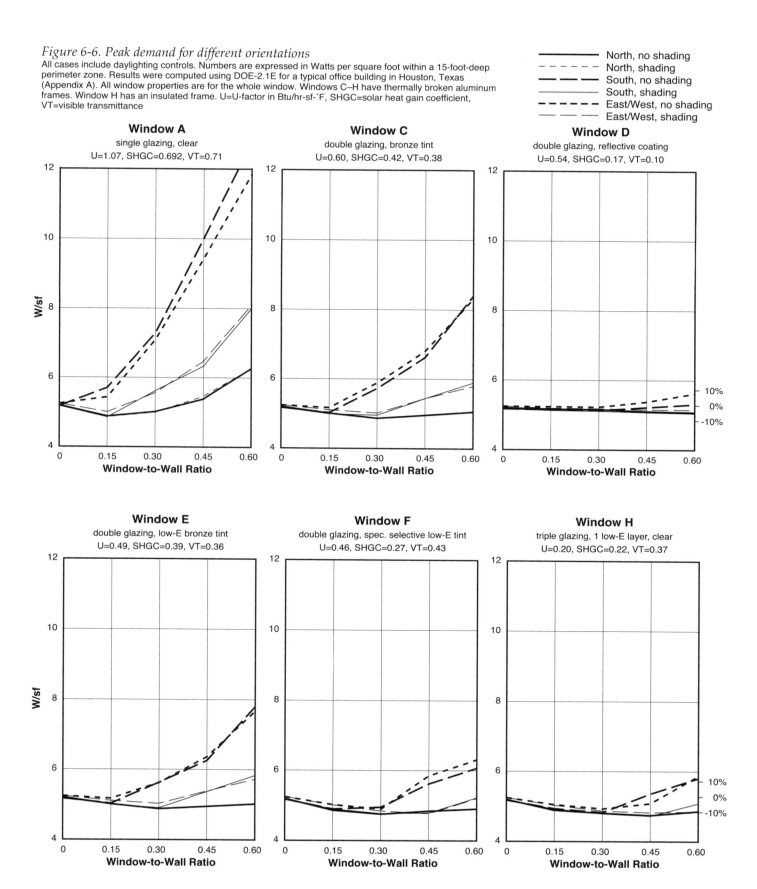

Figure 6-6. Peak demand for different orientations

All cases include daylighting controls. Numbers are expressed in Watts per square foot within a 15-foot-deep perimeter zone. Results were computed using DOE-2.1E for a typical office building in Houston, Texas (Appendix A). All window properties are for the whole window. Windows C–H have thermally broken aluminum frames. Window H has an insulated frame. U=U-factor in Btu/hr-sf-°F, SHGC=solar heat gain coefficient, VT=visible transmittance

**Legend:**
- North, no shading
- North, shading
- South, no shading
- South, shading
- East/West, no shading
- East/West, shading

**Window A**
single glazing, clear
U=1.07, SHGC=0.692, VT=0.71

**Window C**
double glazing, bronze tint
U=0.60, SHGC=0.42, VT=0.38

**Window D**
double glazing, reflective coating
U=0.54, SHGC=0.17, VT=0.10

**Window E**
double glazing, low-E bronze tint
U=0.49, SHGC=0.39, VT=0.36

**Window F**
double glazing, spec. selective low-E tint
U=0.46, SHGC=0.27, VT=0.43

**Window H**
triple glazing, 1 low-E layer, clear
U=0.20, SHGC=0.22, VT=0.37

*Orientation*

227

| Window A | Window E |
|---|---|
| single glazing | double glazing |
| clear | low-E tint |
| U=1.25 | U=0.49 |
| SHGC=0.72 | SHGC=0.39 |
| VT=0.71 | VT=0.36 |
| **Window C** | **Window F** |
| double glazing | double glazing |
| bronze tint | spec. selective low-E tint |
| U=0.60 | U=0.46 |
| SHGC=0.42 | SHGC=0.27 |
| VT=0.38 | VT=0.43 |
| **Window D** | **Window H** |
| double glazing | triple glazing |
| reflective coating | 1 low-E layer, clear |
| U=0.54 | U=0.20 |
| SHGC=0.17 | SHGC=0.22 |
| VT=0.10 | VT=0.37 |

U=U-factor in Btu/hr-sf-°F
SHGC=solar heat gain coefficient
VT=visible transmittance
All window properties are for the whole window.
Windows C–H have thermally broken aluminum
frames. Window A has an aluminum frame.

## Effect of Orientation on Peak Demand

Peak electricity demand follows patterns similar to annual energy use, which was discussed in the previous section. In hot climates, solar heat gains drive demand, which is largely proportional to window area. Window SHGC, U-factor, and shading, if present, impact exactly how the effectively the window addresses the gains. As shown in Figure 6-5, for moderately sized unshaded windows, a north-facing orientation clearly has the lowest peak demand for Windows A, C, and E, while there is relatively little difference between orientations for Windows D, F, and G, which have a low SHGC.

Variation in peak demand between orientations increases significantly with window area for all unshaded window types (Figure 6-6), although the impacts are greater with Windows A, C, and E. Exterior shading reduces peak demand variations between orientations. For moderately sized windows of any type, peak demand declines with shading to the point where variation between orientations is negligible. With large windows, variations also decline, but they are not eliminated for Windows A, C, and E.

*Figure 6-7. Average annual daylight illuminance comparison by orientation*

Average annual daylight illuminance is calculated at a point 10 feet from the window. All cases have a moderate window area (WWR=0.30). Results were computed using DOE-2.1E for a typical office building in Houston, Texas (Appendix A).

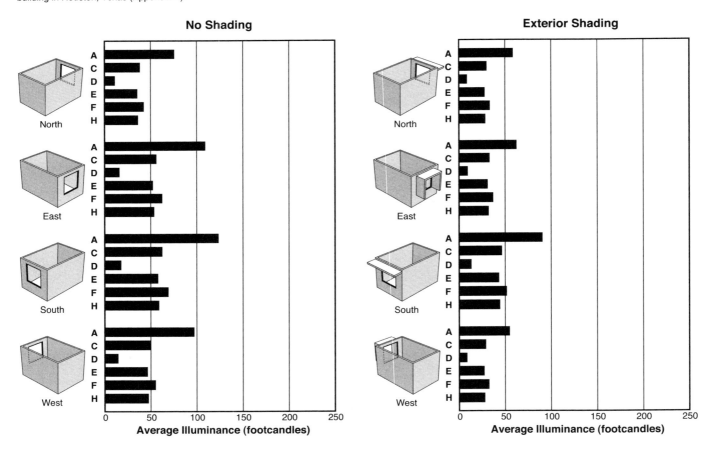

*Window Design for Offices in a Hot Climate*

Utility rates based on peak demand are most applicable during mid- to late- afternoon summer hours, exactly when south- and west-facing zones are most vulnerable. Peak charges can result in electricity costs that are three to five times greater that off-peak periods, so it is worthwhile to consider rate schedules and design affected facades accordingly. It is also noteworthy that peak demand is in direct proportion to the cooling capacity of the building's mechanical system, which impacts capital costs.

### Effect of Orientation on Daylight

Orientation can have a significant effect on interior daylight illuminance levels. Generally, south-oriented perimeter zones have more direct sun and daylight over the year than any other orientation (Figure 6-7). North-facing zones have a lower average annual illuminance than those facing east or west. All orientations provide at least 30 footcandles (fc) on average at a point 10 feet from the window for most window types at WWR=0.30. The impact of orientation is greatest for windows with high VT and least for windows that have low VT (Window D). With exterior shading, differences in average illuminance between orientations declines in all cases (Figure 6-7). The effect of other shading options is shown later in the chapter.

```
GLARE INDEX
 *  = less than 7
 7  = imperceptible glare
10  = just perceptible glare
16  = just acceptable glare
22  = just uncomfortable glare
```

*Figure 6-8. Weighted glare index comparison by orientation*

Weighted glare index is calculated at a point 5 feet from the window for a person facing the side wall. A lower index is better. All cases have a moderate window area (WWR=0.30). Results were computed using DOE-2.1E for a typical office building in Houston, Texas (Appendix A).

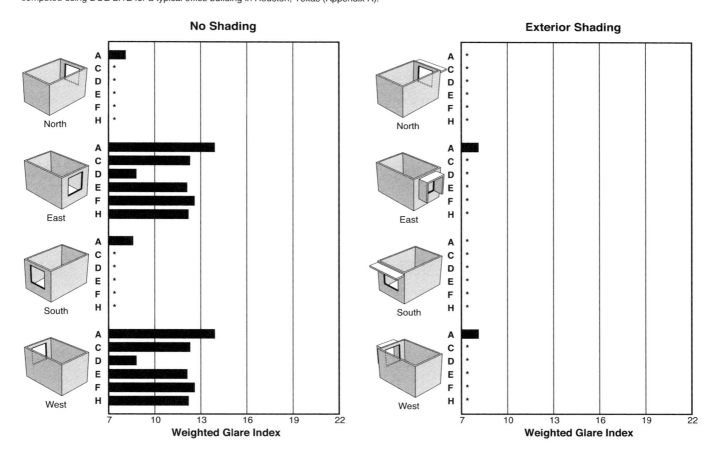

**Window A**
single glazing
clear
U=1.25
SHGC=0.72
VT=0.71

**Window E**
double glazing
low-E tint
U=0.49
SHGC=0.39
VT=0.36

**Window C**
double glazing
bronze tint
U=0.60
SHGC=0.42
VT=0.38

**Window F**
double glazing
spec. selective low-E tint
U=0.46
SHGC=0.27
VT=0.43

**Window D**
double glazing
reflective coating
U=0.54
SHGC=0.17
VT=0.10

**Window H**
triple glazing
1 low-E layer, clear
U=0.20
SHGC=0.22
VT=0.37

U=U-factor in Btu/hr-sf-°F
SHGC=solar heat gain coefficient
VT=visible transmittance
All window properties are for the whole window.
Windows C–H have thermally broken aluminum
frames. Window A has an aluminum frame.

### Effect of Orientation on Glare

North-facing perimeter zones have a low weighted glare index, as illustrated in Figure 6-8. The indices are also low for south-facing windows, with the exception of high-VT Window A. Glare for most windows in the east- and west-facing zones is higher than north and south zones because the former experience low angle sun for extended periods in the early morning and late afternoon. With exterior shading on the east and west, the weighted glare index does not decline significantly because low angle sun still penetrates. Figure 6-8 also illustrates that when overhangs are added to the south, and deep overhangs combined with vertical fins are added to the east and west, glare declines to the point that there is virtually no difference between orientations.

In general, moderate window areas (WWR=0.30) such as these cases result in a relatively low weighted glare index. Glare for the darker, reflective Window D remains low on all orientations because of its very low visible transmittance. The modeling reveals the strong correlation between glare and window size, with later sections illustrating that glare is of much greater concern with larger windows.

*Figure 6-9. View index comparison by orientation*

View index is calculated at a point 10 feet from the window. A higher index is better. All cases have a moderate window area (WWR=0.30). Results were computed using DOE-2.1E for a typical office building in Houston, Texas (Appendix A).

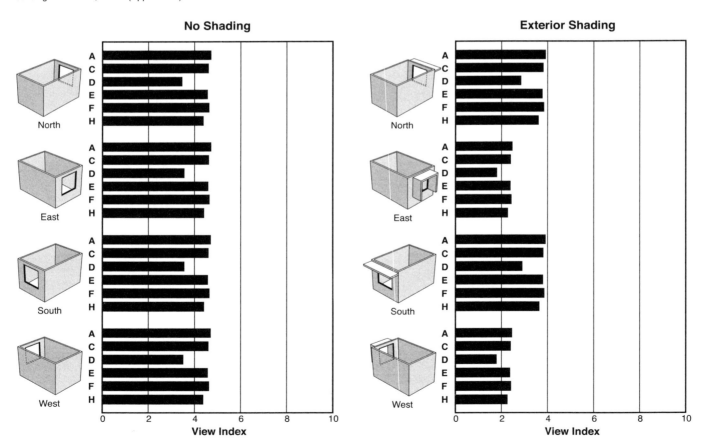

*Window Design for Offices in a Hot Climate*

## Effect of Orientation on View

Orientation does not impact view (Figure 6-9). The appropriate shading for each orientation, however, does impact view. Exterior shading devices such as overhangs reduce view slightly in the north- and south-facing cases. The deeper overhangs and vertical fins on the east- and west-facing cases have a greater effect on view.

## Effect of Orientation on Thermal Comfort

The effect of orientation on thermal comfort with unshaded windows depends on the window type. For most double- and triple-glazed windows (C–H in Figure 6-10) with a moderate area (WWR=0.30), thermal comfort is worse on the north and best on the south, although the index varies no more than 5 predicted percentage dissatisfied (PPD) for a particular window. With the clear single-pane Window A, thermal comfort on the east, south, and west is far worse than on the north (Figure 6-10). Exterior shading affects thermal comfort by blocking direct sun, which has either a positive or negative impact depending on outdoor conditions. If it is cold outside, the direct sun might be welcome, but that same sun might be uncomfortable if hot.

| **Window A** | **Window E** |
|---|---|
| single glazing | double glazing |
| clear | low-E tint |
| U=1.25 | U=0.49 |
| SHGC=0.72 | SHGC=0.39 |
| VT=0.71 | VT=0.36 |
| **Window C** | **Window F** |
| double glazing | double glazing |
| bronze tint | spec. selective low-E tint |
| U=0.60 | U=0.46 |
| SHGC=0.42 | SHGC=0.27 |
| VT=0.38 | VT=0.43 |
| **Window D** | **Window H** |
| double glazing | triple glazing |
| reflective coating | 1 low-E layer, clear |
| U=0.54 | U=0.20 |
| SHGC=0.17 | SHGC=0.22 |
| VT=0.10 | VT=0.37 |

U=U-factor in Btu/hr-sf-°F
SHGC=solar heat gain coefficient
VT=visible transmittance
All window properties are for the whole window.
Windows C–H have thermally broken aluminum frames. Window A has an aluminum frame.

*Figure 6-10. Thermal comfort comparison by orientation*

Thermal comfort is calculated at a point 5 feet from the window. A lower predicted percentage dissatisfied (PPD) is better. All cases have a moderate window area (WWR=0.30). Results were computed using DOE-2.1E for a typical office building in Houston, Texas (Appendix A).

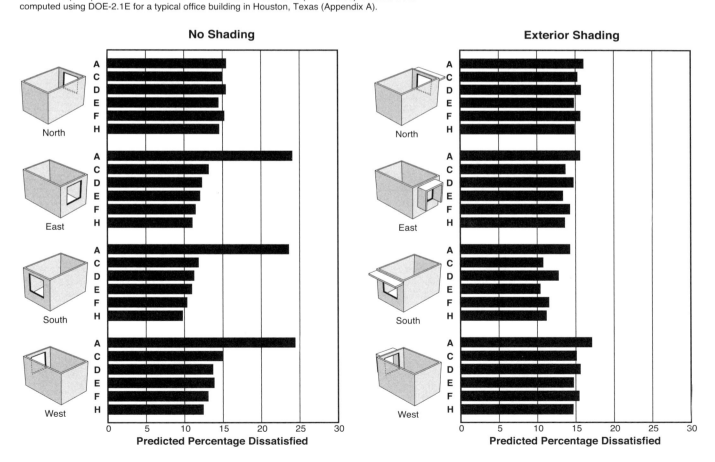

Overall, in most cases the PPD does not change significantly for the double- and triple-glazed windows. Exterior shading does improve thermal comfort considerably for Window A, by up to 10 PPD on the south facade.

### Effect of Orientation on All Attributes Combined

In Figure 6-11, the relative performance of all six attributes for all orientations is shown on a 0-to-10 scale. The window area for all cases in Figure 6-13 is moderate (WWR=0.30). The impact of orientation on each of the individual performance measures is summarized below.

*Energy:* With Windows A, C, and E, north-facing orientations use less energy than other orientations. With low-SHGC Windows D, F, and H, orientation has little effect at moderate areas (WWR=0.30), more with greater areas. Exterior shading diminishes energy use variation between orientations for Windows A, C, and E. Shading has very little impact on energy use with Windows D, F, and H at

### Figure 6-11. Comparison of multiple attributes by orientation

All cases have a moderate window area (WWR=0.30) and include daylighting controls. Results are for a typical office building in Houston, Texas. To compare different window conditions across all attributes, the six measures of window performance are placed on a 0-to-10 scale. See Appendix A for the methodology.

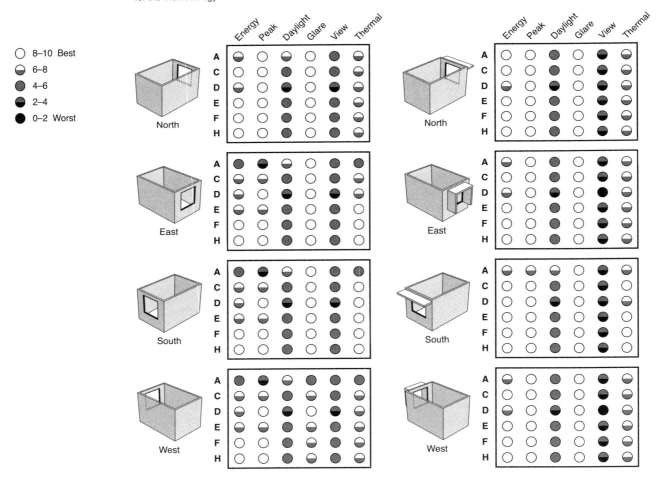

moderate window areas. Energy indices are in the higher range (6–10) in most cases in Figure 6-11 because of the moderate window area.

*Peak Demand:* For window types A, C, and E, north-facing orientations perform better than others. There is less impact on peak demand between different orientations with Windows D, F, and H at a moderate window area (WWR=0.30), but it increases with greater area (Figure 6-6). In most cases, exterior shading reduces peak demand between orientations. Windows F and H perform best overall, with the moderate window area maintaining the peak demand index in Figure 6-11 within the higher range (6–10) for all cases except unshaded Window A.

*Daylight:* Due to direct sun, south-facing zones have greater interior daylight illuminance levels on average than other orientations. North-facing orientations have the least. The impact of orientation on daylight greater with high-VT windows (Window A) and least with low-VT windows (Window D). In reality, north-facing zones will probably capture more useful daylight than other orientations since there is less need to deploy interior shades to control glare and direct sun. Exterior shading reduces daylight but the index in Figure 6-11 remains in the middle range (4-6) for most cases.

*Glare:* For a moderate window area, discomfort glare for north- and south-facing orientations is not problematic. East and west orientations are much worse, given the low sun angles they experience. Exterior shading can reduce glare problems to some extent, as can a glazing like that in Window D.

*View:* View is unaffected by orientation alone. Shading elements, such as overhangs and vertical fins, do reduce view, and these devices are informed by orientation. Glazing also impacts view. Window D has the lowest index because of its low VT. All view indices shown in Figure 6-11 are in the middle range because of the moderate window area.

*Thermal comfort:* For double- and triple-glazed windows (Windows C–H), north-facing zones are less comfortable than other orientations, but differences are small. Exterior shading has little effect. The north orientation is clearly superior to the others for clear single-glazed Window A, however differences significantly decline with exterior shading.

These results reveal that unshaded north-facing perimeter zones yield lower energy use and peak demand without compromising other performance measures when compared to other unshaded orientations in a hot climate like Houston. These differences in orientation can be reduced or eliminated with the proper combination of window type, area, and shading devices. Windows F and H perform best in all cases and are relatively unaffected by orientation. With proper design and window selection, a space may be oriented in any direction without significant energy penalty.

While the advantages of an unshaded north orientation in Houston generally hold true for any window area, the magnitude of the effect corresponds directly to the window area. There is a more significant difference between orientations with larger window areas, as illustrated in later sections.

# North-facing Perimeter Zones

Once the decision has been made to orient perimeter zones to the north, the designer must examine more detailed issues related to window design and selection. The following sections address how lighting controls, window area, and shading affect performance.

## The Effect of Lighting Controls on Annual Energy Use and Peak Demand in a North-facing Perimeter Zone

North-facing zones offer good potential for daylight controls because of the quality of daylight and less potential use of interior shades. In hot climates like Houston, electricity use always declines by installing controls that dim or turn off electric lighting when there is sufficient daylight (Figure 6-12). With daylighting controls, lighting energy use falls to a greater degree as VT rises, while cooling energy use falls slightly because of reduced heat gain from the lights. Since heating energy use is small in Houston, daylighting controls have no significant effect.

Figure 6-13 illustrates that without daylighting controls in a space, total annual energy use increases with window area in proportion to admitted solar heat gains. It rises at a faster rate with higher SHGC and U-factor windows. With daylighting controls, even large window areas (WWR=0.60) generally outperform opaque walls (WWR=0) in terms of total annual energy use.

Daylighting controls also reduce peak electricity demand for all window types (Figure 6-12). Without daylighting controls, Window D with the lowest SHGC has the least peak demand. With daylighting controls, Window D has the highest peak demand at a moderate window area (WWR=0.30). Figure 6-14 illustrates that without daylighting controls, peak demand rises with greater window area.

---

**Window A**
single glazing
clear
U=1.25
SHGC=0.72
VT=0.71

**Window E**
double glazing
low-E tint
U=0.49
SHGC=0.39
VT=0.36

**Window C**
double glazing
bronze tint
U=0.60
SHGC=0.42
VT=0.38

**Window F**
double glazing
spec. selective low-E tint
U=0.46
SHGC=0.27
VT=0.43

**Window D**
double glazing
reflective coating
U=0.54
SHGC=0.17
VT=0.10

**Window H**
triple glazing
1 low-E layer, clear
U=0.20
SHGC=0.22
VT=0.37

U=U-factor in Btu/hr-sf-°F
SHGC=solar heat gain coefficient
VT=visible transmittance
All window properties are for the whole window.
Windows C–H have thermally broken aluminum frames. Window A has an aluminum frame.

---

*Figure 6-12. Annual energy use and peak demand comparison by lighting system*

All cases are north-facing with a 0.30 window-to-wall ratio and no shading. Numbers are expressed per square foot within a 15-foot-deep perimeter zone. Results were computed using DOE-2.1E for a typical office building in Houston, Texas (Appendix A).

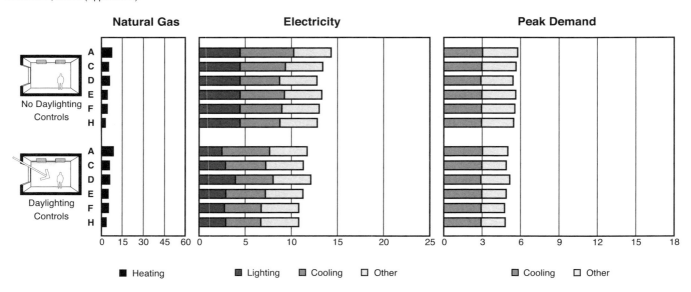

*Window Design for Offices in a Hot Climate*

*Figure 6-13. Total annual energy use comparison by lighting system*

All cases are north-facing with no shading. Numbers are expressed per square foot within a 15-foot-deep perimeter zone. Results were computed using DOE-2.1E for a typical office building in Houston, Texas (Appendix A).

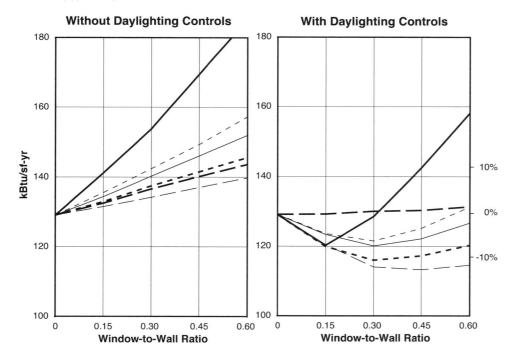

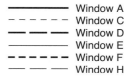

Total annual energy use is calculated by multiplying electricity use by 3 and adding heating energy use. This reflects the 3:1 ratio of primary to end use energy for electricity.

*Figure 6-14. Peak demand comparison by lighting system*

All cases are north-facing with no shading. Numbers are expressed in Watts per square foot within a 15-foot-deep perimeter zone. Results were computed using DOE-2.1E for a typical office building in Houston, Texas (Appendix A).

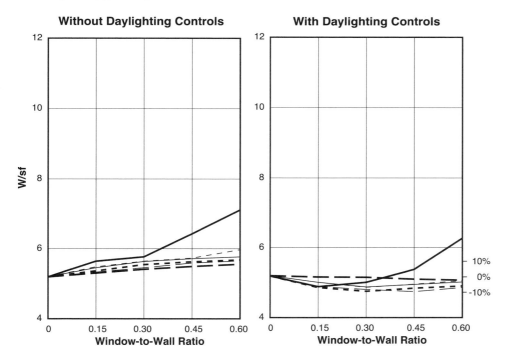

*North-facing Perimeter Zones*

**Window A**
single glazing
clear
U=1.25
SHGC=0.72
VT=0.71

**Window C**
double glazing
bronze tint
U=0.60
SHGC=0.42
VT=0.38

**Window D**
double glazing
reflective coating
U=0.54
SHGC=0.17
VT=0.10

**Window E**
double glazing
low-E tint
U=0.49
SHGC=0.39
VT=0.36

**Window F**
double glazing
spec. selective low-E tint
U=0.46
SHGC=0.27
VT=0.43

**Window H**
triple glazing
1 low-E layer, clear
U=0.20
SHGC=0.22
VT=0.37

U=U-factor in Btu/hr-sf-°F
SHGC=solar heat gain coefficient
VT=visible transmittance
All window properties are for the whole window.
Windows C–H have thermally broken aluminum
frames. Window A has an aluminum frame.

However, with controls, the lowest peak demand falls between WWR=0.30–0.45 for all windows except Window A. Although the north-facing zone has lower peak demand levels than other orientations, it is important to remember that the late afternoon summer sun (the low-angle direct sun from the sky's northwest quadrant) can escalate total building peak demand.

While all the energy-use comparisons in this section show significant savings by using daylighting controls, there is a range of possible performance (see Chapter 2). Lighting controls do not affect daylight, view, glare, and thermal comfort.

## The Effect of Window Area in a North-facing Zone

This section addresses the question of optimal window area on a north-facing perimeter zone. Only the unshaded condition is examined here. Later sections show how shading can mitigate the negative impacts of moderate and large window areas.

*Figure 6-15. Annual energy use and peak demand comparison by window area*

All cases are north-facing with no shading and include daylighting controls. Numbers are expressed per square foot within a 15-foot-deep perimeter zone. Results were computed using DOE-2.1E for a typical office building in Houston, Texas (Appendix A).

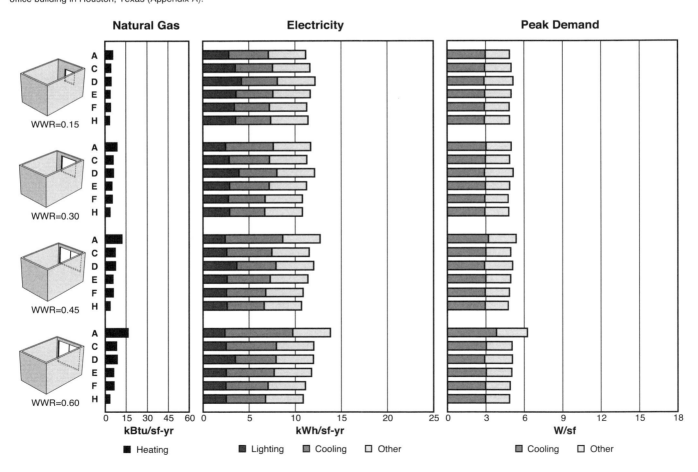

*Window Design for Offices in a Hot Climate*

*Figure 6-16. Annual electricity use*

All cases are north-facing with no shading and include daylighting controls. Numbers are expressed per square foot within a 15-foot-deep perimeter zone. Results were computed using DOE-2.1E for a typical office building in Houston, Texas (Appendix A).

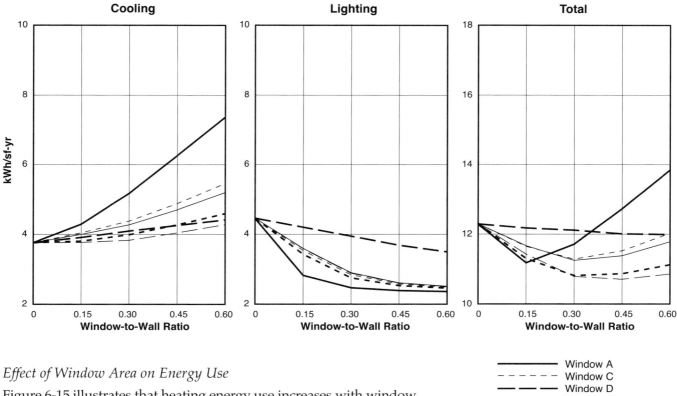

## Effect of Window Area on Energy Use

Figure 6-15 illustrates that heating energy use increases with window area for most window types, but it is a relatively small factor in a hot climate like Houston. With Window H, a very low U-factor is unaffected by greater window area. As shown in the previous heating section (Figure 6-13), annual electricity use does not rise with greater window area when daylighting controls are used (except for Window A). Figure 6-16 illustrates that cooling energy use increases with window area, but electric lighting energy decreases exponentially with greater window area as more daylight enters. When cooling and lighting are combined into total electricity use, each window type yields a different optimal window area (as represented by the low point on the curves in Figure 6-16). The combined effects of heating and electricity use are illustrated in Figure 6-13.

Because electricity use dominates in Houston, the optimal window area based on electricity consumption alone is similar to that based on total energy use. For Window A, a low WWR of 0.15 is optimal, while a higher WWR of 0.45 is optimal for Window H. A moderate WWR of 0.30 is optimal for all other windows except Window D, where area has no impact. The ideal window area is the point where the energy-saving benefits of daylight controls are maximized. The additional lighting energy savings from greater window area does not offset the rising cooling energy use. Windows F and H outperform other conventional windows due to the right combination of a relatively high daylight transmittance (VT) and a low solar heat gain coefficient.

**Window A**
single glazing
clear
U=1.25
SHGC=0.72
VT=0.71

**Window C**
double glazing
bronze tint
U=0.60
SHGC=0.42
VT=0.38

**Window D**
double glazing
reflective coating
U=0.54
SHGC=0.17
VT=0.10

**Window E**
double glazing
low-E tint
U=0.49
SHGC=0.39
VT=0.36

**Window F**
double glazing
spec. selective low-E tint
U=0.46
SHGC=0.27
VT=0.43

**Window H**
triple glazing
1 low-E layer, clear
U=0.20
SHGC=0.22
VT=0.37

U=U-factor in Btu/hr-sf-°F
SHGC=solar heat gain coefficient
VT=visible transmittance
All window properties are for the whole window.
Windows C–H have thermally broken aluminum frames. Window A has an aluminum frame.

### Effect of Window Area on Peak Demand

With north-facing windows, peak demand is relatively low compared to other orientations since there is almost no direct sun. However, the late afternoon summer sun (the low-angle direct sun from the sky's northwest quadrant) can enter north-facing zones and potentially exacerbate peak demand conditions precisely when utility rates may be three to five times higher. The problem may require increased HVAC system capacity as well, impacting capital costs. For most glazing types with daylighting controls, the relationship of peak demand to window area is similar to energy use and window area: neither rise with larger windows. Peak demand declines with greater window area up to 0.35 W/sf (7 percent) with unshaded Windows C–H. Conversely, for clear single-glazed Window A, peak demand rises with greater window area.

### Effect of Window Area on Daylight

Greater window area, for all window types, results in more daylight illuminance for north-facing perimeter zones (Figure 6-17). When the window-to-wall ratio is equal to or exceeds 0.30, the average annual daylight illuminance is at least 40 footcandles for all cases except

```
GLARE INDEX
  *  = less than 7
  7  = imperceptible glare
 10  = just perceptible glare
 16  = just acceptable glare
 22  = just uncomfortable glare
```

*Figure 6-17. Average annual daylight illuminance*

Average daylight illuminance is calculated at a point 10 feet from the window. All cases are north-facing with no shading. Results were computed using DOE-2.1E for a typical office building in Houston, Texas (Appendix A).

*Figure 6-18. Weighted glare index*

Glare index is calculated at a point 5 feet from the window for a person facing the side wall. A lower index is better. All cases are north-facing with no shading. Results were computed using DOE-2.1E for a typical office building in Houston, Texas (Appendix A).

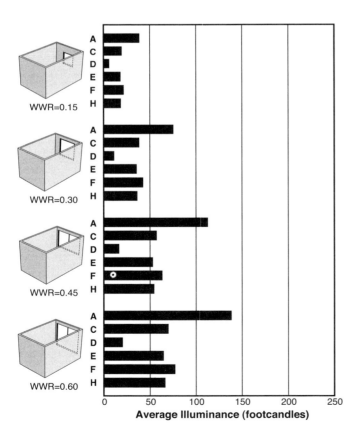

**Average Illuminance (footcandles)**

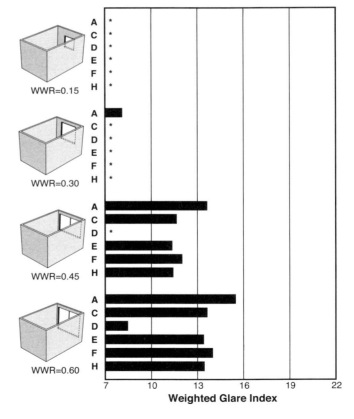

**Weighted Glare Index**

*Window Design for Offices in a Hot Climate*

Window D (VT=0.10), which provides little daylight at any size. Due to infrequent direct sun, daylight from north-facing windows is less compromised by shades compared to other orientations.

## Effect of Window Area on Glare

Figure 6-18 illustrates that there is a low weighted glare index for all window types in north-facing perimeter zones with a small to moderate window area (WWR=0.15–0.30). Weighted glare indices for most windows rise (discomfort glare is more frequent) as the window area climbs above WWR=0.30. The effect is greater with higher VT windows. With large unshaded windows, glare can be significant even in north-facing zones, but interior shading can address this problem. The weighted glare index for the darker, reflective Window D remains low even with large windows because of its very low visible transmittance.

## Effect of Window Area on View

As window area rises, view improves significantly (Figure 6-19). This occurs simply because a major view index component of this analysis is window area. Other factors such as visible transmittance do not change with window area. The lower view index from the reflective

*Figure 6-19. View index*

View index is calculated at a point 10 feet from the window. A higher index is better. All cases are north-facing with no shading. Results were computed using DOE-2.1E for a typical office building in Houston, Texas (Appendix A).

*Figure 6-20. Thermal comfort*

Thermal comfort is calculated at a point 5 feet from the window. A lower PPD is better. All cases are north-facing with no shading. Results were computed using DOE-2.1E for a typical office building in Houston, Texas (Appendix A).

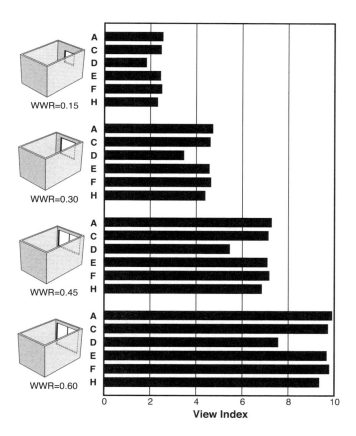

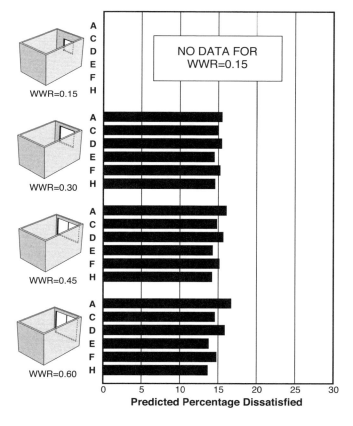

glass (Window D) is due to both its low VT and the greater frequency of reflected images which obscure view during periods of low exterior daylight levels (i.e., winter, early morning, late afternoon).

### Effect of Window Area on Thermal Comfort

The effect of window area on thermal comfort in unshaded north-facing zones in Houston is small because there is almost no direct sun. Figure 6-20 compares the thermal comfort in terms of predicted percentage dissatisfied (PPD) for three different window sizes at a point 5 feet from the window. For all window types, thermal comfort is not significantly affected (less than 2–3 percent difference in PPD) by greater window area.

### Effect of Window Area on All Attributes Combined

In Figure 6-21, the relative performance of all six attributes for a range of window areas is shown on a 0-to-10 scale. All cases have daylighting controls and no exterior or interior shading devices. The impact of window area on each of the individual performance measures is summarized below.

*Energy:* With daylighting controls, there is an optimal window size where lighting energy reduction from daylight is balanced by increased cooling energy use from greater window area. For most window types, a window-to-wall ratio of about 0.30 yields the least total energy use. For Window H, WWR=0.45 is optimal. Energy indices in Figure 6-21 are in the high range for most cases because of the north orientation.

*Peak Demand:* Peak demand changes very little with greater window area on the north (except for Window A). Peak demand indices in Figure 6-23 are in the high range for most cases because of the north orientation.

*Daylight:* Daylight availability and interior brightness rise proportionally with window area and VT. Daylight indices in Figure 6-21 remain in the middle range because of the north orientation.

*Glare:* For most window types, discomfort glare becomes more frequent as window area rises. Window D with a very low VT is the exception.

*View:* For most window types, the view index improves with greater window area.

*Thermal comfort:* There is very little difference in thermal comfort with greater window area.

For north-facing perimeter zones, window size dictates an ideal window type in hot climates like Houston. With moderate window areas (WWR=0.30), the low SHGC and moderate VT of Windows F and H offer optimum energy use and peak demand. These window types also yield good average annual daylight illuminance (about 50 fc), interior brightness, view, and control of glare and thermal discomfort. Windows F and H still offer good overall performance with large window areas (WWR=0.60) if interior shades are used to control discomfort glare, which is an infrequent problem. In short, glass alone cannot optimize total performance of large windows for this climate—even for north-facing windows.

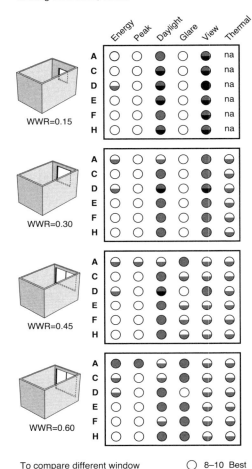

*Figure 6-21. Comparison of multiple attributes by window area*

All cases are north-facing with no shading and include daylighting controls. Results are for a typical office building in Houston, Texas.

To compare different window conditions across all attributes, the six measures of window performance are placed on a 0-to-10 scale. See Appendix A for the methodology.

○ 8–10 Best
◒ 6–8
◓ 4–6
◕ 2–4
● 0–2 Worst

Based on these results, greater window area in north-facing perimeter zones does not have to negatively impact performance. With proper shading design (addressed in the next section) and thoughtful window selection, the benefits of daylight and views offered by large windows need not result in an overall performance penalty.

## The Effects of Shading Conditions in a North-facing Perimeter Zone with Moderate Window Area

This section addresses shading design decisions once a moderate window area (WWR=0.30) has been chosen.

### Effect of Shading Conditions on Energy Use

Generally, shading affects energy loads in three ways: cooling energy declines with control of solar heat gains, lighting energy rises if the shading blocks daylight, and heating energy climbs with less solar gains. In north-facing zones with moderate window area (WWR=0.30), these effects are small, especially for Windows C–H (Figure 6-22).

Given the infrequent, low-angle direct sun on the north, overhangs tend to obstruct more useful daylight than limit solar heat gains. For Windows C–H, overhangs slightly increase annual electricity use compared to an unshaded window; for window A, overhangs decrease electricity use. For most window types, energy use declines more with vertical fins than overhangs. The ideal shading, in terms of energy use, is permanent, low-horizon obstructions from opposing buildings, trees, or mountains. This shading effectively blocks the low-angle direct sun in the early morning and late afternoon, without compromising daylight availability. With obstructions, other exterior shading, like overhangs or vertical fins, add no benefit.

The maximum reductions in annual electricity use between unshaded and all shaded cases is 1 kWh/sf-yr (7–8 percent) for Window A and 0.4 kWh/sf-yr (2–4 percent) for Windows C–H. For an energy efficient building, 1 kWh/sf-yr can represent about 10 percent of the total annual electricity use, so shading has significant benefit in some case. Exterior shading, such as awnings, make particular sense in retrofit applications where the existing glazing is poor, as with Window A, compared to the double- and triple-glazed counterparts.

For north-facing windows, the effect of interior shades is not shown since they are never deployed, given the direct sun and glare thresholds defined in the DOE-2.1E building energy simulation model. Shading devices increase heating energy use slightly, but the amounts are not significant in Houston. Figure 6-23 shows the total energy use (combined heating and electricity use) for five different shading conditions over a range of window areas. The energy-use impact of shading conditions for large windows is discussed in the following section.

---

**Window A**
single glazing
clear
U=1.25
SHGC=0.72
VT=0.71

**Window C**
double glazing
bronze tint
U=0.60
SHGC=0.42
VT=0.38

**Window D**
double glazing
reflective coating
U=0.54
SHGC=0.17
VT=0.10

**Window E**
double glazing
low-E tint
U=0.49
SHGC=0.39
VT=0.36

**Window F**
double glazing
spec. selective low-E tint
U=0.46
SHGC=0.27
VT=0.43

**Window H**
triple glazing
1 low-E layer, clear
U=0.20
SHGC=0.22
VT=0.37

U=U-factor in Btu/hr-sf-°F
SHGC=solar heat gain coefficient
VT=visible transmittance
All window properties are for the whole window.
Windows C–H have thermally broken aluminum frames. Window A has an aluminum frame.

---

**Shading Conditions in North-facing Perimeter Zone with a Moderate Window Area Section**
Figures 6-24 through 6-31
All cases have WWR=0.30.
(6 feet wide x 6 feet high)
See Appendix A for details.

Overhang: 2.8 feet deep
Vertical fins: 3.0 feet deep
Low-rise obstruction: Opposing buildings with a vertical angle of 22.5 degrees.
High-rise obstruction: Opposing buildings with a vertical angle of 45 degrees.

## Effect of Shading Conditions on Peak Demand

For moderately sized Windows C–H, exterior shading does not significantly reduce peak demand—less then 2 percent as illustrated in Figure 6-22. For Window A, exterior shading can reduce peak demand up to 5–6 percent. As window area rises, Figure 6-24 shows that shading on the north does not appreciably impact peak demand.

## Effect of Shading Conditions on Daylight

North zones rely primarily on indirect light from the sky for natural illuminance. Therefore, exterior obstructions that do not block the sky yield higher levels of interior daylight illuminance on average over the year. The degree that exterior shading reduces daylight illuminance depends on the shading device design, as well as window type

*Figure 6-22. Annual energy use and peak demand comparison by shading type*

All cases are north-facing with a 0.30 window-to-wall ratio and include daylighting controls. Numbers are expressed per square foot within a 15-foot-deep perimeter zone. Results were computed using DOE-2.1E for a typical office building in Houston, Texas (Appendix A).

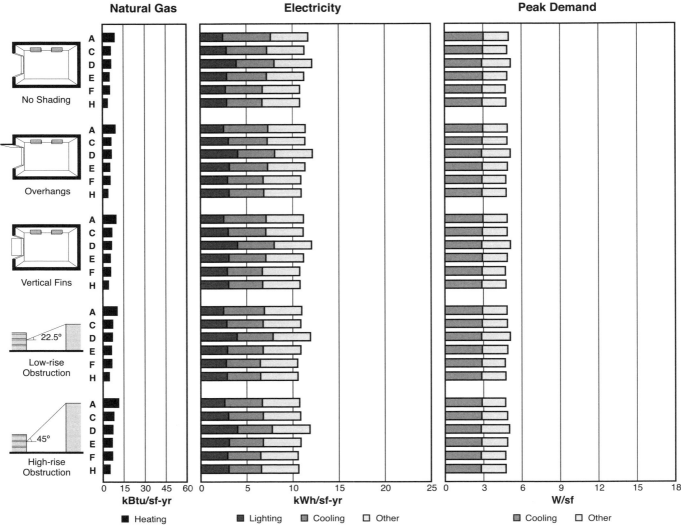

*Window Design for Offices in a Hot Climate*

## Figure 6-23. *Total annual energy use for different shading conditions*

All cases are north-facing and include daylighting controls. Numbers are expressed per square foot within a 15-foot-deep perimeter zone. Results were computed using DOE-2.1E for a typical office building in Houston, Texas (Appendix A). Total annual energy use is calculated by multiplying electricity use by 3 and adding heating energy use. This reflects the 3:1 ratio of primary to end use energy for electricity. All window properties are for the whole window. Windows C–H have thermally broken aluminum frames. Window H has an insulated frame. U=U-factor in Btu/hr-sf-°F, SHGC=solar heat gain coefficient, VT=visible transmittance

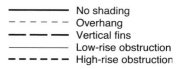

— No shading
--- Overhang
— — Vertical fins
— Low-rise obstruction
— — — High-rise obstruction

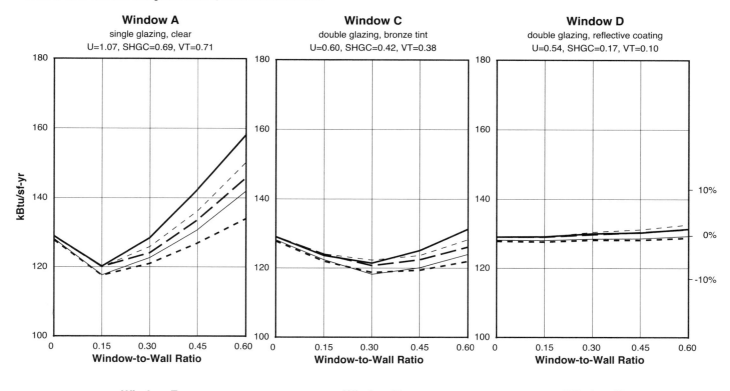

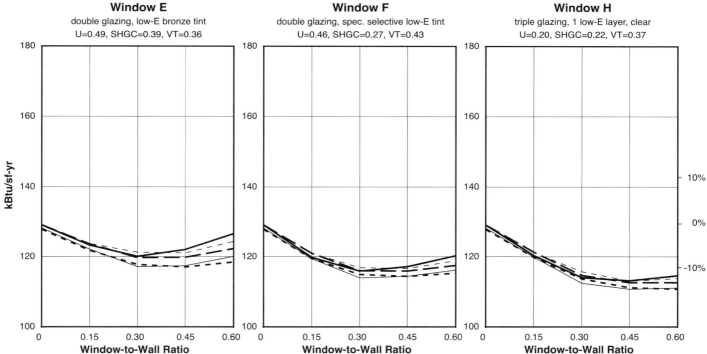

## Figure 6-24. Peak demand for different shading conditions

All cases are north-facing and include daylighting controls. Numbers are expressed in Watts per square foot within a 15-foot-deep perimeter zone. Results were computed using DOE-2.1E for a typical office building in Houston, Texas (Appendix A). All window properties are for the whole window. Windows C–H have thermally broken aluminum frames. Window H has an insulated frame. U=U-factor in Btu/hr-sf-°F, SHGC=solar heat gain coefficient, VT=visible transmittance

| | No shading |
|---|---|
| | Overhang |
| | Vertical fins |
| | Low-rise obstruction |
| | High-rise obstruction |

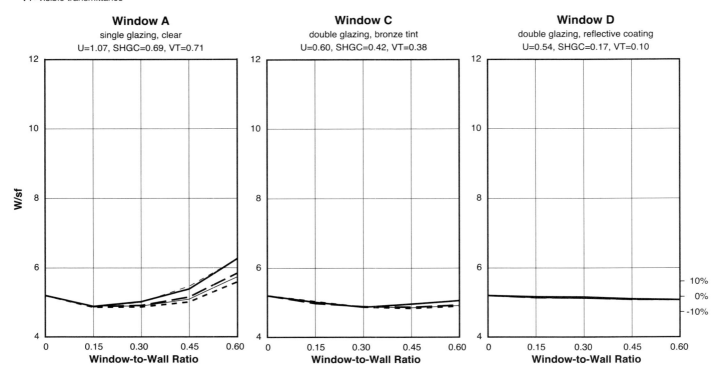

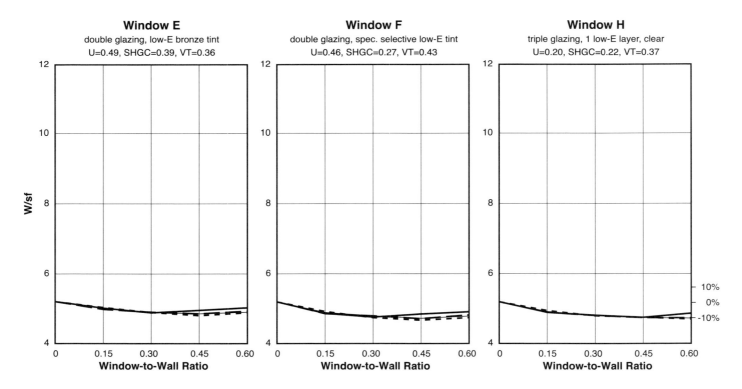

(VT) and area. Compared to the unshaded case, the shading studied in this analysis reduces average annual daylight illuminance up to 10 footcandles for moderately sized Windows C–H (except Window D), and up to 25 footcandles for Window A (Figure 6-25).

## Effect of Shading Conditions on Glare

The northern orientation experiences little direct sun. That fact, combined with a moderate window area (WWR=0.30) translates into a low weighted glare index, with or without shading (Figure 6-26). Exterior shading has an insignificant impact on glare, less than 2 percent reduction, except for Window A, where shading yields a 5 percent reduction. In any case, interior shades can be used to control occasional discomfort glare.

**GLARE INDEX**

| | |
|---|---|
| * | = less than 7 |
| 7 | = imperceptible glare |
| 10 | = just perceptible glare |
| 16 | = just acceptable glare |
| 22 | = just uncomfortable glare |

*Figure 6-25. Average annual daylight illuminance*
Average daylight illuminance is calculated at a point 10 feet from the window. All cases are north-facing. Results were computed using DOE-2.1E for a typical office building in Houston, Texas (Appendix A).

*Figure 6-26. Weighted glare index*
Glare index is calculated at a point 5 feet from the window for a person facing the side wall. A lower index is better. All cases are north-facing with no shading. Results were computed using DOE-2.1E for a typical office building in Houston, Texas (Appendix A).

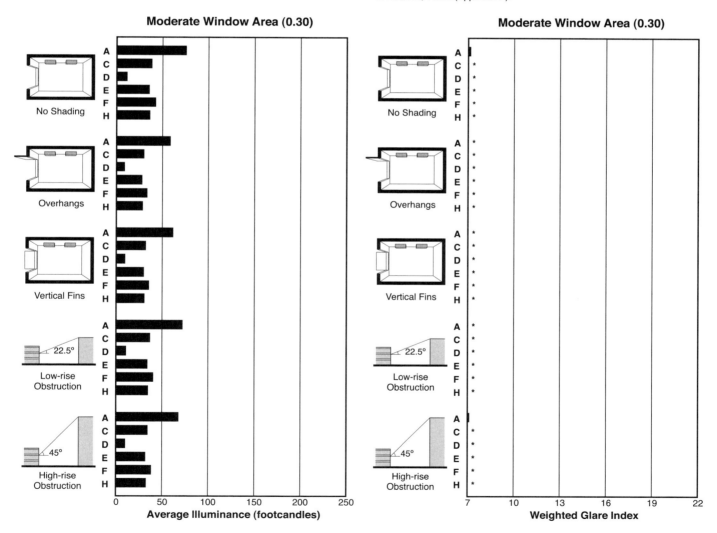

## Effect of Shading Conditions on View

Exterior shading devices, such as overhangs and fins, limit view out north-facing windows (Figure 6-27). For moderately sized windows, the view index drops up to 28 percent with vertical fins. Obstructions such as mountains, trees, and buildings are considered as part of the view and therefore do not reduce the view index. Window D has the lowest view index in all cases because of a low VT.

## Effect of Shading Conditions on Thermal Comfort

Figure 6-28 compares the thermal comfort with and without exterior shading in terms of predicted percentage dissatisfied (PPD) at a point 5 feet from the window. The key factors that affect thermal comfort are hot and cold window surfaces, as well as direct sun. On the north,

*Figure 6-27. View index*
View index is calculated at a point 10 feet from the window. A higher index is better. All cases are north-facing with no shading. Results were computed using DOE-2.1E for a typical office building in Houston, Texas (Appendix A).

*Figure 6-28. Thermal comfort*
Thermal comfort is calculated at a point 5 feet from the window. A lower PPD is better. All cases are north-facing with no shading. Results were computed using DOE-2.1E for a typical office building in Houston, Texas (Appendix A).

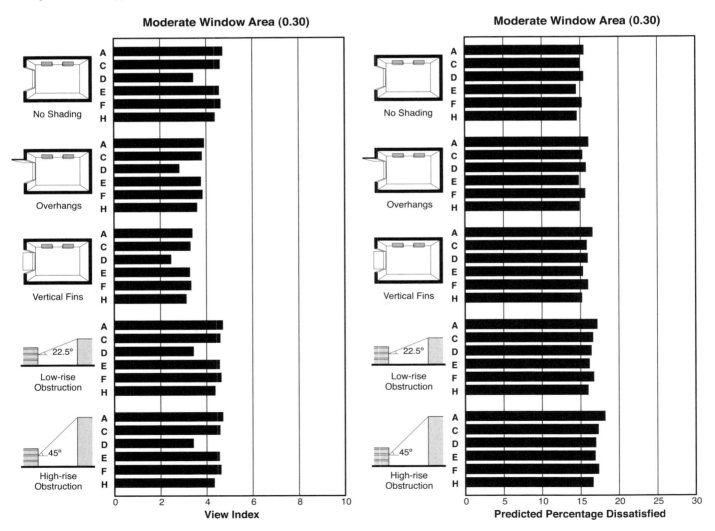

*Window Design for Offices in a Hot Climate*

direct sun has little effect. Glass surface temperatures are also not problematic.

For moderately sized windows (WWR=0.30), exterior shading has very little effect on thermal comfort in north-facing perimeter zones. There is also little difference in thermal comfort between window types in a north-facing zone—less than 3 percent increase from single-pane, clear Window A to triple-pane, low-E Window H. Thermal discomfort remains under 20 PPD for all window and shading types.

### Effect of Shading Conditions on All Attributes Combined

In Figure 6-29, the relative performance of all six attributes for a range of window shading conditions is shown on a 0-to-10 scale. All cases have daylighting controls and a window-to-wall ratio of 0.30. The impact of shading conditions on each of the individual performance measures is summarized below.

*Energy:* For most types of moderately sized windows, exterior shading does not significantly affect annual energy use on a north elevation.

*Peak Demand:* Shading has little effect on peak demand with moderately sized windows.

*Daylight*: Daylight availability and interior brightness decline with exterior shading, although its impact is typically minimal.

*Glare:* Exterior shading does not reduce glare significantly for moderately sized windows on the north.

*View:* For all window types, view declines in proportion to the amount of obstruction from the exterior shading devices.

*Thermal comfort:* Exterior shading has little effect on thermal comfort for windows with moderate area.

For moderately sized, north-facing windows, exterior shading is not recommended in new buildings. Windows C, E, F and H all perform well in this situation. Yet, for retrofit situations with single-pane clear glazing (Window A), exterior shading can reduce annual energy use.

### The Effects of Shading Conditions in a North-facing Perimeter Zone with Large Window Area

This section addresses design decisions about shading once a large window area (WWR=0.60) has been chosen.

### Effect of Shading Conditions on Energy Use

For most types of large, north-facing windows (WWR=0.60), exterior shading can reduce total annual energy use (Figure 6-30). The effect is greater with higher SHGC windows (Windows A, C, and E) and less with lower SHGC windows (Windows F and H). Shading has no impact with very low-SHGC Window D. In general, an overhang is less effective than vertical fins on the north. Opposing buildings, trees, or mountains are the most effective.

The maximum reduction in total annual energy use between the unshaded and all shaded cases is 2.4 kWh/sf-yr (17 percent) for Window A and 1.1 kWh/sf-yr (9 percent) for Windows C–H. Exterior

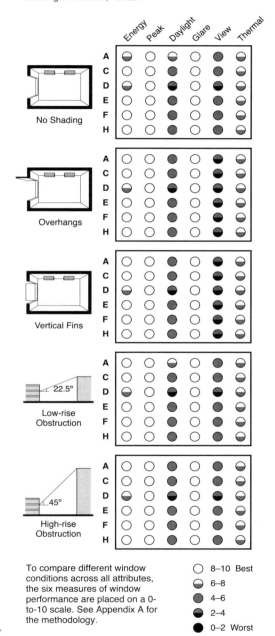

*Figure 6-29. Comparison of multiple attributes by shading condition for moderate window areas*

All cases are north-facing and have WWR=0.30 with daylighting controls. Results are for a typical office building in Houston, Texas.

To compare different window conditions across all attributes, the six measures of window performance are placed on a 0-to-10 scale. See Appendix A for the methodology.

○ 8–10 Best
◔ 6–8
◑ 4–6
◕ 2–4
● 0–2 Worst

**Shading Conditions in North-facing Perimeter Zone with a Large Window Area Section**

Figures 6-32 through 6-37
All cases have WWR=0.60
(10 feet wide x 7.2 feet high)
See Appendix A for details.

Overhang: 3.4 feet deep
Vertical fins only: 2.5 feet deep @ 5 feet O.C. or 5.0 feet deep @ 10 feet O.C.
Low-rise obstruction: Opposing buildings with a vertical angle of 22.5 degrees.
High-rise obstruction: Opposing buildings with a vertical angle of 45 degrees.

shading can benefit large, north-facing windows in a hot climate, although in many cases the impact is relatively small compared to the greater impact shading has on other orientations. The total annual energy (combined heating and electricity) is shown in Figure 6-23.

### Effect of Shading Conditions on Peak Demand

For large Windows C–H (WWR=0.60), exterior shades cut peak electricity demand up to 0.4 W/sf (8 percent). The impact is greatest with Windows C and E (high SHGC glazing) and least with Windows F and H (low SHGC). With Window A, exterior shades reduce peak demand by up to 1.4 W/sf (22 percent) compared to the unshaded case. Shading reflective glass (Window D) impacts peak demand very

*Figure 6-30. Annual energy use and peak demand comparison by shading type*

All cases are north-facing with a 0.60 window-to-wall ratio and include daylighting controls. Numbers are expressed per square foot within a 15-foot-deep perimeter zone. Results were computed using DOE-2.1E for a typical office building in Houston, Texas (Appendix A).

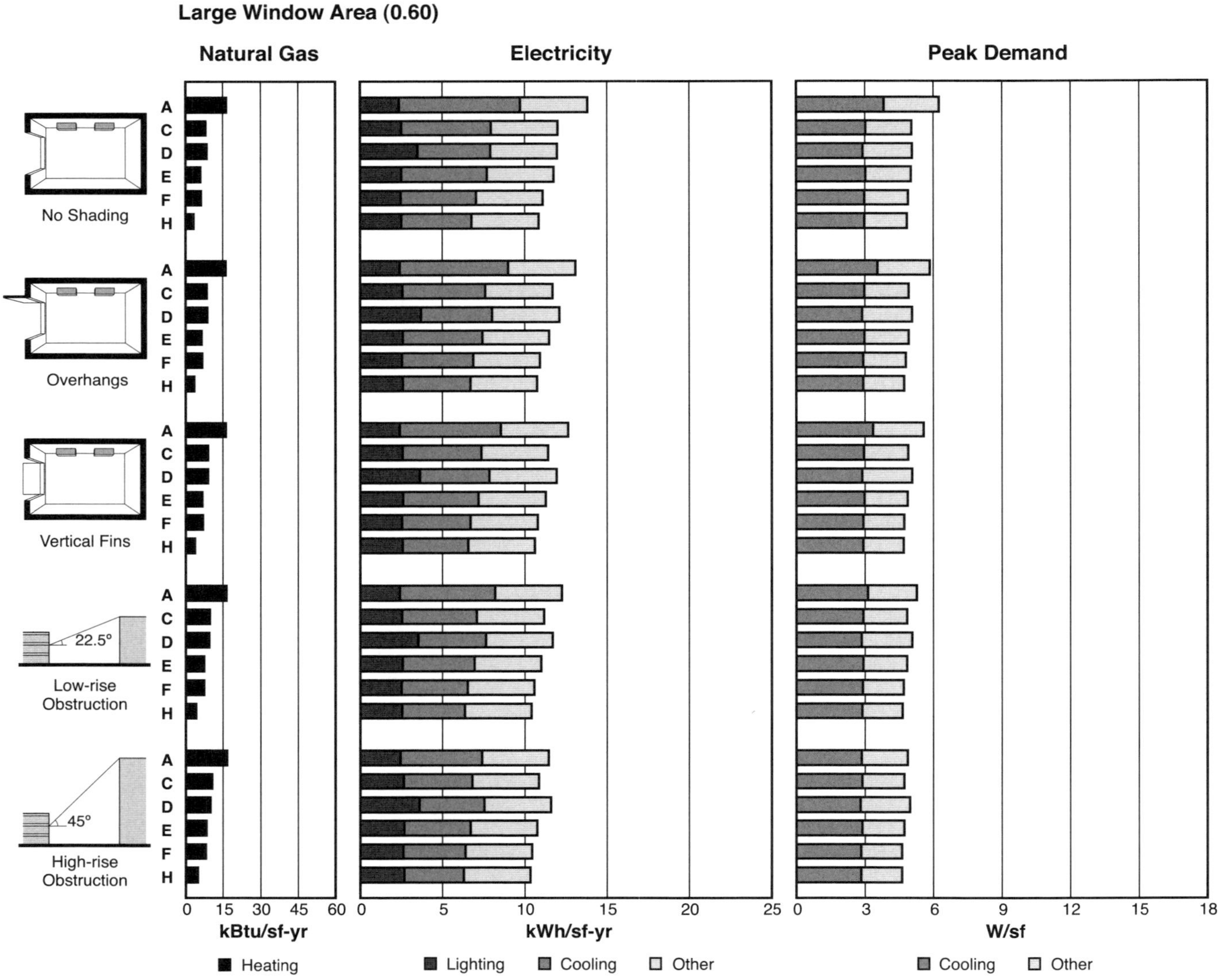

**Large Window Area (0.60)**

little, less than 2 percent. Overall, peak demand for large, north-facing windows declines with shading, although its effect is much greater with other orientations.

## Effect of Shading Conditions on Daylight

Shading limits the sky view, thereby reducing interior daylight illuminance. Thus, a large, north-facing, unshaded window has the greatest average annual illuminance. Overhangs are the most obstructive shading, reducing illuminance slightly more than vertical fins (Figure 6-31). A low- or high-rise obstruction barely impacts illuminance. For all windows except Window D, whose low VT offers little illuminance, shading reduces average illuminance by 25–45 footcandles. However, illuminance remains above 50 footcandles.

*Figure 6-31. Average annual daylight illuminance*

Average daylight illuminance is calculated at a point 10 feet from the window. All cases are north-facing. Results were computed using DOE-2.1E for a typical office building in Houston, Texas (Appendix A).

*Figure 6-32. Weighted glare index*

Glare index is calculated at a point 5 feet from the window for a person facing the side wall. A lower index is better. All cases are north-facing with no shading. Results were computed using DOE-2.1E for a typical office building in Houston, Texas (Appendix A).

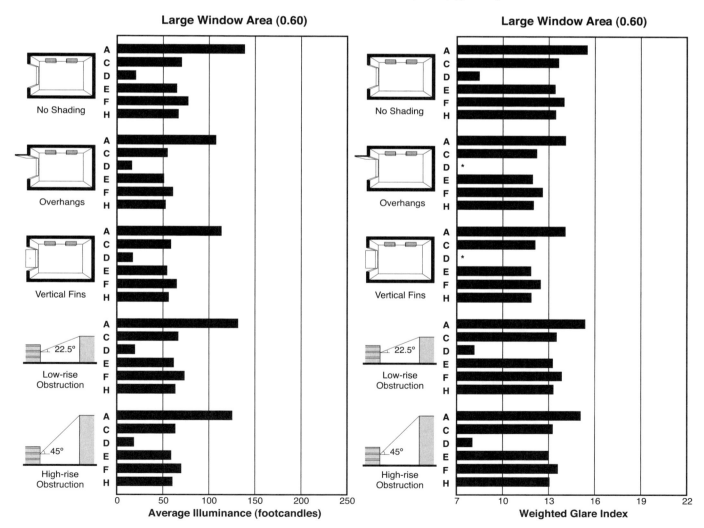

## Effect of Shading Conditions on Glare

Glare can be a problem with large window areas on the north. Exterior overhangs and vertical fins reduce the weighted glare index by 22 to 27 percent for most glazings (Figure 6-32). Window D with low-VT provides good glare control without shading. Low- and high-rise obstructions do not affect glare from the sky significantly.

## Effect of Shading Conditions on View

Overhangs limit the view out north-facing windows. Vertical fins are less obstructive, but block view as well (Figure 6-33). The view index with overhangs or vertical fins drops about 21 percent but remains relatively high given the large window area. Window D has the poorest view index because of its low VT. Obstructions such as

*Figure 6-33. View index*

View index is calculated at a point 10 feet from the window. A higher index is better. All cases are north-facing with no shading. Results were computed using DOE-2.1E for a typical office building in Houston, Texas (Appendix A).

*Figure 6-34. Thermal comfort*

Thermal comfort is calculated at a point 5 feet from the window. A lower PPD is better. All cases are north-facing with no shading. Results were computed using DOE-2.1E for a typical office building in Houston, Texas (Appendix A).

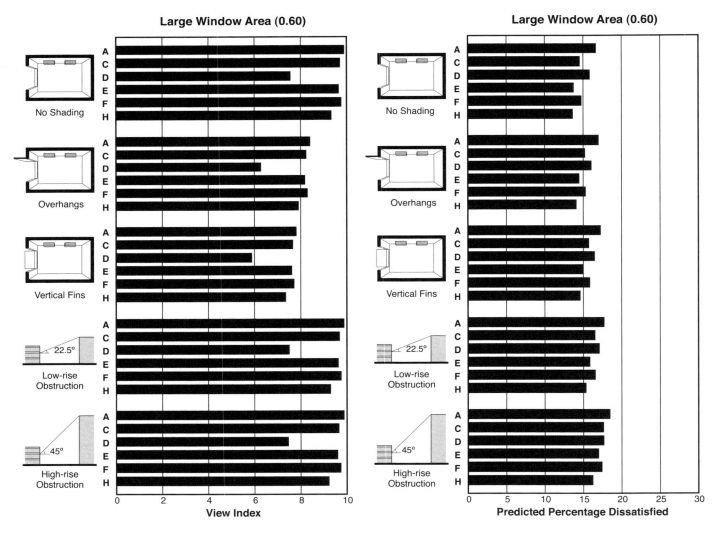

*Window Design for Offices in a Hot Climate*

mountains, trees, and buildings are regarded as part of the view and therefore do not impact the view index.

### Effect of Shading Conditions on Thermal Comfort

For large windows, exterior shading has very little effect on thermal comfort in north-facing perimeter zones (Figure 6-34). There is also little difference in thermal comfort between window types in a north-facing zone—less than 3 PPD increase from single-pane, clear Window A to triple-pane, low-E Window H. Thermal discomfort remains under 20 PPD for all window and shading types.

### Effect of Shading Conditions on All Attributes Combined

In Figure 6-35, the relative performance of all six attributes for a range of window shading conditions is shown on a 0-to-10 scale. All cases have daylighting controls and a window-to-wall ratio of 0.60. The impact of shading conditions on each of the individual performance measures is summarized below.

*Energy:* For large-area windows, exterior shading can reduce annual energy use on the north, although the amounts are relatively small compared to other orientations. The effect is greater with higher SHGC Windows A, C, and E. For Windows D, F, and H, the energy related benefits are very small.

*Peak Demand:* For large window areas on the north, exterior shading can reduce peak demand by 0.4–1.4 W/sf. The effect is greater with higher SHGC Windows A, C, and E.

*Daylight:* Exterior shading can significantly reduce interior daylight illuminance. Shading's impact on light levels depends on the degree to which it obstructs the sky view.

*Glare:* All the large, north-facing window types have moderate glare problems, except for Window D with its low VT. Exterior shading cuts glare, but effective interior shades are likely to provide the best control.

*View:* For all window types, overhangs reduce view. Vertical fins limit view as well, and are more obstructive than overhangs.

*Thermal comfort:* Exterior shading has little effect on thermal comfort for large north-facing windows.

For large-area windows on the north, exterior shading may be recommended to reduce energy use and control glare in some cases, although it is not nearly as important as on other orientations. If shading is used, vertical fins may be preferable because solar heat gain from low-angle direct sun can be controlled with minimal daylight reduction. With low- or high-rise obstructions, exterior shading is not recommended.

For a large north-facing window, Figure 6-35 reveals that Windows F and H perform well across the range of attributes and only require shading for glare control, which is easily addressed with interior shades. Window D most effectively controls glare, but at the expense of energy, daylight, and view.

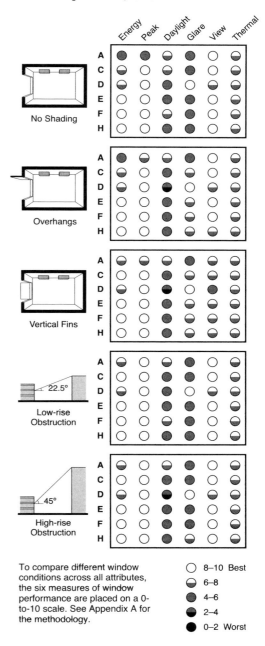

*Figure 6-35. Comparison of multiple attributes by shading condition for large window area*

All cases are north-facing and have WWR=0.60 and include daylighting controls. Results are for a typical office building in Houston, Texas.

To compare different window conditions across all attributes, the six measures of window performance are placed on a 0-to-10 scale. See Appendix A for the methodology.

○ 8–10 Best
◑ 6–8
◕ 4–6
◕ 2–4
● 0–2 Worst

# South-facing Perimeter Zones

Once the decision has been made to orient perimeter zones to the south, the designer must examine more detailed issues related to window design and selection. The following sections address how lighting controls, window area, and shading affect performance.

### The Effect of Lighting Controls on Annual Energy Use and Peak Demand in a South-facing Perimeter Zone

Annual electricity use always declines by installing controls that dim or turn off electric lighting when there is sufficient daylight (Figure 6-36). With daylighting controls, across all sizes of unshaded Windows C–H there is an average reduction of 2.2 kWh/sf-yr (15 percent) compared to a zone without them. Lighting energy use falls to a greater degree as VT increases, while cooling energy use diminishes slightly because of reduced heat gain from the lights. For instance, lighting energy use associated with low-VT Window D does not decline significantly with controls; little light enters Window D, giving little opportunity to dim lights and save energy. With the other window cases, on the other hand, the higher the VT, the greater the lighting load reduction.

Heating energy use rises with daylighting controls, on average 0.47 kBtu/sf-yr (12 percent) compared to a non-daylit zone, but heating represents only about 3 percent of the total annual energy use (assuming an electricity-to-gas fuel ratio of 3:1), so this increase has an insignificant impact on the total perimeter zone performance. Figure 6-37 shows the total annual energy use (combined heating and electricity) across a range of window areas.

**Window A**
single glazing
clear
U=1.25
SHGC=0.72
VT=0.71

**Window E**
double glazing
low-E tint
U=0.49
SHGC=0.39
VT=0.36

**Window C**
double glazing
bronze tint
U=0.60
SHGC=0.42
VT=0.38

**Window F**
double glazing
spec. selective low-E tint
U=0.46
SHGC=0.27
VT=0.43

**Window D**
double glazing
reflective coating
U=0.54
SHGC=0.17
VT=0.10

**Window H**
triple glazing
1 low-E layer, clear
U=0.20
SHGC=0.22
VT=0.37

U=U-factor in Btu/hr-sf-°F
SHGC=solar heat gain coefficient
VT=visible transmittance
All window properties are for the whole window.
Windows C–H have thermally broken aluminum frames. Window A has an aluminum frame.

*Figure 6-36. Annual energy use and peak demand comparison by lighting system*

All cases are south-facing with a 0.30 window-to-wall ratio and no shading. Numbers are expressed per square feet within a 15-foot-deep perimeter zone. Results were computed using DOE-2.1E for a typical office building in Houston, Texas (Appendix A).

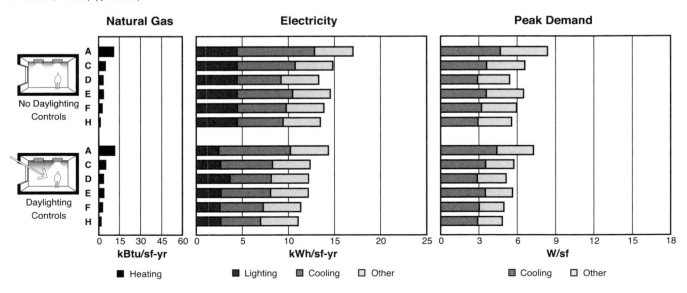

*Window Design for Offices in a Hot Climate*

## Figure 6-37. Total annual energy use by lighting system

All cases are south-facing and have no shading. Numbers are expressed per square feet within a 15-foot-deep perimeter zone. Results were computed using DOE-2.1E for a typical office building in Houston, Texas (Appendix A).

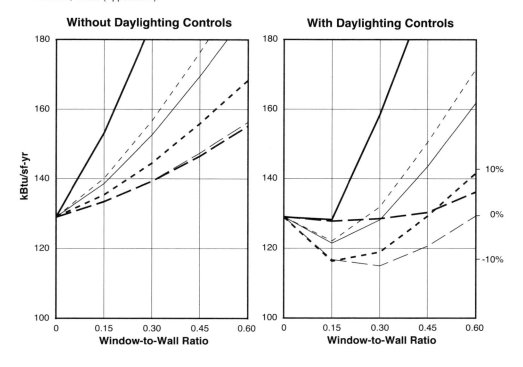

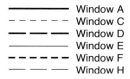

Total annual energy use is calculated by multiplying electricity use by 3 and adding heating energy use. This reflects the 3:1 ratio of primary to end use energy for electricity.

## Figure 6-38. Peak demand by lighting system

All cases are south-facing and have no shading. Numbers are expressed in Watts per square feet within a 15-foot-deep perimeter zone. Results were computed using DOE-2.1E for a typical office building in Houston, Texas (Appendix A).

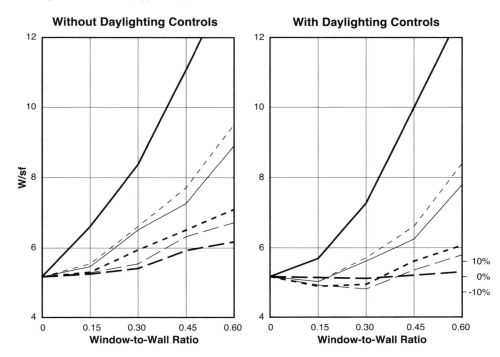

Because of the intense sun on the south facade in hot climates, reductions in energy use stemming from daylighting controls are quickly outweighed by rising energy use caused by solar gains from greater window area increases. Without daylighting controls, annual electricity use rises rapidly with greater window area, as well as higher SHGC and U-factor, in proportion to admitted solar heat gains (Figure 6-37). Daylighting controls reduce lighting and cooling loads, to offset electricity use. The exact energy use profile depends on the window properties. Window types with a very low SHGC and U-factor and a moderate VT generally perform better (Windows F and H). With Window H, total annual energy use can be lower than an opaque insulated wall even for large windows.

Daylight controls also reduce peak electricity demand in south-facing perimeter zones (Figures 6-36 and 6-38). With daylighting controls and a large window area (WWR=0.60), there is an average reduction of 0.77 W/sf (12 percent) compared to a zone without them for Windows C–H.

While all the energy use comparisons in this section that daylight controls offer significant savings, there is a range of possible performance (see Chapter 2). Lighting controls do not affect daylight, view, glare, and thermal comfort.

## The Effect of Window Area in a South-facing Zone

This section addresses the issue of optimal window area on a south-facing perimeter zone. Only the unshaded condition is examined here. See the following sections on how shading conditions can mitigate the negative impacts of moderate and large window areas.

### Effect of Window Area on Energy Use

In south-facing perimeter zones without shading or daylighting controls, annual electricity use increases with window area, SHGC, and U-factor in hot climates like Houston (Figure 6-39). As window area increases from an opaque wall to a large-area window (WWR=0.60), annual electricity use rises by 2.0-5.5 kWh/sf-yr (16–44 percent) for Windows C–H. The rate of increase varies by window type. Electricity use of Windows A, C, and E, with their high SHGC, increases with area at a higher rate than the low-SHGC Windows D, F, and H.

Figure 6-40 illustrates that cooling energy use rises with greater window area. With daylighting controls, electric lighting energy use declines with greater window area to a point where additional daylight produces no significant reductions in lighting energy. When cooling and lighting are combined into total electricity use (as well as all other electricity end uses), the optimal window area (as represented by the low point on the curve in Figure 6-40) depends on window type.

Heating energy use also rises with window area for all window types (Figure 6-39). The increase is great with Window A (high U-factor) compared to Window H (very low U-factor). The combined effects of heating and electricity use are shown in Figure 6-37.

Because electricity use dominates in Houston, optimal window area based on electricity use alone versus total energy use are similar. A small window area (WWR=0.15) is ideal for windows A, C, E, and

F, while WWR=0.30 is ideal for Windows D and H (although electricity use for Window D is affected very little by window area). Greater window area beyond this optimal point yields little additional lighting energy savings, while cooling energy use rises. The optimal window area is the point where the energy-saving benefits of daylight controls are maximized. Window H outperforms other conventional windows due to an ideal combination of a relatively high daylight transmittance (VT) and a low solar heat gain coefficient.

### Effect of Window Area on Peak Demand

With unshaded, south-facing windows, peak demand rises with window area. As WWR climbs from 0 to 0.60 for Windows C–H, the average increase is 2.48 W/sf (48 percent) without daylighting controls and 1.5 W/sf (29 percent) with daylighting controls (Figures 6-38 and 6-39). The rate of increase depends on window type: it is greatest for Windows A, C, and E and least for Windows F and H. A small area (WWR=0.15) is optimal for Windows C and E, while a moderate area (WWR=0.30) has the lowest peak demand for Windows F and H. Window area affects peak demand very little for Window D. Interior

| Window A | Window E |
|---|---|
| single glazing | double glazing |
| clear | low-E tint |
| U=1.25 | U=0.49 |
| SHGC=0.72 | SHGC=0.39 |
| VT=0.71 | VT=0.36 |
| **Window C** | **Window F** |
| double glazing | double glazing |
| bronze tint | spec. selective low-E tint |
| U=0.60 | U=0.46 |
| SHGC=0.42 | SHGC=0.27 |
| VT=0.38 | VT=0.43 |
| **Window D** | **Window H** |
| double glazing | triple glazing |
| reflective coating | 1 low-E layer, clear |
| U=0.54 | U=0.20 |
| SHGC=0.17 | SHGC=0.22 |
| VT=0.10 | VT=0.37 |

U=U-factor in Btu/hr-sf-°F
SHGC=solar heat gain coefficient
VT=visible transmittance
All window properties are for the whole window.
Windows C–H have thermally broken aluminum frames. Window A has an aluminum frame.

*Figure 6-39. Annual energy use and peak demand comparison by window area*

All cases are south-facing with no shading and include daylighting controls. Numbers are expressed per square feet within a 15-foot-deep perimeter zone. Results were computed using DOE-2.1E for a typical office building in Houston, Texas (Appendix A).

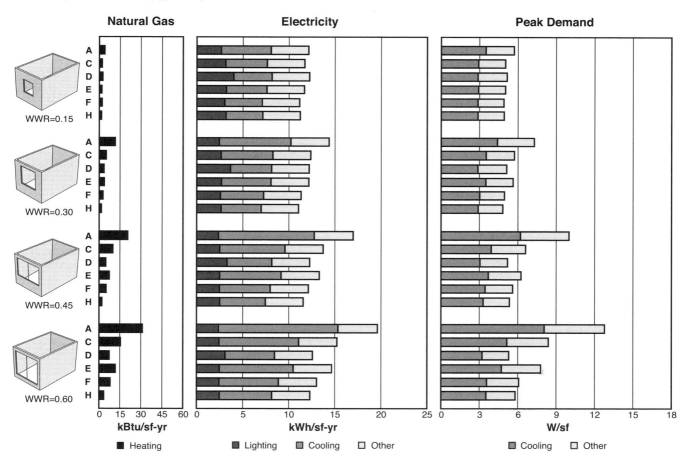

*Figure 6-40. Annual electric use*

All cases are south-facing with no shading and include daylighting controls. Numbers are expressed per square feet within a 15-foot-deep perimeter zone. Results were computed using DOE-2.1E for a typical office building in Houston, Texas (Appendix A).

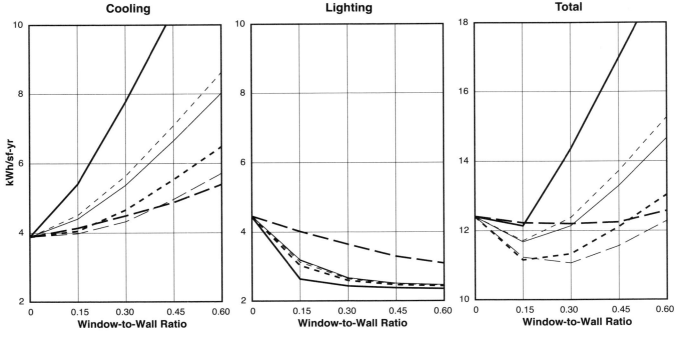

Window A
Window C
Window D
Window E
Window F
Window H

| **Window A** | **Window E** |
|---|---|
| single glazing | double glazing |
| clear | low-E tint |
| U=1.25 | U=0.49 |
| SHGC=0.72 | SHGC=0.39 |
| VT=0.71 | VT=0.36 |
| | |
| **Window C** | **Window F** |
| double glazing | double glazing |
| bronze tint | spec. selective low-E tint |
| U=0.60 | U=0.46 |
| SHGC=0.42 | SHGC=0.27 |
| VT=0.38 | VT=0.43 |
| | |
| **Window D** | **Window H** |
| double glazing | triple glazing |
| reflective coating | 1 low-E layer, clear |
| U=0.54 | U=0.20 |
| SHGC=0.17 | SHGC=0.22 |
| VT=0.10 | VT=0.37 |

U=U-factor in Btu/hr-sf-°F
SHGC=solar heat gain coefficient
VT=visible transmittance
All window properties are for the whole window.
Windows C–H have thermally broken aluminum frames. Window A has an aluminum frame.

and exterior shading can reduce the negative impacts of greater window area (see following sections).

Peak demand typically occurs during mid- to late summer for this south-facing zone. For poorer performing windows, peak demand will occur during the winter due to low-angle direct sun (e.g., November for Window C at WWR=0.45–0.60 or Window E at WWR=0.60 with daylighting controls).

*Effect of Window Area on Daylight*

Greater window area results in increased daylight illuminance in south-facing perimeter zones for all window types (Figure 6-41). When the window-to-wall ratio is equal to or exceeds 0.30, the average annual daylight illuminance is at least 50 footcandles for all cases except Window D (VT=0.10), which provides the least daylight at any size.

For lighting designers, it is useful to note that the average annual daylight illuminance 10 feet from an unshaded window is equal to 521*EA for Houston's latitude and the frequency and degree of its cloud cover. The product of VT and WWR is know as the effective aperture (EA=VT*WWR).

## Effect of Window Area on Glare

Figure 6-42 illustrates that there is a low weighted glare index for all window types in south-facing perimeter zones with a small to moderate window area (WWR=0.15 to 0.30). The weighted glare index for all windows except Window D rises significantly (discomfort glare is more frequent) as the window area increases above WWR=0.30. With unshaded, large windows, glare can be a significant problem. However, this can be controlled with effective exterior shading. Because of its very low visible transmittance, the weighted glare index for the darker, reflective Window D remains low even when unshaded at large window areas.

## Effect of Window Area on View

As window area increases, view improves significantly (Figure 6-43). This occurs simply because a major view index component of this analysis is window area. Window D with its very low visible transmittance (VT) and high visible surface reflectance performs worst with respect to view.

| GLARE INDEX | |
|---|---|
| * | = less than 7 |
| 7 | = imperceptible glare |
| 10 | = just perceptible glare |
| 16 | = just acceptable glare |
| 22 | = just uncomfortable glare |

*Figure 6-41. Average daylight illuminance*

Average daylight illuminance is calculated at a point 10 feet from the window. All cases are south-facing with no shading. Results were computed using DOE-2.1E for a typical office building in Houston, Texas (Appendix A).

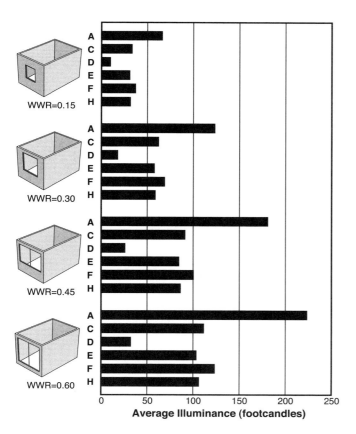

*Figure 6-42. Weighted glare index*

Glare index is calculated at a point 5 feet from the window for a person facing the side wall. A lower index is better. All cases are south-facing with no shading. Results were computed using DOE-2.1E for a typical office building in Houston, Texas (Appendix A).

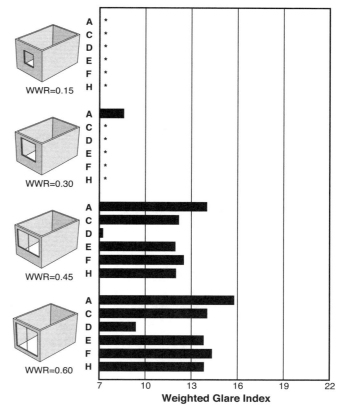

**Window A**
single glazing
clear
U=1.25
SHGC=0.72
VT=0.71

**Window C**
double glazing
bronze tint
U=0.60
SHGC=0.42
VT=0.38

**Window D**
double glazing
reflective coating
U=0.54
SHGC=0.17
VT=0.10

**Window E**
double glazing
low-E tint
U=0.49
SHGC=0.39
VT=0.36

**Window F**
double glazing
spec. selective low-E tint
U=0.46
SHGC=0.27
VT=0.43

**Window H**
triple glazing
1 low-E layer, clear
U=0.20
SHGC=0.22
VT=0.37

U=U-factor in Btu/hr-sf-°F
SHGC=solar heat gain coefficient
VT=visible transmittance
All window properties are for the whole window.
Windows C–H have thermally broken aluminum
frames. Window A has an aluminum frame.

## Effect of Window Area on Thermal Comfort

Thermal discomfort for unshaded south-facing offices in Houston rises slightly with greater window area (Figure 6-44). For all window types, as WWR climbs from 0.30 to 0.60, there is an average increase of 2.5 predicted percentage dissatisfied (PPD). For all window types except Window A, which performs much worse, thermal comfort remains acceptable (below 20 PPD) even at greater window areas.

## Effect of Window Area on All Attributes Combined

In Figure 6-45, the relative performance of all six attributes for a range of window areas is shown on a 0-to-10 scale. All cases have daylighting controls and no exterior or interior shading devices. The impact of window area on each of the individual performance measures is summarized below.

*Energy:* For most unshaded window types, a WWR= 0.15 uses the lowest annual energy, with energy use rising significantly with area. The lowest total energy use for Window H is at WWR=0.30; Window D is affected very little by area.

### Figure 6-43. View index

View index is calculated at a point 10 feet from the window. A higher index is better. All cases are south-facing with no shading. Results were computed using DOE-2.1E for a typical office building in Houston, Texas (Appendix A).

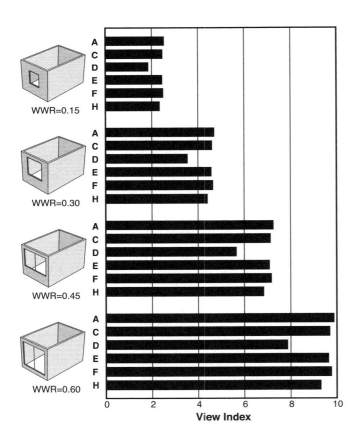

View Index

### Figure 6-44. Thermal comfort

Thermal comfort is calculated at a point 5 feet from the window. A lower PPD is better. All cases are south-facing with no shading. Results were computed using DOE-2.1E for a typical office building in Houston, Texas (Appendix A).

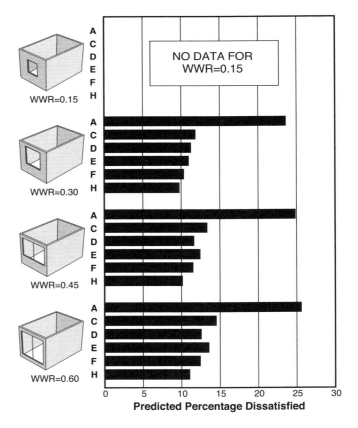

Predicted Percentage Dissatisfied

*Peak Demand:* For most window types, the lowest peak demand is at WWR=0.15. Larger windows increase peak demand significantly. The lowest peak demand for Window H is at WWR=0.30; Window D is unaffected by area.

*Daylight:* Average annual daylight illuminance rises proportionally with greater window area and higher VT.

*Glare:* For all window types except D, the weighted glare index increases significantly (discomfort glare is more frequent) as window area rises above WWR=0.30. Greater window area has less impact on glare with very low-VT Window D.

*View:* For all window types, the view index improves with greater window area.

*Thermal comfort:* Thermal discomfort rises slightly with greater window area. Single-pane, clear Window A offers significantly lower thermal comfort than the other glazings.

For south-facing perimeter zones in Houston, the balance between window size and optimum performance varies by window type. For Windows A, C, and E, the ideal window size is small (WWR=0.15). Windows F and H achieve optimal energy efficiency and peak demand at a moderate window size (WWR=0.30–0.45) with good access to view. For large-area windows (WWR=0.60), Window H and reflective Window D yield the least energy use and peak demand. However, while Window D controls glare well, it does poorly in terms of view, daylight, and interior brightness.

Increasing unshaded, south-facing window areas in a hot climate has a generally negative impact on energy, peak demand, and glare, but a positive effect on daylighting and view. The following sections demonstrate how all issues can be brought into balance through the design and integration of shading devices with glazing.

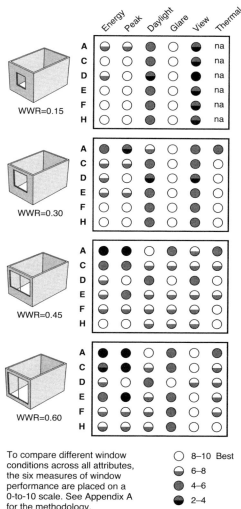

*Figure 6-45. Comparison of multiple attributes by window area*

All cases are south-facing with no shading and include daylighting controls. Results are for a typical office building in Houston, Texas.

To compare different window conditions across all attributes, the six measures of window performance are placed on a 0-to-10 scale. See Appendix A for the methodology.

○ 8–10 Best
◔ 6–8
◑ 4–6
◕ 2–4
● 0–2 Worst

# The Effects of Shading Conditions in a South-facing Perimeter Zone with Moderate Window Area

This section addresses design decisions about shading once a moderate window area (WWR=0.30) has been chosen.

## Effect of Shading Conditions on Energy Use

With moderately sized windows (WWR=0.30), shading devices affect south-facing zone energy use in two ways: cooling energy use declines due to control of solar heat gains, and lighting energy use rises if daylight availability is reduced (Figure 6-46). In a hot climate like Houston, control of solar heat gains is more important than daylight

*Figure 6-46. Annual energy use and peak demand comparison by shading type*

All cases are south-facing with a 0.30 window-to-wall ratio and include daylighting controls. Numbers are expressed per square feet within a 15-foot-deep perimeter zone. Results were computed using DOE-2.1E for a typical office building in Houston, Texas (Appendix A).

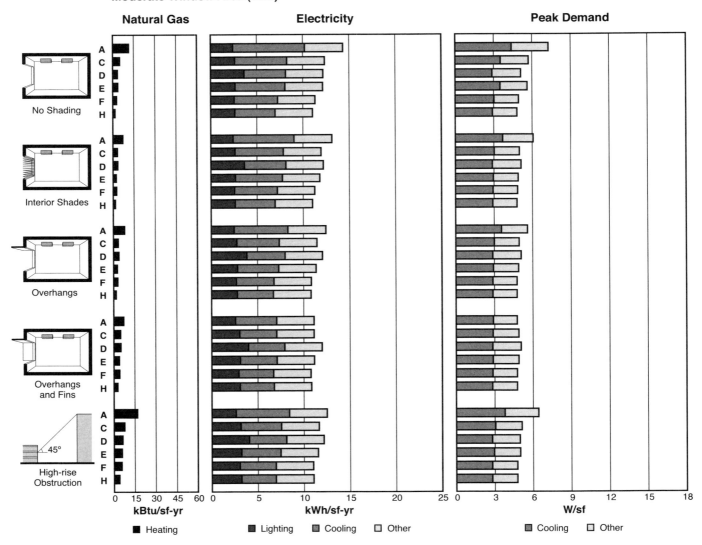

admission for most window types. For Window A with high SHGC and U-factor, shading (including interior or exterior shades or high-rise obstructions) reduces annual electricity use up to 23 percent. Shading Windows C and E yields maximum reductions of 0.6–1.2 kWh/sf-yr (5–10 percent), while for Windows F and H, with their low SHGC and U-factor, shading has little impact (less than 5 percent). Shading offers almost no energy savings for Window D.

There is less than a 3 percent difference in annual electricity use comparing a shallow overhang to a deep overhang combined with vertical fins for Windows C–H (WWR=0.30). With clear glazing (Window A), deep overhangs combined with fins can make a substantial difference (up to 18 percent) in electricity use compared to other shading systems. High-rise obstructions, such as building to the south, reduce energy use—performing similarly to shallow overhangs in that respect—but the obstructions increase heating requirements. Figure 6-46 illustrates that heating energy use declines with attached shading even though the beneficial solar heat gain is reduced in colder periods. This counterintuitive effect occurs because of the mechanical system requiring more heating energy for reheating chilled air during cooling periods in the unshaded condition. Since heating energy use is small in Houston, this has little effect on shading design and window selection.

Figure 6-47 shows the total energy use (heating and cooling combined) for a range of window areas. Exterior shading shifts the optimal window area from WWR=0.15 in the unshaded condition to WWR=0.30 for overhangs to WWR=0.45 and higher for deep overhangs with fins. It is apparent that the magnitude of energy savings from shading devices rises with window area, as illustrated in the following sections for large windows.

### The Effect of Shading Conditions on Peak Demand

For moderately sized windows (WWR=0.30), peak demand reductions follow similar trends to the electricity use reductions described above (Figure 6-46). Their magnitude hinges on the window SHGC and U-factor. For retrofits typical of Window A, shading can cut peak demand up to 2.5 W/sf (34 percent). For Windows C and E, peak demand declines with shading up to 0.84 W/sf (15 percent). In the case of Windows F, D, and H, shading has an insignificant effect on peak demand.

At a moderate window area, Windows C and E benefit from any type of shading illustrated here. Window A greatly benefits from the most extensive shading possible, deep overhangs combined with fins. High-rise obstructions reduce peak demand for all glazings except A, making shading unnecessary. Shading will be most cost effective where peak demand is penalized with significantly higher time-of-use rates. Reductions in peak demand can lead to lower mechanical system size and cost. Figure 6-48 illustrates that the magnitude of peak demand reduction from shading devices increases with window area (see the following section for large window area results).

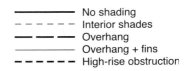

**Figure 6-47.** *Total annual energy use for different shading conditions*

All cases are south-facing and include daylighting controls. Numbers are expressed per square feet within a 15-foot-deep perimeter zone. Results were computed using DOE-2.1E for a typical office building in Houston, Texas (Appendix A). Total annual energy use is calculated by multiplying electricity use by 3 and adding heating energy use. This reflects the 3:1 ratio of primary to end use energy for electricity. All window properties are for the whole window. Windows C–H have thermally broken aluminum frames. Window H has an insulated frame.
U=U-factor in Btu/hr-sf-°F, SHGC=solar heat gain coefficient, VT=visible transmittance

Legend:
— No shading
- - - Interior shades
▬ ▬ Overhang
— Overhang + fins
▬ ▬ High-rise obstruction

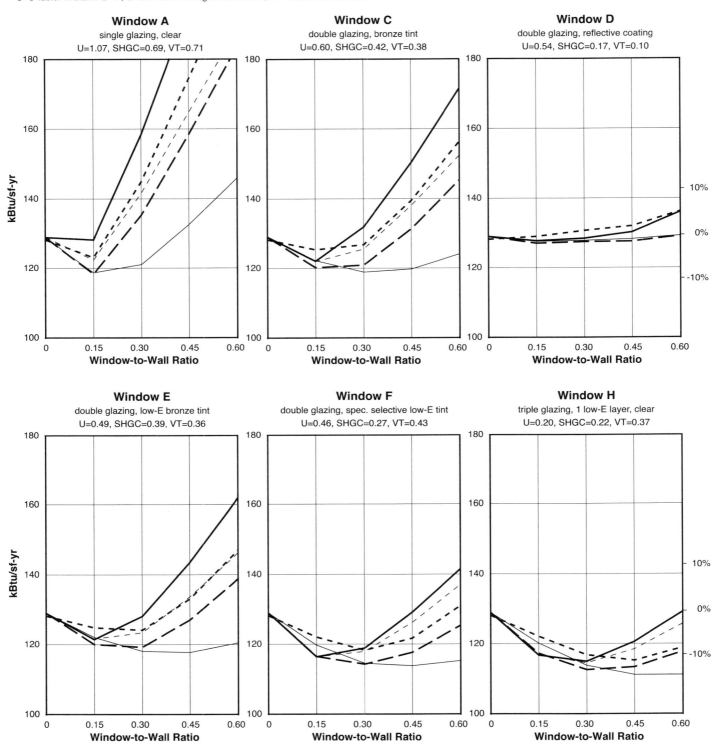

*Window Design for Offices in a Hot Climate*

*Figure 6-48. Peak demand for different shading conditions*

All cases are south-facing and include daylighting controls. Numbers are expressed in Watts per square feet within a 15-foot-deep perimeter zone. Results were computed using DOE-2.1E for a typical office building in Houston, Texas (Appendix A). All window properties are for the whole window. Windows C–H have thermally broken aluminum frames. Window H has an insulated frame. U=U-factor in Btu/hr-sf-°F, SHGC=solar heat gain coefficient, VT=visible transmittance

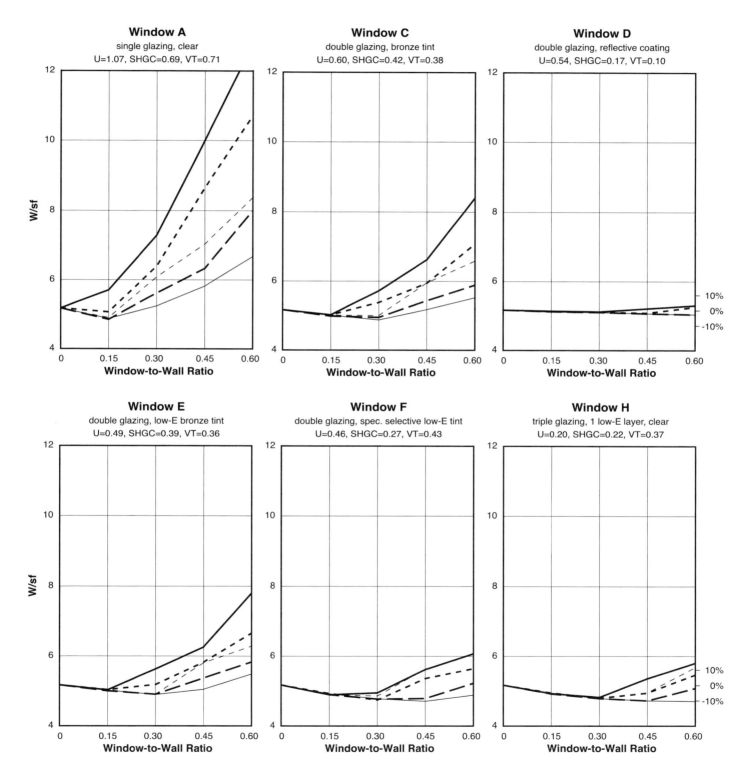

## Effect of Shading Conditions on Daylight

All types of shading reduce the average annual daylight illuminance. In order of least to greatest impact: interior shades, overhangs, deep overhangs combined with fins, and high-rise obstructions. For all window types, the high-rise obstructions cut average illuminance 50 percent compared to an unshaded window. Figure 6-49 shows how shading affects interior daylight illuminance levels for moderate-area windows. For all window types except D and all types of shading, the average illuminance remains above 30 footcandles for WWR=0.30.

**GLARE INDEX**

| | |
|---|---|
| * | = less than 7 |
| 7 | = imperceptible glare |
| 10 | = just perceptible glare |
| 16 | = just acceptable glare |
| 22 | = just uncomfortable glare |

*Figure 6-49. Average annual daylight illuminance*

Average daylight illuminance is calculated at a point 10 feet from the window. All cases are south-facing. Results were computed using DOE-2.1E for a typical office building in Houston, Texas (Appendix A).

*Figure 6-50. Weighted glare index*

Glare index is calculated at a point 5 feet from the window for a person facing the side wall. A lower index is better. All cases are south-facing. Results were computed using DOE-2.1E for a typical office building in Houston, Texas (Appendix A).

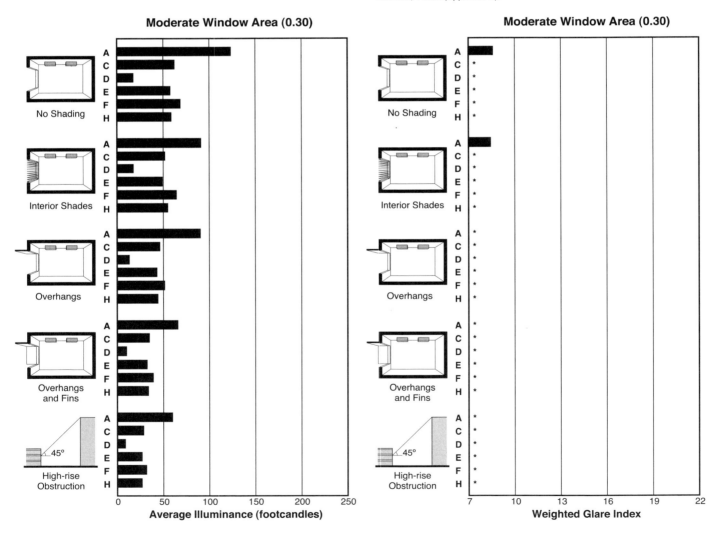

## Effect of Shading Conditions on Glare

For small- to moderately sized windows (WWR=0.30 or less) of all types, the weighted glare index is low for both unshaded and shaded conditions (Figure 6-50). Glare is minimally affected by shades because the size of the glare source, the window, is relatively small.

## Effect of Shading Conditions on View

In this analysis, view is obscured almost completely by interior shades when deployed in response to glare or direct sun heat gain. For a south-facing window with no exterior shading, interior shades are triggered frequently, particularly in a hot climate. Shade use is in fact dictated by window type. High-performance windows with a low

*Figure 6-51. View index*

View index is calculated at a point 5 feet from the window. A higher index is better. All cases are south-facing. Results were computed using DOE-2.1E for a typical office building in Houston, Texas (Appendix A).

*Figure 6-52. Thermal comfort*

Thermal comfort is calculated at a point 5 feet from the window. A lower PPD is better. All cases are north-facing. Results were computed using DOE-2.1E for a typical office building in Houston, Texas (Appendix A).

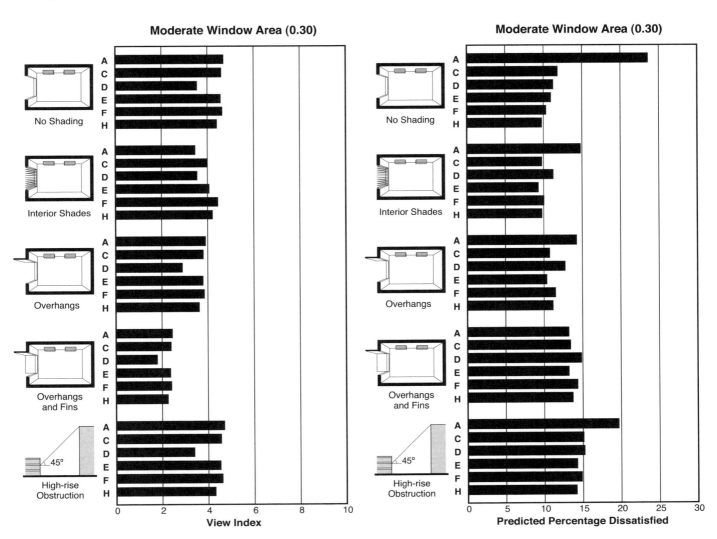

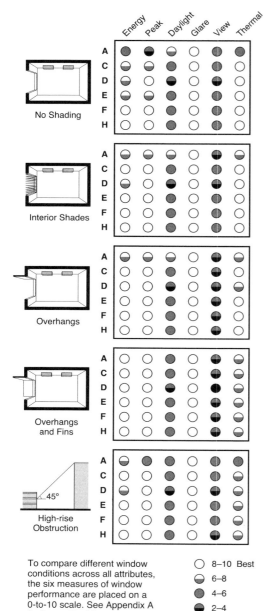

SHGC and U-factor control solar loads for thermal comfort, avoiding the need to use interior shades to control heat gain. For Window A, view is blocked by interior shades for 17–21 percent of annual daylit hours, while Windows D, F, and H require interior shades for less than 3 percent of daylit hours. Windows C and E require shades for 9–11 percent of daylit hours.

View is also partially obstructed by exterior overhangs and/or fins, or blocked by reflections in the window during periods when exterior light levels are low and the interior glass surface reflectance is relatively high. Overhangs reduce the unshaded view index by about one point for moderate area windows across all window types (Figure 6-51). Overhangs combined with fins reduce the index by about 1.5 points.

All window types except Window D have nearly the same view index (within 0.5 points) for any given shade condition except interior shades. The high-rise obstruction is considered part of the view and does not affect the view index. All view indices in Figure 6-51 are in the low to moderate range because of the window area.

## Effect of Shading Conditions on Thermal Comfort

Exterior shading affects thermal comfort by blocking direct sun. Compared to an unshaded window, exterior shading has either a positive or negative impact that hinges on outdoor conditions. If it is hot outside, the direct sun might be uncomfortable, but that same sun might be welcome if cold. With interior shades, thermal comfort improves (Figure 6-52). With overhangs and fins, thermal discomfort increases by up to 4 PPD for Windows C–H. Shading Window A improves thermal comfort by up to 12 PPD; deep overhangs with fins are most effective followed by shallow overhangs and interior shades. For moderately sized, south-facing windows, thermal comfort is within acceptable levels (PPD less than 16) for most window types (Windows C–H) and the variation in PPD produced by shading is small (less than 5 percent).

## Effect of Shading Conditions on All Attributes Combined

In Figure 6-53, the relative performance of all six attributes for a range of window shading conditions is shown on a 0-to-10 scale. All cases have daylighting controls and a window-to-wall ratio of 0.30. The impact of window area on each of the individual performance measures is summarized below.

*Energy:* With Windows A, C, and E, overhangs are recommended to significantly lower total annual energy use. In the case of single-glazed, clear Window A, deep overhangs with fins perform best. With Windows D and H (low SHGC and U-factor), exterior shading reduces energy use less than 2 percent, and is therefore unneeded from an energy standpoint.

*Peak Demand:* Both interior and exterior shading significantly reduce peak demand for moderate area Windows A, C, and E and are therefore recommended. Shading has a smaller effect on peak demand reduction with Windows D, F, and H.

*Daylight:* Interior daylight illuminance and brightness levels decline with all shade types, however, daylight remains at sufficient levels.

For all shading types and window types except Window D, the average annual daylight illuminance remains above 30 footcandles for WWR=0.30.

*Glare:* Discomfort glare is infrequent with moderate window areas for any window type, but interior shades are helpful for glare control in those isolated instances when it is problematic.

*View:* All shading systems reduce view. For moderately sized windows, the view index declines by about 1 point with shallow overhangs, 1.5 points with deep overhangs and fins. Even so, the view index remains in the middle range given the window area.

*Thermal comfort:* Shading does not have a major effect on thermal comfort except for Window A where attached shading offers considerable improvement.

If the building designer or owner wants to avoid exterior shading devices such as overhangs and/or fins on the sunny south facade in a hot climate like Houston, small- to moderately sized (WWR=0.30) high-performance windows (F and H) can be used with interior shades and daylighting controls. This solution offers good energy efficiency, controlled peak demand, adequate interior daylight and brightness levels, low levels of discomfort glare, and acceptable thermal comfort.

For moderately sized windows, exterior shading is recommended in some cases. Overhangs improve the performance of Windows C and E to a level similar to unshaded Windows F and H. Permanent obstructions on the south—mountains, trees, or buildings—do not completely negate the energy-saving benefits of shading Windows A, C, and E. Shading Window D is not recommended because of its negative impact on energy, daylight, and view.

## The Effects of Shading Conditions in a South-facing Perimeter Zone with a Large Window Area

This section addresses design decisions about shading once a large window area (WWR=0.60) has been chosen.

### Effect of Shading Conditions on Energy Use

With large-area windows (WWR=0.60), shading significantly reduces annual electricity use by 1.7–7.0 kWh/sf-yr (14–36 percent) across all window types except Window D (Figure 6-54). The impact of shading is greatest for Windows A, C, and E, but is still significant for Windows F and H. Even with Window D, there is some small benefit.

For all window types, deep overhangs combined with vertical fins offer the most effective shading in terms of electricity use. With this extensive shading, the annual electricity use for Windows D, F, and H is less than that for a smaller unshaded window. Shallower overhangs are also very effective. Interior shades offer 6–9 percent reduction in annual electricity use for Windows C and E–H. It may be possible to avoid the use of exterior shades if high-rise obstructions are present. With such an obstruction, the electricity use for any window (with no interior or attached exterior shades) approximates a window with an overhang and no obstructions.

In Figure 6-54, heating energy use declines with attached shading even though the beneficial solar heat gain is reduced in colder periods. This counterintuitive effect occurs because of the mechanical system requiring more heating energy for reheating chilled air during cooling periods in the unshaded condition. Since heating energy use is relatively small in Houston, this has little effect on shading design and window selection. The total annual energy (combined heating and electricity) is shown in Figure 6-47 in the previous section.

*Figure 6-54. Annual energy use and peak demand comparison by shading type*

All cases are south-facing with daylighting controls. Numbers are expressed per square feet within a 15-foot-deep perimeter zone. Results were computed using DOE-2.1E for a typical office building in Houston, Texas (Appendix A).

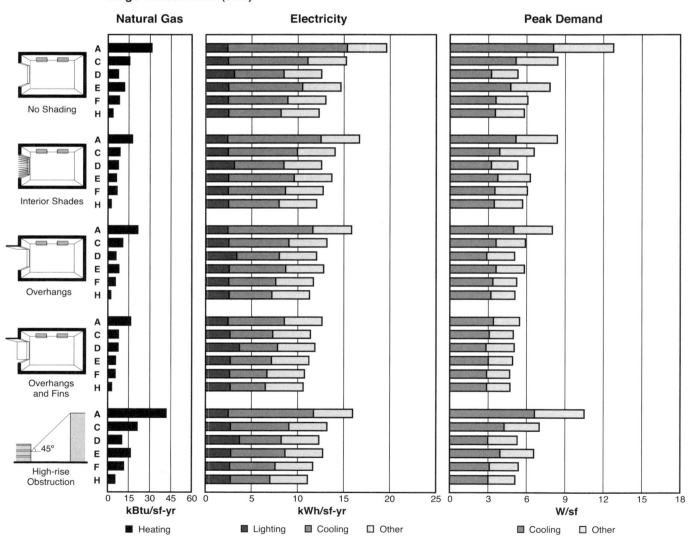

## Effect of Shading Conditions on Peak Demand

For most types of large windows (WWR=0.60), shading significantly reduces peak demand. Shading's impact is greatest with Windows A, C, and E; impact is less with Windows F and H, but still significant. The peak demand with Window D is least affected by shading. Peak demand declines by 1.1–3.5 W/sf (19–41 percent) if Windows C and E–H are shaded (Figure 6-54). Shading reduces peak demand by 0.27 W/sf (5 percent) with Window D. Deep overhangs with vertical fins provide the best performance, but shallower overhangs or interior shades are effective as well. High-rise obstructions cut peak demand somewhat but do not perform as well as attached exterior shading.

| GLARE INDEX | |
|---|---|
| * | = less than 7 |
| 7 | = imperceptible glare |
| 10 | = just perceptible glare |
| 16 | = just acceptable glare |
| 22 | = just uncomfortable glare |

**Figure 6-55. *Average annual daylight illuminance***

Average daylight illuminance is calculated at a point 10 feet from the window. All cases are south-facing. Results were computed using DOE-2.1E for a typical office building in Houston, Texas (Appendix A).

**Figure 6-56. *Weighted glare index***

Glare index is calculated at a point 5 feet from the window for a person facing the side wall. A lower index is better. All cases are south-facing with no shading. Results were computed using DOE-2.1E for a typical office building in Houston, Texas (Appendix A).

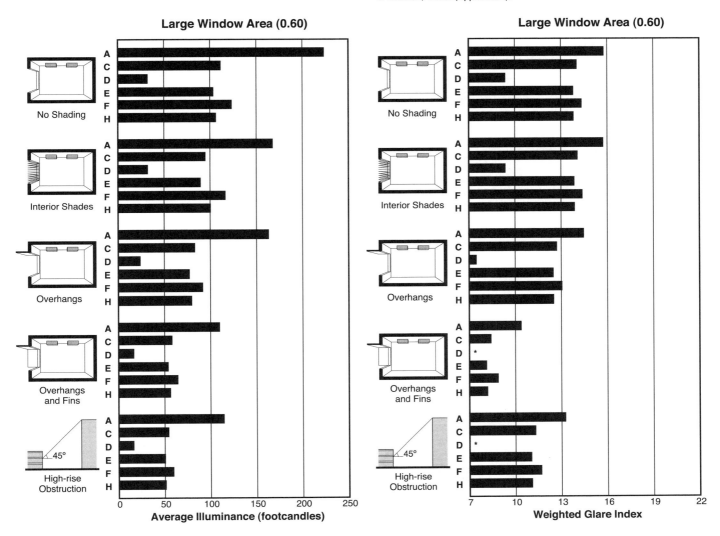

The proper combination of window type, size, and shading significantly cuts peak demand, leading to reduced operating costs, particularly where peak demand is penalized with higher rates, and capital costs savings due to HVAC downsizing.

## Effect of Shading Conditions on Daylight

Figure 6-55 shows how shading affects interior daylight illuminance levels for large area windows. Daylight reduction is greatest with high-rise obstructions or deep overhangs with fins. Moderate reductions occur with smaller overhangs or interior shades. For all window types except D and all types of shading, the average illuminance remains above 50 footcandles for WWR=0.60.

*Figure 6-57. View index*

View index is calculated at a point 10 feet from the window. A higher index is better. All cases are south-facing with no shading. Results were computed using DOE-2.1E for a typical office building in Houston, Texas (Appendix A).

*Figure 6-58. Thermal comfort*

Thermal comfort is calculated at a point 5 feet from the window. A lower PPD is better. All cases are south-facing with no shading. Results were computed using DOE-2.1E for a typical office building in Houston, Texas (Appendix A).

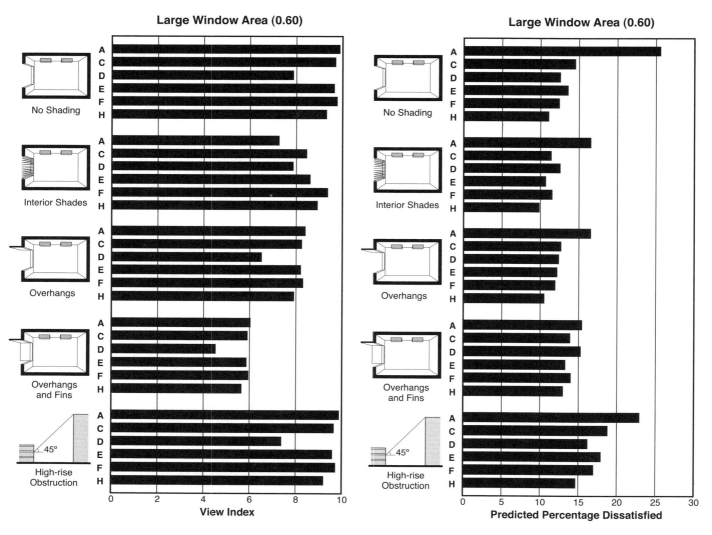

*Window Design for Offices in a Hot Climate*

## Effect of Shading Conditions on Glare

For large windows (WWR=0.45 or more) of most types, shading significantly reduces the weighted glare index (Figure 6-56). Deep overhangs combined with fins produce the lowest weighted glare index. High-rise obstructions or shallower overhangs offer some improvement over no shading, but the translucent interior shades used in this analysis are not opaque enough to reduce the weighted glare index. For Window D, glare is well controlled simply due to its low VT.

## Effect of Shading Conditions on View

Windows D, F, and H, all with a low SHGC, adequately control solar loads and direct sun, reducing the need to use interior shades. Shades are utilized only occasionally to cut glare. For Window A, view is blocked most frequently by interior shades, lowering the view index.

Generally, interior shades or overhangs reduce the unshaded view index by about one point for large-area windows across all window types (Figure 6-57). Deep overhangs combined with fins reduce the unshaded view index by up to 3 points for large-area windows. Window D with a very low VT has the lowest view index of all window types.

## Effect of Shading Conditions on Thermal Comfort

Exterior shading affects thermal comfort by blocking direct sun. Depending on window type and compared to an unshaded window, exterior shading has either a positive or negative impact that hinges on outdoor conditions (Figure 6-58). This is because blocking direct sun can be either negative or positive depending on the outside conditions. The predominant factor used to determine predicted percentage dissatisfied within a particular thermal environment is the asymmetry of mean radiant temperatures near the window due to hot or cold window surfaces and the effect of direct sun on the occupant. In other words, if it is hot outside, the direct sun might be uncomfortable, but that same sun might be welcome if cold.

If interior shades are used, thermal comfort improves. If overhangs combined with fins are used or high-rise obstructions block the sun, thermal comfort actually decreases for some window types. Yet, for large area windows, thermal comfort is within acceptable levels (PPD less than 16) for most window types (Windows C–H) and shading conditions. The variation in PPD produced by shading is small (less than 5 percent). Shading Window A on the interior or exterior reduces thermal discomfort by up to 12 PPD, with overhangs and fins being the most effective.

## Effect of Shading Conditions on All Attributes Combined

In Figure 6-59, the relative performance of all six attributes for a range of window shading conditions is shown on a 0-to-10 scale. All cases have daylighting controls and a window-to-wall ratio of 0.60. The impact of window area on each of the individual performance measures is summarized below.

*Energy:* For large-area windows, deep overhangs combined with fins achieve the lowest energy use for all window types. The impact is

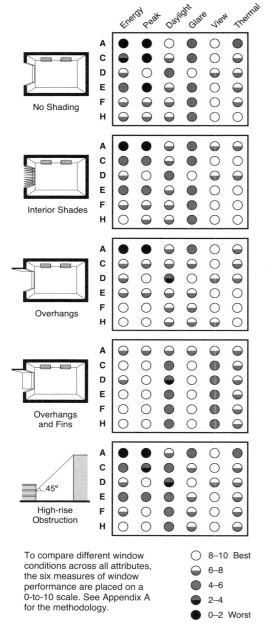

*Figure 6-59. Comparison of multiple attributes by shading condition for large window areas*

All cases are south-facing and have WWR=0.60 and include daylighting controls. Results are for a typical office building in Houston, Texas.

To compare different window conditions across all attributes, the six measures of window performance are placed on a 0-to-10 scale. See Appendix A for the methodology.

○ 8–10 Best
◐ 6–8
◔ 4–6
◑ 2–4
● 0–2 Worst

highest for Windows A, C, and E, and less for Windows F and H, but still justifiable in all cases except for Window D.

*Peak Demand:* Exterior shading significantly reduces peak demand for large-area windows and is therefore recommended in all cases except Window D.

*Daylight:* All types of shade reduce interior daylight illuminance, however, daylight remains at sufficient levels in most cases. For all shading conditions and window types except Window D, the average annual daylight illuminance remains above 50 footcandles for WWR=0.60.

*Glare:* Glare is a significant problem with large south-facing windows. Deep overhangs combined with fins produce the largest improvement in the weighted glare index. Interior shades or shallow overhangs do not offer significant improvements.

*View:* All attached shading reduce view. Across all window types and sizes, interior shades and shallow overhangs lower the view index by about 1 point, while deep overhangs combined with fins lower it by up to 3 points.

*Thermal comfort:* Shading does not have a major effect on thermal comfort except for Window A, where shading offers considerable improvement.

Large south-facing windows in Houston are problematic, and force the designer into challenging trade-offs. If the building designer desires larger windows (WWR=0.60), exterior shading with high-performance windows (F and H) yields the best overall performance by optimizing both energy-efficiency and comfort performance measures. Maximizing exterior shading with deep overhangs with vertical fins provides the best performance in all cases except that view is diminished. Because of the large window area, dark, reflective Window D also performs well in terms of energy and peak demand reduction but at the expense of daylight and view.

If exterior shading is not an option for aesthetic or cost reasons, interior shades with Windows D, F, or H is the best choice, but some energy and peak demand performance is sacrificed. For Windows F and H, high-rise obstructions such as mountains, trees, or opposing buildings perform comparably to overhangs in terms of energy use. Shades can be avoided in those cases, but for other window types, obstructions do not offset the need for attached shading.

*Window Design for Offices in a Hot Climate*

# East- and West-facing Perimeter Zones

Once the decision has been made to orient perimeter zones to the east or west, the designer must examine more detailed issues related to window design and selection. The following sections address how lighting controls, window area, and shading affect performance. All results shown in this section are for west-facing perimeter zones. In most cases, the results for east-facing zones are very similar.

## The Effect of Lighting Controls on Annual Energy Use and Peak Demand in an East- or West-facing Perimeter Zone

Annual electricity use always declines with daylighting controls in east- and west-facing perimeter zones (Figure 6-60). With daylighting controls, for all unshaded window types (except Window A) and all sizes, total annual energy use declines by 2.1 kWh/sf-yr (14 percent) compared to a zone without controls. Accompanying the lighting reduction, cooling energy also declines slightly with reduced heat gain from the lights. The window VT impacts the energy savings. For example, less daylight enters Window D (VT=0.10), providing less opportunity to cut electric lighting or the related cooling loads.

Daylighting controls also impact heating energy use, which rises to make up for lost heat gains from electric lights. Compared to a zones without controls, heating energy use increases 0.24 kBtu/sf-yr or 15 percent on the west, 0.16 kBtu/sf-yr or 13 percent on the east. Since heating contributes to about 3 percent of the total annual energy use (assuming an electricity-to-gas fuel ratio of 3:1), this increase produces an insignificant effect on the total perimeter zone performance.

| Window A | Window E |
|---|---|
| single glazing | double glazing |
| clear | low-E tint |
| U=1.25 | U=0.49 |
| SHGC=0.72 | SHGC=0.39 |
| VT=0.71 | VT=0.36 |
| **Window C** | **Window F** |
| double glazing | double glazing |
| bronze tint | spec. selective low-E tint |
| U=0.60 | U=0.46 |
| SHGC=0.42 | SHGC=0.27 |
| VT=0.38 | VT=0.43 |
| **Window D** | **Window H** |
| double glazing | triple glazing |
| reflective coating | 1 low-E layer, clear |
| U=0.54 | U=0.20 |
| SHGC=0.17 | SHGC=0.22 |
| VT=0.10 | VT=0.37 |

U=U-factor in Btu/hr-sf-°F
SHGC=solar heat gain coefficient
VT=visible transmittance
All window properties are for the whole window. Windows C–H have thermally broken aluminum frames. Window A has an aluminum frame.

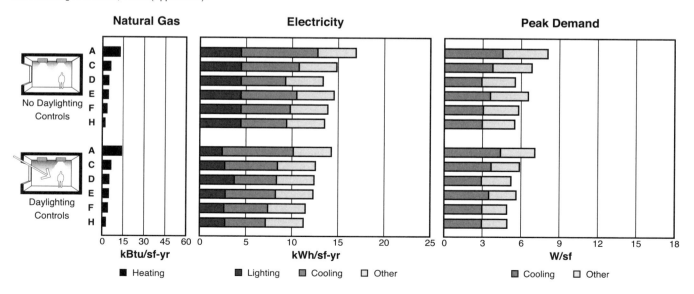

*Figure 6-60. Annual energy use and peak demand comparison by lighting system*

All cases are west-facing with a 0.30 window to wall ratio and no shading. Numbers are expressed per square feet within a 15-foot-deep perimeter zone. Results were computed using DOE-2.1E for a typical office building in Houston, Texas (Appendix A).

## Figure 6-61. *Total annual energy use by lighting system*

All cases are west-facing and have no shading. Numbers are expressed per square feet within a 15-foot-deep perimeter zone. Results were computed using DOE-2.1E for a typical office building in Houston, Texas (Appendix A).

Window A
Window C
Window D
Window E
Window F
Window H

Total annual energy use is calculated by multiplying electricity use by 3 and adding heating energy use. This reflects the 3:1 ratio of primary to end use energy for electricity.

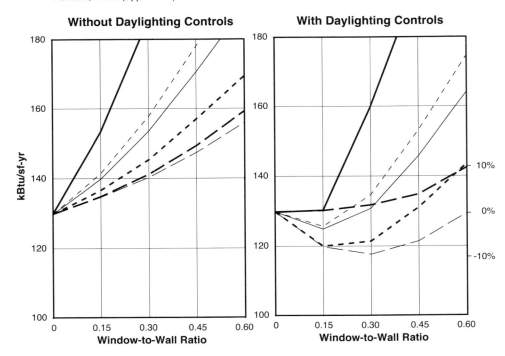

## Figure 6-62. *Peak demand by lighting system*

All cases are west-facing and have no shading. Numbers are expressed in Watts per square feet within a 15-foot-deep perimeter zone. Results were computed using DOE-2.1E for a typical office building in Houston, Texas (Appendix A).

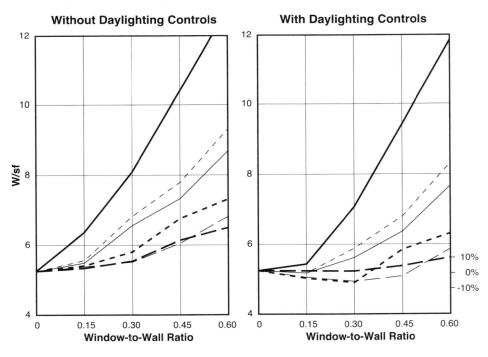

*Window Design for Offices in a Hot Climate*

Figure 6-61 shows the total energy use (combined heating and electricity) across a range of window areas. Because of the intense sun on the east or west facade in hot climates, the energy savings of larger windows with daylight controls are quickly outweighed by increasing energy use caused by greater solar heat gains. Without daylighting controls, annual electricity use rises rapidly with greater window area, as well as higher SHGC and U-factor, in proportion to admitted solar heat gains (Figure 6-39). Daylighting controls reduce lighting and cooling loads, to offset electricity use. The exact energy use profile depends on the window properties. Window types with a very low SHGC and U-factor and a moderate VT, like Windows F and H, generally perform better. With Window H, total annual energy use can be lower than an opaque insulated wall, even for large windows.

With daylighting controls, there is an average peak demand reduction of 0.84 W/sf (13 percent) in the east zone and 0.74 W/sf (11 percent) in the west zone compared to a zone without daylighting controls (Figure 6-62). Peak electricity demand typically falls in late July or August, particularly in the mid- to late afternoon when west - facing windows are most vulnerable to solar heat gains. Thus, it is important to consider the added long-term operating cost of demand charges when evaluating the cost-effectiveness of window options.

While all the energy use comparisons in this section show significant savings by using lighting controls, there is a range of possible performance (see Chapter 2). Lighting controls do not affect daylight, view, glare, and thermal comfort.

## The Effect of Window Area in an East- or West-facing Perimeter Zone

This section is intended to address the question of optimal window area on an east- or west-facing perimeter zone. Only the unshaded condition is examined here. See the following sections on how shading conditions can mitigate the negative impacts of moderate or large window areas.

### Effect of Window Area on Energy Use

As with south-facing perimeter offices, annual electricity use in east- and west-facing zones generally rises with greater window area, SHGC, and U-factor in hot climates like Houston (Figure 6-63). The rate of increase varies depending on window type. Electricity use for Windows A, C, and E with higher SHGC rises with area at a greater rate than lower-SHGC Windows D, F, and H.

Figure 6-64 illustrates that cooling energy use climbs with greater window area. With daylighting controls, electric lighting energy use falls with greater window area to a point where additional daylight produces no significant reductions in lighting energy. When cooling and lighting are combined into total electricity use (as well as all other electricity end uses), the optimal window area (as represented by the low point of the curve on Figure 6-64) varies by window type.

Heating energy use also rises with window area for all window types, though there is great variation (Figure 6-63). The increase is great with Window A ( high U-factor) compared to very little for Window H (very low U-factor). The combined effects of heating and electricity use are shown in Figure 6-61.

| | |
|---|---|
| **Window A**<br>single glazing<br>clear<br>U=1.25<br>SHGC=0.72<br>VT=0.71 | **Window E**<br>double glazing<br>low-E tint<br>U=0.49<br>SHGC=0.39<br>VT=0.36 |
| **Window C**<br>double glazing<br>bronze tint<br>U=0.60<br>SHGC=0.42<br>VT=0.38 | **Window F**<br>double glazing<br>spec. selective low-E tint<br>U=0.46<br>SHGC=0.27<br>VT=0.43 |
| **Window D**<br>double glazing<br>reflective coating<br>U=0.54<br>SHGC=0.17<br>VT=0.10 | **Window H**<br>triple glazing<br>1 low-E layer, clear<br>U=0.20<br>SHGC=0.22<br>VT=0.37 |

U=U-factor in Btu/hr-sf-°F
SHGC=solar heat gain coefficient
VT=visible transmittance
All window properties are for the whole window.
Windows C–H have thermally broken aluminum frames. Window A has an aluminum frame.

Because electricity use dominates in Houston, the optimal window areas based on electricity use alone versus total energy use are similar. A small window area (WWR=0.15) is optimal for windows A, C, E, and F, while WWR=0.30 is optimal for Windows D and H (although energy use for Window D is affected very little by window area). More window area beyond the optimal produces little additional lighting energy savings, while cooling energy use continues to rise. The ideal window area is the point where the energy-saving benefits of daylight controls are maximized. Window H outperforms other conventional windows due to an ideal combination of a relatively high daylight transmittance (VT) and a low solar heat gain coefficient.

### Effect of Window Area on Peak Demand

With unshaded east- or west-facing windows, peak electricity demand rises with window area. For Window C–H, the average increase is 2.54 W/sf (49 percent) without daylight controls and 1.6 W/sf (30 percent) with controls (Figures 6-62 and 6-63). The rate of increase depends on window type. It is greatest for Windows A, C,

*Figure 6-63. Annual energy use and peak demand comparison by window area*

All cases are west-facing with no shading and include daylighting controls. Numbers are expressed per square feet within a 15-foot-deep perimeter zone. Results were computed using DOE-2.1E for a typical office building in Houston, Texas (Appendix A).

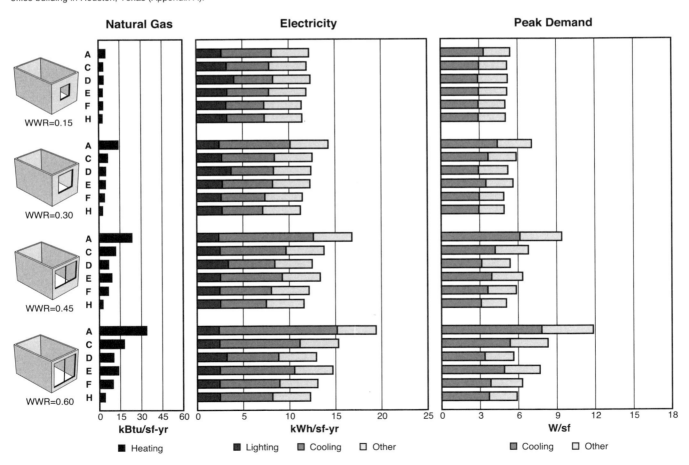

*Window Design for Offices in a Hot Climate*

## Figure 6-64. Annual electrical energy use

All cases are west-facing with no shading and include daylighting controls. Numbers are expressed per square feet within a 15-foot-deep perimeter zone. Results were computed using DOE-2.1E for a typical office building in Houston, Texas (Appendix A).

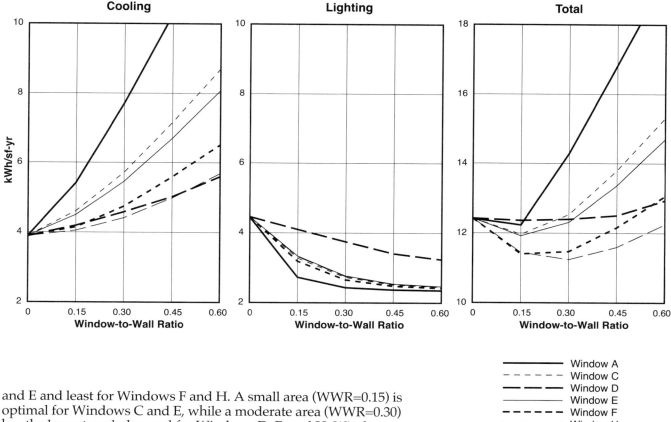

| Window A | Window E |
|---|---|
| single glazing | double glazing |
| clear | low-E tint |
| U=1.25 | U=0.49 |
| SHGC=0.72 | SHGC=0.39 |
| VT=0.71 | VT=0.36 |
| **Window C** | **Window F** |
| double glazing | double glazing |
| bronze tint | spec. selective low-E tint |
| U=0.60 | U=0.46 |
| SHGC=0.42 | SHGC=0.27 |
| VT=0.38 | VT=0.43 |
| **Window D** | **Window H** |
| double glazing | triple glazing |
| reflective coating | 1 low-E layer, clear |
| U=0.54 | U=0.20 |
| SHGC=0.17 | SHGC=0.22 |
| VT=0.10 | VT=0.37 |

U=U-factor in Btu/hr-sf-°F
SHGC=solar heat gain coefficient
VT=visible transmittance
All window properties are for the whole window.
Windows C–H have thermally broken aluminum frames. Window A has an aluminum frame.

and E and least for Windows F and H. A small area (WWR=0.15) is optimal for Windows C and E, while a moderate area (WWR=0.30) has the lowest peak demand for Windows D, F, and H. Window area affects peak demand the least for Window D. Interior and exterior shading can reduce the negative impacts of greater window area (see the following sections).

### Effect of Window Area on Daylight

Greater window area yields more daylight illuminance in east- and west-facing perimeter zones for all window types (Figure 6-65). When the window-to-wall ratio is equal to or exceeds 0.30, the average annual daylight illuminance is at least 50 footcandles for all cases except Window D (VT=0.10), which provides the least daylight at any size.

For lighting designers, it is useful to note that the average annual daylight illuminance at 10 feet from an unshaded window east-facing window is equal to 527*EA, where the product of VT and WWR is known as the effective aperture (EA=VT*WWR). For an unshaded west-facing window, the average annual daylight illuminance is equal to 433*EA.

## Effect of Window Area on Glare

With all small east- or west-facing windows (WWR=0.15), Figure 6-66 illustrates a low weighted glare index. For moderate window area (WWR=0.30), this index increases for all windows except Window D, which remains at a low level because of its low VT. With larger window areas (WWR=0.45 and above), the weighted glare index for all window types, including Window D, increase significantly.

## Effect of Window Area on View

As the window are increases, view improves significantly as a major component of the view index in this analysis is window area (Figure 6-6). Window D with a very low visible transmittance (VT) and high visible surface reflectance performs more poorly than all other window types with respect to view.

**GLARE INDEX**

| | |
|---|---|
| * | = less than 7 |
| 7 | = imperceptible glare |
| 10 | = just perceptible glare |
| 16 | = just acceptable glare |
| 22 | = just uncomfortable glare |

*Figure 6-65. Average daylight illuminance*

Average daylight illuminance is calculated at a point 10 feet from the window. All cases are west-facing with no shading. Results were computed using DOE-2.1E for a typical office building in Houston, Texas (Appendix A).

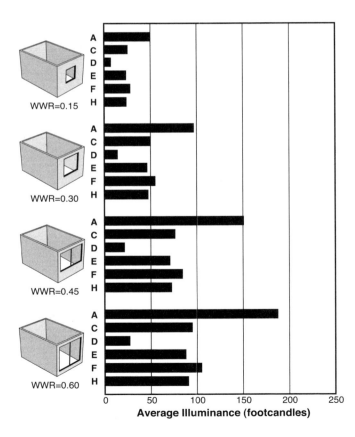

*Figure 6-66. Weighted glare index*

Glare index is calculated at a point 5 feet from the window for a person facing the side wall. A lower index is better. All cases are west-facing with no shading. Results were computed using DOE-2.1E for a typical office building in Houston, Texas (Appendix A).

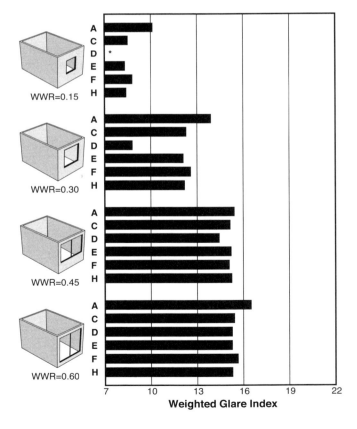

## Effect of Window Area on Thermal Comfort

Thermal discomfort in unshaded east- and west-facing offices in Houston rises slightly with greater window area (Figure 6-68). On average, there is an increase of 1.8 predicted percentage dissatisfied (PPD) with east-facing windows and 2.8 PPD in the west as window area rises from WWR=0.30 to 0.60 for all window types. All windows at all sizes are at an acceptable level (below 20 PPD) except for single-pane clear Window A.

## The Effect of Window Area on All Attributes Combined

In Figure 6-69, the relative performance of all six attributes for a range of window areas is shown on a 0-to-10 scale. All cases have daylighting controls and no exterior or interior shading devices. The impact of window area on each of the individual performance measures is summarized below.

*Energy:* A small window area (WWR=0.15) is optimal for windows A, C, E, and F, while WWR=0.30 is optimal for Windows D and H (although energy use for Window D is affected very little by window area).

| Window A | Window E |
|---|---|
| single glazing | double glazing |
| clear | low-E tint |
| U=1.25 | U=0.49 |
| SHGC=0.72 | SHGC=0.39 |
| VT=0.71 | VT=0.36 |
| **Window C** | **Window F** |
| double glazing | double glazing |
| bronze tint | spec. selective low-E tint |
| U=0.60 | U=0.46 |
| SHGC=0.42 | SHGC=0.27 |
| VT=0.38 | VT=0.43 |
| **Window D** | **Window H** |
| double glazing | triple glazing |
| reflective coating | 1 low-E layer, clear |
| U=0.54 | U=0.20 |
| SHGC=0.17 | SHGC=0.22 |
| VT=0.10 | VT=0.37 |

U=U-factor in Btu/hr-sf-°F
SHGC=solar heat gain coefficient
VT=visible transmittance
All window properties are for the whole window.
Windows C–H have thermally broken aluminum frames. Window A has an aluminum frame.

*Figure 6-67. View index*

View index is calculated at a point 10 feet from the window. A higher index is better. All cases are west-facing with no shading. Results were computed using DOE-2.1E for a typical office building in Houston, Texas (Appendix A).

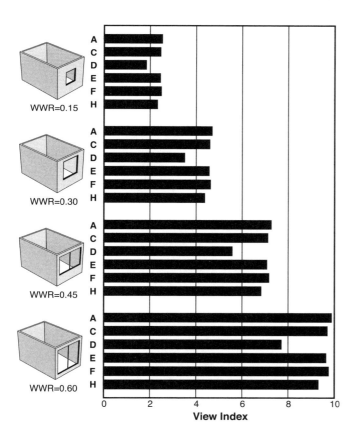

*Figure 6-68. Thermal comfort*

Thermal comfort is calculated at a point 5 feet from the window. A lower PPD is better. All cases are west-facing with no shading. Results were computed using DOE-2.1E for a typical office building in Houston, Texas (Appendix A).

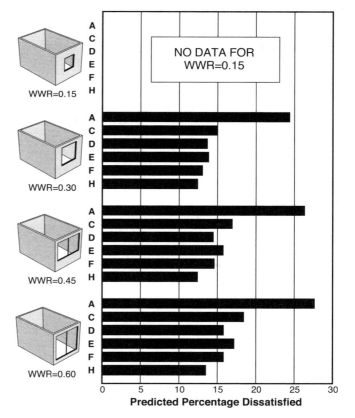

*East- and West-facing Perimeter Zones*

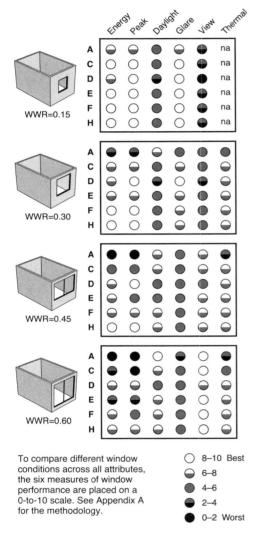

*Figure 6-69. Comparison of multiple attributes by window area*

All cases are west-facing with no shading and include daylighting controls. Results are for a typical office building in Houston, Texas.

To compare different window conditions across all attributes, the six measures of window performance are placed on a 0-to-10 scale. See Appendix A for the methodology.

- ◓ 8–10 Best
- ◔ 6–8
- ◑ 4–6
- ◕ 2–4
- ● 0–2 Worst

*Peak Demand:* A small area (WWR=0.15) is optimal for Windows C and E, while a moderate area (WWR=0.30) has the lowest peak demand for Windows D, F, and H. Window area affects peak demand the least for Window D.

*Daylight:* Daylight increases as window area and VT rise. All windows except Window D provide at least 50 footcandles at WWR=0.30 and above.

*Glare:* For all window types, the weighted glare index increases significantly as window area climbs above WWR=0.15 for unshaded east- and west-facing zones.

*View:* For all window types, the view index improves with greater window area.

*Thermal comfort:* Thermal discomfort rises slightly with greater window area. Comfort is acceptable for all window except single-pane clear Window A, which performs poorly.

For east- and west-facing perimeter zones in a hot climate like Houston, small windows (WWR=0.15) yield the best overall performance—energy use and peak demand are minimized as well as glare and thermal discomfort. Window F and H perform best at small to moderate sizes, but other window types perform adequately.

If larger windows are desired, higher-performance windows are essential. For example, a large triple-pane Window H (WWR=0.60) will yield the same total annual energy use as a small double-pane Window D (WWR=0.15). Peak demand and glare will be significantly worse with the larger window, but view and brightness perception improve significantly, and exterior shading can help balance these performance measures.

## The Effects of Shading Conditions in an East- or West-facing Perimeter Zone with Moderate Window Area

This section addresses design decisions about shading once a moderate window area (WWR=0.30) has been chosen.

### Effect of Shading Conditions on Energy Use

With moderately sized windows (WWR=0.30), shading devices can reduce annual electricity use significantly for some window types and have little effect on others (Figure 6-70). For high-SHGC Window A, annual electricity use declines by 17-19 percent with all types of shading. Shading Windows C and E reduces electricity use by 8–10 percent, and by 3–5 percent for Windows F and H (with low SHGC). Shading has no effect on Window D at a moderate window area.

Comparing vertical fins to deep overhangs combined with fins, there is less than a 5 percent difference in annual electricity use for Windows C–H (WWR=0.30). For retrofit conditions where clear glazing was used (Windows A), deep overhangs combined with vertical fins is the most effective shading type. It should be noted that the vertical fins used in this analysis only extend from the window head to the sill. Continuous vertical fins extending above the window head may perform closer to the deep overhang and fin case.

High-rise obstructions such as mountains, trees, or existing buildings can substantially block low-angle sun on east- and west-facing facades. If there are significant high-rise obstructions, then exterior shading may not be needed. Unshaded windows with a high-rise obstruction have lower annual electricity use than that of any shaded window with no obstructions.

Heating energy use rises slightly with exterior shading and falls slightly with interior shades. Figure 6-71 shows the total energy use (heating and cooling combined) for a range of window areas. Interior shading and vertical fins do not alter the optimal window area from WWR=0.15 for most windows (WWR=0.30 is optimal for Window H). Deep overhangs with vertical fins or high-rise obstructions shift the optimal window area to WWR=0.30 for many windows and up to

*Figure 6-70. Annual energy use and peak demand comparison by shading type*

All cases are west-facing with a 0.30 window-to-wall ratio and include daylighting controls. Numbers are expressed per square feet within a 15-foot-deep perimeter zone. Results were computed using DOE-2.1E for a typical office building in Houston, Texas (Appendix A).

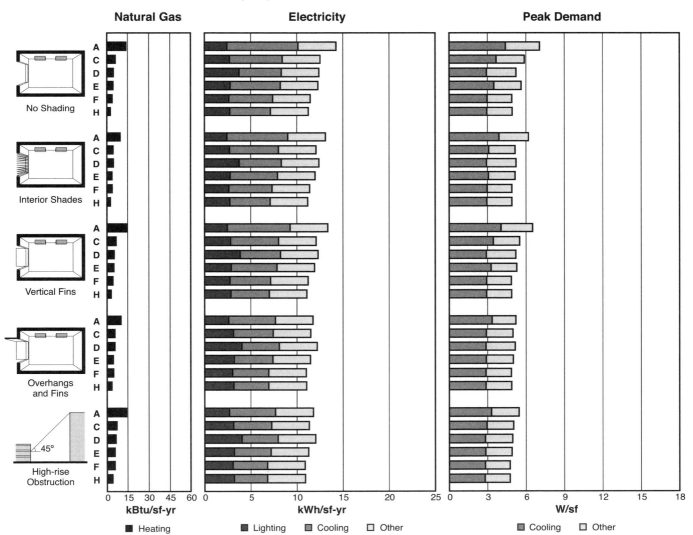

*Figure 6-71. Total annual energy use for different shading conditions*

All cases are west-facing and include daylighting controls. Numbers are expressed per square feet within a 15-foot-deep perimeter zone. Results were computed using DOE-2.1E for a typical office building in Houston, Texas (Appendix A). Total annual energy use is calculated by multiplying electricity use by 3 and adding heating energy use. This reflects the 3:1 ratio of primary to end use energy for electricity. All window properties are for the whole window. Windows C–H have thermally broken aluminum frames. Window H has an insulated frame. U=U-factor in Btu/hr-sf-°F, SHGC=solar heat gain coefficient, VT=visible transmittance

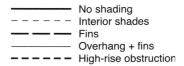

No shading
Interior shades
Fins
Overhang + fins
High-rise obstruction

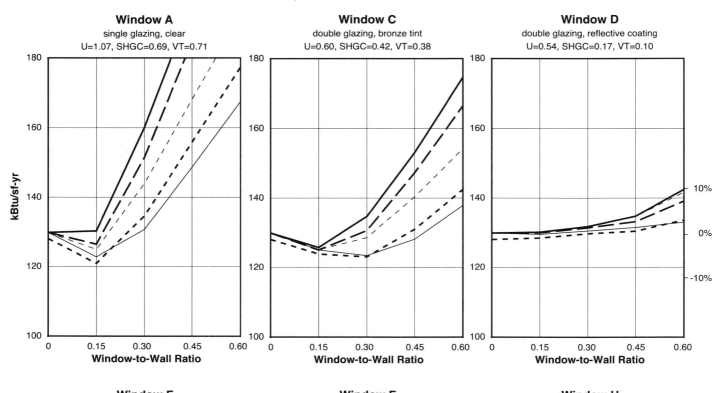

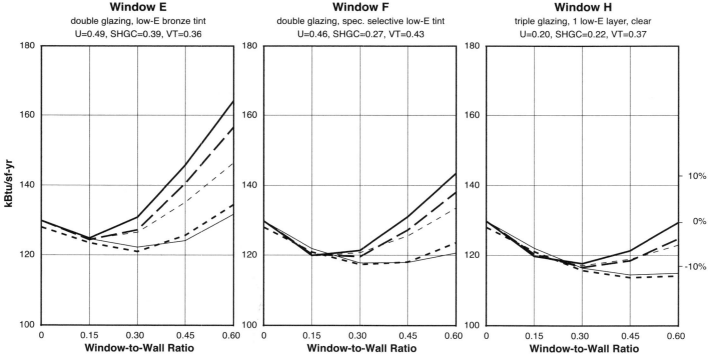

*Window Design for Offices in a Hot Climate*

*Figure 6-72. Peak demand for different shading conditions*

All cases are west-facing and include daylighting controls. Numbers are expressed in Watts per square feet within a 15-foot-deep perimeter zone. Results were computed using DOE-2.1E for a typical office building in Houston, Texas (Appendix A). All window properties are for the whole window. Windows C–H have thermally broken aluminum frames. Window H has an insulated frame. U=U-factor in Btu/hr-sf-°F, SHGC=solar heat gain coefficient, VT=visible transmittance

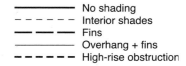

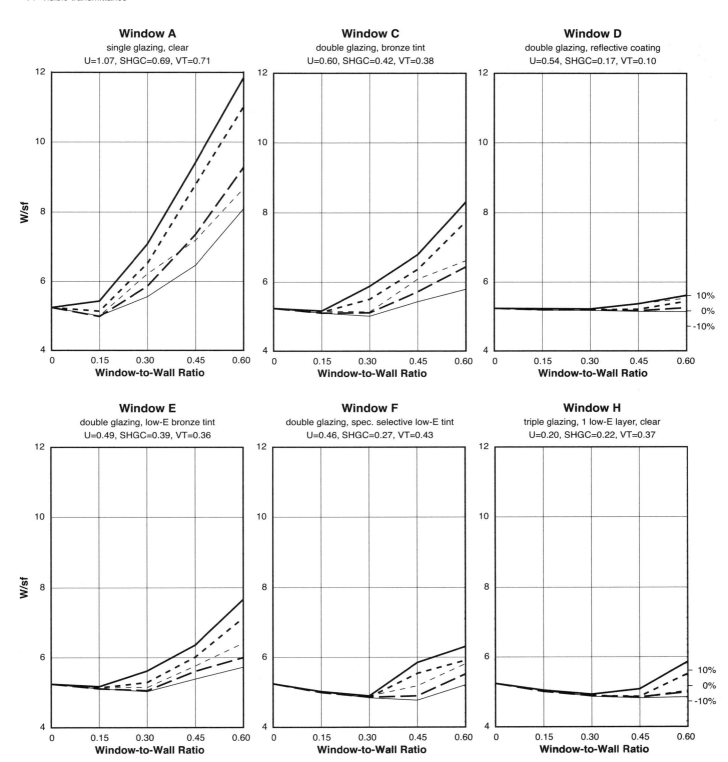

WWR=0.60 for Window H. The magnitude of energy savings from shading devices increases with window area (see the following section for large window area results).

### Effect of Shading Conditions on Peak Demand

For moderately sized windows (WWR=0.30), peak demand reductions are similar to the electricity use patterns described above (Figure 6-70). The magnitude of the reductions, in both cases, is dependent on SHGC and U-factor.

For typical retrofit conditions with Window A, shading can reduce peak demand by up to 1.6-2.0 W/sf (25–27 percent). The most extensive shading possible, deep overhangs and fins, are most beneficial in this case. For Windows C and E, shading can cut peak demand by up to 0.6-0.9 W/sf (12–16 percent). These windows, at moderate area, benefit from any shading type, although vertical fins are the least effective. In the case of Windows F, D, and H, shading has an insignificant effect on peak demand—only 0.1-0.3 W/sf (2–6 percent). For all these examples, peak demand for east-facing zones are within 1 percent of west-facing.

The presence of high-rise obstructions reduces peak demand for all window types, making shading unnecessary. Shading will be most cost effective where peak demand is penalized with significantly higher rates. Reductions in HVAC capacity can offset initial capital costs of the shading system. Figure 6-72 illustrates that the magnitude of peak demand reduction from shading devices increases with window area.

### Effect of Shading Conditions on Daylight

All types of shading reduce the average annual daylight illuminance (Figure 6-73). Overhangs combined with fins or high-rise obstructions cause the greatest reductions: up to 40 percent compared to the unshaded case. Overhangs, fins, or interior shades decrease daylight illuminance moderately, but the actual differences are not great for most window types. Illuminance levels remain above 25 footcandles for WWR=0.30 for all window types (except Window D) and all types of shading.

### Effect of Shading Conditions on Glare

Even for small- to moderately sized windows (up to WWR=0.30), there are potential glare problems in east- and west-facing zones (Figure 6-74). Deep overhangs with fins or high-rise obstructions perform best, with vertical fins ineffective at reducing the weighted glare index. Interior shades have some benefit with Windows A, C, and E.

### Effect of Shading Conditions on View

Interior shade use is dictated by window type, their deployment triggered by a certain level of glare or direct sun heat gain. In this analysis, view is completely blocked when interior shades are drawn. With Windows D, F, and H at WWR=0.30, interior shades block the view for no more that 3 percent of annual daylit hours. Similarly, for Windows C and E shades are deployed for 8–11 percent of daylit hours, and 16–20 percent for Window A.

View is also partially obstructed by exterior overhangs and/or fins, or blocked by reflections in the window during periods when exterior light levels are low and the interior glass surface reflectance is relatively high. The high-rise obstruction is considered to be part of the view and does not affect the view index. For all moderate area window types, vertical fins reduce the view index about one point while overhangs and fins reduce it by 1.5 points (Figure 6-75). Window D has the lowest view index of all window types. All other window types have nearly the same view index (within 0.5 points) for any given shade condition except interior shades. All view indices in Figure 6-75 are in the low to moderate range because of the window area.

*Figure 6-73. Average annual daylight illuminance*

Average daylight illuminance is calculated at a point 10 feet from the window. All cases are east-/west-facing. Results were computed using DOE-2.1E for a typical office building in Houston, Texas (Appendix A).

*Figure 6-74. Weighted glare index*

Glare index is calculated at a point 5 feet from the window for a person facing the side wall. A lower index is better. All cases are east-/west-facing. Results were computed using DOE-2.1E for a typical office building in Houston, Texas (Appendix A).

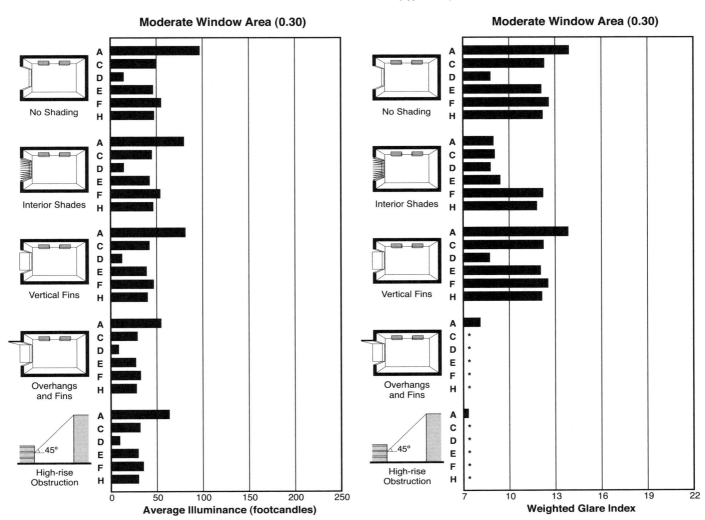

## Effect of Shading Conditions on Thermal Comfort

Compared to an unshaded window, shading can positively or negatively impact thermal comfort (Figure 6-76). For all moderate area window types except A, thermal comfort for both shaded and unshaded windows are acceptable (PPD less than 17), with the variation produced by shading small (less than 3 PPD). With Window A, shading improves thermal comfort by up to 7 PPD. Deep overhangs combined with fins are the most effective shading for Window A, followed by interior shades.

*Figure 6-75. View index*

View index is calculated at a point 5 feet from the window. A higher index is better. All cases are east-/west-facing. Results were computed using DOE-2.1E for a typical office building in Houston, Texas (Appendix A).

*Figure 6-76. Thermal comfort*

Thermal comfort is calculated at a point 5 feet from the window. A lower PPD is better. All cases are east-/west-facing. Results were computed using DOE-2.1E for a typical office building in Houston, Texas (Appendix A).

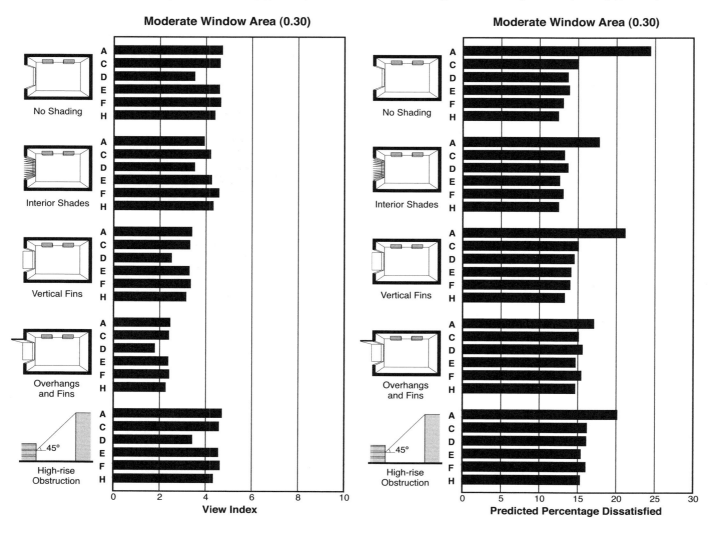

*Window Design for Offices in a Hot Climate*

## Effect of Shading Conditions on All Attributes Combined

In Figure 6-77, the relative performance of all six attributes for a range of window shading conditions is shown on a 0-to-10 scale. All cases have daylighting controls and a window-to-wall ratio of 0.30. The impact of window area on each of the individual performance measures is summarized below.

*Energy:* For Windows A, C, and E (moderate to high SHGC), extensive exterior shading is recommended, but any shading is beneficial. If Windows D, F, and H are used (low SHGC and/or U-factor), exterior shading is not required since the impact on energy use is low (less than 5 percent). With high-rise obstructions, no exterior shading is required for any window type.

*Peak Demand:* Exterior shading is recommended for Windows A, C, and E. Shading is less critical with Windows D, F, and H to reduce peak demand.

*Daylight:* Interior daylight illuminance and brightness levels decline with all types of shading. For all window types except D under any shading condition, the average annual daylight illuminance remains above 25 footcandles for WWR=0.30.

*Glare:* Glare can be a problem even with a moderate window area. Extensive exterior shading is most effective, but properly operated interior shades can be effective as well. Window D with a low VT requires no shading to control glare at a moderate window area.

*View:* All shading systems reduce view. Across all window types, vertical fins lower the view index by about one point, while overhangs combined with fins lower it 1.5. All view indices are low because of the moderate window area.

*Thermal comfort:* Shading does not have a major effect on thermal comfort except for Window A where shading offers considerable improvement.

For moderate area windows (WWR=0.30), interior shades with high-performance Windows F and H result in good energy efficiency, controlled peak demand, adequate interior daylight and brightness levels, low levels of discomfort glare, and acceptable thermal comfort. In contrast, more extensive exterior shading, deep overhangs and vertical fins, are required with Windows C and E to raise their performance to acceptable levels.

If high-rise obstructions such as mountains, trees, or opposing buildings are present, exterior or interior shades are not needed. This type of shading yields the best overall performance across the windows modeled. In any case, Window D is not recommended because of its lower performance in energy, daylight, and view.

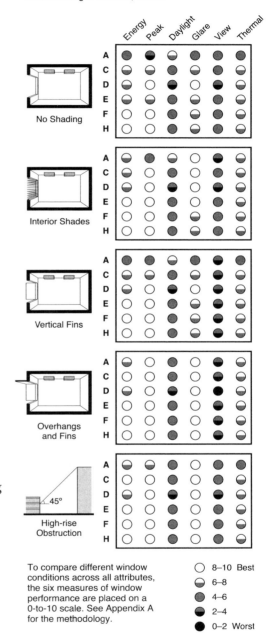

*Figure 6-77. Comparison of multiple attributes by shading condition for moderate window areas*

All cases are west-facing and have WWR=0.30 and include daylighting controls. Results are for a typical office building in Houston, Texas.

To compare different window conditions across all attributes, the six measures of window performance are placed on a 0-to-10 scale. See Appendix A for the methodology.

○ 8–10 Best
◔ 6–8
◑ 4–6
◕ 2–4
● 0–2 Worst

## The Effects of Shading Conditions in an East- or West-facing Perimeter Zone with a Large Window Area

This section addresses design decisions about shading once a large window area (WWR=0.60) has been chosen.

### Effect of Shading Conditions on Energy Use

With large-area windows (WWR=0.60), shading significantly reduces annual electricity use by 1.6–3.2 kWh/sf-yr (13–21 percent) across all window types except Window D (Figure 6-78). The impact of shading is greatest for Windows A, C, and E, but is still significant for Windows F and H. Even with Window D, there is some benefit.

*Figure 6-78. Annual energy use and peak demand comparison by shading type*

All cases are west-facing with a 0.60 window-to-wall ratio and include daylighting controls. Numbers are expressed per square feet within a 15-foot-deep perimeter zone. Results were computed using DOE-2.1E for a typical office building in Houston, Texas (Appendix A).

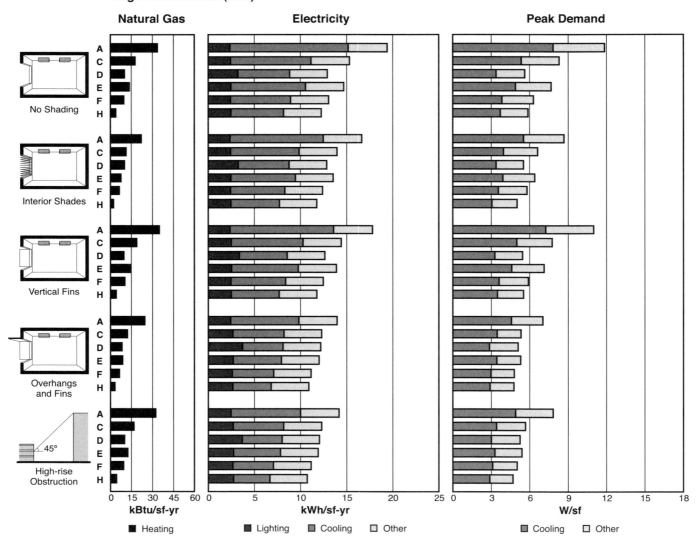

For all window types, deep overhangs combined with vertical fins or high-rise obstructions offer the most effective shading in terms of electricity use. Vertical fins are also effective in reducing energy use, compared to an unshaded window. It must be noted that the vertical fins in this analysis only extend from the window head to the sill. Continuous fins rising above the window head may perform closer to the deep overhang and fin case.

With extensive shading, the annual electricity use for Windows F and H is less than that for a smaller unshaded window. Like moderately sized windows, however, shading is not required on large windows if high-rise obstructions are present. Unshaded windows with these obstructions have annual electricity use nearing that of the most extensive, attached shading. Interior shades cannot effectively substitute for exterior shading, but they do reduce energy use compared to an unshaded window.

Heating energy uses declines with shading in some cases, even though it reduces the beneficial solar heat gain in colder periods (Figure 6-78). This counterintuitive effect occurs because the mechanical system requires more heating energy for reheating chilled air during cooling periods in the unshaded condition. Since these differences are relatively small in Houston, this has little effect on shading design and window selection. The total energy (combined heating and electricity) is shown in Figure 6-71 in the previous section.

### Effect of Shading Conditions on Peak Demand

For large east- or west-facing windows (WWR=0.60), shading can significantly reduce peak demand for all window types. Peak demand falls 1.5–3.0 W/sf (24–36 percent) for Windows C, E, and F compared to the unshaded case. For Windows D and H, shading can reduce peak demand by 0.5–1.2 W/sf (9–20 percent). For retrofit applications (Window A), peak demand reductions of up to 4.0–4.8 W/sf (24–39 percent) are possible.

Deep overhangs with vertical fins perform best but vertical fins or interior shades are effective as well. With peaks stemming from low-angle sun on the east and west, high-rise obstructions reduce peak demand as well or better than any interior or attached exterior shading. In Houston, east-zone peak demand levels can be up to 4 percent greater than west-zone levels.

The proper combination of window type, size, and shading can result in significant peak power demand reductions, decreased operating costs (particularly in regions where peak demand is penalized with higher rates), and capital cost savings, due to HVAC downsizing.

### Effect of Shading Conditions on Daylight

All types of shading reduce the average annual daylight illuminance (Figure 6-79). Overhangs combined with fins or high-rise obstructions cause the greatest reductions. Vertical fins or interior shades have moderate impact. In all cases, daylight illuminance levels remain near 50 footcandles or above for all window types except Window D.

### Effect of Shading Conditions on Glare

For large east- and west- facing windows, glare can be a significant problem and difficult to alleviate. In fact, the glare issue is one reason to avoid large windows facing east or west. Neither the translucent interior shades used in this analysis nor vertical fins offer much improvement (Figure 6-80). Deep overhangs with fins or high-rise obstructions are effective in lowering the weighted glare index, particularly for Window D, which improves more than the others because of its low VT.

### Effect of Shading Conditions on View

As with moderately sized windows, interior shade use with large windows is dictated by window type. With Window D, interior shades block the view 3-7 percent of annual daylit hours. Similarly, for Windows C and E–H, shades are deployed for 9–18 percent of daylit hours, and 19-22 percent for Window A.

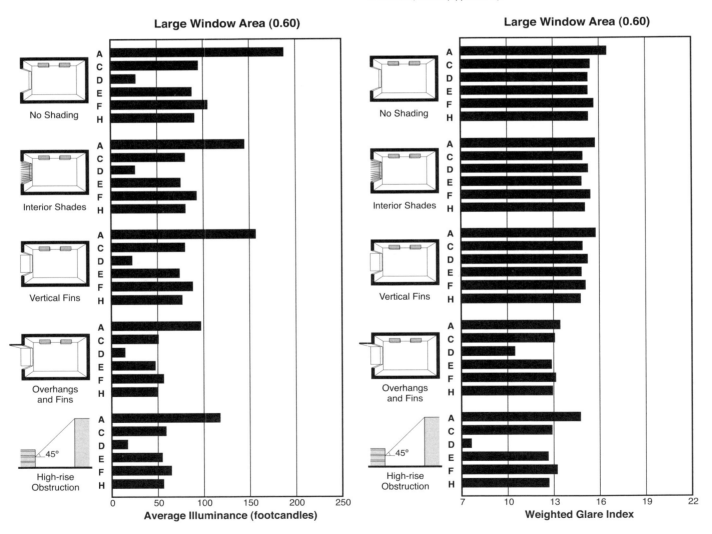

*Figure 6-79. Average annual daylight illuminance*
Average daylight illuminance is calculated at a point 10 feet from the window. All cases are east-/west-facing. Results were computed using DOE-2.1E for a typical office building in Houston, Texas (Appendix A).

*Figure 6-80. Weighted glare index*
Glare index is calculated at a point 5 feet from the window for a person facing the side wall. A lower index is better. All cases are west-facing with no shading. Results were computed using DOE-2.1E for a typical office building in Houston, Texas (Appendix A).

*Window Design for Offices in a Hot Climate*

For all large area window types, interior shades reduce the view index about one point and vertical fins about two points, while deep overhangs and fins reduce it up to four points (Figure 6-81). Window D has the lowest view index of all window types.

## Effect of Shading Conditions on Thermal Comfort

Compared to an unshaded window, shading can positively or negatively impact thermal comfort. For all large window types except Window A, thermal comfort for both shaded and unshaded windows are acceptable (PPD less than 20), with the variation produced by shading small (less than 5 PPD). With Window A, shading improves thermal comfort by up to 8 PPD, with interior shades or deep overhangs with fins being most effective.

*Figure 6-81. View index*

View index is calculated at a point 10 feet from the window. A higher index is better. All cases are west-facing with no shading. Results were computed using DOE-2.1E for a typical office building in Houston, Texas (Appendix A).

*Figure 6-82. Thermal comfort*

Thermal comfort is calculated at a point 5 feet from the window. A lower PPD is better. All cases are west-facing with no shading. Results were computed using DOE-2.1E for a typical office building in Houston, Texas (Appendix A).

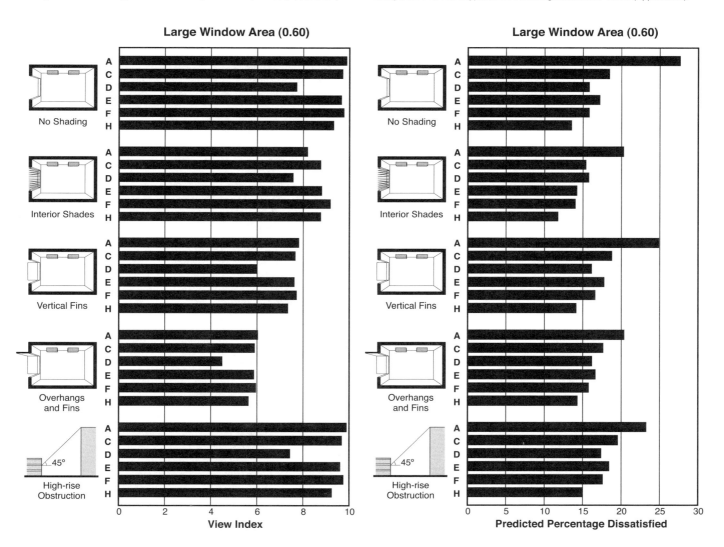

*East- and West-facing Perimeter Zones*

## Effect of Shading Conditions on All Attributes Combined

In Figure 6-83, the relative performance of all six attributes for a range of window shading conditions is shown on a 0-to-10 scale. All cases have daylighting controls and a window-to-wall ratio of 0.60. The impact of window area on each of the individual performance measures is summarized below.

*Energy:* For large windows, exterior or interior shading is recommended for all window types. Deep overhangs combined with fins yield the greatest energy efficiency. If high-rise obstructions are present, attached shading is not required.

*Peak Demand:* Exterior shading is highly recommended for all types of large-area windows, especially where peak demand is penalized with significantly higher time-of-use rates. Reductions in HVAC capacity can offset initial capital costs.

*Daylight:* All shade types reduce interior daylight illuminance and brightness levels. Yet, for all shading types and window types except Window D, the average annual daylight illuminance remains near 50 footcandles or above.

*Glare:* Glare is a significant problem with large window areas. Interior shades and vertical fins have little effect. Deep overhangs with fins glare the most, but the problem is not alleviated.

*View:* All shading systems reduce view. Across all window types, interior shades lower the view index by about one point, vertical fins about 2 points, and overhangs with fins by up to 4 points.

*Thermal comfort:* Shading does not have a major impact on thermal comfort except for Window A, where shading offers considerable improvement.

Large east- or west-facing windows in Houston are problematic, and force the designer into challenging trade-offs. If large windows (WWR=0.60) are desired, higher-performance Windows F or H with extensive shading (deep overhangs and fins) provide the best overall performance by optimizing both energy-efficiency and comfort. This shading option offers the best performance in all cases, but view is sacrificed somewhat. Vertical fins alone do not perform as well in this analysis, although they might be designed to extend above the windows with better results.

If high-rise obstructions are present, exterior shades are not necessary. If exterior shading is not an option for aesthetic or cost reasons, and there are no exterior obstructions, Windows F and H with interior shades are the best solution. Window D, with its dark reflective glazing, also performs well in terms of energy and peak demand, but at the expense of daylight and view.

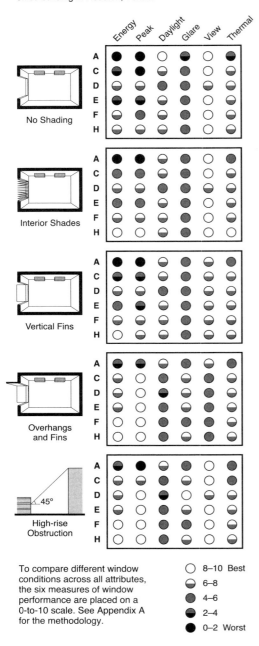

*Figure 6-83. Comparison of multiple attributes by shading condition for large window areas*

All cases are west-facing and have WWR=0.60 and include daylighting controls. Results are for a typical office building in Houston, Texas.

To compare different window conditions across all attributes, the six measures of window performance are placed on a 0-to-10 scale. See Appendix A for the methodology.

○ 8–10 Best
◔ 6–8
◑ 4–6
◕ 2–4
● 0–2 Worst

*Window Design for Offices in a Hot Climate*

# Summary

This section summarizes the window comparisons found in Chapter 6. Guidelines are given for window orientation (Figure 6-84), and then for window type, size and shading within each orientation: north, south, and east/west (Figures 6-85 through 87).

## Summary of Guidelines for Window Orientation

In a hot climate, north-facing windows are recommended with the unshaded condition to reduce energy, peak demand and glare for Windows A, C, and E (moderate to high SHGC). With effective exterior shading on Windows A, C, and E, there is no difference between orientations. Orientation has little effect on low-SHGC Windows D, F, and H with or without shading.

*Figure 6-84. Summary of window performance by orientation*

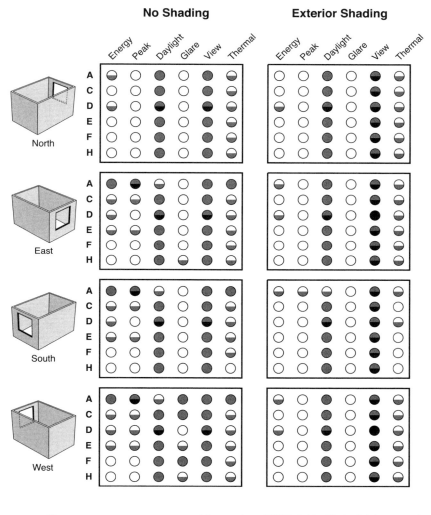

**Window A**
single glazing
clear
U=1.25
SHGC=0.72
VT=0.71

**Window C**
double glazing
bronze tint
U=0.60
SHGC=0.42
VT=0.38

**Window D**
double glazing
reflective coating
U=0.54
SHGC=0.17
VT=0.10

**Window E**
double glazing
low-E tint
U=0.49
SHGC=0.39
VT=0.36

**Window F**
double glazing
spec. selective low-E tint
U=0.46
SHGC=0.27
VT=0.43

**Window H**
triple glazing
1 low-E layer, clear
U=0.20
SHGC=0.22
VT=0.37

U=U-factor in Btu/hr-sf-°F
SHGC=solar heat gain coefficient
VT=visible transmittance
All window properties are for the whole window.
Windows C–H have thermally broken aluminum frames. Window A has an aluminum frame.

○ 8–10 Best
◐ 6–8
◓ 4–6
● 2–4
● 0–2 Worst

All cases have WWR=0.30 with daylighting controls. Windows are 6 feet wide x 6 feet high. Results are for a typical office building in Houston, Texas.

Shading conditions:
North:  2.8-foot-deep overhang
East:   4.2-foot-deep overhang + 3.0-foot-deep fins
South:  2.8-foot-deep overhang
West:   4.2-foot-deep overhang + 3.0-foot-deep fins

To compare different window conditions across all attributes, the six measures of window performance are placed on a 0-to-10 scale. See Appendix A for the methodology.

## Summary of Guidelines for North-facing Perimeter Zones

*Daylighting Controls: Recommended.*

Daylighting controls reduce total annual energy use with all window types, although there is less impact with Window D that has a low visible transmittance (VT). Peak demand also declines with daylighting controls but it typically is small on the north in any case.

*Window Area: No recommendation, not a major factor in most cases.*

When daylighting controls are used, window area is not a significant factor in energy use or peak demand on the north (except with single glazing). Greater window area provides more daylight and view but increases glare problems.

*Shading: No shading recommended.*

Shading has no significant effect on north-facing perimeter zones with moderate window areas. Exterior shading can improve glare with larger areas, and interior shades may be desirable to control infrequent glare in any case.

*Window Type: Select windows with low SHGC and relatively high VT.*

Avoid windows with a high SHGC (above 0.40 for the whole unit). When daylighting controls are used, a combination of a low SHGC (below 0.40 for whole unit) and a high VT (above 0.35 for whole unit) perform best. For moderate window areas, Windows C, E, F, and H all perform well. With larger areas, Windows E, F, and H are best.

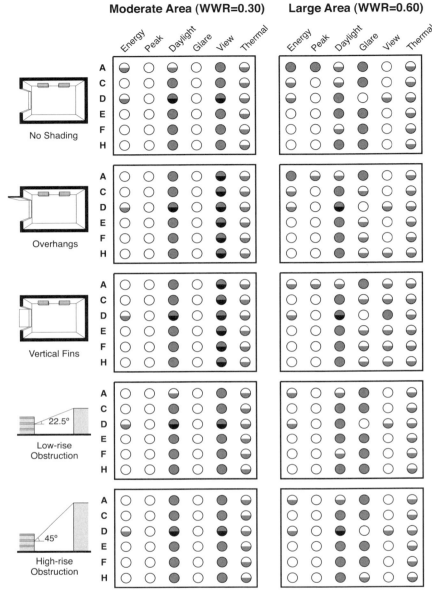

*Figure 6-85. Summary of north-facing window performance*

○ 8–10 Best
◔ 6–8
◑ 4–6
◕ 2–4
● 0–2 Worst

To compare different window conditions across all attributes, the six measures of window performance are placed on a 0-to-10 scale. See Appendix A for the methodology.

All cases have with daylighting controls. Results are for a typical office building in Houston, Texas.

**WWR=0.30** (6 feet wide x 6 feet high)
Overhang only: 2.8 feet deep
Vertical fins: 3.0 feet deep
Low-rise obstruction: Opposing buildings with a vertical angle of 22.5 degrees.
High-rise obstruction: Opposing buildings with a vertical angle of 45 degrees.

**WWR=0.60** (10 feet wide x 7.2 feet high)
Overhang only: 3.4 feet deep
Vertical fins only: 2.5-foot-deep @ 5 feet O.C. or 5.0-foot-deep @ 10 feet O.C.
Low-rise obstruction: Opposing buildings with a vertical angle of 22.5 degrees.
High-rise obstruction: Opposing buildings with a vertical angle of 45 degrees.

*Figure 6-86. Summary of south-facing window performance*

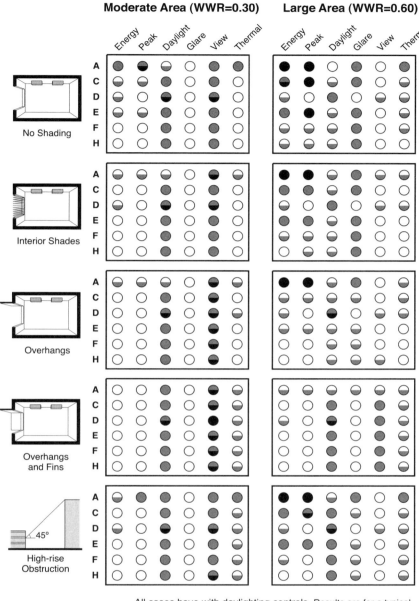

## Summary of Guidelines for South-facing Perimeter Zones

*Daylighting Controls: Recommended.*

Daylighting controls reduce total annual energy use and peak demand with all window types, although there is less impact with windows that have a low visible transmittance (VT).

*Window Area: Moderate window area recommended (WWR=0.30 or less).*

Energy use and peak demand rise with window area in an unshaded condition. Greater glazing area provides more daylight and view but increases glare problems.

*Shading for Moderate Window Area: Recommended for some window types.*

Interior and exterior shading devices significantly reduce energy and peak demand for Windows A, C, and E. Shading has less effect with Windows D, F, and H. High-rise obstructions do not offset the need for shading.

*Shading for Large Window Area: Recommended in all cases.*

Interior and exterior shading devices reduce energy and peak demand in all cases. Deep overhangs with fins outperform interior shades and shallow overhangs. High-rise obstructions are equivalent to shading with shallow overhangs.

*Window Type: Always select windows with low SHGC.*

Avoid windows with a high SHGC (above 0.40 for the whole unit). Windows with both a low SHGC and a reasonably high VT (above 0.35 for whole unit) are recommended if daylight and view are desired. Windows F and H perform best across all conditions.

All cases have with daylighting controls. Results are for a typical office building in Houston, Texas.

**WWR=0.30** (6 feet wide x 6 feet high)
Overhang only: 2.8 feet deep
Overhang + Vertical fins:
    4.2-foot-deep overhang + 3.0-foot-deep fins
High-rise obstruction: Opposing buildings with a vertical angle of 45 degrees.

**WWR=0.60** (10 feet wide x 7.2 feet high)
Overhang only: 3.4 feet deep
Overhang + Vertical fins: 5.0-foot-deep overhang + 2.5-foot-deep fins @ 5 feet O.C. or 5.0-foot-deep fins @ 10 feet O.C.
High-rise obstruction: Opposing buildings with a vertical angle of 45 degrees.

8–10  Best
6–8
4–6
2–4
0–2  Worst

To compare different window conditions across all attributes, the six measures of window performance are placed on a 0-to-10 scale. See Appendix A for the methodology.

## Summary of Guidelines for East- or West-facing Perimeter Zones

*Daylighting Controls: Recommended.*

Daylighting controls reduce total annual energy use and peak demand with all window types, although there is less impact with windows that have a low visible transmittance (VT) like Window D.

*Window Area: Small window area recommended (WWR=0.15 or less).*

Energy use and peak demand rise with window area in an unshaded condition. Greater glazing area provides more daylight and view but increases glare problems.

*Shading for Moderate Window Area: Recommended for some window types.*

Interior and exterior shading devices significantly reduce energy and peak demand for Windows A, C, and E. Shading has less effect with Windows D, F, and H. High-rise obstructions offset the need for shading for all window types.

*Shading for Large Window Area: Recommended in all cases.*

Interior and exterior shading devices reduce energy and peak demand in all cases. Deep overhangs with vertical fins outperform interior shades and vertical fins alone. High-rise obstructions offset the need for shading for all window types.

*Window Type: Always select windows with low SHGC.*

Avoid windows with a high SHGC (above 0.40 for the whole unit). Windows with both a low SHGC and a reasonably high VT (above 0.35 for whole unit) are recommended if daylight and view are desired. Windows F and H perform best across all conditions.

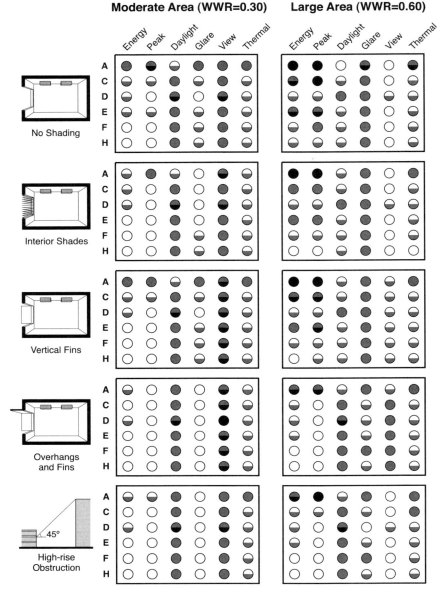

*Figure 6-87. Summary of east-/west-facing window performance*

All cases have with daylighting controls. Results are for a typical office building in Houston, Texas.

**WWR=0.30** (6 feet wide x 6 feet high)
Vertical fins only: 3.0 feet deep
Overhang + Vertical fins:
    4.2-foot-deep overhang + 3.0-foot-deep fins
High-rise obstruction: Opposing buildings with a vertical angle of
    45 degrees.

**WWR=0.60** (10 feet wide x 7.2 feet high)
Vertical fins only: 2.5-foot-deep @ 5 feet O.C. or 5.0-foot-deep @ 10 feet O.C.
Overhang + Vertical fins: 5.0-foot-deep overhang + 2.5-foot-deep fins @ 5 feet O.C. or 5.0-foot-deep fins @ 10 feet O.C.
High-rise obstruction: Opposing buildings with a vertical angle of
    45 degrees.

To compare different window conditions across all attributes, the six measures of window performance are placed on a 0-to-10 scale. See Appendix A for the methodology.

# CHAPTER 7

# Window Design for Schools

## Introduction

The analysis in this chapter guides the designer in making decisions about windows for schools in two U.S. cities with different climates. Unlike the previous chapters on office perimeter zones, this analysis of school classrooms is limited to energy use and peak demand and does not include indoor environmental factors such as daylight, glare, view, and thermal comfort. Chapters 5 and 6 can be used for guidance on these issues since they are similar across building types. This information can then be placed into a larger decision-making framework that includes appearance, cost, technical requirements, and environmental issues.

The chapter is divided into two main parts—window selection for schools in a cold climate (Chicago, Illinois) and a hot climate (Houston, Texas). Since some schools operate only nine months a year, while others operate year-round, the impact of schedule is explored at the beginning of each section. Then issues are addressed beginning with large-scale issues progressing down to individual zone design. For each climate, the impact of window orientation is considered, followed by analysis and design guidance for north-, south-, and east-/west-facing zones. Within each of these sections, the effects of daylighting controls and window size and type are studied, with interior shades assumed in all cases.

Throughout this chapter, a set of six representative window types is used for comparison. The sets are different for the two climates. In Chicago, a clear double-pane window is the base case, while in Houston it is a clear single-pane window—both bases reflecting some existing window norms in their region. Other differences in window types reflect greater use of tinted glazings in warmer climates. Window types are discussed in detail in Chapter 3. Annual energy use and peak demand per square foot of perimeter floor area are shown for each set of conditions being compared.

This analysis pertains only to classroom perimeter zones (30 feet by 30 feet with one exposed facade). The degree to which these perimeter zones contribute to overall building energy use and peak demand depends on the size, shape, and use of the whole school building.

*Figure 7-1. Elementary school. Photo: Courtesy of TRACO*

# School Window Design in a Cold Climate

## THE IMPACT OF SCHEDULE

Table 2-29 in Chapter 2 shows which windows comply with ASHRAE 90.1-99 for this climate.

Unlike most other building types, schools are often not occupied twelve months a year. A nine-month school year is common, but schools are increasingly used for summer classes, community education, and special events. Both the number of months and the hours of operation may be extended. Even if the entire school is not in use during these extended periods, some classrooms are likely to be.

To illustrate the impact of schedule, Figure 7-2 compares nine-versus twelve-month operating schedules in a south-facing classroom in Chicago. As expected, the three additional months of occupation in summer have a small effect (3 percent increase on average) on annual heating energy use, but significantly increase annual electricity use (35 percent on average across all window types). Although the magnitude of energy use changes with schedule, the relative performance between different window types remains the same. Window D always performs more poorly than the others because its low VT limits daylight and increases lighting energy use.

When heating and cooling are combined into total annual energy use, there is a 20 percent increase on average (with all window types) due to the twelve-month building occupancy period. Because peak electricity demand occurs in the summer for a south-facing zone, demand rises with a twelve-month operating schedule. On average for all windows, it increases 0.34 W/sf or 9 percent compared to the nine-month schedule.

With the unpredictability of future use and operating schedules of schools, it is wise to design as if there will be twelve-month use at some time in the future. In the remainder of this section, all comparisons are based on a twelve-month operating schedule.

*Figure 7-2. Annual energy use and peak demand comparison by schedule*
All cases are south-facing with a 0.30 window-to-wall ratio with interior shading and include daylighting controls. Numbers are expressed per square foot within a 30-foot-deep perimeter zone. Results were computed using DOE-2.1E for a typical school building in Chicago, Illinois (see Appendix B).

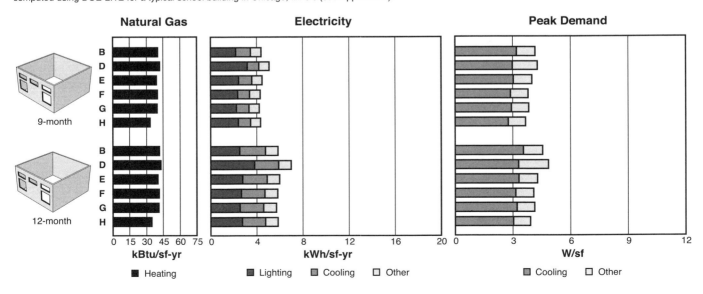

# THE IMPACT OF ORIENTATION

This section addresses the question of how window orientation impacts energy use and peak demand of a school classroom with moderate window area in a cold-climate city.

In Chicago, differences in annual electricity use between orientations are driven by solar gain affecting cooling energy use and daylight affecting electric lighting energy use. On average, between all orientations and window types, there is a small difference (2 percent or less) in annual electricity use with moderately sized windows (Figure 7-3).

Windows influence heating energy use in three ways—a lower U-factor results in less heat loss, a higher SHGC provides more solar heat gain, and a higher VT allows more daylight, which may reduce electric lighting resulting in less heat gain from lights, increasing heating loads. When these three factors combine, south-facing zones with interior shades and moderate window areas use 13 percent less annual heating energy compared to northern zones, while eastern and western orientations use 6–8 percent less heating than a northern orientation (Figure 7-3).

*Figure 7-3. Annual energy use and peak demand comparison by orientation*

All cases have a 0.30 window-to-wall ratio with interior shading and include daylighting controls. Numbers are expressed per square foot within a 30-foot-deep perimeter zone for a twelve-month operating schedule. Results were computed using DOE-2.1E for a typical school building in Chicago, Illinois (see Appendix B).

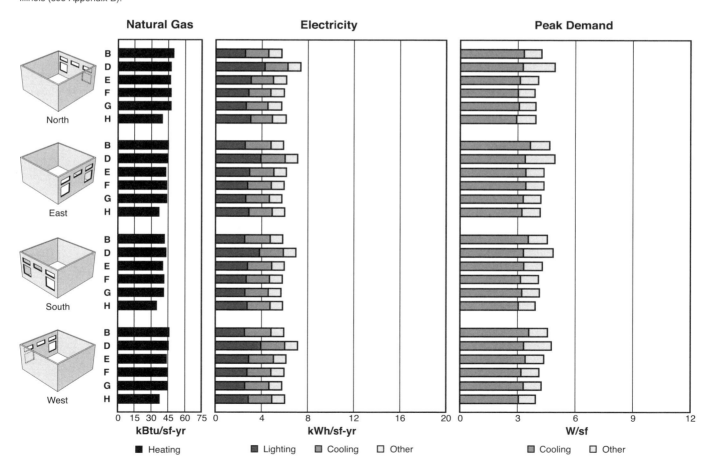

## Figure 7-4. *Total annual energy use comparison by orientation*

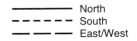

All cases have interior shading and daylighting controls. Numbers are expressed per square foot within a 30-foot-deep perimeter zone for a twelve-month operating schedule. Results were computed using DOE-2.1E for a typical school classroom in Chicago, Illinois (Appendix A). Total annual energy use is calculated by multiplying electricity use by 3 and adding heating energy use. This reflects the 3:1 ratio of primary to end use energy for electricity. All window properties are for the whole window. Windows B–H have thermally broken aluminum frames. Window H has an insulated frame. U=U-factor in Btu/hr-sf-°F, SHGC=solar heat gain coefficient, VT=visible transmittance

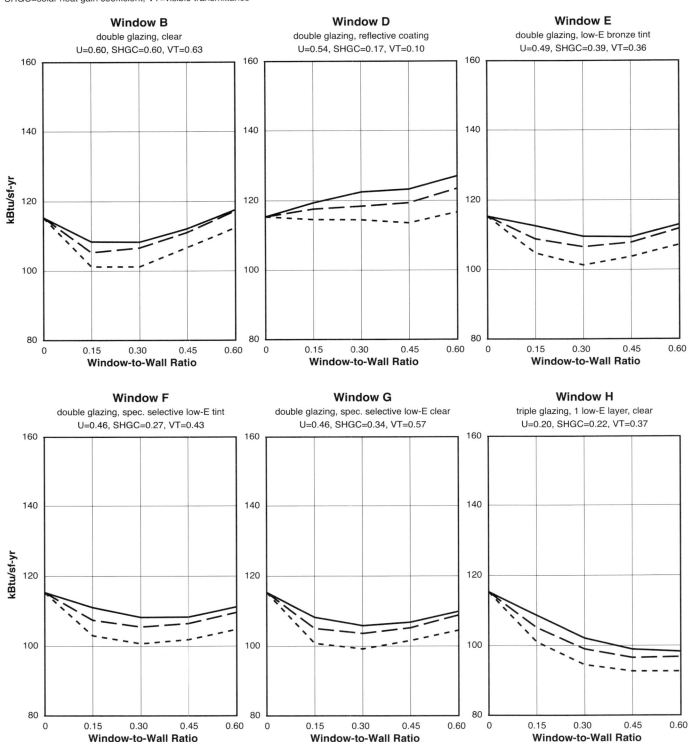

*Window Design for Schools*

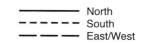

*Figure 7-5. Peak demand comparison by orientation*

All cases have interior shading and include daylighting controls. Numbers are expressed in Watts per square foot within a 30-foot-deep perimeter zone for a twelve-month operating schedule. Results were computed using DOE-2.1E for a typical school classroom in Chicago, Illinois (Appendix A). All window properties are for the whole window. Windows B–H have thermally broken aluminum frames. Window H has an insulated frame. U=U-factor in Btu/hr-sf-°F, SHGC=solar heat gain coefficient, VT=visible transmittance

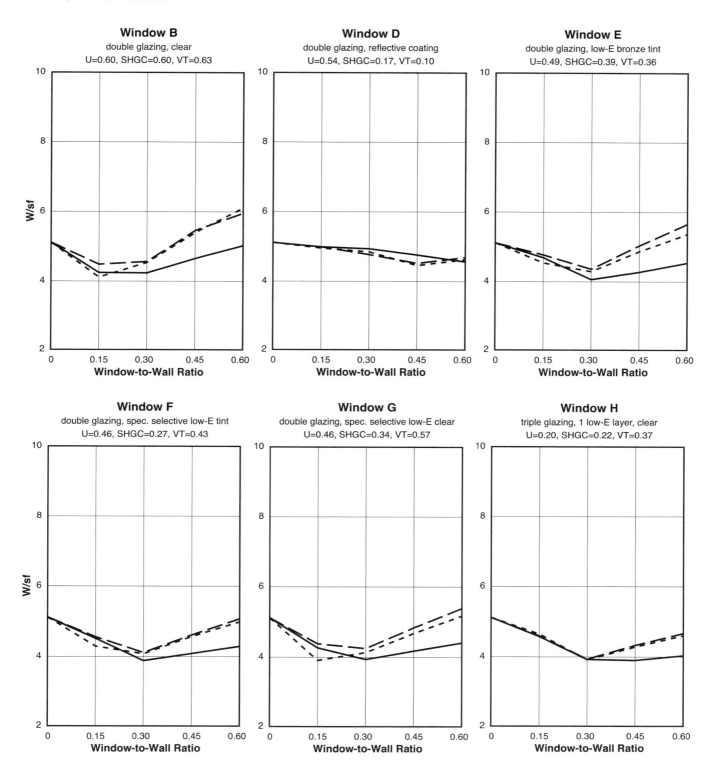

Figure 7-4 shows the total annual energy use (combined heating and electricity) over a range of window areas. For all window types, sizes, and orientations, a southern orientation performs best and a northern orientation worst. For moderately sized windows (WWR=0.30), there is a 7 percent average difference between north- and south-facing orientations. East- and west-facing orientations fall in between, with 3–4 percent lower total annual energy use than the north.

The effect of orientation on peak electricity demand depends on the window type. As shown in Figure 7-3 for moderately sized windows with interior shades, a north-facing orientation has the lowest peak demand for Windows B, E, F, and G. On average, peak demand levels of south-, east-, and west-facing orientations are 5–12 percent greater than the north. These differences diminish with Windows D and H.

The difference in peak demand between orientations increases significantly with window area for all window types except D (Figure 7-5). If applicable, utility rates based on time of use usually penalize high-demand use from south- and west-facing zones during mid- to late-afternoon summer hours, so it is worthwhile to consider local utility rate schedules. Demand charges can result in electricity costs that are three to five times greater than off-peak periods. It is also noteworthy that peak demand is in direct proportion to the cooling capacity of the building's mechanical system and can impact capital costs.

## NORTH-FACING CLASSROOMS

Once the decision has been made to orient classrooms to the north, the designer must examine more detailed issues related to window design and selection. The following sections address how lighting controls and window area affect performance.

### The Effect of Lighting Controls on Annual Energy Use and Peak Demand in a North-facing Classroom

In a cold climate like Chicago, daylighting controls in north-facing classrooms are recommended. The combined total annual energy use declines 12 percent on average with daylighting controls. Annual electricity use in north-facing classrooms falls significantly by installing dimmable light fixtures and controls that reduce electric lighting when there is sufficient daylight (Figure 7-6). Cooling energy use also decline because of diminished heat gain from the lights. The total annual electricity use reduction is 24 percent (2.0 kWh/sf-yr) on average across all window types with daylighting controls. However, heating energy use increase 12 percent (4.77 kBtu/sf-yr) on average because the lighting contributes less heat.

Figure 7-7 illustrates that without daylighting controls, total annual energy use rises with window area in proportion to admitted solar heat gains. It increases at a faster rate with higher SHGC and U-factor windows. With daylighting controls, total energy use generally falls then rises with greater window area. For most window types, the energy consumption in a zone with a large window (WWR=0.60) can be lower than one with an opaque wall (WWR=0). At window areas above WWR=0.15, triple-pane Window H performs the best while Window D always performs the worst.

With moderately sized windows, daylighting controls can significantly reduce peak electricity demand for all window types by 1.4 W/sf or 25 percent on average (Figure 7-6). Without daylighting controls, Window D (low VT and SHGC) has nearly the lowest peak demand. With daylighting controls, Window D has the highest peak demand with a moderate window area (WWR=0.30). Figure 7-8 illustrates that without daylight controls, peak demand increases with window area. With controls, peak demand falls and then rises with greater window area for all windows except Window D.

While all the energy-use comparisons in this section show significant savings by using daylighting controls, there is a range of possible performance (see Chapter 2).

## The Effect of Window Area on Annual Energy Use and Peak Demand in a North-facing Classroom

This section addresses the question of the optimal window area in a north-facing perimeter zone. In a cold climate city like Chicago, energy use does not necessarily increase with greater window area. The relationship between window area and energy use depends on several factors. Figure 7-9 shows that heating energy use in a north-facing space climbs significantly with increased window area— 55 percent on average between window types as window area rises from WWR=0 to WWR=0.60.

With daylighting controls, cooling energy use rises with window area, but lighting energy use falls with increased window area and daylight, resulting in a net decline in annual electricity use (26 percent decrease on average by increasing window area from WWR=0 to 0.60). Total annual energy use falls on average by 2 percent as win-

| Window B | Window F |
|---|---|
| double glazing | double glazing |
| clear | spec. selective low-E tint |
| U=0.60 | U=0.46 |
| SHGC=0.60 | SHGC=0.27 |
| VT=0.63 | VT=0.43 |
| **Window D** | **Window G** |
| double glazing | double glazing |
| reflective coating | spec. selective low-E clear |
| U=0.54 | U=0.46 |
| SHGC=0.17 | SHGC=0.34 |
| VT=0.10 | VT=0.57 |
| **Window E** | **Window H** |
| double glazing | triple glazing |
| low-E, bronze tint | 1 low-E layer, clear |
| U=0.49 | U=0.20 |
| SHGC=0.39 | SHGC=0.22 |
| VT=0.36 | VT=0.37 |

U=U-factor in Btu/hr-sf-°F
SHGC=solar heat gain coefficient
VT=visible transmittance
All window properties are for the whole window. Windows B–H have thermally broken aluminum frames. Window H has an insulated frame.

*Figure 7-6. Annual energy use and peak demand comparison by daylighting controls*

All cases are north-facing with a 0.30 window-to-wall ratio and interior shading. Numbers are expressed per square foot within a 30-foot-deep perimeter zone for a twelve-month operating schedule. Results were computed using DOE-2.1E for a typical school building in Chicago, Illinois (see Appendix B).

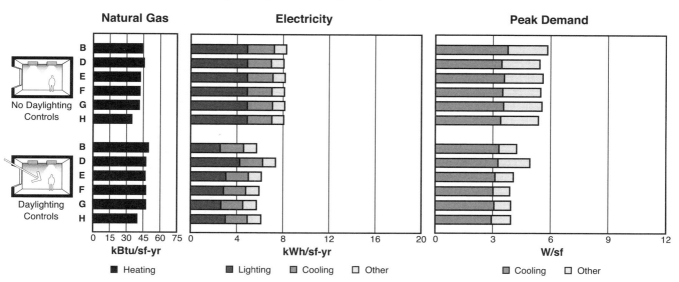

## Figure 7-7. Annual energy use comparison by daylighting controls

All cases are north-facing with interior shading. Numbers are expressed per square foot within a 30-foot-deep perimeter zone for a twelve-month operating schedule. Results were computed using DOE-2.1E for a typical school building in Chicago, Illinois (see Appendix B).

——————— Window B
– – – – – – Window D
— — — — Window E
——————— Window F
– – – – – Window G
— — — — Window H

Total annual energy use is calculated by multiplying electricity use by 3 and adding to heating energy use. This reflects the 3:1 ratio of primary to end use energy for electricity compared to natural gas.

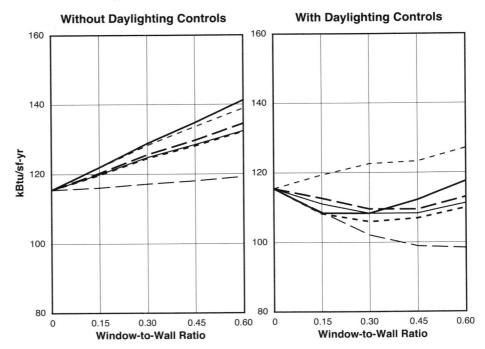

## Figure 7-8. Peak demand comparison by daylighting controls

All cases are north-facing with interior shading. Numbers are expressed in Watts per square foot within a 30-foot-deep perimeter zone for a twelve-month operating schedule. Results were computed using DOE-2.1E for a typical school building in Chicago, Illinois (see Appendix B).

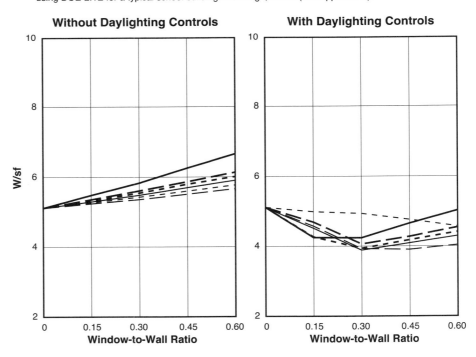

dow area rises from WWR=0 to 0.60, however, there is great variation depending on window type. For Window D, energy consumption rises by 10 percent as window area increases from WWR=0 to 0.60, for Window H it falls by 15 percent. The other windows change 5 percent or less.

For the combined electricity and heating energy use (assuming a fuel ratio of 3:1), the optimal window area is dependent on the window type. For each window this occurs (the low point on Figure 7-7) where the energy-saving benefits of daylight controls are realized and increasing the window area produces little additional lighting energy savings while the cooling and heating energy use continue to rise. For Window B, this occurs at WWR=0.15 and for Window G at WWR=0.30. The lowest total energy use for Windows E and F lies between WWR=0.30 and 0.45. For Window D, the optimum is WWR=0 (no windows). The lowest total annual energy use with Window H is optimized at a window-to-wall ratio (WWR) of 0.60—this is the least total energy use for any window type at any area.

Similar to total energy use, there is an optimal window area with respect to peak demand (the low point on Figure 7-8). For Window B,

*Figure 7-9. Annual energy use and peak demand comparison by window area*

All cases are north-facing with interior shading and include daylighting controls. Numbers are expressed per square foot within a 30-foot-deep perimeter zone for a twelve-month operating schedule. Results were computed using DOE-2.1E for a typical school building in Chicago, Illinois (see Appendix B).

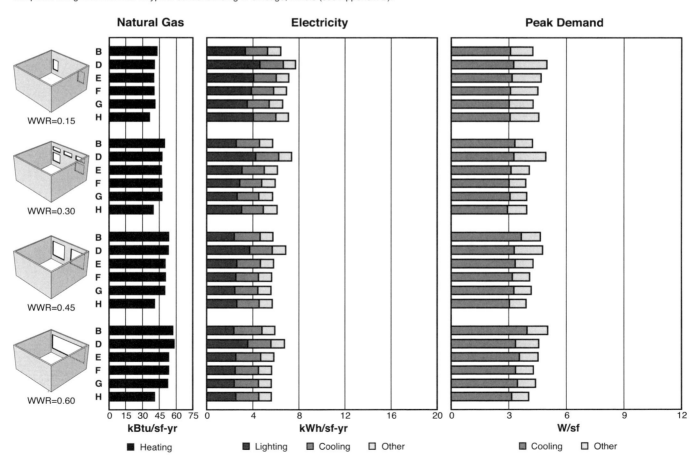

**Window B**
double glazing
clear
U=0.60
SHGC=0.60
VT=0.63

**Window F**
double glazing
spec. selective low-E tint
U=0.46
SHGC=0.27
VT=0.43

**Window D**
double glazing
reflective coating
U=0.54
SHGC=0.17
VT=0.10

**Window G**
double glazing
spec. selective low-E clear
U=0.46
SHGC=0.34
VT=0.57

**Window E**
double glazing
low-E, bronze tint
U=0.49
SHGC=0.39
VT=0.36

**Window H**
triple glazing
1 low-E layer, clear
U=0.20
SHGC=0.22
VT=0.37

U=U-factor in Btu/hr-sf-°F
SHGC=solar heat gain coefficient
VT=visible transmittance
All window properties are for the whole window.
Windows B–H have thermally broken aluminum
frames. Window H has an insulated frame.

the lowest peak demand lies in the range of WWR=0.15–0.30, while the best performance for Windows E, F, and G occurs at WWR=0.30. The optimal for Window H is between WWR=0.30–0.45. The peak demand for Window D falls continuously with increased area so the optimal area is WWR=0.60. On average, peak demand declines 1.0 W/sf or 19 percent when area climbs from WWR=0 to 0.30, but this difference diminishes to 12 percent at WWR=0.60. Similar to energy use, peak demand varies considerably between window types.

## SOUTH-FACING CLASSROOMS

Once the decision has been made to orient classrooms to the south, the designer must examine more detailed issues related to window design and selection. The following sections address how lighting controls and window area affect performance.

### The Effect of Lighting Controls on Annual Energy Use and Peak Demand in a South-facing Classroom

In a cold climate like Chicago, daylighting controls in south-facing classrooms are recommended. The combined total annual energy use falls 15 percent on average with daylighting controls. Annual electricity use in south-facing classrooms declines significantly by installing dimmable light fixtures and controls that reduce electric lighting when there is sufficient daylight (Figure 7-10). Cooling energy use also declines because of reduced heat gain. The total annual electricity use falls 27 percent on average across all window types with daylighting controls. However, energy use rises 13 percent on average because of reduced heat gain from the lights.

*Figure 7-10. Annual Energy use and peak demand comparison by daylighting controls*
All cases are south-facing with a 0.30 window-to-wall ratio and interior shading. Numbers are expressed per square foot within a 30-foot-deep perimeter zone for a twelve-month operating schedule. Results were computed using DOE-2.1E for a typical school building in Chicago, Illinois (see Appendix B).

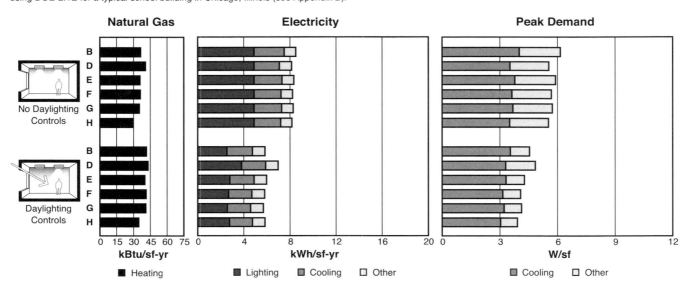

## Figure 7-11. *Annual energy use comparison by daylighting controls*

All cases are south-facing with interior shading. Numbers are expressed per square foot within a 30-foot-deep perimeter zone for a twelve-month operating schedule. Results were computed using DOE-2.1E for a typical school building in Chicago, Illinois (see Appendix B).

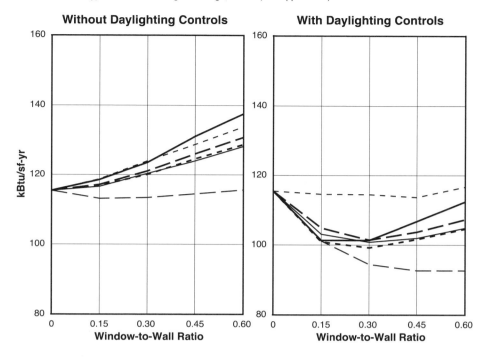

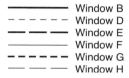

Total annual energy use is calculated by multiplying electricity use by 3 and adding to heating energy use. This reflects the 3:1 ratio of primary to end use energy for electricity.

## Figure 7-12. *Peak demand comparison by daylighting controls*

All cases are south-facing with interior shading. Numbers are expressed in Watts per square foot within a 30-foot-deep perimeter zone for a twelve-month operating schedule. Results were computed using DOE-2.1E for a typical school building in Chicago, Illinois (see Appendix B).

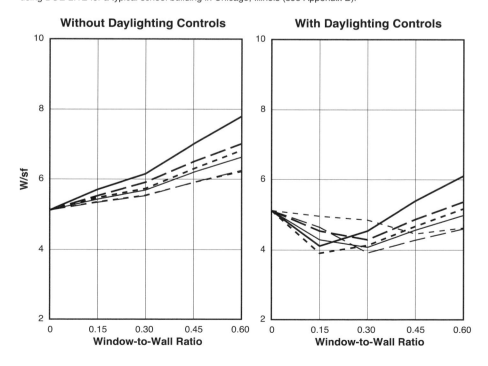

Figure 7-11 illustrates that without daylighting controls, total annual energy use increases with window area in proportion to admitted solar heat gains. It climbs at a faster rate with higher SHGC and U-factor windows. With daylighting controls, total annual energy use generally falls and then rises with greater window area. For most window types, the energy consumption in a zone with a large window (WWR=0.60) can be lower than an opaque wall (WWR=0). At window areas above WWR=0.15, triple-pane Window H performs best while Window D always performs worst.

With moderately sized windows on the south (WWR=0.30), daylighting controls can significantly reduce peak electricity demand for all window types by 1.5 W/sf or 25 percent on average (Figure 7-10). Without daylighting controls, Window D (low VT and SHGC) has nearly the lowest peak demand. With daylighting controls, Window D has the highest peak demand with a moderate window area (WWR=0.30). Figure 7-12 illustrates that without daylight controls, peak demand increases with window area. With controls, peak demand declines and then climbs with greater window area for all windows except D.

*Figure 7-13. Annual energy use and peak demand comparison by window area*

All cases are south-facing with interior shading and include daylighting controls. Numbers are expressed per square foot within a 30-foot-deep perimeter zone for a twelve-month operating schedule. Results were computed using DOE-2.1E for a typical school building in Chicago, Illinois (see Appendix B).

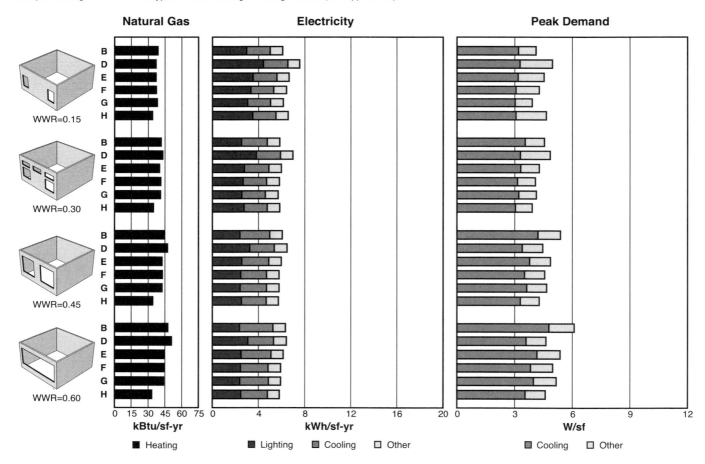

While all the energy-use comparisons in this section show significant savings by using daylighting controls, there is a range of possible performance (see Chapter 2).

## The Effect of Window Area on Annual Energy Use and Peak Demand in a South-facing Classroom

This section addresses the question of the optimal window area in a south-facing perimeter zone. In a cold climate city like Chicago, energy use does not necessarily rise with greater window area, as the relationship between window area and energy use depends on several factors. Figure 7-13 shows that heating energy use in a south-facing space increases significantly with greater window area—30 percent on average between window types as window area rises from WWR=0 to WWR=0.60.

With daylighting controls, cooling energy use climbs with window area, but lighting energy use declines with increased window area and daylight, resulting in a net decrease in annual electricity use (23 percent decrease on average by increasing window area from WWR=0 to 0.60). Total annual energy use declines 8 percent on average as window area increases from WWR=0 to 0.60, however there is great variation among the window types. Window D remains relatively constant while Window H decreases by 20 percent. Total annual energy for Windows E, F, and G decreases by 7–9 percent as window area increases from WWR=0 to 0.60.

For the combined electricity and heating energy use (assuming a fuel ratio of 3:1), the optimal window area is dependent on the window type (Figure 7-11). For each window, this occurs (the low point on Figure 7-11) where the energy-saving benefits of daylight controls are realized and increasing the window area produces little additional lighting energy savings while the cooling and heating energy use continue to increase. For Window B, the optimum energy use lies between WWR=0.15–0.30. For Windows E, F, and G the lowest energy use is at WWR=0.30 and at WWR=0.45 for Window D, with little variation between WWR=0–0.45. The lowest total annual energy use with Window H in between WWR= 0.45–0.60—the lowest total energy use for any window type at any area.

Similar to total energy use, there is an optimal window area (the low point on Figure 7-12) with respect to peak demand. For windows B and G, the optimal window area is WWR=0.15, while for Windows E, F, and H it is WWR=0.30. The optimal area in terms of peak demand for Window D is WWR=0.45. On average across all windows, peak demand falls by 0.8 W/sf or 16 percent when area increases from WWR=0 to 0.30, but demand increases by 8 percent at WWR=0.45 and there is no change on average comparing WWR=0 and 0.60. Similar to energy use, peak demand varies considerably between window types.

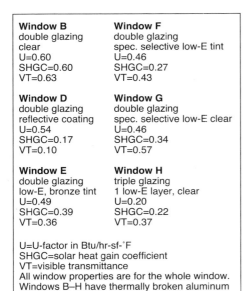

**Window B**
double glazing
clear
U=0.60
SHGC=0.60
VT=0.63

**Window F**
double glazing
spec. selective low-E tint
U=0.46
SHGC=0.27
VT=0.43

**Window D**
double glazing
reflective coating
U=0.54
SHGC=0.17
VT=0.10

**Window G**
double glazing
spec. selective low-E clear
U=0.46
SHGC=0.34
VT=0.57

**Window E**
double glazing
low-E, bronze tint
U=0.49
SHGC=0.39
VT=0.36

**Window H**
triple glazing
1 low-E layer, clear
U=0.20
SHGC=0.22
VT=0.37

U=U-factor in Btu/hr-sf-°F
SHGC=solar heat gain coefficient
VT=visible transmittance
All window properties are for the whole window.
Windows B–H have thermally broken aluminum
frames. Window H has an insulated frame.

## EAST- AND WEST-FACING CLASSROOMS

Once the decision has been made to orient classrooms to the east or west, the designer must examine more detailed issues related to windows. The following sections address how lighting controls and window area affect performance. All results shown in this section are for west-facing perimeter zones. In most cases, the results for east-facing zones are very similar.

### The Effect of Lighting Controls on Annual Energy Use and Peak Demand in an East- or West-facing Classroom

In a cold climate like Chicago, the average combined total annual energy use declines 14 percent on average in east- or west-facing classrooms with daylighting controls. Annual electricity use is cut significantly by installing dimmable light fixtures and controls that reduce electric lighting when there is sufficient daylight (Figure 7-14). This lighting load decline reduces heat gains, which in turn reduces cooling loads. Total annual electricity uses falls 26 percent on average across all window types with daylighting controls. Total annual electricity use reduction is 26 percent on average across all window types with daylighting controls. The heating energy use rises 12 percent on average because of reduced heat gain from the lights.

Figure 7-15 illustrates that without daylighting controls in a space, total annual energy use increases with window area in proportion to admitted solar heat gains. It climbs at a faster rate with higher SHGC and U-factor windows. With daylighting controls, total energy use generally falls and then rises with greater window area. For most window types, the energy consumption in a zone with a large window (WWR=0.60) can be lower than one with an opaque wall (WWR=0). At window areas above WWR=0.15, triple-pane Window H performs the best while Window D always performs the worst.

*Figure 7-14. Annual energy use and peak demand comparison by daylighting controls*

All cases are west-facing with a 0.30 window-to-wall ratio and interior shading. Numbers are expressed per square foot within a 30-foot-deep perimeter zone for a twelve-month operating schedule. Results were computed using DOE-2.1E for a typical school building in Chicago, Illinois (see Appendix B).

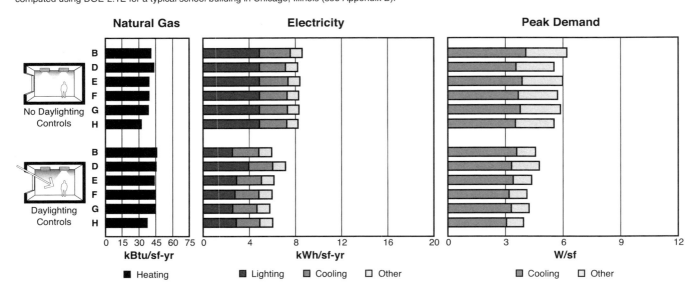

## Figure 7-15. Annual energy use comparison by daylighting controls

All cases are west-facing with interior shading. Numbers are expressed per square foot within a 30-foot-deep perimeter zone for a twelve-month operating schedule. Results were computed using DOE-2.1E for a typical school building in Chicago, Illinois (see Appendix B).

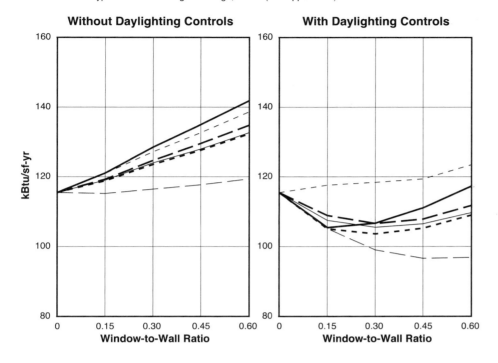

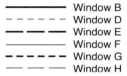

Total annual energy use is calculated by multiplying electricity use by 3 and adding to heating energy use. This reflects the 3:1 ratio of primary to end use energy for electricity.

## Figure 7-16. Peak demand comparison by daylighting controls

All cases are west-facing with interior shading. Numbers are expressed in Watts per square foot within a 30-foot-deep perimeter zone for a twelve-month operating schedule. Results were computed using DOE-2.1E for a typical school building in Chicago, Illinois (see Appendix B).

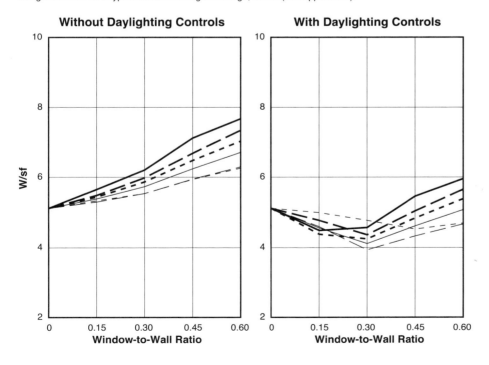

With moderately sized windows on the east or west, daylighting controls can significantly cut peak electricity demand for all window types by 1.5 W/sf or 25 percent on average (Figure 7-14). Without daylighting controls, Window D (low VT and SHGC) has nearly the lowest peak demand. With daylighting controls, Window D has the highest peak demand with a moderate window area (WWR=0.30). Figure 7-16 illustrates that without daylight controls, peak demand increases with window area. With controls, peak demand falls and then rises with greater window area for all windows except D.

While all the energy-use comparisons in this section show significant savings by using daylighting controls, there is a range of possible performance (see Chapter 2).

*Figure 7-17. Annual energy use and peak demand comparison by window area*

All cases are west-facing with interior shading and include daylighting controls. Numbers are expressed per square foot within a 30-foot-deep perimeter zone for a twelve-month operating schedule. Results were computed using DOE-2.1E for a typical school building in Chicago, Illinois (see Appendix B).

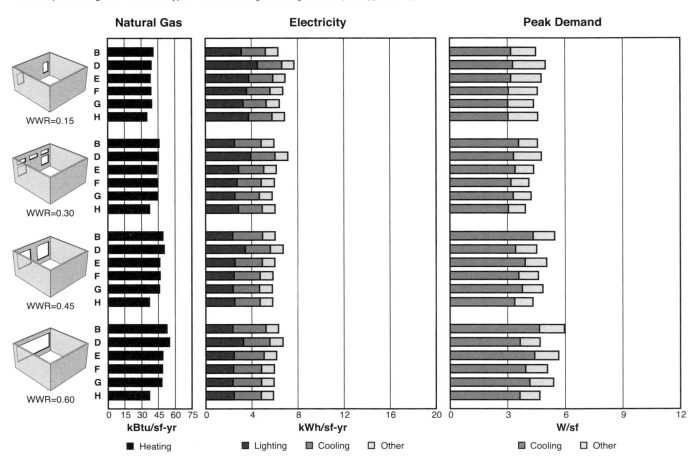

## The Effect of Window Area on Annual Energy Use and Peak Demand in an East- or West-facing Classroom

This section addresses the question of the optimal window area for an east- or west-facing perimeter zone. In a cold climate city like Chicago, energy use does not necessarily increase with greater window area. The relationship between window area and energy use depends on several factors. Figure 7-17 shows that heating energy use in an east- or west-facing space rises significantly with greater window area—43 percent on average between window types as window area increases from WWR=0 to WWR=0.60.

With daylighting controls, cooling energy use increases with window area, but lighting energy use falls with greater window area and the daylight it yields, resulting in a net decline in annual electricity use (23 percent decrease on average by increasing window area from WWR=0 to 0.60). Total annual energy use decreases on average by 4 percent as window area increases from WWR=0 to 0.60, however, there is great variation depending on window type. With Window D, energy use rises by 7 percent, while with Window H it falls by 16 percent.

For the combined electricity and heating energy use (assuming a fuel ratio of 3:1), the optimal window area hinges on the window type. For each window this occurs (the low point on Figure 7-15) where the energy-saving benefits of daylight controls are realized and increasing the window area produces little additional lighting energy savings while the cooling and heating energy use continue to rise. For Window B, the optimum is WWR=0.15 and for Windows E, F, and G it is WWR=0.30. For Window D, the optimum is WWR=0 (no windows). The lowest total annual energy use with Window H is between WWR=0.45–0.60—the lowest total annual energy use for any window type at any area.

Similar to total energy use, there is an optimal window area (the low point on Figure 7-16) with respect to peak demand. For Window B, the lowest peak demand is WWR=0.15, while the lowest for Windows E, F, G, and H is WWR=0.30. The optimal area for Window D is WWR=0.45. On average, peak demand declines 0.8 W/sf or 15 percent when area rises from WWR=0 to 0.30, but the average actually increases by 2 percent at WWR=0.60. Similar to energy use, peak demand varies considerably between window types.

# School Window Design in a Hot Climate

## THE IMPACT OF SCHEDULE

As noted in the previous section on cold climates, a nine-month school year is common, however, schools are increasingly used for summer classes, community education, and special events. Both the number of months and the hours of operation may be extended.

To illustrate the impact of schedule, Figure 7-18 compares nine-versus twelve-month operating schedules in a south-facing classroom in Houston. Compared to Chicago, there is much less heating energy use and greater electricity use for cooling. School occupancy in summer does not impact annual heating energy consumption, but of course it does significantly increase electricity consumption for cooling (33 percent on average across all window types). Although the magnitude of electricity use changes with schedule, the relative performance of different windows remains the same. Window D always performs worse than the others because its low VT limits daylight and increases electric light use.

When heating and cooling are combined into total annual energy use, there is a 29 percent rise on average (with all window types) due to the twelve-month operating schedule. Peak electricity demand rises slightly with a twelve-month operating schedule in Houston. On average for all windows, it climbs 0.12 W/sf or 2 percent compared to the nine-month schedule.

With the unpredictability of future use and operating schedules of schools, it is wise to design as if there will be twelve-month use at some time in the future. In the remainder of this section, all comparisons are based on a twelve-month operating schedule.

---

**Window A**
single glazing
clear
U=1.25
SHGC=0.72
VT=0.71

**Window C**
double glazing
bronze tint
U=0.60
SHGC=0.42
VT=0.38

**Window D**
double glazing
reflective coating
U=0.54
SHGC=0.17
VT=0.10

**Window E**
double glazing
low-E tint
U=0.49
SHGC=0.39
VT=0.36

**Window F**
double glazing
spec. selective low-E tint
U=0.46
SHGC=0.27
VT=0.43

**Window H**
triple glazing
1 low-E layer, clear
U=0.20
SHGC=0.22
VT=0.37

U=U-factor in Btu/hr-sf-°F
SHGC=solar heat gain coefficient
VT=visible transmittance
All window properties are for the whole window.
Windows C–H have thermally broken aluminum frames. Window A has an aluminum frame.

Table 2-30 in Chapter 2 shows which windows comply with ASHRAE 90.1-99 for this climate.

---

*Figure 7-18. Annual energy use and peak demand comparison by schedule*

All cases are south-facing with a 0.30 window-to-wall ratio with interior shading and include daylighting controls. Numbers are expressed per square foot within a 30-foot-deep perimeter zone. Results were computed using DOE-2.1E for a typical school building in Houston, Texas (Appendix B).

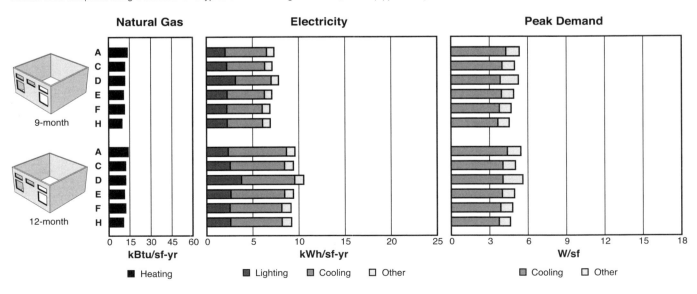

# THE IMPACT OF ORIENTATION

This section addresses the question of how window orientation impacts energy use and peak demand for a school classroom in a hot-climate city.

In Houston, differences in annual electricity use between orientations are driven primarily by solar gain affecting cooling and daylight affecting electric lighting. These two factors offset each other however, so orientation has a less than 2 percent effect on electricity use on average across all windows (Figure 7-19).

Although heating is less important in a hot climate, windows can influence heating energy use—a lower U-factor results in less night-time heating loss and a higher SHGC provides more solar heat gain during occasional cool periods. Additionally, a higher VT allows more daylight, which may reduce electric lighting, which in turn reduces heat gain and therefore increases the need at times for space heating. In Houston's climate, south-facing classrooms have 22 percent less annual heating energy use compared to north-facing

*Figure 7-19. Annual energy use and peak demand comparison by orientation*
All cases have a 0.30 window-to-wall ratio with interior shading and include daylighting controls. Numbers are expressed per square foot within a 30-foot-deep perimeter zone for a twelve-month operating schedule. Results were computed using DOE-2.1E for a typical school building in Houston, Texas (see Appendix B).

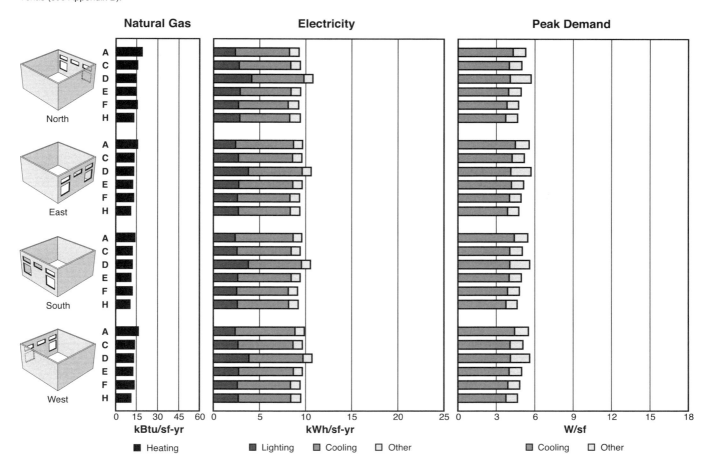

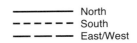

*Figure 7-20. Total annual energy use comparison by orientation*

All cases have interior shading and daylighting controls. Numbers are expressed per square foot within a 30-foot-deep perimeter zone for a twelve-month operating schedule. Results were computed using DOE-2.1E for a typical school classroom in Houston, Texas (Appendix A). Total annual energy use is calculated by multiplying electricity use by 3 and adding heating energy use. This reflects the 3:1 ratio of primary to end use energy for electricity. All window properties are for the whole window. Windows C–H have thermally broken aluminum frames. Window H has an insulated frame. U=U-factor in Btu/hr-sf-°F, SHGC=solar heat gain coefficient, VT=visible transmittance

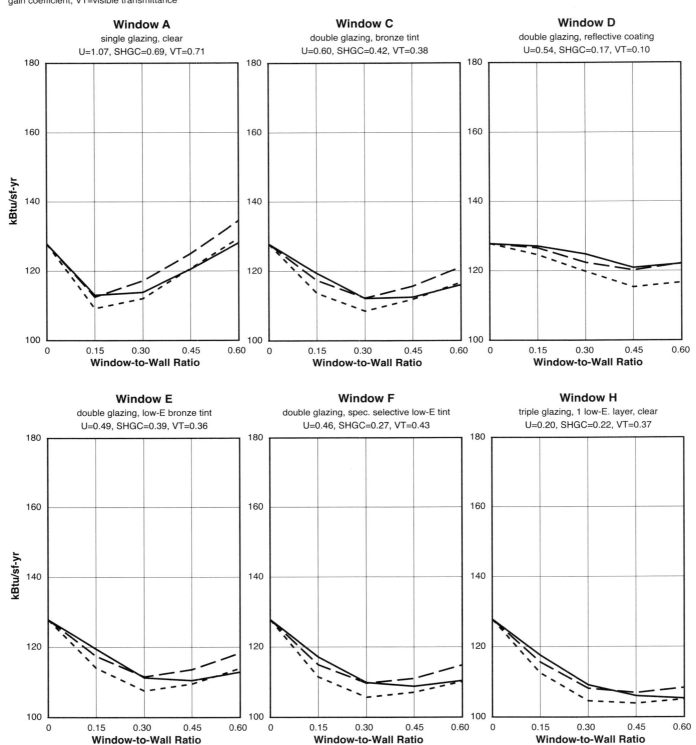

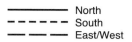

*Figure 7-21. Peak demand comparison by orientation*

All cases have interior shading and include daylighting controls. Numbers are expressed in Watts per square foot within a 30-foot-deep perimeter zone for a twelve-month operating schedule. Results were computed using DOE-2.1E for a typical school classroom in Houston, Texas (Appendix A). All window properties are for the whole window. Windows C–H have thermally broken aluminum frames. Window H has an insulated frame. U=U-factor in Btu/hr-sf-˚F, SHGC=solar heat gain coefficient, VT=visible transmittance

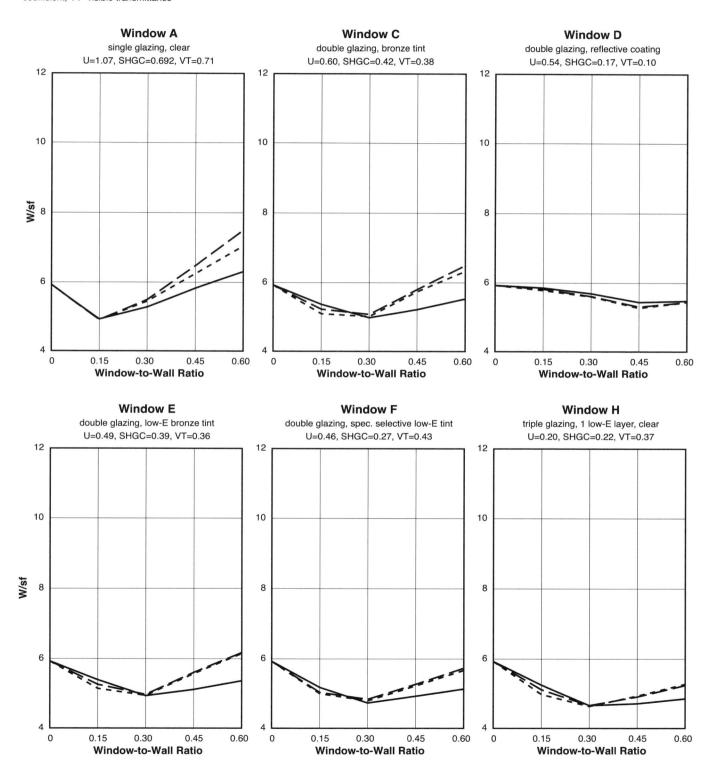

classrooms. But heating loads are relatively minor in the climate, minimizing the impact of orientation with respect to heating.

Figure 7-20 shows the total annual energy use (combined heating and electricity) over a range of window areas. For all window types, a southern orientation performs best overall for all window areas (WWR=0–0.60). With window areas in the WWR=0.45–0.60 range, the northern orientation provides comparable performance. In Houston, different orientations do not result in great variations in total energy use—less than a 4 percent average difference at a moderate window area (WWR=0.30).

The effect of orientation on peak electricity demand depends on the window type. As shown in Figure 7-19 for moderately sized windows with interior shades, there is little difference between orientations for most window types (C–H). North has a 3–5 percent lower peak demand on average compared to other orientations. The difference in peak demand between orientations increases significantly with window area for all window types except D (Figure 7-21). At window areas above WWR=0.30, a northern orientation always performs best for all window types except D.

If applicable, utility rates based on time of use usually penalize high-demand use from south- and west-facing zones during mid- to late-afternoon summer hours. It is worthwhile to consider local utility rate schedules because demand charges can result in electricity costs that are three to five times greater than off-peak periods. It is also noteworthy that peak demand is in direct proportion to the cooling capacity of the building's mechanical system and can impact capital costs.

## NORTH-FACING CLASSROOMS

Once the decision has been made to orient classrooms to the north, the designer must examine more detailed issues related to window design and selection. The following sections address how lighting controls and window area affect performance.

### The Effect of Lighting Controls on Annual Energy Use and Peak Demand in a North-facing Classroom

In Houston as well as Chicago, daylighting controls in north-facing classrooms are recommended. The combined total annual energy use declines 16 percent on average with daylighting controls. Annual electricity use in north-facing classrooms falls significantly by installing dimmable light fixtures and controls that cut electric lighting when there is sufficient daylight (Figure 7-22). Cooling energy use also declines because of reduced heat gain. The total annual electricity use reduction is 20 percent (2.3 kWh/sf-yr) on average across all window types with daylighting controls. Heating energy use rises 22 percent on average because of reduced heat gain from the lights.

Figure 7-23 illustrates that without daylighting controls, total annual energy use increases with window area in proportion to admitted solar heat gains, rising at a faster rate with higher SHGC and U-factor windows. With daylighting controls, total annual energy use generally falls and then rises with greater window area. The energy consumption in a zone with a large window (WWR=0.60) can be lower than one with an opaque wall (WWR=0) for most window types, with triple-pane Window H outperforming the others.

With moderately sized windows, daylighting controls can significantly reduce peak electricity demand for all window types by 1.4 W/sf or 21 percent on average (Figure 7-22). Without daylighting controls, Window D (low VT and SHGC) has nearly the lowest peak demand. With daylighting controls, Window D has the highest peak demand with a moderate window area (WWR=0.30). Figure 7-24 illustrates that without daylight controls, peak demand increases with window area. With controls, peak demand falls and then rises with greater window area for all windows except D.

While all the energy-use comparisons in this section show significant savings by using daylighting controls, there is a range of possible performance (see Chapter 2).

## The Effect of Window Area on Annual Energy Use and Peak Demand in a North-facing Classroom

This section addresses the question of the optimal window area for a north-facing perimeter zone. In a hot-climate city like Houston, energy use does not necessarily increase with greater window area. The relationship between window area and energy use depends on several factors. Figure 7-25 shows that heating energy use in a north-facing space rises significantly with greater window area—81 percent on average between window types as window area rises from WWR=0 to WWR=0.60.

With daylighting controls, cooling energy use rises with window area, but lighting energy use falls with greater window area and daylight resulting in a net reduction in annual electricity use (17 percent decrease on average by increasing window area from

| Window A | Window E |
|---|---|
| single glazing | double glazing |
| clear | low-E tint |
| U=1.25 | U=0.49 |
| SHGC=0.72 | SHGC=0.39 |
| VT=0.71 | VT=0.36 |
| | |
| Window C | Window F |
| double glazing | double glazing |
| bronze tint | spec. selective low-E tint |
| U=0.60 | U=0.46 |
| SHGC=0.42 | SHGC=0.27 |
| VT=0.38 | VT=0.43 |
| | |
| Window D | Window H |
| double glazing | triple glazing |
| reflective coating | 1 low-E layer, clear |
| U=0.54 | U=0.20 |
| SHGC=0.17 | SHGC=0.22 |
| VT=0.10 | VT=0.37 |

U=U-factor in Btu/hr-sf-°F
SHGC=solar heat gain coefficient
VT=visible transmittance
All window properties are for the whole window.
Windows C–H have thermally broken aluminum frames. Window A has an aluminum frame.

*Figure 7-22. Annual energy use and peak demand comparison by daylighting controls*

All cases are north-facing with a 0.30 window-to-wall ratio and interior shading. Numbers are expressed per square foot within a 30-foot-deep perimeter zone for a twelve-month operating schedule. Results were computed using DOE-2.1E for a typical school building in Houston, Texas (see Appendix B).

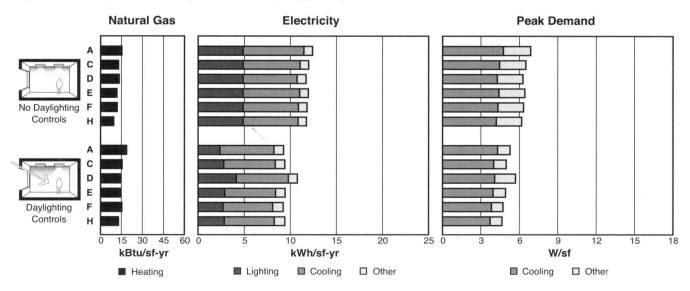

## Figure 7-23. *Annual energy use comparison by daylighting controls*

All cases are north-facing with interior shading. Numbers are expressed per square foot within a 30-foot-deep perimeter zone for a twelve-month operating schedule. Results were computed using DOE-2.1E for a typical school building in Houston, Texas (see Appendix B).

Window A
Window C
Window D
Window E
Window F
Window H

Total annual energy use is calculated by multiplying electricity use by 3 and adding heating energy use. This reflects the 3:1 ratio of primary to end use energy for electricity.

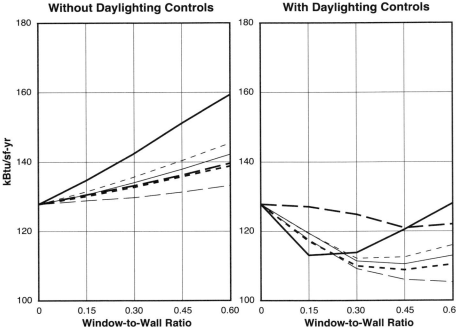

## Figure 7-24. *Peak demand comparison by daylighting controls*

All cases are north-facing with interior shading. Numbers are expressed in Watts per square foot within a 30-foot-deep perimeter zone for a twelve-month operating schedule. Results were computed using DOE-2.1E for a typical school building in Houston, Texas (see Appendix B).

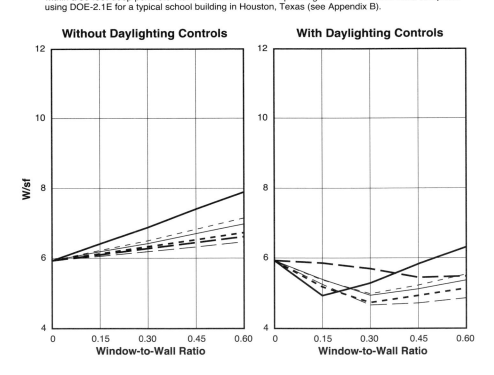

*Window Design for Schools*

WWR=0 to 0.60). Total annual energy use declines on average by 9 percent as window area rises from WWR=0 to 0.60, however, there is great variation depending on window type. There is little change with Window A as window area rises from WWR=0 to 0.60, while Window H decreases by 18 percent.

For the combined electricity and heating energy use (assuming a fuel ratio of 3:1), the optimal window area is dependent on the window type. For each window this occurs (the low point on Figure 7-23) where the energy-saving benefits of daylight controls are realized and increasing the window area produces little additional lighting energy savings while the cooling and heating energy use continue to rise. For Window A, the optimum is WWR=0.15 and for Windows C, E, and F, it lies between WWR=0.30 and 0.45. For Window D, the optimum is WWR=0.45. The lowest total annual energy use with Window H occurs at a window-to-wall ratio (WWR) of 0.60—this is the least total energy use for any window type at any area.

*Figure 7-25. Annual energy use and peak demand comparison by window area*

All cases are north-facing with interior shading and include daylighting controls. Numbers are expressed per square foot within a 30-foot-deep perimeter zone for a twelve-month operating schedule. Results were computed using DOE-2.1E for a typical school building in Houston, Texas (see Appendix B).

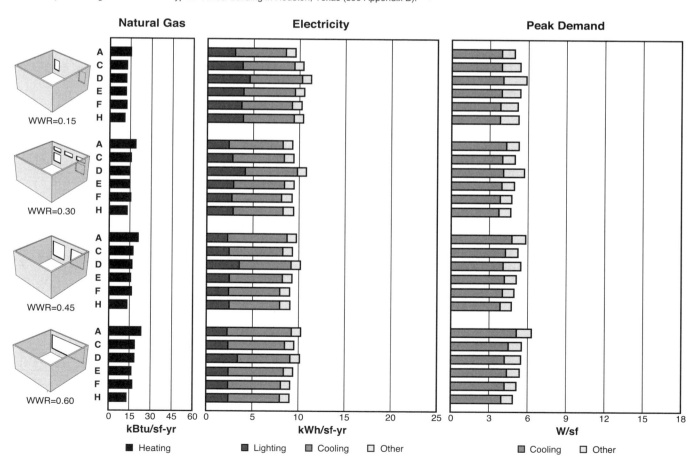

| Window A | Window E |
|---|---|
| single glazing | double glazing |
| clear | low-E tint |
| U=1.25 | U=0.49 |
| SHGC=0.72 | SHGC=0.39 |
| VT=0.71 | VT=0.36 |

| Window C | Window F |
|---|---|
| double glazing | double glazing |
| bronze tint | spec. selective low-E tint |
| U=0.60 | U=0.46 |
| SHGC=0.42 | SHGC=0.27 |
| VT=0.38 | VT=0.43 |

| Window D | Window H |
|---|---|
| double glazing | triple glazing |
| reflective coating | 1 low-E layer, clear |
| U=0.54 | U=0.20 |
| SHGC=0.17 | SHGC=0.22 |
| VT=0.10 | VT=0.37 |

U=U-factor in Btu/hr-sf-°F
SHGC=solar heat gain coefficient
VT=visible transmittance
All window properties are for the whole window.
Windows C–H have thermally broken aluminum
frames. Window A has an aluminum frame.

Similar to total energy use, there is a an optimal window area with respect to peak demand (the low point on Figure 7-24). For Window A, the lowest peak demand occurs at WWR=0.15, while for Windows E, F, and H the optimum is at WWR=0.30, although Window H performs as well up to WWR=0.60. The optimal peak demand for Window D is in the range of WWR=0.45–0.60. On average, peak demand is reduced 0.5 W/sf or 15 percent when area is increased from WWR=0 to 0.30, but this difference diminishes to 8 percent at WWR=0.60. Similar to energy use, peak demand varies considerably between window types.

## SOUTH-FACING CLASSROOMS

Once the decision has been made to orient classrooms to the south, the designer must examine more detailed issues related to window design and selection. The following sections address how lighting controls and window area affect performance.

### The Effect of Lighting Controls on Annual Energy Use and Peak Demand in a South-facing Classroom

In Houston as well as Chicago, daylighting controls in south-facing classrooms are recommended. The combined total annual energy use declines 19 percent on average with daylighting controls. Annual electricity use in south-facing classrooms falls significantly by installing dimmable light fixtures and controls that reduce electric lighting when there is sufficient daylight (Figure 7-26). Cooling energy use also declines because of reduced heat gain. The total annual electricity use reduction is 22 percent on average across all window types with daylighting controls. However, heating energy use rises 23 percent on average because of the reduced heat gain from the lights.

*Figure 7-26. Annual energy use and peak demand comparison by daylighting controls*

All cases are south-facing with a 0.30 window-to-wall ratio and interior shading. Numbers are expressed per square foot within a 30-foot-deep perimeter zone for a twelve-month operating schedule. Results were computed using DOE-2.1E for a typical school building in Houston, Texas (see Appendix B).

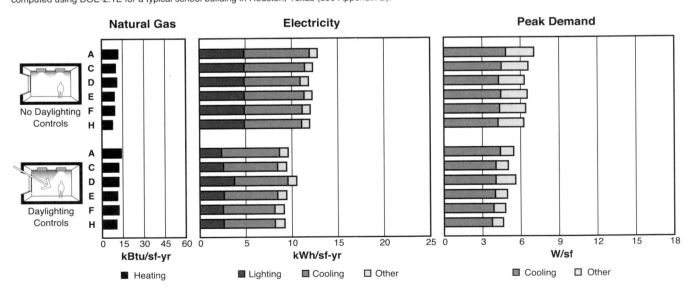

## Figure 7-27. Annual energy use comparison by daylighting controls

All cases are south-facing with interior shading. Numbers are expressed per square foot within a 30-foot-deep perimeter zone for a twelve-month operating schedule. Results were computed using DOE-2.1E for a typical school building in Houston, Texas (see Appendix B).

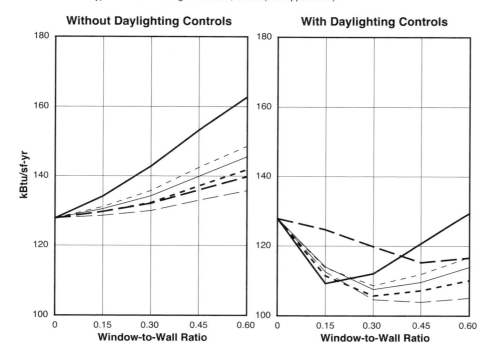

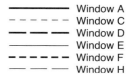

Total annual energy use is calculated by multiplying electricity use by 3 and adding heating energy use. This reflects the 3:1 ratio of primary to end use energy for electricity.

## Figure 7-28. Peak demand comparison by daylighting controls

All cases are south-facing with interior shading. Numbers are expressed in Watts per square foot within a 30-foot-deep perimeter zone for a twelve-month operating schedule. Results were computed using DOE-2.1E for a typical school building in Houston, Texas (see Appendix B).

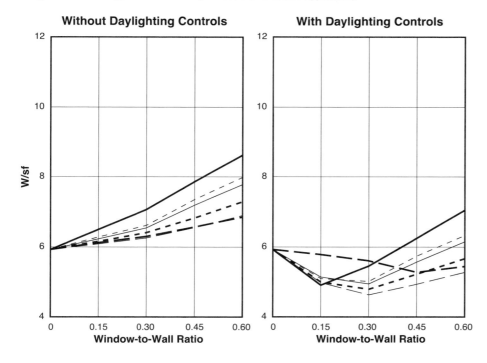

*School Window Design in a Hot Climate*

Figure 7-27 illustrates that without daylighting controls, total annual energy use increases with window area in proportion to admitted solar heat gains. It rises at a faster rate with higher SHGC and U-factor windows. When daylighting controls are used, total annual energy use generally falls and then rises with greater window area. The energy consumption in a zone with a large window (WWR=0.60) can be lower than one with an opaque wall (WWR=0) for most window types, with triple-pane Window H outperforming others.

With moderately sized, south-facing windows, daylighting controls can significantly reduce peak electricity demand for all window types by 1.5 W/sf or 22 percent on average (Figure 7-26). Without daylighting controls, Window D (low VT and SHGC) has nearly the lowest peak demand. With daylighting controls, Window D has the highest peak demand with a moderate window area (WWR=0.30) but is more effective at larger areas. Figure 7-28 illustrates that without daylight controls, peak demand increases with window area. With controls, peak demand falls and then rises with greater window area for all windows except Window D.

*Figure 7-29. Annual energy use and peak demand comparison by window area*

All cases are south-facing with interior shading and include daylighting controls. Numbers are expressed per square foot within a 30-foot-deep perimeter zone for a twelve-month operating schedule. Results were computed using DOE-2.1E for a typical school building in Houston, Texas (see Appendix B).

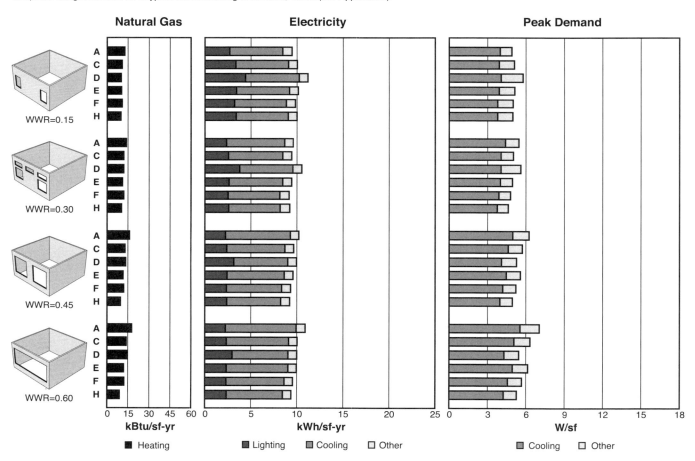

*Window Design for Schools*

While all the energy-use comparisons in this section show signifi-cant savings by using daylighting controls, there is a range of possible performance (see Chapter 2).

## The Effect of Window Area on Annual Energy Use and Peak Demand in a South-facing Classroom

This section addresses the question of the optimal window area in a south-facing perimeter zone. In a hot climate city like Houston, energy use is not necessarily increased with greater window area. The relationship between window area and energy use depends on several factors. Figure 7-29 shows that heating energy use in a south-facing space climbs significantly with increased window area—35 percent on average between window types as window area rise from WWR=0 to WWR=0.60.

With daylighting controls, cooling energy use rises with window area, but lighting energy use falls with increased window area and daylight resulting in a net reduction in annual electricity use (14 percent decrease on average by increasing window area from WWR=0 to 0.60). Total annual energy use declines on average by 10 percent as window area rises from WWR=0 to 0.60, however, there is great variation depending on window type. Window A changes very little while Window H decreases by 18 percent. Total annual energy for Windows E, F, and G falls by 7–9 percent as window area rises from WWR=0 to 0.60.

For the combined electricity and heating energy use (assuming a fuel ratio of 3:1), the optimal window area is dependent on the window type. For each window this occurs (the low point on Figure 7-27) where the energy-saving benefits of daylight controls are realized and increasing the window area produces little additional lighting energy savings while the cooling and heating energy use continue to rise. For Window A, the optimum is WWR=0.15, for Windows C, E, and F it is WWR=0.30, and for Window D it is WWR=0.45. The lowest total annual energy use with Window H is at a window-to-wall ratio (WWR) of 0.45—this is the least total energy use for any window type at any area—although the performance is similar from WWR=0.30–0.45.

Similar to total energy use, there is an optimal window area (the low point on Figure 7-28) with respect to peak demand. For Window A, the lowest peak demand is with a WWR=0.15, while the low point for Windows C, E, F, and H is WWR=0.30. The optimal area in terms of peak demand for Window D is WWR=0.45. On average across all windows, peak demand falls by 0.9 W/sf or 14 percent when area increases from WWR=0 to 0.30, but there is no change on average comparing WWR=0 and 0.60. Similar to energy use, peak demand varies considerably between window types.

## EAST- AND WEST-FACING CLASSROOMS

Once the decision has been made to orient classrooms to the east or west, the designer must examine more detailed issues related to window design and selection. The following sections address how lighting controls and window area affect performance. All results shown in this section are for west-facing perimeter zones. In most cases, the results for east-facing zones are very similar.

### The Effect of Lighting Controls on Annual Energy Use and Peak Demand in an East- or West-facing Classroom

In a hot climate like Houston, the average combined total annual energy use declines 17 percent on average in east- or west-facing classrooms by using daylighting controls. Annual electricity use falls significantly by installing dimmable light fixtures and controls that cut electric lighting when there is sufficient daylight (Figure 7-30). The lighting load reduction in turn lessens the cooling load because of reduced heat gain. Total annual electricity use falls 21 percent on average across all window types with daylighting controls. However, heating energy use climbs 21 percent on average because of reduced heat gain from the lights.

Figure 7-31 illustrates that without daylighting controls, total annual energy use increases with window area in proportion to admitted solar heat gains. It rises at a faster rate with higher SHGC and U-factor windows. With daylighting controls, total annual energy use generally falls and then climbs with greater window area. The energy consumption in a zone with a large window (WWR=0.60) can be lower than one with an opaque wall (WWR=0) for most window types, with triple-pane Window H outperforming others.

---

**Window A**
single glazing
clear
U=1.25
SHGC=0.72
VT=0.71

**Window E**
double glazing
low-E tint
U=0.49
SHGC=0.39
VT=0.36

**Window C**
double glazing
bronze tint
U=0.60
SHGC=0.42
VT=0.38

**Window F**
double glazing
spec. selective low-E tint
U=0.46
SHGC=0.27
VT=0.43

**Window D**
double glazing
reflective coating
U=0.54
SHGC=0.17
VT=0.10

**Window H**
triple glazing
1 low-E layer, clear
U=0.20
SHGC=0.22
VT=0.37

U=U-factor in Btu/hr-sf-°F
SHGC=solar heat gain coefficient
VT=visible transmittance
All window properties are for the whole window.
Windows C–H have thermally broken aluminum frames. Window A has an aluminum frame.

---

*Figure 7-30. Annual energy use and peak demand comparison by daylighting controls*

All cases are west-facing with a 0.30 window-to-wall ratio and interior shading. Numbers are expressed per square foot within a 30-foot-deep perimeter zone for a twelve-month operating schedule. Results were computed using DOE-2.1E for a typical school building in Houston, Texas (see Appendix B).

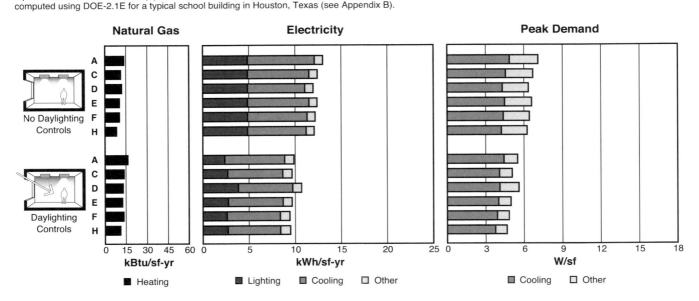

## Figure 7-31. *Annual energy use comparison by daylighting controls*

All cases are west-facing with interior shading. Numbers are expressed per square foot within a
30-foot-deep perimeter zone for a twelve-month operating schedule. Results were computed using
DOE-2.1E for a typical school building in Houston, Texas (see Appendix B).

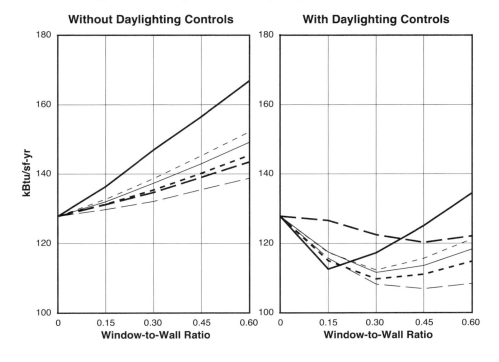

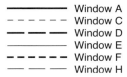

Total annual energy use is
calculated by multiplying electricity
use by 3 and adding heating energy
use. This reflects the 3:1 ratio of
primary to end use energy for
electricity.

## Figure 7-32. *Peak demand comparison by daylighting controls*

All cases are west-facing with interior shading. Numbers are expressed in Watts per square foot
within a 30-foot-deep perimeter zone for a twelve-month operating schedule. Results were computed
using DOE-2.1E for a typical school building in Houston, Texas (see Appendix B).

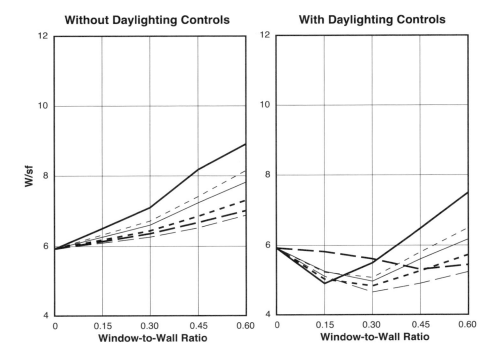

With moderately sized windows on the east or west, daylighting controls can significantly reduce peak electricity demand for all window types by 1.5 W/sf or 22 percent on average (Figure 7-30). Without daylighting controls, Window D (low VT and SHGC) has nearly the lowest peak demand. With daylighting controls, Window D has the highest peak demand with a moderate window area (WWR=0.30) but is more effective at larger areas. Figure 7-32 illustrates that without daylight controls peak demand increases with window area. With controls, peak demand falls and then rises with greater window area for all windows except Window D.

While all the energy-use comparisons in this section show significant savings by using daylighting controls, there is a range of possible performance (see Chapter 2).

*Figure 7-33. Annual energy use and peak demand comparison by window area*

All cases are west-facing with interior shading and include daylighting controls. Numbers are expressed per square foot within a 30-foot-deep perimeter zone for a twelve-month operating schedule. Results were computed using DOE-2.1E for a typical school building in Houston, Texas (see Appendix B).

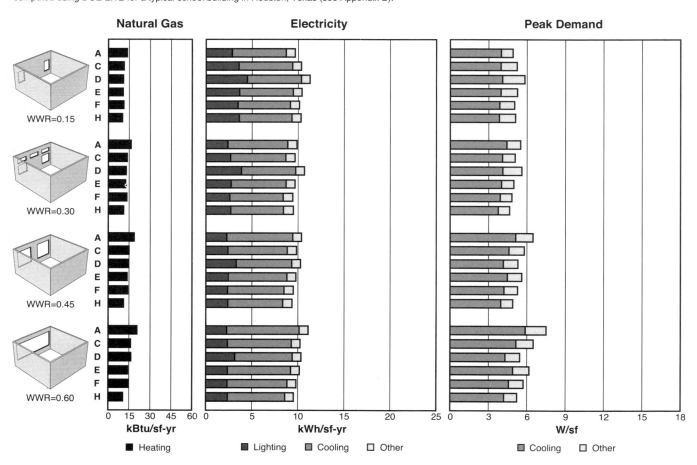

## The Effect of Window Area on Annual Energy Use and Peak Demand in an East- or West-facing Classroom

This section addresses the question of the optimal window area in an east- or west-facing perimeter zone. In a hot-climate city like Houston, energy use does not necessarily increase with greater window area. The relationship between window area and energy use depends on several factors. Figure 7-33 shows that heating energy use in an east- or west-facing space rises significantly with increased window area—58 percent on average between window types as window area is increased from WWR=0 to WWR=0.60.

With daylighting controls, cooling energy use climbs with window area, but lighting energy use falls with greater window area and the daylight it yields, resulting in a net decline in annual electricity use (12 percent decrease on average by increasing window area from WWR=0 to 0.60). Total annual energy use decreases on average by 6 percent as window area increases from WWR=0 to 0.60, however, there is great variation depending on window type. With Window A, energy use rises by 5 percent while with Window H it falls by 15 percent.

For the combined electricity and heating energy use (assuming a fuel ratio of 3:1), the optimal window area is dependent on the window type (Figure 7-31). For each window this occurs (the low point on Figure 7-31) where the energy-saving benefits of daylight controls are realized and increasing the window area produces little additional lighting energy savings while the cooling and heating energy use continue to rise. For Window A, the optimum is WWR=0.15, for Windows C, E, and F it is WWR=0.30, and for Window D it is WWR=0.45. The lowest total annual energy use with Window H is at WWR=0.45—this is the least total energy use for any window type at any area—although the performance varies little from WWR=0.30–0.45.

Similar to total energy use, there is an optimal window area (the low point on Figure 7-32) with respect to peak demand. For Window A, the lowest peak demand is at WWR=0.15, while the low point for Windows C, E, F, and H is at WWR=0.30. The optimal area for Window D is WWR=0.45. On average peak demand is reduced 0.8 W/sf or 14 percent when area increases from WWR=0 to 0.30, but the average actually rises by 3 percent at WWR=0.60. Similar to energy use, peak demand varies considerably between window types.

# CHAPTER 8

# Case Studies

## Introduction

This chapter includes seven case studies of buildings in a variety of climate and site conditions, and a range of sizes and uses that demonstrate innovative uses of windows or illustrate important design approaches related to windows and glazing.

The Hoffmann-La Roche Ltd. Office Building in New Jersey uses several design strategies to bring daylight into a massive central core building. These include small interior atriums, light shelves, and prismatic glazing that transmits daylight to the building core.

The Seattle Justice Center deals with a very restricted site where only the southwest orientation is available for windows. The response is an advanced double-envelope facade that provides a thermal buffer while allowing sunlight to penetrate deep into the building.

The Debis Tower in Berlin is an example of another advanced facade concept, with an outer envelope of operable glass panels functioning as a thermal buffer when needed. The inner glass wall with operable windows provides excellent control and comfort for the occupants in a high-rise building.

The Phoenix Central Library is an example of how a building can reflect its site and climate through different window and shading approaches on each orientation. The building effectively responds to the sun path of its particular latitude.

The Florida Solar Energy Center reflects the use of glazing and daylighting techniques to reduce energy in a hot-humid climate. Light shelves, shading systems and skylights provide benefits that are documented by the researchers who inhabit the building.

The Cambria Office Facility in Pennsylvania demonstrates the benefits of integrated design. By using triple-glazed, high-performance windows, the designers eliminated perimeter heating and downsized the mechanical system. This more than offset the cost of improved windows and saved energy as well.

The designers of the Xilinx Development Center in Colorado had the freedom to extend the building on an east-west axis, resulting in mostly north- and south-facing windows that bring light and view into the perimeter spaces. An innovative light redirection device on the transoms reflects sunlight into the spaces.

*Figure 8-1. Debis Tower, Berlin, Germany. Photo: COLT International*

330

# Hoffmann-La Roche Ltd. Office Building
## Nutley, New Jersey

Maximizing building surface area is one response to designing for effective daylighting, and this approach was necessary before the advent of reliable electric lighting, extensive mechanical services, and cheap energy. Traditionally, building designers were mindful that spaces had to be in close proximity to windows, with daylighting only possible within 15 to 25 feet of a window—given a standard window head height of 8 feet. This "daylight dimension" limited building depth.

Designing with such a precept in mind, however, has drawbacks. Long, thin buildings are more expensive to construct because their shape requires more exterior wall area to enclose the same volume of space compared to a structure with a square plan. For instance, a floor of 40,000 square feet can be enclosed in an area of 200 by 200 feet, or 80 by 500 feet. The latter requires a 1,160-foot perimeter, while the former only requires an 800-foot perimeter, significantly impacting initial building cost.

A common challenge, given the economic realities of construction, is to design a deep-plan building while still offering daylighting. The Hoffmann-La Roche Ltd. Office Building in Nutley, New Jersey, by Hillier, is a seven-story building with a 185-by-185-foot footprint—a square administration building. The goal of designing with effective daylight in mind is addressed through several basic strategies:

- The building is planned with a central core to maximize the perimeter for daylighting. In addition, the core is offset at the north side where daylight penetrates the least and to accommodate the design of a skylit atrium stair to the south of the core where the occupiable office space is furthest from the wall.

- Two-story work studios anchor each of the building's four sides. With their tall glass openings, these spaces admit daylight deep into the building's center. As a more conventional 13-foot floor-to-floor height predominates (9.5 feet from floor to finish ceiling), the work studios increase daylight penetration to adjacent spaces.

- Within the standard office areas, interior and exterior light shelves redirect light onto the ceiling, bouncing light back further into space, as well as offering shade and glare protection. Prismatic glazing in the transom window is angled to redirect sunlight and ambient light onto the ceiling plane, so that it becomes an indirect light source.

These basic design decisions were made recognizing the sun's movement throughout the year and the impact adjacent buildings would have—both in terms of shading or reflecting light upon the new facility.

The project does not feature any active elements such as heliostats tracking the sun to maximize daylight. Rather, passive daylighting strategies work in concert to provide a comfortable work environment. Computer modeling and other studies helped

*Figure 8-2. Exterior view of southeast corner of the Hoffmann-La Roche Ltd. Office Building. The projecting "work studios"—two-story spaces to facilitate daylight penetration—are evident on each elevation. Photo: Hillier*

**Project**
*Hoffmann-La Roche Ltd. Office Building*
*U.S. Headquarters, Nutley, NJ*

**Owner**
*Hoffmann-La Roche Ltd.*
*Basel, Switzerland*

**Architect**
*Hillier, Princeton, NJ*
*Core and shell architect, including the lobby interior design and upper story work studios*

**Interior Architects**
*Gensler, New York, NY*

**Mechanical and Electrical Engineer**
*RG Vanderweil Engineers, Boston, MA*

**Daylighting Consultant**
*Carpenter Norris Consulting, New York, NY*

refine the strategies, which were reinforced throughout the design process. For instance, at the interior design level, careful attention was given to interior finishes, which were designed to optimize brightness and reduce glare and contrast. Similarly, the open interior was planned without perimeter offices in order to maximize daylight penetration.

*Figure 8-3. Two-story work studios effectively increase the "daylight dimension"—the depth of space that light can penetrate the building. Interior roller blinds help control brightness and glare in these spaces. The blind fabric has a 2–3 percent openness factor. The fabric is light in color toward the outside, providing greater reflectivity for heat gain reduction. Conversely, its inner face is darker to reduce surface brightness. Photo: Mario Carrieri*

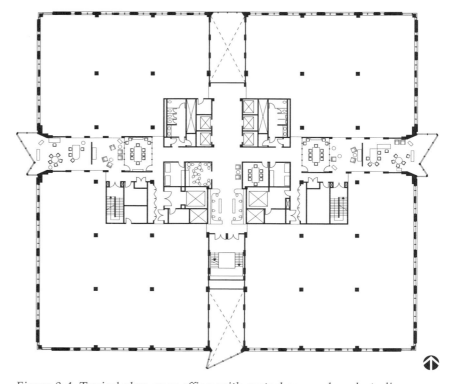

*Figure 8-4. Typical plan, open offices with central core and work studios*

*Figure 8-5. North-south section through two-story work studios and the skylit atrium stair; these features help admit more daylight to the building center*

*Case Studies*

Given the emphasis on daylighting, glazing selection and specification, and even window mock-ups, required thoughtful consideration.

- The standard glazing is low-E insulating glass, with a U-factor of 0.29 Btu/hr-sf-°F, a shading coefficient of 0.44 (SHGC=0.38), and visible light transmittance of 0.70. It was used on all the building faces, in the vision glass panels of the regular office windows and in the work studio curtain walls.

- The specialty glass for transom windows is ECOSS glass type—an acronym for "Ecological Sunlight System" manufactured by Figla. The window assembly is a set of acrylic prisms sandwiched between two sheets of glass.

Attention to all these details has seemingly paid off. The building has not been monitored since its occupation in the late 1990s, but Philippe Dordai of Hillier notes: "We have strong anecdotal evidence and evidence from photographs that the daylight penetrates at least 35 feet, and up to 45 feet under ideal conditions, from the building perimeter."

Dordai also comments that daylight sensors engage roller shades to help control brightness and glare when there is too much daylight entering the curtain walls in the work studios. On the other hand, photosensors do not control the electrical lighting, to tune down or turn off the lights when there is sufficient daylight in the space. Such elements were not integrated into the final design.

Despite this, overall the design illustrates an integrated lighting solution and how design decisions must work in concert to yield such a result. Client and design team interest and proper use of daylighting studies and tools contribute to a design where daylighting supplements electric lighting in a dynamic and energy-efficient manner.

*Figure 8-6. Interior view of windows—exterior light shelf, vision glass below and prismatic transom panel above. The light shelf and transom panel direct light up to the ceiling and back into the space. In mock-ups, the team found that direct sunlight coming in through unfiltered clear glass was too bright and directional. Acid etching on the inner pane provided the right amount of diffusion. Photo: Philippe Dordai*

*Figure 8-7. The trapezoidal prisms in the ECOSS system can be angled to deflect light in the summer and redirect it inside a building in other seasons. Through their studies, the design team recognized that varying the prism angles according to their orientation would optimize performance—the prisms on the south facade should ideally be angled differently from those on the west. This "tuning" proved to be cost prohibitive at the time. Photos: Figla*

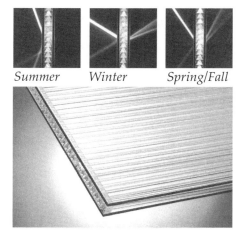

Summer    Winter    Spring/Fall

*The horizontal light control panel in the ECOSS IG unit floats in the air space between the glass lights.*

# The Seattle Justice Center
## Seattle, Washington

*Figure 8-8. Seattle Justice Center, from the southwest. The innovative double-envelope facade is ventilated to cool the large southwest-facing glazed area. Photo: Tim Griffith*

Architects must be mindful of multiple concerns in designing building facades. There are always trade-offs that must be made in optimizing building facade performance and the challenge lies in balancing conflicting criteria. A desire to maximize transparency, daylight, and views, for instance, can often be at odds with the need to minimize solar heat gain and reduce air-conditioning loads. Orientation is also an important factor. Site constraints or features, such as surrounding buildings or vistas, often dictate easterly or westerly facades, which are difficult to shade from low-angle morning or afternoon sun.

For the design of the Seattle Justice Center, NBBJ had a public client with high expectations. The project brief emphasized daylight penetration, views, and outdoor connections, but they were not to be achieved at the expense of increased air-conditioning or energy expenditure. The project goals were to create a work environment that provided high occupant satisfaction, set an appropriate, open image for the City of Seattle, and address sustainable building design principles.

The City of Seattle recently mandated that new buildings must meet a Silver rating from the U.S. Green Building Council's Leadership in Energy and Environmental Design (LEED™) program. The Justice Center features many green elements including a planted roof, the use of recycled materials, a rainwater recycling program, and energy conservation. All the sustainable building features were chosen and developed to express and emphasize good building practices. The City of Seattle set the goal to demonstrate and encourage such strategies for other projects.

These programmatic goals had to be addressed on a difficult site. Constrained on three adjacent blocks by high-rise buildings and sharing the block with an existing six-level parking structure,

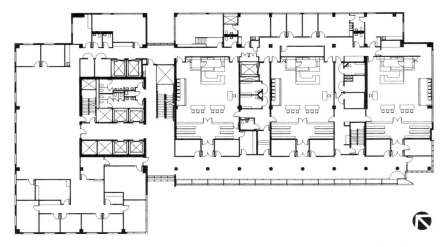

*Figure 8-9. Typical courtroom floor with circulation space between double envelope and courtrooms*

*Case Studies*

the Seattle Justice Center opens to potential daylight and views, of the new City of Seattle campus and Elliot Bay, only to the south-west. Lot depth also made it difficult to provide daylight deep in the building. NBBJ therefore explored the use of a double-skin *glazed thermal buffer* to offset these site conditions.

Existing research illustrates that vented, double-skin facades are an appropriate approach to maximizing the positive qualities of glazing while minimizing its negative energy impact and potential for thermal discomfort, especially on easterly or westerly glazed facades. Simply put, a shading device within the double skin can absorb solar gain and re-radiate it as heat trapped in the cavity. Exterior apertures at the wall's top and bottom induce air move-ment. The heat's natural tendency to rise pulls fresh, cool air in at the bottom while exhausting hot air out the top. Controlling the capture or venting of this trapped heat dictates cavity air tempera-ture and, in turn, the inner glass surface temperature.

A related advantage of double-envelope facades—especially when external shading elements are not possible for technical, aesthetic, or maintenance reasons—is the control they offer against direct solar gains, particularly in a building's perimeter zone. For instance, operable shading located in the double-envelope cavity, as opposed to internal blinds located in the internal perimeter zone, stop direct solar heat gain before it enters the perimeter zone space and becomes an air-conditioning load. When open, the shades provide high transparency when direct sunlight is not an issue, and they can be closed to provide shade from low-angle sun. Direct solar heat is absorbed and re-radiated when trapped within the cavity of the double skin, inducing a *thermal stack*, which is the driving mechanism for the cavity ventilation.

The double envelope, in short, can offer significant advantages with regard to thermal energy control and daylighting if properly designed and operated. Yet, just as external shading devices reflect a particular building site, climate, and orientation, a vented double-skin facade must be matched to the climate, orientation, and building program in order for it to perform well. Double-skin systems are prevalent in European climates, but less common in the United States. NBBJ studied the overall building envelope in light of local energy codes and standards, and the specifics of different building facades and their impact on the adjacent interior perimeter zones, to demonstrate their applicability.

The design had to be adapted to the Seattle context and climate. NBBJ teamed with Arup in developing their preliminary facade proposal. With sophisticated computer modeling, interdependent parameters could be understood to keep the facade's initial cost in alignment with the building budget, as well as meeting all the other criteria established in the building program.

Experience has shown that in benign climates such as Seattle's and in projects like the Justice Center, with a high percentage of core floor area to perimeter zone floor, saving significant amounts of energy from advanced facade design is difficult to achieve. The low cost of energy typically inhibits realization of overall building energy savings, offsetting the anticipated additional facade system's first costs. Not surprisingly, while the highly effective facade system proposed for the southwest-facing facade indicated a

*Figure 8-10. View of double envelope with interior light shelf. Photo: Kerry Hegedus*

**Project**
*Seattle Justice Center*

**Owner**
*City of Seattle*

**Architect**
*NBBJ*
*Seattle, WA*

**Mechanical Engineer**
*CDi Mechanical Engineers*
*Seattle, WA*

**Electrical Engineer**
*Abacus Engineering Systems*
*Seattle, WA*

**Sustainability Consultant**
*Ove Arup & Partners*
*San Francisco, CA*

**Lighting Design**
*J. Miller & Associates*
*Seattle, WA*

**Daylighting Study**
*Seattle Lighting Design Lab*
*Seattle, WA*

33 percent energy savings in the adjacent perimeter zone, preliminary estimates indicate this to result in only a 2 percent overall building energy savings.

As with any project, the quality of the environment desired must be weighed against cost. In this case, the impact was felt in the initial cost of the final vented, double-skin facade. Cost estimates indicate that the final vented, double-skin solution would be $320,000 ($17.50 per square foot of facade) greater than a traditional glazed facade. The previous technical analyses allowed the design team to achieve the aesthetic goals of the project, increase perimeter floor-to-ceiling heights, and bring more daylight deep into the building; these variables were ultimately difficult to quantify in a life cycle cost analysis.

Measured on its own, the double-envelope, thermal-flue facade has limited energy benefits (considering the limited area and orientation). But considering the orientation, client goals, aesthetic considerations, and the Seattle Justice Center's overall sustainability strategy, the thermal-flue concept is seen as an essential feature of the project, extending beyond its measurable qualities.

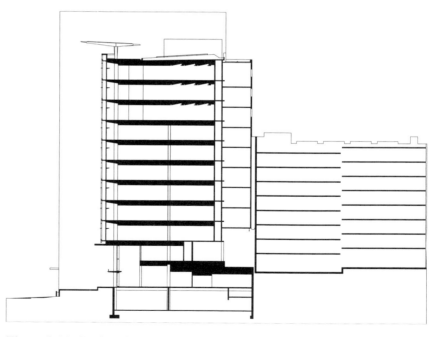

*Figure 8-11. Section showing the nine-story double envelope. Courtrooms are on the upper three levels, open offices on the lower six. Note the existing parking garage to the right of the Justice Center*

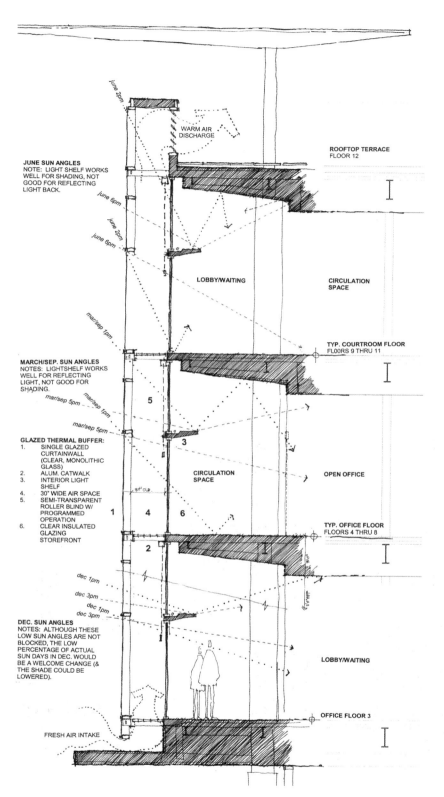

**JUNE SUN ANGLES**
NOTE: LIGHT SHELF WORKS WELL FOR SHADING, NOT GOOD FOR REFLECTING LIGHT BACK.

june 2pm
june 6pm
june 2pm
june 6pm

WARM AIR DISCHARGE

ROOFTOP TERRACE
FLOOR 12

LOBBY/WAITING

CIRCULATION SPACE

mar/sep 1pm

**MARCH/SEP. SUN ANGLES**
NOTES: LIGHTSHELF WORKS WELL FOR REFLECTING LIGHT, NOT GOOD FOR SHADING.

mar/sep 5pm
mar/sep 1pm
mar/sep 5pm

TYP. COURTROOM FLOOR
FLOORS 9 THRU 11

**GLAZED THERMAL BUFFER:**
1. SINGLE GLAZED CURTAINWALL (CLEAR, MONOLITHIC GLASS)
2. ALUM. CATWALK
3. INTERIOR LIGHT SHELF
4. 30" WIDE AIR SPACE
5. SEMI-TRANSPARENT ROLLER BLIND W/ PROGRAMMED OPERATION
6. CLEAR INSULATED GLAZING STOREFRONT

CIRCULATION SPACE

OPEN OFFICE

TYP. OFFICE FLOOR
FLOORS 4 THRU 8

dec 1pm
dec 3pm
dec 1pm
dec 3pm

**DEC. SUN ANGLES**
NOTES: ALTHOUGH THESE LOW SUN ANGLES ARE NOT BLOCKED, THE LOW PERCENTAGE OF ACTUAL SUN DAYS IN DEC. WOULD BE A WELCOME CHANGE (& THE SHADE COULD BE LOWERED).

LOBBY/WAITING

OFFICE FLOOR 3

FRESH AIR INTAKE

*Figure 8-13. Wall section of double envelope, illustrating daylighting and ventilation strategies for floor levels 3 through 11. Source: Kerry Hegedus*

*Figure 8-12. Interstitial space in the double envelope. Photo: Kerry Hegedus*

---

**Glazing Properties**

**Double envelope**
*Outer layer: ³⁄₈-inch tempered clear glass curtain wall*
*Inner layer: insulating glass storefront with low-E coating*
*U-factor=0.31 Btu/hr-sf-°F*
*SHGC=0.53*
*VT=0.76*

**Other curtain wall glazing**
*Insulating glass with low-E coating*
*U-factor=0.29 Btu/hr-sf-°F*
*SHGC=0.37*
*VT=0.70*

# Debis Tower
## Berlin, Germany

**Project**
*Debis Tower*
*Potsdamer Platz*
*Berlin, Germany*

**Client and Owner**
*Daimler-Chrysler AG*

**Architect**
*Renzo Piano Building Workshop,*
*Genoa, Italy*
*in association with Christoph*
*Kohlbecker*

**Engineers**
*IGH/Ove Arup & Partners, Schmidt-*
*Reuter & Partner (HVAC); IBB Burrer,*
*Ove Arup & Partners (electrical*
*engineering)*

Buildings are static objects. While they are fixed in space, the sun is in constant motion throughout the day and year. Many daylighting strategies do not account for the sun's motion, but some address it brilliantly, allowing building occupants to control and tune their environment. Berlin's Debis Tower is an example of a building using operable elements to supplement the basic design decisions that support good daylighting.

The attitude that occupants should have a high degree of control over their environment with an operable, layered facade impacted building development and detailing. Codes and site also shaped form. For instance, German building regulations mandate that all office workers must be less than 25 feet from a window and natural light. This norm impacts building form, giving rise to the atrium. Debis's important site—Potsdamer Platz, the historic center of Berlin—meant that urbanistic concerns had to be addressed. It was critical to maintain the traditional street edge and take cues from the city fabric. Debis Tower is essentially a full city block, with a center atrium hollowed out of building mass to provide light and fresh air.

Debis's office spaces—totaling 482,000 square feet—are within relatively thin building volumes accessible to light and fresh air. Throughout the complex, occupants can open their windows for

*Figure 8-14. Exterior of the Debis Tower at street level. Six- and seven-story low-rise buildings in foreground, with twenty-story tower beyond. Photo: Enrico Cano*

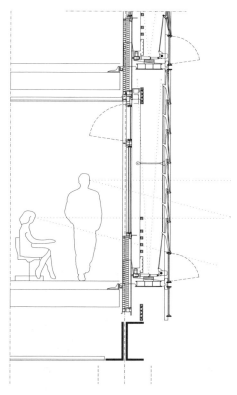

Figure 8-16. Section of the tower's double envelope, showing the outer skin closed in its winter position.

Figure 8-15. Double envelope of the tower with operable window inside, and an outer glazed skin. In this photo, the outer skin is open in the summer position. Photo: Colt International

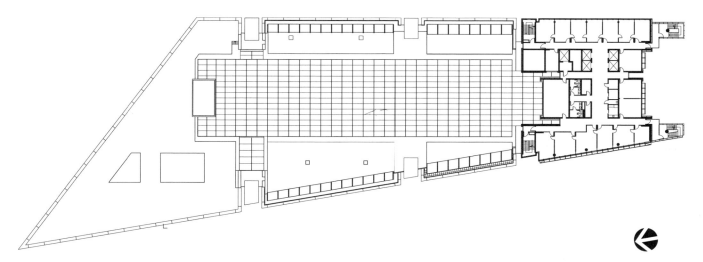

Figure 8-17. Typical tower plan. The twenty-story tower is at the south end of the block. The plan also shows the roof of the atrium and the roofs of the surrounding six- and seven-story low-rise buildings.

*Figure 8-18. The atrium is at the heart of the complex, with overlooking office spaces. Photo: Gianni Berengo Gardin*

*Figure 8-19. A detail of the fritted louvers which diffuse the daylight entering the space. The windows overlooking the atrium also have fritted louvers to temper the light. The frit density decreases on the lower level windows, to let in more light. Photo: Gianni Berengo Gardin*

ventilation. External aluminum sun blinds, which the occupant controls electronically from the interior, control light and glare on all exterior facades. Beyond this, the complex's twenty-story tower proper, the adjacent, lower six- and seven-story buildings and the spaces fronting the six-story atrium employ different key environmental control measures:

- On the tower's east, south and west elevations—which have high solar gains—an outer layer of glass panels sits 27 inches outside the inner wall of operable glass windows. The panels, controlled by sensors, pivot open in summer. In the closed position in winter, they offer thermal protection. Along with the external blinds, maintenance platforms within the double envelope function as horizontal sunshades.

- Within the complex's lower buildings—six and seven stories—the outer wall of pivoting glass panels is replaced by fixed terra cotta rods, which act as a sunscreen. These elements cut off high sun angles, supplementing the operable external sun blinds just outside the window.

- If blocking or tuning light with operable blinds is the external facade strategy, the atrium is about filtering. Fritted glass fins diffuse and temper light entering the skylight. Windows overlooking the atrium receive fritted fins with glare control curtains used also on the office windows.

Maximizing building surface area is one response to designing for daylighting, with the corollary that sun control is also necessary. At Debis, glare and other light control issues are addressed within a building envelope featuring substantial user control. The tower's double envelope and the layered facade on the lower buildings also addresses thermal and ventilation issues, resolved in a sustainable manner with occupant control.

This is especially important in the tower proper, with its high internal gains. The double facade's summer and winter modes are just the start to thermal control measures. For instance, the upper light opens automatically at night when the weather is warm enough to flush out the heat accumulated during the day. The concrete floor slab is exposed at floor perimeter to radiate out heat accumulated during the day. These measures, along with the combination of shading and double wall, reduce heat loads to make air-conditioning supplementary.

The project is clad in a very elaborate, maintenance-intensive curtain wall that, along with other energy-efficient, sustainable measures, is projected to reduce primary energy consumption by 50 percent compared to normally air-conditioned offices. With the opportunity to control light and ventilation, occupants can control their environment in a way not possible in sealed, air-conditioned buildings.

Debis, a Daimler-Chrysler subsidiary created to engage in real estate development and management, among other business services, views the project as a model or prototype for future real estate endeavors. The complex is a test for innovations in energy conservation and sustainable building design. As project managers and occupants, Debis is in the position to learn—with the complex becoming a teaching tool.

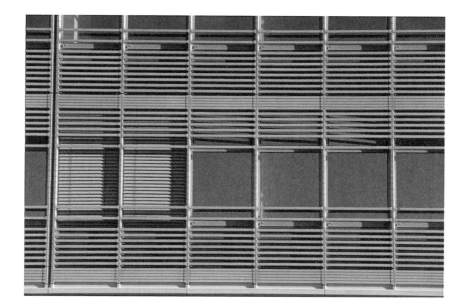

*Figure 8-20. Detail of cladding on the six- and seven-story buildings. Fixed, terra cotta rods act as a sun screen, with operable sun blinds behind. These external elements provide two layers of sun protection, with the operable windows offering another means of occupant control. Photo: Gianni Berengo Gardin*

*Figure 8-21. Background, the Debis Tower stair, with the double envelope in open summer position in the foreground. The photo clearly shows the maintenance platforms within the double envelope, grates which also offer sun control. Photo: Gianni Berengo Gardin*

*There is a gradation of layered facades over the buildings at Potsdamer Platz. They start with a terra cotta rainscreen facade, as in the upper image, and work through a series of solutions with increasing areas of glass until they reach the double-skin, fully glazed system on the tower, shown in the lower image.*

*All the double-glazed windows have a selective coating, with a visible transmittance of 0.63. The additional glass skin on the tower's double envelope reduces the visible transmittance to 0.54.*

# Phoenix Central Library
## Phoenix, Arizona

With a total area of 280,000 square feet spread out over five floors in a basic rectangular form, the Phoenix Central Library is outwardly an air-conditioned big box. However, underpinning this simple form is a design wed to the hot-dry desert at 33 degrees North latitude. Facades and roof are designed to control solar heat gains, a significant factor in this climate; building faces were conceived mindful of sun angles and sun path.

Context and climate have the capacity to shape design. In fact, the design team initially studied an Adobe concept—a library with thick walls and small windows—a nod to the lessons from traditional vernacular architecture of the region. An architecture of thermal mass and minimal openings has advantages in the desert. However, such a strategy did not yield good contact with the outdoors, and the team wanted to capitalize on vistas of Phoenix's mountains enjoyed at the library site. The library design had to limit solar gains and glare while admitting light and views.

The design resolution ultimately recognized that it is possible to let in light on the facades where it can be tempered and controlled, but it is not feasible to harness light on all orientations. For instance, at Phoenix's latitude (and others for that matter) low sun angles, characteristic in the rising and setting sun, are the most difficult to control. Neither overhangs nor vertical fins fully block the intense sun on building elevations facing east or west. This fact shaped the design.

On the east and west facades, copper-clad saddlebags—mechanical rooms, emergency stairs, toilets, service elevators, and

### Project
*Phoenix Central Library*
*Phoenix, AZ*

### Owner
*City of Phoenix*

### Architect
*bruderDWLarchitects, New River, AZ.*
*The project was a joint venture between*
*william p. bruder, architect, ltd. and*
*DWL Architects & Planners.*

### Mechanical and Electrical Engineer
*Ove Arup & Partners California*
*Los Angeles, CA*

### Daylighting Consultant
*Tait Solar Company*
*Tempe, AZ*

### Structural Fabric Consultant
*FTL/Happold*
*New York, NY*

*Figure 8-22. View of the north and west facades of the Phoenix Central Library. The east and west cladding consists of perforated copper sheets, which reduce the solar gains normally associated with those orientations. In contrast, the west entry point—the incision that curves into the building—is clad in highly reflective stainless steel, a surface that accentuates heat and light. On the north facade, "saddlebags" jut out to protect the glazing. These, along with the fabric "sails," fully shade the glazing. The elevations, with their diverse palette of materials, explore the issues of shade, reflectivity, and solar gains, all executed mindful of orientation. Photo: Bill Timmerman*

other servant spaces—buffer the primary, served spaces of the main library block. The auxiliary areas bear the brunt of the intense summer sun, offering protection from the sun's light and heat. Their reflective copper cladding provides the first line of sun defense, with their depth—about 25 feet at the widest—also providing protection. The saddlebags are naturally ventilated, unconditioned spaces (except in the rest rooms), with the mass of 12-inch concrete panel walls acting as a thermal damper.

The saddlebags, on multiple levels, are designed to protect the main library spaces from the early morning and late afternoon sun. In contrast, the north and south facades are designed to admit light and views, but are again conceived with orientation in mind. The fully glazed north face is fitted with external, fixed vertical shading—Teflon-coated acrylic fabric sails. The saddlebags also jut out to protect the glazing. As the rising and setting summer sun strikes the north facade, both elements shield glazing from direct sun penetration in the critical time frame of March through September.

In contrast, the south facade is fitted with adjustable, horizontal louvers. Externally mounted, the aluminum louvers are computer controlled to eliminate direct sun penetration, while maximizing

Figure 8-24. Shade "sails" located on north facade. These sails help reduce sky glare and undesirable direct-beam solar radiation during the summer months in the morning and evening, when the rising and setting sun actually strikes the north facade. See the azimuth angle on the sun path diagram for Phoenix's latitude below. Photo: Bill Timmerman

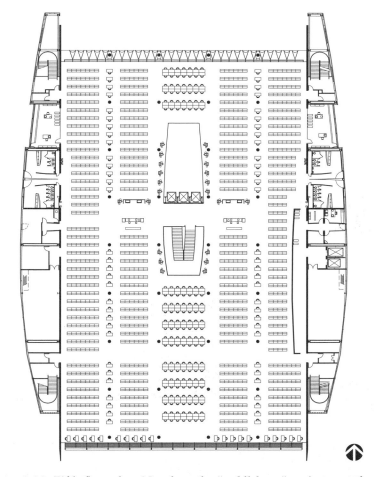

Figure 8-23. Fifth-floor plan. Note how the "saddlebags" project past the north facade glazing to shield the glass from summer's rising and setting sun

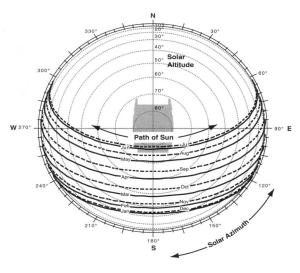

Figure 8-25. Sun path diagram for Phoenix, Arizona. Source: Solar Tool, Square One Research Pty Ltd., www.squ1.com

343

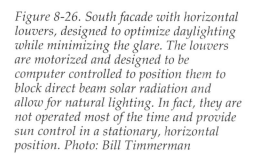

views and daylight. High sun angles on the south facade make horizontal elements effective means to control and temper sunlight, and even drive light deeper into space if properly positioned to act as light shelves. These customized louvers are integrated with the conventional window system, offering a cost-effective, striking solution to sun control.

Toplighting for the fifth-floor reading room is also important, and is accomplished with narrow, linear skylights running along the saddlebag walls and circular skylights set above each column. These small, simple skylights are not fitted with louvers or other controls, but their depth limits direct sun penetration. Only the high sun at solar noon fully enters the reading room through the linear skylights. Direct sun fully penetrates the deep circular oculi only at solar noon on the summer solstice. The atrium skylights, however, are fitted with reflective louvers that track the sun and direct appropriate amounts downwards, with a lower set that diffuses the light and eliminates direct glare within the spaces below.

The Phoenix Central Library illustrates how the sun path and facade orientation can shape design decisions. Daylight is important in library spaces, yet it must be tempered within the desert context. As the north and south facade glazing is shading appropriately for each orientation, a relatively high-VT glazing is possible—to offer light and views. Toplighting is also carefully considered and controlled.

While the east and west facades lack glazing, on each face a vertical opening in the copper cladding reveals the public entry. A curved stainless steel surface reflects the desert sun onto the arriving library patrons, focusing the scorching heat. The cool air and tempered light of the interior lies beyond this entry, which heightens the qualities of the geography and climate.

*Figure 8-26. South facade with horizontal louvers, designed to optimize daylighting while minimizing the glare. The louvers are motorized and designed to be computer controlled to position them to block direct beam solar radiation and allow for natural lighting. In fact, they are not operated most of the time and provide sun control in a stationary, horizontal position. Photo: Bill Timmerman*

*Figure 8-27. Fifth-floor reading room with view of the south facade louvers. Vistas of the city and mountains beyond drove the decision to open up this facade with full glazing. Photo: Bill Timmerman*

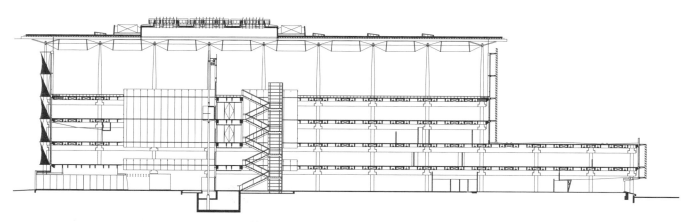

*Figure 8-28. North-south section. Note shading devices on north and south elevations. Shading is also integral with the atrium glazing*

# Florida Solar Energy Center

## Cocoa, Florida

Figure 8-29. Overall view of Florida Solar Energy Center. The Visitor Center is in foreground, with office beyond. Photo: Steven Spencer

In the design of their new facility, the Florida Solar Energy Center's goal was to create "the world's most energy-efficient building" within climatic limits. Beyond this, a Center mission to educate the public, and their affiliation with the University of Central Florida, meant that the building must also be a didactic design demonstrating its energy efficiency. The building itself had to be a teaching tool, one monitored long after commissioning to ensure that it meets efficiency standards.

The Energy Center design starts with the premise that in most office buildings, electric lighting is the largest energy load, and much of it is unnecessary. In Florida's warm and humid climate, excess electric lighting only adds to air-conditioning loads. If a building is to keep occupants cool and dry without consuming much energy, it must effectively address daylighting in its basic form and development.

With this concept as a starting point, the Energy Center office and lab building is designed as a long, thin rectangle oriented on an east-west axis. This basic design gesture accomplishes three energy-efficiency objectives:

- Orientation exposes the smallest east- and west-facing building surfaces to hot morning and afternoon sun. By design, daylight principally enters through the south and north facades.

- Form maximizes usable space on the building perimeter, to capitalize on sidelighting. With a building depth of 60 feet, toplighting must light the deep interior, non-perimeter zones. Roof monitors can provide daylight within the building core.

**Project**
*Florida Solar Energy Center*
*Cocoa, FL*

**Owner**
*University of Central Florida*
*Orlando, FL*

**Architect**
*Architects Design Group*
*Winter Park, FL*

**Mechanical and Electrical Engineer**
*Brian Cumming & Associates Inc.*
*Maitland, FL*

Figure 8-30. View of the Visitor Center window wall, facing southeast. Photo: Steven Spencer

*Case Studies*

- The design facilitates the development of independent north and south HVAC zones, so interior air temperatures can be controlled based on solar exposure. South-facing zones can thus be cooled without wasting energy cooling the north side.

Design development, such as glazing specifications, reinforces these form decisions. For instance, in the Visitor Center, the south-east-facing window wall receives significant solar exposure, yet little solar gain. The insulated glass unit—and the thin, almost-transparent metallic, spectrally selective film sandwiched inside it—provides a relatively high 56 percent visible transmittance, with a solar heat gain coefficient of 0.28. The glazing admits sunlight but minimizes solar heat. This high-performance window system costs more than conventional ones, but energy savings—from reducing air-conditioning costs and using daylight rather than electric light for illumination—paid back that additional expense in about two years.

Linked with the window system are the shading devices, which were monitored with regard to their ability to reduce electric lighting loads. The architects designed exterior light shelves as an integral facade element, but FSEC staff added interior light shelves too, after significant testing. Interior light shelves, traditional blinds and a control window without blinds or light shelves were all tested for half a year to gauge relative performance. The data indicated that the light shelves increase daylight penetration, thereby reducing electric light loads and giving glare reduction (Figure 8-34). In contrast, more traditional interior blinds had a negative impact on daylighting. Based on the monitoring, all south-facing offices were subsequently fitted with interior light shelves.

Monitoring also revealed the importance of the window frames. The window unit's overall U-factor of 0.31 Btu/hr-sf-°F provides effective control of conductive gains under peak load conditions but the highly conductive metal window frames seriously degrade

*Figure 8-31. South facade and exterior light shelves. Photo: Steven Spencer*

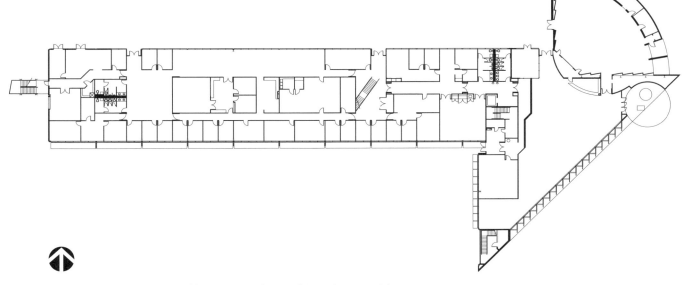

*Figure 8-32. Plan showing the office wing as long, thin volume, with public areas toward the east*

**Glazing Properties**

*Spectrally selective tinted insulating glass with low-E coating*
*U-factor=0.31*
*SHGC=0.28*
*VT=0.56*

the assumed U-factor. Monitoring reveals that the actual overall assembly U-factor cannot be less than about 0.7 Btu/hr-sf-°F. In short, the window assembly's assumed U-factor—used in DOE-2 runs and operational energy assumptions—was erroneous, as learned in documenting the building's actual energy use. As the glazing system in each office—approximately 56 square feet—is about 44 square feet of glass and 12 square feet of frame, the high-performance glazing could be improved with better, less conductive frames. A key lesson is that window specification must address frame as well as glazing, unless a serious compromise in performance can be accepted.

Figure 8-33. *South offices, with interior light shelves. Photo: Steven Spencer*

Figure 8-34. *Within south-facing offices, the FSEC monitored lighting performance of interior light shelves, blinds, and a control office with no window treatment. The electric lights—two T8 lamps per office, with electronic dimming ballasts linked to photosensors—were left on 24 hours a day during the evaluation. Monitoring the electric usage revealed how the interior light shelf reduced electric lighting loads compared to the office with no window treatment, especially during the early morning and late afternoon. The blinds had a negative impact on lighting. Graph from FSEC, Danny Parker*

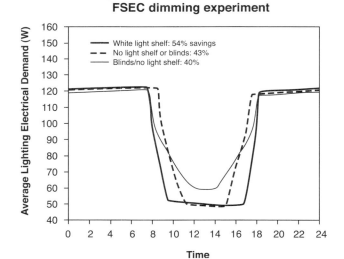

**Comparative lighting demand profiles**
**FSEC dimming experiment**

— White light shelf: 54% savings
- - No light shelf or blinds: 43%
— Blinds/no light shelf: 40%

*Case Studies*

Moving from the perimeter offices and exterior spaces, in the building core, roof monitors (also referred to as lightscoops) replace windows to provide daylight. Florida's solar-intense climate make skylights problematic—they cause hot spots from direct-beam sunlight, fade interior furnishings, and create too much internal heat in general. Roof monitors, projecting 10 feet above the flat roof, provide light without the drawbacks of skylights. Each monitor's north-facing surface is a highly efficient glazing system that lets in cool light from the northern sky but no hot, direct-beam sunlight. The light is directed downward into the building's core, reducing electrical lighting loads.

If the overall design strategy is to turn the building itself into a daylight fixture that captures light, there is certainly a need to reject light too. With cooling loads dominating the building in this hot-humid climate, the facility envelope cannot be a heat sink for solar gains. To keep the Energy Center's air-conditioning load down, the facility's white roof reflects almost 80 percent of the sun's energy. Even though the building's walls are blue, rather than white, they still block heat gain through the use of a radiant barrier. This aluminum foil surface in the air space behind the exterior finish blocks the transfer of solar-generated heat.

Within the Center's climate, a typical single-story office building has 30 percent of its annual cooling load attributed to heat produced by electric lighting, 20 percent to solar gain through windows, 15 percent to roof heat gain, and 13 percent to heat from internal equipment. The lighting system is not only the largest cooling load component, but second only to the HVAC in electric consumption. By directly tackling lighting improvements—through glazing, daylight and occupancy sensors, and good design strategies—as well as other energy saving measures, the facility uses half the energy of a similar building.

*Figure 8-36. North-facing roof monitors and white roof. Photo: Steven Spencer*

*Figure 8-37. Looking up to the roof monitor. Splayed surfaces around the monitor increase the toplighting efficiency of glazing and provide a more gradual visual transition to the brighter view of the sky. Photo: Steven Spencer*

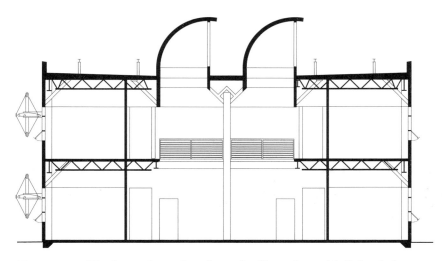

*Figure 8-35. North-south section through office wing with light shelves on south facade. The roof monitor glazing faces north.*

# Cambria Office Facility
## Ebensburg, Pennsylvania

**Project**
*Cambria Office Facility*
*Ebensburg, PA*

**Owner**
*Commonwealth of Pennsylvania*

**Architect**
*L. Robert Kimball & Associates*
*Harrisburg, PA*

**Mechanical Engineer**
*Beardsley Design Associates*
*Auburn, NY*

**Electrical Engineer**
*Design/build through various*
*vendors and designers*

**Sustainable Design Consultant**
*Energy Opportunities, Inc.*
*Wellsville, PA*

**Sustainable Materials Consultant**
*Horst, Inc.*
*Kutztown, PA*

Buildings and occupants rely ever more on mechanical services. Traditionally, a building's basic structure accounted for about 80 percent of its costs. With the transition to skeleton frame structures over the last hundred years—as opposed to load-bearing masonry—that cost has fallen to some 20 percent. On the other hand, the cost of building services has ballooned, with mechanical systems typically consuming 35 percent of the building budget. Today, more is spent on services than on any other building component.

We place tremendous importance on environmental comfort, leading to these profound changes within building expenditures. But these broad distinctions between costs for a building's basic structure and mechanical services do not sufficiently address the interplay between building components. Structure, which encompasses envelope, impacts services. For instance, consider Pennsylvania's Cambria Office Facility in Ebensburg, where investment in a high-performance, triple-glazed window system eliminates the need for perimeter heating—reducing mechanical system first costs, to say nothing of operational energy.

The Cambria project is an internally load-dominated building. It is cooled year round, even in Pennsylvania's harsh winters. Despite this, perimeter heating in this and similar buildings is invariably needed to temper the cold surface of typical glazing assemblies. Instead of perimeter heating, however, the Cambria design team addressed this issue with triple-pane windows. Triple glazing cost about $15,000 more than double-glazed windows. However, with triple glazing, a perimeter heating system, priced out at $25,000, was not needed.

*Figure 8-38. South elevation of the Cambria Office Facility. Photo: Jim Schafer*

Figure 8-39. South elevation with exterior light shelves on the ground level. Overhangs help control light on the first floor. Photo: Jim Schafer

Figure 8-40. Note the daylight directed to the ceiling from the reflective surface in the light shelves. There is no electric lighting in these elements. The light shelf side and front "wings" block direct sunlight early in the morning and late in the afternoon at certain times of the year. Photo: Jim Schafer

The project, a 34,500-square-foot facility, constructed for and leased by the Commonwealth of Pennsylvania, was designed utilizing a systems-integration process to minimize redundancies and maximize efficiencies. The end result is that systems, like perimeter heating, were entirely eliminated or downsized. Beyond this, the triple glazing had other advantages:

- The project air-conditioning system was reduced from 120 to 60 tons, saving $40,000. A tight, well-insulated building envelope, attention to daylighting, and other factors contributed to these savings. But project engineers and architects calculate that about 25 percent of this reduction—15 tons or $10,000—is attributable simply to better, more energy-efficient windows. The triple glazing saved capital costs associated with the HVAC system.

- Regarding comfort, the standards for this building require that the interior surface temperature of the windows remain 62 degrees Fahrenheit or higher when the exterior temperature is 20 degrees Fahrenheit. Triple-glazed windows meet this requirement. Though not a prime issue with this project, triple glazing is also very resistant to sound infiltration. Triple glazing also limits condensation. With their warmer surface temperatures, less moisture forms on triple-glazed windows.

Glazing innovations and shading or light redirection elements can reduce electric lighting needs and their associated mechanical loads. However, daylight never totally supplants electric lighting; rather, the glazing and envelope help daylight complement the electric lighting. Lighting fixtures are needed when there is insufficient daylight or for night occupation. The Cambria project illustrates that triple glazing can eliminate a building component, in this case perimeter heating, thus reducing capital as well as operational costs.

> **Glazing Properties**
>
> *Aluminum-clad wood-framed awning windows, triple-glazed, low-E, argon U=0.26, SHGC=0.27, VT=0.44*
>
> *Aluminum-clad wood-framed fixed windows, triple-glazed, low-E, argon U=0.24, SHGC=0.27, VT=0.44*
>
> *Storefront windows, 3 element, low-E U=0.26, SHGC=0.33, VT=0.49*

The Cambria project also illustrates designers using triple glazing in concert with traditional daylighting strategies, to achieve energy consumption goals. The project is oriented longitudinally along an east-west axis, to maximize south and north exposures. Light shelves on the south-facing windows provide shade and reflect light inside, with an ultra-reflective ceiling driving daylight

*Figure 8-41. First-floor office space, with clerestory windows. Photo: Jim Schafer*

*Figure 8-42. Map room on the first floor. Glass in large map table allows light to penetrate through to the lobby on the ground level. High clerestory windows ring the room. Photo: Jim Schafer*

into the building. Roof overhangs shade second-floor south-facing windows to reduce cooling loads. Clerestory windows over the center of the second floor provide daylight from two directions, which increases daylight and distributes it more evenly to reduce glare.

The integrated manner in which the project team addressed envelope, daylight, and other issues led to Cambria's LEED™ Gold certification. The building uses about half the energy of similar facilities, yet it was constructed for approximately $90 per square foot, well within the cost range of conventionally constructed office buildings in the area.

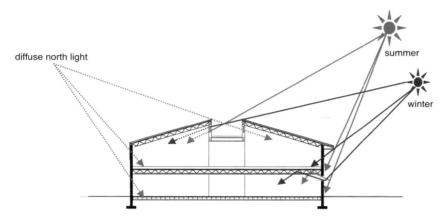

*Figure 8-43. Section showing the office wing and varying lighting strategies on the north and south elevations, and through the clerestory*

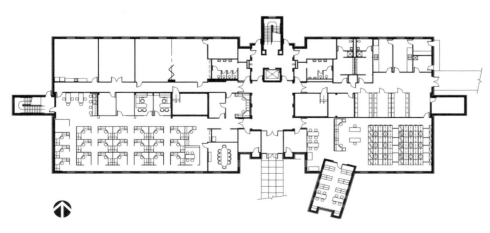

*Figure 8-44. Plan, ground level*

# Xilinx Development Center
## Longmont, Colorado

**Project**
*Xilinx Development Center*
*Longmont, CO*

**Owner**
*Xilinx Corporation*
*San Jose, CA*

**Architect**
*Downing Thorpe James*
*(Design Architect)*
*Boulder, CO*
*The Neenan Company*
*(Architect-of-Record and General*
*Contractor)*
*Fort Collins, CO*

**Energy, Daylighting, and**
**Sustainable Design Consultant**
*Architectural Energy Corporation*
*Boulder, CO*

**Mechanical and Electrical Engineer**
*BCER*
*Arvada, CO*

Effective daylighting requires attention to a myriad of issues, with building orientation and massing, site climate, interior spatial organization, appropriate glazing location and selection, and integration with the electric lighting and HVAC systems among the more important considerations. The Xilinx Development Center is an excellent example of how these factors were addressed by the design team, especially the "details," which often do not receive adequate attention.

The Center houses the software development activities of Xilinx Corporation. It is the first building on Xilinx's new Colorado research campus, and established a design benchmark for architectural, landscape, and sustainable design. Sustainable design concepts incorporated into the Center include indigenous landscaping, underfloor air distribution, direct/indirect evaporative cooling, and low-environmental impact materials.

Campus master planning placed the Development Center in the center of the site on an east-west axis. This building orientation resulted in perimeter open offices on the south and the north, with a core zone of support spaces and common areas, facilitating the use of daylight to provide ambient lighting of the perimeter open office areas.

Within the integrated design approach, perimeter windows were conceived as "vision" glass from 3 to 7 feet above the floor, and "daylight" glass from 7 feet above the floor to the 10-foot ceiling. The vision glass has a relatively low visible light transmission (0.29) and a low solar heat gain coefficient (0.24). The U-factor is 0.31 Btu/hr-sf-°F (winter). The daylight glass has the same U-factor, but a high visible light transmission (0.76) and a high solar heat gain coefficient (0.53).

*Figure 8-45. Exterior view of the Xilinx Development Center from the southwest. Photo: DTJ Design*

The high visible light transmission of the daylighting glass provides adequate daylight onto Architectural Energy Corporation's innovative, patented Mini Optical Light Shelf (MOLS) daylighting system, which shades occupants from direct sunlight while redirecting daylight deep into the open office space. Each MOLS unit consists of a frame which supports a series of fixed horizontal reflective louvers, of a unique compound geometry, that redirects daylight uniformly across the ceiling surface. The illuminated ceiling surface provides ambient light to the space below. Photosensors determine the ambient light from daylight and raise or lower the indirect electric lighting to maintain the minimum ambient lighting level.

Architectural Energy Corporation tested two south-facing open office areas: one on the first floor with unobstructed vision and daylight (with MOLS) windows, and one on the second floor with only the vision glass unobstructed. The MOLS units were covered by black plastic. Illuminance measurements were taken in various cubicles at set distances away from the window plane. Figure 8-51 presents the workplane—30 inches above the finished floor—illuminance values for these two areas on a sunny December day. The addition of the MOLS daylighting system essentially doubles the illumination levels.

This comparison clearly demonstrates the ambient lighting potential of optical daylighting systems. The excellent daylighting strategies within the overall Xilinx architectural scheme were reinforced through effective window design and glazing selection, integration with the electric lighting design, and implementation of effective shading and lighting control elements, including the MOLS daylighting system. The rigorous approach of the design team was carried forward through subsequent improvements in the MOLS design, as demonstrated in Figure 8-51.

*Figure 8-46. Exterior view of south fenestration with shading device between the lower "vision" glass and upper "daylighting" glass. Photo: DTJ Design*

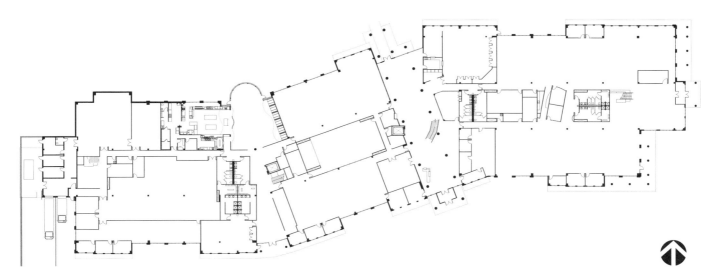

*Figure 8-47. First-floor plan of the 127,000 square foot two story Xilinx Development Center. The U.S. Green Building Council's Leadership in Energy and Environmental Design (LEED™) rating system guided the overall sustainable design of the campus master plan and the Development Center*

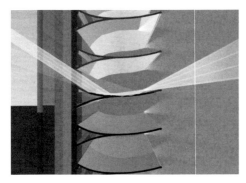

Figure 8-48. Detail of Mini Optical Light Shelf daylighting system—MOLS 51 Design. Source: Architectural Energy Corporation

An important factor in Xilinx's energy efficiency is the lighting approach. Beyond the careful integration of daylighting and electric lighting, the design team employed an ambient, task, accent lighting strategy to provide only the required amount of light:

- Daylighting and indirect (pendant) electric lighting provide 20–25 fc of ambient illumination, with photosensors raising or lowering electric light levels as required to maintain the minimum ambient light level.

- Furniture-mounted fluorescent lighting provides task lighting requirements of 40–50 fc with accent lighting highlights on specific areas, such as break rooms and wall-mounted art.

Figure 8-51. Since the Xilinx MOLS 51 installation, design refinements have led to a final, optimized design—MOLS 100. Using the results of Xilinx testing and computer model validation, the performance of the MOLS 100 design compared to MOLS 51 and the base case are shown here. The MOLS 100 design doubles the illuminance levels in the office cubicles compared to the MOLS 51 design, and quadruples the illuminance levels compared to the base case. Graph: Architectural Energy Corporation

Figure 8-49. Interior view of Architectural Energy Corporation's patented Mini Optical Light Shelf daylighting system—MOLS 51 Design. Photo: Architectural Energy Corporation

Figure 8-50. Interior view of open office area, with redirected daylight illuminating the ceiling. Photo: Architectural Energy Corporation

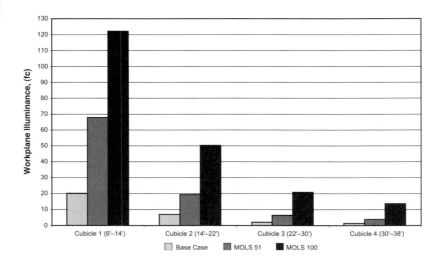

# Appendix A

# Method for Generating Performance Data

## INTRODUCTION

Window performance was analyzed with computer simulations. Inputs to the simulation included a building module which could be analyzed with different sizes and types of windows. The analysis was based on a default set of window and lighting conditions that includes various climates, window sizes, window types, shading, and daylighting controls. Alternate analyses looked at window frame types, switchable windows, and variations in daylighting controls. The computer model calculated a number of performance measures such as glare, brightness, illuminance, thermal comfort, view, energy use, and peak demand. This appendix provides a detailed description of the assumptions in the building simulation, the input parameter values, and the performance measures. These methods and assumptions apply to all office performance results throughout the book. A smaller set of results for schools was modeled separately. Those assumptions are discussed in the last section of the appendix.

Building energy simulations of commercial window systems were performed using the U.S. Department of Energy's DOE-2.1E building energy simulation program (Winkelmann et al. 1993). The DOE-2.1E program is the building industry standard that requires as input a geometrical description of the building and a physical description of the building construction, mechanical equipment, end-use load schedules, utility rates, and hourly weather data to determine the energy consumption of the building. DOE-2 has been used to develop American Society of Heating, Refrigerating and Air-Conditioning Engineers (ASHRAE) 90.1 and California Title-24 Energy-Efficiency Standards and to design many commercial buildings over the past twenty years. EnergyPlus is a new building performance simulation program, released in April 2001, that combines the best capabilities and features from BLAST and DOE-2.1E with new capabilities (Winkelmann et al. 2001, http://gundog.lbl.gov/). While there are differences between the two programs, EnergyPlus and DOE-2.1E use the same basic WINDOW4 algorithms for the window load calculations. Relative performance trends and conclusions drawn from this analysis with DOE-2.1E are expected to be the same as those from EnergyPlus. In the future, further improvements in EnergyPlus modeling will add new capabilities that we will

use for fenestration analysis. As these results emerge, we will provide updates to modeling results in later versions of this book or on the commercial windows web site (Appendix C).

## COMMERCIAL BUILDING PROTOTYPE

A generic commercial office building prototype originally developed by the Lawrence Berkeley National Laboratory (LBNL) for ASHRAE SP-41 was used for this study. The prototype was modified by the Pacific Northwest National Laboratory (PNNL) (Friedrich and Messinger 1995) in support of the ASHRAE Standard 90.1-1989 nonresidential building

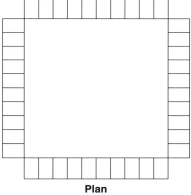

**Plan**
Ten 10 x 15 ft offices on all four sides

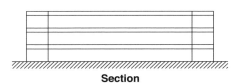

**Section**

*Figure A-1. Floor plan and section of the three-story prototype*

energy standards (ASHRAE 1989). The prototype was further modified by LBNL for this study to reflect ASHRAE Standard 90.1-1999 (changes to the ASHRAE Standard 90.1-2001 were not substantive) and to isolate relative differences in energy performance between different window design strategies. The prototype is a synthetic hypothetical building, not a physically real building, with size, shell construction, heating, ventilating, and air-conditioning (HVAC) system type, operating schedules, etc. based on the mean prevailing condition among statistical samples and engineering judgment. The analysis in this book relies on relative performance differences between window systems; the intention is not to provide absolute data from which a reader may determine energy performance for a specific building.

The three-story prototype consists of a ground, intermediate, and rooftop floor (Figure A-1). Each floor has four 1500 square foot perimeter zones, each consisting of ten 10 by 15 feet private offices, and a 100 by 100 feet square core zone with a floor area of 10,000 square feet. The floor-to-floor height is 12 feet with a 9-foot-high ceiling and a 3-foot-high unconditioned plenum. The total floor area of the model is 48,000 square feet. The building was oriented to true north with each facade facing the four cardinal directions. Six climates were modeled (Table A-1) corresponding roughly to the five climate zones defined by the U.S. DOE's Energy Information Administration (EIA 1998).

Lightweight construction was used for the building and was the same for each climate: 4-inch brick exterior facade, built-up roofing over a 0.75-inch plywood deck, and a carpeted, 6-inch heavyweight concrete slab on grade. Insulation values for the exterior wall, roof, and floor were obtained from ASHRAE Standard 90.1-1999 for each climate and are summarized in Table A-2. An effective U-value was applied to account for the slab-to-ground-contact temperature variations of the soil.

The interior was specified with adiabatic walls between perimeter offices and standard walls between the perimeter and core zone. These walls were composed of 0.625-inch gypsum and metal studs. A 0.5-inch acoustical tile ceiling was specified for all occupied zones and 0.167-inch lightweight concrete floors with a carpet were specified for the two upper level floors.

Peak occupant density was 390 square feet per person in the core zones and 275 square feet per person in the perimeter zones. Peak equipment loads were 0.75 W/sf. Scheduling corresponded to data from ASHRAE 90.1-1989, ELCAP, and PG&E (Friedrich and Messinger 1995).

## Windows

Flush-mounted, non-operable windows were modeled in the exterior wall of each perimeter zone office. Five window sizes were modeled with a fenestration window-to-wall area ratio (WWR) (which includes the area of the whole window with frame), of 0.0, 0.15, 0.30, 0.45, and 0.60, where the wall area was defined as the floor-to-floor exterior wall area and the floor-to-floor height was 12 feet. Note, the ASHRAE Standard 90.1-1999 uses this same definition for WWR; however in previous research, WWR was based on the glazed window area (see Table A-3 for equivalent WWR values). Figure A-2 gives the position of the window in the window wall as seen from the exterior. Window position can influence the distribution of heat flux to interior room surfaces and the distribution

of daylight within the room. The head height of the framed window was set flush with the ceiling at 9 feet for all window areas except WWR=0.15.

Several types of commercially available windows were modeled in order to determine relative performance impacts for both retrofit and new construction. Glass layers were all 0.25 inches thick. Spectral properties of the glass were obtained from the Optics5 (version 2.0.2) database and input into WINDOW4.1 (http://windows.lbl.gov/software/default.htm) to derive the whole window properties shown in Table A-4. The single-pane window (type A) was modeled with a non-thermally broken, aluminum frame (assuming a retrofit condition) while all double-pane windows were modeled with a thermally broken, aluminum frame. The three-pane and four-pane windows were modeled with aluminum inner and outer frames with a polyamide thermal break between the inner and outer frames. Multipane windows were modeled with aluminum or insulated spacers, as indicated in Table A-4. Frame width increased with window area (i.e., window-to-wall-ratio). For WWR=0.15, the frame width was 1.25 inches wide and for WWR=0.30–0.60, the frame width was 3 inches wide. For multipane windows, all gaps were filled with air. The gap width was 0.5 inches for double-pane windows and 0.79 inches for triple-pane. For the four-pane window, the outer gap was 1 inch and the remaining were 0.79 inches wide. The intermediate layers for the three- and four-layer windows were suspended, clear polyethylene (PET) films.

Additional window frame types were modeled to illustrate the effect of frame conductance on energy performance (see Chapter 3): 1) wood or vinyl window frames, 2) external flush glazed aluminum window frames, and 3) non-thermally broken frames. U-values including the outside air film coefficient at a 15 mph wind speed were 0.3, 0.7, and 1.9 Btu/h-sf-°F, respectively. Spacers remained the same as the default case: aluminum for double-pane windows and insulated for the special triple- and quadruple-pane windows. See Table A-5 for whole window properties.

To illustrate the potential of switchable windows, electrochromic windows were modeled. Electrochromic (EC) windows switch between a transparent clear and colored state with a small applied voltage (see Chapter 3). The windows were modeled with the clear and colored solar-optical properties given in Table A-4. The window was modeled to switch linearly between clear and colored states. The EC glazing had an emissivity of 0.84 on the exterior surface and 0.15 on the interior. The EC glazing was combined with a 0.5-inch interior clear glazing layer with a 0.5-inch air gap. The electrochromic window was switched so as to provide 50 footcandles at 10 feet from the window wall, centered on the window, and at a work plane height of 2.5 feet every hour during daylight hours. If there was insufficient daylight, the window was switched to its clearest state. If there was too much daylight, the window was switched to fully colored. This daylight control strategy optimizes cooling and lighting energy use.

## Interior Shades

The windows were modeled with and without an interior shade. The shade was manually operated where it was drawn down completely by the occupant for daylight hours if direct sun or glare was present. The shade was deployed if the heat gain per square foot of window area from direct (beam) solar radiation transmitted through the window exceeded 30 Btu/hr-sf or if the daylighting glare index computed using the Hopkinson Cornell-BRS formula exceeded 22 ("just uncomfortable," maximum recommended for general office work). With the shade drawn, the visible transmittance of the glazing is reduced by 65 percent (translucent light white drape) and the solar heat gain coefficient (SHGC) by 40 percent. The maximum number of hours that the shade could be deployed is given in Table A-1.

The shade was modeled as a planar, ideally diffuse, translucent layer parallel to the glass layers and interior to the window. The effectiveness of a shading system to moderate heat flux through a fenestration system varies with the type of window it is combined with, solar incident angle, and other factors. However, the present state of available measured data on shading devices does not permit greater accuracy in the calculation of heat flow through shaded fenestration and prior measurements predate modern developments in fenestration systems. Also, the shade algorithms in the DOE-2.1E program do not facilitate the modification of angle-dependent solar-optical properties or the inward-flowing fraction to enable one to conduct a detailed separation of transmitted and absorbed fluxes and the distribution of absorbed energy among multiple fenestration layers. Therefore, the shade modeled in DOE-2.1E represents an approximation at best. Note, however that the SHGC multiplier has been applied to the solar heat flux at the appropriate angle of incidence, as is standard in DOE-2.1E.

## Exterior Shades

Fins, overhangs, and a setback window were modeled in DOE-2.1E as opaque, non-reflective surfaces. These obstructions block diffuse light from the sky and direct sun but reflect no light from the ground.

*Setback.* The window is recessed from the exterior plane of the facade, so that a 1-foot-deep overhang, fin, and sill shade the glazing.

*Overhangs.* The depth of the overhang was set to provide a profile angle of 65 degrees or 55 degrees for a fully shaded window (Figure A-2 and Table A-6). These solar profile angles roughly correspond to the cooling season of a south-facing perimeter zone in the cold and hot climates and were constrained to depths deemed acceptable by standard practice. The width of the overhang was made the same width as the office module (not the window): 10 feet. The overhang height was set so that its lower surface was flush with the top of the framed window opening.

*Fins.* A single case was modeled for fins (Figure A-2 and Table A-7). The fin depth yields an azimuthal cutoff angle of 26.6° for shading the full window width ("100 percent-shade" condition) and 45 degrees for shading half the window width ("50 percent-shade" condition). The fin was made the full height of the window and placed flush with the left and right edges of the framed window opening.

*Overhangs and Fins.* When the overhang and fins were combined, the overhang width was the width of the window. The overhang depth was that for the 55 degree profile angle case.

*Horizon Obstructions.* Horizon obstructions due to opposing buildings or mountains were modeled so that the window was fully shaded when solar profile angles were less

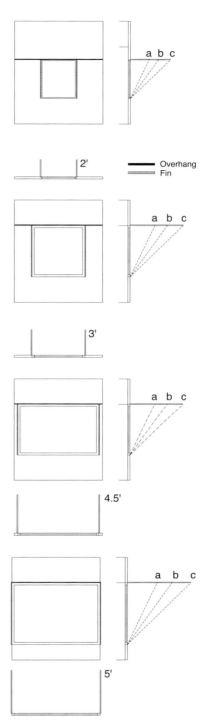

*Figure A-2. Interior elevation of window wall for window-to-wall ratios (WWR) of 0.15, 0.30, 0.45, and 0.60 (top to bottom); sections through the overhang and fin are given as well (see Tables 6 and 7)*

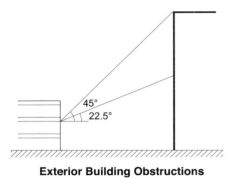

**Exterior Building Obstructions**

*Figure A-3. Section view of horizon building obstruction*

than 22.5 degrees or 45 degrees. These obstructions were modeled as a 54-foot- or 101-foot-high opaque plane set 80 feet from each perimeter zone's window, with 80 feet being an average facade-to-facade distance across an urban street (Figure A-3, Table A-8). These obstructions surrounded the three-story commercial building entirely on all four sides and were of infinite length. The heights of the exterior obstructions were calculated to yield profile angles of 22.5 degrees or 45 degrees from the second floor window head. The exterior obstruction was modeled with a visible surface reflectance of 0.50 and had a luminance due to daylight from the sky and ground. The ground had a surface reflectance of 0.20.

## Lighting

Recessed fluorescent lighting systems were modeled with a lighting power density of 1.2 W/sf throughout the building. Heat from the lighting system was apportioned to the interior space (60 percent) and to the unconditioned plenum (40 percent). If no daylighting controls were specified, the lighting was assumed to be at 100 percent power, and governed, as in the daylighting case, by the occupancy schedule.

If daylighting controls were specified, the perimeter zone electric lights were dimmed linearly (continuous dimming) so as to provide 50 footcandles at 10 feet from the window wall, centered on the window, and at a work plane height of 2.5 feet.

The design work plane illuminance level of 50 footcandles is recommended for performing typical office tasks by the Illuminating Engineering Society. The recommended illuminance level in modern buildings has been changing. The current recommendation is for 30 footcandles where there is intensive visual display terminal (VDT) use and 50 footcandles for filing, intermittent VDT use, and private offices. The reduction in the recommended light level where VDT use is intensive is a response to the reflection problems with cathode-ray terminal (CRT) based VDTs. It is generally assumed that higher light levels would be preferred if there were not problems with the VDTs. The recent increase in availability and popularity of flat screen liquid crystal display (LCD) VDTs is likely to change lighting practice and recommendations as these screens are much less prone to veiling reflection problems. The recommendations may return to 50 footcandles, even for intensive VDT use.

The electronic dimmable ballasts were modeled with a minimum power consumption of 33 percent and 10 percent

minimum light output. Surface reflectances were 70 percent for ceilings, 50 percent for walls, and 20 percent for floors.

Several alternate lighting systems and control conditions were modeled to illustrate the impact of the electric lighting design on overall energy performance (Chapter 2).

- Pendant lighting fixtures were modeled, where 100 percent of the heat from the lighting system was apportioned to the interior space and none to the unconditioned plenum.

- Lighting power density levels of 0.8 and 2.7 W/sf were used, as opposed to the default 1.2 W/sf.

- The setpoints for daylight dimming were set at 30 and 80 footcandles, compared to the default 50 footcandles, and modeled with the default continuous daylighting controls.

- A more efficient dimming electronic ballast, typical of newer products on the market, was modeled with a 100–20 percent power dimming range with a light output range of 100–5 percent.

- Stepped, as opposed to continuous dimming, daylighting controls were modeled with a probability factor of 100 percent and 50 percent to model the behavior of a dedicated versus semi-dedicated energy-conscious occupant. If the stepped control was one step, then power was either on or off. If the stepped controls had two or three steps, then power was 100–50–0 percent or 100–66—33–0 percent, respectively, in proportion to the amount of required electric lighting required to top up the daylight illuminance to meet the 50 footcandle setpoint within the space.

## Mechanical System

Five variable-air-volume systems with economizers were employed: one each for perimeter zones facing a particular orientation (i.e., north-facing perimeter zones on all three floors were controlled by one system) and one for the three core zones. Such zoning facilitated an analysis of window orientation on heating and cooling energy use. The heating thermostat setpoint was 70°F during occupied hours with a night setback temperature of 55°F; the cooling thermostat setpoint was 75°F with a night setback temperature of 99°F. Heating was provided by a gas boiler and cooling was provided by a hermetic centrifugal chiller and cooling tower.

## OFFICE PERFORMANCE PARAMETERS

### Annual Energy Use and Peak Demand

All annual energy performance data are given as energy use per perimeter zone floor area (e.g., kWh/sf-yr or kBtu/sf-yr), unless otherwise noted.

Perimeter zone lighting electric energy use data are given without modification.

Perimeter zone cooling electric use data were determined using system-level extraction loads converted to plant-level electric use with a fixed coefficient of performance (COP) of 3.0. Fan electric energy use for hours when only cooling is required was then added to this quantity to arrive at total

*Method for Generating Performance Data*

perimeter zone cooling electric use.

Perimeter zone "other" electric use data are all electric end uses that are not included in lighting and cooling, such as convenience outlets, and supply and return fans for heating, heating and cooling, and float periods.

Total annual electricity use includes all electricity end uses: lighting, cooling, and other electric end uses.

Perimeter zone heating energy use data were determined using system-level extraction loads converted to plant-level energy use with a fixed heating efficiency factor (HEF) of 0.8. Fan electric energy use for hours when only heating is required was not added to this quantity to enable total energy performance comparisons based on fuel type.

The COP and HEF efficiency factors represent system-to-plant efficiency, not component-level equipment efficiencies such as those given in ASHRAE 90.1. Such a procedure was necessary since the DOE-2.1E program does not separate zonal energy at the plant level. These perimeter zone data enable equitable comparisons to be made across the entire data set.

Total annual energy use (electricity and heating energy use) was computed using a source-site efficiency of 0.33 for electricity and 1.0 for natural gas. The source-site efficiency indicates the generating efficiency of the fuel or utility prior to its use in the simulated commercial building.

Peak electric demand data are given for the peak condition that occurs in each perimeter zone and are non-coincident with the whole building's peak condition. Like total annual electricity use, peak demand data includes all electricity end uses: lighting, cooling, and other electric end uses.

The trends that occur with annual heating energy use are counterintuitive. A reduction in heating loads between cases does not necessarily result in a reduction in heating energy. For example, when one compares an unshaded south window to a shaded window, there is a reduction in solar heat gains during the winter and therefore one expects an increase in heating energy use. The reverse of these trends is seen in Chapters 5 and 6. This is due to the inefficiencies of the variable-volume (VAV) system. Outside air is brought in and heated to 55°F by central cooling and heating coils then distributed by a supply fan to individual zones. At each zone, reheat coils raise the supply air temperature from 55∞to 70°F (room temperature) then raise the temperature again by some amount needed to offset zone heating requirements. When in the heating mode, the supply airflow rate is held at a constant minimum volume equal to 30 percent of the maximum flow rate.

The supply fan is sized based on the maximum heating or cooling requirement; typically cooling requirements are greater than heating. Therefore, the supply fan size for an unshaded south window (using the above example) will be greater than that for a shaded window. During heating conditions, the reheat energy needed to raise the supply air temperature from 55 to 70°F is greater for the unshaded case simply due to the larger volume of air delivered by the larger fan. This reheat energy use tends to swamp out the differences in heating requirements due to differences in loads from windows.

A more efficient VAV system that turns off the economizer and cooling coils during the winter would more closely track changes in perimeter zone heating loads. However, humidity control then becomes a factor. Most commercial buildings with central systems are run more conservatively and inefficiently (i.e., as modeled in this book) because of the concerns over humidity control.

## Whole-Building HVAC System Capacity

The HVAC capacity of the heating and cooling systems was determined at the whole-building plant level. DOE-2 was allowed to automatically size the plant equipment for each parametric run to ensure realistic part-load-ratio operations. For these comparisons, note that the perimeter zone window and lighting condition is the same for all orientations.

## Visual Environment

Four types of data are given related to the visual environment: 1) annual average work plane illuminance due to daylight, 2) percent hours that the daylight illuminance is greater than 50 footcandles, 3) annual average glare index, and 4) percent hours that the glare index is greater than 22. These data are given at 5 feet and 10 feet from the window wall, 2.5 feet above the second story floor, and centered on the window wall. The data are based on occupied hours from 7:00 to 17:00 each day of the year exclusive of Saturdays, Sundays, and holidays. A brightness index and weighted glare index were computed based on these data and are described in the Bubble Diagram section below.

## Thermal Comfort

Thermal comfort was determined in the perimeter zone of the second, intermediate story. The DOE-2.1E program generated hourly mean radiant (MRT) and room air temperatures for a variety of geographic locations, building space orientations, and window size and type configurations. These data were used in conjunction with the ASHRAE Thermal Comfort Program (Fountain and Huizenga 1994) to determine levels of thermal comfort.

The ASHRAE Thermal Comfort Program is a computer program that is based on the work by Fanger (1970). The Predicted Percentage Dissatisfied (PPD) within a particular environment can be obtained as a function of the mean radiant temperature (MRT), room air temperature, relative humidity, air speed, activity level, and amount of clothing. Fixed values for the following variables were assumed: (1) relative humidity = 50 percent; (2) air speed = 19.7 ft/min; (3) activity level = 1.0 met (sitting quietly) (ASHRAE Standard 55); and (4) clothing = 0.67 clo (pants, shirt, panty hose, slip, shoes (ASHRAE Standard 55), Summer = 0.50, Winter = 0.90). By obtaining the hourly variation in MRT and room air temperatures during occupied hours (occupancy was assumed from 7:00–17:00 each day of the year exclusive of Saturdays, Sundays, and holidays) from the DOE-2 simulations, hourly PPD values were computed. These values were then averaged over the course of the year to obtain an annual average PPD.

With the focus being on the comfort effects of windows, hourly PPD values accounted for both short wavelength radiation from solar radiation striking an occupant in the space and the long wavelength radiation due to all surrounding interior surfaces including the window. (Fanger 1970) provides such a procedure: initially, an unirradiated MRT due to long wavelength sources is determined, then an irradiated MRT is defined based on the amount of solar radiation absorbed by the occupant. Thus for each occupied hour and each space with a window, two PPDs are computed, one for an unirradiated occupant and one for an irradiated occupant.

The resultant PPD is the larger of the two, which is then summed and eventually averaged at the end of the year.

Fanger indicates that the mean radiant temperature of an irradiated occupant due to a high-intensity short wavelength source is a function of: (1) the mean radiant temperature of an unirradiated occupant, (2) the amount of high intensity radiation striking the occupant, (3) the absorptance of the occupant, and (4) the projected area factor which varies with source altitude and azimuth, window orientation, and position within the space. The DOE-2 simulations provided the hourly MRTs of an unirradiated occupant. An assumption was made that if there was incident direct solar radiation on a window during a particular occupied hour, then the transmitted solar radiation through the window was striking an occupant. Such an assumption is most accurate for large window-to-wall area ratios (therefore, thermal comfort was not determined for small windows (WWR=0.15). The absorptance of the clothed human body was assumed to be 0.80 (Fanger 1970). A constant projected area factor of 0.25 was selected. The projected area is the area of the surface times the cosine of the angle between the surface normal and the source. The cosine corrects the flux density normal to the beam of radiation to the flux density at the surface orientation. Fanger indicates that for an adult occupant directly facing a source at 0° altitude, the factor would be 0.29. For a source directly overhead, the factor is about 0.18 and does not vary with source azimuth. The largest projected area factor is about 0.33 for an altitude of 15° at an azimuth of 30°. (Note: PPD data are for average adults. No PPD data are presented for school children in Chapter 7, for example.)

## BUBBLE DIAGRAMS

Bubble diagrams were designed to visually provide information about several different attributes or performance indices of a window at the same time. The diagrams typically show six performance indices with a range in value from 0 (worst) to 10 (best):

- brightness level
- glare
- view
- thermal comfort
- energy use
- peak power demand.

To provide the maximum information to the user, each index needs to describe an important attribute of the window, while being relatively independent of the other five indices. Each index currently has the same visual weight as the other indices so each attribute should, as much as possible, have a similar importance. Finally, there should be a well-defined way of evaluating the index value for each axis, and the value of each index should represent an increasing merit in equal steps.

The first two indices, brightness level and glare, represent the visual/psychological response to the amount of light that the windows admit. The IESNA recommends light levels for spaces, but provides no guidance as to the relative merit of light levels below or above the recommended level. Furthermore, it is common to operate commercial spaces with electric light sources that fill in the deficit of having too little daylight.

Although the ability to do visual work increases with light level, the response is very nonlinear, with almost all the benefit occurring at levels of 10 lux or less, which are levels far below those generally considered to be acceptable for commercial or residential spaces. At the higher light levels, people judge light in terms of gloom/brightness, and glare/comfort. The sensation of overall brightness is known to follow a power law versus the luminance of the scene, while glare has been fit by a variety of formulas that compare the intensity of a glare source to the surround level. These formulas are both well defined, and easily adaptable to a 0 to 10 scale for the bubble diagrams.

## Brightness Index

Work by Stevens and others (Bodmann 1992) have shown that brightness sensation follows a power-law of about 0.31 exponent versus the luminance of the source. For any given surface, luminance is just illuminance multiplied by the reflectance. In the brightness formula, reflectance just acts as a constant multiplier. Therefore, the difference between using luminance or illuminance becomes irrelevant when brightness is scaled to the bubble index range of 0 to 10. DOE-2 runs have been made where the hourly work plane illuminance, E, is calculated at a distance of 10 feet into the office (see section on Visual Environment above). This provides a measure of the penetration of daylight into the space. Based on these measurements, an average brightness index for a space can be calculated from the following formula (Figure A-4):

$$\text{Index} = \text{minimum } [\text{average}(0.80 * E^{0.31}), 10]. \tag{1}$$

The constant 0.80 controls what illuminance corresponds to the maximum brightness index of 10. A value of 0.58 would correspond to a value of 10,000 lux as initially intended, but this value tended to depress the sensitivity to cases shown in the bubble diagrams. The value of 0.80 gave the best sensitivity to the range of illuminances given in the simulation database and corresponds to 3,455 lux. Hourly values of the brightness index based on this formula can exceed 10, but the average value over the year for the parametric runs do not. The use of the minimum function assures that values will still not exceed 10 even for extreme conditions outside the range of those that have been considered.

## Weighted Glare Index

DOE-2 computes the hourly daylighting glare indices based on the Hopkinson Cornell-BRS formula (see section on Visual Environment above). There are two issues that need to be dealt with. The first is the occupant's view orientation. Glare will be worse facing a window, but research has shown that people tend to be more tolerant of glare through a window. Glare on a sidewall will be the best case condition in that if the glare is unacceptable on a sidewall, it will only be worse facing the window. It is not clear which orientation is better for this index, as long as the results are scaled appropriately. The index was therefore based on the glare facing the sidewall at 5 feet from the window.

The second issue is the question of how to evaluate the individual hourly values to get an overall yearly index. Numerical values of the glare index cover a range of values where glare is rated imperceptible by most people on up to

*Figure A-4. Brightness index versus hourly work plane daylight illuminance (lux)*

values where it is rated uncomfortable. A simple average could easily result in a value of imperceptible glare from individual values that cover the range up to uncomfortable glare. It should be clear that a weighted glare index should be sensitive to fairly infrequent periods of perceptible or uncomfortable glare.

The manner in which the glare sensation responds to multiple spatial sources provides a guide as to how to make the weighted glare index sensitive to extreme values. The Hopkinson Cornell-BRS glare index is actually the logarithm of a glare value. When there are multiple glare sources, the glare sensation is the logarithm of the sum of the glare values. A straight adoption of this transformation for the temporal average results in a weighted glare index that is actually too sensitive, in that even a single excursion returns almost the maximum value, allowing almost no discrimination between this case and one with more excursions. This procedure also gives a single large excursion a worse overall weighted glare index value than a case with multiple just slightly smaller excursions. However, the procedure can be modified by the inclusion of a constant in the transformation to reduce the sensitivity of the average to what seems to be a reasonable compromise. The following formula gives an average that is sensitive to excursions from a base value if they occur at a frequency of 1 percent or more (Figure A-5):

$$\text{Gavg} = 4*\log 10(\text{average G' over year}) \qquad (2)$$
where the G' are

$$\text{G'} = 10^{(\text{GI}/4)} \qquad (3)$$
and GI are the hourly glare index values from the DOE-2 runs.

To provide an appropriate scaling from the range of glare index values found in the data set to the desired 0 to 10 range, the value of 0 was assigned the glare index value of "just

uncomfortable" (22), which was the maximum value in the data set, and the value of 10 was assigned the glare index value of 7. The glare index value of 7 represents imperceptible glare, as it is one half a subjective step below the glare index value of 10, which is "just imperceptible". Since it represents imperceptible glare, there is no difference in the subjective responses for glare index values of 7 and below. It is therefore the effective minimum value for the data set.

**Bubble glare index (BGI) = max[10–(2/3)\*max(Gavg–7,0), 0].   (4)**

The BGI scale was set so that glare is worse as the value decreases, corresponding to way the other five bubble indices are presented. When comparisons are made to the original glare index values it is more convenient re-scale the BGI back to the original glare index range and direction so that values of 7 correspond to imperceptible glare and a value of 22 corresponds to "just uncomfortable" glare:

**Weighted Glare Index (WGI) = 22 – 3\*BGI/2   (5)**

Gavg values less than 7 are represented by a WGI value of 7 and Gavg values greater than 22 are represented by a WGI value of 22.

## View Index

The view index is defined as the fraction of area available as view times a factor near 1 that corrects for excessive reflectance from the window as seen by the occupant:

**Index = WWRi \* %Exterior Shade \* %Interior Shade \* R \* 10   (6)**

The area factor is the product of the window-to-interior-window-wall ratio times the fraction of solid angle of the window that is unobstructed by fins and/or overhangs as computed from the midpoint between the side walls 5 feet from the window, times a factor representing the fraction of the year the window is unobstructed by shades. The window-to-interior-window-wall ratio was multiplied by a factor of 1.414 so that the largest window (WWR=0.60) modeled in this book would yield a value of 10 (if all other factors were 1).

A reflectance factor is designed to lower the view index of windows that show interior reflections when exterior light levels are moderately low. The view out is diminished by reflections of interior light sources (electric lights, etc.) off the interior glass surface when it is relatively dark outside. This factor is computed with the following formula (Figure A-6):

**R = Tvis\*Eglo / [Tvis\*Eglo + Et\*Rbvis]   (7)**

where both visible transmittance (Tvis) and interior visible reflectance (Rbvis) of the window are computed at normal incidence. Before discussing the illuminance values, it is useful to note that the actual visibility of any particular reflectance will depend upon the luminance ratios of the transmitted and reflected images. The formula uses illuminances in place of luminances, because the latter depend upon reflectances which are not under the designer's control. The R factor provides a benchmark value for clarity, it is not an average over all the possible reflectances that might apply to a particular design situation. Et is the work plane lighting level from daylight and electric lighting at 10 feet from the window wall. A minimal value of 500 lux was selected for fluorescent lighting. If continuous dimming controls were used, this value was varied in proportion to fractional light output. Eglo is the horizontal exterior global illuminance. The R factor ranged from 0.999 to 0.637 over the range of window parametrics between all six climates. The limited range in this case is desirable, because this factor should not be as important in the final calculation as the area of the window, yet there should be some loss in rating for glazing which reduces the clarity of the view.

The initial proposal for the view index also included the color rendering index (CRI) as a factor, but the values varied little over the windows examined. Worse, to the extent that they did vary, they did not vary in a manner that seemed to

*Figure A-5. Bubble glare index versus fraction of time that the hourly Hopkinson Cornell-BRS glare index is 16 (left) or 20 (right). The solid line (labeled "GR(.25)") is the relationship used for this study, where a bubble glare index value of 4 is given if the hourly glare index is 20 for 10 percent of the time, assuming a base glare index of 7*

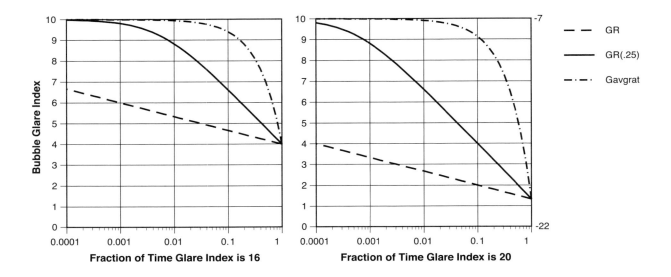

*Figure A-6. Reflectance factor (R) as a function of hourly total (daylight plus fluorescent lighting) work plane illuminance (lux) for three types of glazing: single-pane clear, double-pane bronze, and double-pane reflective glass; two exterior horizontal illuminance levels are given: Eglo = 10 klux and 150 klux*

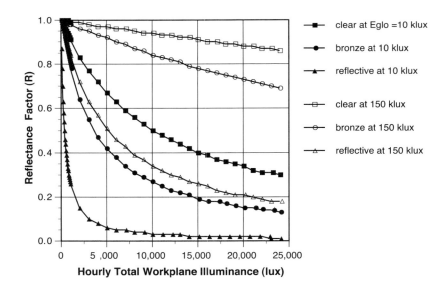

*Method for Generating Performance Data*

correspond to the intuitive feeling of how disturbing the color distortion of the window might be. This term has been dropped until a better correspondence can be obtained.

## Thermal Comfort Index

ASHRAE provides a method of calculating thermal comfort in terms of the Predicted Percentage Dissatisfied (PPD) with a given thermal environment. This calculation has been modified to include the influence of solar radiation from the window. Higher probabilities of discomfort are associated with higher average levels of discomfort. A calculation of the average level of discomfort as a function of PPD found that the relationship was essentially linear. It is possible to compute a bubble index directly as a linear transformation of PPD, or as some nonlinear transformation of the average level of discomfort. The latter procedure is analogous to what is done for glare, but in this case it produces a rating that varies very little until the average discomfort level (or PPD) is very high, which seems exactly the opposite of what is desired. The procedure for simply converting the average annual PPD to the 0–10 scale of the bubble index produces values which directly reflect the fraction of people dissatisfied over time, which seems reasonable. This procedure is given by the formula:

$$\text{Index} = (10/(95\text{-}60))*(100\text{-PPD}) - 60*(10/35). \qquad (8)$$

The constants in the equation keep the rating in the range of 0 to 10 over the range of values of PPD that were found in the data set. The minimum PPD is always 5, as there is always some fraction of people who are dissatisfied with any given thermal environment. The maximum value of PPD in the data set was 40. (The inverses of these PPD values (i.e., predicted percentage satisfied) are 95 and 60, respectively, as shown in equation (8).)

## Annual Energy Use and Peak Demand Indices

The annual energy use or peak electricity demand indices are meaningful and easy to compute. The issue for these factors is how to convert these energy and demand values to a bubble index value. The relative importance of the other axes is not climate dependent. The potential for a view, for instance, is the same in one climate as it is in another. This is not true for energy or peak demand. For example, the range of the amount of energy used by a building with the best and worst windows will depend on the climate. The range of the bubble index should also depend on climate, as follows:

$$\text{Index} = 10 * \{1 - [E(i,j) - Emin(i)]/[\max(Emax(i) - Emin(i))]\}. \qquad (9)$$

In this equation, the index **i** stands for climate, and **j** for window type. The variable **E(i,j)** is the energy use in the **i**th climate with the **j**th window. The variables **Emin(i)** and **Emax(i)** are the minimum and maximum energy uses as determined by window type differences in the **i**th climate. The maximum determination (of **Emax(i)** minus **Emin(i)**) is over the six climates. The bubble index will return a value of 10 for the best window in each climate. It will return a value of 0 for the worst window in the climate that shows the biggest range of energy usage (in this case, Phoenix). It will return a value between 0 and 10 for all other climates and energy usages. A similar expression for peak demand shows the same properties.

Because retrofit glazings were included in this database (e.g., single-pane clear), the maximum determination over the six climates was quite broad (Tables 9 and 10) and tended to swamp out the bulk of the data which represented desired practice. Therefore, the maximum determination was adjusted so that **Emax(i)** was defined by 20 percent above the ASHRAE 90.1-1999 prescriptive energy budget. ASHRAE 90.1-1999 compliant energy budgets were determined for all window areas and orientations using the prescribed maximum SHGC and U-values with the base model defined with no interior or exterior shading and no lighting controls (Tables A-11 and A-12).

## SCHOOL MODELING ASSUMPTIONS

### Introduction

Window performance for schools was analyzed using a methodology very similar to that used in the modeling of the commercial buildings in this book. These results are discussed in Chapters 4 and 7. However, since the building types analyzed are not the same, different inputs and approaches were necessary. This section summarizes the differences.

### Differences

Although the DOE-2 model outputs can be used to analyze thermal and visual comfort indices, the school analysis only looks at the impact of the windows on energy use and peak demand.

### Architectural

The analysis looks at the impact of windows on perimeter classrooms. The hypothetical model consists of two 30-foot-by-30-foot classrooms in a two-story arrangement with a roof above, slab-on-grade, and one exterior wall for each. The classrooms have 10-foot-high ceilings. A total of 18 occupants, including a teacher, are assumed for each classroom.

This configuration was tested for each orientation separately. The school analysis tested the same window-to-wall ratios as the office model. However the arrangement of the windows on the exterior wall was optimized to bring daylight in to the classrooms. All variations were analyzed for a nine-month operation with summer vacation, and a twelve-month year-round operation. The matrix of all variables modeled is shown in Table A-13.

### Lighting

The classrooms are modeled with a lighting power density of 1.6 watts per square foot based on ASHRAE 90.1-1999 and an equipment power density of 0.2 watts per square foot. Two light sensors were modeled to measure light, one at 10 feet away from the exterior wall and the other at 20 feet. Each sensor controls half the light fixtures in the classroom. The daylight factor calculations for DOE-2 were checked against those in Lumen Micro. Lumen micro is a software package that only simulates light. Assuming the lighting results of

Lumen Micro to be more robust that those of DOE-2, the light setpoints in DOE-2 were adjusted to 52 footcandles for the first sensor and 56 footcandles to compensate for the error. This method would cause the dimming control algorithm of DOE-2 to dim the lights for Lumen Micro equivalent of 50 footcandles throughout the room.

## Mechanical

The mechanical schedules assume a 12-hour operation of the fans in an occupied mode. Both classrooms are served by one variable-air-volume (VAV) air handling system; the most common configuration for classrooms is a rooftop air-cooled direct expansion system that serves at least an entire wing of classrooms in a school building. Variable frequency drives are common and required by ASHRAE 90.1 1999 for fans with motors larger than 25 horsepower. Fixed outside air controls deliver outside air of 15 cfm per person. Supply air is at 1.25 cfm per person with minimum supply air during occupied hours at 30 percent of that. Supply fan static is at 3.25 inches and return fans static is at 1.2 inches. The heating thermostat setpoint was 72°F during occupied hours with a night setback temperature of 65°F; the cooling thermostat setpoint was 76°F with a night setback temperature of 82°F.

*Figure A-7. Perimeter classroom window layouts*

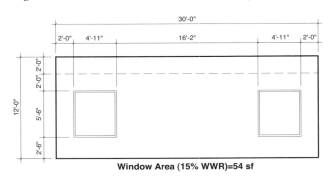

Window Area (15% WWR)=54 sf

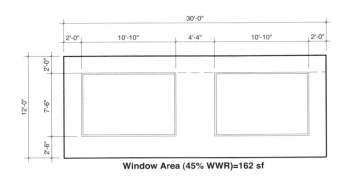

Window Area (45% WWR)=162 sf

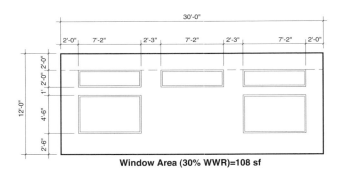

Window Area (30% WWR)=108 sf

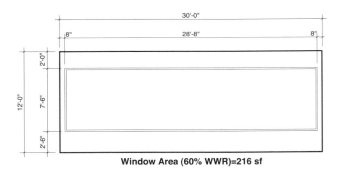

Window Area (60% WWR)=216 sf

*Table A-1. Weather data*

| City | HDD65 | CDD50 | Latitude (°) | Longitude (°) | Elevation (ft) | HDT (°F) | WBT (°F) | DBT (°F) | N | Hrs Sun Up Shade Hrs |
|---|---|---|---|---|---|---|---|---|---|---|
| Minneapolis | 7981 | 2680 | 44.88 | 93.22 | 834 | -16 | 88 | 71 | 566 | 4756 |
| Chicago O'Hare | 6536 | 2941 | 41.98 | 87.90 | 674 | -6 | 88 | 73 | 613 | 4757 |
| Washington, DC | 4820 | 3709 | 38.90 | 77.00 | 14 | 11 | 91 | 74 | N.A. | 4750 |
| Los Angeles | 1458 | 4777 | 33.93 | 118.38 | 100 | 43 | 81 | 64 | 1849 | 4747 |
| Houston Hobby | 1599 | 6876 | 29.97 | 95.35 | 96 | 29 | 93 | 77 | N.A. | 4755 |
| Phoenix | 1350 | 8425 | 33.43 | 112.02 | 1110 | 34 | 108 | 70 | 746 | 4756 |

HDT: heating design temperature, WBT: wet-bulb temperature, DBT: dry-bulb temperature
N: number of hours between 8:00–16:00 where 55<DBT<69°F
N.A.: not available
Washington, DC's HDT, WBT, DBT, and N values are for Baltimore, Maryland.
Hrs Sun Up: number of hours sun is up and maximum number of hours shade could be deployed.

*Method for Generating Performance Data*

*Table A-2. ASHRAE 90.1-1999 insulation values*

| City | HDD65 | CDD50 | ASHRAE Table No. | Assembly Maximum (Btu/h-sf-°F) | | |
|------|-------|-------|------------------|------|-------|-------|
| | | | | Uow | Uroof | Fslab |
| Minneapolis | 7981 | 2680 | B-19 | 0.084 | 0.063 | 0.73 |
| Chicago O'Hare | 6536 | 2941 | B-17 | 0.084 | 0.063 | 0.73 |
| Washington, DC | 4820 | 3709 | B13 | 0.124 | 0.063 | 0.73 |
| Los Angeles | 1458 | 4777 | B-7 | 0.124 | 0.093 | 0.73 |
| Houston Hobby | 1599 | 6876 | B6 | 0.124 | 0.063 | 0.73 |
| Phoenix | 1350 | 8425 | B5 | 0.124 | 0.063 | 0.73 |

*Table A-3. Window placement*

| WWR | Window Height (ft) | Window Width (ft) | Sill Height (ft) | Window Area (sf) | Frame Width (in) | Glass Area (sf) | WWRg |
|------|------|------|------|------|------|------|------|
| 0.00 | 0.0 | 0.0 | 0.0 | 0 | 0.00 | 0.00 | 0.00 |
| 0.15 | 4.5 | 4.0 | 3.0 | 18 | 1.25 | 16.27 | 0.14 |
| 0.30 | 6.0 | 6.0 | 3.0 | 36 | 3.00 | 30.25 | 0.25 |
| 0.45 | 6.0 | 9.0 | 3.0 | 54 | 3.00 | 46.75 | 0.39 |
| 0.60 | 7.2 | 10.0 | 1.8 | 72 | 3.00 | 63.65 | 0.53 |

*Table A-4. Window properties*

| Window | Outer Layer | Inner Layer | U-factor (Btu/h-sf-°F) | | SHGC | | VT | | CRI | Frame U-factor | Spacers |
|------|------|------|------|------|------|------|------|------|------|------|------|
| | | | (Overall) | (COG) | (Overall) | (COG) | (Overall) | (COG) | | | |
| A | Clear | | 1.25 | 1.09 | 0.72 | 0.82 | 0.71 | 0.88 | 97.9 | 1.90 | none |
| B | Clear | Clear | 0.60 | 0.48 | 0.60 | 0.70 | 0.63 | 0.78 | 95.7 | 1.00 | alum |
| C | Bronze tint | Clear | 0.60 | 0.48 | 0.42 | 0.49 | 0.38 | 0.48 | 95.2 | 1.00 | alum |
| D | Reflective | Clear | 0.54 | 0.40 | 0.17 | 0.17 | 0.10 | 0.13 | 96.1 | 1.00 | alum |
| E | Bronze tint | Clear low-E | 0.49 | 0.33 | 0.39 | 0.44 | 0.36 | 0.44 | 94.1 | 1.00 | alum |
| F | Evergreen tint | Clear Selective low-E | 0.46 | 0.29 | 0.27 | 0.29 | 0.43 | 0.53 | 85.2 | 1.00 | alum |
| G | Clear with selective low-E | Clear | 0.46 | 0.29 | 0.34 | 0.38 | 0.57 | 0.71 | 95.4 | 1.00 | alum |
| H | Clear with 1 low-E layer | Clear low-E | 0.20 | 0.15 | 0.22 | 0.26 | 0.37 | 0.46 | 88.2 | 0.35 | insul |
| I | Clear with 2 low-E layers | Clear low-E | 0.14 | 0.13 | 0.20 | 0.24 | 0.34 | 0.42 | 89.4 | 0.18 | insul |
| J1 | Clear electrochromic | Clear | 0.49 | 0.33 | 0.37 | 0.42 | 0.45 | 0.56 | 92.7 | 1.00 | alum |
| J2 | Colored electrochromic | Clear | 0.49 | 0.33 | 0.10 | 0.09 | 0.02 | 0.02 | 52.3 | 1.00 | alum |

COG: center-of-glass; CRI: color rendering index; EC: electrochromic glazing; low-E: low emissivity; PET: spectrally selective polyethylene layer; SHGC: solar heat gain coefficient; SS: spectrally selective; Alum: aluminum; Insul: insulating. U-values are given for ASHRAE winter conditions. Overall U-values are given for a window whose overall dimensions including frame are 4x6 ft (3-in frame). SHGC computed for ASHRAE summer conditions. All properties determine using WINDOW4.1 and Optics5 (v.2.0.2).

*Table A-5. Overall window properties with varying frame U-values*

| U-factor (Btu/h-sf-°F) | | | 1.90 | 1.90 | 1.90 | 0.70 | 0.70 | 0.70 | 0.30 | 0.30 | 0.30 |
|------|------|------|------|------|------|------|------|------|------|------|------|
| Window | Outer Layer | Inner Layer | U-factor | SHGC | VT | U-factor | SHGC | VT | U-factor | SHGC | VT |
| A | Clear | | 1.25 | 0.72 | 0.71 | 1.01 | 0.68 | 0.71 | 0.93 | 0.66 | 0.71 |
| B | Clear | Clear | 0.78 | 0.63 | 0.63 | 0.54 | 0.59 | 0.63 | 0.46 | 0.57 | 0.63 |
| C | Bronze tint | Clear | 0.78 | 0.45 | 0.38 | 0.54 | 0.41 | 0.38 | 0.46 | 0.40 | 0.38 |
| D | Reflective | Clear | 0.72 | 0.20 | 0.10 | 0.48 | 0.16 | 0.10 | 0.40 | 0.15 | 0.10 |
| E | Bronze tint | Clear low-E | 0.67 | 0.42 | 0.36 | 0.43 | 0.38 | 0.36 | 0.35 | 0.36 | 0.36 |
| F | Evergreen tint | Clear Selective low-E | 0.64 | 0.30 | 0.43 | 0.40 | 0.26 | 0.43 | 0.32 | 0.24 | 0.43 |
| G | Clear with selective low-E | Clear | 0.64 | 0.37 | 0.57 | 0.40 | 0.33 | 0.57 | 0.32 | 0.31 | 0.57 |
| H | Clear with 1 low-E layer | Clear low-E | 0.54 | 0.27 | 0.37 | 0.30 | 0.23 | 0.37 | 0.22 | 0.22 | 0.37 |
| I | Clear with 2 low-E layers | Clear low-E | 0.52 | 0.26 | 0.34 | 0.28 | 0.22 | 0.34 | 0.20 | 0.20 | 0.34 |

*Table A-6. Overhang depths (ft)*

| | Angle (°) | WWR 0.15 | WWR 0.30 | WWR 0.45 | WWR 0.60 |
|---|---|---|---|---|---|
| Case A | 65 | 2.10 | 2.80 | 2.80 | 3.36 |
| Case B | 55 | 3.15 | 4.20 | 4.20 | 5.04 |

Case B was used for the combined overhang and fin case.

*Table A-7. Fin depths (ft)*

| | WWR 0.15 | WWR 0.30 | WWR 0.45 | WWR 0.60 |
|---|---|---|---|---|
| Window width | 4.00 | 6.00 | 4.50 | 5.00 |
| Fin depth | 2.00 | 3.00 | 4.50 | 5.00 |

Shallower depths can be accomplished by subdividing height or width of window.

*Table A-8. Horizon obstruction profile angles at each floor level*

| | Floor 1 | Floor 2 | Floor 3 |
|---|---|---|---|
| 22.5° Obstruction | 14.8 | 22.5 | 29.1 |
| 45° Obstruction | 40.0 | 45.0 | 49.0 |

*Table A-9. Range of total annual energy use (kWh/sf-yr) and bubble indices*

| City | | Zone (kWh/sf-yr) | | | | Data set (kWh/sf-yr) | | Bubble index for data set range |
|---|---|---|---|---|---|---|---|---|
| | | North | East | South | West | | | |
| Minneapolis | max | 61.07 | 78.59 | 77.44 | 81.48 | avg+sd: | 46.82 | 3.56 |
| | min | 31.81 | 31.91 | 29.89 | 31.59 | avg-sd: | 33.15 | 8.76 |
| Chicago | max | 56.25 | 74.45 | 72.05 | 76.10 | avg+sd: | 44.57 | 4.15 |
| | min | 30.27 | 31.30 | 29.17 | 30.38 | avg-sd: | 32.41 | 8.77 |
| Washington, DC | max | 54.63 | 71.28 | 72.22 | 73.87 | avg+sd: | 44.11 | 4.41 |
| | min | 30.44 | 30.86 | 29.41 | 30.70 | avg-sd: | 32.63 | 8.77 |
| Los Angeles | max | 42.12 | 66.04 | 77.80 | 68.99 | avg+sd: | 40.50 | 5.36 |
| | min | 28.29 | 28.91 | 28.29 | 28.60 | avg-sd: | 29.44 | 9.56 |
| Houston | max | 54.37 | 73.29 | 75.69 | 75.35 | avg+sd: | 45.78 | 4.81 |
| | min | 32.13 | 33.22 | 32.48 | 33.20 | avg-sd: | 34.58 | 9.07 |
| Phoenix | max | 59.15 | 88.35 | 89.91 | 92.19 | avg+sd: | 50.83 | 2.92 |
| | min | 32.19 | 34.36 | 33.10 | 33.74 | avg-sd: | 35.56 | 8.72 |

*Table A-10. Range of peak demand (W/sf) and bubble indices*

| City | | Zone (W/sf) | | | | Data set (W/sf) | | Bubble index for data set range |
|---|---|---|---|---|---|---|---|---|
| | | North | East | South | West | | | |
| Minneapolis | max | 6.50 | 13.46 | 13.48 | 12.68 | avg+sd: | 6.01 | 3.16 |
| | min | 3.28 | 3.42 | 3.39 | 3.37 | avg-sd: | 3.30 | 9.97 |
| Chicago | max | 6.72 | 13.01 | 12.22 | 12.91 | avg+sd: | 5.95 | 3.96 |
| | min | 3.54 | 3.58 | 3.61 | 3.61 | avg-sd: | 3.44 | 10.25 |
| Washington, DC | max | 6.86 | 12.97 | 12.67 | 12.86 | avg+sd: | 6.20 | 4.62 |
| | min | 4.05 | 4.11 | 4.13 | 4.12 | avg-sd: | 4.04 | 10.02 |
| Los Angeles | max | 5.47 | 12.36 | 14.69 | 12.38 | avg+sd: | 5.79 | 2.54 |
| | min | 2.82 | 3.11 | 2.98 | 3.07 | avg-sd: | 2.89 | 9.82 |
| Houston | max | 7.11 | 12.84 | 13.86 | 12.77 | avg+sd: | 6.65 | 4.84 |
| | min | 4.59 | 4.67 | 4.62 | 4.69 | avg-sd: | 4.60 | 9.96 |
| Phoenix | max | 8.49 | 15.22 | 15.53 | 15.18 | avg+sd: | 7.56 | 2.95 |
| | min | 4.75 | 4.83 | 4.88 | 4.87 | avg-sd: | 4.78 | 9.92 |

*Method for Generating Performance Data*

*Table A-11. ASHRAE 90.1-1999 annual energy use budgets (kWh/sf-yr) and bubble ratings*

| City | ASHRAE energy budget (kWr/sf-yr) | Bubble Index | ASHRAE (kWr/sf-yr) | | Bubble Index | |
|---|---|---|---|---|---|---|
| Minneapolis | 42.21 | 5.32 | +20%: | 50.65 | +20%: | 2.11 |
| | | | -20%: | 33.77 | -20%: | 8.52 |
| Chicago | 40.66 | 5.63 | +20%: | 48.79 | +20%: | 2.54 |
| | | | -20%: | 32.53 | -20%: | 8.72 |
| Washington, DC | 40.36 | 5.84 | +20%: | 48.43 | +20%: | 2.77 |
| | | | -20%: | 32.29 | -20%: | 8.90 |
| Los Angeles | 42.15 | 4.73 | +20%: | 50.58 | +20%: | 1.53 |
| | | | -20%: | 33.72 | -20%: | 7.93 |
| Houston | 44.21 | 5.41 | +20%: | 53.05 | +20%: | 2.05 |
| | | | -20%: | 35.37 | -20%: | 8.77 |
| Phoenix | 48.75 | 3.71 | +20%: | 58.50 | +20%: | - |
| | | | -20%: | 39.00 | -20%: | 7.41 |

*Table A-12. ASHRAE 90.1-1999 peak demand budgets (kWh/sf-yr) and bubble ratings*

| City | ASHRAE energy budget (W/sf) | Bubble Index | ASHRAE (W/sf) | | Bubble Index | |
|---|---|---|---|---|---|---|
| Minneapolis | 5.58 | 4.23 | +20%: | 6.70 | +20%: | 1.43 |
| | | | -20%: | 4.47 | -20%: | 7.03 |
| Chicago | 5.47 | 5.15 | +20%: | 6.57 | +20%: | 2.40 |
| | | | -20%: | 4.38 | -20%: | 7.90 |
| Washington, DC | 5.66 | 5.97 | +20%: | 6.79 | +20%: | 3.13 |
| | | | -20%: | 4.53 | -20%: | 8.81 |
| Los Angeles | 5.67 | 2.84 | +20%: | 6.81 | +20%: | 0.00 |
| | | | -20%: | 4.54 | -20%: | 5.69 |
| Houston | 5.68 | 7.26 | +20%: | 6.82 | +20%: | 4.41 |
| | | | -20%: | 4.54 | -20%: | 10.11 |
| Phoenix | 7.01 | 4.32 | +20%: | 8.41 | +20%: | 0.80 |
| | | | -20%: | 5.61 | -20%: | 7.84 |

*Table A-13. School variations modeled*

| Variations | 1 | 2 | 3 | 4 | 5 | 6 | 7 | 8 |
|---|---|---|---|---|---|---|---|---|
| Location | Chicago | Houston | | | | | | |
| Orientation | North | South | East | West | | | | |
| Window/Wall Ratio (WWR) | 0.15 | 0.3 | 0.45 | 0.6 | | | | |
| Glass Types | Single clear | Double clear | Double bronze tint | Double reflective | Double bronze tint low-E | Double Evergreen tint low-E | Clear spec. selective low-E | Double low-E + 1 PET |
| Daylighting Controls | None | Dimming | | | | | | |
| Operating Schedule | 12 mth 12 hr | 9 mth 12 hr | | | | | | |

# Appendix B

# Lighting Controls

Lighting controls have evolved significantly over the past two decades. In the 1980s, lighting controls consisted of high-cost daylight dimming systems that didn't work well and often ended up being disabled by the occupant due to poor reliability. Occupancy sensors were also unreliable, switching off at the most inconvenient of times and requiring people to wave at the sensor to "prove" occupancy. Today, lighting controls are considered not just for saving energy but also as an amenity for enhancing lighting quality, for providing tailored lighting conditions according to task, preferences, or time of day workplace conditions, and to provide flexibility as space configuration or use changes over the long-term life of the building. Manual and automated lighting control systems have improved significantly in terms of sophistication, reliability, and integration with the whole building controls infrastructure. Today, facility managers are increasingly motivated to use lighting controls to reduce electric lighting energy use, reduce peak demand charges, downsize HVAC equipment, reduce HVAC operating costs, and achieve greater occupant satisfaction with the built environment. Energy codes are also enforcing stricter requirements on the installed lighting equipment power density, zoning, and type of controls used in commercial buildings.

The basic control strategies for lighting include:

- occupancy sensing: turn lights off when there are no occupants in the space
- scheduling: turn lights off using a time clock device after scheduled work hours
- daylighting: reduce power in the presence of daylight from windows or skylights
- tuning: adjust lighting levels according to user preferences or needs
- demand limiting: reduce lighting levels in the event of a regional emergency power alert to curtail energy use
- adaptive compensation: reduce light levels for night time lighting preferences

In this book, the use of daylighting controls has been assumed in the performance analysis given for Chapters 5 through 7 (savings due to occupancy sensors and scheduling were also included through the use of a lighting schedule (based on field studies) in the DOE-2 simulations). Savings by daylighting controls can be achieved using manual or automated controls, as shown in Chapter 2. Manual control is inexpensive and has been successfully used in private offices or classrooms where the occupant can adjust the lighting to their preferences. For example, in a 6-month field study (Jennings et al. 2000) of 30 daylit perimeter offices, it was found that occupants elected to set their lights at less than full lighting 45 percent of the time and that for 28 percent of the time, the occupants only used one-third of the available lighting, thereby achieving significant lighting energy use savings of 24 percent. Automatic control delivers more reliable energy savings and, if designed and calibrated well, can respond to daylight availability without causing occupant dissatisfaction. In the same field study (Jennings et al. 2000), annual lighting energy savings of 41 percent and 30 percent for the area nearest the window (south- and north-facing windows, respectively) and 22 percent and 16 percent for areas further from window were obtained in a San-Francisco open-plan office building with large-area windows and interior venetian blinds (VT=~0.40, WWR=~0.45).

Manual control involves the use of simple wall-mounted dimmers or switches that are wired to groups of lamps or fixtures. With bi-level switching, two wall switches can control either 2-lamp or 3-lamp fixtures (luminaries). In a typical 2-lamp installation of multiple fixtures, one switch controls one of the lamps in each the fixtures, while the other controls the second lamp in each of the fixtures, so that light levels are 0, 50, or 100 percent of full light output. In a typical 3-lamp installation of multiple fixtures, one switch controls the center lamp in each fixture, while the second switch controls the two outboard lamps in each fixture, so that light levels are 0, 33 percent, 66 percent, and 100 percent. Dimming controls using a manual slider switch or knob, common in homes, are also available for commercial applications. Hand-held remote controllers or PC- or web-based individual controls are also becoming increasingly available.

Automated controls can implement either switching or dimming control strategies. Switching strategies involve the same hardware setup as manual bi-level switching except that the lights are automatically switched via a signal from a photosensor or occupancy sensor. This type of switching results in abrupt, noticeable changes in light levels and can be annoying so application of this type of strategy must be carefully applied to situations where daylight does not fluctuate over the day (e.g., climates with predominantly clear skies) or where switching is unlikely to be noticed (e.g., circulation areas). Four-level switching with 3-lamp installations (or even greater levels of switching) can also reduce the disturbance since the drop in illuminance level is less.

Automated dimming control strategies are by far the most acceptable to building occupants since light is modulated smoothly in response to changes in daylight levels over the course of the day and seasons. This type of control involves the use of dimming ballasts coupled to dimmable lamps (typically fluorescent lamps in commercial office applications), photosensors which measure the light level in the space, and ballast controllers which translate the photosensor signal into a command to the dimming ballast. The perimeter zone of a building is typically divided into sub-zones that run parallel to the window wall and have similar average daylight levels. Bright areas closest to the window wall can be dimmed separately from the darker areas further from the window wall. After installation of the lighting equipment, the daylighting controls must be commissioned to ensure that each piece of equipment has been installed correctly, is in good working order, and has been calibrated to meet the design specifications. Depending on the type of system, calibrating typically involves tuning the response of the control photosensor to the output of the electric lights. Procedures are typically provided by the manufacturer. Additional procedures can be found in "Tips for Daylighting with Windows" listed in the resources section below. Systems that enable remote-control or web-based commissioning are increasingly being developed and offered by manufacturers so that performance of these systems can be maintained over the life of the installation.

# RESOURCES

**Manufacturers**  This is generally the only source of assistance available for calibration of daylighting controls and commissioning of advanced HVAC control systems. It is advisable to make an agreement with the supplier regarding proper installation and calibration to design specifications. In fact, manufacturer selection might be based on the level of calibration support promised.

**Design Professionals**  Use a lighting specialist whenever daylighting controls are planned. Lighting designers (as opposed to electrical engineers) are recommended in general for a higher quality end result. Cost for added service is easily recouped in ensured performance and occupant satisfaction, and gives the best chance at gaining energy savings.

**Utility Companies**  Many utilities offer incentives for energy efficient lighting equipment. Inquire at your local utility about new construction or retrofit programs. Some utilities offer incentives for commissioning in both new and retrofit projects. Inquire at your local utility about these programs.

**Calculation Methods**  Well-established methods exist for calculating light levels with a proposed design. The best source for reference material on this topic is the IESNA.

Many lighting designers use software such as Lumen Micro or Luxicon in place of tedious hand calculations. A package which is capable of addressing daylight and electric light integration is recommended. For a list of lighting design software with daylight capabilities, request a "Daylighting Design Tool Survey" from the Windows and Daylighting Group at the Lawrence Berkeley Laboratory (510) 486-5605.

**Publications**  There are many titles available on general lighting design, but little to assist high performance lighting design with daylight controls. The IES may be the best source for literature. Controls are changing so rapidly, especially in DDC (direct digital controls) and HVAC applications, that books on the topic are often quickly out of date. The most current information comes from manufacturers, the IES, and ASHRAE.

*ASHRAE Applications Handbook* (American Society of Heating, Refrigerating and Air Conditioning Engineers 1991) is a good source for testing, adjusting and balancing procedures. See also *ASHRAE Guideline 1-1989, Guideline for Commissioning of HVAC Systems.*

Control Systems for Heating, Ventilating and Air Conditioning, 5th Ed., *by R. Haines and D. Little (Van Nostrand Reinhold 1993).*

O'Connor, J., E. S. Lee, F. R. Rubinstein, S. E. Selkowitz. "Tips for Daylighting with Windows." *Lawrence Berkeley Laboratory Report 39945* (1997). http://eetd.lbl.gov/btp/pub/designguide.

Rundquist, R., T. McDougall, and J. Benya, *Lighting Controls: Patterns for Design,* Electric Power Research Institute, 1996 (available from IESNA).

Wilson, A., "Lighting Controls: Beyond the Toggle Switch," *Environmental Building News,* Vol. 12, No. 6, June 2003.

## Organizations

**IESNA**  The Illuminating Engineering Society is a resource for literature, standards, codes, guidelines and a monthly journal covering lighting, daylighting and visual comfort. These materials provide useful and up-to-date technical information. Local chapters also may offer classes or other resources. For publications, call (212) 248-5000, ext. 112.

Illuminating Engineering Society of North America (IESNA)
120 Wall Street, Floor 17
New York, NY 10005
Phone: (212) 248-5000
Fax: (212) 248-5017
www.iesna.org

**EPRI**  The Electric Power Research Institute has a strong collection of fact sheets, brochures, guidelines and software available. Call EPRI Lighting Information Office (800) 525-8555.

Electric Power Research Institute (EPRI)
3412 Hillview Avenue, Palo Alto, CA 94304-1395
Website: www.epri.com

# Appendix C

# Tools and Resources

## Procedures and Ratings

**National Fenestration Rating Council** provides procedures for rating window systems that are often required by state energy codes:

    http://www.nfrc.org

See also a useful flowchart describing procedures for site-built or custom projects:

    http://www.nfrc.org/sb_outline.html

## Computer Simulation Programs

**WINDOW 5.0** is a publicly available computer program for calculating total window thermal performance indices (i.e. U-values, solar heat gain coefficients, shading coefficients, and visible transmittances). WINDOW 5.0 provides a versatile heat transfer analysis method consistent with the updated rating procedure developed by the National Fenestration Rating Council (NFRC) that is consistent with the ISO 15099 standard. The program can be used to design and develop new products, to assist educators in teaching heat transfer through windows, and to help public officials in developing building energy codes.

**THERM** is a state-of-the-art, Microsoft Windows™-based computer program developed at Lawrence Berkeley National Laboratory (LBNL) for use by building component manufacturers, engineers, educators, students, architects, and others interested in heat transfer. Using THERM, you can model twodimensional heat-transfer effects in building components such as windows, walls, foundations, roofs, and doors; appliances; and other products where thermal bridges are of concern. THERM's heat-transfer analysis allows you to evaluate a product's energy efficiency and local temperature patterns, which may relate directly to problems with condensation, moisture damage, and structural integrity.

**Optics5** allows the user to view and modify glazing data in many new and powerful ways. Optical and radiative properties of glazing materials are primary inputs for determination of energy performance in buildings. Properties of composite systems such as flexible films applied to rigid glazing and laminated glazing can be predicted from measurements on isolated components in air or other gas. Properties of a series of structures can be generated from those of a base structure. For example, the measured properties of a coated or uncoated substrate can be extended to a range of available substrate thickness without the need to measure each thickness. Similarly, a coating type could be transferred by calculation to any other substrate.

WINDOW 5.0, THERM, and Optics5 have been developed by LBNL and are available over the web:

    http://eetd.lbl.gov/btp/software.html

The tools are accepted by NFRC for rating window systems. In some cases, these tools can be applied by NFRC-certified simulators, test labs and inspection agencies to determine ratings for non-standard products.

**Daylighting algorithms and tools** are described in detail in the International Energy Agency Task 21 Daylight in Buildings publication: "Daylight in Buildings: A Source Book on Daylighting Systems and Components".

    See http://eetd.lbl.gov/Bookstore.html under Practical Guides & Tools for Energy Users for "Daylight in Buildings: A Source Book on Daylighting Systems and Components".

    For those residing outside of U.S. or Canada, please visit: http://www.iea-shc.org. Download the hyperlinked report 8.9.3 "Daylight Simulation: Methods, Algorithms, and Resources" from the CD-ROM directory.

**RADIANCE** is a lighting and daylighting visualization tool developed by LBNL and is available over the web:

    http://eetd.lbl.gov/btp/software.html

This program can model very sophisticated window systems and complex systems, given BTDF measured data.

**Daylighting and Electric Lighting Simulation Engine (DElight)** is a simulation engine for daylight and electric lighting system analysis in buildings. The program's origin was the LBNL SUPERLITE program from the 1980s, but the new version has updated the code and added new capabilities. It accepts a bidirectional transmittance distribution function (BTDF) and calculates daylight factors. The program can analyze complex systems, where the daylighting window aperture is treated as a directional light fixture and coupled to the interior space. An exterior radiance model is being developed that takes into account how exterior obstructions modify the BTDF incoming flux.

> http://eande.lbl.gov/Task21/DElightWWW.html

**DOE-2 and EnergyPlus** are public domain programs developed by LBNL and other team members:

> http://eetd.lbl.gov/btp/software.html

The **DOE-2** program for building energy use analysis provides the building construction and research communities with an up-to-date, unbiased, well documented public-domain computer program for building energy analysis. DOE-2 is a portable FORTRAN program that can be used on a large variety ofcomputers, including PC's. Using DOE-2, designers can quickly determine the choice of building parameters which improve energy efficiency while maintaining thermal comfort. A user can provide a simple or increasingly detailed description of a building design or alternative design options and obtain an accurate estimate of the proposed building's energy consumption, interior environmental conditions and energy operation cost. DOE-2 has been used by national labs, universities, and industry for hundreds of studies of products and strategies for energy efficiency and electric demand limiting. Examples include advanced insulating materials, evaporative cooling, low-E windows, switchable glazing, daylighting, desiccant cooling, cogeneration, gas-enginedriven cooling, cool storage, effect of increased ventilation, sizing of thermal energy storage systems, gas heat pumps, thermal bridges, thermal mass, variable exterior solar and IR absorptance, and window performance labeling.

**EnergyPlus** is a new-generation building energy simulation program based on DOE-2 and BLAST, with numerous added capabilities. The initial version of the program, EnergyPlus 1.0, was released in April 2001. EnergyPlus includes a number of innovative simulation features – such as sub-hour time steps, built-in template and external modular systems that are integrated with a heat balance-based zone simulation – and input and output data structures tailored to facilitate third party module and interface development. Other capabilities include multi-zone airflow, moisture adsorption/desorption in building materials, radiant heating and cooling, and photovoltaic simulation.

A general list of tools offered by the U.S. Department of Energy are available over the web at:

> **http://www.eren.doe.gov/buildings/tools_directory/ software.html**

## American Professional and Manufacturer's Organizations

American Architectural Manufacturers Association (AAMA)
1827 Walden Office Square, Suite 104
Schaumberg, IL 60173-4268
Phone: (847) 303-5664/Fax: (847) 303-5774
www.aamanet.org

American Institute of Architects (AIA)
1735 New York Ave.. N. W.
Washington, DC 20006
Phone: (202) 626-7300
www.aia.org

American National Standards Institute (ANSI)
11 West 42nd Street, 13th Floor
New York, NY 10036
Phone: (212) 642-4900/Fax: (212) 398-0023
www.ansi.org

American Society of Heating, Refrigerating and Air Conditioning Engineers, Inc. (ASHRAE)
1791 Tullie Circle, NE
Atlanta, GA 30329-2305
Phone: (404) 636-8400/Fax: (404) 321-5478
www.ashrae.org

American Society for Testing and Materials (ASTM)
100 Barr Harbor Drive
West Conshohocken, PA 19428-2959
Phone: (610) 832-9598/Fax: (610) 832-9599
www.astm.org

American Solar Energy Society
2400 Central Avenue, G-1
Boulder, CO 80301-2843
Phone: (303) 443-3130/Fax: (303) 443-3212
www.ases.org

Illuminating Engineering Society of North America (IESNA)
120 Wall Street, Floor 17
New York, NY 10005
Phone: (212) 248-5000
Fax: (212) 248-5017
www.iesna.org

International Code Council (ICC)
5203 Leesburg Pike, Suite 708
Falls Church, VA 22041
Phone: 703-931-4533
www.intlcode.org

National Fenestration Rating Council (NFRC)
1300 Spring Street, Suite 500
Silver Spring, MD USA 20910
Phone: (301) 589-NFRC/Fax: (301) 588-0854
www.nfrc.org

Window and Door Manufacturers Association (WDMA)
1400 East Touhy Avenue, Suite G-54
Des Plaines, IL 60018
Phone: (847) 299-5200/Fax: (847) 299-1286

## Canadian and International Organizations

Canadian Standards Association
178 Rexdale Boulevard
Rexdale, Ontario M9W 1R3
Phone: (416) 747-4000

Canadian Window and Door Manufacturers
Association
27 Goulbourn Avenue
Ottawa, Ontario K1N 8C7
Phone: (613) 233-9804

International Energy Agency
Solar Heating and Cooling Programme
1808 Corcoran Street, NW
Washington, DC 20009
Phone: (202) 483-2393/Fax: (202) 265-2248
www.arch.vuw.ac.nz/iea/index.html

International Energy Agency
Center for the Analysis and Dissemination of
Demonstrated Energy Technologies (CADDET)
www.ornl.gov/CADDET/caddet.html

International Standards Organization (ISO)
1, rue de Varembe
Case postale 56
CH-1211 Geneva 20
Switzerland
Phone: + 41 22 749 01 11/Fax: + 41 22 733 34 30
www.iso.ch/welcome.html

National Research Council of Canada
Institute for Research in Construction (IRC)
1500 Montreal Road, Building M-24
Ottawa, Ontario K1A 0R6
www.cisti.nrc.ca:80/irc/irccontents.html

Standards Council of Canada
45 O'Connor Street, Suite 1200
Ottawa, Ontario K1P 6N7
Phone: (613) 238-3222/Fax: (613) 995-4564
www.scc.ca

## Government, Research, and Educational Organizations

Center for Sustainable Building Research
College of Architecture and Landscape Architecture
University of Minnesota
1425 University Avenue SE
Minneapolis, MN 55455
Fax: 612-626-7424
www.csbr.umn.edu

Electric Power Research Institute (EPRI)
3412 Hillview Avenue, Palo Alto, CA 94304-1395
EPRI Lighting Information Office: (800) 525-8555
Website: www.epri.com

Florida Solar Energy Center (FSEC)
1679 Clearlake Road
Cocoa, FL 32922
Phone: (407) 638-1000/Fax: (407) 638-1010
www.fsec.ucf.edu

Lawrence Berkeley National Laboratory (LBNL)
Building Technologies Department
Environmental Energy Technologies Division
Lawrence Berkeley Laboratory, Berkeley, CA 94720
Phone: (510) 486-6845/Fax: (510) 486-4089
eetd.lbl.gov/BT.html

Lighting Research Center
Rensselaer Polytechnic Institute
21 Union St.
Troy, NY 12180 USA
Phone: 518-687-7100
Fax: 518-687-7120 or 518-687-7121
www.lrc.rpi.edu

National Renewable Energy Laboratory
Center for Buildings and Thermal Energy Systems
1617 Cole Blvd.
Golden, CO 80401
(303) 384-7520
Fax: (303) 384-7540
www.nrel.gov

National Technical Information Service (NTIS)
www.fedworld.gov/ntis/ntishome.html

Oak Ridge National Laboratory (ORNL)
Building Envelope Systems and Materials
P.O. Box 2008
Oak Ridge, TN 37831-6070
Phone: 423-574-4345
www.ornl.gov/roofs+walls

U.S. Department of Energy's EREN: Energy Efficiency and
Renewable Energy Network
www.eren.doe.gov

U.S. Department of Energy
www.doe.gov

U.S. Government's Federal Information Network
www.fedworld.gov

# Glossary

**Abrasion resistance.** The ability to withstand scuffing, scratching, rubbing or wind-scouring.

**Absorptance.** The ratio of radiant energy absorbed to total incident radiant energy in a glazing system.

**Absorption.** Transformation of radiant energy to a different form of energy by interaction with matter.

**Acoustic performance.** The ability of a window to attenuate sound transmission in noisy environments, normally expressed as the sound transmission coefficient (STC) in decibels; the ratio of transmitted to incident sound intensity.

**Acid embossing/etching.** A process where the surface of flat or bent glass is obscured by treatment with hydrofluoric acid or its compounds.

**Acid polishing.** The polishing of a glass surface by acid treatment.

**Acrylic.** A noncrystalline thermoplastic with good weather resistance, shatter resistance, and optical clarity; sometimes used for glazing.

**Aerogel.** A microporous, transparent silicate foam which has a low thermal conductivity; used as a glazing cavity fill material. *See also* Transparent Insulation Material.

**Accent lighting.** Directional lighting designed to emphasize a particular object or to draw attention to a part of the field of view

**Air change rate.** The rate of replacement of air in a space, usually due to infiltration of outdoor air through cracks around windows and doors. Commonly expressed in air changes per hour.

**Air film.** The layer of air next to a surface, such as a glass pane, which offers some resistance to heat flow. The R-value of a still-air film is about 0.68, while that for the air film associated with a 15-mile-per-hour wind velocity is 0.17. *See also* R-value.

**Air gap** (also **air space**). The space in the cavity between two panes of glass in an insulated glass unit.

**Air leakage.** The flow of air which passes through cracks in closed and locked fenestration products.

**Air leakage rating.** A measure of a fenestration system's rate of air leakage in the presence of a specific pressure difference. It is expressed in units of cubic-feet-per-minute per square foot of window area (cfm/sq ft) or cubic-feet-per-minute per foot of window perimeter length (cfm/ft). The lower a window's air leakage rating, the better its airtightness.

**Altitude (solar).** The vertical angular distance of a point in the sky above the horizon. Altitude is measured positively from the horizon to the zenith, from 0 to 90 degrees.

**Aluminum.** A light, strong, noncorrosive metal that can either be extruded into shapes or used in sheet or coil form and bent into shapes (capping). It has a very high thermal conductivity.

**Aluminum-clad window.** Window consisting mainly of wood that is covered externally with aluminum sheet to deter the elements.

**Aluminum spacer.** A rectangular or contoured hollow aluminum bar filled with a desiccant (or moisture-absorbing material) that is traditionally used to separate the panes in double-pane glass units.

**Ambient lighting.** Lighting throughout an area for general illumination. *See* task lighting.

**Angular-selective window.** A glazed window whose visible and solar transmittance varies with angle of incidence. For example, high transmittance at near-normal incidence (to retain the view) and low transmittance for high angle of incidence (beam component of sunlight from near the zenith).

**Annealed glass.** Standard sheet of float glass, which is heat-treated to increase its impact resistance.

**Annealing.** Heat treatment that involves the heating of metal, glass, or other materials above the critical or recrystallization temperature, followed by controlled cooling to eliminate the effects of cold-working, relieve internal stresses, or improve strength, ductility, or other properties.

**Anodized aluminum.** Aluminum that is treated by electrolysis to develop a finished surface (an extremely hard, noncorrosive oxide film). The electrochemical process produces an anodic coating by converting aluminum into aluminum oxide by electrolytic action. The resulting finish may be either clear or colored, and is an integral part of the aluminum.

**Anti-glare coating.** A treatment applied to a glazing system to reduce the amount of unwanted diffuse visible transmittance.

**Anti-reflective coating.** A transparent coating, typically 150 nm thick, which reduces surface reflectance by using destructive interference between light reflected at the substrate surface and light reflected at the coating surface.

**Argon gas (argon filled).** An inert, nontoxic gas placed between glass panes in insulated glass units in order to improve the insulating value of sealed glass units.

**Atrium.** Traditionally, the central space of a building open to the sky; today, the atrium is usually multistory and glazed. An atrium differs from a court, also an outdoor area, but which is surrounded partially or entirely by buildings or walls.

**Attenuation.** The sound reduction process in which sound energy is absorbed or diminished in intensity as the result of energy conversion from sound to motion or heat.

**Awning window.** A window with a sash hinged at the top, which projects outward from the plane of the frame. *See also* Projected or projecting windows.

**Azimuth (solar).** Compass bearing, relative to true (geographic) north, of a point on the horizon. The horizon is defined as a huge, imaginary circle centered on the observer. Bearings are measured clockwise in degrees from north, ranging from 0 degrees (north) through 90 (east), 180 (south), 270 (west), and up to 360 (north again).

**Blinding glare**. Glare that is so intense that, for an appreciable length of time after it has been removed, no object can be seen.

**Borate glass.** A glass whose essential glass former is boron oxide rather than silica.

**Brightness**. The subjective perception of luminance.

**Brise-soleil.** An architectural device on a building (such as a projection, louvers, or a screen) that blocks unwanted sunlight.

**Btu.** An abbreviation for British thermal unit—a standard measure of the amount of energy required to raise the temperature of one pound of water by one degree Fahrenheit.

**Building envelope.** The outer elements of a building, both above and below ground, that divide the external and internal environments.

**Casement.** A window sash which swings open on side hinges.

**Casement window.** A window containing one or more side-hinged sashes hinged that project outward or inward from the plane of the window in the vertical plane. A conventional casement window in North America swings outward, while in Europe it swings inward.

**Casting.** A process of shaping glass by pouring hot glass into or onto molds or tables.

**Caulk, caulking compound.** A mastic compound for filling joints and sealing cracks to prevent leakage of water and air; commonly made of silicone, bituminous, acrylic or rubber-based material.

**Caulking.** Filling joints, cracks, voids, or crevices with a sealant (caulk) in order to prevent the passage of air or water.

**Ceramic glass enamel (**also **ceramic enamel** or **glass enamel).** A vitreous inorganic coating bonded to glass by fusion at a temperature generally above 500 degrees Celsius.

**Chromogenic glazing.** A broad class of switchable glazings including active materials (e.g. electrochromic) and passive materials (photochromic and thermochromic).

**Clear glass.** Architectural clear glass is mostly of the soda-lime-silica type, and composition varies between manufacturers, but is generally 70–74 percent silica, 5–12 percent lime, and 12–16 percent soda, with small amounts of magnesium, aluminum, iron, and other elements.

**Clerestory.** That part of a building rising clear of the roof or other parts, whose walls contain windows for lighting the interior.

**Clerestory window.** A venting or fixed window positioned above other windows or doors on an upper outside wall of a room.

**Coating.** A thin layer applied to the surface of a glass in either a chemical deposition technology (i.e., vapor, liquid, etc.) or a vacuum sputtering process. After application it is converted to a solid protective, decorative, or functional adherent film.

**Color of transmitted light.** The human eye's and brain's subjective interpretation of the spectral distribution of transmitted visible radiation. Transmitted light is said to be colorless (white) if it matches the spectrum of the external incident light, while any imparted color is due to the subtraction of the complementary wavelengths by absorption or reflection of those wavelengths by the glazing system.

**Commercial entrance system.** Products used for ingress and egress in nonresidential buildings. Commercial entrance systems typically utilize panic hardware, automatic closers, and relatively large amounts of glass.

**Composite frame.** A frame consisting of two or more materials—for example, an interior wood element with an exterior fiberglass element.

**Condensation.** The deposit of water vapor from the air on any cold surface whose temperature is below the dew point, such as a cold window glass or frame that is exposed to humid indoor or outdoor air.

**Conduction.** Transfer of heat through a material via molecular contact; heat flows from a higher-temperature area to a lower-temperature one.

**Conductivity, thermal.** The time rate of steady state heat flow through a unit area of homogenous material induced by a unit temperature gradient in a direction perpendicular to that unit area.

**Convection.** A heat transfer process involving motion of a fluid (such as air) caused by either the difference in density of the fluid and the action of gravity (natural convection) or by mechanical forces such as blowers, fans, etc. (forced convection). Convection affects heat transfer from the surface to air, whether it is for enclosed spaces (like insulated glazing unit cavity) or open spaces (like indoor glass surface to room air).

**Cool daylight glazing.** Spectrally selective glazing that employs tinting and/or surface coatings to achieve a visible transmittance that exceeds the solar heat gain coefficient (total solar energy transmittance). *See also* Light-to-solar-gain ratio.

**CR.** Condensation Resistance index; an indication of a window's ability to resist condensation developed by NFRC. The higher the CR, the less likely condensation is to occur.

**CRF.** Condensation Resistance Factor; an indication of a window's ability to resist condensation developed by AAMA. The higher the CRF, the less likely condensation is to occur.

**Crown glass.** Large panes that first became available in the seventeenth century and were incorporated in wooden sash windows. The glass was hand-blown through a pipe (pontil) into a circular disc, leaving a bubble or bullion where the pipe was inserted. Also known as *bottle glass* or *bull's eye glass*.

**Curtain wall.** An external non-load bearing wall, applied in front of a frame structure, thereby bypassing floor slabs. The cladding is intended to separate the internal and external environments, and is distinct from the building structure. There are now many curtain walls systems manufactured from a variety of materials; the systems typically include both windows and spandrel sections.

**Cylinder glass.** A glass that is blown in the shape of a cylinder and flattened into a sheet.

**Daylight distribution.** The distribution of illuminance due to sunlight and sky light within a room, generally measured on a horizontal plane at typical workplane height (0.8 m, or 2.5 feet above the floor). Units: lux (lx=lm/m²) or footcandles (fc) where 1 fc=10.764 lx.

**Daylight factor.** The ratio, in percent, of workplane illuminance (at a given point) to the outdoor illuminance on a horizontal plane. It is only evaluated under cloudy sky conditions (no direct solar beam).

**Daylighting.** A building energy conservation measure involving the deliberate displacement of artificial lighting by dispersed sunlight or diffuse sky light. Switching, dimming, or other light control strategies must be employed. The mere admission of natural light without a compensating reduction in electric lighting density will not result in a net energy or environmental benefit, although it might improve visual amenity.

**Debridge.** The process of cutting away the metal on the bottom of a thermal-break cavity once the two-part polyurethane has reached full strength, thus creating a thermally broken extrusion.

**Decibel.** A unit for expressing the relative intensity of sounds on a scale from 0 for average least perceptible sound to about 130 for the average pain level.

**Desiccant.** An extremely porous crystalline substance (hygroscopic or water-absorbing) used in granulated or bulk form inside the spacer of an insulating glass unit in order to keep the gas(es) within the sealed space dry and prevent condensation and fogging.

**Design heat loss.** The calculated values, expressed in units of Btu per hour (abbreviated Btu/h), for the heat transmitted from a warm interior to a cold outdoor condition under prescribed extreme weather conditions. The values are useful for selecting heating equipment and estimating seasonal energy requirements. Infiltration heat loss is a part of the design heat loss.

**Design life.** The period of time during which a system or component is expected to perform its intended function, without significant degradation of performance and without requiring major maintenance or replacement.

**Design Pressure (DP).** The wind-load pressure to which a product is tested and rated to withstand.

**Design wind load.** The wind-load pressure a product is required by the specifier to withstand in its end use application.

**Dewpoint (temperature).** The temperature at which water vapor in air will condense at a given state of humidity and pressure.

**Diffuse light.** Lighting on a workplane or object that is not predominantly incident from any particular direction.

**Diffusing glass.** Glass with an irregular surface for scattering light; used for privacy or to reduce glare.

**Diffuser.** A translucent glazing layer or window accessory designed to intercept direct-beam radiation and transmit it diffusely (i.e. in many directions at the same time); also provides privacy.

**Diffusivity, thermal.** Thermal conductivity per unit of heat capacity.

**Direct glare.** Glare resulting from high illuminance or insufficiently shielded light sources in the field of view. Direct glare is usually associated with bright areas, such as the sky, that are outside the visual task or region being viewed.

**Direct sunlight (beam sunlight).** Daylight directly from the sun without any diffusion.

**Disability glare.** Glare resulting in reduced visual performance and visibility. Often accompanied by discomfort glare.

**Discomfort glare.** Glare producing discomfort. It does not necessarily interfere with visual performance or visibility.

**Distortion.** The optical effect due to the variation of sheet glass thickness.

**Divided light.** A window with a number of small panes of glass separated and held in place by muntins.

**DOE2.1E.** A building-simulation computer program used to calculate total annual energy use.

**Double envelope.** A facade comprised of a pair of "skins" separated by an air space, which acts as a buffer against temperature extremes, wind and sound. The cladding can be designed into a multiple permutations of solid and diaphanous members, operable or fixed. Sun-shading devices are often located within the cavity. The system goes by many names, including Double-Leaf Facade, Double-Skin Facade and Ventilated Facade.

**Double glazing.** In general, any use of two layers of glass separated by an air space within an opening to improve insulation against heat transfer and/or sound transmission. In factory-made double glazing units, the air between the glass sheets is thoroughly dried and the space is sealed airtight, eliminating possible condensation and providing superior insulating properties. It also allows for between-glass shading options such as muntins, blinds, and pleated shades. *See also* Insulating Glass, Dual-seal Unit.

**Double glazing unit.** Two panes of glass separated by a permanently sealed cavity.

**Double-hung (window).** A window consisting of a pair of vertical sliding sashes with either sash opening independently of the other. It can use either a counterbalance mechanism to hold the sash in place or spring-loaded side bars that keep sash in place by friction. *See also* Single-hung window.

**Drawn glass.** Glass made by a continuous mechanical drawing operation.

**Drip.** A projecting fin or a groove at the outer edge of a sill, soffit, or other projecting member in a wall, designed to interrupt the flow of water downward over the wall or inward across the soffit.

**Dual-seal unit.** A sealed multiple-pane glazing unit with two independent materials used in the edge seal for bonding the glass layers to the spacer. The dual seal reduces the possibility of mechanical failure (i.e., separation of glass from spacer and loss of dry air or other gas(es) used in the cavity).

**Dynamic glazing.** *See* Switchable glazing.

**Egress window.** A window providing egress, as defined in applicable building codes. Also referred to as *emergency exit window, escape window,* and *fire-escape window.*

**Effective thermal conductivity.** The combined effects of conduction, convection, and radiation in fluid-filled (gas-filled) enclosures and cavities, converted into an apparent or effective conductivity of a solid.

**Electrochromic(s) (glazing).** Glazing with optical properties that can be varied continuously from clear to dark with a low-voltage signal. Ions are reversibly injected or removed from an electrochromic material.

**Electromagnetic spectrum.** Radiant energy over a broad range of wavelengths.

**Emissivity.** The relative ability of a surface to reflect or emit heat by radiation. Emissivity factors range from 0 to 1; the lower the emissivity, the less heat is emitted through a window system. Emissivity is typically measured by U-factor (or its inverse, R-value).

**Etch.** To attack the surface of glass with hydrofluoric acid or other agents, generally for marking or decoration.

**Evacuated glazing.** An insulating glazing composed of two glass layers, hermetically sealed at the edges, with a hard vacuum between (< 10-3 Pascals) to eliminate convection and conduction. A spacer system (commonly referred to as "pillars") throughout the surface of glass (rather than just at the edges) is needed to keep the panes from touching.

**Exterior stop.** The removable glazing bead that holds the glass or panel in place when it is on the exterior side of the light or panel, as contrasted to an interior stop located on the interior side of the glass.

**Extrusion.** The process of producing aluminum shapes by forcing heated material through an orifice in a die by means of a pressure ram. Also, any item made by this process. An example is the complex cross-section of an extruded aluminum or PVC window frame.

**Fenestration.** The placement of openings in a building wall, such as windows, doors, skylights, etc., designed to permit the passage of air, light, or people; one of the important aspects of a building's exterior appearance. Also, associated interior or exterior elements, such as shades or blinds. From the Latin word, *fenestra,* meaning "window."

**Fiberglass.** A composite material made by embedding glass fiber in a polymer matrix. It may be used as a diffusing material in sheet form, or as a standard sash and frame element.

**Film conductance.** The time rate of heat flow from a unit area of a surface to its surroundings, induced by a unit temperature difference between the surface and the environment.

**Fire resistance.** As applied to buildings, the property of a material or assembly to withstand fire or give protection from it, characterized by the ability to confine a fire or to continue serving a structural function, or both.

**Fixed (window)**. A single sash fastened permanently in a frame so that it cannot be raised, lowered, or swung open; a non-venting or non-operable window unit.

**Flashing**. (1) Sheet metal or other material applied to seal and protect the joints formed by different materials or surfaces. (2) Applying a thin layer of opaque or colored glass to the surface of clear glass, or vice versa.

**Flat glass**. A general term covering sheet glass, plate glass, float glass, window glass, and various forms of rolled glass, and named according to the method used in its manufacture. *See also* Float glass, Plate glass, Rolled glass, Sheet glass.

**Float glass**. Glass formed by a process of floating the molten glass (at approximately 1000 degrees Celsius) on a shallow bed of molten tin. Thickness is controlled by the speed at which the solidifying glass ribbon is drawn off the tin bath. The surfaces of the glass do not come into contact with any rollers or mechanisms that could cause damage until the glass has solidified; therefore it produces a high-optical-quality glass with parallel surfaces without polishing and grinding.

**Flush glazing**. A method of glazing wherein the surfaces of the glass retaining members (stops or beads) are in the same plane normal to the glass as the side faces of the frame members; often achieved by providing pockets in these faces.

**Foam spacer**. Nonconductive, foam material (often closed-cell silicone foam) used to separate the double- and triple-pane insulating glass units; improves the thermal performance of the window.

**Fogging**. A deposit of contamination left on the inside surface of a sealed insulating glass unit due to extremes of temperatures or failed seals.

**Fourcault process**. The method of making sheet glass by drawing vertically upward from a slotted debiteuse block.

**Frame**. The fixed, enclosing structure of a window or other fenestration system which holds the sash, casement, door panels, etc., as well as hardware. Frames can be constructed from aluminum extrusions, steel, PVC extrusions, wood, composite materials, or a combination of these materials.

**Freeze-thaw resistance**. Resistance to cycles of freezing and thawing that could affect application, appearance, or performance

**Frit**. Ceramic frit opacification is one or more coats of durable colored ceramic material fire-fused onto compatible base glass. The firing also produces a heat-treated product. Since the basic purpose is generally to render the glass opaque, the frit is typically applied to the second surface of monolithic glass or the fourth surface of an insulating unit (counting from the outside surface in). The opacity can be improved with thicker or multiple coats, which are available in a wide range of colors.

**Gasochromic glazing**. Glazing which uses the phenomenon of chromism due to tin injection/ejection to color the window. The application of gas flow transporting ions to the surface (catalyst), which changes solar and visible transmittance. *See also* Switchable glazing.

**Gas fill, Gas-filled IGU**. A gas, usually argon or krypton, placed between window or skylight glazing panes to reduce the U-factor by suppressing conduction and convection.

**Gasket**. A pre-formed section, generally of neoprene or rubber-like composition, that provides a continuous sealing for the glass or frame members. It provides a weather-tight seal when compressed.

**Gas retention**. The ability of a sealed insulating glazing unit to retain its original gas-filled composition. In the long term, diffusion through frame and edge-seal materials allows air to progressively replace the original gas(es).

**g-factor**. Same as solar heat gain coefficient (SHGC). This quantity is related to total solar energy transmittance (TSET). In some countries, it is formally applied to only the glazing, but generally applies to both transparent and opaque parts of a fenestration system. *See* Solar Heat Gain Coefficient (SHGC).

**Glare**. High luminosity values from a point, line, or area source that may affect the visual amenity, depending on luminosity, background illumination, adaptation of the eye, and area size. There are upper limits for physiological glare (damage to the eyes) and psychological glare (feeling of discomfort).

**Glare-veiling**. Diffuse scattering from a glazing system, which obscures (masks) the visibility of objects beyond the glazing system.

**Glass**. An inorganic, hard, brittle substance, usually transparent, that is made by fusing silicates (sand), soda (sodium carbonate), and lime (calcium carbonate) with small quantities of alumina, boric, or magnesia oxides under high temperatures, without crystallizing. Contrary to common belief, glass is not solid, but is rather a very hard fluid which flows slowly.

**Glazing**. A generic term used to describe an infill material, such as glass or window assemblies in general. Also refers to the process of applying or installing glass into a window or door sash.

**Glazing bar**. *See* Muntin.

**Glazing bead**. A small, applied molding used to hold a pane of glass, or substitute for it, in a frame.

**Ground glass**. A light-diffusing glass, usually sandblasted or ground.

**Hard coat(ing)**. A low-emittance (low-E), thin-film surface coating on sheet glass which is deposited at a high temperature during the final stage of glass production. It is resistant to abrasion and attack by moisture, atmospheric pollutants, etc. *See also* Pyrolytic coating.

**Haze**. The scattering of visible light, resulting in a decrease in the transparency of a window system and a cloudy appearance.

**Head**. The main horizontal member forming the top of a window or door frame.

**Heat-absorbing glass**. Glass having the property of absorbing a substantial percentage of radiant energy in the near-infrared range of the spectrum. *See also* Tinted glass.

**Heat flow rate (Q)**. The quantity of heat transferred to or from a system in unit time.

**Heat Gain**. Instantaneous rate of heat gain at which heat enters into and/or is generated within a space. Latent heat gain occurs when moisture is added to the space (from occupants or equipment). Sensible heat gain is added directly to the space by conduction, convection, and/or radiation.

**Heating degree-day**. Term used to relate the typical climate conditions to the amount of energy needed to heat a building. The base temperature is usually 65 degrees Fahrenheit. A heating degree-day is counted for each degree below 65 degrees that the average daily outside temperatures reach in the winter.

**Heat loss**. The transfer of heat from inside to outside by means of conduction, convection, and radiation through all surfaces of a building.

**Heat loss rate**. The rate at which heat is lost from a system or component of a system, per degree of temperature difference between its average temperature and the average ambient air temperature

**Heat Mirror™**. A thin, transparent-coated (low-e) polymer film that is inserted between double or triple glazing, which permits transmission of visible light but reflects far-infrared (and sometimes near-infrared) radiation. Heat Mirror™ is a commercial trademark of Southwall Technologies for their proprietary soft-coated, low-e polyester glazing films.

**Heat-strengthened glass**. Glass that has been subjected to a thermal treatment characterized by rapid cooling to produce a compressively stressed surface layer somewhat less stressed than that produced in tempered glass. Heat-strengthened glass is approximately twice as strong as annealed glass of the same thickness when exposed to uniform static pressure loads. Heat-strengthened glass is not considered safety glass and will not completely dice as with fully tempered glass.

**Heat-treated (glass).** A term sometimes used for both fully tempered and heat-strengthened glass.

**Heliostat.** A sun tracking device. Typically, an instrument consisting of a mirror or other reflective surface moved by clockwork, by which a sunbeam is made apparently stationary, by being steadily directed to one spot during the whole of its diurnal period. A heliostat, for instance, might be used with a skylight, reflecting direct sunlight through the aperture throughout the day to increasing illuminance.

**High-transmission glass.** Glass that transmits an exceptionally high percentage of visible light.

**Holographic glazing.** Glazing with a thin-film microstructure coating that refracts incident light in some advantageous way, e.g. as a light-redirecting glazing for daylighting applications.

**Hopper window.** A partially movable sash that is hinged at the bottom and opens inward.

**Horizontal-pivoted window.** A window fitted with a ventilator; it opens by rotating on centrally located pivots on upright frame members.

**Horizontal-sliding window (horizontal slider).** A window fitted with one or more sashes that opens by sliding horizontally in grooves provided in horizontal frame members. An operating sash with a fixed light (comprising a unit) is termed a single slider.

**Humidity, absolute.** The mass of water vapor per unit of volume.

**Humidity, relative.** The percentage of moisture in the air in relation to the amount of moisture the air could hold at that given temperature.

**Impact resistance.** The ability to withstand mechanical blows or shock without damage seriously affecting the effectiveness of the material or system.

**Inert gas.** Refers to the use of chemically nonreactive gas(es) within the cavity of a sealed insulating glass unit for the purpose of reducing conductive/convective heat transfer. *See* Gas fill.

**Infiltration (air).** The movement of outdoor air into the interior of a building through cracks around windows, doors, and the building envelope in general.

**Infiltration heat loss.** The heat loss due to infiltration. The loss depends upon the indoor and outdoor temperatures, the crack perimeter, and the rate of air leakage per foot of crack.

**Infrared Radiation (IR).** Invisible electromagnetic radiation, beyond red light on the spectrum, with wavelengths greater than 0.7 microns. Short-wave infrared radiation is from 770 nm to 2500 nm (0.77 to 2.5 microns), while long-wave infrared is from 2.5 microns and beyond.

**Insulating Glass (IG) Insulating Glass Unit (IGU).** A combination of two or more panes of glass with a hermetically sealed air space between the panes of glass, separated by a spacer. This space may or may not be filled with an inert gas, such as argon.

**Interior venetian blinds.** A venetian blind installed between two panes of glass and remotely controlled.

**Jal-awning window.** A window consisting of multiple top-hinged ventilators arranged in a vertical series and operated by one or more control devices that swing the bottom edges of the ventilator outward. The window does not contain a cross shaft or torque bar, but does have an individually operated locking mechanism.

**Jalousie (window).** Window made up of horizontally mounted, louvered glass slats that tightly abut each other when closed and rotate outward when cranked open. *See also* Louvered window.

**Jamb.** The main vertical members forming the sides of a window or door frame.

**Krypton.** An inert, nontoxic gas used in insulating windows to reduce heat transfer.

**kWh.** Kilowatt-hour; a unit of energy equal to one thousand watt-hours.

**Laminated glass.** Two or more sheets of glass bonded together with one or more inner layers of transparent plastic (interlayer) to which the glass adheres if broken. The bonding is achieved by heating the glass/interlayer sandwich under pressure in an autoclave. The glass is used for overhead, safety glazing, and sound reduction.

**LCD switchable.** Form of chromogenic (switchable) glazing that employs a liquid crystal device to modulate transmittance of solar radiation.

**Light.** A window; or a pane of glass within a window. Double-hung windows are designated by the number of lights in the upper and lower sashes, as in six-over-six. Also, spelled informally, *lite*.

**Lightscoops.** Clerestory roof monitors oriented away from the sun, utilized when and where indirect light is desired or solar heat gains are undesirable.

**Light pipe.** A generic term for a system employing bulk optics (lenses, mirrors, reflective ducts, or other optical waveguide technology) designed to transport light (natural or artificial) to parts of a building remote from the envelope. Also known as *tubular daylighting devices (TDD)*.

**Light-redirection system.** A glazing unit or panel, possibly retrofitted, which intercepts incident sunlight and sky light and specularly reflects it in another direction, usually toward the ceiling. *See also* Prismatic glazing *and* Holographic glazing.

**Light shaft.** An insulated shaft built to direct the light from a roof window or skylight through the attic to the room below.

**Light shelf.** A daylight-enhancement device; an internal and/or external overhang with a reflecting upper surface normally above head height. Designed to reduce glare near the window and improve illuminance uniformity along an axis normal to the window wall.

**Light-to-solar-gain ratio (LSG).** A measure of the ability of a glazing to provide light without excessive solar heat gain. It is the ratio between the visible transmittance of a glazing and its solar heat gain coefficient.

**Lightwell.** An open shaft in a building that provides air and light to windows opening onto the shaft.

**Liquid crystal glazing.** Glass in which the optical properties of a thin layer of liquid crystals are controlled by an electric current, changing from a clear state to a diffusing state.

**Litrium (also Literium).** An atrium designed to optimize daylighting in adjacent spaces. *See* also atrium.

**Load.** The amount of energy that must be added to or extracted from a space to thermal comfort. Sensible or latent cooling or heating loads are due to accumulated heat gains or losses through the building envelope, window, infiltration or ventilation, and occupancy.

**Long-wave infrared radiation.** Invisible radiation, beyond red light on the electromagnetic spectrum (above 2.5 micro meters or microns), emitted by warm surfaces such as a body at room temperature radiating to a cold window surface.

**Louvered window.** A window having louvers or slats that fill all or part of the opening.

**Louvers.** Slanted fins or slats in a window, ventilator, or venetian blind; the slats may be fixed or adjustable, and made of wood, metal, glass, or plastic.

**Low-conductance spacers.** An assembly of materials designed to reduce heat transfer at the edge of an insulating window. Spacers are placed between the panes of glass in a double- or triple-glazed window.

**Low-E (low-emittance) coating.** A microscopically thin (less than 100 nm) metal, metal oxide, or multilayer coating deposited on a glazing surface to reduce its thermal infrared emittance and radiative heat transfer. Near-infrared emittance may also be reduced depending on whether solar heat is to be rejected or admitted. Low-emissivity glass is used to increase a window's insulating value, block heat flow, and reduce fading

**Low-iron glass.** Glass with a low concentration of ferrous compounds, which are absorbing in the near-infrared part of the solar spectrum. Particularly used for solar collector covers and equator-facing windows in cold-climate, passive-solar buildings where solar transmittance must be maximized.

**Luminous efficacy ($K_e$).** The ratio of the visible transmittance to the shading coefficient; it is a measure of the light-to-heat ratio of the transmitted energy. *See also* Light-to-solar-gain ratio.

**Metal-clad window.** Exterior wood parts covered with extruded aluminum, or other metal, with a factory-applied finish for protection.

**Metal window.** A window composed of a metal frame and sash; the metals are commonly aluminum, steel, stainless steel, and bronze, but the vast majority of metal frames are made of aluminum.

**Micron.** One millionth ($10^{-6}$) of a metric meter.

**Mil.** One thousandth of an inch, or 0.0254 millimeters.

**Moisture migration.** The passage of moisture into or through a material or construction, in the form of water vapor, due to a difference in vapor pressure at the two faces.

**Molded glass.** Glass that is formed in a mold, as distinct from cast, rolled, drawn, or offhand ware.

**Monitor.** A raised section of roof that includes a vertical, or nearly vertical, glazed aperture for daylighting.

**Mullion.** A major structural vertical or horizontal member connecting windows, sliding glass doors, or frames.

**Muntin, Muntin bars, Muntin grilles.** Small, secondary horizontal or vertical framing members that divide glazing into separate vision areas within the basic framework of a door, window, sash, or ventilator. Sometimes referred to as: *sash bar, window bar,* or *glazing bar.*

**Natural convection.** A heat transfer process involving motion in a fluid (such as air) that is caused by a difference in the density of the fluid and the action of gravity. This is an important part of heat transfer from the glass surface to room air.

**Natural ventilation.** Air movement into and out of a building due to wind or differences in air pressure or temperature.

**Obscure glass.** Any textured glass (frosted, etched, fluted, ground, etc.) used for privacy, light diffusion, or decorative effects. Also knows as *vision-proof glass.*

**Operable window.** A window that can be opened for ventilation.

**Optical glass.** High-quality glass with closely specified optical properties; it is used in the manufacture of optical systems.

**Outdoor-Indoor Transmission Class (OITC).** A single-number rating calculated in accordance with ASTM E 1332, using values of outdoor-indoor transmission loss. It provides an estimate of the sound insulation performance of a facade or building elements. The frequency range used is typical of outdoor traffic noises.

**Pane.** One of the compartments of a door or window consisting of a single sheet of glass in a frame; also, a sheet of glass, or a substitute for it, cut to size and shape and ready for glazing. Often called a *square* or a *light.*

**Panning.** In replacement window work, the outside aluminum trim that can extend around the perimeter of the window opening; it is used to cover up the old window material. Panning can be installed in the opening or attached directly to the window before installation.

**Particle-dispersed glazing.** Glazing in which the orientation of small particles between two sheets of glass is controlled electrically, thus changing its optical properties.

**Passive solar heat gain.** The direct admittance of solar heat to a building (usually deliberately and in winter) through windows to reduce or eliminate the need for additional heating energy.

**Passive system.** A solar heating or cooling system that uses no external mechanical power to move the collected solar heat.

**Patterned glass.** One or both surfaces of glass with a rolled design; it is used for privacy and light diffusion.

**Peak demand.** The maximum hourly total building electricity use in the year. Electricity uses include space conditioning equipment such as chillers, fan coil units, electrical reheat coils, auxiliary equipment such as pumps and fans, electric lighting, and other office equipment (computers, copy machines, etc.).

**Peak load.** The maximum hourly total building heating or cooling load in the year.

**Performance (energy).** The thermal, solar, and visual properties of a product influence the building energy balance due to solar gains, heat loss, and daylight, and require auxiliary energy from artificial lighting, heating, and cooling; ventilation energy (fans) may also be affected. Therefore, a product has an impact on the overall primary energy use in a building.

**Performance class.** There are five window performance classes; R–Residential, LC–Light Commercial, C–Commercial, HC–Heavy Commercial, and AW–Architectural. This classification system provides for several levels of performance so the purchaser or specifier may select the appropriate level of performance depending on climatic conditions, height of installation, type of building, etc.

**Performance grade (design pressure).** The minimum level of design pressure (air, water, wind) a product must be tested at to achieve a particular rating.

**Perimeter heating.** A system of heating in which radiators or registers are located along the exposed wall, usually below windows; heated air from the heating devices counteracts the cold convection flow from the windows.

**Perm.** Empirical unit of water-vapor permeance (mass flow rate), equal to one grain (avoirdupois) of water vapor per hour flowing through one square foot of material or construction induced by a vapor-pressure difference of one inch of mercury between the two surfaces.

**Permeability.** The ability of a porous material to permit transmission of water vapor.

**Permeance.** A measure of the transmission of water vapor through a material expressed in units of "perms."

**Photochromic glazing, photochromics.** Glazing which changes its thermal, solar, and visible transmittance in response to outdoor illuminance or ultraviolet (UV) radiation. *See also* Switchable glazing.

**Photopic response function.** *See* V-lambda curve.

**Photovoltaic.** A device that produces electricity (voltage) directly from sunlight (photons).

**Pivot (pivoted) window.** A window with a sash that swings open or shut by revolving on pivots at either side of the sash, or at the top and bottom.

**Plastic film.** A thin, plastic substrate sometimes used as the inner layers in a triple- or quadruple-glazed window.

**Plate glass.** Flat glass with surfaces that are essentially plane and parallel; it is formed by a rolling process, ground, and polished on both sides. It is available in thicknesses varying from 1/8" to 1-1/4" (3.2 mm to 31.8 mm), but has been replaced by float glass.

**Point fixings.** In contrast to mullions or patch fittings, which project beyond the plane of the glazing, point fixings are interior. Typically, holes are drilled into the glass, and bolts or screws attach the glass in an interior frame structure.

**Polished wire glass.** Wire glass that is ground and polished on both sides.

**Polyvinylchloride.** *See* PVC.

**Prismatic glazing.** A daylighting device that consists of a light-redirecting glazing with a fine-structure, sawtooth cross-section, designed to refract incident sunlight and sky light toward the ceiling.

**Projected window.** A window fitted with one or more sashes opening on pivoted arms or hinges. The term refers to casements, awnings, and hoppers.

**Protected opening.** A window with a fire-resistance rating suitable for the wall in which it is located.

**Psychrometric chart**. A chart which shows various psychrometric quantities, like dry bulb and wet bulb temperatures, moisture content, partial pressure of water vapor, etc.

**PVC**. A polymer known as polyvinylchloride made by combining several chemicals, fillers, plasticizers, and pigments. It is often used as an extruded or molded plastic material for window framing or as a thermal barrier for aluminum windows.

**Pyrolytic coating**. A low-E, thin-film coating applied at high temperature. *See also* Hard coating.

**Radiant temperature**. The temperature describes the infrared radiant field at a certain position and is the weighted average of surface temperatures surrounding the location; the weighting is dependent on surface emissivity and the view factors to the measurement point.

**Radiation**. The transfer of heat, in the form of electromagnetic waves, from one surface to another. For example, energy from the sun reaches the earth by radiation, and a person's body can lose heat to a cold window or skylight surface in a similar way.

**Rail**. A horizontal member of a window sash or door panel. Also known as *head rail, top rail, bottom rail, meeting rail*.

**Rebate**. Part of a surround, the cross-section of which forms an angle into which the edge of the glass is received.

**Reflectance**. The fraction of incident radiation upon a surface that is reflected from that surface.

**Reflection**. The process by which incident flux leaves a surface or medium form the incident side, without change in frequency.

**Reflective glass**. Window glass that is coated to reflect radiation striking the surface of the glass.

**Reflectivity**. The reflectance of a microscopically homogeneous sample with a clean, optically smooth surface and of thickness sufficient to be completely opaque.

**Refraction**. The deflection of a light ray from a straight path when it passes at an oblique angle from one medium (such as air) to another (such as glass).

**Relative humidity**. The percentage of moisture in the air in relation to the amount of moisture the air could hold at that given temperature. At 100 percent relative humidity, moisture condenses and water droplets are formed.

**Ribbon window (window band)**. A series of windows in a row across the face of a building.

**Rolled glass**. A flat glass with a patterned or irregular surface, produced by rolling, and having varying transparency. Types include flat wire glass, corrugated glass, patterned glass, obscured glass, cast glass, and figured glass.

**Roll-up shade**. A window shade installed on inside of building that rolls up around a cylindrical holder at the top. These shades serve to maintain privacy, reflect some solar radiation, and reduce convection flow when fully extended. Also known as *roller shade*.

**Roof window**. A fixed or operable window similar to a skylight that is placed in the sloping surface of a roof. *See also* Skylight.

**Rough opening**. The framed opening in a wall into which a window or door unit is installed.

**R-value**. A measure of resistance to heat flow of a material or construction (insulating ability). The higher the R-value, the better the insulating effect and the lower the rate of heat flow.

**Safety glass**. Glass constructed, treated, or combined with other materials to reduce the likelihood of injury to persons in the broken or unbroken state. Types of safety glass include laminated safety glass, tempered glass, and wire glass.

**Sandblasting**. A method for creating a decorative effect on glass. Sandblasting consists of blasting an abrasive at the surface of the glass under pressure. Matte and peppered effects are achieved using different pressures and shading is achieved by changing the distance and pressure of blasting during application.

**Sash**. The portion of a window that includes the glass and framing sections which are directly attached to the glass. Not to be confused with the master frame into which the sash sections are fitted.

**Sealant**. A flexible material placed between two or more parts of a structure with adhesion to the joining surfaces to prevent the passage of certain elements such as air, moisture, water, dust, and other matter. Sealants are commonly made of silicone, butyl tape, or polysulfide.

**Selective surface**. A surface for which the spectral optical properties of reflectance, absorptance, emittance, or transmittance vary significantly with wavelength, enhancing the collection (or rejection) of radiant energy in a restricted portion of the spectrum.

**Setting block**. Small blocks made of neoprene, vinyl, etc., to distribute the weight of glass to the strong point of a sash or frame, to aid in centering the glass, and to prevent glass-to-metal contact.

**Shading Coefficient (SC)**. The ratio of solar heat gain through a window to the solar heat gain through a single layer of 3mm clear glass under the same environmental conditions. This is meaningful for near-normal incidence only. This quantity has been replaced by the Solar Heat Gain Coefficient (SHGC).

**Sheet glass**. Flat glass made by continuous drawing and whose surface has a characteristic waviness. Because of the long usage of the term, much thin float glass is still incorrectly referred to as sheet glass.

**Short-wave Infrared Radiation**. Short-wave infrared radiation is from 770 nm to 2500 nm (0.77 to 2.5 microns).

**Sidelighting**. Lighting from windows and translucent walls. Sidelighting historically was encouraged by the need for exterior views as well as light, and is best accomplished in buildings with narrow plans.

**Silk-screen process**. A decorating process in which a design is printed on glass through a silk mesh, woven wire, or similar screen. *See* Frit.

**Sill**. The lowest horizontal member in a door, window, sash, or ventilator frame. Also known as *sill plate, inside sill, outside sill*.

**Single-glazed, single glazing**. Glazing that is just one layer of glass or other glazing material (as opposed to sealed insulating glass which offers far superior insulating characteristics).

**Single-hung window**. A window consisting of two sashes, the top one stationary and the bottom movable. This window is similar to a double-hung window except that the top sash is stationary. *See also* Double-hung window.

**Skylight**. A sloped or horizontal application of a fenestration product which allows for daylighting. Skylights may be either fixed (non-operable) or venting (operating). Unlike roof windows, skylights need not provide provisions for the cleaning of exterior surfaces from the interior of the building. *See also* Sloped glazing, Roof window.

**Sliding window**. A window fitted with one or more sashes opening by sliding horizontally or vertically in grooves provided by frame members. Vertical sliders may be single- or double-hung.

**Sloped glazing**. A glass and framing assembly that is sloped more than 15 degrees from the vertical and essentially forms the entire roof of the structure. This is generally a single-slope construction. Also, any glazed opening in a sloped roof or wall, such as a stationary skylight or fully operable roof window.

**Smart window**. The generic term for windows with switchable coatings to control solar gain.

**Soft coat(ing)**. Generally refers to silver-based, low-E coating; see above. So called due to its susceptibility to damage through abrasion. The coating generally consists of a multilayer structure of alternate dielectric and thin transparent metal layers which are deposited in a vacuum chamber. Also known as *sputtered coating*.

**Solar absorptance**. The fraction of incident solar radiation absorbed by glazing.

**Solar control coatings**. Thin film coatings on glass or plastic that absorb or reflect solar energy, thereby reducing solar gain.

**Solar-control glazing**. Glazing modified to reduce its total solar energy transmittance by means of tinting, selective surface coating, or the application of a retrofit film.

**Solar heat gain**. Heat from solar radiation that enters a building.

**Solar Heat Gain Coefficient (SHGC)**. The fraction of solar radiation admitted through a window or skylight, both directly transmitted and absorbed, and subsequently released inward. The solar heat gain coefficient has replaced the shading coefficient as the standard indicator of a window's shading ability. It is expressed as a number between 0 and 1. The lower a window's solar heat gain coefficient, the less solar heat it transmits, and the greater its shading ability. SHGC can be expressed in terms of the glass alone or can refer to the entire window assembly. For near-normal incidence only, SHGC = 0.86 x SC. *See also* Shading Coefficient (SC).

**Solar radiation**. The total radiation of energy from the sun, including ultraviolet and infrared wavelengths as well as visible light.

**Sound-insulating glass**. Glazing that is fixed on resilient mountings and separated so as to reduce sound transmission. Also known as *sound-resistive glass*.

**Sound Transmission Class (STC)**. A single-number rating calculated in accordance with ASTM E 413 using sound transmission loss values. It provides an estimate of the sound insulation performance of an interior partition in common sound insulation situations. The frequency range used is typical of indoor office noises.

**Spacer**. The linear object that separates and maintains the space between the glass surfaces of insulating glass.

**Spandrel**. An exterior wall panel filling the space beneath a window sill that usually extends to the top of the window below in multistory construction.

**Spandrel glass**. Architectural glass that is used in spandrel panels.

**Spectrally selective coating**. A low-E coating with optical properties that are transparent to some wavelengths of energy and reflective to others. Typical spectrally selective coatings are transparent to visible light and reflect short-wave and long-wave infrared radiation.

**Spectrally selective tint**. A tinted glazing with optical properties that are transparent to some wavelengths of energy and reflective to others. Typical spectrally selective tints are transparent to visible light and reflect short-wave and long-wave infrared radiation.

**Spectrally selective glazing**. A specially engineered low-E coated or tinted glazing whose optical properties vary with wavelength. *See* Spectrally selective coating *and* Spectrally selective tint.

**Specular surface**. A mirrored surface which reflects light at the same angle as the light falling on the surface.

**Stile**. The main vertical members of the framework of a sash or door panel.

**Storefront**. A nonresidential system of doors and windows mulled as a composite structure. Typically designed for high use/abuse and strength. The storefront system is usually installed between floor and ceiling.

**Structural glass**. (1) Flat glass that is usually colored or opaque and frequently ground and polished, used for structural purposes. (2) Glass block, usually hollow, that is used for structural purposes.

**Structural glazing**. Glazing which is part of the structural design of a building.

**Substrate**. The underlying hard structure supporting a special purpose surface treatment (e.g. thin-film coating).

**Sun-control film**. A tinted or reflective film applied to the glazing surface to reduce visible, ultraviolet, or total transmission of solar radiation. It reduces solar heat gain and glare and, in some cases, can be removed and reapplied with changing seasons.

**Sunscoops**. Clerestory roof monitors oriented toward the sun, utilized when and where capturing direct light or solar gains are desired.

**Superwindow**. A window with a very low U-factor (typically less than 0.15) achieved through the use of multiple glazings, low-E coatings, and gas fills.

**Surface coating**. The deposition of a thin-film coating on a surface.

**Suspended film**. Polymer-based, optically clear glazing layer mounted between glass layers in a multiple-glazed system.

**Suspended glazing**. Glazing system suspended from above. This innovation, first achieved in projects of the 1960s, made possible continuous glass facades, without mullions.

**Switchable glazings**. Glazings with optical properties that can be reversibly switched from clear to dark or reflective with the application of an external stimulus, e.g. heat, light, electric signal, etc. Also known as *dynamic glazing*. *See also* Electrochromic glazing, Photochromic glazing, *and* Gasochromic glazing.

**Task lighting**. Light used to illuminate visually demanding activities, such as reading.

**Tempered glass**. Treated glass that is strengthened by reheating it to just below the melting point and suddenly cooling it. When shattered, it breaks into small pieces. Since these particles do not have the sharp edges and dagger points of broken annealed glass, tempered glass is regarded as a safety glass and safety glazing material. Tempered glass is also approximately five times stronger than standard annealed glass. The glass must be cut to size and have any other processing (such as edge polishing and hole drilling) completed before being subjected to toughening, because attempts to work the glass after tempering will cause it to shatter. Also known as *toughened glass*.

**Thermal barrier, thermal break**. An element, made of a material with relatively low thermal conductivity, which is inserted between two members having high thermal conductivity in order to reduce the heat transfer. Such elements are often used in aluminum windows.

**Thermal conductance (C)**. The same as thermal conductivity except that thickness is "as stated" rather than one inch.

**Thermal conduction**. The mode of heat transfer through a material by molecular contact. Heat flows from a high-temperature area to one of lower temperature.

**Thermal conductivity (k)**. The heat transfer property of materials, expressed in units of power per area and degree of temperature (e.g., Btu-per-hour per inch of thickness per square foot of surface per one degree F temperature difference).

**Thermal emissivity**. Similar to thermal emittance, except that the suffix "-ivity" refers to a property of general material, while "-ance" refers to a specific material with a certain thickness, surface finish, etc.

**Thermal emittance**. The ability of a surface to emit long-wave radiation relative to that of a perfect black body. Also known as the *long-wave infrared emittance*. A perfect black body has an emittance equal to 1.0, while a perfect reflector has an emittance equal to zero.

**Thermal mass**. The mass in a building (furnishings or structure) that is used to absorb solar gain during the day and release the heat as the space cools in the evening.

**Thermal radiation**. The heat transfer by radiation from surfaces at or near the room temperature (i.e., wavelengths in the range 2.5–50 microns). It is often referred to as far IR radiation or long-wave IR radiation.

**Thermal resistance.** A property of a substance or construction which retards the flow of heat; one measure of this property is R-value.

**Thermal shock.** A rapid change in temperature imposed on a glass body.

**Thermal stress.** Stress caused by the temperature differential across a glazing layer; e.g. for a tinted or switchable glazing in its darkened state, the sunlit side of the glazing will be hotter than the reverse side.

**Thermochromic glazing, thermochromics.** Glazing which changes its thermal, solar, and visible transmittance in response to its temperature. Because of absorption, the temperature of the glazing may differ from the ambient temperature.

**Thermogram.** An image of an object taken with an infrared camera that shows surface temperature variation.

**Tinted glass.** Glass that is colored by incorporation of a mineral admixture, by surface coating, or by the application of retrofit film. Any tinting reduces both visual and radiant transmittance.

**Toplighting.** Lighting from skylights, roof monitors or clerestories. Toplighting historically has been utilized when floor areas are too large to be illuminated adequately by sidelighting.

**Translucent.** Permitting light to pass through, but with differing degrees of obscuration and diffusion.

**Transmission.** The quantity of heat flowing through a unit area due to all modes of heat transfer induced by the prevailing conditions.

**Transmittance.** The percentage of radiation that can pass through glazing. Transmittance can be defined for different types of light or energy, e.g. visible light transmittance, UV transmittance, or total solar energy transmittance.

**Transom window.** The window sash located above a door. Also called *transom light.*

**Transparent.** Permitting light to pass through with clear vision.

**Transparent Insulation Material (TIM).** A generic name for a class of glazing materials having high visible transmittance and very low thermal transmittance. Includes so-called geometric media (honeycomb structures, aerogels, etc.). Some TIMs are translucent (diffusely transmitting) rather than transparent.

**Triple glazing, Triple-pane glass.** A window with three panes of glass or two outer panes of glass with a suspended plastic film in between. The layers are separated by two gas-filled spaces (usually Argon or Krypton) to increase energy efficiency and provide other performance benefits.

**UBC.** Uniform Building Code.

**U-factor.** The heat transmission in unit time through unit area of a material or construction and the boundary air films, induced by unit temperature difference between the environments on each side. A measure of the rate of non-solar heat loss or gain through a material or assembly. The lower the U-factor, the greater a window's resistance to heat flow and the better its insulating value. Also known as *U-value.*

**U-Factor (total).** The area-weighted average thermal transmittance of a complete window, including center-of-glass, edge-of-glass, and frame U-factors.

**Ultraviolet Radiation (UV).** Extremely short wavelength invisible radiation at the violet end of the visible spectrum. UV rays are found in everyday sunlight and can cause fading, chalking of dark paint finishes, or other damage. Extreme UV exposure can cause certain plastic materials to distort and can cause sunburn.

**Ultraviolet transmittance-weighted.** A measure of non-visible solar transmittance between 280 and 380 nanometers in wavelength.

**Vacuum glazing (window).** *See* Evacuated glazing.

**Vapor barrier.** A membrane or coating which resists the passage of water vapor from a region of high vapor pressure to low pressure, more accurately called a *vapor retarder.*

**Vapor retarder.** A material (usually in the form of a membrane or coating) that reduces the diffusion of water vapor across a building assembly, from a region of high vapor pressure to low vapor pressure.

**Venetian blind.** A light-controlling shading device consisting of overlapping thin, horizontal slats which can be raised or adjusted from wide open to closed positions by varying the tilt of the slats.

**Vinyl.** *See* PVC.

**Vinyl-clad window.** A window with exterior wood parts that are covered with extruded vinyl.

**Visible light.** The portion of the electromagnetic spectrum yielding light that can be seen. Wavelengths range from 380 to 720 nanometers.

**Visible Transmittance (VT).** The fraction of visible radiation transmitted by a glazing system between the limits of 380 and 770 nanometers (0.38–0.77 micrometers). It is weighted according to the photopic response of the human eye (V-lambda curve) and is expressed as a number between 0 and 1. Also known as *visible light transmittance (VLT).*

**Visible reflectance.** The measured amount of energy in the visible wavelength range that is reflected by a window system; it is expressed as a percentage.

**Visible spectrum.** That portion of the total radiation that is visible to the human eye and which lies between the ultraviolet and infrared portions of the electromagnetic spectrum. The colors associated with the visible spectrum range from violet, indigo, blue, green, yellow, orange, through red.

**Visual comfort.** A set of qualities associated with the amenity of a window, such as freedom from glare and excessive contrast.

**V-lambda curve.** A bell-shaped function describing the relative response of the human eye to solar radiation as a function of wavelength under bright light conditions. Also known as *photopic response function.*

**Warm edge.** Term used to describe technology that uses insulating spacers to achieve better thermal performance of an insulating glass unit, particularly evident in the increase of edge surface temperatures on the indoor side in the winter.

**Weatherstrip, weatherstripping.** A strip of resilient and flexible material for covering the joint between the window sash and frame in order to reduce air leaks and prevent water from entering the structure. Also, the process of applying such material.

**Window.** The frame, equipped with sash(es), ventilator(s) or louvers, if any, and their fittings, which, when glazed with glass or substitute for it, closes an opening for the admission of air and/or light in the wall of a building. (From the old Norse word "*vindauga,*" which is formed from "*vinder,*" wind, and "*auga,*" eye. Therefore, a window is an "eye for the wind" or "wind-eye.")

**Window-to-wall ratio (WWR).** The ratio of the total area of a building facade which is occupied by windows (glass area and frame).

**Window unit.** A complete window with sash and frame.

**Window wall.** A metal curtain wall of the commercial type in which windows are the most prominent element.

**Wind pressure.** The pressure produced by stopping the wind velocity; the main cause of air infiltration.

**Wire glass.** A glass with inner wire mesh for strength and fire-retardant qualities.

**Xerogel.** A type of transparent insulation material similar to aerogel but simpler to manufacture. It has both a higher visible transmittance and higher thermal conductivity than aerogel.

**Zenith.** The point on the skydome directly overhead, a 90 degree solar altitude.

# References and Bibliography

## GENERAL REFERENCES

AAMA. *Glass and Glazing.* Schaumberg, IL: American Architectural Manufacturers Association, 1997.

———. *Industry Statistical Review and Forecast.* Schaumberg, IL: American Architectural Manufacturers Association, 1995.

———. *Skylight Handbook: Design Guidelines.* Schaumberg, IL: American Architectural Manufacturers Association, 1988.

———. *Window Selection Guide.* Schaumberg, IL: American Architectural Manufacturers Association, 1988.

Advanced Lighting Technologies, Applications Guidelines: 1990, EPRI, CEC (EPRI TR-101022s).

Advanced Lighting Guidelines: 1993, EPRI, CEC, and DOE.

Al-Sahhaf, Nasr. "Contributions of Windows and Isovists to the Judged Spaciousness of Simulated Crew Cabins." Unpublished Masters Thesis, Dept. of Mechanical & Systems Engineering, The University of Washington. Seattle, WA: 1987.

American Institute of Architects. "Daylighting Design." *Architect's Handbook of Energy Practice.* Washington, DC: 1982.

———. "Shading and Sun Controls." *Architect's Handbook of Energy Practice.* Washington, DC: 1982.

Amstock, J.S. *Handbook of Glass in Construction.* New York: McGraw Hill, 1997.

Ander, Gregg D. *Daylighting Performance and Design.* New York: Van Nostrand Reinhold, 1995

———. *Daylighting Performance and Design,* 2nd ed. New York: John Wiley & Sons, 2003.

*Applications Manual: Window Design.* London: The Chartered Institution of Building Services Engineers (CIBSE), 1987.

Arasteh, D. "Advances in Window Technology: 1973–1993." *Advances in Solar Energy, An Annual review of Research and Development 9.* Boulder, CO: American Solar Energy Society, Inc.,1994. *Lawrence Berkeley Laboratory Report 36891.*

———. "Super Windows." *Glass Magazine* 5 (1989): 82–83.

Baird, George. *Architectural Expression of Environmental Control Systems.* London: Spon Press, 2001.

Baird, C. L., P. A. Bell. "Place attachment, isolation, and the power of a window in a hospital environment: a case study." *Psychol Rep,* 76, 3 Pt 1, (1995): 847–50.

Baker, N., A. Fanchiotti, K. Steemers, eds. *Daylighting in Architecture: A European Reference Book.* Brussels: James & James, 1993.

Banham, Reyner. *The Architecture of the Well-Tempered Environment,* London: Architectural Press, 1969.

———. *The Architecture of the Well-Tempered Environment* 2nd ed. Chicago: University of Chicago Press, 1984.

Behling, Sophia and Stefan. *Sol Power: The Evolution of Solar Architecture.* Munich: Prestel-Verlag, 1996.

———, eds. *Glass: Structure and Technology in Architecture.* Munich: Prestel-Verlag, 1999.

Benson, D. and E. Tracy. "Wanted: Smart Windows that Save Energy," *NREL in Review,* June 1992.

Benson, D.K. et al. *Solid-state Electrochromic Switchable Window Glazing.* Colorado: Solar Research Institute, 1996.

Benton, Charles and Marc Fountain. "Successfully Daylighting a Large Commercial Building: A Case Study of Lockheed Building 157." *Progressive Architecture* (November 1990): 119–21.

Boyce, Peter, Claudia Hunter and Owen Howlett. *The Benefits of Daylight through Windows,* Troy, NY: Lighting Research Center, Rensselaer Polytechnic Institute, 2003.

Bradshaw, V. *Building Control Systems.* New York: John Wiley and Sons, 1985.

Brown, G.Z. *Sun, Wind, and Light: Architectural Design Strategies* 2nd ed. New York: John Wiley and Sons, 2000.

Bryan, H. "Seeing the Light." *Progressive Architecture* (Sept. 1982).

Bryan, H., W. Kroner, and R. Leslie. *Daylighting: A Resource Book, Center for Architectural Research.* Troy, NY: Rensselaer Polytechnic Institute, 1981.

Buchanan, Peter *Renzo Piano Building Workshop,* vol. 3, *Complete Works.* London: Phaidon, 1997, 60.

Button, D. et al, ed.s *Glass in Building: A Guide to Modern Architectural Glass Performance.* Boston: Butterworth Architecture, 1993.

Byrd, H. and A. Hildon. "Daylighting: Appraisal at the Early Design Stages." *Lighting Research Technology* 11, no.2 (May 1979).

Carmody, John, Stephen Selkowitz, Dariush Arasteh and Lisa Heschong. *Residential Windows.* New York: W. W. Norton, 2000.

Caron, Julien. "A Villa of Le Corbusier, 1916." trans. Joan Ockmann. *Oppositions,* 15/16 (1979): 186–97, 196. Originally published as "Une villa de Le Corbusier 1916." *L'Esprit Nouveau,* no. 6, n.d., 679–704.

CEA. *Energy-Efficient Residential and Commercial Windows Reference Guide.* Montreal, PQ: Canadian Electricity Association, 1995.

Cerver, Francisco Asensio. *The Architecture of Glass: Shaping Light.* New York: Hearts Books, 1997.

Chong, C. V. Y. *Properties of Materials.* Plymouth: MacDonald and Evans, 1977.

CIE Technical Committee 4.2, E. Ne'eman and N. Ruck, eds. *Guide on Daylighting of Building Interiors, Part 1.* Vienna, Austria.

Collins, B. *Windows and People: A Literature Survey, Psychological Reaction with and without Windows.* National Bureau of Standards Building Science Series 70, 1975.

Compagno, Andrea. *Intelligent Glass Facades: Material, Practice, Design.* Basel: Birkhauser, 1999.

Cooper J. R., T. J. Wiltshire and A. C. Hardy. "Attitudes toward the use of heat rejecting/low light transmission glasses in office buildings." CIE TC-4.2 *Proceedings of the Symposium on Windows and their Function in Architectural Design.* Brussels: Committee Nationale Belge de l'Eclairage, 1973, V1–7.

Cuttle, Kit. "Subjective assessments of the appearance of special performance glazing offices." *Lighting Research and Technology* 11 no. 3 (1979): 140–49.

———. "People and Windows in Workplaces." *Conference on People and Physical Environment Research Proceedings.* Duncan Joiner, G. Brimilcombe, J. Daish, J. Gray, and D. Kernohan, eds. Wellington, New Zealand: New Zealand Ministry of Works and Development, 1983.

*Daylighting Manual.* Hull, Quebec: Public Works Canada, March 1990.

Dolden, M. "James Carpenter Profile" *Progressive Architecture* (May 1988).

Dordai, Philippe C. "Integrated Solutions for Daylighting." *Architectural Lighting* (April/May 1997): 64-66.

Douglas, R. and Susan Frank. *A History of Glass Making.* Henley-on-Thames: G. T. Foulis and Co. Ltd., 1972.

Dutton, H. "Structural Glass Design from La Villette, Paris and After" *Symposium Proceedings.* Technische Universiteit Delft, 1992.

Edwards, L. and P. Torcellini. *A Literature Review of the Effects of Natural Light on Building Occupants.* National Renewable Energy Laboratory Report (NREL/TP-550-30769), 2002.

Egan, M. D. *Concepts in Architectural Lighting.* New York: McGraw-Hill, 1983.

Egan, M. D. and V. Olgyay *Architectural Lighting* 2nd ed. New York: McGraw-Hill, 2001.

Energy Information Administration. *A Look at Commercial Buildings in 1995: Characteristics, Energy Consumption, and Energy Expenditures.* DOE/EIA-0625(95). (October 1998). U.S. Department of Energy, Washington, D.C. 20585.

Evans, B. *Daylighting in Architecture.* New York: McGraw-Hill, 1981.

Fanger, P. O. *Thermal Comfort.* New York: McGraw-Hill, 1970.

Flynn, J. E., A. W. Segil, and G. R. Steffy. *Architectural Interior Systems: Lighting, Acoustics, Air Conditioning* 2nd ed. New York: Van Nostrand Reinhold, 1988.

Fricke, J. "Aerogels." *Scientific American.* 258-5 (1988): 92–97.

Geller, H., and J. Thorne. *U.S. Department of Energy's Office of Building Technologies: Successful Initiatives of the 1990s.* Washington, DC: American Council for an Energy-Efficient Economy, 1999.

Gilmore, V. E. "Superwindows." *Popular Science* 3 (1986): 76.

Guzowski, Mary. *Daylighting for Sustainable Design.* New York: McGraw-Hill, 2000.

Harriman, L., G. Brundrett, and R. Keittler. *Humidity Control Design Guide for Commercial and Institutional Buildings.* Atlanta: American Society of Heating, Refrigerating and Air-Conditioning Engineers, 2001.

Hathaway, Warren E., J. A. Hargreaves, G. W. Thompson, and D. Novitsky. "A study into the effects of light on children of elementary school age—A case of daylight robbery" Edmonton: Policy and Planning Branch, Planning and Information Services Division, Alberta Education, 11160 Jasper Avenue, Edmonton, Alberta, T5K 0L2 (1993).

Herzog, Thomas, ed. *Solar Energy in Architecture and Urban Planning.* Munich: Prestel-Verlag, 1996.

Heschong Mahone Group. *Daylighting in Schools, An Investigation into the Relationship Between Daylighting and Human Performance.* A Report to Pacific Gas and Electric, 1999.

———. *Skylighting and Retail Sales, An Investigation into the Relationship Between Daylighting and Human Performance.* A Report to Pacific Gas and Electric, 1999.

Hill, B. *Small Office Building Handbook: Design for Reducing First Costs and Utility Costs.* New York: Van Nostrand Reinhold, 1985.

Hinrichs, Robert A. *Energy.* Fort Worth: Saunders College Publishing, 1991.

Hoke, John ed. *Architectural Graphic Standards* 9th ed. New York: AIA and John Wiley & Sons, 1994.

Humm, Othmar and Peter Toggweiler. *Photovoltaics in Architecture.* Basle: Birkhauser, 1993.

Illumination Engineering Society of North America. *Lighting Handbook.* 8th ed. New York: IESNA, 1993.

———. *Recommended Practice of Daylighting.* New York: IESNA, 1979.

International Code Council. International energy conservation code. International Code Council, Falls Church, VA. (2000).

International Energy Agency Report. "Daylight in Buildings: A Source Book on Daylighting Systems and Components." *Lawrence Berkeley Laboratory Report* 47493 (2000).

International Energy Agency Solar Heating and Cooling Programme. *Passive Solar Commercial and Institutional Buildings: A Sourcebook of Examples and Design Insights.* West Sussex, England: John Wiley & Sons, Ltd., 1994.

Johnson, Timothy. *Low-E Glazing Design Guide.* Boston: Butterworth-Heinemann, 1991.

Kaufman, J. and H. Haynes, eds. *IES Lighting Handbook: Reference Volume.* New York: Illuminating Engineering Society of North America, 1981.

Krewinkel, Heinz. *Glass Buildings: Material, Structure, and Detail.* Boston: Birkhauser, 1998.

Lam, William, *Perception and Lighting as Formgivers for Architecture.* New York: McGraw-Hill, 1987.

———. *Sunlighting as Formgiver for Architecture.* New York: Van Nostrand Reinhold, 1986.

Leather, Phil, Mike Pyrgas, Di Beale and Claire Lawrence. "Windows in the workplace: sunlight, view, and occupational stress." *Environment & Behavior* 30, no. 2. (Nov. 1998): 739–62.

Lee, E. S. "Spectrally Selective Glazings." *Federal Technology Alert,* New Technology Energy Management Program, Federal Energy Management Program, DOE/EE-0173, August 1998. http://www.eren.doe.gov/femp/prodtech/fed_techalert.html

Lee, E. S., S. Selkowitz, V. Bazjanac, V. Inkarojrit, C. Kohler. *High-Performance Commercial Building Facades.* Lawrence Berkeley Laboratory Report 50502 (2002).

*Life Cycle Cost Analysis—A Guide for Architects.* Washington, D. C.: AIA, 1977.

Lstiburek, Joseph and John Carmody. *Moisture Control Handbook.* New York: John Wiley & Sons, 1993.

Longmore, J. "The Engineering of Daylight." In Lynes, J.,ed.. *Developments in Lighting.* Essex: Applied Science Publishers, Ltd., 1978.

Lynes, J. "A Sequence for Daylighting Design," *Lighting Research and Technology.* (1979).

———. "Architects' Journal Handbook, Building Environment, Section 2: Sunlight: Direct and Diffused." *The Architects' Journal* Information Library. London: The Architectural Press, 1968.

McCluney, R. *Choosing the Best Window for Hot Climates.* Cape Canaveral, FL: Florida Solar Energy Center, 1993.

———. *Introduction to Radiometry and Photometry.* Boston: Artech House, 1994.

———. *Fenestration Solar Gain Analysis.* Cape Canaveral, FL: Florida Solar Energy Center, 1996.

———. "Let there be Daylight." *Window Rehabilitation Guide for Historic Buildings.* The Window Conference and Exposition for Historic Buildings II, National Park Service, Washington, DC (20 Feb. 1997): IV-45–54.

McCluney, R., M. Huggins, and C. Emrich. *Fenestration Performance: An Annotated Bibliography.* Cape Canaveral, FL: Florida Solar Energy Center, 1990.

McGowan, A. *Energy-Efficient Residential and Commercial Windows Reference Guide.* Montreal, Quebec: Canadian Electricity Association, 1995.

McKenna, Sean. "Let the Light Shine In." *Glass Magazine.* (March 1997): 43–45.

Mendler, S and W. Odell. *The HOK Guide to Sustainable Design.* New York: John Wiley & Sons, 2000.

Michael Hopkins and Partners. "Engineering Research and Prototype Development for Low-energy Buildings." Interim Report, Commission of the European Communities, CEC DGXII, Joule Programme, March 1994.

Moore, Fuller. *Concepts and Practice in Architectural Daylighting.* New York: Van Nostrand Reinhold, 1991.

National Research Council of Canada. "Window Performance and New Technology." *Proceedings of Building Science Insight Conference.* Ottawa, Ontario: National Research Council of Canada, 1988.

Natural Resources Canada. *Consumer's Guide to Buying Energy-Efficient Windows and Doors.* Ottawa, Ontario: Minister of Supply and Services, 1994.

Ne'eman, E. "A Comprehensive Approach to the Integration of Daylight and Electric Light in Buildings." *Energy and Buildings* 6 (1984).

Ne'eman, Light, and Hopkinson. "Recommendation for Admission and Control of Sunlight in Buildings," *Building and Environment,* no. 11 (1976): 91–101.

Neumann, Dietrich. "The Century's Triumph in Lighting: The Luxfer Companies and their Contribution to Early Modern Architecture." *Journal of the Society of Architectural Historians* (March 1995).

Nicklas, Michael H. and Gary B. Bailey. "Analysis of the performance of students in daylit schools." (l996). Report available from Innovative Design, 850 West Morgan St., Raleigh, NC 27603.

O'Connor, J., E. S. Lee, F. R. Rubinstein, S. E. Selkowitz. "Tips for Daylighting with Windows." *Lawrence Berkeley Laboratory Report 39945* (1997). http://eetd.lbl.gov/btp/pub/designguide.

Oesterle E., R. Lieb, M. Lutz, and W. Heusler. *Double-Skin Facades.* Munich: Prestel-Verlag, 2001.

Ojeda, Oscar Riera, ed. *Phoenix Central Library.* Gloucester, MA: Rockport Publishers, 1999.

Olgyay and Olgyay. *Solar Control and Shading Devices.* Princeton, NJ: Princeton University Press, 1957.

Othmar, Humm and Peter Toggweiler. *Photovoltaics in Architecture: The Integration of Photovoltaic Cells in Building Envelope.* Basel: Birkhauser, 1993.

Parker, Danny S., Philip W. Fairey III and Janet E. R. McIlvaine. "Energy Efficient Office Building Design for Florida's Hot and Humid Climate." *ASHRAE Journal* (April 1997): 49–58.

Rice, P. and H. Dutton. *Structural Glass* 2nd ed. New York: E & FN Spon, 1995.

Robbins, C. *Daylighting: Design and Analysis.* New York: Van Nostrand Reinhold, 1986.

Rundquist, R., T. McDougall, and J. Benya. *Lighting Controls: Patterns for Design.* Palo Alto, CA: Electric Power Research Institute, 1996 (available from IESNA).

Rush, R. *The Building System Integration Handbook.* New York: John Wiley & Sons, 1986.

Russell, James S. "Debis Tower, Berlin, Germany" *Architectural Record* (October 1998): 124–35.

Scheerbart, Paul. *Glasarchitektur (Glass Architecture)* (1914). New York: Praeger, 1972.

Schittich, C., G. Staib, D. Balkow, M. Schuler, W. Sobek. *Glass Construction Manual.* Basel: Birkhauser, 1999.

Schulitz, H. C., W. Sobek and K. J. Habermann. *Steel Construction Manual.* Basel: Birkhauser, 2000.

Schuman, J. "Cool Glazing." *Progressive Architecture* (April 1992).

Selkowitz, S. "High-Performance Glazing Systems: Architectural Opportunities for the 21st Century" Presented at the Glass Processing Days (GPD), Tampere, Finland, June 1999. *Lawrence Berkeley Laboratory Report 42724.*

———."Influence of Windows on Building Energy Use." Presented at Windows in Building Design and Maintenance, Gothenburg, Sweden, June 1984.

Stein, B., J. Reynolds and W. McGuinness, *Mechanical and Electrical Equipment for Buildings,* 7th ed. New York: John Wiley and Sons, 1986.

———. "Smart Windows." *Glass Magazine* (August 1986).

Selkowitz, S. and S. LaSourd. "Amazing Glazing." *Progressive Architecture* (June 1994).

Terman, M., S. Fairhurst, B. Perlman, J. Levitt, and R. McCluney. "Daylight Deprivation and Replenishment: A Psychobiological Problem with a Naturalistic Solution." Proceedings of International Daylighting Conference, Long Beach, CA, 1986.

Thayer, Burke Miller. "Daylit Durrant Middle School." *Solar Today* (November/December 1995): 36.

Tuluca, Adrian. *Energy Efficient Design and Construction for Commercial Buildings.* New York: McGraw-Hill, 1997.

Turner, D.P. *Window Glass Design Guide.* London: The Architectural Press, 1977.

Turner, W. *Energy Management Handbook.* Lilburn, GA: Fairmont Press, 1993.

Villecco, M., S. Selkowitz and J. Griffith. "Strategies of Daylight Design." *AIA Journal* (September 1979).

Watson, D., ed. *The Energy Design Handbook.* Washington, DC: AIA Press, 1993.

Wigginton, Michael. *Glass in Architecture.* London: Phaidon Press Limited, 1996.

———. "Glass Today" *Report and Proceedings of the Glass in the Environment Conference.* London: London Crafts Council, 1986.

Wigginton, M. and Battle McCarthy. 2000. *Environmental Second Skin Systems.* http://www.battlemccarthy.demon.co.uk/research/doubleskin/doubleskinhomepage.htm

Willmert, Todd. "Prismatic Daylighting Systems." *Architectural Record* (August 1999): 177–79.

Wilson, A. "Lighting Controls: Beyond the Toggle Switch." *Environmental Building News* 12, no. 6 (June 2003).

Winheim, L., R. Riegel and M. Shanus. "Case Study: Lockheed Building 157: An Innovative Deep Daylighting Design for Reducing Energy Consumption." Presented at 6th World Energy Engineering Congress, Atlanta, December 1993.

## TECHNICAL REFERENCES AND STANDARDS

AAMA 501. "Test Methods for Exterior Walls." Schaumburg, IL: American Architectural Manufacturers Association.

AAMA 501.4, 501.6. "Recommended Static Test Method for Evaluating Curtain Wall and Storefront Systems Subjected to Seismic and Wind Induced Interstory Drifts" and "Recommended Dynamic Test Method for Determining a Seismic Drift Causing Glass Fallout From a Wall System." Schaumburg, IL: American Architectural Manufacturers Association.

AAMA 502-90. "Voluntary Specification for Field Testing of Windows and Sliding Glass Doors." Schaumburg, IL: American Architectural Manufacturers Association.

AAMA 503-92. "Voluntary Specification for Field Testing of Metal Storefronts, Curtain Walls and Sloped Glazing Systems." Schaumburg, IL: American Architectural Manufacturers Association.

AAMA 701/702-01. "Voluntary Specifications for Pile Weatherstripping and Replaceable Fenestration Weatherseals." Schaumburg, IL: American Architectural Manufacturers Association.

AAMA 850-91. *Fenestration Sealants Guide Manual.* Schaumburg, IL: American Architectural Manufacturers Association.

AAMA 1503-98. "Voluntary Test Method for Thermal Transmittance and Condensation Resistance of Windows, Doors and Glazed Wall Sections." Schaumburg, IL: American Architectural Manufacturers Association.

AAMA 1504-97. "Voluntary Standard for Thermal Performance of Windows, Doors and Glazed Wall Sections." Schaumburg, IL: American Architectural Manufacturers Association.

AAMA 1801-97. "Voluntary Specification for the Acoustical Rating of Windows, Doors and Glazed Wall Sections." Schaumburg, IL: American Architectural Manufacturers Association.

AAMA CW-11. "Design Wind Loads and Boundary Layer Wind Tunnel Testing." Schaumburg, IL: American Architectural Manufacturers Association.

AAMA CW-12. "Structural Properties of Glass." Schaumburg, IL: American Architectural Manufacturers Association.

AAMA CW-RS-1. "The Rain Screen Principle and Pressure-Equalized Wall Design." Schaumburg, IL: American Architectural Manufacturers Association.

AAMA SFM-87. "Aluminum Storefront and Entrance Manual." Schaumburg, IL: American Architectural Manufacturers Association.

AAMA TIR A1–02. "Sound Control for Fenestration Products." Schaumburg, IL: American Architectural Manufacturers Association.

AAMA and CMHC/SCHL, CW-RS-2. "Rain Penetration Control—Applying Current Knowledge." Schaumburg, IL: American Architectural Manufacturers Association.

AAMA and WDMA 101/I.S. 2-97. "Voluntary Specifications for Aluminum, Vinyl (PVC) and Wood Windows and Glass Doors." Schaumburg, IL: American Architectural Manufacturers Association.

AAMA and WDMA 1600/I.S. 7. "Voluntary Specification for Skylights." Schaumburg, IL: American Architectural Manufacturers Association.

AGSL. 1992. "Vision3, Glazing System Thermal Analysis — User Manual." Dept. of Mechanical Engineering, University of Waterloo, Waterloo, Ontario, N2L 3G1 Canada, Aug. 1992.

Allen, C. W. *Astrophysical Quantities.* London: The Athlone Press, University of London, 1973.

ASCE 7. "Minimum Design Loads for Buildings and Other Structures." Reston, VA: American Society of Civil Engineers.

ASHRAE. *ASHRAE Applications Handbook*. Atlanta: American Society of Heating, Refrigerating and Air-Conditioning Engineers, 1995.

———. *ASHRAE Handbook of Fundamentals*. Atlanta: American Society of Heating, Refrigerating and Air-Conditioning Engineers, 1993.

———. "Energy Efficient Design of New Buildings Except Low-Rise Residential Buildings." ASHRAE/IES Standard 90.1-1989. Atlanta: American Society of Heating Refrigerating and Air-Conditioning Engineers, Inc., 1989.

———. "Energy Efficient Design of New Buildings Except Low-Rise Residential Buildings." ASHRAE/IES Standard 90.1-1999. Atlanta: American Society of Heating, Refrigerating and Air-Conditioning Engineers, Inc., 1999.

———. "Energy-Efficient Window Design." *ASHRAE Technical Data Bulletin* 66, no. 2 (1990).

———. "Fenestration." *ASHRAE Handbook of Fundamentals*. Atlanta: American Society of Heating, Refrigerating, and Air-Conditioning Engineers, 1997.

———. Method of measuring solar-optical properties of materials. ANSI/ASHRAE Standard 74-1988.

———. "Standard Method for Determining and Expressing the Heat Transfer and Total Optical Properties of Fenestration Products." Draft of ASHRAE Standard, February 1996.

———. "Thermal Environmental Conditions for Human Occupancy." ANSI/ASHRAE Standard 55-1992. Atlanta: American Society of Heating, Refrigerating and Air-Conditioning Engineers, Inc., 1992.

ASTM E 84. "Test Method for Surface Burning Characteristics of Building Materials." Philadelphia, PA: American Society of Testing Materials.

ASTM E 90-81. "Recommended practice for laboratory measurements of airborne sound transmission loss of building partitions." Philadelphia, PA: American Society for Testing and Materials.

ASTM E 90-94. "Test method of Laboratory Measurement of Airborne Sound Transmission Loss of Building Partitions." Philadelphia, PA: American Society of Testing Materials.

ASTM E 283-91. "Standard Test Method for Determining Rate of Air Leakage Through Exterior Windows, Curtain Walls, and Doors Under Specified Pressure Differences Across the Specimen." Philadelphia, PA: American Society for Testing and Materials.

ASTM E 330. "Standard Test Method for Structural Performance of Exterior Windows, Curtain Walls, and Doors by Uniform Static Air Pressure Difference." Philadelphia, PA: American Society of Testing Materials.

ASTM E 331. "Standard Test Method for Water Penetration of Exterior Windows, Skylights, Doors, and Curtain Walls by Uniform Static Air Pressure Difference." Philadelphia, PA: American Society of Testing Materials.

ASTM E 413-87(94). "Classification for Rating Sound Insulation." Philadelphia, PA: American Society of Testing Materials.

ASTM E 546. "Standard Test Method for Frost Point of Sealed Insulating Glass Units." Philadelphia, PA: American Society of Testing Materials.

ASTM E 547. "Standard Test Method for Water Penetration of Exterior Windows, Skylights, Doors, and Curtain Walls by Cyclic Static Air Pressure Difference." Philadelphia, PA: American Society of Testing Materials.

ASTM E 576. "Standard Test Method for Frost Point of Sealed Insulating Glass Units in the Vertical Position." Philadelphia, PA: American Society of Testing Materials.

ASTM E 773-88. 1988. "Standard Test Method for Seal Durability of Sealed Insulated Glass Units." Philadelphia, PA: American Society for Testing and Materials.

ASTM E 774-92. 1992. "Standard Specification for Sealed Insulated Glass Units." Philadelphia, PA: American Society for Testing and Materials.

ASTM E 891-87. 1987a. "Standard Tables for Terrestrial Direct Normal Solar Spectral Irradiance for Air Mass 1.5." Philadelphia, PA: American Society for Testing and Materials (now part of standard ASTM G 159-98).

ASTM E 892-87. 1987b. "Standard Tables for Terrestrial Solar Spectral Irradiance at Air Mass 1.5 for a 37∞Tilted Surface." Philadelphia, PA: American Society for Testing and Materials (now part of standard ASTM G 159-98).

ASTM E 903-82. 1982. Standard test method for solar absorptance, reflectance, and transmittance of materials using integrating spheres. Philadelphia, PA: American Society for Testing and Materials.

ASTM E 971-88. 1988a. Standard practice for calculation of photometric transmittance and reflectance of materials to solar radiation. Philadelphia, PA: American Society for Testing and Materials.

ASTM E 972-88. 1988b. Standard test method for solar photometric transmittance of sheet materials using sunlight. Philadelphia, PA: American Society for Testing and Materials.

ASTM E 997. "Standard Test Method for Structural Performance of Glass in Exterior Windows, Curtain Walls, and Doors Under the Influence of Uniform Static Loads by Destructive Methods." Philadelphia, PA: American Society of Testing Materials.

ASTM E 998. "Standard Test Method for Structural Performance of Glass in Windows, Curtain Walls, and Doors Under the Influence of Uniform Static Loads by Nondestructive Method." Philadelphia, PA: American Society of Testing Materials.

ASTM C 1036. "Standard Specification for Flat Glass."Philadelphia, PA: American Society of Testing Materials.

ASTM C 1048. "Standard Specification for Heat-Treated Flat Glass-Kind HS, Kind FT Coated and Uncoated."Philadelphia, PA: American Society of Testing Materials.

ASTM E 1084-86. 1986. Standard test method for solar transmittance (terrestrial) of sheet materials using sunlight. Standard. Philadelphia, PA: American Society for Testing and Materials.

ASTM E 1105. "Standard Test Method for Water Penetration of Installed Exterior Windows, Curtain Walls and Doors by Uniform or Cyclic Static Air Pressure Difference." Philadelphia, PA: American Society of Testing Materials.

ASTM E 1233. "Standard Test Method for Structural Performance of Exterior Windows, Curtain Walls, and Doors by Cyclic Static Air Pressure Differential." Philadelphia, PA: American Society of Testing Materials.

ASTM E 1300. "Standard Practice for Determining the Minimum Thickness of Annealed Glass Required to Resist a Specified Load." Philadelphia, PA: American Society of Testing Materials.

ASTM E 1300-00. "Standard Practice for Determining Load Resistance of Glass in Buildings." Philadelphia, PA: American Society of Testing Materials.

ASTM E 1300-94. "Standard Practice for Determining the Minimum Thickness and Type of Glass Required to Resist a Specific Load." Philadelphia, PA: American Society for Testing and Materials.

ASTM E 1332-90. "Classification for Determination of Outdoor-Indoor Transmission Class." Philadelphia, PA: American Society of Testing Materials.

ASTM E 1425-91. "Practice for Determining the Acoustical Performance of Exterior Windows and Doors." Philadelphia, PA: American Society of Testing Materials.

ASTM E 1887. "Standard Test Method for Fog Determination." Philadelphia, PA: American Society of Testing Materials.

ASTM E 1887. "Standard Test Method for Performance for Exterior Windows, Curtain Walls, Doors, and Storm Shutters Impacted by Missiles and Exposed to Cycle Pressure Differentials." Philadelphia, PA: American Society of Testing Materials.

ASTM E 1996. "Standard Specification for Performance of Exterior Windows, Curtain Walls, Doors and Storm Shutters Impacted by Windborne Debris in Hurricanes." Philadelphia, PA: American Society of Testing Materials.

ASTM E 2074. "Standard Test Method for Fire Test of Door Assemblies, Including Positive Pressure Testing of Side-Hinged and Pivoted Swinging Door Assemblies." Philadelphia, PA: American Society of Testing Materials.

ASTM E 2010. "Standard Test Method for Positive Pressure Fire Test for Window Assemblies." Philadelphia, PA: American Society of Testing Materials.

ASTM E 2188. "Standard Test Method for Insulating Glass Unit Performance." Philadelphia, PA: American Society of Testing Materials.

ASTM E 2189 ."Standard Test Method for Testing Resistance to Fogging in Insulating Glass Units." Philadelphia, PA: American Society of Testing Materials.

ASTM E 2190. "Standard Specification for Insulating Glass Unit Performance and Evaluation." Philadelphia, PA: American Society of Testing Materials.

ASTM F 1642. "Standard Test Method for Glazing and Glazing Systems Subject to Air Blast Loadings." Philadelphia, PA: American Society of Testing Materials.

ANSI/American Society of Heating, Refrigerating, and Air-Conditioning Engineers. 1988. "Method of measuring solar-optical properties of materials." Standard 74-88.

Arasteh, D. "Advances in Window Technology: 1973–1993." In *Advances in Solar Energy, An Annual Review of Research and Development* Vol. 9. Karl W. Böer, ed. Boulder, CO: American Solar Energy Society, Inc., 1994. *Lawrence Berkeley Laboratory Report 36891* (1995).

Arasteh, D., F. Beck, N. Stone, W. duPont, and M. Koenig. "Phase I Results of the NFRC U-Value Procedure Validation Project." *ASHRAE Transactions* 100, no. 1 (1994). *Lawrence Berkeley Laboratory Report 34270.*

Arasteh, D.; E. U. Finlayson, D. Curcija, J. Baker, C. Huizenga. "Guidelines For Modeling Projecting Fenestration Products." *ASHRAE Transactions* 104, pt. 1. (1998).

Arasteh, D., J. Hartman and M. Rubin. "Experimental Verification of a Model of Heat Transfer Through Windows," Proceedings of the ASHRAE Winter Meeting, *Symposium on Fenestration Performance,* New York, NY, 1987.

Arasteh, D., R. Johnson, S. Selkowitz and R. Sullivan. "Energy Performance and Savings Potentials with Skylights." *ASHRAE Transactions* 91, no. 1 (1984):154–79. *Lawrence Berkeley Laboratory Report 17457.*

Arasteh, D., R. Mathis and W. duPont. "The NFRC Window U-Value Rating Procedure." Proceedings of Thermal Performance of the Exterior Envelopes of Buildings V. Clearwater Beach, FL, 1992. *Lawrence Berkeley Laboratory Report 32442.*

Arasteh, D., S. Reilly and M. Rubin. "A Versatile Procedure for Calculating Heat Transfer Through Windows." Presented at ASHRAE Meeting. Vancouver, British Columbia, June 1989. *Lawrence Berkeley Laboratory Report 27534.*

Arasteh, D. and S. Selkowitz. "Prospects for Highly Insulating Window Systems." Presented at Conservation in Buildings: Northwest Perspective, Butte, MT, May 1985. (sponsored by the National Center for Appropriate Technology). *Lawrence Berkeley Laboratory Report 19492.*

———. "A Superwindow Field Demonstration Program in Northwest Montana." Proceedings of Thermal Performance of the Exterior Envelopes of Buildings IV, Orlando, FL, Dec. 1989. *Lawrence Berkeley Laboratory Report 26069.*

Arasteh, D., S. Selkowitz and J. Hartman. "Detailed Thermal Performance Data on Conventional and Highly Insulating Window Systems." Proceedings of the BTECC Conference, Clearwater Beach, FL, 1985. *Lawrence Berkeley Laboratory Report 20348.*

Arasteh, D., S. Selkowitz and J. Wolfe. "The Design and Testing of a Highly Insulating Glazing System for Use with Conventional Window Systems." *Journal of Solar Energy Engineering* 111 (1989): 44–53. *Lawrence Berkeley Laboratory Report 24903.*

Arasteh, D., E. Finlayson, J. Huang, C. Huizenga, R. Mitchell and M. Rubin. "State-of-the-Art Software for Window Energy-Efficiency Rating and Labeling." Proceedings of the ACEEE 1998 Summer Study on Energy Efficiency in Buildings. *Lawrence Berkeley Laboratory Report 42151.*

Arasteh, D., E. Finlayson, D. Curcija, J. Baker and C. Huizenga. "Guidelines for Modeling Projecting Fenestration Products." *ASHRAE Transactions* 104, no.1 (1998). *Lawrence Berkeley Laboratory Report 40707.*

Arasteh, D. et al. "Recent Technical Improvements to the WINDOW Computer Program." Proceedings of the Windows Innovations Conference, Toronto, Ontario, CANMET, June 1995.

———. "WINDOW 4.1: A PC Program for Analyzing Window Thermal Performance in Accordance with Standard NFRC Procedures." Publ. LBL-35298. Berkeley, CA: Lawrence Berkeley Laboratory, Energy & Environment Division, 1993.

Arens, E. A., R. Gonzalez, L. Berglund. "Thermal Comfort Under an Extended Range of Environmental Conditions." *ASHRAE Trans* 9286, Part 1 (1986).

Aschehoug, O., M. Thyholt, I. Andresen, and B. Hugdal. "Frame and Edge Seal Technology: A State of the Art Survey." Trondheim, Norway: IEA Solar Heating and Cooling Program, Norwegian Institute of Technology, 1994.

Bass, Michael, ed. *Handbook of Optics, Vol. I –Fundamentals, Techniques, and Design* 2nd ed. Optical Society of America, New York. New York: McGraw-Hill, 1995.

Beason, W.L. "A Failure Prediction Model for Window Glass." PhD dissertation. Lubbock, TX: Texas Tech University, 1980.

Beason, W.L., T.L. Kohutek, and J.M. Bracci. "Basis for ASTM E 1300 Annealed Glass Thickness Selection Charts." *Journal of Structural Engineering* vol. 124, no.2 (1998).

Beck, F. "A Validation of the WINDOW4/FRAME3 Linear Interpolation Methodology," *ASHRAE Transactions* 100, no.1 (1994).

Beck, F., B. Griffith, D. Turler, and D. Arasteh. "Using Infrared Thermography for the Creation of a Window Surface Temperature Database to Validate Computer Heat Transfer Models." Proceedings of the Windows Innovations Conference, Toronto, Ontario, CANMET, June 1995. *Lawrence Berkeley Laboratory Report 36975.*

Bell, L. H. *Industrial Noise Control, Fundamentals and Applications.* New York: Marcel Dekker, Inc., 1982.

Beltrán, L.O., E.S. Lee, K.M. Papamichael, S.E. Selkowitz. "The Design and Evaluation of Three Advanced Daylighting Systems: Light Shelves, Light Pipes and Skylights." Proceedings of the Solar '94, Golden Opportunities for Solar Prosperity, American Solar Energy Society, June 25–30, 1994, San Jose, CA. *Lawrence Berkeley Laboratory Report 34458.*

Beltrán, L.O., E.S. Lee, S.E. Selkowitz. "Advanced Optical Daylighting Systems: Light Shelves and Light Pipes." *Journal of the Illuminating Engineering Society* 26, no. 2 (1997): 91–106. *Lawrence Berkeley Laboratory Report 38133.*

———. "Advanced Optical Daylighting Systems: Light Shelves and Light Pipes," Proceedings of the 1996 IESNA Conference, Cleveland, OH.

Bird, R.E. and R.L. Hulstrom. *Terrestrial solar spectral data sets.* SERI/TR-642-1149. Solar Energy Research Institute, 1982.

Bliss, R. W. "Atmospheric Radiation Near the Surface of the Ground." *Solar Energy* 5, no. 3 (1961):103.

Bodmann, H. W. "Elements of Photometry, Brightness and Visibility." *Lighting Research and Technology* 24 (1992): 29–42.

Brambley, M. and S. Penner. "Fenestration Devices for Energy Conservation I: Energy Savings During the Cooling Season." *Energy* (Feb. 1979).

Brandle, K. and R. Boehm. "Air-Flow Windows: Performance and Applications." Proceedings of Exterior Envelopes of Buildings Conference II: ASHRAE, Dec. 1982.

Braun, R. and FIRST INITIAL?] Meisel. "Large Scale Electrochromic Glazings," *SPIE* 1728 (1992).

"Building Systems Automation-Integration." Proceedings of the 1991 and 1992 International Symposiums, University of Wisconsin–Madison, 1993.

Burt, W., D. A. Button, P. Foulkes, J. A. Lynes, T. A. Markus, P. G. Owens, and P. H. Parkin. *Windows and Environment.* Pilkington Brothers Ltd. Newton-le-Willows, England: McCorquodale & Co Ltd, 1969.

Byars, N., and D. Arasteh. "Design Options for Low-Conductivity Window Frames." *Solar Energy Materials and Solar Cells* 25 (1992). Elsevier Science Publishers B.V. and *Lawrence Berkeley Laboratory Report 30498.*

Canadian Standards Association. *Windows.* Publication CAN/CSA-A440. Rexdale, Ontario: Canadian Standards Association, 1990.

———. *Windows/User selection guide to CSA standards.* Publication CAN/CSA A440-M90/A440.1-M90. Rexdale, Ontario: Canadian Standards Association, 1991.

———. *Energy Performance Evaluation of Windows and Sliding Glass Doors.* Publication CAN/CSA A440.2-93. Rexdale, Ontario: Canadian Standards Association, 1993.

———. *Energy Performance Evaluation of Swinging Doors.* Publication CSA A453-95. Rexdale, Ontario: Canadian Standards Association, 1995.

CANMET. *A Study of the Long Term Performance of Operating and Fixed Windows Subjected to Pressure Cycling.* Ottawa, Ontario: Efficiency and Alternative Energy Technology Branch, CANMET. M91-7/214-1993E.

———. *Long Term Performance of Operating Windows Subjected to Motion Cycling.* Ottawa, Ontario: CANMET. M91-7/235-1993E.

Carpenter, S., and A. McGowan. "Frame and Spacer Effects on Window U-Value." *ASHRAE Transactions* 95, no. 1 (1989).

———. "Effect of Framing Systems on the Thermal Performance of Windows." *ASHRAE Transactions* 99, no. 1 (1993).

Carpenter, S. and A. Elmahdy. "Thermal Performance of Complex Fenestration Systems." *ASHRAE Transactions* 100, no. 2 (1994).

Carpenter, S. and J. Hogan. "Recommended U-factors for Swinging, Overhead and Revolving Doors." *ASHRAE Transactions* [vol??no.??] (1996).

Collins, R., and S. Robinson. *Evacuated Glazing.* Sydney, Australia: University of Sydney Press, 1996.

Curcija, D., and W. P. Goss. "Two-Dimensional Finite Element Model of Heat Transfer in Complete Fenestration Systems." *ASHRAE Transactions* 100, no. 2 (1994).

———. "Three-Dimensional Finite Element Model of Heat Transfer in Complete Fenestration Systems." Proceedings of Window Innovations Conference, Toronto, Ontario, 1995.

———. "New Correlations for Convective Heat Transfer Coefficient on Indoor Fenestration Surfaces: Compilation of More Recent Work." Proceedings of Thermal Performance of the Exterior Envelopes of Buildings VI, Clearwater Beach, FL, 1995.

Curcija, D., W. P. Goss, J. P. Power and Y. Zhao. *Variable-h' Model for Improved Prediction of Surface Temperatures in Fenestration Systems.* Amherst, MA: University of Massachusetts, 1996.

de Abreu, P., R. A. Fraser, H. F. Sullivan, and J. L. Wright. "A Study of Insulated Glazing Unit Surface Temperature Profiles Using Two-Dimensional Computer Simulation." *ASHRAE Transactions* 102, no. 2 (1996).

DiBartolomeo, D.L., E.S. Lee, F.M. Rubinstein, S.E. Selkowitz. "Developing a Dynamic Envelope/Lighting Control System with Field Measurements." *Journal of the Illuminating Engineering Society* 26 no. 1 (1997): 146–64. *Lawrence Berkeley Laboratory Report 38130.*

Dietrich, U. "Partly Transparent Shading Systems Based on Holografic-optical Elements," *Solar Energy in Architecture and Urban Planning* 3. European Conference CEC in Florence, Italy. Felmersham, Bedford, UK: H.S. Stephens and Associates, May 1993.

Duffie, J. A. and W. A. Beckman. *Solar Engineering of Thermal Processes.* New York: John Wiley & Sons, Inc., 1980.

Elmahdy, A. H. "A Universal Approach to Laboratory Assessment of the Condensation Potential of Windows." Presented at the 16th Annual Conference of the Solar Energy Society of Canada, Ottawa, Ontario, 1990.

———. "Air Leakage Characteristics of Windows Subjected to Simultaneous Temperature and Pressure Differentials." Proceedings of the Windows Innovations Conference, Toronto, Ontario, CANMET, 1995.

———. "Surface temperature measurement of insulating glass units using infrared thermography." *ASHRAE Transactions* 102, Part 2 (1996).

Elmahdy, A. H., and S. A. Yusuf. "Determination of Argon Concentration and Assessment of the Durability of High Performance Insulating Glass Units Filled with Argon Gas." *ASHRAE Transactions* 101, Part 2 (1995).

ElSherbiny, S. M. et al. "Heat Transfer by Natural Convection Across Vertical and Inclined Air Layers." *Journal of Heat Transfer* 104 (1982): 96–102.

EN 1279. "Insulating Glass Units." European glazing durability standard.

Enermodal Engineering Ltd. *FRAME/VISION Window performance modelling and sensitivity analysis.* Ottawa, Ontario: Institute for Research in Construction, National Research Council of Canada, 1990.

———. "The Effect of Frame Design on Window Heat Loss: Phase 1." Ottawa, Ontario: Enermodal Engineering Ltd., 1987.

———. *The FRAMEplus Toolkit for Heat Transfer Assessment of Building Components.* Kitchener, Ontario and Denver, CO: Enermodal Engineering Ltd., 1995.

Ewing, W. B. and J. I. Yellott. "Energy Conservation through the Use of Exterior Shading of Fenestration. *ASHRAE Transactions* 82, no. 1 (1976):703–33.

Finlayson E., D. Arasteh, C. Huizenga, D. Curcija, M. Beall and R. Mitchell. "THERM 2.0: Program Description." *Lawrence Berkeley Laboratory Report 37371 Rev.*

Finlayson, E. U. et. al. *Window 4.0: Documentation of Calculation Procedures.* Berkeley, CA: Lawrence Berkeley Laboratory, 1993. *Lawrence Berkeley Laboratory Report 33943.*

Fountain, M. and C. Huizenga. ASHRAE Thermal Comfort Program Version 1.0. Berkeley, CA: Center for Environmental Design Research, University of California, Berkeley, CA 94720, 1994.

Friedrich, M. and M. Messinger. "Method to Assess the Gross Annual Energy-Saving Potential of Energy Conservation Technologies Used in Commercial Buildings." *ASHRAE Transactions* 101 no.1 (1995): 444–53.

Galanis, N. and R. Chatiguy. "A Critical Review of the ASHRAE Solar Radiation Model." *ASHRAE Transactions* 92, no. 1 (1986).

Galitz, C. L. and A. R. Whitlock. "Simulating Design Storms with Water Chamber Testing." Water Problems in Building Exterior Walls: Evaluation, Prevention, and repair, Third Volume, ASTM STP 1352. J. A. Boyd and M.J Scheffler, eds. Philadelphia, PA: American Society of Testing Materials.

Galitz, C. L. and A. R. Whitlock. "The Application of Local Weather Data to the Simulation of Wind-Driven Rain." Water Leakage Through Building Facades, ASTM STP 1314. R. J. Kudder and J. L. Erdly, eds. Philadelphia, PA: American Society of Testing Materials.

Gates, D. M. "Spectral Distribution of Solar Radiation at the Earth's Surface." *Science* 151, no. 2 (1966): 3710.

Glass Association of North America. *GANA Glazing Manual, 1997 Edition.* Topeka, KS: Glass Association of North America, 1997.

Granqvist, C.G. "Electrochromic Coatings for Smart Windows: a Status Report." *Renewable Energy, Second World Energy Congress,* vol.1. Oxford: Pergamon Press, 1992.

———. *Handbook of Inorganic Electrochromic Materials.* Amsterdam: Elsevier, 1995.

Griffith, B., F. Beck, D. Arasteh, and D. Turler. "Issues Associated with the Use of Infrared Thermography for Experimental Testing of Insulated Systems." Proceedings of Thermal Performance of the Exterior Envelopes of Buildings VI, Clearwater Beach, FL, December 1995. *Lawrence Berkeley Laboratory Report 36734.*

Griffith, B., D. Curcija, D. Turler and D. Arasteh. "Improving Computer Simulations of Heat Transfer for Projecting Fenestration Products: Using Radiation View-Factor Models." *ASHRAE Transactions* 104, no. 1 (1998). *Lawrence Berkeley Laboratory Report 40706.*

Griffith, B.; E. Finlayson, M. Yazdanian and D. Arasteh. "The Significance of Bolts in the Thermal Performance of Curtain-Wall Frames for Glazed Facades." *ASHRAE Transactions,* 105, Part 1 (1998).

Griffith, B., D. Turler and D. Arasteh. "Surface Temperature of Insulated Glazing Units: Infrared Thermography Laboratory Measurements." *ASHRAE Transactions* 102, no. 2 (1996).

Griffith, B. and D. Arasteh. "Buildings Research Using Infrared Imaging Radiometers with Laboratory Thermal Chambers." *Proceedings of the SPIE* 3700 (April 6–8, 1999). *Lawrence Berkeley Laboratory Report 42682.*

GSA. "Standard Test Method for Glazing and Glazing Systems Subject to Air Blast Loadings." Washington, DC: U. S. General Services Administration.

Gueymard, C. A. "An Anisotropic Solar Irradiance Model for Tilted Surfaces and Its Comparison with Selected Engineering Algorithms." *Solar Energy* 38 (1987): 367–86.

———. "Development and Performance Assessment of a Clear Sky Spectral Radiation Model." Proceedings of the 22nd Annual Solar Conference. Washington, DC: American Solar Energy Society, 1993.

———. "A Simple Model of the Atmospheric Radiative Transfer of Sunshine: Algorithms and Performance Assessment." Cape Canaveral, FL: Florida Solar Energy Center, 1995. *Florida Solar Energy Center Report FSEC-PF-270-95.*

———. "Critical analysis and performance assessment of clear sky solar irradiance models using theoretical and measured data." *Solar Energy* (1993)

Harris, D. A. *Noise Control Manual for Residential Buildings.* New York: McGraw-Hill, 1997.

Harrison, S., and S. van Wonderen. "A Test Method for the Determination of Window Solar Heat Gain Coefficient." *ASHRAE Transactions* 100, no. 1 (1994).

Hartman, J., M. Rubin, and D. Arasteh. "Thermal and Solar-Optical Properties of Silica Aerogel for Use in Insulated Windows." Presented at the 12th Annual Passive Solar Conference, Portland, OR, July 1987. *Lawrence Berkeley Laboratory Report 23386*.

Hawthorne W., Reilly M. S. "The Impact of Glazing Selection on Residential Duct Design and Comfort." *ASHRAE Transactions* 106, Part 1 (2000).

Hickey, J. R. et al. "Observations of the Solar Constant and Its Variations: Emphasis on Nimbus 7 Results." Presented at the Symposium on the Solar Constant and the Special Distribution of Solar Irradiance, Hamburg, Germany, IAMAP 1981.

Hogan, J. F. "A summary of tested glazing U-values and the case for an industry wide testing program." *ASHRAE Transactions* 94, no. 2 (1988).

Hollands, K. G. T. and J. L. Wright. "Heat loss coefficients and effective ta products for flat plate collectors with diathermous covers." *Solar Energy* 30 (1982): 211–16.

Huizenga, C., D. Arasteh, E. Finlayson, R. Mitchell, B. Griffith and D. Curcija. "Teaching Students About Two-Dimensional Heat Transfer Effects in Buildings, Building Components, Equipment, and Appliances Using THERM 2.0." *ASHRAE Transactions* 105, no. 1 (1999). *Lawrence Berkeley Laboratory Report 42102*.

———. "THERM 2.0: A Building Component Model For Steady-State Two-Dimensional Heat Transfer." Building Simulation September 1999. IBSPA. *Lawrence Berkeley Laboratory Report 43991*.

IGMA A-6001-01. "Technical Manual for Acoustical Glass." Ottawa, Ontario: Insulating Glass Manufacturers Alliance, www.igmaonline.org.

IGMA TM-4000-02. "Insulating Glass Manufacturing Quality Procedure Manual." Ottawa, Ontario: Insulating Glass Manufacturing Alliance, www.igmaonline.org.

International Symposium on Optical Materials Technology for Energy Efficiency and Solar Energy Conversion XIII, Friedrichsbau, Freiburg, Germany, April 1994.

Iqbal, M. *An Introduction to Solar Radiation*. Toronto: Academic Press, 1983.

Johnson, R. et al. "The Effects of Daylighting Strategies on Building Cooling Loads and Overall Energy Performance." (January 1986) Presented at ASHRAE/DOE/BTECC Conference on Thermal Performance of the Exterior Envelopes of Buildings III, Florida, December 1985.

Jennings, Judith D., Francis M. Rubinstein, Dennis DiBartolomeo. "Comparison of Control Options in Private Offices in an Advanced Lighting Controls Testbed." (2000) Proceedings of the 1999 IESNA Annual Conference, New Orleans, LA, August 9, 1999. LBNL-43096REV.

Johnson, B. *Heat Transfer through Windows*. Stockholm, Sweden: Swedish Council for Building Research, 1985.

Keyes, M. W. Analysis and Rating of Drapery Materials Used for Indoor Shading. *ASHRAE Transactions* 73, no. 1 (1967).

Klems, J. H. "Method of Measuring Nighttime U-Values Using the Mobile Window Thermal Test (MoWitt) Facility." *ASHRAE Transactions* 98, no. 2 (1992). *Lawrence Berkeley Laboratory Report 30032*.

———. "Methods of Estimating Air Infiltration through Windows." *Energy and Buildings* 5 (1983): 243–52. *Lawrence Berkeley Laboratory Report 12891*.

———. "A New Method for Predicting the Solar Heat Gain of Complex Fenestration Systems: I. Overview and Derivation of the Matrix Layer Calculation." *ASHRAE Transactions* 100, no. 1 (1994a): 1065–72.

———. "A New Method for Predicting the Solar Heat Gain of Complex Fenestration Systems: II. Detailed Description of the Matrix Layer Calculation." *ASHRAE Transactions* 100, no. 1 (1994a): 1073–86.

———. "Solar Heat Gain Through Fenestration Systems Containing Shading: Procedures for Estimating Performance From Minimal Data." Berkeley, CA: Windows and Daylighting Group, Lawrence Berkeley National Laboratory, 2000.

———. "U-values, solar heat gain, and thermal performance: Recent studies using the MoWitt." *ASHRAE Transactions* 95, no. 1 (1989).

Klems J. H. and J. L. Warner. "Solar Heat Gain Coefficient of Complex Fenestrations with a Venetian Blind for Differing Slat Tilt Angles." *ASHRAE Transactions* 103, no.1 (1997). *Lawrence Berkeley Laboratory Report 39248*.

Klems, J. H. and H. Keller. "Thermal Performance Measurements of Sealed Insulating Glass Units with Low-E Coatings Using the MoWitt Field Test Facility." Presented at the ASHRAE Winter Meeting, Symposium on Fenestration Performance, New York, January 1987. *Lawrence Berkeley Laboratory Report 21583*.

Klems, J. H. and G. O. Kelley. "Calorimetric Measurements of Inward-Flowing Fraction for Complex Glazing and Shading Systems." *ASHRAE Transactions* (1995).

Klems, J. H. and J. L. Warner. "Measurement of Bidirectional Optical Properties of Complex Shading Devices." *ASHRAE Transactions* 101, no. 1 (1995): 791–801.

Klems, J. H., M. Yazdanian and G. Kelley. "Measured Performance of Selective Glazings." Proceedings of Thermal Performance of the Exterior Envelopes of Buildings VI, Clearwater Beach, FL, 1995. *Lawrence Berkeley Laboratory Report 37747*.

Klems J. H., J. Warner and G. Kelley. "A comparison between calculated and measured SHGC for complex glazing systems." *ASHRAE Transactions* 102, no.1 (1996). *Lawrence Berkeley Laboratory Report 37037*.

Kopec, J. W. *The Sabines at Riverbank, Their Role in the Science of Architectural Acoustics*. Woodbury, NY: Acoustical Society of America, 1997.

Lampert, C. "Chromogenic Switchable Glazing: Towards the Development of the Smart Window." Proceedings of Window Innovations Conference. Toronto, Canada: CANMET, 1995. *Lawrence Berkeley Laboratory Report 37766*.

Lampert, C.M. "Large-area smart glass and integrated photovoltaics." *Solar Energy Materials and Solar Cells* 76 (2003): 489–99.

Lawrence Berkeley National Laboratory. "Windows for Energy Efficient Buildings" U.S. Department of Energy 1, no. 2 (January 1980).

———. "WINDOW 4.1 — A PC Program for Analyzing Window Thermal Performance of Fenestration Products." LBL – 35298. Berkeley, CA: Windows and Daylighting Group, Lawrence Berkeley Laboratory, 1994.

———. "THERM 1.0: A PC Program For Analyzing The Two-Dimensional Heat Transfer Through Building Products." LBL-37371. Berkeley, CA: Windows and Daylighting Group, Lawrence Berkeley Laboratory, 1996.

Lee, E. S., L. O. Beltrán, S. E. Selkowitz, H. Lau, and G. D. Ander. "Demonstration of a Light-Redirecting Skylight System at the Palm Springs Chamber of Commerce." Proceedings from the ACEEE 1996 Summer Study on Energy Efficiency in Buildings, 4:229-241. Washington, D.C.: American Council for an Energy-Efficient Economy. *Lawrence Berkeley Laboratory Report 38131*.

Lee, E. S., D. L. DiBartolomeo. "Application issues for large-area electrochromic windows in commercial buildings." *Solar Energy Materials & Solar Cells* 71 (2002): 465–91. *Lawrence Berkeley Laboratory Report 45841*.

Lee, E. S., D. L. DiBartolomeo, S. E. Selkowitz. "The Effect of Venetian Blinds on Daylight Photoelectric Control Performance." *Journal for the Illuminating Engineering Society* 28, no. 1. (1998): 3–23. *Lawrence Berkeley Laboratory Report 40867*.

———. "Thermal and Daylighting Performance of an Automated Venetian Blind and Lighting System in a Full-Scale Private Office." *Energy and Buildings* 29, no. 1 (1998):47–63. *Lawrence Berkeley Laboratory Report 40509*.

———. "Electrochromic windows for commercial buildings: Monitored results from a full-scale testbed." Presented at the ACEEE 2000 Conference and published in the *Proceedings from the ACEEE 2000 Summer Study on Energy Efficiency in Buildings: Energy Efficiency in a Competitive Environment, August 20–25, 2000, Asilomar, Pacific Grove, CA*. Washington, D. C.: American Council for an Energy-Efficient Economy, 2000. *Lawrence Berkeley Laboratory Report 45415*

Lee, E. S., D. L. DiBartolomeo, E. L. Vine, S. E. Selkowitz. "Integrated Performance of an Automated Venetian Blind/Electric Lighting System in a Full-Scale Private Office." Thermal Performance of the Exterior Envelopes of Buildings VII, Conference Proceedings, Clearwater Beach, FL, December 7–11, 1998. *Lawrence Berkeley Laboratory Report 41443.*

Lee, E. S. and S. E. Selkowitz. "The Design and Evaluation of Integrated Envelope and Lighting Control Strategies for Commercial Building." *ASHRAE Transactions* 95 no.101. (1995): pt. 1, 326–42. *Lawrence Berkeley Laboratory Report 34638.*

———. "Establishing the Value of Advanced Glazings." Proceedings of Glass in Buildings: An international conference on the use of glass as an architectural/engineering form and material, March 31–April 1, 1999, University of Bath, U.K. *Lawrence Berkeley Laboratory Report 42761.*

———. "Design and Performance of an Integrated Envelope/Lighting System." *ICBEST '97 Proceedings*, International Conference on Building Envelope Systems and Technology, 15–17 April 1997, University of Bath, U.K: 375–80. *Lawrence Berkeley Laboratory Report 39729.*

———. "Integrated Envelope and Lighting Systems for Commercial Buildings: A Retrospective." *Proceedings from the ACEEE 1998 Summer Study on Energy Efficiency in Buildings: Energy Efficiency in a Competitive Environment, August 23–28, 1998. Asilomar, Pacific Grove, CA.* Washington, D.C.: American Council for an Energy-Efficient Economy. *Lawrence Berkeley Laboratory Report 40967.*

Lee, E. S., S. E. Selkowitz, M. S. Levi, S. L. Blanc, E. McConahey, M. McClintock, P. Hakkarainen, N. L. Sbar, M. P. Myser. "Active Load Management with Advanced Window Wall Systems: Research and Industry Perspectives." *Proceedings from the ACEEE 2002 Summer Study on Energy Efficiency in Buildings: Teaming for Efficiency, August 18–23, 2002, Asilomar, Pacific Grove, CA.* Washington, D. C.: American Council for an Energy-Efficient Economy, 2002. *Lawrence Berkeley Laboratory Report 50855.*

Lingnell, A.W. "Glass and Glazing Relative to Curtainwall Design." *U. S. Glass* (Feb., 1994).

———. "Glass Deflection Characteristics for Wall System Design." *U. S. Glass* (Oct. ,1994).

Lingnell, A.W. and W. L. Beason."A Thermal Stress Evaluation Procedure for Monolithic Glass." ASTM Symposium on Use of Glass in Buildings. Pittsburgh, PA: April, 2002.

Lyons, P., D. Arasteh and C. Huizenga. "Window Performance for Human Comfort." ASHRAE, February 2000. *Lawrence Berkeley Laboratory Report 44032.*

Meyer-Arendt, J. R. "Radiometry and Photometry: Units and Conversion Factors." *Applied Optics* 7 (1968): 2081–84.

McCabe, M. E. et al. "U-value measurements for windows and movable insulations from hot box tests in two commercial laboratories." *ASHRAE Transactions* 92, no. 1 (1986).

McCluney, R. "Determining Solar Radiant Heat Gain of Fenestration Systems." *Passive Solar Journal* 4, no. 4 (1987): 439–87.

———. "Awning Shading Algorithm Update," *ASHRAE Transactions* 96, Part 1 (1990).

———. "The Death of the Shading Coefficient?" *ASHRAE Journal* (March 1991): 36–45.

———. *Introduction to Radiometry and Photometry.* Boston: Artech House, 1994.

———. "Sensitivity of Optical Properties and Solar Gain of Spectrally Selective Glazing Systems to Changes in Solar Spectrum" Proceedings of the 22nd Annual Solar Conference. Washington, DC: American Solar Energy Society, 1993.

———. "Angle of Incidence and Diffuse Radiation Influences on Glazing System Solar Gain," Proceedings of the Annual Solar Conference. San Jose, CA: American Solar Energy Society, 1994.

———. "Sensitivity of Fenestration Solar Gain to Source Spectrum and Angle of Incidence." *ASHRAE Transactions* 10 (1996).

McCluney, R. and C. Gueymard. "SUNSPEC 1.0, Operating Manual," Florida Solar Energy Center report number FSEC-SW-3-92, September 17, 1992. Florida Solar Energy Center, 1679 Clearlake Rd., Cocoa, FL 32922

McCluney, R. and L. Mills. "Effect of Interior Shade on Window Solar Gain." *ASHRAE Transactions* 99, no. 2 (1993).

Moeck, M., E. S. Lee, R. Sullivan, S. E. Selkowitz. "Visual Quality Assessment of Electrochromic and Conventional Glazings." *Solar Energy Materials and Solar Cells* 54 no.1/4 (Aug. 1998): 157–64. *Lawrence Berkeley Laboratory Report 38132.*

Moon, P. "Proposed standard solar radiation curves for engineering use." *Journal of the Franklin Institute* 11 (1940): 583.

Moore, G. L. and C. W. Pennington. "Measurement and Application of Solar Properties of Drapery Shading Materials." *ASHRAE Transactions* 73, no. 1 (1967).

Nagai, J. "Recent Development in Electrochromic Glazings," *SPIE* 1728 (1992).

NFRC 100-97. "NFRC 100-97: Procedure for Determining Fenestration Product U-Factors." National Fenestration Rating Council, Silver Spring, Maryland, 1997.

NFRC 100-97a. "NFRC 100-97 Attachment A: NFRC Test Procedure for Measuring the Steady-State Thermal Transmittance of Fenestration Systems." National Fenestration Rating Council, Silver Spring, Maryland, 1997.

NFRC 100-99. "NFRC 100 Section B: Procedure for Determining Door System Product Thermal Properties (Currently Limited to U-values)." National Fenestration Rating Council, Silver Spring, Maryland, 1999.

NFRC 200-95. "NFRC 200-95: Procedure for Determining Fenestration Product Solar Heat Gain Coefficients at Normal Incidence,." National Fenestration Rating Council, Silver Spring, Maryland, 1995.

NFRC 300-94. "NFRC 300-94: Procedures for Determining Solar Optical Properties of Simple Fenestration Products." National Fenestration Rating Council, Silver Spring, Maryland, 1994.

NFRC 301-93. "NFRC 301-93: Standard Test Method for Emittance of Specular Surfaces Using Spectrometric Measurements." National Fenestration Rating Council, Silver Spring, Maryland, 1993.

NFRC 400-95. "NFRC 400-95: Procedure for Determining Fenestration Product Air Leakage." National Fenestration Rating Council, Silver Spring, Maryland, 1995.

NFRC 500. "NFRC 500-2001: Procedure for Determining Fenestration Product Condensation Resistance Values." National Fenestration Rating Council, Silver Spring, Maryland, 2001.

NFRC. "User Guide to NFRC 500: Procedure for Determining Fenestration Product Condensation Resistance Values." NFRC Special Publication 500UG-2002. National Fenestration Rating Council, Silver Spring, Maryland, 2002.

NFRC. Spectral Data Library available through www.nfrc.org/software.html, 2000.

Nicodemus, F. E. "Radiance." *American Journal of Physics* 31 (1963): 368.

Nicodemus, F. E. et al. "Self-study manual on optical radiation measurements, Part I—Concepts." NBS Technical Notes 910-1, 910-2, 910-3, and 910-4. National Bureau of Standards (now National Institute of Standards and Technology), 1976–84

———. "Geometrical considerations and nomenclature for reflectance." NBS Monograph 160, NBS (now NIST), October 1977.

Norville, H. S. and E. J. Conrath. "Consideration for blast-resistant glazing design." *Journal of Architectural Engineering* (September 2001).

Ozisik, N. and L. F. Schutrum. "Solar Heat Gain Factors for Windows with Drapes." *ASHRAE Transactions* 66 (1960).

Papamichael, K. "New Tools for the Analysis and Design of Building Envelopes." In the proceedings of Thermal Performance of the Exterior Envelopes of Buildings VI, Clearwater Beach, FL (1995). *Lawrence Berkeley Laboratory Report 36281.*

Papamichael, K., L. Beltrán, R. Furler, E. S. Lee, S. Selkowitz, and M. Rubin. "The Energy Performance of Prototype Holographic Glazings." (1994). Proceedings SPIE International Symposium on Optical Materials Technology for Energy Efficiency and Solar Energy Conversion XIII, April 18–22, 1994, Freiburg, Germany. *Lawrence Berkeley Laboratory Report 34367.*

Parmelee, G. V. and R. G. Huebscher. "Forced Convection Heat Transfer from Flat Surfaces." *ASHRAE Transactions* 53 (1947).

Parmelee, G. V. and W. W. Aubele. "Radiant Energy Emission of Atmosphere and Ground." *ASHRAE Transactions* 58 (1952).

Patenaude, A. "Air Infiltration Rate of Windows Under Temperature and Pressure Differentials." Proceedings of Window Innovation Conference. Toronto, Ontario: CANMET, 1995.

Pennington, C. W. "How Louvered Sun Screens Cut Cooling, Heating Loads." *Heating, Piping, and Air Conditioning* (Dec. 1968).

Pennington, C. W. et al. "Experimental Analysis of Solar Heat Gain through Insulating Glass with Indoor Shading." *ASHRAE Journal* 2 (1964).

Pennington, C. W. and G. L. Moore. "Measurement and Application of Solar Properties of Drapery Shading Materials." *ASHRAE Transactions* 73, no. 1 (1967).

Pennington, C. W., C. Morrison and R. Pena. "Effect of Inner Surface Air Velocity and Temperatures Upon Heat Loss and Gain through Insulating Glass." *ASHRAE Transactions* 79, no. 2 (1973).

Perez, R. et al. "An Anisotropic Hourly Diffuse Radiation Model for Sloping Surfaces—Description, Performance Validation, and Site Dependency Evaluation." *Solar Energy* 36 (1986): 481–98.

Pierpoint, W. and J. Hopkins. "The derivation of a new area source equation." Presented at the Annual Conference of the Illuminating Engineering Society, Atlanta, August 1982.

Raswick, Jerry. "Specifying Fire Rated Glass and Framing." *Construction Specifier* (July 2002): 48–53.

Reilly, M.S. "Spacer Effects on Edge-of Glass and Frame Heat Transfer." *ASHRAE Transactions* 31, no. 3 (1994).

Reilly, M. S., D. Arasteh and S. Selkowitz. "Thermal and Optical Analysis of Switchable Window Glazings." *Solar Energy Materials* 22 (1991). Elsevier Science Publishers B.V. *Lawrence Berkeley Laboratory Report 29629.*

Reilly S., F. Winkelmann, D. Arasteh and W. Carroll. "Modeling Windows in DOE-2.1E." Thermal Performance of the Exterior Envelopes of Buildings V Conference Proceedings, December 7–10, 1992, Clearwater Beach, FL. *Lawrence Berkeley Laboratory Report 33192.*

Rousseau, J. and R. L. Quiroutte. "Rainscreen Computer Program." Water Leakage Through Building Facades, ASTM STP 1314. J. A. Boyd and M.J Scheffler, eds. Philadelphia, PA: American Society of Testing Materials.

———. "A Review of Pressure Equalization and Compartmentalization Studies of Exterior Walls for Rain Penetration Control." Water Leakage Through Building Facades, ASTM STP 1314. J. A. Boyd and M.J Scheffler, eds. Philadelphia, PA: American Society of Testing Materials.

Rubin, M. "Calculating heat transfer through windows." *International Journal of Energy Research* 6 (1982): 341–49. *Lawrence Berkeley Laboratory Report 12246.*

———. "Optical Constants and Bulk Optical Properties of Soda Lime Silica Glasses for Windows." Berkeley, CA: Lawrence Berkeley Laboratory, 1984. *Lawrence Berkeley Laboratory Report 13572.*

———. "Optical Properties of Soda Lime Silica Glasses." *Solar Energy Materials* 12 (1985).

———. "Solar Optical Properties of Windows." *International Journal of Energy Research* 6 (1982): 123–33. *Lawrence Berkeley Laboratory Report 12246.*

Rubin, M., R. Powles and K. von Rottkay. "Models for the Angle-Dependent Optical Properties of Coated Glazing Materials." *Solar Energy* 66, no. 4 (1999): 267–76.

Rudoy, W. and F. Duran. "Effect of Building Envelope Parameters on Annual Heating/Cooling Load." *ASHRAE Journal* 7 (1975).

Rundquist, R. A. "Calculation procedure for daylighting and fenestration effects on energy and peak demand." *ASHRAE Transactions* 97, no 2 (1991).

Selkowitz, S. "Thermal Performance of Insulating Window Systems." *ASHRAE Transactions* 85, no. 2 (1981). *Lawrence Berkeley Laboratory Report 08835.*

———. "Window Performance and Building Energy Use: Some Technical Options for Increasing Energy Efficiency." Proceedings of Energy Sources: Conservation and Renewables, AIP Conference, Washington, DC, April 1985. *Lawrence Berkeley Laboratory Report 20213.*

Selkowitz, S. and Bazjanac, V. "Thermal Performance of Managed Window Systems." *ASHRAE Transactions* 85, no. 1 (1981): 392–408. *Lawrence Berkeley Laboratory Report 09933.*

Selkowitz, S., M. Rubin, E. Lee, and R. Sullivan. "A Review of Electrochromic Window Performance Factors." Proceedings of SPIE International Symposium on Optical Materials Technology for Energy Efficiency and Solar Energy Conversion XIII, Friedrichsbau, Freiburg, Germany, April 1994. *Lawrence Berkeley Laboratory Report 35486.*

Selkowitz, S. and C. Lampert. "Application of Large-Area Chromogenics to Architectural Glazings." In *Large Area Chromogenics: Materials and Devices for Transmittance Control*, C. Lampert, ed. SPIE, 1989. *Lawrence Berkeley Laboratory Report 28012.*

Selkowitz, S. E., E. S. Lee. "Advanced Fenestration Systems for Improved Daylight Performance." Proceedings of the International Daylighting Conference, May 10–13, 1998, Ottawa, Ontario, Canada: 341–348. *Lawrence Berkeley Laboratory Report 41461.*

Shewen, E. C. "A Peltier-effect technique for natural convection heat flux measurement applied to the rectangular open cavity." Ph.D. thesis, Department of Mechanical Engineering, University of Waterloo, Ontario, 1986.

Simko T., R. Collins, F. Beck and D. Arasteh. "Edge Conduction in Vacuum Glazing. Thermal Performance of the Exterior Envelopes of Buildings." VI Conference Proceedings, December 4–8, 1995, Clearwater Beach, FL. *Lawrence Berkeley Laboratory Report 36958.*

Smith, Joseph L. *Designing for Antiterrorism*. Vicksburg, MS: Applied Research Associates, Inc., 2002: 1–19.

Smith, W. A. and C. W. Pennington. "Shading Coefficients for Glass Block Panels." *ASHRAE Journal* 5 (Dec. 1964).

Sodergren, D. and T. Bostrom. "Ventilating with the Exhaust Air Window." *ASHRAE Journal* 13, no. 4 (1971).

Sterling, E. M. A., Arundel, T. D. Sterling. "Criteria for Human Exposure in Occupied Buildings." *ASHRAE Transactions* 91, no. 1 (1985).

Sullivan, R., L. Beltran, M. Rubin and S. Selkowitz. "Energy and Daylight Performance of Angular Selective Glazings." Proceedings of Thermal Performance of the Exterior Envelopes of Buildings VII, Clearwater Beach, FL, December 7–11, 1998. *Lawrence Berkeley Laboratory Report 41694.*

Sullivan, R., E. Lee, K. Papamichael, M. Rubin, and S. Selkowitz. "Effect of Switching Control Strategies on the Energy Performance of Electrochromic Windows." Proceedings of SPIE International Symposium on Optical Materials Technology for Energy Efficiency and Solar Energy Conversion XIII, Friedrichsbau, Freiburg, Germany, April 1994. *Lawrence Berkeley Laboratory Report 35453.*

Sullivan, R., E. S. Lee, M. Rubin, S. Selkowitz. "The Energy Performance Of Electrochromic Windows In Heating-Dominated Geographic Locations." Proceedings of SPIE International Symposium on Optical Materials Technology for Energy Efficiency and Solar Energy Conversion XV, September 16–19, 1996, Konzerthaus, Freiburg, Germany. *Lawrence Berkeley Laboratory Report 38252.*

Sullivan, R.; E. S. Lee; and S. Selkowitz. 1992. "A Method of Optimizing Solar Control and Daylighting Performance in Commercial Office Buildings." Proceedings of Thermal Performance of the Exterior Envelopes of Buildings V, December 7–10, 1992, Clearwater Beach, FL. *Lawrence Berkeley Laboratory Report 32931.*

Sullivan, R. and F. Winkelmann. "Validation Studies of the DOE-2 Building Energy Simulation Program." August 1998. *Lawrence Berkeley Laboratory Report 42241.*

Sullivan, H. F. and J. L. Wright. "Recent improvements and sensitivity of the VISION glazing system thermal analysis program." Proceedings of the 12th Passive Solar Conference, ASES/SESCI, Portland, OR, 1987. 145–49.

Sullivan, H. F., J. L. Wright and R. A. Fraser. "Overview of a Project to Determine the Surface Temperatures of Insulated Glazing Units: Thermographic Measurement and 2-D Simulation." *ASHRAE Transactions* 102, no. 2 (1996).

Sweitzer, G., D. Arasteh, and S. Selkowitz. "Effects of Low-E Glazing on Energy Use Patterns in Nonresidential Daylighting Buildings." *ASHRAE Transactions* 93, no. 1 (1986): 1553–566. *Lawrence Berkeley Laboratory Report 21577.*

TSC. "WinSARC: Solar Angles and Radiation Calculation for MS Windows." *User's Manual.* Tempe, AZ: Tait Solar Co., Inc., 1996.

Threlkeld, J. L. and R. C. Jordan. "Direct solar radiation available on clear days." *ASHRAE Transactions* 64 (1958): 45.

Threlkeld, J. L. "Thermal environmental engineering." 321. New York: Prentice Hall, 1962.

Turler D., B. Griffith and D. Arasteh. "Laboratory Procedures for Using Infrared Thermography to Validate Heat Transfer Models." ASTM Third Symposium on "Insulation Materials: Testing and Applications: Third Volume," ASTM STP 1320. R.S. Graves and R. R. Zarr, eds. Quebec City, Quebec, Canada : American Society for Testing and Materials, 1997. *Lawrence Berkeley Laboratory Report 38925.*

Van Dyke, R. L. and T. P. Konen. *Energy Conservation through Interior Shading of Windows: An Analysis, Test and Evaluation of Reflective Venetian Blinds.* Berkeley, CA: Lawrence Berkeley Laboratory, March 1982. *Lawrence Berkeley Laboratory Report 14369,*

Vild, D. J. "Solar Heat Gain Factors and Shading Coefficients." *ASHRAE Journal* 10 (1964): 47.

Vine, E., E. S. Lee, R. Clear, D. DiBartolomeo, S. Selkowitz. "Office Worker Response to an Automated Venetian Blind and Electric Lighting System: A Pilot Study." *Energy and Buildings* 28 no. 2 (1998): 205–18. *Lawrence Berkeley Laboratory Report 40134.*

Warner, J., S. Reilly, S. Selkowitz, and D. Arasteh. "Utility and Economic Benefits of Electrochromic Smart Windows." Proceedings of the ACEEE 1992 Summer Study on Energy Efficiency. Pacific Grove, CA: ACEEE, June 1992. *Lawrence Berkeley Laboratory Report 32638.*

Wehrli, "Extraterrestrial Solar Spectrum." Publ. No. 615. Davos, Switzerland: Physikalisch Metrologisches Observatorium and World Radiation Data Center, 1985.

Wilson, H. R. "Potential of Thermotropic Layers to Prevent Overheating." *SPIE* 2255 (1994).

Winkelmann, F. C. Modeling Windows in EnergyPlus. Proceedings of IBPSA, Building Simulation 2001, Rio de Janeiro, September 2001. *Lawrence Berkeley Laboratory Report 47972.*

Winkelmann, F. C, B. E. Birdsall, W. F. Buhl, K. L. Ellington, and A. E. Erdem. 1993. DOE-2 Supplement: Version 2.1E. *Lawrence Berkeley Laboratory Report 34947.*

Wittwer, V., W. Graf and A. Georg. "Gasochromic glazings with a large dynamic range in total solar energy transmittance." Proceedings of *Glass Processing Days* (2001): 18–21.

Wright, J. L. "Summary and Comparison of Methods to Calculate Solar Heat Gain." *ASHRAE Transactions* 101, no. 1 (1995).

———. "VISION4 Glazing System Thermal Analysis: User Manual." *Advanced Glazing System Laboratory.* Waterloo, Ontario: University of Waterloo, 1995.

———. "VISION4 Glazing System Thermal Analysis: Reference Manual." *Advanced Glazing System Laboratory.* Waterloo, Ontario: University of Waterloo, 1995.

———. "A Correlation to Quantify Convective Heat Transfer between Window Glazings." *ASHRAE Transactions* 102, Part 1 (1996).

Wright, J. L., R. Fraser, P. de Abreu and H. F. Sullivan. "Heat Transfer in Glazing System Edge-Seals: Calculations Regarding Various Design Options." *ASHRAE Transactions* 100, no. 1 (1994).

Wright, J. L., and H. F. Sullivan. "A 2-D numerical model for natural convection in a vertical, rectangular window cavity." *ASHRAE Transactions* 100, no. 2 (1995).

———. "A 2-D numerical model for glazing system thermal analysis." *ASHRAE Transactions* 100, no. 1 (1995).

———. "A Simplified Method for the Numerical Condensation Resistance Analysis of Windows." Proceedings of Window Innovations Conference, Toronto, Ontario, June 1995.

Yazdanian, M., and J. Klems. "Measurement of the Exterior Convective Film Coefficient for Windows in Low-Rise Buildings." *ASHRAE Transactions* 100, no. 1 (1994). *Lawrence Berkeley Laboratory Report 34717.*

Yellott, J. I. "Selective reflectance: A New Approach to Solar Heat Control." *ASHRAE Transactions* 69 (1963): 418.

———. "Drapery Fabrics and Their Effectiveness in Sun Control." *ASHRAE Transactions* 71, no. l (1965): 260–72.

———. "Shading Coefficients and Sun-Control Capability of Single Glazing." *ASHRAE Transactions* 72, no. l (1966): 72.

———. "Effect of Louvered Sun Screens upon Fenestration Heat Loss." *ASHRAE Transactions* 78, no. l (1972): 199–204.

Zhao, Y., D. Curcija and W. P. Goss."Condensation resistance validation project." A detailed computer simulation using finite element methods. *ASHRAE Transactions* 102, Part. 2 (1996).

———. "Prediction of the Multicellular Flow Regime of Natural Convection in Fenestration Glazing Cavities." *ASHRAE Transactions* 103, Part. 1 (1997).

Zhao, Y., D. Curcija, W. P. Goss and J. P. Power. "A New Set of Correlations for Predicting Convective Heat Transfer in Fenestration Glazing Cavities Based on Computer Simulations Using Finite Element Method." CLIMA 2000 conference in Brussels, Belgium, September, 1997.

# Index

zone models, 31
  *see also* daylight
lightscoops, 127, 349
light shelves, 47, 118–19, 331, 347–49, 351–53, 356
light-to-solar-gain ratio, 28–29
liquid crystal technology, 95–96
litrium, 119, 128
load and stress analysis, 59–61
low-E coatings, 14, 188–90
  emissivity, 22, 89
  manufacturing process, 82, 89–90
luminous efficacy, 28–29

## M

manufactured window units, 15–16
  materials of construction, 102–5
  performance comparison of frame types, 105–6
Mass Law, 55
materials selection
  for acoustic performance, 55
  curtain walls, 106
  frames, 61
  insulated glazing units, 81–85
  manufactured window units, 102–6
  smart windows, 94–101
  storefronts, 106
  sunlight shading strategies, 110–14
matte finish glass, 91
mechanical systems
  cost, 350
  in double-envelope buildings, 121–22, 124
  windows and, 13, 38–39
  zone models, 31
mini optical light shelf system (MOLS), 119, 355
motorized
  louvres, 77, 117, 131, 344
  shades, 101, 112–14

## N

National Fenestration Rating Council, 13, 25, 27, 58, 71–72, 73, 102
NFRC. *see* National Fenestration Rating Council

## O

Occidental Chemical Corporation, 121, 123
occupancy, life cycle process, 14
office buildings, 147
  energy use, 138–43
operable windows, 10, 30, 52, 58, 59, 330, 339, 341
organizaion of book, 15
orientation of windows, 45, 111, 114
  in cold climates, 218
      all attributes, 157–59
      daylight, 153–54
      energy use, 148–51
      glare, 154–55
      peak demand, 151–53
      thermal comfort, 156
      view, 155
  in hot climates, 293
      all attributes, 232–33
      daylight, 229
      energy use, 223–24
      glare, 230
      peak demand, 228–29
      thermal comfort, 232–33
      view, 231
  school design, 299–302, 315–19

  *see also* cold climate designs, east-/west-facing perimeter zones; cold climate designs, north-facing perimeter zones; cold climate designs, south-facing perimeter zones; hot climate designs, east-/west-facing perimeter zones; hot climate designs, north-facing perimeter zones; hot climate designs, south-facing perimeter zones
Outdoor-Indoor Transmission Class, 56
overhangs, 40, 108
  shading role, 111, 112, 114, 127

## P

peak demand. *see* cold climate designs; hot climate designs; school design in cold climates; school design in hot climates
Pei, I. M., 125
perimeter zones, 25, 27, 31–33, 34, 39, 42, 45
  design decision-making process, 131
  east-/west-facing, 198–221, 273–75
  north-facing, 158–61, 234–36
  south-facing, 178–97, 252–54
Phoenix Central Library, 111, 125, 126, 330, 342–44
photochromics, 95
photosensors, 34, 333, 355
photovoltaics, 14, 81, 93, 98, 101
plastic films, 14, 81, 84–85, 87, 89, 92, 95
polycarbonate glass products, 75
polyethylene terephthalate, 75
polymer dispersed liquid crystal device, 95–96
polyvinyl butryl (PVB), 55, 75, 92
polyvinyl chloride (PVC), 55, 103–4
Potsdamer Platz, 13. *see also* Debis Tower (Berlin, Germany)
predesign, life cycle process, 12
predicted percentage dissatisfied (PPD), 52
pressure-equalization, 67
prismatic glazing, 118, 119–20, 126, 331, *333*
projections. *see* overhangs
purpose of windows, 7–8
PVB. *see* polyvinyl butryl
PVC. *see* polyvinyl chloride
pyrolytic coatings, 90

## R

radiant asymmetry, 51
radiation heat transfer, 18, 19–22
  long-wave, 19, 22
  short-wave, 19, 22
reflectance, 19, 132
  definition, 21
  light shelves, 118–19
  ratios, 47
reflective coatings, 87–88
refraction, 119
retrofits and replacements
  for acoustic performance, 58–59
  for blast resistance, 75
  evacuated windows, 94
  low-E coatings, 90
  tinted glass, 87
roller shades, 101, 112, 113, 333
roof monitors, 34, 349
R-value, 24